WITHDRAWN

# An Index to Literature
## in
## The New Yorker

### Volumes XXXI-XLV, 1955-1970

by

## Robert Owen Johnson

# The Scarecrow Press, Inc.
# Metuchen, N. J.      1971

# Table of Contents

I wish to dedicate this volume to those who have helped me the most with its preparation: Jani S. Adams, William H. Day, Susan L. Johnson, Susan J. Umberger.

R. O. J.

# Introduction

This third volume indexes Volumes **XXXI** through **XLV** of The New Yorker (February 19, 1955 through February 14, 1970). Like its predecessors, it is divided into three sections: Original Material, Reviews, and Name Index. The first section lists all poetry and fiction, in addition to factual material found in departments such as A Reporter at Large, Profiles, The Wayward Press, and the like. In addition, subject references to literary figures and their work also appear here.

In the second section I have listed all signed book, theatre, current cinema and television reviews, and anonymous book reviews of over twenty lines. Entries for signed reviews include the reviewer's last name in parenthesis; a complete listing of reviewers may be found beginning on page 165. Reviewers are listed in the Name Index, as are authors of works reviewed. The small letter r after each identifying number in the Name Index signifies that the reference is to a review.

As is the case in the first two volumes, each title in the Original Material and Review sections is identified by a number, with original material in numbers 1 to 5579, and reviews in numbers 5580 to 13,090. The user will find in the Name Index a complete listing of an author's original material, reviews that he has written, and reviews by others of books and plays that he has published or produced.

An asterisk in the volume, page and date designator indicates that the citation is from the Out-of-Town edition; page numbers may vary widely between this and the New York edition. The Out-of-Town edition, which went out of existence in April 1960, can be identified by a small five-pointed star on the cover, just before the date. The matter of the two editions is discussed in detail on pages vi-viii of the Introduction to the first volume.

The first forty-five years of The New Yorker have now been indexed, and the project is up to date; it is my sincere wish that the work has benefited literary scholars. I intend to keep the index current, and shall decide at a future date the frequency with which supplements are published. Perhaps librarians and scholars will be kind enough to express their opinion. The New Yorker's recently established Table of Contents eases the search for material, but an index assures accuracy and completeness, as well as speed.

Recently it occurred to me that a separate index for The New Yorker's renowned Profiles could aid biographers, as well as students in many fields other than literature, and that volume is now in preparation. It will list all Profiles published from 1925 to 1971 by title, by subject's name, by subject's profession or reason for notoriety, and by author.

I wish to express my appreciation to my wife Barbara, to my daughter Susan, and to Nancy Carlson and Judy Haswell for helping me with the incredibly tedious job of reading proof.

Pullman, Washington
January 1971

## Symbols and Abbreviations

*      Citation is from Out-of-Town edition
AC     Annals of Crime
AF     Annals of Finance
AM     Annals of Medicine
AS     Annals of Science
FFT    Further Fables for Our Time
NFG    Notes for a Gazetteer
OFC    Our Footloose Correspondents
OFFC   Our Far-Flung Correspondents
OPH    Other People's Houses
OUWA   Onward and Upward with the Arts
PR     Profile
REF    Reflections
RL     A Reporter at Large
TT     Talk of the Town
TWNY   That Was New York
TWW    That Was the War
WP     The Wayward Press

# Original Material

1

The bath. Prose. Mary Cable.
31:86-93 Ap23'55.          383
The bathing beach. Verse.
John Hall Wheelock. 41:36
Jy17'65.                   384
Bathrooms remembered. Prose.
Sylvia Townsend Warner.
39:33-6 Ja11'64.           385
Bathtubs. Verse. Richmond
Lattimore. 41:30 Jy31'65.386
Bats. Verse. George MacBeth.
42:159 S17'66.             387
A battle against the bewitchment
of our intelligence. OUWA.
Ved Mehta. 37:59-159
D9'61.                     388
The battle of Harlem Heights.
TWNY. Bruce Bliven, Jr.
31:93-128*N12'55.          389
Battle problem. Verse. William
Meredith. 31:52*D3'55.     390
Battles long ago. Prose.
Patrick Kinross. 34:154-63
D13'58.                    391
Baucis & Philemon. Verse.
Jean Farley. 42:49 F18'67.
                           392
Baudelaire, Charles. Janet
Flanner. 35:131-2 Mr22'69.
                           393
Baudelaire, Charles. Anthony
West. 45:149-58 Ap12'58.394
The bay at West Falmouth.
Verse. Barbara Howes.
42:44 My14'66.             395
Bay memory. Verse. William
Jay Redding. 31:42*O22'55.
                           396
The bay stone. Verse. Howard
Moss. 44:34 Je8'68.        397
Be a cat's-paw! lose big
money! Prose. S.J.
Perelman. 45:31-3 Jy26'69.
                           398
Beach glass. Verse. Howard
Moss. 43:40 Jy1'67.        399
Beach letter. Verse. John
Hollander. 37:26 F3'62.    400
The beam. Prose. Nancy Hale.
32:32-40 O27'56.           401
A bear at large. RL. E.J.
Kahn, Jr. 33:118-24 Mr23'57.
                           402

The bear on the Delhi Road.
Verse. Earle Birney. 36:101
O22'60.                    403
Bearings. Verse. Jack
Marshall. 43:56 Mr18'67.
                           404
The beating. Prose. H.L.
Mountzoures. 42:30-2
Ag20'66.                   405
The beating. Verse. Ann
Stanford. 45:48 S13'69.    406
Beatrice Trueblood's story.
Prose. Jean Stafford.
31:24-32 F26'55.           407
The Beats. TT. 36:36-7
Ap16'60.                   408
Beautiful. PR (Rich). Whitney
Balliett. 42:35-66 Ja21'67.
                           409
The beautiful blue horse.
Prose. Niccolò Tucci.
33:42-71 Ap13'57.          410
The beautiful day. Prose.
Edith Iglauer. 42:53-6
Mr19'66.                   411
The beautiful flower. PR
(Campion). Joseph Mitchell.
31:39-89 Je4'55.           412
Beauty in high dudgeon. Verse.
R.P. Lister. 33:137
D7'57.                     413
The beaver's story. Verse.
Vernon Watkins. 42:198
O15'66.                    414
Because of the waters of the
flood. Prose. Mark Henry
Helprin. 45:35 S27'69.     415
Bech in Rumania. Prose.
John Updike. 42:54-63
O8'66.                     416
Bech takes pot luck. Prose.
John Updike. 44:28-36
S7'68.                     417
Beckett, Samuel. George
Steiner. 44:164-74
Ap27'68.                   418
Beds and boards. Prose.
Alfred Chester. 38:
34-7 Mr10'62.              419
Bedtime in Autumn. Verse.
Michael Goldman. 31:48
*N12'55.                   420
Beerbohm, Max. PR.

S.N. Behrman. 35:45-88
F6'60; 35:40-86 F13'60; 36:
50-98 F20'60; 36:43-99
F27'60; 36:47-119 Mr5'60;
36:59-108 Mr12'60; 36:50-
112 Mr19'60.          421
Beersheba, Eilat, and Sodom.
OFFC. Joseph Wechsberg.
36:182-202 N19'60.          422
Beetle on the Shasta Daylight.
Verse. Shirley Kaufman.
42:48 Ap2'66.          423
Before crowned heads. Prose.
Dean Doner. 33:91-100
Ap20'57.          424
Before dawn. Verse. Horace
Hamilton. 39:62 N30'63.          425
Before the cashier's window in
a department store. Verse.
James Wright. 41:50
Mr13'65.          426
Before the end of Summer.
Prose. Grant Moss, Jr. 36:
173-91 O15'60.          427
Before the wedding. Prose.
R. Prawer Jhabvala. 33:28-
32 D28'57.          428
The beginning. Verse. Marcia
Carlson. 31:100 Ap30'55. 429
The beginning of a long story.
Prose. Maeve Brennan.
36:28-35 F4'61.          430
Behan, Brendan. John Lardner.
35:192-3 D12'59.          431
Behavior that gives who away?
or whom? Verse. W.W.
Watt. 35:22 Ag1'59.          432
Behind the glass panel. OFFC.
A.J. Liebling. 33:100-21
S14'57.          433
Beisbol in Central Park. Verse.
Wallace White. 40:46 My16
'64.          434
The bell of charity. Prose.
Calvin Kentfield. 31:23-30
Jy16'55.          435
Bella. Tom O'Malley and Jane
Douglass. (Oliver) T. 37:95-6
N25'61.          435a
The bella lingua. Prose. John
Cheever. 34:34-55 Mr1'58 436
Bellow, Saul (Parody).
Thomas Meehan. 40:26-7
Ja9'65.          437

Bellow, Saul (Parody). S.J.
Perelman. 40:26-8
D26'64.          438
The bells at Denton. Verse.
F.D. Reeve. 41:46 Ap17
'65.          439
Bendix. Verse. John Updike.
33:30 F15'58.          440
Benediction. Prose. Patricia
Collinge. 33:25-31 Jy13'57.          441
The benefactress. Prose.
Elizabeth Taylor. 35:50-6
D5'59.          442
The bequest. Verse. James
Merrill. 38:26 Ag11'62.          443
The bequest. Prose. Edith
Templeton. 33:46-9 D7'57.          444
Bergman, Ingmar. Janet
Flanner. 35:102-103 Je13'59.          445
Bernadette. Prose. Mavis
Gallant. 32:24-34 Ja12'57.          446
Berryman, John (Parody).
John Updike. 32:28-9 Ja26'57.          447
Besoyan, Rick. TT. 35:26-7
Ja16'60.          448
Best. RL. Fred C. Shapiro.
42:181-98 O22'66.          449
The best four years. Prose.
St. Clair McKelway.
32:28-31 O27'56.          450
The best I know how. PR
(Gibbs). Winthrop Sargeant.
40:49-84 Je6'64.          451
The best of the best. PR
(Donon). Geoffrey T.
Hellman. 38:47-78 Mr10'62.          452
Bestiary. Verse. John Updike.
38:228 D1'62.          453
Betjeman, John. PR. John
Betjeman. 36:31-42 Ag27'60.          454
Betjeman, John. TT. 33:
22-4 Mr16'57.          455
Better than dead. Prose.
R. Prawer Jhabvala. 34:
30-6 My24'58.          456
Better times. Prose. Mavis

Flanner. 31:129-31 Ap23'55.
534
Book show, contemporary
Russian. Janet Flanner. 32:
60-2*Je2'56. 535
Bookkeeping. Prose. Harold
Brodkey. 44:44-83 Ap27'68.
536
Books from the wood. Prose.
H. F. Ellis. 44:81-3 Ja18'69.
537
Books published, number of.
TT. 34:23-4 Mr29'58. 538
The bootlegger. Prose. Robert
Froman. 39:176-81 S14'63.
539
Bootless speculations. Verse.
Phyllis McGinley. 33:49
O5'57. 540
Borges, Jorge Luis. John
Updike. 41:223-46 O30'65.
541
Borrowed light. RL. Alan
Moorehead. 40:39-76
Je27'64. 542
A Bostonian's ode to Central
and Prospect. Verse. Ham-
lin Hunt. 31:75*S17'55. 543
Both banks of the Mekong. RL.
Robert Shaplen. 40:78-114
Ja16'65. 544
Botsford, Stephen B. (Obituary).
43:92 Ja6'68. 545
A bottle of cold perrier. OFFC.
Hoyt Fuller. 39:35-57
Ja4'64. 546
Bottles. Prose. Natacha Stewart.
41:33-7 Jy17'65. 547
Bounty. Prose. Bentz
Plagemann. 31:137-48*S17'55.
548
A bouquet from a fellow-rose-
man. Verse. Robert Graves.
32:30*Je30'56. 549
Bourchier, Arthur. S.N.
Behrman and Max
Beerbohm. 36:72-6
Mr5'60. 550
The bow. Prose. Ted Walker.
43:34-7 S2'67. 551
Bowwow, dingdong, and pooh-
pooh. Verse. Ormonde

deKay, Jr. 44:50 O5'68. 552
A box at the opera. Verse.
Howard Moss. 31:30
Mr12'55. 553
Boy. Verse. John Ciardi.
42:30 Jy23'66. 554
The boy. Prose. L.
Woiwode. 44:32-53
Ag31'68. 555
The boy and the ball. Prose.
Sonia Rollnick. 35:37-41
Ap4'59. 556
Boy at target practice: a
contemplation. Verse.
W.R. Moses 36:135
Je11'60. 557
Boy in a boater. Prose.
Susan Gillespie. 40:207-28
N14'64. 558
The boy who used foul
language. Prose. Julian
Mazor. 44:30-42 Mr30'68.
559
The bracelet. Prose. Mina
Lewiton Simon. 44:32-8
F8'69. 560
The bragdowdy and the busy-
body. FFT. James Thurber.
32:28-9*Je9'56. 561
Brassens, Georges. Janet
Flanner. 43:98-9 Ja20'68.
562
Brazil, January 1,1502. Verse.
Elizabeth Bishop. 35:26
Ja2'60. 563
Brazilian happenings. Verse.
Richard O'Connell. 42:58
S17'66; 42:60 O22'66;
42:62 N19'66. 564
The bread is rising. RL.
Francine du Plessix Gray.
44:37-75 Ja25'69. 565
Bread, love, and neo-realismo.
PR (De Sica). Winthrop
Sargeant. 33:35-58 Je29'57;
33:35-53 Jy6'57. 566
A break with tradition. RL.
Bernard Taper. 41:58-86
Jy 24'65. 567
Breakdown. Verse. Howard
Moss. 31:98*D10'55.
568

$CH_3CO_2C_6H_4CO_2H$    -19-   

A city of speech. Prose. Jon
Swan. 39:125-8 Ap6'63. 814
A city of stone. PR (Florence,
Italy). Mary McCarthy.
35:36-75 Ag8'59; 35:32-79
*Ag15'59; 35:38-94 Ag22'59.
815
City of the baroque. PR (Vienna).
Joseph Wechsberg. 44:50-87
S28'68; 44:58-90 O5'68; 44:
60-100 O12'68. 816
City on a tilting plain. OFFC.
Christopher Rand. 31:35-62
Ap 30'55. 817
City science. Verse. Morris
Bishop. 32:62*Mr31'56. 818
City without walls. Verse.
W. H. Auden. 44:43 Ap27'68.
819
A civilized thing. OFFC. John
Bainbridge. 40:136-51 F13'65.
820
Clair de lune. Verse. Anthony
Hecht. 36:86 Ag13'60. 821
Clair, René. TT. 34:44-5
N29'58. 822
The clamdiggers. Verse. Gene
Baro. 39:103 S7'63. 823
Clamming. Verse. Reed.
Whittemore. 41:30 Ag28'65.
824
Clarke, Arthur C. TT.
43:25-6 My27'67. 825
The classless society. Prose.
Elizabeth Hardwick. 32:30-
52 Ja19'57. 826
Claudel, Paul. Janet Flanner.
31:78-80 Mr12'55. 827
Claus. Prose. Thomas
Meehan. 40:26-7 Ja9'65. 828
A clean sweep. Prose.
Montgomery Newman. 31:84-5
Ap2'55. 829
The cleanup man. PR (Bru-
beck). Robert Rice. 37:41-89
Je3'61. 830
Clear Haven. Prose. John
Cheever. 32:50-111 D1'56.
831
The clearing. Verse. Robert
Graves. 31:33 Ap30'55. 832
Clementina. Prose. John

Cheever. 36:40-8
My7'60. 833
Clerihews. Verse. Clifton
Fadiman. 32:37*My5'56.
834
Cleveland, Ohio. Verse.
Hawley Truax. 43:24
Ja6'68. 835
Cliffs of Fall. Prose.
Shirley Hazzard. 38:38-46
S22'62. 836
The clock runs out at Stur-
bridge Watch & Clock.
Prose. Michael J. Arlen.
39:39-40 My4'63. 837
Close, but no cigar. Prose.
Ray Irwin. 42:86-92
Ja21'67. 838
Close shave. Prose. Dwight
Taylor. 32:209-16 N17'56.
839
Close to Mom. Prose. St.
Clair McKelway. 41:28-31
Ag21'65. 840
A closer look. WP. E.J. Kahn,
Jr. 34:116-26 Ap5 '58. 841
Closing time. Verse. R.P.
Lister. 40:38 Mr21'64. 842
Closing time. Verse. David
Wagoner. 39:48 Mr16'63. 843
The clothes moth and the luna
moth. FFT. James Thurber.
32:29-30*My19'56. 844
A cloud of smoke. RL.
Thomas Whiteside. 39:67-
108 N30'63. 845
The clown. Verse. Donald
Hall. 36:174 N26'60. 846
The coast recedes. WP.
A.J. Liebling. 36:124-30
My21'60. 847
The coasts of New England.
Prose. Nancy Hale.
31:37-42*S10'55. 848
Cock. Verse. Peter Kane
Dufault. 39:38 S7'63. 849
The cockatoo. Prose. St.
Clair McKelway. 33:48-78
O19'57. 850
Cockcrow. Prose. Robert
Henderson. 44:22-7 Jy6'68.
851

A day in the city. Verse.
L. E. Sissman. 42:64 D3'66.
                                    1032
A day in the country. Prose.
H. L. Mountzoures.
43:29-35 F10'68.          1033
A day in the country. Prose.
Edith Templeton. 34:25-32
Jy19'58.                        1034
A day in the life of Roger
Angell. Prose. Roger Angell.
43:28-31 Ag19'67.        1035
A day in town. Prose. Faye
Riter. 31:94-100 Je4'55.
                                    1036
The day of Miss Durbin's. Prose.
Nora Johnson. 32:28-33
*My5'56.                       1037
The day of the dog. Prose.
Emily Hahn. 38:111-14 Mr10
'62.                            1038
The day of the dying rabbit.
Prose. John Updike. 45:22-6
Ag30'69.                      1039
The day of the lion. Prose.
Ralph Blum. 36:33-67
Ja14'61.                       1040
Day on kind continent. Verse.
Robert David Cohen.
41:52 S25'65.               1041
A day on Ragged. Prose.
Donald Hall. 37:23-31
Ag12'61.                      1042
A day on the river. RL.
Berton Roueché. 39:48-68
Ap6'63.                       1043
The day the redcoats left. Prose.
Florence Codman. 33:162-78
S21'57.                        1044
Daybreak. Verse. Jorge
Luis Borges. Norman
Thomas di Giovanni, trans.
45:133 My24'69.           1045
Daydreams. Prose. Frank
O'Connor. 33:28-32 Mr23'57.
                                    1046
The days and the neighbors.
Prose. Robert Henderson.
40:44-7 Ap25'64.          1047
Days at the races. OFFC.
A. J. Liebling. 32:50-60
*Jy21'56.                     1048

Days at the zoo. RL.
Emily Hahn. 43:38-73
S2'67; 43:96-133 S23'67;
43:117-56 S30'67; 43:170-
207 O14'67.               1049
Days of grace. Verse. Hawley
Truax. 45:21 Jy19'69.    1050
Days without you. Verse. Anne
Sexton. 44:34-5 Je29'68.
                                    1051
Dayton, O. NFG. Philip
Hamburger. 35:94-8*D19'59.
                                    1052
de la Mare, Walter. Mollie
Panter-Downes. 32:72
*Jy7'56.                       1053
de la Ramée, Marie Louise.
Mollie Panter-Downes.
33:208-209 D14'57.       1054
De Sica, Vittorio. PR.
Winthrop Sargeant.
33:35-58 Je29'57; 33:35-53
Jy6'57.                         1055
DeVoto, Bernard. TT.
31:41*N26'55.              1056
Dead center. Verse. Ruth
Whitman. 41:43
My8'65.                        1057
The dead fiddler. Prose.
Isaac Bashevis Singer.
44:42-72 My25'68.        1058
A dead leaf. Verse. Howard
Moss. 44:34 Mr30'68.     1059
The dead mosquitoes. AM.
Berton Roueché. 45:123-42
O11'69.                        1060
Dead Negro. Verse. Paris
Leary. 36:48 Mr19'60.   1061
The dead of the house. Prose.
Hannah Green. 45:54-82
O11'69.                        1062
Dead of Winter. Verse.
Anthony Towne. 37:30
Ja20'62.                      1063
The Dead Sea scrolls: 1969
RL. Edmund Wilson. 45:45-84
Mr22'69; 45:45-96 Mr29'69;
45:45-94 Ap5'69.          1064
Dear Alexandros. Prose. John
Updike. 35:40-1 O31'59.
                                    1065
Dear Elizabeth. Verse.

Department of amplification.
Prose. Naomi Bliven.
36:162-7 S24'60.        1103
Department of amplification.
Robert Clurman. 35:166-70
Mr14'59.        1104
Department of amplification.
Alistair Cooke. 35:89-93
*Ag15'59.        1105
Department of amplification.
John J. Espey. 33:147-51
My11'57.        1106
Department of amplification.
John Kenneth Galbraith.
42:50-2 Ja14'67.        1107
Department of amplification.
William M. Gibson.
34:63 Jy26'58.        1108
Department of amplification.
Brendan Gill. 36:136
D3'60; 39:136-8 Mr9'63.1109
Department of amplification.
Nancy Hale. 32:124-32
O13'56.        1110
Department of amplification.
Geoffrey T. Hellman.
31:89-90 Mr26'55; 42:171-3
Ap16'66.        1111
Department of amplification.
Mary Hemingway. 39:160-3
Mr16'63.        1112
Department of amplification.
Nat Hentoff. 41:102
S11'65.        1113
Department of amplification.
Gerald Jonas. 38:108-12
Mr31'62.        1114
Department of amplification.
E.J. Kahn, Jr. 31:48-50
*D24'55; 32:144-5 S29'56;
38:133 Ap28'62; 40:159-63
Je6'64.        1115
Department of amplification.
Richard Lemon. 32:212-14
*N10'56.        1116
Department of amplification.
St. Clair McKelway.
34:63-4 Jy26'58; 34:81-2
Ja17'59.        1117
Department of amplification.
Faith McNulty. 37:94-106
F25'61.        1118
Department of amplification.

Donald Malcolm.
42:101-103 Ja28'67.        1119
Department of amplification.
Marianne Moore. 33:140-6
Ap13'57.        1120
Department of amplification.
Noel Perrin. 34:126-8
My10'58; 34:81-3 F14'59;
37:158-60 O28'61; 38:
157-8 D8'62; 39:63-5
Jy6'63.        1121
Department of amplification.
Alastair Reid. 40:194-5
N14'64.        1122
Department of amplification.
Richard H. Rovere.
39:119 My11'63.        1123
Department of amplification.
Edward Teller. 32:164-6
D15'56.        1124
Department of amplification.
Eli Waldron. 32:168-75
O6'56.        1125
Department of amplification.
Joyce Warren. 36:76-9 Ag13
'60; 38:157-63 S22'62.        1126
Department of amplification.
E.B. White. 37:42-5
Ag5'61.        1127
Department of amplification.
Katharine S. White.
41:70-1 Jy10'65; 42:112-
14 Je18'66.        1128
Department of amplification,
correction, and abuse.
Richard Lockridge.
32:69-70*D22'56.        1129
Department of correction.
James Thurber. 34:77
F7'59.        1130
Department of correction
and amplification.
Editors. 39:108 Ap27'63.
        1131
Department of correction
and amplification. Ved
Mehta. 40:87 Ja9'65.        1132
Department of correction
and amplification. Frank
O'Connor. 34:112-13 My17
'58.        1133
Department of correction
and amplification. John

O'Hara. 40:164-5
S19'64. 1134
Department of correction and
amplification. Richard H.
Rovere. 38:119 Ap7'62. 1135
Des Moines, Ia. NFG. Philip
Hamburger. 36:107-110
O29'60. 1136
The descent of Mr. Aldez.
Verse. John Updike.
37:132 Je3'61. 1137
A description of presumption.
Prose. Gilbert Rogin. 39:29
Ja18'64. 1138
The desert in the oasis. Prose.
Niccolò Tucci. 38:56-93
O6'62. 1139
A deserted barn. Verse.
L. Woiwode. 44:191 D14'68.
1140
The deserted nation. Verse.
E.B. White. 42:53 O8'66.
1141
Despair. Verse. Richard
Eberhart. 45:35 F14'70.
1142
Destroying angel. Verse.
Hilary Corke. 38:42 S8'62.
1143
The deterrent. Prose. Gene
Williams. 41:141-9 F20'65.
1144
Deturtling. Prose. Richard
F. Graber. 36:156-62
O29'60. 1145
The devil and angels. Verse.
R.P. Lister. 34:88
Mr8'58. 1146
Dhery, Robert. TT.
34:22-3 Ja10'59. 1147
Dial "H" for heartburn.
Prose. S.J. Perelman.
36:56-8 D3'60. 1148
The dial tone. Verse.
Howard Nemerov. 38:50
N24'62. 1149
Diamond. RL. Emily Hahn.
32:57-91*Ap7'56; 32:83-
101*Ap14'56; 32:116-32*Ap
28'56; 32:108-24*My19'56;
32:94-108*My26'56; 32:102-
32 S22'56; 32:39-85
S29'56. 1150

Diamonds in the vault.
Prose. Sylva Grossman.
33:113-27*N30'57. 1151
The diaries and letters of
Sir Gerald Woolton. Prose.
Philip Hamburger. 43:52-3
O28'67. 1152
Dickens, Charles. TT.
38:17-18 Jy7'62. 1153
Dictionaries and grammars.
Edmund Wilson. 39:165-
208 Ap20'63. 1154
A dictionary of contemporary
American usage. Bergan Evans.
(Macdonald) B. 34:136-53 My
17'58. 1154a
The dictionary ounce. Verse.
Robert A. Wallace.
37:44 Mr11'61. 1155
Die mauer. PR (Berlin Wall).
John Bainbridge. 38:57-144
O27'62. 1156
A different time, a different
place. Prose. Robert M.
Coates. 40:45-52 S26'64. 1157
Dinesen, Isak. Hannah Arendt.
44:223-36 N9'68. 1158
The dinner party. Prose.
Viola Meynell.
32:35-8*Ap7'56. 1159
Dinosaurs. Verse. Carolyn
Stoloff. 40:30 F29'64. 1160
Diplomacy at Flushing
Meadow. OUWA. John
Brooks. 39:41-59 Je1'63. 1161
Diplomacy über alles. Prose.
E.J. Kahn, Jr. 33:199-
202 D14'57. 1162
Directed to the product. PR
(Restaurant Association).
Geoffrey T. Hellman.
40:59-107 O17'64. 1163
Directions to the armorer.
Verse. Elder Olson. 35:
191 N14'59. 1164
Director of research. Prose.
W.J.J. Gordon. 37:48-
52 N4'61. 1165
Directors' director. PR
(Weinberg). E.J. Kahn, Jr.
32:39-63*S8'56; 32:49-74
*S15'56. 1166
Dirt. Prose. Roy Bongartz.
37:124-9 S9'61. 1167

Disasters of war: Goya at the museum. Verse. Babette Deutsch. 33:132 Ap27'57. 1168

Disorder in the Roman Hills. Prose. Nika Standen Hazelton. 34:112-32 N29'58. 1169

The dispersal. Prose. Clifford Aucoin. 38:180-93 D1'62. 1170

Dissection of a poll. WP. Joseph Alsop. 36:170-84 S24'60. 1171

Distances. Verse. Jeremy Kingston. 40:95 Ja23'65. 1172

Distinctions. Verse. Barbara Lawrence. 40:126 F6'65. 1173

The divine fireplace. Prose. Maeve Brennan. 32:34-40 *Ap21'56. 1174

The divine insect. Verse. John Hall Wheelock. 35:30 S5'59. 1175

The diviner. Prose. Brian Friel. 38:36-42 Mr31'62. 1176

Division. Verse. John Ratti. 37:111 F17'62. 1177

Divorce. Verse. Heather McHugh. 45:110 Mr1'69. 1178

Do good works, up to twenty per cent of adjusted gross income. Verse. Morris Bishop. 34:144 Ap12'58. 1179

Do you belong in journalism? WP. A.J. Liebling. 36:105-12 My14'60. 1180

The doctor. Prose. André Dubus. 45:38-9 Ap26'69. 1181

Doctor in a red truck. OFFC. Christopher Rand. 35:114-43 Ap18'59. 1182

Dr. Parkhurst's crusade. TWNY. M.R. Werner. 31:189-210*N19'55; 31:93-131*N26'55. 1183

Dr. Salaam. Prose. Padma Perera. 40:54-63 N28'64. 1184

The doctor's wife. Prose. John Updike. 36:35-8 F11'61. 1185

Dodd, Edward H., Jr. TT. 43:47-8 O28'67. 1186

Does anyone look his age? Prose. Geoffrey T. Hellman. 36:28 Jy16'60. 1187

The dog at the Plaza fountain. Prose. Robert Henderson. 38:34-7 My26'62. 1188

The dogs in the Great Glen. Prose. Benedict Kiely. 36:42-8 O8'60. 1189

Dogs, mah-jongg, and Americans. Prose. David Kidd. 34:89-109 Ap19'58. 1190

The dolt. Prose. Donald Barthelme. 43:56-8 N11'67. 1191

The dome car. Prose. Robert Henderson. 34:40-5 S20'58. 1192

The dominant house. Verse. Jean Garrigue. 43:30 Jy 29'67. 1193

The dominant kite in Bangkok. Prose. George J.W. Goodman. 32:188-95 N3'56. 1194

Donovan's boots. Prose. Ted Walker. 45:51-3 N8'69. 1195

Don't bite the hand that puts its foot in your mouth. Verse. Ogden Nash. 37:40 My27'61. 1196

Don't call us, we'll recall you. Prose. Gordon Cotler. 43:65 D2'67. 1197

Don't give me none of your lip. Verse. W.W. Watt. 31:22 Jy9'55. 1198

Don't give me one dozen roses, give me a nosegay. Prose. Noel Perrin.

35:126-9 Ap4'59.          1199
Don't give my body to science,
the dying mother said.
Prose. Katinka Loeser.
41:57-62 O30'65.          1200
Don't look now, but there's
something behind the
curtain. Verse. Ogden
Nash. 33:36 F1'58.        1201
Don't quote me. Prose.
Robert J. Schoenberg.
37:145-8 O28'61.          1202
Don't sit under the family
tree. Verse. Ogden Nash.
36:44 Je4'60.             1203
Don't take notes on the boy
friend. Prose. Geoffrey T.
Hellman. 31:33*Ag20'55.
                          1204
The door on West Tenth
Street. Prose. Maeve
Brennan. 43:54-7 O7'67.
                          1205
Doors. Verse. Grover Amen.
38:105 Je2'62.            1206
Dostoevsky, Fyodor (Parody).
Woody Allen. 44:38-9
Mr16'68.                  1207
The double. Verse. Irving
Feldman. 40:52 S26'64.    1208
Double bluff. Verse. Alastair
Reid. 42:190 N26'66.      1209
The double bollix. Prose.
Philip Hamburger. 44:24-6
Je22'68.                  1210
Double darkness and worst of
all. TWNY. Andy Logan.
34:81-113 F22'58.         1211
Doubt. Prose. Deborah Pease.
42:186-7 S24'66.          1212
Down the line with the annual.
Prose. Donald Barthelme.
40:34-5 Mr21'64.          1213
Down to the ice. RL. John
Brooks. 34:88-132 Ap12'58.
                          1214
Downstairs no upstairs. Prose.
Brian Friel. 39:82-5 Ag24'63.
                          1215
A dragon is not a flower.
Prose. Frederick L. Keefe.
36:71-2 Ja7'61.           1216

The drawback. Prose.
Richard T. Gill.
32:47-9 S22'56.           1217
Drawing and quartering.
Prose. Jeremy Kingston.
40:177-92 S26'64.         1218
Drawing of a little girl by
a little boy. Verse.
Dorothy Donnelly.
34:38 Mr15'58.            1219
Dream. Verse. Marianne
Moore. 41:52 O16'65.      1220
The dream. Verse. Theodore
Roethke. 31:34 Je4'55.    1221
The dream. Verse. Mark
Strand. 43:34 Ag19'67.    1222
A dream, dreamed between
midnight and 1 a.m.,
July 8, 1969. Prose.
L. E. Sissman. 45:36
D20'69.                   1223
Dream objects. Verse. John
Updike. 44:54 O26'68.     1224
A dream of Albany. Prose.
St. Clair McKelway.
37:139-43 Ap15'61.        1225
A dream of gifties. Verse.
Phyllis McGinley. 36:30
Jy9'60.                   1226
A dream of governors.
Verse. Louis Simpson.
33:40 S21'57.             1227
A dream of innocent orgies.
Verse. Ogden Nash. 44:24
Jy6'68.                   1228
A dreamer of wine. PR
(Lichine). Joseph
Wechsberg 34:48-86
My17'58; 34:37-72
My24'58.                  1229
Dreaming with a friend.
Verse. Stephen Berg.
45:40 Mr15'69.            1230
Dreams. Verse. Howard
Moss. 35:56 N7'59.        1231
Dreams of water. Verse.
Donald Justice. 41:233
N20'65.                   1232
Dreamscape in kümmel. Verse.
Harold Witt. 38:107
Je16'62.                  1233
The Dress rehearsal. Prose.
Edith Templeton.

Je3'67                          1269
Dylan (Play). TT. 39:30-1
  F8'64.                        1270
Dynamics. PR (General
  Dynamics Corp.). John
  Brooks.  33:29-47 Ja4'58.
                               1271

E

ESP. Verse. R.P. Lister.
  39:40 S21'63.               1272
Each one had a home. Verse.
  Joan Thorne. 43:28
  Ja6'68.                      1273
Ear-driven. PR(Cook). Daniel
  Lang. 32:39-58*Mr3'56;
  32:45-65*Mr10'56.           1274
Earliness at the Cape. Verse.
  Babette Deutsch. 32:71
  *Je30'56.                    1275
The early flower. Verse.
  Theodore Roethke. 35:44
  Ap25'59.                     1276
Early journeys. Prose. Maddy
  Vegtel. 32:129-41
  O27'56.                      1277
Early morning dream. Verse.
  Rosemary Thomas. 37:117
  F18'61.                      1278
Early morning of a motion-
  picture executive. Prose.
  Thomas Meehan. 37:39-40
  My6'61.                      1279
The early settler. Prose. Amy
  Witting. 44:42-4 My18'68.
                               1280
Early supper. Verse. Barbara
  Howes. 32:56*N10'56.        1281
Early tea at the castle. Prose.
  Edith Templeton. 37:42-50
  S30'61.                      1282
Earth and fire. Verse.
  Vernon Watkins. 36:48
  O8'60.                       1283
Earth satellite no. 1. RL.
  Daniel Lang. 33:108-32
  My11'57.                     1284
Earth tremor in Lugano. Verse.
  James Kirkup. 42:62
  S24'66.                      1285
Earthquakes, Kona, Hawaii.
  Verse. Edith Shiffert.

35:138 Ap25'59.               1286
Earthworm. Verse. John
  Updike. 38:145 My12'62.
                               1287
East River. Verse. Whitney
  Balliett. 32:80*Mr10'56.
                               1288
Easter eggs and enterprise.
  Prose. Jane Cassels
  Record. 36:130-5 Ap9'60.
                               1289
The easy way. Prose.
  William Murray. 34:112-
  22 S13'58.                   1290
The easygoing method. PR
  (Burrows). E.J. Kahn,
  Jr.  33:51-81 My11'57;
  33:41-67 My18'57.           1291
Eat, drink, and be wary.
  Prose. S.J. Perelman.
  40:53-5 N21'64.              1292
The echo of the whistle.
  RL.  Richard Harris.
  34:112-41 S20'58.           1293
The eclipse.  Prose.
  Elizabeth Spencer. 34:25-30
  Jy12'58.                     1294
Ecstasy at the onion. OFFC.
  Whitney Balliett. 45:175-90.
  O18'69.                      1295
The ecstasy of Mr. Price.
  Verse. Morris Bishop.
  31:120*D17'55.              1296
Eddychan.  Prose. Emily
  Hahn. 44:33-9 Ja18'69. 1297
Eden must go--or must he?
  WP. A.J. Liebling. 32:
  131-8 N24'56.               1298
The edge of the sea. PR
  (Edge of sea).  Rachel
  Carson. 31:34-61*Ag20'55;
  31:36-67 *Ag27'55.          1299
The Edinburgh caper. RL.
  St. Clair McKelway. 38:
  50-179 O13'62.              1300
Edinburgh villanelle. Verse.
  Muriel Spark. 43:24
  Ag26'67.                     1301
Edouard. Verse. W.S.
  Merwin. 45:166 N8'69. 1302
An educated American
  woman. Prose. John
  Cheever. 39:46-54 N2'63. 1303

The education. Verse. David
Posner. 43:148 N18'67. 1304
An education in Georgia. RL.
Calvin Trillin. 39:30-67
Jy13'63; 39:32-71 Jy20'63;
39:34-77 Jy27'63. 1305
Edward and Pia. Prose.
Donald Barthelme. 41:46-9
S25'65. 1306
Effort at speech. Verse.
William Meredith. 45:58
D6'69. 1307
Ego. Verse. Philip Booth.
31:98*F11'56. 1308
Eh? Verse. Ogden Nash.
37:20 Jy29'61. 1309
Eichmann in Jerusalem. RL.
Hannah Arendt. 38:40-113
F16'63; 39:40-111 F23'63;
39:40-91 Mr2'63; 39:48-
131 Mr9'63; 39:58-134 Mr
16'63. 1310
The eighteenth of August.
Prose. Edith Templeton.
39:27-33 Ag17'63. 1311
Eighty-six-storied pomp. Prose.
Geoffrey T. Hellman.
32:87-90*My12'56. 1312
Eileen. Prose. John
Jurkowski. 38:24-9 Ag11'62.
1313
Eine kleine mothmusik.
Prose. S.J. Perelman. 36:28-
30 Ag13'60. 1314
Eino. Prose. Ella Leffland.
36:115-34 N26'60. 1315
The ekistic world. PR
(Doxiadis). Christopher
Rand. 39:49-87 My11'63.
1316
The eldest child. Prose.
Maeve Brennan. 44:30-3
Je29'68. 1317
The elected. Prose. R.
Prawer Jhabvala. 36:40-5
Ap30'60. 1318
Electrical storm. Verse.
Elizabeth Bishop. 36:48
My14'60. 1319
The elegance of stately
measures. Verse. Richard
Eberhart. 36:34 F4'61.
1320

Elegant economy. Prose.
Edith Templeton.
34:40-8 O4'58. 1321
Elegy: E.W. Verse.
L.E. Sissman. 42:36
My28'66. 1322
Elegy for a nature poet.
Verse. Howard Nemerov.
35:50 D12'59. 1323
Elegy in Big Sur. Verse.
Lyon Phelps. 39:56
N23'63. 1324
An elegy long after. Verse.
Constance Carrier. 33:30
Mr2'57. 1325
The elephants pass Carnegie
Hall. Verse. Rosemary
Thomas. 31:48 My14'55.
1326
1109 Klingenstein. Prose.
Gilbert Rogin. 40:45-8
Ap18'64. 1327
Eliot, T.S. (Parody).
William Jay Smith.
33:36 Mr2'57. 1328
Eliot, T.S. Edmund Wilson.
34:119-50 My24'58. 1329
The Elizabethan maid.
Verse. Helen Bevington.
32:140 O20'56. 1330
Elmira, N.Y. NFG. Philip
Hamburger. 37:194-7
D16'61. 1331
The embarkment for Cythera.
Prose. John Cheever.
38:59-106 N3'62. 1332
Emblems. Verse. Luke Zilles.
31:80 F19'55. 1333
An emergency case. Prose.
Mavis Gallant. 32:34-6
F16'57. 1334
Emerita Anna's daughters.
Prose. Antonio Barolini.
32:37-8 F2'57. 1335
An emotion of weirdness. AM.
Berton Roueché. 39:34-51
Ag17'63. 1336
Emotion recollected in late-
Cenozoic tranquillity.
Verse. John Sack. 33:38
Ag24'57. 1337
The empire of things. Prose.
H.L. Mountzoures.

31:68-82 Jy9'55.  1372
Equality cake. Prose.
Edith Templeton. 42:56-67
N12'66.  1373
The equilibrist. Verse. James
Kirkup. 31:147*O15'55.
1374
Equinox. Verse. Whitney
Balliett. 32:115*Mr24'56.
1375
Equus caballus. Prose.
Calvin Tomkins. 45:28-9
Ja24'70.  1376
Erie, Pa. NFG. Philip
Hamburger. 35:62-5
Ag1'59.  1377
Ernest observes. Prose.
Gilbert Rogin. 39:44-7
O26'63.  1378
Ernst in civilian clothes.
Prose. Mavis Gallant.
39:54-8 N16'63.  1379
Escape. Prose. Grover
Amen. 39:138-63 Ap20'63.
1380
The escape. Verse. James
Dickey. 40:30 Jy18'64. 1381
The escape. Prose. Emily
Hahn. 39:125-46 N2'63. 1382
An essay on a premonition and
eight heads. Prose. James
McConkey. 38:28-33
Mr3'62.  1383
Estates of the Loire. Verse.
Jean Garrigue. 43:30 Ag19'67.
1384
Estuary. Verse. Ted Walker.
40:46 Ap11'64.  1385
Et quid amabo nisi quod
aenigma est. Verse. Stephen
Sandy. 42:54 D3'66.  1386
The eternal return. Verse.
Robert Hillyer. 33:30
Mr9 '57.  1387
Eternities. Verse. Norman
Mailer. 37:200 N11'61. 1388
The ethnocentrics. RL.
E.J. Kahn, Jr. 36:98-133
Ap2'60.  1389
Eton bookie. Prose. John
Godley. 31:31-3 Je25'55.1390
Eugene, Ore. NFG. Philip
Hamburger. 39:95-9

Je1'63.  1391
Eugénie Grandet. Prose.
Donald Barthelme. 44:24-5
Ag17'68.  1392
European diary. REF. Lewis
Mumford. 44:30-43 Jy6'68.
1393
A European from America
in Europe. REF. Leopold
Tyrmand. 44:38-60
D21'68.  1394
Eva. Verse. Howard Moss.
40:30 Ja2'65.  1395
Eve's Eden. Verse.
Katherine Hoskins.
34:28 Ag16'58.  1396
Even egrets err. Verse.
John Updike. 33:74
S7'57.  1397
Even his feet look sad.
PR (Russell). Whitney
Ballett. 38:30-45
Ag11'62.  1398
Even the crocodile and the
hyena. RL. Alan
Moorehead. 42:154-77
O29'66.  1399
Evening. Verse. James
Wright. 33:61*Jy27'57. 1400
The evening of the holiday.
Prose. Shirley Hazzard.
41:44-157 Ap17'65.  1401
An evening with the horse.
OFFC. Joseph Wechsberg.
34:173-91 O25'58.  1402
An evening with Virginia
Woolf. Prose. Evelyn
Irons. 39:115-21
Mr30'63.  1403
The events in May: a Paris
notebook. REF. Mavis
Gallant. 44:58-124 S14'68;
44:54-134 S21'68.  1404
The events of that Easter.
Prose. John Cheever.
35:40-8 My16'59.  1405
Ever let the fancy. Prose.
Nancy Hale. 32:35-8
*Mr31'56.  1406
Ever popular am I, mammoth,
wilt resistant. Verse. E.B.
White. 31:36 Mr26'55.
1407

Evergreen. Verse. Joseph
Langland. 31:34*F18'56. 1408
The everlasting delight. Prose.
Shirley Hazzard. 43:32-7
Ag19'67.                      1409
Every cloud has a silver
lining. Prose. Geoffrey T.
Hellman. 38:26-7 Ja19'63.
                             1410
Every day requires an atlas
and more. Prose. James
McConkey. 41:64-105
D4'65.                       1411
Every dog has his day in
court. Prose. Burton
Bernstein. 36:74-83 Ag20'60.
                             1412
Everything neat and tidy.
Prose. Brian Friel. 40:39-
42 Ap11'64.                  1413
Evidence of affluence. Prose.
Robert Graves. 33:38-42
O12'57.                      1414
Evolution of a mesa. RL.
Daniel Lang. 34:39-63
Je7'58.                      1415
Evolution of a term. OUWA.
Henry Fairlie. 44:173-206
O19'68.                      1416
Evolution of an iron-toed boy.
PR (Barstow). Robert
Lewis Taylor. 33:41-76
Ap20'57; 33:39-65
Ap27'57.                     1417
Exactly eight thousand dollars
exactly. Prose. John
O'Hara. 36:24-6 D31'60.
                             1418
An examination. Prose.
H.L. Mountzoures. 43:28-34
Ja20'68.                     1419
Ex-basketball player. Verse.
John Updike. 33:62 Jy6'57.
                             1420
The executor. Prose. H.L.
Mountzoures. 45:44-7 S20'69.
                             1421
The exegesis of St. Nick.
Prose. Roger Angell. 42:
28-9 D24'66.                 1422
Exorcism. Verse. Robert
Friend. 33:113 My25'57. 1423

Exotic departures. Prose.
Muriel Spark. 42:31-2
Ja28'67.                     1424
Expectation of life. Prose.
Frank O'Connor. 31:20-5
*Ag13'55.                    1425
An expedient--Leonardo da
Vinci's (and a query). Verse.
Marianne Moore. 40:52
Ap18'64.                     1426
The experience of forms. PR
(Moore). Donald Hall.
41:66-141 D11'65;
41:59-151 D18'65.            1427
The expert. Prose. John
Watney. 33:209-16*N30'57.
                             1428
The explanation. Prose.
Donald Barthelme.
44:44-6 My4'68.              1429
Explorers. Verse. Howard
Moss. 35:24 Ja9'60.          1430
Expo. OFFC. E.J. Kahn,
Jr. 43:119-37 Je10'67.       1431
Exposé. Verse. John Updike.
39:40 My25'63.               1432
Exposure. Verse. John
Updike. 38:49 D8'62.         1433
Extravaganza. Verse.
George Starbuck. 42:36
Jy30'66.                     1434
The ex-untouchables. RL.
Harold R. Isaacs. 40:60-
150 D12'64; 40:75-138
D19'64.                      1435
Eyes and no ears; or, the
art of seeing. Prose.
Nancy Hale. 41:52-9
N20'65.                      1436
Eyes of an eagle. Verse.
Vernon Watkins. 40:56
D12'64.                      1437
The eyes of the drowned.
Verse. W.S. Merwin.
32:37*Mr3'56.                1438

F

Façade collapsing. Prose.
Elizabeth Taylor. 38:40-6
My19'62.                     1439
The face. Prose. Virginia

Sorenson. 39:114-30
My25'63.                          1440
A face in the crowd (film).
  TT. 32:42 D1'56.                1441
The face in the mirror. Verse.
  Robert Graves. 32:34 Ja12'57.
                                  1442
The face of the enemy. Prose.
  Montgomery Newman.
  41:132-7 My22'65.               1443
A fact in the fable. Verse.
  Harold Witt. 40:148 Ap18'64.
                                  1444
Fact of crystal. Verse.
  Abbie Huston Evans. 36:40
  Mr19'60.                        1445
Faeseya's Mrs. Scipio. Prose.
  Sonia Rollnick. 34:45-8
  N8'58.                          1446
The failure. Verse. Jackson
  Morris. 31:54*D10'55.           1447
Faint heart. Prose. John van
  Druten. 31:46-50 My7'55.
                                  1448
The fair that was. Prose.
  Frank Zachary. 40:122-9
  Ap11'64.                        1449
Fairbanks, Alas. NFG.
  Philip Hamburger. 42:219-
  28 N5'66.                       1450
Fairground. Verse. W.H.
  Auden. 42:32 Ag20'66.           1451
Fairy story. Verse. Robert
  Penn Warren. 43:123
  Mr18'67.                        1452
The fall. Verse. Howard
  Moss. 40:32 F6'65.              1453
The fall. Prose. V.S.
  Pritchett. 36:35-40
  My28'60.                        1454
The fall. Verse. Alastair
  Reid. 44:106 Je1'68.            1455
Fall. Verse. Jon Swan. 43:
  156 N25'67.                     1456
The fall. Prose. Arturo
  Vivante. 37:22-3 Jy1'61.
                                  1457
Fall classic. Verse. Roger
  Angell. 37:49-51 O14'61.
                                  1458
Fall comes in back-country
  Vermont. Verse. Robert

Penn Warren. 41:56-7
  O23'65.                         1459
Fall of snow. Verse. Katinka
  Loeser. 31:28*Ja14'56.          1460
Falling. Verse. James
  Dickey. 42:38-40 F11'67.
                                  1461
The falling dog. Prose.
  Donald Barthelme. 44:28-9
  Ag3'68.                         1462
Fallout. RL. Daniel Lang.
  31:31-55 Jy16'55.               1463
The falls. Verse.
  F.D. Reeve. 40:64
  D5'64.                          1464
False youth: Winter. Verse.
  James Dickey. 42:44
  F26'66.                         1465
Family. Verse. Josephine
  Miles. 45:36 Ag16'69.           1466
Family evening. Verse.
  Daniel Huws. 34:115 Ap5
  '58.                            1467
A family feud. Prose.
  Winifred Williams. 31:134-
  44*N26'55.                      1468
The family meadow. Prose.
  John Updike. 41:24-5
  Jy24'65.                        1469
The family tree. Verse.
  Laurence Lieberman. 40:52
  D12'64.                         1470
Fan-piece. Verse. Hilary
  Corke. 33:30 D28'57.            1471
A fantasy of little waters.
  Verse. James Scully.
  39:44 N2'63.                    1472
A far cry after a close call.
  Verse. Richard Howard.
  41:107 Jy17'65.                 1473
A far cry from the Corybantes.
  OUWA. J.M. Flagler.
  34:135-63 D6'58.                1474
Farewell: a long farewell to
  figure skating. Prose.
  Robert Henderson.
  31:23-4*Jy30'55.                1475
Farewell to Fargo: selling
  the house. Verse. Karen
  Swenson. 45:54 O18'69. 1476
Farewell to the dacha. Prose.
  Ivy Litvinov. 43:47-54 S16'67.
                                  1477

Farewell to the shopping district
of Antibes. Verse. John
Updike. 39:50 Ap20'63. 1478
A farm in Minnesota. Verse.
Louis Simpson. 37:121 Feel free.
S9'61. 1479
Farmington revisited. OUWA.
Geoffrey T. Hellman.
35:156-72 O31'59. 1480
The fashion show. Prose.
Arturo Vivante. 38:28-31
D22'62. 1481
Father. Verse. Milton
Kaplan. 33:115 Je15'57. 1482
The father. Prose. John
O'Hara. 37:48-9 O28'61.1483
The father and his daughter.
FFT. James Thurber.
32:37*My26'56. 1484
Father father son and son.
Verse. Jon Swan. 42:204
N19'66. 1485
Fathers. Prose. H.L.
Mountzoures. 42:24-6 Ja21'67.
1486
Fatimas and kisses. Prose.
John O'Hara. 42:44-53
My21'66. 1487
Faulkner, William. Janet
Flanner. 38:74 Jy21'62. 1488
Fawcett Publications. TT.
36:36-7 Ap16'60. 1489
The fawn pup. Prose. Brian
Friel. 36:42-6 Ap2'60. 1490
The fear. Verse. Francis
King. 34:81 Jy12'58. 1491
Fear beyond reason. Prose.
Ida Treat. 31:138-59
*N12'55. 1492
Fear of falling. Verse.
Walker Gibson. 32:58
D29'56. 1493
The feast. Verse. Howard
Moss. 35:39 O24'59. 1494
The feather behind the rock.
Prose. Anne Tyler.
43:26-30 Ag12'67. 1495
February. Verse. W.S.
Merwin. 44:32 Ja18'69. 1496
February 22. Verse. John
Updike. 37:40 F18'61.
1497

Fee fi ho hum, no wonder
baby sucks her thumb.
Verse. Ogden Nash.
32:30*Mr24'56. 1498
OFC. John
Bainbridge. 39:105-38
N9'63. 1499
Feel me. Verse. May
Swenson. 44:58 O12'68. 1500
A feeling of intense concen-
tration. PR (Rudel).
Winthrop Sargeant. 38:57-
82 O20'62. 1501
The feet of the Mayor of Clay.
Verse. E.B. White
32:32 S29'56. 1502
Fellini, Federico. PR.
Lillian Ross. 41:63-107
O30'65. 1503
A fellow of infinite jest.
Prose. Wolcott Gibbs.
33:37-40 Ap13'57. 1504
Fellow-American. Prose.
Richard Berczeller. 41:
50-6 S25'65. 1505
Fellow-creatures, Tray and outré.
Verse. Ogden Nash.
33:42 O12'57. 1506
Fence wire. Verse. James
Dickey. 38:36 F24'62. 1507
The ferry to Vermont. Prose.
Donald Stewart. 40:26-7
Ja30'65. 1508
Festival international d'art
dramatique. Janet Flanner.
31:61-4 Jy16'55. 1509
Festivities at the philosophical.
OUWA. Geoffrey T.
Hellman. 35:62-94
Jy18'59. 1510
Feuer, Cy. PR. E.J. Kahn,
Jr. 31:29-47*Ja7'56;
31:33-55*Ja14'56. 1511
A few moments of sleeping
and waking. Prose.
Donald Barthelme. 43:24-6
Ag5'67. 1512
A few puffs on Mr. Su's
pipe. OFFC. Noel F.
Busch. 35:162-72 N28'59.
1513
The fiasco. Prose. Emily

Hahn. 31:89-96 Je18'55.1514
The field glasses. Prose.
  Frederick L. Keefe.
  37:149-56 My6'61.          1515
Field Marshall, retired. Verse.
  Louis O. Coxe. 35:34
  S5'59.                     1516
Fielding, Temple Hornaday.
  PR. John McPhee. 43:32-67
  Ja6'68.                    1517
Fielding's progress. Prose.
  Gilbert Rogin. 39:58-66
  N30'63.                    1518
Fifteen thousand quarts of
  air. RL. Edith Iglauer.
  40:54-117 Mr7'64.          1519
The fifth of November. Prose.
  Sylvia Townsend Warner.
  35:48-51 N14'59.           1520
Fifty-two people on a
  continent. RL. John
  McPhee. 42:101-50  Mr5'66.
                             1521
The fight game. Prose. Scott
  Corbett. 37:156-63 Ap8'61.
                             1522
Figure in an imaginary land-
  scape. PR (Cage). Calvin
  Tomkins. 40:64-128 N28'64.
                             1523
Figures in a garden. Verse.
  Ernest Kroll. 35:160
  Ap4'59.                    1524
Figures of authority. Verse.
  Edward Watkins. 36:62
  D3'60.                     1525
The figures on the frieze.
  Verse. Alastair Reid.
  38:32 F9'63.               1526
Filling station. Verse.
  Elizabeth Bishop. 31:48
  *D10'55.                   1527
The film club. TT.
  43:19-21 Ja13'68.          1528
Film festival at Lincoln Center
  (Parody). Roger Angell.
  40:42-3 S26'64.            1529
The final fate of the
  alligators. Prose. Edward
  Hoagland. O18'69.
                             1530
A final report. Prose. William

Maxwell. 39:37-43
  Mr9'63.                    1531
Finders keepers. Verse.
  Albert Newgarden. 31:128
  My7'55.                    1532
Finding by the referee. Prose.
  Jeffrey Potter. 40:204-16
  N7'64.                     1533
A fine old gentleman. Prose.
  Ken Kraft. 33:63-9*Jy
  20'57.                     1534
Fingers in the nesting box.
  Verse. Robert Graves.
  34:104 Mr29'58.            1535
The fipple flute. Prose.
  Robert Henderson.
  43:44-7 Ap22'67.           1536
The fire balloons 1906.
  Verse. David McCord.
  31:27*Jy2'55.              1537
The fire fountain. Verse.
  Howard Moss. 37:52
  D16'61.                    1538
Fire Island walking song.
  Verse. E.F.K. 33:53
  Ag31'57.                   1539
A fire truck. Verse.
  Richard Wilbur. 34:44
  O25'58.                    1540
Fireflies. Verse. Ernest
  Kroll. 32:61*Jy28'56.      1541
The fireflies. Prose.
  St. Clair McKelway.
  37:32-6 F3'62.             1542
Firelight and lamp.
  Verse. Gene Baro.
  38:104 F24'62.             1543
The fires of Olympus.
  Prose. Charles Bracelen
  Flood. 36:139-42
  Ap2'60.                    1544
Fireworks. Verse. Babette
  Deutsch. 38:48 O20'62. 1545
Fireworks. Verse. John
  Updike. 40:28 Jy4'64.      1546
A firm word or two. Prose.
  Nathaniel Benchley. 34:24-
  30 Ja31'59.                1547
First boat to King Island.
  OFFC. Berton Roueché. 42:
  98-139 O22'66.             1548
First dark. Prose. Elizabeth

Spencer. 35:31-40
Je20'59.                              1549
The first day of school. Prose.
Nancy Hale. 31:32-5
F19'55.                               1550
First death in Nova Scotia.
Verse. Elizabeth Bishop.
38:36 Mr10'62.                        1551
The first editions of T.J.
Wise. AC. Dwight
Macdonald. 38:168-205
N10'62.                               1552
The first kiss. Prose. Arturo
Vivante. 38:84-9 Ja12'63.
                                      1553
First love and other sorrows.
Prose. Harold Brodkey. 33:
32-69 Je15'57.                        1554
First marriage. Prose. St.
Clair McKelway. 36:36-9
Ap2'60.                               1555
The first rain of Spring. Verse.
Maxine W. Kumin. 35:30
Mr28'59.                              1556
First reader. Verse. Paris
Leary. 38:40 Ap21'62.      1557
First snow. Prose. Nathaniel
Benchley. 41:194-8
N20'65.                               1558
First things first. Verse.
W.H. Auden. 33:38
Mr9'57.                               1559
Fish. Verse. Emily
Townsend. 35:113 F21'59.
                                      1560
Fish for Friday. Prose. Frank
O'Connor. 31:23-9 Je18'55.
                                      1561
The fisher. Verse. Lyle
Glazier. 32:117*Je2'56. 1562
Fisherman . Verse. Peter
Kane Dufault. 41:203
My15'65.                              1563
The fisherman's gift. Verse.
Beverly Baff Quint. 38:138
O20'62.                               1564
Fisherman's terrace. Prose.
Arturo Vivante. 37:38-41
S30'61.                               1565
The fisherman's wife. Verse.
David Wagoner. 45:30
Ag23'69.                              1566

The fishermen. Verse. W.S.
Merwin. 31:32*Ja28'56.
                                      1567
The fishing lake. Prose.
Elizabeth Spencer. 40:24-5
Ag29'64.                              1568
Fissures of men. Verse.
W.W. Watt. 36:30
Jy2'60.                               1569
Fists across the sea. Prose.
Nancy Hale. 35:36-8
Ja16'60.                              1570
Fitzgerald, F. Scott.
Geoffrey T. Hellman.
33:28-31 Mr9'57.           1571
Fitzgerald, F. Scott.
Andrew Turnbull. 32:92-
103*Ap7'56; 32:153-65
N17'56.                               1572
Fitzgerald, F. Scott.
Edmund Wilson. 34:115-24
Ja24'59.                              1573
Fitzgerald, Robert
(Apology to). TT.
33:23 Mr2'57.                         1574
Five birds rise. Verse.
William Hayward.
38:42 D15'62.                         1575
Five horses. Verse. May
Swenson. 44:54 N2'68.      1576
Five little biceps and how
they flew. Prose. S.J.
Perelman. 44:53-4 O19'68.
                                      1577
Five minutes before sleep.
Prose. William Wertenbaker.
39:28-9 Je15'63.                      1578
Five poems. Verse. W.S.
Merwin. 45:62-3 N15'69.
                                      1579
Five poems. Verse. J.D.
Reed. 45:38 Jy12'69.       1580
Five poems. Verse. Karl
Shapiro.    43:38 Ag12'67.
                                      1581
Five poems. Verse. William
Walden. 40:52 Ap25'64.
                                      1582
Five poems. Verse. Ted
Walker. 40:56-7 O3'64. 1583
Five-ten on a sticky June day.
RL. John Brooks.

31:39-75 My28'55.        1584
A fixture. Verse. May
Swenson. 35:132 N14'59.
                         1585
Flagpole. Verse. Hayden
Carruth. 33:74 Ja18'58.
                         1586
Flanders, Michael. TT.
35:45-6 D12'59.          1587
The flatted saxophone. Prose.
John O'Hara. 39:28-9
Je1'63.                  1588
Flatten your wallet--high style
ahead. Prose. S.J.
Perelman. 41:34-6 F20'65.
                         1589
Flea dance. Verse. Frederick
Bock. 44:28 Je22'68.     1590
Fledglings. Verse. William
Meredith. 45:40 My10'69.
                         1591
Flee on your donkey. Verse.
Anne Sexton. 42:44-5
My7'66.                  1592
Fleischmann, Raoul (Obituary).
45:27-8 My17'69.         1593
Fleming, Ian. TT.
38:32-4 Ap21'62.         1594
Flight. Verse. Barbara
Howes. 41:28 Jy10'65.    1595
Flight. Prose. John Updike.
35:30-7 Ag22'59.         1596
The flight of crook-taloned
birds. OUWA. Ved Mehta.
38:59-147 D8'62; 38:47-
129 D15'62.              1597
A flock of guinea hens seen
from a car. Verse. Eudora
Welty. 33:35 Ap20'57.    1598
A floral tribute. Prose.
Frank Tuohy. 41:40-4 Ap10'65.
                         1599
Florida. Verse. Howard
Moss. 34:26 Ja31'59.     1600
Flotsam. Prose. Nancy Hale.
35:32-8 S5'59.           1601
The flower gully. Prose.
Berry Morgan. 44:35-7
Ag24'68.                 1602
Flowers. Verse. Gene Baro.
37:193 O14'61.           1603
Flowers in crannied Wall

Street. Verse. W.W.
Watt. 38:38 Mr31'62.     1604
The flowers of sorrow.
Prose. Shirley Hazzard.
40:52-4 O17'64.          1605
The fluctuation. AF. John
Brooks. 39:35-55
Ag31'63.                 1606
Flute solo with figured bass.
Prose. Mina Lewiton Simon.
39:44-7 Mr9'63.          1607
Fly in December. Verse.
Robert A. Wallace.
41:190 D18'65.           1608
Fly Trans-love Airways.
RL. Renata Adler.
43:116-31 F25'67.        1609
Flying home from Utah. Verse.
May Swenson. 41:50
My15'65.                 1610
A flying start. Prose. Sylvia
Townsend Warner. 39:40-1
Ap20'63.                 1611
The foal of Medusa. Verse.
Martha Keller. 33:44
S28'57.                  1612
Fog. Verse. David Galler.
36:119 Mr5'60.           1613
Foghorn. Verse. W.S.
Merwin 34:99 My24'58.    1614
The foghorn. Prose. Arturo
Vivante. 34:58-9
Ag2'58.                  1615
Folk songs from the oblivian.
Verse. William Walden.
38:40 Ap28'62.           1616
The foolhardy mouse and the
cautious cat. FFT. James
Thurber. 32:38-9*My12'56.
                         1617
For a gentleman of fortune.
Prose. H.F. Ellis. 37:22-4
D30'61.                  1618
For an old friend. Verse.
Barbara Howes. 43:139
S9'67.                   1619
For Benny * * * much loved.
Prose. Roy Bongartz.
39:38-46 S14'63.         1620
For Epiphany. Verse. Robert
Fitzgerald. 42:77
Ja7'67.                  1621

For God, country, Yale, and
Garden. PR (Kilpatrick).
E. J. Kahn, Jr. 31:35-51
*Ja28'56. 1622
For Guillaume Apollinaire.
Verse. William Meredith.
39:140 Ap13'63. 1623
For my lover, returning to
his wife. Verse. Anne
Sexton. 43:91 F3'68. 1624
For Nicholas, born in September.
Verse. Tom Perry. 38:44
S29'62. 1625
For ring-givers. Verse.
Alastair Reid. 32:108 F9'57.
1626
For sale at auction. Prose.
Carlton Lake. 31:134-53
*N5'55. 1627
For spacious skies and ample
waves of green. Prose.
Calvin Trillin. 39:24-5
Ja4'64. 1628
For the bride. Verse.
Kathleen Raine. 44:34
Ag17'68. 1629
For the marsh's birthday.
Verse. James Wright. 41:71
Jy10'65. 1630
For the nightly ascent of the
hunter Orion over a forest
clearing. Verse. James
Dickey. 37:58 D2'61. 1631
For whom the bell doesn't toll.
Prose. Thomas Meehan.
43:47-9 Mr18'67. 1632
For worse is better and sick-
ness is in health. Prose.
Calvin Trillin. 45:53-6
N22'69. 1633
A forager. PR(Gibbons).
John McPhee. 44:45-104
Ap6'68. 1634
Forecast. Verse. Howard
Nemerov 31:38*F11'56. 1635
Foreign affairs. Verse.
Stanley Kunitz. 34:47 Mr15'58.
1636
Forest. Verse. Mary Swenson.
33:30 Ag24'57. 1637
Forest murmurs. Verse. R.P.
Lister. 36:99 F27'60. 1638

Forever painting. Prose.
Peter DeVries. 39:169-75
S28'63. 1639
The forgery of art. RL.
Richard Harris. 37:112-45
S16'61. 1640
Forster, Edward Morgan.
PR. Mollie Panter-Downes.
35:51-86 S19'59. 1641
Fort Wayne, Ind. NFG.
Philip Hamburger.
35:104-107 O3'59. 1642
The fortress. Verse. Anne
Sexton. 38:44 S22'62. 1643
Fortune. Verse. Jon Swan.
45:30 Ja10'70. 1644
Forward six, balance six,
side gents do-si-do. PR
(Keeler). Robert Lewis
Taylor. 32:39-69
F9'57. 1645
No entry. 1646
Forty. Verse. Donald
Stewart. 41:160 Ap10'65.1647
The fossils. Verse. Galway
Kinnell. 41:58 O16'65. 1648
Foundation. PR (Ford Founda-
tion). Dwight Macdonald.
31:57-89*N26'55; 31:55-103
*D3'55;31:57-95*D10'55;
31:40-69*D17'55. 1649
Foundry house. Prose. Brian
Friel. 37:50-7 N18'61. 1650
Four academic fantasies.
Prose.Noel Perrin. 41:205-14.
D4'65. 1651
Four dialogues. Prose.
Niccolò Tucci. 38:34-6
Ag18'62. 1652
Four for the T-bird. Prose.
Roger Angell. 34:28-30
Mr29'58. 1653
Four hours by rail from
Jakarta. OFFC. Christopher
Rand. 31:39-78 Je11'55.
1654
Four hundred and forty vibra-
tions. Pr (Allers).
Joseph Wechsberg. 36:47-80
Ap2'60. 1655
Four hundred and twenty. Prose.
Ved Mehta. 39:56-62 D7'63.
1656

The frog grass problem.
Prose. Faith McNulty. 35:130-
3 My16'59.                 1691
Frog week at the 7-11, near
West Hollywood. Prose.
F.P. Tullius. 43:40-2
S9'67.                     1692
From an observation tower.
Verse. Lisel Mueller. 36:42
Ap16'60.                   1693
From an offshore island.
Verse. Abbie Huston Evans.
36:40 S24'60.              1694
From backwoods to bois. WP.
E.J. Kahn, Jr. 32:52-7
Je30'56.                   1695
From Canto CXIII. Verse.
Ezra Pound. 44:64 N30'68.
                           1696
From dance cards to the ivy-
league look. OUWA. John
Brooks. 33:76-103 My18'57.
                           1697
From morning-glory to
Petersburg. Verse. Adrienne
Cecile Rich. 33:34 Jy13'57.
                           1698
From St. George's day. Prose.
Al Newman. 35:96-101 Mr7'59.
                           1699
From sassafras branches. PR
(Stone). Winthrop Sargeant.
34:32-49 Ja3'59.           1700
From the sweet to the bitter.
OFFC. Christopher Rand.
31:100-15 F19'55.          1701
From the window down. Verse.
Louis O: Coxe. 32:20*Jy
14'56.                     1702
From under the hill of night.
Verse. Paul Petrie. 41:30
Ja8'66.                    1703
Front Street. Verse. Howard
Moss. 42:26 Jy2'66.        1704
The frontier. Verse. Hilary
Corke. 32:30 F2'57.        1705
The frosting's on the dry goods,
the customer's in shock.
Prose. S.J.Perelman. 32:
29-31 O20'56.              1706
Frueh, Alfred (Obituary).
44:184 S28'68.             1707

The fruit of the tree. Verse.
David Wagoner. 40:34
Ag22'64.                   1708
Fry, Christopher (Parody).
Patricia Collinge. 32:46
D8'56.                     1709
Fuchs, Daniel. Howard Moss.
37:231-42 N11'61.          1710
Fugue in three voices.
Prose. Mina Lewiton Simon.
42:133-48 O1'66.           1711
The full impact of parting.
Prose. Mohamed
Mehdevi. 31:23-8*Ja7'56.
                           1712
Full text. Prose. St. Clair
McKelway. 37:24-5
Ja20'62.                   1713
The full-length portrait.
Prose. Donald Windham.
36:39-43 My14'60.          1714
The fundament is shifted.
Verse. Abbie Huston
Evans. 36:56 N5'60.        1715
Funeral of a slave. Prose.
Bowen Ingram. 34:40-4
My10'58.                   1716
A funny thing happened...
Prose. Nathaniel Benchley.
41:78-83 Ja15'66.          1717
The furnace of colors.
Verse. Vernon Watkins.
38:28 Jy28'62.             1718
Furniture. Verse. Phyllis
Harris. 43:34 F3'68.       1719
Furnivall's hoopoe. Prose.
Sylvia Townsend Warner.
45:28-31 Ja3'70.           1720
Further notes on Fitzgerald
at La Paix. Prose.
Andrew W. Turnbull.
32:153-65 N17'56.          1721
Further tales about men
and women. Prose.
William Maxwell.
41:22-7 Ag7'65; 41:50-4
O16'65; 41:51-6 N13'65;
41:54-60 D11'65; 41:26-33
D25'65.                    1722
The fury. PR (Sahl). Robert
Rice. 36:31-53 Jy30'60.
                           1723

G

The gallery. Verse. Barbara
Howes. 34:32 Ap5'58.          1724
The galvanized-iron roof. RL.
Alan Moorehead. 38:37-55
S1'62.          1725
The gambler. Prose. John
O'Hara. 41:40-2 My1'65.
1726
The gamblers--Cape Town.
Verse. Anthony Delius. 34:
116 Je14'58.          1727
Game. Prose. Donald
Barthelme. 41:29-30 Jy31'65.
1728
A game of chess. Prose. Gifford
Brown. 41:37-46 Je12'65.
1729
A game of glass: Spain. Verse.
Alastair Reid. 31:30
Ap23'55.          1730
A game on a hill. OFFC.
John Hersey. 33:57-90
D7'57.          1731
Game resumed. Verse.
Richmond Lattimore. 39:145
My11'63.          1732
Games. Prose. Howard Webber
39:42-6 Mr30'63.          1733
Garden: before snowfall. Verse.
John Fandel. 34:159
O4'58.          1734
A garden of flowers. Prose.
George H. Freitag.
45:28-30 F7'70.          1735
The garden snail. Verse.
Robert A. Wallace. 32:92
*S8'56.          1736
The gardener. Verse. John
Hall Wheelock. 33:29*Jy27
'57.          1737
The gardener outside a college
window. Verse. Barbara
Gibbs. 32:138 N24'56.          1738
The gardens of Mont-Saint-
Michel. Prose. William
Maxwell. 45:30-9 Ag9'69.
1739
Garland for the Winter solstice.
Verse. Ruthven Todd.
31:34*D17'55.          1740

Garrison. RL. Edward Jay
Epstein. 44:35-81
Jy13'68.          1741
Gather. Verse. Michael
Dennis Browne. 45:44 My10
'69.          1742
Gather ye rosebuds, but
watch ye step. Prose.
S.J. Perelman. 36:24-6
Ja7'61.          1743
The gauger. Prose. Walter
Macken. 31:22-5*F4'56. 1744
Gelber, Jack. TT. 36:24-5
Jy9'60.          1745
The general manager. PR
(Bing). Joseph Wechsberg.
42:65-124 S17'66.          1746
The general's wife. Prose.
Sonia Rollnick. 34:35-40
Mr22'58.          1747
Geneva. Verse. Alastair Reid.
39:30 Ja25'64.          1748
Gentian. Prose. Donald
Windham. 38:53-8 N17'62.
1749
The gentile Jewesses. Prose.
Muriel Spark. 39:31-4
Je22'63.          1750
Gentle gardener. Verse.
Jean Sewell Standish. 31:
62 Jy9'55.          1751
Gentle lamb. Verse. Arthur
Gregor. 42:78 Ja28'67. 1752
The gentle yes. Verse.
Paul Squires. 31:81
*F4'56.          1753
The gentleman in the pink-and-
white striped shirt. Prose.
Maeve Brennan. 31:40-4
My7'55.          1754
The gentlemanly junket. RL.
John Brooks. 45:97-138
Ap26'69.          1755
Gentles all. OUWA. J. M.
Flagler. 33:56-70 Ag31'57.
1756
Geography: a song. Verse.
Howard Moss. 43:34
Ja20'68.          1757
Gerdy, Robert S. (Obituary).
41:112 Ja8'66.          1758
Getaway. Prose. Robert M.

Giving blood. Prose. John
Updike. 39:36-41 Ap6'63.
1796
Glade walker. Verse. John
Clarke. 45:38 Ja31'70. 1797
A glare into the future. Prose.
F.P. Tullius. 40:24-5
Jy11'64.                   1798
The glass blower. Verse.
James Scully. 37:26 Ja13'62.
1799
Glass world. Verse. Dorothy
Donnelly. 36:155 Mr12'60.
1800
Glasses. Verse. John Updike.
33:139 Ap20'57.            1801
The glimpse of pathos. Prose.
Albert Hubbell. 37:63-8 D2
'61.                       1802
Glimpse of three children on
a picnic. Verse. Peter
Kane Dufault. 32:28*Je23'56.
1803
Gloria. Prose. Roy Bongartz.
39:42-70 Mr23'63.         1804
Glory,. Verse. Marianne
Moore. 36:37 Ag13'60. 1805
The glove. Verse. Harold
Bond. 43:60 N4'67.        1806
Glove and palette. PR (Walker).
Robert Lewis Taylor.
31:57-84*N12'55.          1807
Go be insulted when a fella
hands you a compliment!
Prose. Arthur Kober.
32:20-2 D29'56.           1808
Go it, tortoise. Prose. Robert
Henderson. 39:39-40 S28'63.
1809
Go where glory waits thee.
Prose. Frank O'Connor.
36:35-77 Mr26'60.         1810
God bless the Gideons. Verse.
Ogden Nash. 43:30 Jy1'67.
1811
God writes a bad hand. Prose.
J.F. Powers. 36:44-68
O15'60.                   1812
Godard, Jean-Luc. TT.
41:43-6 O9'65.            1813
Godchildren. Verse. William
Meredith. 32:134 F16'57.
1814

Gods: Jocotepec, Mexico.
Verse. Lysander Kemp.
31:114*S10'55.            1815
Going home, 1945. Verse.
L.E. Sissman. 43:31-3
Je24'67.                  1816
Going to sleep in the
country. Verse. Howard
Moss. 37:42 My13'61.      1817
Going to the bakery. Verse.
Elizabeth Bishop. 44:40
Mr23'68.                  1818
The gold in the sea. Prose.
Brian Friel. 41:32-7
Jy31'65.                  1819
Gold standard on the booze.
AF. John Brooks. 45:107-
26 S13'69.                1820
The golden age. Prose.
John Cheever. 35:46-50
S26'59.                   1821
The golden fan. Verse.
Gillian Stone. 41:42
Ap3'65.                   1822
A golden legend. Prose.
Sylvia Townsend Warner.
33:28-30 F8'58.           1823
The golden lily. Verse.
E.N. Sargent. 44:128
My25'68.                  1824
Golden-voiced on the lobby
floor. Prose. Noel Perrin.
35:109-16 Je13'59.        1825
The goldfish wife. Verse.
Sandra Hochman. 43:128
O21'67.                   1826
Golgotha. Verse. X.J.
Kennedy. 44:58 N9'68.  1827
Good deed. Prose. Mavis
Gallant. 45:35-41 F22'69.
1828
Gomillion vs. Lightfoot.
RL. Bernard Taper.
37:37-93 Je10'61;
37:39-77 Je17'61.         1829
"Gone with the wind," maybe.
Lillian Ross. Prose.
36:47-50 N19'60.          1830
The good children. Prose.
Katinka Loeser. 38:33-4
Ag4'62.                   1831
The good earth. Prose. John
Sack. 35:23-4 Jy4'59.  1832

A good example. Prose.
Calvin Kentfield. 34:29-56
Ag30'58. 1833
The good humor man. Prose.
Rebecca Morris. 43:29-36
Je17'67. 1834
A good light. Prose. Nancy
Hale. 44:100-20 S28'68.
1835
A good location. Prose. John
O'Hara. 41:29-31 S4'65. 1836
Good manners and common
sense. PR (Duke). E.J.
Kahn, Jr. 40:34-83 Ag15'64.
1837
The good news. Prose. Mitsu
Yamamoto. 33:209-22
N23'57. 1838
Good of you to do this for us,
Mr. Truman. RL. Philip
Hamburger. 31:120-39
*N19'55. 1839
A good old message like the
golden rule. Prose. Calvin
Kentfield. 32:30-7
F9'57. 1840
Good speed for southward
voyagers. Verse. Richmond
Lattimore. 31:28 Je25'55.
1841
Goodbye, Ady, goodbye, Joe.
Prose. Amy Witting. 41:51-8
N6'65. 1842
The goodbye land. Prose.
Jose Yglesias. 43:51-118
Mr18'67; 43:48-114
Mr25'67. 1843
Goodbye, Mr. McCollum!
Prose. E.J. Kahn, Jr.
32:78-80 Ja26'57. 1844
Goodbye to Regal. Verse.
Daniel Huws. 37:30 Jy15'61.
1845
Goodbye to serpents. Verse.
James Dickey. 39:47
S21'63. 1846
Goodness is as goodness does.
Prose. Stewart Johnson.
36:38-41 Mr19'60. 1847
The goodnight. Verse. Louis
Simpson. 34:38 Ja24'59.
1848

The goof-offs. Prose. George
J.W. Goodman. 31:76-8
Je25'55. 1849
The goose pits. Prose.
Vance Bourjaily. 37:58-92
N25'61. 1850
The goose that laid the gilded
egg. FFT. James Thurber.
32:18-19*Jy7'56. 1851
Gorey, Edward. Edmund
Wilson. 35:60-6 D26'59.
1852
The Gossage-Vardebedian
papers. Prose. Woody
Allen. 41:26-8 Ja22'66. 1853
Gottmann, Jean. TT.
37:52-4 D2'61. 1854
Gourmandise. Verse.
Norman Mailer. 37:107
S16'61. 1855
The governess. Prose.
Francine du Plessix Gray.
42:28-45 Ja14'67. 1856
The government and the people.
OFFC. E.J. Kahn, Jr.
36:104-24 O15'60. 1857
The grace of the moment. PR
(Szell). Joseph Wechsberg.
41:59-112 N6'65. 1858
A grackle observed. Verse.
Lisel Mueller. 34:103 S20
'58. 1859
"The graduate." OUWA.
Jacob Brackman. 44:34-66
Jy27'68. 1860
Grammar. TT. 33:23-4
F23'57. 1861
Grandfather and the cold
year. Prose. Samuel
Hopkins Adams. 32:88-103
*My19'56. 1862
Grandfather and the turnout.
Prose. Samuel Hopkins
Adams. 31:153-63 My14'55.
1863
The grandson. Verse. James
Scully. 43:42 My20'67. 1864
Granite and steel. Verse.
Marianne Moore. 42:32
Jy9'66. 1865
Granville-Barker, Harley.
S.N. Behrman and

Max Beerbohm. 36:97-
108 Mr5'60.                      1866
Grass. Verse. Ted Walker.
44:65 Je29'68.                   1867
The grasses are cut down.
Verse. Norma Farber.
35:40 S26'59.                    1868
Grasset publishing house.
Janet Flanner. 42:65-6
D31'66.                          1869
A grasshopper. Verse.
Richard Wilbur. 34:34 Ag22'59.
                                 1870
The great bear. Verse. John
Hollander. 33:30 F1'58.
                                 1871
The great bird barbecue of
Cousin Canal. Prose.
Antonio Barolini. 33:93-107
S7'57.                           1872
Great Britain. Verse.
R.P. Lister. 41:61 D25'65.
                                 1873
Great Central Railway, Sheffield
Victoria to Banbury. Verse.
John Betjeman. 38:34
Mr31'62.                         1874
A great god's angel standing.
Prose. Benedict Kiely.
44:28-34 Ag24'68.                1875
A great green cloud. PR
(American elm). Berton
Roueché. 37:35-53
Jy15'61.                         1876
The great healer. Verse.
Walker Gibson. 32:73
D15'56.                          1877
A great man. Prose.
Frank O'Connor. 34:34-8
My10'58.                         1878
Great oafs from little monsters
grow. Prose. S.J.
Perelman. 40:44-6 My16'64.
                                 1879
The great scarf of birds.
Verse. John Updike.
38:52 O27'62.                    1880
Great simplicity. PR (Suzuki).
Winthrop Sargeant. 33:34-53
Ag31'57.                         1881
The great starch debate. Prose.
Roger Angell. 38:36-8
My19'62.                         1882

The great state. RL.
A.J. Liebling. 36:41-91
My28'60; 36:48-94
Je4'60; 36:95-135
Je11'60.                         1883
The great wave. Prose.
Mary Lavin. 35:28-37
Je13'59.                         1884
A great wondering goony
bird. Prose. Calvin
Kentfield. 36:39-46
Mr5'60.                          1885
Great-and-a-half champion.
RL. A.J. Liebling.
31:86-98 Mr12'55.                1886
The greater the lie, the
sooner is it found out.
Verse. Robert David
Cohen. 42:32 Ag27'66.            1887
Grecian calendar. RL.
Christopher Rand. 38:32-
63 Jy7'62; 38:39-59
Jy14'62; 38:40-63
Jy21'62.                         1888
The Greeks had a word for
it, so why speak English?
Verse. Ogden Nash.
31:46*S24'55.                    1889
The green and the black.
Verse. Anthony Bailey./
32:56 N24'56.                    1890
Green as the vice at Humpty
Doo. Verse. R.P. Lister.
34:116 Ap19'58.                  1891
The green banana. Prose.
J.F. Powers. 32:48-58
*N10'56.                         1892
The green berets (film).
TT. 44:24-7 Je29'68.             1893
Green girls. Verse.
Harvena Richter. 33:32
Je29'57.                         1894
Green grass, blue sky,
white house. Prose.
Wright Morris. 45:56-62
O25'69.                          1895
The green shepherd. Verse.
Louis Simpson. 32:36
O20'56.                          1896
Green song. Verse. May
Sarton. 32:50*Ag11'56.           1897
The green tree grows. Verse.
R.P. Lister. 34:87 Ag16'58.
                                 1898

Green water, green sky.
Prose. Mavis Gallant.
35:22-9 Je27'59.          1899
Greetings, friends! Verse.
Frank Sullivan.    31:23*D24'55;
32:20*D22'56; 33:27 D21'57;
34:21 D27'58; 35:22 D26'59;
36:27 D24'60; 37:24 D23'61;
38:33 D22'62; 39:30 D21'63;
40:29 D26'64; 41:25 D25'65;
42:31 D24'66; 43:27 D23'67;
44:33 D21'68; 45:27 D27'69.
                         1900
No entry                 1901
The gregarious age. Verse.
Robert Hillyer. 33:101
F8'58.                   1902
The grizzly and the gadgets.
FFT. James Thurber.
32:18*Jy7'56.            1903
Growing, flying, happening.
Verse. Alastair Reid.
34:34 My24'58.           1904
Growth with truth. Prose.
Molly Ramshaw. 34:90-5
Mr1'58.                  1905
The guest. Prose. Esther
Evarts. 31:49-52*Jy30'55.
                         1906
Guests. Prose. Peter
Taylor. 35:48-92 O3'59.1907
Guests on a Winter night.
Prose. Isaac Bashevis
Singer. Dorothea Straus,
trans. 45:31-8 Ja24'70.
                         1908
Gunbar Downs. Prose.
Alwyn Lee. 33:32-8 F8'58.
                         1909
Gunther, John. John
Lardner. 35:166-7 O24'59.
                         1910
The gypsy moth. Verse. Stephen
Berg. 35:54 N28'59.      1911

                 H

The habit. Prose. John
Cheever. 40:45-7
Mr7'64.                  1912
The habits of childhood.
Verse. Maxine W. Kumin.
37:65 Jy22'61.           1913

Haiku. TT. 34:24-5
Ja10'59.                 1914
Hail to the chief, at two-
thirds off. Prose. S.J.
Perelman. 38:38-40
S15'62.                  1915
The haircut. Prose. Ted
Walker. 43:50-4 S23'67.
                         1916
Half out of our tree. REF.
Richard H. Rovere. 43:60-
100 O28'67.              1917
Half-bent man. Verse.
Richard Eberhart. 34:38
Je7'58.                  1918
Hamilton, Edith. TT.
33:36-7 My11'57.         1919
Handicapped children
swimming. Verse. Michael
Dennis Browne. 43:36
Jy22'67.                 1920
The handkerchiefs of Khaibar
Khan. Verse. John Updike.
37:172 N25'61.           1921
Hanged ancestors. Prose.
Christopher Hollis.
33:146-53 D14'57.        1922
Hanging on. Prose. Frank
Conroy. 42:58-63
D10'66.                  1923
Hanna. Prose. Kenneth
Lamott. 35:52-8 N14'59.
                         1924
Hansberry, Lorraine. TT.
35:33-5 My9'59.          1925
The happiest I've been.
Prose. John Updike.
34:24-31 Ja3'59.         1926
Happiness. Prose. Mary
Lavin. 44:60-7 D14'68.   1927
Happiness. Prose. Sylvia
Townsend Warner.
38:24-7 Ag18'62.         1928
Happiness of 6 a.m. Verse
Harvey Shapiro. 45:134
My17'69.                 1929
The happy ending. Prose.
Sylva Grossman. 31:
120-37*D10'55.           1930
The happy hour. Prose.
Robert M. Coates. 33:
44-8 O12'57.             1931

The happy Indian laughter.
Prose. Oliver LaFarge.
31:20-6*Ag6'55.          1932
The happy venture. PR
(Bullock). John Brooks.
34:47-83 Mr8'58.         1933
Hapworth 16, 1924. Prose.
J.D. Salinger. 41:32-113
Je19'65.                 1934
Hare Park. Prose Elizabeth
Taylor. 32:35-9*Ap14'56.
                         1935
Hark, hark, the bark. Verse.
Morris Bishop. 34:96
Mr22'58.                 1936
Hark the Herald Tribune,
Times, W.O.R., and all
other angels sing! Prose.
James Thurber. 32:40-1
*Ap14'56.                1937
Hark! Whence came those
pear-shaped drones? Prose.
S.J. Perelman. 45:46-8
N1'69.                   1938
The Harkness Pavilion. Verse.
Barbara Howes.
45:48 N1'69.             1939
The harmonies of heaven.
OUWA. Suyin Han. 39:38-51
D28'63.                  1940
Harmony. Prose. William
Fain. 31:31-40 Ap9'55.   1941
Harold. Prose. Shirley
Hazzard. 38:46-9 O13'62.
                         1942
Harper's Bazaar (Magazine).
Geoffrey T. Hellman. 31:29
Ap30'55.                 1943
The harpooning. Verse. Ted
Walker. 45:42 O4'69.     1944
Harris, Frank. S.N. Behrman
and Max Beerbohm.
36:55-61 F27'60.         1945
Harris, George Washington.
Edmund Wilson. 31:150-9
My7'55.                  1946
The harsh country. Verse.
Theodore Roethke. 35:39
Ap18'59.                 1947
Hart, Moss. TT. 31:29
Ap2'55.                  1948
Harv is plowing now. Prose.

John Updike. 42:46-8
Ap23'66.                 1949
Harvard Square. Verse.
Robert A. Brooks. 41:54
N13'65.                  1950
Harvest. Verse. Andrew
Oerke. 32:48 O13'56.     1951
Harvest. Verse. Eda Lou
Walton. 35:47 N28'59.    1952
Has anybody seen Miss
Dora Dean? Prose.
Ann Petry. 34:41-8 O25'58.
                         1953
Hastily, R. Prose. James
Reid Parker. 31:63-5
*Ja7'56.                 1954
Hastings and prairie. RL.
Robert Shaplen. 42:129-
93 D17'66.               1955
Hat bar. Verse. Mildred
Weston. 32:138 D15'56.
                         1956
The hats of overgrown gnomes.
Prose. St. Clair
McKelway. 35:28-30
Mr7'59.                  1957
A haunting. Prose. Nancy
Hale. 33:44-8 O26'57.    1958
Hauptmann, Gerhart. S.N.
Behrman and Max
Beerbohm. 36:60-1
Mr12'60.                 1959
Having one wonderful time.
WP. E.J. Kahn, Jr.
33:94-106 My25'57.       1960
Hawk on the roadside. Verse.
Andrew Oerke. 34:97
F14'59.                  1961
The hawk's victim. Verse.
Ruthven Todd. 32:86
F2'57.                   1962
Hayes, Joseph. TT.
31:26-7 Mr5'55.          1963
The headmaster. PR (Boy-
den). John McPhee. 42:
57-159 Mr19'66.          1964
Heads I trim, frails you
lose. Prose. S.J. Perel-
man. 43:38-40 F25'67.    1965
Heads of houses. Prose.
Peter Taylor. 35:52-89
S12'59.                  1966

Healthy landscape with dor-
mouse. Prose. Sylvia
Townsend Warner. 38:30-6
S1'62.                          1967
Hearst, William Randolph, Jr.
A.J. Liebling. 31:64-75
F26'55.                         1968
Heart. Prose. Peter DeVries.
37:46-9 N18'61.                 1969
Heart of darkness. Prose.
F.P. Tullius. 41:125-6
F27'65.                         1970
Heart of gold. Prose. Mary
Lavin. 40:29-38 Je27'64.
                                1971
Hearth. Verse. Maxine W.
Kumin. 37:232 N25'61.           1972
The heart-shaped frame. Prose.
Robert Henderson. 31:32-6
Mr5'55.                         1973
Heat yeggs in vessel and sprinkle
with hazard. Prose. S.J.
Perelman. 32:38-41*S15'56.
                                1974
The heaven of animals. Verse.
James Dickey. 37:48
N18'61.                         1975
Heavy parent. Prose.
Emily Hahn. 38:165-73 My5'62.
                                1976
Hector the dog. Verse.
Kate Barnes. 37:155 Ap8'61.
                                1977
Hedge life. Verse. James
Dickey. 41:34 S4'65.            1978
The hedgerows in England.
Prose. Ruth Stone. 38:127-41
Mr17'62.                        1979
Heirloom for a ranch house.
Prose. Jean Fritz. 33:106-13.
O26'57.                         1980
Hellas bent. Verse. Felicia
Lamport. 40:81 Ag8'64.
                                1981
Hell-diver. Verse. Conrad
Hilberry. 35:79 Ap11'59.
                                1982
Hello, Central, give me that
jolly old pelf. Prose.
S.J. Perelman. 39:27-9
D21'63.                         1983
Hello great people! Prose.
Roy Bongartz. 38:24-30

Jy28'62.                        1984
Help! Prose. Geoffrey T.
Hellman. 37:50-9 S2'61.
                                1985
Help! Help! My son the
doctor is drowning! Prose.
Lillian Ross. 37:31-9 Ap
1'61.                           1986
Hemingway, Ernest. Mary
Hemingway. 39:160-3
Mr16'63.                        1987
Henley, July 4: 1914-1964.
Verse. L.E. Sissman.
40:55 Jy4'64.                   1988
Henry Agard Wallace. WATN.
Kevin Wallace. 36:60-75
Ag13'60.                        1989
The Henry James papers.
Prose. Noel Perrin.
36:191-8 N12'60.                1990
Henry, O. TT. 34:33-4
Ap19'58.                        1991
Her last sickness. Verse.
Sandra M. Gilbert. 45:98
Je21'69.                        1992
Heraclitus. Verse. Jorge
Luis Borges. Norman
Thomas di Giovanni, trans.
45:34 Ag9'69.                   1993
Herbert Blossom and the
colored ball players. Prose.
Wilfrid Sheed. 33:94-104
Ag17'57.                        1994
The herds. Verse. W.S.
Merwin. 41:36 Ja15'66.
                                1995
The herdsmen. RL.
Elizabeth Marshall Thomas.
41:51-119 My1'65; 41:50-
119 My8'65; 41:61-157
My15'65; 41:54-113
My22'65.                        1996
Here and there. Verse.
Jean Farley. 31:140
Ap16'55.                        1997
Here, dear library, are the
papers. Prose. Stanley
Walker. 32:52 N24'56.           1998
Here live your life out!
Verse. Robert Graves.
35:34 Mr28'59.                  1999
The hermit. Prose. John
Updike. 41:38-46 F20'65.
                                2000

The hermit crab. Prose.
S.J. Perelman. 43:26-7
Jy15'67. 2001
The heroes in the dark house.
Prose. Benedict Kiely.
34:28-32 Ja17'59. 2002
Heroes in their prime. Verse.
Robert Graves. 35:42
My23'59. 2003
Heron. Verse. Ted Walker.
41:30 F27'65. 2004
Hero's Winter. Verse. Louis
O. Coxe. 32:44 N3'56. 2005
Herzen, Alexander. George
Steiner. 44:114-26
F8'69. 2006
Hesse, Hermann. George
Steiner. 44:87-97
Ja18'69. 2007
Hey, what's wriggling around
that caduceus? Prose.
S.J. Perelman. 42:32-5
Je18'66. 2008
Hibben, Sheila (Obituary).
40:183-4 Mr7'64. 2009
The hiccups. AM. Berton
Roueché. 45:107-17.
Ap5'69. 2010
Hidden persuasion. Verse.
Robert Hale. 35:105
F6'60. 2011
Hiding from Walter. Prose.
Daniel Gordon. 42:159-65
My21'66. 2012
High dive. Verse. Robert
Watson. 45:85 Je14'69. 2013
A high life or two in Ghana.
OFFC. Norman Lewis.
33:134-56 N23'57. 2014
High opinions. Prose.
F.P. Tullius. 44:131-2 Je8'68.
2015
High wind at the Battery. Verse.
Ralph Pomeroy. 43:30 F3'68.
2016
The high-hearts. Verse. John
Updike. 38:30 F24'62. 2017
A highly inbred species. Prose.
Rosemary Edisford. 37:53-9
N4'61. 2018
A hill. Verse. Anthony Hecht.
40:36 F29'64. 2019

The hillies. Prose. John
Updike. 45:33-5 D20'69.
2020
Hilltop. Verse. Ted Hughes.
41:103 F27'65. 2021
Hindsight and foresight.
Prose. Linda Grace
Hoyer. 44:30-7 F1'69. 2021a
Hippoprognosis in England.
OFFC. A.J. Liebling.
32:94-105*S15'56. 2022
Hiroshige. Verse. Mark
Perlberg. 38:44 Ap28'62.
2023
Hirschfeld, Albert. TT.
34:42-4 D6'58. 2024
His finest hour. Prose.
John Updike. 32:26-31
*Je23'56. 2025
Historical footnote. Verse.
David Daiches. 32:137
O13'56. 2026
History. Verse. James L.
Montague. 31:145*N26'55.
2027
History in the balance.
Prose. Calvin Tomkins.
34:38-9 O4'58. 2028
The history lesson. Prose.
L. Woiwode. 43:47-83
S30'67. 2029
The history of the Russian
Revolution. Prose.
S.N. Behrman. 32:47-51
N24'56. 2030
Hitchhiker. Verse. Jack
Marshall. 39:52 O26'63.
2031
The hit's the thing. PR
(Martin & Feuer). E.J.
Kahn Jr. 31:29-47*Ja7
'56; 31:33-55*Ja14'56. 2032
Ho Farragut! Verse. Andrew
Glaze. 31:34 My21'55. 2033
The hoarder. Prose. Louise
Field Cooper. 33:28-9
Ap6'57. 2034
Hoeing. Verse. John Updike.
39:142 Ap27'63. 2035
Hofstedt and Jean--and others.
Prose. Harold Brodkey.
44:26-36 Ja25'69. 2036

The holborn. Prose. Arturo
Vivante. 44:57 S14'68.
                                        2037
The hole. Prose. Barbara
Vroom. 42:96-7 Ag6'66.
                                        2038
A hole in the floor. Verse.
Richard Wilbur. 37:32 Jy1
'61.                               2039
The hole in the sea. Verse.
Marvin Bell. 41:149 Mr6'65.
                                        2040
The holes. Verse. Stephen
Berg. 44:34 F1'69.        2041
A holiday ramble. Prose.
James Thurber. 31:34-7 Ap2'55.
                                        2042
Holroyd, Michael. TT.
44:27-8 My25'68.             2043
Holy smokestacks, what a mess!
PR (Fraad). Thomas White-
side. 32:39-73 Mr24'56.
                                        2044
Homage. Verse. David
Wagoner. 37:47
S2'61.                             2045
Homage to Don Marquis.
Verse. W.W. Watt.
34:30 Je7'58.                  2046
Homage to Emerson, on a
night flight to New York.
Verse. Robert Penn Warren.
42:30-1 Jy16'66.           2047
Homage to Rodin. Verse.
Brendan Gill. 44:80
Je22'68.                          2048
Home. Prose. John Updike.
36:26-31 Jy9'60.           2049
Home in Summer. Verse.
Edward Parone. 31:68
*Ag20'55.                        2050
Home is the sailor. Prose.
Nathaniel Benchley.
33:91-9 Ag24'57.           2051
Home is where the heart was.
Prose. Robert Henderson.
31:46-8*D3'55.               2052
Home sweet home. PR (Far-
rell). Winthrop Sargeant.
35:47-71 My23'59.         2053
Home town. RL. Christopher
Rand. 40:109-40 N7'64.   2054

Homecoming. Verse.
Maxine W. Kumin. 36:30
F4'61.                             2055
Homecoming. RL. Ved
Mehta. 36:123-66 My7'60.
                                        2056
Homecoming. Verse. Jon
Swan. 35:30 Ag8'59.       2057
Homecoming. Verse. Charles
Wright. 42:108 Ag27'66.
                                        2058
Homing pigeons. Verse.
Ted Walker. 42:54 Ap16
'66.                               2059
Honey, don't you mix, Honey,
you butt out. Prose.
Arthur Kober. 32:35-7
*My5'56.                         2060
Honolulu, Hawaii. NFG.
Philip Hamburger.
41:90-100 Ap3'65.         2061
The honored society.
PR (Mafia). Norman
Lewis. 39:42-105 F8'64;
39:39-111 F15'64; 40:35-
91 F22'64.                     2062
The Horations. Verse.
W.H. Auden. 45:44 My24'69.
                                        2063
Horizon (Magazine). TT.
34:34-5 S20'58.             2064
Hors concours. PR (Point).
Joseph Wechsberg. 39:57-
130 O5'63.                     2065
A horse and two goats.
Prose. R.K. Narayan.
40:30-2 Ja23'65.           2066
The horses. Prose.
L. Woiwode. 44:24-6
D28'68.                          2067
Hospitality. Prose.
Sally Benson. 31:37-40
Mr19'55.                         2068
Hospitality. Prose. Robert
Henderson. 35:22-4
*Ag15'59.                        2069
The hot potato. Prose.
Frank Sullivan. 34:129-
39 O4'58.                       2070
Hot Springs, Ark. NFG.
Philip Hamburger.
40:170-81 N7'64.           2071

The ice skin. Verse. James
Dickey. 39:37 D28'63.      2170
The ice wagon going down the
street. Prose. Mavis
Gallant. 39:54-79 D14'63.
                           2171
The iceberg. Verse. W.S.
Merwin. 32:30*My5'56.      2172
"Ich am of Irlaunde."
Verse. John Malcolm
Brinnin. 32:30*Ag25'56.    2173
I'd like to talk to you for a
minute. RL. Richard
Harris. 32:72-105*Je16'56.
                           2174
Idyll. Verse. Dabney Stuart.
41:94 Ag9'69.              2175
Idyll. Verse. John Updike.
45:50 O10'59.             2176
If a boder meet a boder, need
a boder cry? Yes. Verse.
Ogden Nash. 43:58 O28'67.
                           2177
If a man answers, he's crazy.
Prose. Arthur Hoppe.
36:218-23 N26'60.         2178
If a slicker meet a slicker.
Prose. S.J. Perelman.
39:24-7 Ja25'64.          2179
If I should die before I wake.
Verse. Robert Mezey.
33:47 S14'57.             2180
If it please your honor.
Prose. S.J. Perelman.
38:37-8 Ap28'62.          2181
If there were no England,
"Country Life" could invent
it. Verse. Ogden Nash.
43:54 O14'67.             2182
If you can. Verse. Howard
Moss. 35:24*Ag15'59.      2183
If you want to save twenty
minutes, skip this. Prose.
Geoffrey T. Hellman. 31:
40-3*N5'55.               2184
Il ploe:r da mo koe:r.
Prose. Hortense Calisher.
32:34-8*S8'56.            2185
Il talento mysterioso.
Prose. Thomas Meehan.
43:27-8 Je17'67.          2186
Ill and exiled to the desert.
Verse. Josephine Saunders.

39:134 My18'63.           2187
Ill met by zenith. Verse.
Ogden Nash. 43:40
Ap1'67.                   2188
I'll trade you an elk.
Prose. Charles A.
Goodrum. 38:115-27
Ap14'62.                  2189
Ill-met by fluorescence.
Verse. Ogden Nash.
42:36 F26'66.             2190
Ilya. Prose. J.L. Stampfer.
37:26-36 Ja20'62.         2191
I'm glad you asked that
question, because it
shows you in your true
colors. Verse. Ogden
Nash. 35:36 F21'59.       2192
I'm here. Verse. Theodore
Roethke. 32:39
D15'56.                   2193
Imagine kissing Pete. Prose.
John O'Hara. 36:43-134
S17'60.                   2194
An imaginable conference.
Verse. John Updike.
31:24*Ag6'55.             2195
Imaginary beings. Prose.
Jorge Luis Borges and
Margarita Guerrero.
Norman Thomas diGiovanni,
trans. 45:39-46 O4'69.
                           2196
The imminence of a nation.
OFFC. Robert Shaplen.
39:130-71 Ap6'63.         2197
Immortality. Prose. Robert
Henderson. 34:33-8
F7'59.                    2198
The immortals. Prose. Jorge
Luis Borges and Adolfo Bioy
Casares. Norman Thomas di
Giovanni, trans. Prose.
45:34-5 F14'70.           2199
The impeccable glass. PR
(Frey). Joseph Wechsberg.
31:29-46*Ag13'55.         2200
Imperturbable noble. PR
(d'Harnoncourt). Geoffrey
T. Hellman. 36:49-112
My7'60.                   2201
The importer. AC. E.J.
Kahn, Jr. 38:126-54
S15'62.                   2202

Impression: essentially normal.
AM. Berton Roueché.
34:71-90 Ap5'58.　2203
Improve the game better
than how it is. Prose.
John McNulty. 31:46-7
*O15'55.　2204
In a boat on Glienicker See.
Verse. Joel Agee. 44:77
Jy20'68.　2205
In a café. Prose. Mary
Lavin. 35:32-9 F13'60.　2206
In a churchyard. Verse.
Richard Wilbur. 44:66
N23'68.　2207
In a different light. Prose.
Elizabeth Taylor. 37:51-60
O28'61.　2208
In a field. Verse. Robert
Pack. 37:155 O7'61.　2209
In a foreign city. Prose.
Robert M. Coates. 31:39-44
My14'55.　2210
In a museum cabinet. Verse.
May Swenson. 41:36
F20'65.　2211
In a northern wood. Verse.
Gene Baro. 41:180 N27'65.
　2212
In a pergola. Verse.
Adrienne Cecile Rich. 34:43
S27'58.　2213
In a shaken house. Prose.
Sylvia Townsend Warner.
37:43-50 S16'61.　2214
In a Summer cabin, Autumn.
Verse. Otis Kidwell Burger.
38:173 O27'62.　2215
In a very modest and
abbreviated way. WP. E.J.
Kahn, Jr. 33:81-4 Jy14'57.
　2216
In a word. Prose. Nancy
Hale. 39:80-3 Jy27'63.　2217
In and out. Verse. L.E.
Sissman. 42:50-1 My14'66.
　2218
In and out of never-never
land. Prose. Maeve Brennan.
39:28-40 Jy6'63.　2219
In cold blood. Truman
Capote. AC. 41:57-166
S25'65; 41:57-175 O2'65;

41:58-183 O9'65; 41:62-
193 O16'65.　2220
In Colorado. Verse. Howard
Moss. 41:50 Ap3'65.　2221
In conclusion. Verse.
William J. Murphy.
34:71 Ja3'59.　2222
In defense of self-pity.
Prose. Peter DeVries.
38:28-31 F24'62.　2223
In defense of sterling.
AF. John Brooks.
44:44-96 Mr23'68;
44:43-101 Mr30'68.　2224
In defense of superficiality.
Verse. Elder Olson.
33:46 O26'57.　2225
In football season. Prose.
John Updike. 38:48-9
N10'62.　2226
In her song she is alone.
Verse. Jon Swan. 33:30
*Ag10'57.　2227
In Hurricane Canyon. Verse.
William Stafford. 45:70
D20'69.　2228
In India. Verse. Karl
Shapiro. 32:42 S22'56.　2229
In Italy. Prose. Mavis
Gallant. 32:32-6
*F25'56.　2230
In love with a beautiful girl.
Prose. R. Prawer
Jhabvala. 41:31-9
Ja15'66.　2231
In love with the bears.
Verse. Greg Kuzma. 45:48
Ap12'69.　2232
In memoriam: A.C.,
R.J.O., K.S. Verse. John
Betjeman. 38:28 Jy14'62.
　2233
In memory of H.G. Grand
(5-10¢ to $1.00). Verse.
Marvin Bell. 45:36
Je21'69.　2234
In Montecito. Verse. Randall
Jarrell. 39:50 O5'63.　2235
In passing. Verse. Gerald
Jonas. 42:207 O1'66.　2236
In perpetuum. RL. Alastair
Reid. 41:38-53 Jy31'65.
　2237

Intellectuals. Harold
Rosenberg. 41:98-105
Je26'65.                    2305
Intercession. Prose. John
Updike. 34:24-7 Ag30'58.
                           2306
An interesting case of too
much food in "Life," or vice
versa. Prose. St. Clair
McKelway. 38:68-73
D22'62.                    2307
Interior with figures. Prose.
Peter DeVries. 44:37
S7'68.                     2308
International Exhibition of
Book Design. Mollie
Panter-Downes.31:130*S24'55.
                           2309
The international wilderness.
Prose. John Cheever.
39:43-7 Ap6'63.            2310
The interpreter. Prose.
Frederick L. Keefe. 42:178-
97 D10'66.                 2311
Interval for metaphysics.
Prose. Sylvia Townsend
Warner. 34:38-40
O25'58.                    2312
The interview. Prose.
R. Prawer Jhabvala.
33:25-9*Jy27'57.           2313
Intimations of mortality.
Prose. Robert M. Coates.
34:30-43 Jy26'58.          2314
An introduction to glamour.
Prose. Nancy Hale. 33:28-31
Mr2'57.                    2315
The invasion. Verse. Otis
Kidwell Burger. 35:68 Je27'59.
                           2316
The invasion planners. Prose.
James Reid Parker. 35:89-95
My23'59.                   2317
Invitation to the harvest.
Prose. Colleen Brooks. 41:86-
92 Ap10'65.                2318
Ionesco, Eugene. TT.
36:46-7 D10'60.            2319
Iowa. Verse. Michael Dennis
Browne.43:36 F17'68.       2320
Iris, at the piano. Verse.
May Swenson. 34:44 Ap19'58.
                           2321

Irish hotel. Verse. David
Wevill. 40:164
O24'64.                    2322
The Irish mail and the
Kaiser's war. Prose.
Stanton M. Meyer.
39:74-7 D21'63.            2323
Irish sketches. Prose.
John McCarten. 44:96-
100 F24'68; 45:95-
100 F22'69.                2324
The iron, the charcoal, the
woods. OFFC. Christopher
Rand. 39:31-59 Ag10'63.
                           2325
The irony of it all. Prose.
Peter DeVries. 32:33-7
O20'56.                    2326
Irreconcilables. Verse.
Arthur Gregor. 41:36
F5'66.                     2327
An irreplaceable treasure.
OFFC. E.J. Kahn, Jr.
35:92-128 S19'59.          2328
Is Fabian too young to kiss?
Prose. Faith McNulty.
36:38-40 S24'60.           2329
Is Paris burning? (Film).
Janet Flanner. 41:142-3
S18'65.                    2330
Is the oyster overworked?
Prose. Frank Sullivan.
32:40-3*My12'56.           2331
Is there a doctor in the
cast? Prose. S.J.
Perelman. 31:46-9*N26'55.
                           2332
Is there a Dr. Johnson in the
house? Verse. Ogden Nash.
44:30 D21'68.              2333
Is you is or is you ain't,
goober man? Prose. S.J.
Perelman. 34:52-5 N15'58.
                           2334
Isidoro Acevedo. Verse. Jorge
Luis Borges. Norman
Thomas di Giovanni, trans.
45:60 N8'69.               2335
The island of the crofter and
the laird. PR (Colonsay Island).
John McPhee. 45:69-165
D6'69; 45:61-112 D13'69.
                           2336

44:26-9 Ag31'68. 2371
The Jewish New Year.
Verse. Adrienne Cecile
Rich. 32:28 S1'56. 2372
Jimmy Bennett doesn't work
here any more. Prose. J.Q.
Purcell. 40:38-9 Mr14'64.
2373
Joan and Darby. Verse.
Robert Graves. 35:54 D12'59.
2374
The Job Corps. RL. John
Bainbridge. 42:112-58 My
21'66. 2375
Jocelyn. Prose. Mary Nash.
31:106-17 Je11'55. 2376
Joe Gould's secret. PR (Gould).
Joseph Mitchell. 40:61-125
S19'64; 40:53-159 S26'64.
2377
John Barrow Rosedale, actor's
actor. Prose. John O'Hara.
39:46-53 Mr16'63. 2378
John Knox rides again. Prose.
Richard H. Rovere. 34:74-9
Ag16'58. 2379
John Otto. Verse. W.S.
Merwin. 34:30 Mr29'58. 2380
John Peel, shake hands with
37 mamas. Verse. Ogden
Nash. 40:42 Mr14'64. 2381
John Smith, U.S.A., buys the
new family bus. Prose.
Thomas Meehan. 35:38-40
My9'59. 2382
Johnnie Brewer. Prose. Sylvia
Townsend Warner. 41:45-50
Ap10'65. 2383
Jorinda and Jorindel. Prose.
Mavis Gallant. 35:38-42
S19'59. 2384
Josephine. Prose. Richard H.
Rovere. 33:48-52 N9'57.
2385
Journal of a pseudo-event.
OFFC. Richard H. Rovere.
39:76-88 Jy13'63. 2386
The journal of an old gent.
Prose. John Cheever.
31:32-55*F18'56. 2387
Journey back. Verse. Ted
Walker. 43:64 N25'67. 2388

Journey in a circle. Prose.
Arturo Vivante. 36:157-65
D10'60. 2389
Journey in remembering.
Prose. Oliver LaFarge. 36:
140-51 N5'60. 2390
Journey of a lady, on horse
back and, later, by water.
Verse. Jane Hayman.
43:28 Je17'67. 2391
Journey of the snowmen.
Verse. Howard Nemerov.
37:81 Ja13'62. 2392
A journey to Crete. Prose.
Ruth M. Adams. 32:132-8
D15'56. 2393
A journey to seven streams.
Prose. Benedict Kiely.
37:42-8 My6'61. 2394
Journey to the center of the
room. Prose. Peter De
Vries. 44:56-7 O5'68. 2395
Journey to the interior.
Verse. Theodore Roethke.
36:27 Ja7'61. 2396
Journey toward a sense of
being treated well. RL.
John Hersey. 33:39-87
Mr2'57. 2397
Journey toward evening.
Verse. Phyllis McGinley.
34:115 F7'59. 2398
Joyce, James. Dwight
Macdonald. 35:213-34
D12'59. 2399
Joyce, James. TT. 34:26-7
F14'59; 40:34-6 Mr14'64.
2400
Joyous gard. Prose. Nancy
Hale. 44:175-90 O12'68.
2401
Judging Keller. Prose.
Gilbert Rogin. 40:40-7
Mr14'64. 2402
Julie. Prose. Geoffrey Bush.
32:21-5*Jy21'56. 2403
July. Verse. Rolfe Humphries.
31:19*Jy2'55. 2404
July in Indiana. Verse. Robert
Fitzgerald. 42:36 Jy16'66.
2405
The junction: a warm afternoon.

Kindness. Verse. Catherine
Davis. 31:105 Mr19'55. 2442
The king in May. Verse.
Michael Dennis Browne.
42:40 My28'66. 2443
The king of fancy's daughter.
Prose. Nancy Hale.
33:28-33 Ap27'57. 2444
The king of kissingdom. Prose.
Penelope Mortimer. 36:42-9
Mr19'60. 2445
The kingdom. Verse. Jon
Swan. 41:197 D4'65. 2446
The kingfisher and the phoebe.
FFT. James Thurber. 32:
22*S1'56. 2447
Kingsman. PR (Forster).
Mollie Panter-Downes.
35:51-86 S19'59. 2448
Kipling, Rudyard. S.N. Behrman
and Max Beerbohm.
35:70-86 F13'60. 2449
The kiss. Prose. Walter
Macken. 39:130-5 S7'63.
2450
The kite. Verse. Mark
Strand. 41:50 Mr20'65. 2451
The kite. Verse. May
Swenson. 39:36 My18'63.
2452
Knight, with umbrella. Verse.
Elder Olson. 33:72
F1'58. 2453
Knock. Verse. James Dickey.
44:92 Ja25'69. 2454
The knowing. Verse.
Theodore Roethke. 37:38
Ap15'61. 2455
The knowledge. OFFC. John
Bainbridge. 41:62-9 Jy3'65.
2456
Known for her frankness.
Prose. Penelope Gilliatt.
43:26-31 F3'68. 2457
Knoxville, Tenn. NFG. Philip
Hamburger. 36:96-103
Ja14'61. 2458
Koheleth who? Prose. Susan
M. Black. 37:91-5 F3'62.
2459
The kokuteru house. Prose.
Allan R. Bosworth. 34:94-111
My17'58. 2460

The Krankenhaus of
Leutkirch. Verse.
Richmond Lattimore.
37:28 Ag26'61. 2461
Kreuger. AC. Robert
Shaplen. 35:51-91 S26'59;
35:108-41 O3'59; 35:51-
118 O10'59. 2462
Krutch, Joseph Wood
(Parody). Samuel French
Morse. 34:26 Je28'58. 2463
Kubrick, Stanley. PR.
Jeremy Bernstein. 42:70-
110 N12'66. 2464
Kudzu. Verse. James
Dickey. 39:44 My18'63. 2465
Kuwait. OFFC. Welles
Hangen. 37:35-53 Jy22'61.
2466
Kyoto days. OFFC. Anthony
West. 34:113-28*Ap26'58;
34:100-16 My10'58. 2467

L

LM. RL. Henry S.F. Cooper,
Jr. 44:37-54 Ja11'69. 2468
The LP catalog: an apprecia-
tion. Verse. Curt Leviant.
32:57*Je23'56. 2469
La bagarède. Verse.
Galway Kinnell. 42:58
S24'66. 2470
La belle dame sans merci.
PR. Robert Lewis Taylor.
(Hurricane Donna).
36:39-70 F11'61; 37:45-90
F18'61. 2471
La plume de mon ami est
dans le flapdoodle. Prose.
S.J. Perelman. 34:38-41
O11'58. 2472
The ladder. Verse. Gene
Baro. 34:93 Je7'58. 2473
The ladies of Orlon. Prose.
James Thurber. 31:28-9
Je11'55. 2474
Ladies should not shoot.
Prose. Florence Codman.
33:73-8 F15'58. 2475
The lady at the Old Bailey.
OUWA. Mollie Panter-
Downes. 36:159-71 N19'60.
2476

A last poem. Verse. Robert
Graves. 40:39 Je6'64.    2512
The last repository. Prose.
H.F. Ellis. 37:29-30
F17'62.                  2513
A last ride with coachman Lin.
Prose. Antonio Barolini.
35:149-56 My9'59.        2514
Last rites. Prose. Arturo
Vivante. 41:42-3 My22'65.
                         2515
The last skill acquired. RL.
Calvin Tomkins. 39:127-57
S14'63.                  2516
Last things. Verse. William
Meredith. 44:48 S21'68. 2517
The last to go. Prose.
Penelope Gilliatt. 45:38-46
Ap19'69.                 2518
The last trespassers. Verse.
Joseph Francis Murphy.
36:163 Ap23'60.          2519
The last wilderness. RL. Peter
Matthiessen. 37:30-57
Jy8'61; 37:35-67 Ag12'61;
37:51-111 S9'61.         2520
Last words for a sunken ship.
Verse. Edward Parone. 32:50
N24'56.                  2521
Last year at Marienbad
(Parody). 38:38-9 My12'62.
                         2522
Last year at Miami Beach.
Prose. Thomas Meehan.
38:28-9 My12'62.         2523
Late afternoon, riverhouse.
Verse. Robert Mezey.
41:189 Ap24'65.          2524
A late aubade. Verse.
Richard Wilbur. 44:32
Ag3'68.                  2525
Late butterflies. Verse.
Howard Nemerov. 45:38
O4'69.                   2526
Late dandelions. Verse. Ben
Belitt. 41:197 O23'65.   2527
Late light. Verse. Barbara
Bellow Watson. 41:36
F12'66.                  2528
Late reflections. Verse.
Babette Deutsch. 37:40
Mr18'61.                 2529

Late show. Prose. Robert
Hemenway. 39:46-9
N9'63.                   2530
Late snow. Verse. Louise
Glück.43:189 Mr25'67.    2531
Late Spring. Verse. Nancy
Wilson Ross. 32:87
*Ap21'56.                2532
A late Spring. Verse. James
Scully. 38:48 Ap21'62.   2533
Latitude. Prose. Merrill
Joan Gerber. 40:24-7
Ag8'64.                  2534
The laughing Dutchman and
the devil dancers. Prose.
Santha Rama Rau. 33:119-40
N2'57.                   2535
Laundry. Verse. Ruth Stone.
34:30 Je28'58.           2536
Lavallière. Prose. Robert M.
Coates. 34:23-5 D27'58.
                         2537
The lawns of Wimbledon. PR
(Twynam). John McPhee.
44:32-57 Je22'68.        2538
Lawrence, D.H. S.N.
Behrman and Max Beer-
bohm. 36:79 Mr19'60.     2539
Le Chopin to Moscow.
OFFC. Alan Moorehead.
38:118-36 O6'62.         2540
Le gamin. Janet Flanner.
PR (Buffet). 35:57-112
N21'59.                  2541
Le hibou et la poussiquette.
Verse. Francis Steegmuller.
35:38 Je20'59.           2542
Le meneur de jeu. PR (Renoir).
Penelope Gilliatt. 45:34-61
Ag23'69.                 2543
Le petit déjeuner. Prose.
Elizabeth Cullinan. 36:32-7
Ag13'60.                 2544
Le Quang. RL. Susan Sheehan.
42:137-49 N5'66.         2545
Lead, damsel, and I follow.
Prose. Edward Newhouse.
34:39-46 Mr8'58.         2546
Lead player. PR (Glow).
William Whitworth. 45:43-54
D20'69.                  2547
Leaflight. Verse. Dorothy

Donnelly. 36:132 O1'60.
2548
The leafy air. Verse. Charles
Norman. 42:42 Ap9'66. 2549
Lear, Edward (Parody).
William Jay Smith 33:36
Mr2'57. 2549A
Least said. Prose. Louise
Field Cooper. 33:92-7 Mr9'57.
2550
A leave-taking. Prose. Shirley
Hazzard. 39:20-3 Jy13'63.
2551
Leaves. Prose. John Updike.
40:52-3 N14'64. 2552
The leaves of a tree. PR
(Lhevinne). Winthrop Sargeant.
38:37-72 Ja12'63. 2553
Leaves of three. AM. Berton
Roueché. 40:158-70
S12'64. 2554
The leaving. Verse. Elizabeth
Hawes. 41:118 Ag14'65.
2555
A lecture. Prose. H.L.
Mountzoures. 42:170-6
Ap23'66. 2556
Led astray. Prose. Dan
Jacobson. 40:34-9 Ja23'65.
2557
Left for me. Verse. Margoret
Smith. 43:42 My27'67. 2558
The legend of success, the
salesman's story. Verse. Louis
Simpson. 35:26 F28'59.
2559
Lekha. Prose. R. Prawer
Jhabvala. 33:38-44
S14'57. 2560
Lemons. Verse. Ted Walker.
42:58 N26'66. 2561
Lemuel's blessing. Verse. W. S.
Merwin. 38:54 D8'62. 2562
A lemur in the supermarket at
night: a view of the after-
life. Verse. George Mac-
Beth. 40:154 Mr14'64. 2563
Leonard. Prose. John
O'Hara. 42:33-7 F26'66.
2564
The Leonardo da Vinci traffic
jam. Prose. Robert
Henderson. 40:24-6 Ag15'64.
2565

Leonardo da Vinci's. Verse.
Marianne Moore. 35:22 Jy18'59.
2566
Les chasse-neige. Verse.
Ralph A. Lewin. 34:134
F22'58. 2567
Les enfants du Thalia.
Prose. Gene Williams. 40:28-
9 F6'65. 2568
Lesser married. Prose.
Gilbert Rogin. 41:32-40
F27'65. 2569
A lesson for beautiful
women. Verse. Alastair
Reid. 34:40 Ap19'58. 2570
A lesson in handwriting.
Verse. Alastair Reid.
37:40 S30'61. 2571
Lessons and lessons and
then more lessons. Prose.
Maeve Brennan. 38:155-6
N10'62. 2572
Lester, Richard. TT. 43:50-1
O28'67. 2573
Let a snarl be your umbrella.
Prose. S.J. Perelman.
42:26-7 Ja14'67. 2574
Let old acquaintance be
forgot. Prose. S.J.
Perelman. 36:38-40
O8'60. 2575
Let x equal the amount.
Prose. David Daiches.
32:88-97 *Ap21'56. 2576
Let's play portraits. Prose.
Natacha Stewart. 37:32-71
Ja27'62. 2577
The letter. Prose. Dinah
Brooke. 40:52-7 N7'64. 2578
A letter. Verse. Anthony
Hecht. 38:42 Mr17'62. 2579
Letter. Verse. Mark Strand.
45:119 Mr22'69. 2580
Letter (delayed) from the
North. Prose. E.B. White.
37:47-110 Mr25'61. 2581
A letter for Allhallows.
Verse. Peter Kane Dufault.
32:30 O27'56. 2582
Letter from a region in my
mind. Prose. James
Baldwin. 38:59-144 N17'62.
2583
Letter from Algeria.

Letter from Milan. William
Murray. 38:128-38
S8'62.                              2653
Letter from Nagasaki. E.J.
Kahn, Jr.37:52-60 Jy29
'61.                               2654
Letter from New Delhi.
Christopher Rand. 31:118-32
Ap16'55; 32:81-97 Mr3'56.
                                   2655
Letter from Paris. Janet
Flanner. 31:54-60 F26'55;
31:78-85 Mr12'55; 31:112-19
Mr26'55; 31:112-19 Ap9'55;
31:127-32 Ap23'55; 31:140-4
My7'55; 31:120-8 My21'55; 31:
103-108 Je4'55; 31:72-5 Je
25'55; 31:54-60*Jy2'55; 31:
60-5 Jy16'55; 31:44-8*Jy30'55;
31:64-8*Ag13'55; 31:85-91
*Ag27'55; 31:78-82*S10'55;
31:145-9*N19'55; 31:114-18
*D3'55; 31:121-5*D17'55;
31:38-42*D31'55; 31:79-83
*Ja14'56; 31:76-80*Ja28'56;
31:103-108*F11'56; 32:115-20
*F25'56; 32:127-31*Mr10'56;
32:76-81*Mr31'56;32:106-12
*Ap7'56; 32:98-107*Ap21'56;
32:134-8 *My5'56; 32:60-7
*Je2'56; 32:110-16*Je9'56;
32:72-7*Jy14'56; 32:68-72
*Jy21'56; 32:58-62*Ag4'56;
43:74-80*Ag25'56; 32:81-5
*S15'56; 32:117-21 S29'56;
32:143-8 O20'56; 32:77-87
N3'56; 32:227-9*N10'56;32:219-
22 N17'56; 32:230-7 D1'56; 32:
167-75 D15'56; 33:62-7 Je29'57;
33:56-62*Jy20'57; 33:62-8
Ag3'57; 33:82-8 Ag24'57;
33:76-83 S7'57; 33:111-18
S21'57; 33:178-84 O5'57;
33:124-31 O19'57; 33:144-51
N2'57; 33:152-7 N16'57; 33:
104-10*N30'57; 33:132-40
D14'57; 33:52-7 Ja4'58; 33:
80-5 Ja18'58; 33:67-72 F1'58;
33:123-8 F15'58; 34:75-85
Mr1'58; 34:116-21 Mr15'58;
34:62-8 My31'58; 34:66-70
Je7'58; 34:100-105 Je14'58;
34:117-24 O4'58; 34:187-92

O11'58; 34:164-70 O25'58;
34:186-94 N8'58; 34:109-15
N22'58; 34:197-202 D6'58;
34:105-10 D20'58; 34:104-
109 Ja10'59; 34:90-5 Ja24'59;
34:127-33 F7'59; 35:105-13
F21'59; 35:102-11 Mr7'59;
35:154-60 Mr21'59; 35:117-
25 Ap4'59; 35:153-61 Ap18'59;
35:148-53 My2'59; 35:92-8
My30'59; 35:100-106 Je13'59;
35:57-63 Je27'59; 35:78-83
Jy11'59; 35:60-6 Jy25'59;
35:90-4 Ag8'59; 35:104-108
Ag22'59; 35:92-100 S5'59;
36:149-55 Ap2'60; 36:94-104
Ap9'60; 36:141-6 Ap23'60;
36:182-9 My7'60; 36:131-6
My21'60; 36:145-51 Je4'60;
36:112-16 Je18'60; 36:65-9
Jy2'60; 36:72-7 Jy16'60;
36:68-72 Jy30'60; 36:87-94
Ag13'60; 36:83-8 Ag27'60;
36:186-92 S10'60; 36:163-71
O29'60; 36:134-41 N12'60;
36:210-17 N26'60; 36:147-52
D10'60; 36:42-5 D24'60;
36:64-70 Ja7'61; 36:90-7
Ja21'61; 36:69-77 F4'61;
37:106-11 F18'61; 37:95-100
Mr4'61; 37:130-7 Mr18'61;
37:133-8 Ap15'61; 37:132-40
Ap29'61; 37:125-8 My6'61;
37:148-56 My13'61; 37:123-30
My27'61; 37:150-4 N25'61;
37:104-109 D16'61; 37:64-7
D23'61; 37:73-7 Ja6'62;
37:104-109 Ja20'62; 37:79-85
F3'62; 37:120-9 F17'62;
38:124-8 Mr3'62; 38:173-8
Mr17'62; 38:115-22 Mr31'62;
38:165-71 Ap14'62; 38:151-9
Ap28'62; 38:146-50 My12'62;
38:147-52 My26'62; 38:84-9
Je9'62; 38:92-100 Je23'62;
38:66-72 Jy7'62; 38:70-4
Jy21'62; 38:140-6 S22'62;
38:115-16 O6'62; 38:194-9
O13'62; 38:186-92 O20'62;
38:196-203 N3'62; 38:170-9
N17'62; 38:127-31 D1'62;
38:174-8 D15'62; 38:64-8
D29'62; 38:102-109 Ja12'63;

O20'62; 38:34-59 D29'62;
39:120-45 My11'63; 39:41-53
Je15'63; 39:74-85 Jy20'63;
39:179-91 S28'63; 39:123-43
O26'63; 39:144-63 N30'63;
39:88-106 Ja18'64; 40:166-
73 S19'64; 40:90-103 Ja9'65;
41:135-52 S11'65; 41:34-49
D25'65; 42:140-63 O22'66;
43:119-39 S9'67; 44:131-47
N2'68.                                    2692
Letter from Vienna. Joseph
Wechsberg. 31:178-98
*N26'55; 34:140-57 O4'58;
36:104-25 Je4'60.            2693
Letter from Wales. Anthony
Bailey. 36:168-92
D3'60.                                    2694
Letter from Warsaw. Joseph
Wechsberg. 34:33-69
Jy12'58; 38:106-26 F9'63.
                                               2695
Letter from Washington. Richard
H. Rovere. 31:90-100
F26'55; 31:79-84 Mr26'55;
31:103-12 Ap30'55; 31:125-35
Je11'55; 31:68-75 Jy16'55;
31:167-77*O8'55; 31:74-88
*D17'55; 31:96-104*Ja21'56;
32:122-9*F25'56; 32:68-80
*Mr10'56; 32:72-87*Ap21'56;
32:128-37*My19'56; 32:68-80
*Je23'56; 32:135-43 S29'56;
32:95-100 N17'56; 32:73-81
*D22'56; 32:84-93 Ja26'57;
33:108-15 F23'57; 33:125-35
Mr23'57; 33:70-84 Ap27'57;
33:117-24 My25'57; 33:65-72
Jy6'57; 33:72-82 Ag31'57;
33:167-72 O5'57; 33:175-80
N2'57; 33:149-52 D7'57;
33:94-105 Ja25'58; 34:97-103
Mr1'58; 34:131-42 Mr22'58;
34:79-86 Ap19'58; 34:131-7
My10'58; 34:122-8 Je14'58;
34:86-97 Jy12'58; 34:91-8
S20'58; 34:108-16 O11'58;
34:141-6 N15'58; 34:85-93
Ja17'59; 34:104-12 F14'59;
35:159-63 Mr14'59; 35:93-
100 Ap25'59; 35:90-103 My
16'59; 35:119-26 Je13'59;
35:31-40 Ag1'59; 35:96-100

Ag29'59; 35:201-207 N14'59;
35:107-13*D19'59; 35:87-93
Ja30'60; 36:120-8 F27'60;
36:138-47 Mr26'60; 36:90-8
Ap30'60; 36:85-92 Je25'60; 36:
118-24 S10'60; 36:90-101 O29
'60; 36:203-10 N19'60; 36:52-
60 D24'60; 36:108-20 Ja21'61;
36:106-12 F4'61; 37:103-11 Mr4
'61; 37:131-6 Mr25'61; 37:156-
61 Ap15'61; 37:139-46 My6'61;
37:125-32 Je3'61; 37:32-6
Ag5'61; 37:64-70 S2'61; 37:82-8
S23'61; 37:201-206 N11'61; 37:
204-10 D9'61; 37:85-93 Ja27'62;
38:117-22 F24'62; 38:151-8
Ap14'62; 38:166-75 My12'62;
38:118-23 Je9'62; 38:78-84
Jy 21'62; 38:101-107 Ag25'62;
38:148-57 O6'62; 38:118-23
N3'62; 38:200-207 N17'62;
38:103-10 F2'63; 39:125-31
Mr2'63; 39:163-9 Mr30'63;
39:155-62 My4'63; 39:100-108
Je1'63; 39:90-8 Je22'63;
39:159-66 S14'63; 39:149-56
O5'63; 39:113-20 N2'63;
39:78-87 D21'63; 39:35-9
Ja25'64; 39:133-8 F15'64;
40:178-88 Mr21'64; 40:149-
55 Ap11'64; 40:193-8 My16'64;
40:111-18 Je13'64; 40:101-
11 Ag22'64; 40:235-43 N14
'64; 40:156-62 D19'64;
40:122-7 Ja16'65; 41:131-6
F20'65; 41:177-86 Mr20'65;
41:160-9 Ap17'65; 41:204-13
My15'65; 41:143-50 Je12'65;
41:99-107 Jy17'65; 41:108-
18 Ag14'65; 41:116-30
S11'65; 41:233-44 O16'65;
41:201-206 N20'65; 41:
191-9 D18'65; 41:88-95
Ja22'66; 41:146-58 F19'66;
42:167-72 Mr19'66; 42:180-
5 Ap23'66; 42:167-74
My21'66; 42:118-43 Je18'66;
42:108-22 S10'66; 42:197-
203 O8'66; 42:197-201
N19'66; 42:200-206 D17'66;
42:94-104 Ja21'67; 43:176-
83 Mr18'67; 43:153-60
Ap22'67; 43:90-9 Je24'67;

Light poem. Verse. Theodore Roethke. 41:21 Jy10'65. 2724

The lighthouse. Prose. Arturo Vivante. 43:26-7 Ja20'68. 2725

Lighting the lamps. Verse. James Atlas. 45:30 F7'70. 2726

Lik. Prose. Vladimir Nabokov. Dmitri Nabokov, trans. 40:64-90 O10'64. 2727

Like a homesick angel. PR (Blackburn). John Bainbridge. 38:61-145 N10'62. 2728

"Like a wave at the curl." Verse. Marianne Moore. 45:50 N29'69. 2729

The likeness. Verse. Arthur Gregor. 42:134 F18'67. 2730

Lilies don't bloom at Easter. Prose. James G. McClure. 40:176-218 O24'64. 2731

Lilith (Film). TT. 39:23 Ag17'63. 2732

The lime umbrella. Verse. Michael Goldman. 39:38 Je8'63. 2733

Lines. Verse. E.B. White. 33:32 Ag31'57. 2734

Lines to be carved on Coogan's Bluff. Verse. Ogden Nash. 33:39 S28'57. 2735

L'inglese. Verse. John Ciardi. 39:78 Ja18'64. 2736

Links in a chain. Verse. Samuel French Morse. 34:26 Je28'58. 2737

The lion and the lizard. FFT. James Thurber. 32:23*S1'56. 2738

A lion comes to dine. Verse. Josephine Saunders. 37:64 Jy1'61. 2739

Lions at the gate. Verse. William David Roberts. 32:105 Ja19'57. 2740

Lippmann, Walter. Richard H. Rovere. 33:66-70 Jy13'57. 2741

Listen, Son. Prose. Robert Henderson. 35:46-8 D5'59. 2742

Listen to the lambs. Prose. Peter DeVries. 31:26-7 *Ag13'55. 2743

A listener's guide to the birds. Verse. E.B. White. 35:28-9 Jy4'59. 2744

Listening to foxhounds. Verse. James Dickey. 36:48 N26'60. 2745

The little ark. Prose. Arturo Vivante. 42:61-3 N19'66. 2746

A little Brahms, a little beer. Prose. Sari Magaziner. 33:154-60 O19'57. 2747

The little brown girl. Prose. Elizabeth Spencer. 33:27-9 *Jy20'57. 2748

The little dressmakers of Vicenza. Prose. Antonio Barolini. 34:201-207 N22'58. 2749

Little elegy. Verse. X.J. Kennedy 36:100 Je4'60. 2750

Little girl, my stringbean, my lovely woman. Verse. Anne Sexton. 41:30 Ag7'65. 2751

The little heiress. Prose. Rhys Davies. 40:31-6 Ag29'64. 2752

Little joy poem. Verse. Kathleen Fraser. 42:114 Ja14'67. 2753

Little Kwanda does it again. Prose. Gordon Cotler. 43:26-7 Jy8'67. 2754

The little lives. Prose. Robert Henderson. 36:36-9 O22'60. 2755

A little louder, please. Prose. Woody Allen. 42:39-41 My28'66. 2756

Little Love Lane. Verse. R.P. Lister. 34:75 S13'58. 2757

Little lullaby. Verse.

Irving Feldman. 40:51
S12'64.                                    2758
Little Mrs. Perkins. Prose.
Penelope Mortimer.
36:45-50 Ap23'60.                          2759
A little morning music.
Verse. Delmore
Schwartz. 35:44 Ap18'59.
                                           2760
A little mystery out of
Maupassant. Prose.
Francis Steegmuller.
34:104-107 S6'58.                          2761
A little ode. Verse. F.
Pratt Green. 33:30 My4'57.
                                           2762
Little poems. Verse. John
Updike. 32:67 *Jy21'56.
                                           2763
The little rapids. Verse. May
Swenson. 42:141 My7'66.
                                           2764
A little retarded boy on the
Lexington Avenue Express.
Verse. Ralph Pomeroy.
44:36 Mr23'68.                             2765
The little stone man. Prose.
Oliver LaFarge. 36:32-8
Je25'60.                                   2766
Little Willie. Prose. Nadine
Gordimer. 33:28-31
Mr30'57.                                   2767
The living. Prose. Mary
Lavin. 34:52-6 N22'58.                     2768
Living in Hong Kong. Verse.
Sandra Hochman. 43:32-3
F17'68.                                    2769
Living on the box. Prose.
Penelope Gilliatt. 42:48-52
D17'66.                                    2770
Living well is the best
revenge. PR (The Murphys).
Calvin Tompkins. 38:31-69
Jy28'62.                                   2771
The lizard. Verse.
Theodore Roethke. 37:36
Je17'61.                                   2772
L'lapse. Prose. Donald
Barthelme. 39:29-31
Mr2'63.                                    2773
Llorona. Prose. Calvin
Kentfield. 40:28-36
Ag8'64.                                    2774

Lobrano, G.S. (Obituary).
32:143*Mr10'56.                            2775
L'observatoire. Verse.
Hawley Truax. 45:40
Mr8'69.                                    2776
Lobsters in the window.
Verse. W.D. Snodgrass.
38:36 F2'63.                               2777
Local places. Verse.Howard
Moss. 32:36*Ap21'56.                       2778
Lock lips--monkeyshines
in the bridgework. Prose.
S.J. Perelman. 43:47-9
O7'67.                                     2779
The Locomobile. Prose.
John O'Hara. 39:22-7
Jy20'63.                                   2780
The locum tenens. Prose.
Sylvia Townsend Warner.
34:32-8 Mr29'58.                           2781
L'oeil (Magazine).
Janet Flanner. 31:55-8
F26'55.                                    2782
Lolita. Prose. Dorothy
Parker. 31:32-5*Ag27'55.
                                           2783
The London fog. RL. Joseph
Wechsberg. 37:137-62
N11'61.                                    2784
The lonesome dream. Verse.
Lisel Mueller. 40:141
My23'64.                                   2785
Long, Darwin and others. Verse.
Peter Kane Dufault. 35:98
My9'59.                                    2786
The long green puddle.
RL. Mollie Panter-
Downes. 38:71-96 Ag25'62.
                                           2787
The long journey. Verse.
R.P. Lister. 33:140
N2'57.                                     2788
The long letter. Prose.
Robert Henderson. 42:36-
40 Je18'66.                                2789
A long night. Prose. Sylvia
Townsend Warner. 40:44-
51 My2'64.                                 2790
The long of it. Prose.
Francis Steegmuller. 35:52-
4 D26'59.                                  2791
The long phrase. PR (Stern).
Joseph Wechsberg. 41:49-117
Je5'65.                                    2792

Long song, a wife song, a
cat song, a rain song.
Verse. Barry Spacks.
43:32 S 2'67.                    2793
The long trip. Prose. L.
Woiwode. 44:26-34
Jy13'68.                         2794
The long walk. Verse.
David Galler. 33:24
*Jy20'57.                        2795
The long waters. Verse.
Theodore Roethke. 38:34
Je2'62.                          2796
A long way from London.
Prose. Dan Jacobson.
31:50-6*D10'55.                  2797
The long way home. Prose.
Joe Savage. 33:131-45
S14'57.                          2798
The longest day. Prose.
Shirley Ann Grau. 31:30-4
*S3'55.                          2799
The longest nickle ride in
mule-car history. Prose.
Marcia Darrah Buchanan.
34:151-61 N1'58.                 2800
Look at me. Prose. Peter
Gray. 39:133-45 Mr23'63.
                                 2801
A look at the record. WP.
A.J. Liebling. 37:187-93
O14'61.                          2802
A look at the Spring suits.
Prose. F.P. Tullius.
42:86-90 F26'66.                 2803
Look, lady! Prose. Patricia
Collinge. 35:183-92
S12'59.                          2804
The look: lines after
Kalidasa. Verse. Leonard
Nathan. 44:206 N16'68.           2805
Looking for mushrooms at
sunrise. Verse. W.S.
Merwin. 43:32 My27'67.
                                 2806
Looking into psi. RL.
Kevin Wallace. 35:126-51
Mr14'59.                         2807
Looking out to sea. Verse.
Anthony Ostroff. 44:36
Ag31'68.                         2808
Looking straight. Verse.
John Moffitt. 37:36
F17'62.                          2809
Looking up. Verse. Howard

Moss. 40:48 Ap18'64.             2810
Looking uptown. Verse.
May Swenson. 32:48
D1'56.                           2811
The loom. Prose.
Morton Grosser. 40:72-4
Ag1'64.                          2812
Loovis, David. TT.
35:18-20 Jy11'59.                2813
The Lord did the rest. Prose.
John Day. 33:58-60*Jy27'57.
                                 2814
The Lord in the air. Verse.
James Dickey. 44:56 O19'68.
                                 2815
Losers weepers. Prose.
Carlton Lake. 31:73-84
Mr19'55.                         2816
Losing a falcon. Prose.
T.H. White. 34:30-4
Ja24'59.                         2817
A losing game. Prose.
J.F. Powers. 31:44-8
*N5'55.                          2818
Lost and found. Verse. Rose-
mary Thomas. 35:46
Je6'59.                          2819
Lost in translation. RL.
Alastair Reid. 39:43-
74 S7'63.                        2820
The lost, strayed,
stolen. Prose. M.F.K.
Fisher. 41:47-80
Mr20'65.                         2821
A lost world. Verse.
Robert Graves. 37:39
Ap1'61.                          2822
Love and wisdom. Prose.
H.L. Mountzoures.
41:50-7 S18'65.                  2823
Love, Edmund G. TT.
38:34-5 Ap28'62.                 2824
Love in the city. Verse.
Louis Simpson. 38:28
Jy7'62.                          2825
Love in the marble foot.
Prose. Julie O'Faolain.
33:99-109 Ap27'57.               2826
The love object. Prose. Edna
O'Brien. 43:42-52 I
My13'67.                         2827
A love song. Verse. Rolfe
Humphries. 31:121 Ap23'55.
                                 2828

The loved one. Verse. Joseph
Hansen. 38:139 S22'62. 2829
Lovely to look at, delightful
to hold. Prose. Edna
O'Brien. 40:38-44
Mr28'64. 2830
The lover and his lass.
FFT. James Thurber.
32:36*My26'56. 2831
A lover of cities.PR (Abrams).
Bernard Taper. 42:39-91
F4'67; 42:45-115 F11'67.
2832
The lovers. Verse. Josephine
Jacobsen. 44:155
Ap27'68. 2833
The lovers. Prose. Edna
O'Brien. 38:28-34
F16'63. 2834
The lover's ghost. Verse.
Louis Simpson. 33:107 S7'57.
2835
The lovers go fly a kite. Verse.
W. D. Snodgrass. 38:36
F9'63. 2836
Love's island. Verse.
Walter Kaiser. 32:142
*Mr17'56. 2837
Loves of the puppets. Verse.
Richard Wilbur. 33:40
Ap13'57. 2838
Love's old sweet musical-
therapy song. Prose.
Richard Lemon. 31:103-105
Mr12'55. 2839
Love's stratagems. Verse.
Donald Justice. 34:196
D6'58. 2840
Loving memory. Prose.
Mary Lavin. 36:32-8 Ag20'60.
2841
The lowboy. Prose. John
Cheever. 35:38-42
O10'59. 2842
Low fields and light. Verse.
W. S. Merwin 31:42
*N5'55. 2843
The lowering (Arlington
Cemetery, June 8, 1968).
Verse. May Swenson. 45:46
Je7'69. 2844
Loyalty. Prose. Edith
Templeton. 34:25-32

Ag2'58. 2845
Lüchow's and after. Verse.
L. E. Sissman. 44:64
N2'68. 2846
Lucien, Octave, Victoire,
Emile. Prose. Francine
du Plessix Gray. 43:26-
34 Jy29'67. 2847
Lucienne. Prose. Robert
Riskin. 35:26-9 Jy25'59.2848
Lucky, lucky me. Prose.
John Sack. 33:63-5
D28'57. 2849
The lucky pair. Prose.
Mary Lavin. 38:39-46
Ap28'62. 2850
The lug wrench. Prose.
Berton Roueché. 45:32-4
Je7'69. 2851
Lullaby. Verse. Robert
Beverly Hale. 31:52
*Jy30'55. 2852
A lullaby for small boats.
Verse. Frances Higginson
Savage. 31:74*N5'55. 2853
Lullaby to two growing old. Verse.
Irving Feldman. 34:44 O4'58.
2854
The lung-gom runner.
Prose. Kenneth Lamott.
36:151-63 Ap23'60. 2855
Lux et veritas. Prose.
Milton White. 38:213-22
N17'62. 2856
The Luzhin defense. Prose.
Vladimir Nabokov. Michael
Scammell, trans. 40:40-
140 My9'64; 40:48-163
My16'64. 2857
Lying awake. Verse.
W. D. Snodgrass. 35:36
Je13'59. 2858
The lyre. Prose. Vladimir
Nabokov. 39:44-139
Ap13'63. 2859

M

Mac and chief. Prose.
John McNulty. 31:16-17
*D31'55. 2860
McCabe, John. TT.
35:23-4 Je20'59. 2861

McLuhan, Marshall. TT.
41:43-4 My15'65;
44:33-4 My11'68.                    2862
McNulty, John (Obituary).
32:72*Ag4'56.                        2863
A Mack Sennett comedy.
Prose. Natacha Stewart.
41:46-8 O2'65.                       2864
Mad day in March. Verse.
Philip Levine. 34:38
Mr29'58.                             2865
Mme. de Braye. Prose.
Mary Mian. 31:31-8*F11'56.
                                     2866
Mme. Shamsi. Prose. Anne
Sinclair Mehdevi. 31:116-
24*S10'55.                           2867
A madman. Prose. John
Updike. 38:34-8 D22'62.
                                     2868
Madness. Verse. James
Dickey. 45:40 Ap26'69.               2869
A madrigal, as it were, of
modifiers. Verse. Fred R.
Miller. 37:36 Ag26'61.               2870
Maestro de costruzione.
PR(Nervi). - Winthrop
Sargeant. 36:40-64
Je11'60.                             2871
Maggie Meriwether's rich ex-
perience. Prose. Jean
Stafford. 31:24-30
Je25'55.                             2872
The Magi hangup. Prose.
William Cox. 43:44-6
D23'67.                              2873
Magic. Verse. Jean Pedrick.
36:52 Mr12'60.                       2874
The magic lantern. Prose.
Robert Henderson. 36:48-51
D10'60.                              2875
The magic mineral. RL.
Paul Brodeur. 44:117-65
O12'68.                              2876
The magpie. Verse. Jon
Swan. 35:48 N21'59.                  2877
The magpie's treasure. FFT.
James Thurber. 32:45
S22'56.                              2878
The magus. Verse. James
Dickey. 36:30 D24'60.                2879
The maiden ladies. Prose.
Nika Standen Hazelton.

39:162-77 S21'63.                    2880
The mail in Majorca. Prose.
Anne Sinclair Mehdevi.
32:66-71*Je30'56.                    2881
Mailer, Norman. Dwight
Macdonald. 36:154-66
O8'60.                               2882
Makassar robbery. Prose.
Santha Rama Rau. 31:76-
83*O1'55.                            2883
The makers. Verse. David
Galler. 41:32 Ja15'66.               2884
Makers. Verse. Richard
Moore. 40:54 O31'64.                 2885
Making marks. Verse. Peter
Davison. 45:38 My17'69.
                                     2886
The making of a pastime:
1971. Prose. F.P. Tullius.
41:212-14 O16'65.                    2887
The making of paths. Prose.
Wallace Stegner. 34:37-8
S6'58.                               2888
Making the customers whole.
AF. John Brooks.
40:160-93 N14'64.                    2889
Malcolm and Bea. Prose.
Mavis Gallant. 44:35-43
Mr23'68.                             2890
Malraux, André. Janet
Flanner. 34:100-103 Je14'58;
35:154-6 Ap18'59.                    2891
The mammoth. Verse.
Robert A. Wallace. 33:71
F23'57.                              2892
Man. Verse. Arturo Vivante.
43:99 F10'68.                        2893
Man and daughter in the
cold. Prose. John Updike.
44:34-6 Mr9'68.                      2894
A man and his matrix. Prose.
Gordon Cotler. 43:164-7
S9'67.                               2895
Man and whose world? Prose.
Calvin Tomkins. 43:24
Ag26'67.                             2896
A man can complain, can't
he? Verse. Ogden Nash.
39:40 Ap27'63.                       2897
Man decides where. OFFC.
Emily Hahn. 36:163-83
Mr12'60.                             2898

A man in a mirror. RL.
Joseph Alsop. 31:35-63
Je25'55.                          2899
Man in black. Verse. Sylvia
Plath. 36:40 Ap9'60.       2900
The man in black. Verse. Mark
Strand. 42:34 Ag6'66.    2901
Man in space. RL. Daniel
Lang. 34:111-38 N15'58.
                                  2902
The man in the dead machine.
Verse. Donald Hall.
42:195 N19'66.              2903
The man in the mirror. Verse.
Mark Strand. 43:50 Mr11'67.
                                  2904
The man in the tree. Verse.
Mark Strand. 43:30
D30'67.                          2905
The man Jones. Prose.
Frances Gray Patton.
31:31-8 Mr26'55.          2906
A man named Hoffman. AM.
Berton Roueché. 41:51-80
Ap24'65.                         2907
A man of habit. Prose.
C.Y. Lee. 33:33-8 Mr30'57.
                                  2908
The man of the world. Prose.
Frank O'Connor. 32:19-22
*Jy28'56.                        2909
The man on the tractor.
Prose. John O'Hara. 39:25-
30 Je22'63.                    2910
Man waiting. Prose. Warren
Miller. 35:27-35 Ag8'59.
                                  2911
A man who. Prose. E.J.
Kahn, Jr. 31:36-8*D17'55.
                                  2912
The man who could not come
into the house. Prose.
Donald Windham. 36:21-4
Jy30'60.                         2913
The man who cried wolf.
Prose. E.J. Kahn, Jr.
31:62-3*Ag13'55.           2914
Man who is happening now.
PR (Scull). Jane Kramer.
42:64-120 N26'66.          2915
The man who jumped into the
water. Prose. Laurie Col-
win. 45:38-42 D20'69.    2916

The man who vanished.
Prose. Robert M. Coates.
31:38-42*O22'55.           2917
The man with the broken
arm. Prose. John O'Hara.
37:42-7 Ap22'61.           2918
The man with the dog.
Prose. R. Prawer Jhabvala.
42:52-60 N19'66.           2919
Man-about-town. Prose.
Nathaniel Benchley.
38:96-105 F9'63.           2920
The manager. Prose. John
O'Hara. 39:42-8
My4'63.                          2921
Mandarins in a farther field.
Prose. John Casey.
45:34-42 Je14'69.          2922
The Mandelbaum Gate: a
delightful English atmos-
phere. Prose. Muriel
Spark. 41:26-54 Jy24'65.
                                  2923
The Mandelbaum Gate:
Abdul's orange groves. Prose.
Muriel Spark. 41:28-65
Ag7'65.                          2924
The Mandelbaum Gate:
Barbara Vaughn's identity.
Prose. Muriel Spark.
41:25-52 Jy10'65.          2925
The Mandelbaum Gate:
Freddy's walk. Prose.
Muriel Spark. 41:54-9
My15'65.                         2926
The mandolin. Verse.
Dorothy Gilbert. 35:92
My9'59.                          2927
Manhole covers. Verse. Karl
Shapiro. 37:36 F10'62.   2928
The manic in the moon.
Prose. James Thurber.
37:22-4 Ag19'61.           2929
Manifesto. Verse. C.M.
Fair. 35:122 F13'60.      2930
Manners. Verse. Elizabeth
Bishop. 31:48*N26'55.    2931
Manners makyth man. Prose.
Patrick Kinross. 34:
34-7 My3'58.                   2932
Man's castle. Prose. James
Reid Parker. 31:56-9
*S3'55.                          2933

Man's face. Prose. Donald
Barthelme. 40:29
My30'64. 2934
Mansfield, Katherine.
Mollie Panter-Downes.
33:208-209 D14'57. 2935
Man-song, river-song. Verse.
Robert David Cohen.
41:48 Mr27'65. 2936
Manuelzinho. Verse.
Elizabeth Bishop. 32:32
*My26'56. 2937
Ms. found under a serviette
in a lovely home. Verse.
Ogden Nash. 32:49 S22'56.
2938
Many arrivals. Verse.
Theodore Roethke. 35:29
Jy25'59. 2939
The map. Verse. Mark
Strand. 39:30 Jy20'63. 2940
A map of Europe: some paintings
by Vermeer. Verse.
Anthony Bailey. 33:32 Je8'57.
2941
The mapmaker on his art.
Verse. Howard Nemerov.
33:54*N30'57. 2942
Marat /Sade (Play). TT.
41:21-3 Ja29'66. 2943
The marauders. Verse.
Robert Hillyer. 33:67
Je29'57. 2944
Marceau, Marcel. Whitney
Balliett. 36:138-9
S17'60. 2945
Marcel Proust and his time
(Exhibition) Mollie Panter-
Downes. 31:167*N5'55. 2946
March. Verse. Jane Cooper.
44:36 Mr2'68. 2947
March 1st. Verse. Kathleen
Spivack. 41:40 Mr6'65. 2948
March, my lion. Verse.
Margaret Thomson. 35:111
Mr21'59. 2949
March twilight. Verse. Louise
Bogan. 33:32 Mr23'57. 2950
March weather. Verse. Jon
Swan. 39:42 Mr9'63. 2951
Marching through Boston.
Prose. John Updike. 41:
34-8 Ja22'66. 2952

A mare. Verse. Kate
Barnes. 34:79 Ja17'59. 2953
Margaret's choice. Verse.
John Holmes. 37:62
O7'61. 2954
Margins. Prose. Donald
Barthelme. 40:33-4 F22
'64. 2955
Marie, Marie, hold on tight.
Prose. Donald Barthelme.
39:49-51 O12'63. 2956
Marietta, O. NFG.
Philip Hamburger.
37:91-4 Je17'61. 2957
Marin. Verse. Philip
Booth. 35:182 S12'59. 2958
Marito in Città. Prose.
John Cheever. 40:26-31
Jy4'64. 2959
Marmee. Prose. Katinka
Loeser. 42:28-32
Je25'66. 2960
Marquand, John P. Geoffrey T.
Hellman. 33:28-31 Mr9'57.
TT. 36:19 Ag6'60. 2961
Marquis, Don. W.W. Watt.
34:30 Je7'58. 2962
Marriage counsel. Verse.
John Updike. 37:103
Ja20'62. 2963
The marriage of heaven and
Earth. Verse. Howard
Nemerov. 42:146
D10'66. 2964
The marriage of mankind.
Verse. H.P.F.
33:193 O26'57. 2965
The married couple. OPH.
Lore Segal. 37:25-34
Jy22'61. 2966
The marrow. Verse.
Theodore Roethke. 38:42
My19'62. 2967
Martin, Ernest H. PR.
E.J. Kahn, Jr.
31:29-47*Ja7'56;
31:33-55*Ja14'56. 2968
Mary and Norma. Prose.
John O'Hara. 37:22-6
Ag5'61. 2969
The mass island. Prose.
Frank O'Connor. 34:26-31
Ja10'59. 2970

Massachusetts vs. Mailer.
OFFC. Dwight Macdonald.
36:154-67 O8'60.          2971
Master. PR (Braque).
Janet Flanner. 32:49-89
O6'56; 32:50-97 O13'56.
                         2972
The masterpiece. Prose.
John Haase. 36:146-52
O8'60.                   2973
A match. Prose. Mary Cable.
31:191-8*D3'55.          2974
The matin pandemoniums.
Verse. Richard Eberhart.
41:42 Ap10'65.           2975
Matlock Bath. Verse. John
Betjeman. 35:40 Mr14'59.
                         2976
The matriarch. Prose.
Alexander Frater. 42:53-6
Ap16'66.                 2977
A matter of taste. Prose.
John Collier. 31:18-21
*Ja7'56.                 2978
The mattress mender. Verse.
Kathleen Fraser. 39:201
O12'63.                  2979
Maugham, W. Somerset.
S.N. Behrman and
Max Beerbohm. 36:96-8
Mr19'60.                 2980
Mauna. Prose. Padma
Perera. 42:205-31 O29'66.
                         2981
Mauriac, François. A.J. Lieb-
ling. 34:39-67 Je21'58.  2982
The May Day dancing.
Verse. Howard Nemerov.
40:48 My2'64.            2983
May, Elaine. PR. Robert
Rice. 37:47-75 Ap15'61.
                         2984
May 10th. Verse. Maxine W.
Kumin. 40:46 My9'64.     2985
May you live in interesting
times. Prose. Gene
Williams. 45:27-9 Ag2'69.
                         2986
Maybe alone on my bike.
Verse. William Stafford.
40:94 Ap4'64.            2987
Maybe like mosaics. Prose.
Patricia Collinge.

35:201-208 O17'59.       2988
The mayor. PR (Wagner).
Philip Hamburger.
32:39-67 Ja26'57;
32:39-69 F2'57.          2989
The mayor. PR (Lindsay).
Nat Hentoff. 43:58-128
O7'67; 43:61-148 O14'67;
45:44-104 My3'69;
45:42-118 My10'69.       2990
Me to you. Verse. Alastair
Reid. 38:36 Ja19'63;
39:36 D21'63.            2991
Mea culpa. Prose. John
Updike. 39:137-40
N16'63.                  2992
The meadow. Verse. Joyce
Horner. 33:71 Je29'57.   2993
The meadows. RL. John
Brooks. 33:98-115
Mr9'57; 33:108-27
Mr16'57.                 2994
Means of protection. Verse.
Vernon Watkins. 40:158
Je6'64.                  2995
Mecca, La. OFC. Whitney
Balliett. 42:128-66
Je11'66.                 2996
Mechanics Library. TT.
31:13-14*D31'55.         2997
The medical scene. Prose.
Lillian Ross. 36:40-50
O29'60.                  2998
Meditation at a stop light.
Verse. Mildred Weston.
36:166 My7'60.           2999
Meditation at Oyster River.
Verse. Theodore Roethke.
36:54 N19'60.            3000
Meditation on a news item.
Verse. John Updike.
36:38 Jy16'60.           3001
Mediterranean. Verse.
May Sarton. 31:131
*O29'55.                 3002
Mediterranean. Verse.
Louis Simpson. 35:41
My2'59.                  3003
Mediterraniam. Verse.
Alastair Reid. 43:151
My20'67.                 3004
The meeting. Verse. Louise
Bogan. 32:36 F9'57.      3005

A meeting. Verse. C. Day
Lewis. 33:42 O19'57.        3006
The meeting. Prose.
Shirley Hazzard. 42:26-31
Jy23'66.                    3007
The meeting. Verse. Howard
Moss. 42:36 Ag20'66.       3008
Meeting again. Verse.
Ruthven Todd. 44:159
My18'68.                   3009
A meeting at Dors River.
Prose. Dan Jacobson.
40:52-9 D5'64.             3010
A meeting in Atlanta. RL.
Bernard Taper. 32:78-121
*Mr17'56.                  3011
Memento. Prose. Robert M.
Coates. 31:50-4*D3'55.
                           3012
Memo. Verse. Hildegarde
Flanner. 44:100 F8'69.     3013
Memoir. Prose. George S.
Kaufman. 36:39 Je11'60.
                           3014
Memoirs of a feeder in France.
OUWA. A.J. Liebling.
35:51-79 Ap11'59; 35:49-76
Ap18'59; 35:108-35 Ap25'59;
35:108-27 My2'59.          3015
Memoirs of a short-wave prophet.
Prose. Willie Morris.
39:117-32 N30'63.          3016
Memoirs of an anti-Semite.
Prose. Gregor von Rezzori.
45:42-83 Ap26'69.          3017
Memorandum. Verse. William
Stafford. 42:104 F26'66. 3018
A memory. Verse. Robert
Hillyer. 34:44 S13'58.     3019
Men on the moon. RL. Henry
S. F. Cooper, Jr. 45:53-
129 Ap12'69; 45:47-97 Ap19
'69.                       3020
Ménage à trois. Verse.
Howard Moss. 45:56 O11'69.
                           3021
Mene, mene, tekel, upharsin.
Prose. John Cheever.
39:38-41 Ap27'63.          3022
Mercifully, . Verse. Marianne
Moore. 44:34 Jy20'68.
                           3023

Merioneth, Wales. Verse.
Rolfe Humphries. 32:133
*My5'56.                   3024
Merrimack County. Verse.
Donald Hall. 35:96
Ag22'59.                   3025
Merry*Christmas*from*the*
Smiths! Prose. Frances
Lanahan. 39:32-3 D21'63.
                           3026
The mesa land. Verse.
Reeve Spencer Kelley.
32:157 O27'56.             3027
Messages. Verse. James
Dickey. 45:30 Ag2'69.      3028
The messenger. Verse.
Kathleen Raine. 44:188
D7'68.                     3029
The messengers. Verse.
Muriel Spark. 43:44
S16'67.                    3030
Messieurs, faites vos jeux.
Prose. E.J. Kahn, Jr.
33:144-8 O12'57.           3031
Metamorphoses. Prose.
John Cheever 39:32-9
Mr2'63.                    3032
Metamorphosis. PR (Rubin-
stein). Joseph Wechsberg.
34:47-95 N1'58.            3033
Metamorphosis in the
Gorbals. OFFC. Stephen
Watts. 35:137-64
O24'59.                    3034
The metamorphosis of Philip
Musica. AC. Robert
Shaplen. 31:49-81*O22'55;
31:39-79*O29'55.           3035
The Metterling lists. Prose.
Woody Allen. 45:34-5
My10'69.                   3036
Mice and birds and boy.
Prose. Elizabeth Taylor.
38:28-32 F9'63.            3037
Michener, James A. John
Lardner. 35:167-9
O24'59.                    3038
Micromutations. Verse.
James Wright. 41:97
Je26'65.                   3039
Micronesia. RL. E.J. Kahn,
Jr. 42:42-111 Je11'66;

42:42-109 Je18'66; 42:56-
104 Je25'66.                     3040
Middle age: a Chinese
restaurant. Verse. John
Malcolm Brinnin. 45:58
N22'69.                          3041
Middle-aged man without a
horn. PR (Shaw) Robert
Lewis Taylor. 38:47-98
My19'62.                         3042
Midnight at Tim's place.
Prose. James Thurber.
34:46-7 N29'58.                  3043
Midsummer. Verse. James
Scully. 38:28 Ag4'62.            3044
Midsummer night. Verse.
Helen Bevington. 35:61
Jy18'59.                         3045
A mild attack of locusts. Prose.
Doris Lessing. 31:80-7
F26'55.                          3046
The milk train stops at
Tiffany's. Verse. Andy
Logan. 39:194 Mr16'63.
                                 3047
The mill at the bottom of the
sea. Prose. Robert
Henderson. 36:35-7 Mr5'60.
                                 3048
Miller, Jonathan. TT. 38:30-1
S8'62.                           3049
Milwaukee, Wis. NFG. Philip
Hamburger. 36:150-4
Ap9'60.                          3050
The mind, intractable thing.
Verse. Marianne Moore.
41:60 N27'65.                    3051
Mine. Verse. Frank Polite.
43:64 D2'67.                     3052
Minimax, minimax, tekel,
uphilton. Prose. E.J.
Kahn, Jr. 32:141-6 N24'56.
                                 3053
The minor cavalier. Prose.
John D. Stewart. 36:225-30
D3'60.                           3054
A minor change. Verse.
Mark McCloskey. 42:96
Mr5'66.                          3055
A minority. Prose. Frank
O'Connor. 33:36-9
S28'57.                          3056
Minuet in four rounds. Prose.

Robert Henderson. 38:20-1
Jy21'62.                         3057
Miriam. Verse. Howard
Moss. 40:62 N28'64.              3058
The mirroring transparencies.
Verse. D.C. Brown.
35:24 Jy11'59.                   3059
The miser. Prose. Robert
Henderson. 31:44-8
*O22'55.                         3060
Miserere. Verse. Lawrence
Kramer. 45:140 S13'69.
                                 3061
Miss Berry and the mushroom.
Prose. Grover Amen.
34:113-16 Je14'58.               3062
Miss Douglas and Mrs.
Dillon. OPH. Lore Segal.
38:23-36 Jy21'62.                3063
Miss Idella, the travelling
hoe lady. Prose. Berry
Morgan. 42:53-5 D10'66.
                                 3064
Miss Lenora when last seen.
Prose. Peter Taylor.
36:52-90 N19'60.                 3065
Miss Millard. Prose. Anthony
West. 43:132-79 N11'67.
                                 3066
Miss Wapshot. Prose. John
Cheever. 32:40-3 S22'56.
                                 3067
The missing person. Verse.
Donald Justice. 42:202
O15'66.                          3068
The Missouri. Verse. Ernest
Kroll. 37:157 O28'61.            3069
The misstep. Verse. E.B.
White. 34:28 Jy12'58.
                                 3070
Mr. Clarke. Prose.
Burton Bernstein. 36:169-
76 My7'60.                       3071
Mr. Collier. Prose. Berry
Morgan. 45:58-60
O18'69.                          3072
Mr. Considine's wake. Prose.
Frank Sullivan. 32:114-25
O20'56.                          3073
Mr. Dock. Prose. Berry
Morgan. 44:34-6 Ja11'69.
                                 3074
Mr. Engel's eye. Prose.

Patricia Collinge. 34:69-77
Ag23'58.                         3075
Mr. ex-resident. Prose.
John Updike. 37:27 Ag5'61.
                                 3076
Mr. Fingerhood's bill of goods.
Prose. Burton Bernstein.
36:100-17 S10'60.         3077
Mr. Harty. Prose. Arturo
Vivante. 41:81-7 Ja22'66.
                                 3078
Mr. High-mind. Verse. John
Updike. 32:44*Ap28'56. 3079
Mr. Hunter's grave. PR
(Hunter). Joseph Mitchell.
32:50-95 S22'56.         3080
Mr. Keogh. Prose. Anthony
West. 43:29-51 Jy8'67.
                                 3081
Mr. Mauriac's automobile.
RL. A.J. Liebling. 34:39-
67 Je21'58.               3082
Mr. Nyedly. Prose. Eleanor
L. Glaze. 36:132-42
Je4'60.                   3083
Mr. Roundy. Prose. Anne
Sinclair Mehdevi. 37:
141-3 Mr25'61.            3084
Mr. Smith. Verse. William
Jay Smith. 33:36 Mr2'57.
                                 3085
Mr. Snowden among the
people. RL. Edith Iglauer.
38:105-54 Ap21'62.        3086
Mr. Wharton. Prose.
Elizabeth Taylor. 39:36-40
Je8'63.                   3087
Mistral. Verse. Barbara
Howes. 32:36 F16'57.      3088
Mrs. Barker. Prose. Anthony
West. 42:52-113 My14'66.
                                 3089
Mrs. Beeton. Prose. Calvin
Tomkins. 36:84-90
Je11'60.                  3090
Mrs. Billingsby's wine.
Prose. Peter Taylor.
43:56-60 O14'67.          3091
Mrs. Cleaver, exorcised.
Prose. Mary Nash. 33:109-26
My18'57.                  3092
Mrs. Gentry. Prose. Anthony
West. 37:32-40 F17'62.
                                 3093

Mrs. Harcourt's mare.
Prose. Nancy Hale.
38:20-3 Jy28'62.          3094
Mrs. Julia Wolfe. Prose.
Stewart Johnson. 34:39-44
Ap12'58.                  3095
Mrs. Kane's illness. Prose.
Viola Meynell. 31:37-42
My21'55.                  3096
Mrs. Levine's house. OPH.
Lore Segal. 37:82-106
My27'61.                  3097
Mrs. Rogers. Prose.
Joyce Warren. 38:177-8
N3'62.                    3098
The Moabitess. Prose.
Mavis Gallant. 33:42-6
N2'57.                    3099
Mobile, Ala. NFG.
Philip Hamburger.
37:141-6 O7'61.           3100
Mobile of birds. Verse.
John Updike. 35:32
*D19'59.                  3101
The Moccasin River. Verse.
Joseph Hansen. 34:27
Ag30'58.                  3102
The mockingbird. Verse.
Randall Jarrell. 39:48
N2'63.                    3103
The model. Prose. Nancy
Hale. 32:30-53
*Ag4'56.                  3104
The moderate. Verse. John
Updike. 34:103 Ja10'59.
                                 3105
Modigliani's death mask.
Verse. John Updike.
36:34 Mr26'60.            3106
Modrone, Luchino Visconti
di. TT. 44:25-8
Jy20'68.                  3107
Molière. TT. 31:43-5
N12'55.                   3108
Molnár, Ferenc. Edmund Wilson.
42:118-26 Je4'66.         3108a
Moment. Verse. Howard
Nemerov. 36:27 Ag20'60.3109
A moment. Prose. Arturo
Vivante. 44:195-6 N9'68.3110
A moment of equilibrium among
the islands. Verse. Richard
Eberhart. 36:64 Jy16'60.
                                 3111

Moment of truth. Verse. Ethel
Barnett deVito. 31:32
*Ja21'56.                         3112
Momentum. Prose. Patricia
Collinge. 35:20-3 Jy18'59.
3113
Monday. Verse. William
Stafford. 41:184 D11'65. 3114
Money. Prose. John O'Hara.
38:38-46 Mr24'62.        3115
Money and the generations of
mankind. Prose. St. Clair
McKelway. 36:29-32
D24'60.                          3116
Money-building. OFFC.
E.J. Kahn, Jr. 37:167-77
O7'61.                           3117
The mongoose. PR (Moore).
Jack Murphy. 37:61-112
N11'61.                          3118
Monica. Prose. Emily Hahn.
34:121-37 O11'58.        3119
Monody. Verse. Robert
David Cohen. 41:66 N27'65.
3120
Monomania, you and me is
quits. Prose. S.J.
Perelman. 36:46-8 N26'60.
3121
Monsieur Flandin's domaine.
RL. A.J. Liebling. 34:90-
111 S13'58.              3122
M. Mauriac's automobile.
RL. A.J. Liebling.
34:39-67 Je21'58.        3123
M. Zuckerberg's heart. Prose.
Richard Berczeller. 41:98-
106 S4'65.               3124
Monsoon. Verse. David Wevill.
38:56 N17'62.            3125
Montana eclogue. Verse.
William Stafford. 42:56 D17'66.
3126
Montegutoni. Prose. Eyre
de Lanux. 42:198-204
S10'66.                  3127
Montraldo. Prose. John
Cheever. 40:37-9 Je6'64.
3128
Moods. Verse. T.S.
Matthews. 33:114 F15'58.
3129

The moon. Verse. Luke Zilles.
32:53 Ja5'57.                    3130
Moon in a box. OFFC.
Daniel Lang. 33:50-7
D28'57.                          3131
The moon in your hands.
Verse. H.D. 33:29
*Jy20'57.                        3132
Moon landing. Verse.
W.H. Auden. 45:38
S6'69.                           3133
Moon song. Verse. Anne
Sexton. 44:32 S7'68.     3134
Moonstruck at sunset. Prose.
S.J. Perelman. 45:28-31
Ag16'69.                         3135
Moontan. Verse. Mark
Strand. 41:152 S11'65.   3136
Moore, George. S.N. Behr-
man and Max Beerbohm.
36:64-70 Mr19'60.        3137
Moore, Marianne. PR.
Winthrop Sargeant. 32:38-
77 F16'57.                       3138
Moore, Marianne. TT.
41:24-6 Ja29'66.         3139
Moravia, Alberto. TT.
31:39 My7'55.            3140
Moray eels. Verse. David
Galler. 45:34 Ja24'70.   3141
More, and still more,
memories of the Nineteen-
twenties. Prose. Michael
J. Arlen. 35:22-3
Ja2'60.                          3142
More big news from out
there. Prose. Gordon Cotler.
42:28-9 F4'67.           3143
A more complete cross-
section. Prose. John
Casey. 44:55-64 O19'68.
3144
More fellow-creatures. Verse.
Ogden Nash. 34:38
S27'58.                          3145
More film fun. Prose.
Roger Angell. 40:42-3
S26'64.                          3146
More friend than lodger.
Prose. Angus Wilson.
33:28-49*Ag10'57.        3147
More old tales about men and

women. Prose. William
Maxwell. 34:36-40 O18'58.
                  3148
More old tales about women.
Prose. William Maxwell.
34:20-2 Ag23'58.      3149
Morels. Verse. William Jay
Smith. 40:44 My23'64.  3150
Morgantown, W.Va. NFG.
Philip Hamburger. 37:108-11
S16'61.                  3151
The moribundant life, or, grow
old along with whom? Prose.
James Thurber. 31:31-4
*O1'55.                3152
The moritorium and the new
mobe. RL. Francine du
Plessix Gray. 45:32-42
Ja3'70.                3153
Morituri. Verse. Barbara
Bellow Watson. 44:38
Mr30'68.              3154
Morning. Verse. Hilary
Corke. 38:30 Ja5'63.  3155
The morning. Prose. John
Updike. 40:24-6 Jy18'64.
                  3156
Morning exercises. Prose.
Robert M. Coates. 36:108-14
F27'60.                3157
Morning, noon, and ...
Verse. Hawley Truax. 43:47
Mr25'67.              3158
Morning notebook. Verse.
Edward Kessler. 36:174
O8'60.                3159
Morning on the St. John's.
Verse. Jane Cooper. 33:36
Je15'57.              3160
A morozhenoe a day keeps
the M.V.D. away. Prose.
John Sack. 36:82-7 Ja28'61.
                3161
The morphinist. Prose. Richard
Berczeller. 42:141-53
Ap16'66.              3162
Mortality. Prose. Calvin
Kentfield. 31:44-9*O8'55.
                3163
Mosby's memoirs. Prose. Saul
Bellow. 44:36-49 Jy20'68.
                3164

Moses cussed me. Verse.
Howard Cushman. 38:87
Ag11'62.              3165
Mosquito. Verse. John
Updike. 36:32 Je11'60. 3166
The most delicate thing in
the world. AM. Berton
Roueché. 33:146-61
My4'57.                3167
The most elegant drawing
room in Europe. Prose.
Nancy Hale. 42:55-64
S17'66.                3168
The most singular place.
Prose. Susan Gillespie.
33:151-66 O5'57.      3169
A most valuable accident.
RL. Daniel Lang. 35:49-
92 My2'59.           3170
The most wonderful bed in
the world. Prose. Sonia
Rollnick. 34:43-8
O11'58.                3171
The moth. Verse. Van K.
Brock. 42:38 Ap9'66.  3172
Mother Taft's chickens (cont.)
Prose. Geoffrey T.
Hellman. 31:34-5 Mr19'55.
                3173
Mother tongue. Verse.
Richard Armour. 32:68*My26
'56.                 3174
The mother tongue. Verse.
Ogden Nash. 33:46
N9'57.                3175
Mother Westminster's
chickens. Prose. Geoffrey
T. Hellman. 31:18-19
*Jy2'55.              3176
Mother's Day at Porte de
Vanves. Prose. Francis
Steegmuller. 34:31-2
Jy12'58.              3177
Mount Rushmore. Verse.
Sheridan Baker. 31:30
*Ag20'55.             3178
Mountain. Verse. Maxine W.
Kumin. 37:133 F10'62. 3179
The mountain day. Prose.
Jean Stafford. 32:24-32
*Ag18'56.            3180
The mountain of miracles.

A new place. Prose. Nancy
Hale. 34:41-58 My3'58. 3284

No entry. 3285
A new situation in the world.
REF. Richard H. Rovere.
44:43-72 F24'68. 3286
The new sound. OUWA. Renata
Adler. 41:63-105 F20'65.
3287
A new system of water
purification. Verse. Nathan
Fast. 33:139 Ap13'57. 3288
The new theologian. PR (New
Theology). Ved Mehta.
41:63-153 N13'65; 41:60-
144 N20'65; 41:65-169 N27'65.
3289
New Year's Eve. Prose.
Mavis Gallant. 45:25-30 Ja
10'70. 3290
New Year's Eve. Verse.
Richard Shelton. 45:26 Ja3'70.
3291
New Year's, 1948. Verse.
L. E. Sissman. 44:34-5
D28'68. 3292
New York. OPH. Lore Segal.
40:30-55 Jy25'64. 3293
New York: a prayer. Verse.
George S. Kaufman. 31:34
*S3'55. 3294
New York film festival.
Brendan Gill. 40:134-6 O3'64.
3295
New York Herald Tribune
(Parody). St. Clair
McKelway. 39:34-5 My25'63.
3296
New York Review of Books
(Parody). Roger Angell.
42:28-9 D24'66. 3297
New York revisited. WP.
A.J. Liebling. 31:94-104
*O29'55. 3298
New York surprised. Verse.
Alastair Reid. 42:42 Ap2'66.
3299
New York Times (Parody).
St. Clair McKelway. 39:
34-5 My25'63. 3300

New York Times Book
Review (Parody). St.
Clair McKelway. 38:36-7
Ja26'63. 3301
New York Times Magazine
(Parody). Roger Angell.
41:40-1 Mr27'65. 3302
New York Times Magazine
(Parody). St. Clair
McKelway. 39:20-1 Je29'63.
3303
Newark, O. NFG. Philip
Hamburger. 37:118-23
F18'61. 3304
Newley, Anthony (Parody).
Emerson Beauchamp.
41:68-71 Jy17'65. 3305
The newlyweds. Verse.
John Updike. 31:142
*N19'55. 3306
Newman, James R. TT.
32:43-4*N10'56. 3307
News. Prose. Lillian Ross.
38:36-8 Jy14'62. 3308
News from the cabin. Verse.
May Swenson. 34:29 Jy
26'58. 3309
News from the house. Verse.
Michael Dennis Browne.
44:34 Ja4'69. 3310
News from the islands. Verse.
John Malcolm Brinnin. 34:
38 F22'58. 3311
The news of the week in
review. Prose. Gifford
Brown. 39:66-9 Ja4'64.
3312
Newstead, Helaine. PR.
Morton M. Hunt. 33:
39-80 Mr30'57. 3313
Next day. Verse. Randall
Jarrell. 39:58 D14'63. 3314
Next door. Verse. Richard
Wilbur. 37:40 My6'61. 3315
Next week at the Prado:
Frankie Goya plus monster
cast. Prose. S.J.Perelman.
31:28-30 Mr26'55. 3316
Next-to-last stand, maybe.
RL. A.J. Liebling.
31:90-106 Ap16'55. 3317
A nice, big, surprising city.
RL. A.J. Liebling.

34:117-24 Ap19'58.      3318
The nicest girl in Cook County.
    Prose. Allan Seager.
    32:42-7*S15'56.      3319
A niche for the architect.
    Verse. John Nixon, Jr.
    33:110 F8'58.      3320
Nichols, Mike. PR. Robert
    Rice. 37:47-75 Ap15'61.
                      3321
Nicolson, Harold. TT.
    38:24-6 F9'63.      3322
Night and day. Prose. Mavis
    Gallant. 38:48-50 Mr17'62.
                      3323
Night and day, day and night.
    Prose. Lillian Ross. 38:
    48-58 N3'62.      3324
The night crawler. Prose.
    Charles B. Finney. 35:132-
    47 D5'59.      3325
The night face up. Prose.
    Julio Cortázar. Paul Black-
    burn, trans. 43:49-52
    Ap22'67.      3326
Night foray. Prose. Robert
    M. Coates. 33:22-6*Ag10'57.
                      3327
The night mirror. Verse.
    John Hollander. 41:111
    Ag28'65.      3328
Night of souls. Verse. Ann
    Stanford. 44:44 My25'68.
                      3329
The night of the sad women.
    Verse. David Wagoner. 40:56
    S19'64.      3330
Night passage. Verse. David
    Wagoner. 42:54 Mr19'66.
                      3331
Night poem. Verse. Gene
    Baro. 41:87 Ja22'66.      3332
Night talk. Verse. Jean
    Garrigue. 33:30 Jy13'57.
                      3333
Night thought. Verse. Gerald
    Jonas. 40:205 O17'64.      3334
Night thoughts in age. Verse.
    John Hall Wheelock.
    31:26*Jy23'55.      3335
Night walk. Verse. Donald
    Finkel. 45:52 N1'69.      3336

Night walk. Verse. Sylvia
    Plath. 34:40 O11'58.      3337
Night walk. Verse. Stanley
    Young. 31:66*O1'55.      3338
Nightfall at twenty thousand
    feet. Verse. Robert
    Graves. 36:50 N19'60.      3339
The nightingale. Prose.
    Elizabeth Cullinan. 37:
    26-30 D30'61.      3340
Nightingale. Verse. Charles
    Tomlinson. 39:76
    Je1'63.      3341
The nightingale. Prose.
    Arturo Vivante. 39:136-8
    My18'63.      3342
The nightingale song.
    Prose. Noel Perrin.
    33:26-7 Mr16'57.      3343
Nights away from home. Prose.
    Frank Conroy. 42:56-80
    O22'66.      3344
Nine decades after Stanley.
    RL. Thomas Sterling.
    36:146-80 My14'60;
    36:49-114 My21'60.      3345
The 1930 Olympics. Prose.
    H.L. Mountzoures. 45:127-
    30 Ap5'69.      3346
Ninety-nine years is not
    forever. Prose. F.P. Tul-
    lius. 45:20-1 Jy19'69.      3347
No autographs, please--I'm
    invisible. Prose. S.J.
    Perelman. 41:46-9 S18'65.
                      3348
No conformity to enormity!
    Verse. Ogden Nash. 34:34
    F22'58.      3349
No entry. Prose. Patricia
    Collinge. 33:24-5 Ja18'58.
                      3350
No feeling of falling. PR
    (Istel) Robert Lewis
    Taylor. 34:42-73 Ja24'59.
                      3351
No larger than life. Prose.
    Wendell Wilcox. 32:51-6
    N17'56.      3352
No medal for Matt. Prose.
    Walter Macken. 34:70-6
    Je28'58.      3353

No moon, no star. Verse.
  Babette Deutsch. 38:66
  Ag4'62.                      3354
No more elegies. Verse.
  Jane Cooper. 43:30 Ja13'68.
                               3355
No news is bad news. Verse.
  Dorothy Lobrano. 39:47
  Mr9'63.                      3356
No sale. Prose. Joyce
  Warren. 33:187-92 O12'57.
                               3357
No telling, no summing up.
  OUWA. Calvin Trillin. 42:
  118-26 Je11'66.              3358
No trouble at all, it's as easy
  as falling off a loggerhead.
  Verse. Ogden Nash. 45:34
  Mr8'69.                      3359
Nobody here 'cep' us riffraff.
  Prose. S.J. Perelman.
  37:32-4 Ap29'61.            3360
Nobody knows the muggin' I've
  seen. Prose. S.J. Perelman.
  38:22-4 Jy7'62.              3361
Nobody's fool. Prose. Peter
  DeVries. 38:28-9 Je16'62.
                               3362
Noctuary. Verse. R.P. Lister.
  35:162 O17'59.               3363
Nocturne. Prose. Katinka
  Loeser. 39:44-6 O5'63.      3364
Nodehportsuob. Verse.
  R.P. Lister. 34:138 N15'58.
                               3365
Noisy flushes the birds. Prose.
  V.S. Pritchett. 37:44-80
  S23'61.                      3366
Noisy in the doghouse. Prose.
  V.S. Pritchett. 38:50-60
  N10'62.                      3367
Non troppo with Topo. RL.
  Joseph Wechsberg. 34:179-
  92 N22'58.                   3368
None are so blind. Prose.
  John Collier. 32:29-34
  *Mr31'56.                    3369
Noon. Verse. Whitney
  Balliett. 31:70*Ag27'55.
                               3370
North Philadelphia, Trenton,
  and New York. Verse.
  Richmond Lattimore.31:30

Mr5'55.                        3371
Northeast acre. Verse. Constance
  Carrier. 31:175 D3'55.
                               3372
A norther--Key West. Verse.
  Elizabeth Bishop. 37:25
  Ja20'62.                     3373
Not another word. Prose.
  Richard Thurman. 33:37-44
  My25'57.                     3374
Not counting rhizopods and
  flagellates. Prose. H.F.
  Ellis. 34:20-1 Jy26'58.
                               3375
Not for dogs. Prose. Sylva
  Grossman. 32:80-93
  *My26'56.                    3376
Not seen and/or less seen.
  PR (Duchamp). Calvin
  Tomkins. 40:37-93 F6'65.
                               3377
The not so tangled web.
  Verse. Jessica Nelson North.
  31:116*O22'55.               3378
Not valid in Macao. Prose.
  H.F. Ellis. 40:218-24
  O31'64.                      3379
A note from the coast. Verse.
  Alastair Reid. 32:192
  D15'56.                      3380
Note on a certain statesman.
  Verse. C.M. Fair. 34:23
  Ja3'59.                      3381
A note to La Fontaine. Verse.
  Jean Garrigue. 40:171
  Mr21'64.                     3382
Note to Wang Wei. Verse.
  John Berryman. 34:59
  Ag2'58.                      3383
Notebook of a dilettante.
  REF. Leopold Tyrmand.
  44:68-112 N9'68.             3384
Notes. Prose. John Updike.
  32:28-9 Ja26'57.             3385
Notes for a New England
  road map. Verse. Phyllis
  McGinley. 34:27 Ag23'58.
                               3386
Notes for the chart in 306.
  Verse. Ogden Nash. 42:30
  Je25'66.                     3387
Notes from a bottle. Prose.
  James Stevenson. 44:31
  F8'69.                       3388

The oak and the axe. Prose.
Elizabeth Hardwick. 32:49-72
*My12'56. 3423

An o/b m/b overdue, a c/c
in distress. RL. John
Brooks. 31:98-114*S10'55.
3424

The object. Prose. Nancy
Hale. 32:46-75*Mr17'56.
3425

Observation on skiers. Verse.
Louise Darcy. 33:86 D21'57.
3426

Observer Film Exhibition.
Mollie Panter-Downes. 32:
71-2*Jy7'56. 3427

An obstacle or two. AC. E.J.
Kahn, Jr. 35:126-61
Ap11'59. 3428

The ocean. Prose. John
Cheever. 40:30-40 Ag1'64.
3429

Ocean. Verse. Adrien Stoutenburg. 38:58 O13'62. 3430

October. Verse. Ralph
Pomeroy. 35:42 O10'59.
3431

October maples. Verse.
Richard Wilbur. 36:46
O22'60. 3432

October's face. Verse. John
Moffitt. 33:144 O5'57. 3433

An ode. Verse. John Updike.
31:47*O15'55. 3434

Ode to a model. Verse.
Vladimir Nabokov. 31:48
*O8'55. 3435

Ode to Poseidon. Verse.
Barbara Howes. 41:60 O30
'65. 3436

Oë, Kenzaburo. TT. 44:25-6
Je8'68. 3437

Of history more like myth.
Verse. Jean Garrigue. 39:44
S28'63. 3438

Of inhuman bondage. Prose.
E.J. Kahn, Jr. 33:72-9
Ja11'58. 3439

Of puddings (Yorks.). Prose.
Anthony Bailey. 36:112-16
My28'60. 3440

Off Marblehead. Verse. John
Hollander. 35:34 Ag29'59.
3441

An offering. Verse. Louis
O. Coxe. 44:52 S14'68.
3442

Offers and demands. WP.
A.J. Liebling. 38:110-20
Ja26'63. 3443

Official life. Prose. Shirley
Hazzard. 43:24-30
Je24'67. 3444

O'Gorman, Ned. TT.
43:54-5 D2'67. 3445

Oh, I am a cook and a house-
boy bland. Prose. S.J.
Perelman. 37:34-7
F18'61. 3446

O'Hara, John. Geoffrey T.
Hellman. 33:28-31
Mr9'57. 3447

Oklahoma City, Okla. NFG.
Philip Hamburger. 37:210-
14 N4'61. 3448

The old Adam. Prose. Rhys
Davies. 36:40-8 O22'60.
3449

Old amusement park. Verse.
Marianne Moore. 40:34
Ag29'64. 3450

Old copy-desk editor. Verse.
J.U. 33:73*Jy20'57. 3451

Old faces of '56. Verse.
John Updike. 32:36
O27'56. 3452

The old familiar faces. Verse.
R.P. Lister. 32:216
N17'56. 3453

An old field mowed. Verse.
William Meredith. 37:48
S30'61. 3454

Old folks at the home. Verse.
Morris Bishop. 33:106
Ja11'58. 3455

The old friends. Prose.
Mavis Gallant. 45:27-30
Ag30'69. 3456

The old glory. Prose.
Robert Hemenway. 35:25-33
Jy4'59. 3457

Old gramaphone records.
Verse. James Kirkup.
31:36 My28'55. 3458

The old guy. Prose. Sylva
Grossman. 41:207-17
O30'65. 3459

## ONE

Verse. C.M. Fair. 37:78
Ag12'61.                                3529

On the wagon. Verse. Adrien
Stoutenburg. 44:154
My11'68.                                3530

On the waves. Prose. Harold
Brodkey. 41:24-7 S4'65.3531

On the way to school. Prose.
John Updike. 38:32-67
Ja5'63.                                 3532

On the Welsh marches. Verse.
Walter Stone. 35:161
S26'59.                                 3533

On the youth of England corrupted
by coffee. Verse. R.P.
Lister. 32:60 Ja5'57.     3534

On this day. Prose. L.
Woiwode. 43:44-9 S9'67.
                                        3535

On turtles. Verse. John
Malcolm Brinnin. 39:30
Je29'63.                                3536

Once a lady. Prose. Angus
Wilson. 33:23-9 Ag31'57.
                                        3537

Once more unto the breach.
Prose. Patricia Collinge.
36:48-9 N5'60.               3538

Once over lightly, and please
hush your bazoo. Prose. S.J
Perelman. 39:50-2 D14'63.
                                        3539

One aspect of a rainy day.
Prose. Mavis Gallant. 38:38-
9 Ap14'62.                  3540

One beat to the bar. PR
(Evans). Robert Lewis
Taylor. 31:47-73 Ap16'55;
31:39-64 Ap23'55.          3541

One comely babe, piping
hot. Prose. S.J. Perelman.
32:18-20*Jy14'56.          3542

One day in the life of James
Hoover. Prose. James
Hoover. 39:76-80 Ag17'63.
                                        3543

The one day of the year.
Prose. Frank O'Connor.
35:31-3*D19'59.            3544

One dollar for the lot. AF.
John Brooks. 33:110-32
Ap27'57.                                3545

One more new botched
beginning. Verse. Stephen

Spender. 40:42 My2'64.
                                        3546

One morning in New Hampshire.
Verse. May Swenson.
37:85 Ag19'61.             3547

104 Boulevard Saint-
Germain. Verse. Kenneth
Pitchford. 34:46 My17'58.
                                        3548

One of my generation. Prose.
John Updike. 45:57-8
N15'69.                                 3549

One of the lucky ones. AM.
Berton Roueché. 31:35-49
F26'55.                                 3550

One of their kings. Verse.
Louis Simpson. 41:46
My1'65.                                 3551

One Summer. Prose. Mary
Lavin. 41:50-98
S11'65.                                 3552

One thing leading to another.
Prose. Sylvia Townsend
Warner. 37:34-43
F10'62.                                 3553

One touch of nature. REF.
Mary McCarthy. 45:39-57
Ja24'70.                                3554

One volume, soiled. Verse.
John M. Ridland. 32:85
*S15'56.                                3555

One with Nineveh. Prose.
Wolcott Gibbs. 32:28-32
*Mr24'56.                               3556

One-man think tank. PR
(Scammon). William
Whitworth. 45:50-89
S20'69.                                 3557

The one-ton pencil. PR
(Friendly). Thomas
Whiteside. 37:41-88
F17'62.                                 3558

Onward and upward with
science: go on, investi-
gators! scrutinize! Prose.
Geoffrey T. Hellman.
38:142-76 N3'62.          3559

Onward and upward with the
sciences: blazing the trail
for the alpha and omega.
Prose. Geoffrey T. Hellman.
40:97-155 D5'64.          3560

Onward and upward with the
sciences: the tail of taxonomy.

Prose. Geoffrey T. Hellman.
40:41-77 My30'64.        3561
Onward and upward with tech-
nology: giving up the gun.
Prose. Noel Perrin.
41:211-28 N20'65.        3562
Onward, Christian soldier.
Prose. Sally Benson. 31:35-40
*O1'55.                  3563
Onward, upward, backward,
forward, and sideways with
the RX-550. Prose. Michael
J. Arlen. 39:37-8 My11'63.
                         3564
Ooty. PR (Ootacamund).
Mollie Panter-Downes. 43:48-
131 Mr4'67; 43:57-124
Mr11'67.                 3565
Open and shut. Prose. Colleen
Brooks. 45:34-5 Jy5'69.
                         3566
Open entry for a "Time &
Tide" competition. Prose.
Patricia Collinge. 32:46
D8'56.                   3567
Open letter to a cold-slough
mob. Prose. S.J.
Perelman. 35:49-52
N7'59.                   3568
Open letter to the Le Goarnics.
Verse. C.M. Fair. 39:32
Je1'63.                  3569
Open season on Turks. Prose.
William Murray. 34:95-107
O25'58.                  3570
Open to the public. Prose. Julia
Siebel. 36:36-40 Ap9'60.
                         3571
The opening. Verse. Jon
Swan. 36:146 Ap2'60.    3571a
Opera after midnight. RL.
Joseph Wechsberg. 31:43-77
My21'55.                 3572
The optimist's daughter. Prose.
Eudora Welty. 45:37-128
Mr15'69.                 3573
The orange man. AM. Berton
Roueché. 43:110-23
My27'67.                 3574
Oranges. Verse. George
Amabile. 44:44 S28'68.
                         3575

Oranges. RL. John McPhee.
42:142-81 My7'66;
42:144-99 My14'66.       3576
The orchard. Prose. Arturo
Vivante. 44:24-7 Je15'68.
                         3577
The ordeal of Dr. Blauber-
man. Prose. Lillian Ross.
37:39-88 My13'61.        3578
An ordinary evening in
Cleveland. Verse. Lewis
Turco. 44:40 Mr2'68.     3579
An Oregon message. Verse.
William Stafford. 44:194
N23'68.                  3580
The organ piece. Prose.
Berry Morgan. 42:24-6
Ag13'66.                 3581
Organizer. PR (Chavez).
Peter Matthiessen.
45:42-85 Je21'69;
45:43-71 Je28'69.        3582
No entry.                3583
Orientals are stoic. Prose.
André M. Tao-Kim-Hai.
33:105-23 S28'57.        3584
Origins. Prose. Alice
Marriott. 34:106-15. Ap5
'58.                     3585
O'Riley's late-bloomed little
son. Verse. X.J. Kennedy.
45:142 Ap19'69.          3586
Orlando in Monte Kisco. PR
(Menotti). Winthrop
Sargeant. 39:49-89
My4'63.                  3587
The ormolu clock. Prose.
Muriel Spark. 36:38-41
S17'60.                  3588
Ornamental sketch with
verbs. Verse. May Swenson.
31:91 My7'55.            3589
Orphans' progress. Prose.
Mavis Gallant. 41:49-51
Ap3'65.                  3590
Orpheus before Hades.
Verse. James Dickey. 35:
52 D5'59.                3591
Orpheus' song. Verse. Irving
Feldman. 38:135 Mr24'62.
                         3592

Orwell, George. Mollie
Panter-Downes. 31:84-5
F19'55. 3593
Osborne, John. TT.
33:36-7 O26'57; 42:47-8
O8'66. 3594
The other death. Prose. Jorge
Luis Borges. Norman
Thomas di Giovanni, trans.
44:52-5 N2'68. 3595
The other side. Prose.
Nancy Hale. 45:82-93 Mr1'69.
3596
The other side of the island.
Prose. Sally Benson. 31:33-
7 My28'55. 3597
The other times. Prose. Peter
Taylor. 33:36-64 F23'57.
3598
Other times, other teen-agers.
Prose. Helene Hanff.
37:213-21 D9'61. 3599
Ouida. See de la Ramée,
Marie Louise. 3600
Our Bovary. Prose. Nadine
Gordimer. 33:41-6
S28'57. 3601
Our local correspondents:
Central Park bird walk.
Prose. Eugene Kinkead.
45:58-66 Ag2'69. 3602
Our Maximilian. Prose.
Richard Berczeller. 39:45-55
Ja25'64. 3603
Our plunging correspondents.
Prose. John Brooks. 31:
100-14 My21'55. 3604
Our rural correspondents: the
changing landscape. Prose.
Christopher Rand. 38:200-
17 O13'62. 3605
Out here again. PR (Williams).
Whitney Balliett. 40:52-85
My2'64. 3606
Out in the cold. Verse.
George Starbuck. 39:41 Ap20
'63. 3607
Out of darkness. Prose.
Mitchell Alland. 40:178-88
Ap25'64. 3608
Out of Itea. Prose. Shirley
Hazzard. 41:125-38
My1'65. 3609

Out of the death bag in West
Hollywood. Prose. F.P.
Tullius. 42:57-8 N5'66. 3610
Out of the ego chamber.
PR (Clarke). Jeremy
Bernstein. 45:40-65
Ag9'69. 3611
Out of the sea, early.
Verse. May Swenson. 42:
58 O29'66. 3612
Out of the walls. Prose.
Nadine Gordimer. 42:34-7
F11'67. 3613
Out of this nettle, danger ...
Prose. S.J. Perelman.
45:49-51 N29'69. 3614
An out-and-out free gift.
Prose. Frank O'Connor.
33:38-42 O26'57. 3615
Outing. Prose. John Updike.
34:28-9 Je14'58. 3616
An outlook. Prose. Alfred
M. Goodale. 38:221-4
O13'62. 3617
Outpost of Christendom. Prose.
Bruce Grant. 35:39-69
Ja23'60. 3618
The outrage. Prose. Mary D.
Rudd. 36:28-9 Ag27'60. 3619
The outrageously blessed.
Verse. Barry Spacks.
43:40 S30'67. 3620
Outside. Prose. Nancy Hale.
32:29-33 S29'56. 3621
Outward. Verse. Louis
Simpson. 40:36 F13'65. 3622
Over and out. Verse. Bianca
Bradbury. 31:159*N12'55.
3623
Over my head. Prose.
Roger Angell. 37:22-5 Je
24'61. 3624
Over the Mad River. RL.
John Hersey. 31:109-31
*S17'55. 3625
Overview. Verse. Sue Smart.
31:74*O1'55. 3626
Ovibos moschatus. Peter
Matthiessen. RL. 41:
94-123 F5'66. 3626a
Ovid on the Dacian coast.
Verse. Dunstan Thompson.
40:63 Ja2'65. 3627

The owl. Prose. Nathaniel
Benchley. 34:33-6 Jy19'58.
3628
Oxenhope. Prose. Sylvia
Townsend Warner. 42:25-9
Jy9'66. 3629
Oxygen. Verse. Joan Swift.
38:40 My5'62. 3630

P

Packed dirt, churchgoing, a
dying cat, a traded car. Prose.
John Updike. 37:59-92
D16'61. 3631
Paean. Verse. C.M. Fair
34:163 D13'58. 3632
Pageant Bible. TT. 36:33-4
Mr19'60. 3633
A pageant in sack suits. RL.
Christopher Rand. 32:68-87
Ja19'57. 3634
Pain for a daughter. Verse.
Anne Sexton. 42:50 Mr26'66.
3635
Paint me a pinion immortal,
limner dear. Prose. S.J.
Perelman. 43:41-3 My6'67.
3636
Painting a wave. Verse.
Howard Moss. 40:51 S19'64.
3637
A pair of bright-blue eyes.
Prose. Peter Taylor. 34:33-8
Je7'58. 3638
A pair of duelling pistols.
Prose. Sylvia Townsend Warner.
43:29-31 F17'68. 3639
The palace of delight. TWNY.
Andy Logan. 41:41-93 F27'65.
3640
Palace thoughts. Verse. E.B.
White. 31:102 Mr12'55. 3641
Pan. Prose. Emily Hahn.
38:72-8 Ag11'62. 3642
Pandora's boxes. Prose.
Sonia Rollnick. 37:48-53
D16'61. 3643
Paola. Prose. John Cheever.
34:22-9 Jy26'58. 3644
The papal broth. Prose.
Antonio Barolini. 35:98-115
Mr28'59. 3645

Paper tiger, burning
bright. Prose. Gene
Williams. 41:52-4 O30'65.
3646
Papermill graveyard. Verse.
Ben Belitt. 43:46 My20'67.
3647
Paphos. Verse. Lawrence
Durrell. 42:57 Mr26'66.
3648
A parable of love. Prose.
Robert M. Coates. 32:36-42
*Ap28'56. 3649
The parachutist. Verse. Jon
Anderson. 45:36 Mr22'69.
3650
Paradise for sale. Verse.
Ogden Nash. 35:34 Jy25'59.
3651
Paraguay. Prose. Donald
Barthelme. 45:32-4
S6'69. 3652
Pargellis, Stanley. TT.
34:26-7 F7'59. 3653
The pariah. Prose. Frank
O'Connor. 32:28-32
*S8'56. 3654
Parody, Literary. John
Updike. 37:163-76
S16'61. 3655
The Parsis. OFFC. Emily
Hahn. 34:116-53 O18'58.
3656
The parson. Prose.
Penelope Mortimer. 33:20-5
*Jy20'57. 3657
Part of an afternoon. Prose.
Laura Tennen. 38:69-70
D29'62. 3658
Parthenope. Prose. Rebecca
West. 35:53-86 N7'59. 3659
Particular beauties. Verse.
Howard Moss. 43:188
My13'67. 3660
The parting. Verse. Harry
Brown. 33:34 Ag17'57. 3661
Partners. PR (Harrigan and
Hart). E.J. Kahn, Jr.
31:42-67 Mr19'55; 31:39-72
Mr26'55; 31:45-67 Ap2'55;
31:41-81 Ap9'55. 3662
Part-time city. RL. John
Brooks. 34:76-92 Ja10'59.
3663

The party. Prose. Shirley
Hazzard. 38:46-9 D8'62.3664
The party. Prose. Frank
O'Connor. 33:44-8
D14'57.                          3665
Party knee. Verse. John
Updike. 34:46 D13'58.            3666
Pas devant les enfants.
Prose. Viola Meynell.
32:41-3*Ap21'56.                 3667
Passage. Verse. Babette
Deutsch. 37:138 S30'61.          3668
Passeggiata archeologica.
Prose. Arturo Vivante.
35:63-4 Jy4'59.                  3669
The passengers. Verse. David
Antin. 41:60 N13'65.             3670
The passing of Alpheus W. Hal-
liday. Verse. E.B. White.
31:19*D4'55.                     3671
Passion. Prose. R. Prawer
Jhabvala. 43:56-64
D2'67.                           3672
The passionate semanticist
to his offspring. Verse.
Morris Bishop. 32:19*Jy21'56.
                                 3673
The past. Verse. R.P. Lister.
32:128 D1'56.                    3674
Pasternak, Boris. Janet
Flanner. 34:113-15
N22'58.                          3675
Pasternak, Boris. TT. 34:33
N8'58.                           3676
Pastiche of the author in
sweet disarray. Prose. S.J.
Perelman. 40:26-8 D26'64.
                                 3677
Pastoral. Verse. Kate
Barnes. 35:46 S19'59.            3678
Pastoral. Verse. David
Wright. 39:56 N30'63.            3679
Paterfamilias. PR (Ginsberg).
Jane Kramer. 44:32-73
Ag17'68; 44:38-91 Ag24'68.
                                 3680
The path. Verse. Robert
David Cohen. 43:136 S16'67.
                                 3681
Patrick Kavanagh: an annotated
exequy. Verse. L.E.
Sissman. 44:51 My4'68.
                                 3682

Patriotic tour and postulate
of joy. Verse. Robert
Penn Warren. 41:28 Ja22'66.
                                 3683
Patrum propositum. Verse.
Robert Fitzgerald. 43:28
F10'68.                          3684
The pattern of perfection.
Prose. Nancy Hale. 31:16-
22*D24'55.                       3685
The patterned fields. Verse.
R.P. Lister. 33:145
S14'57.                          3686
A pause for breath. Verse.
Ted Hughes. 42:90
Ag27'66.                         3687
Pawpaw pie. Prose. Emily
Hahn. 43:47-54 Ap15'67.
                                 3688
Paysage de crépuscule. RL.
A.J. Liebling. 39:95-106
Ja11'64.                         3689
Peace march. Verse. Lisel
Mueller. 45:24 Jy19'69.
                                 3690
The peaceable gypsies. RL.
Daniel Lang. 39:34-61
D21'63.                          3691
The peacelike mongoose.
FFT. James Thurber.
32:25*Je23'56.                   3692
Peacemaker. PR (Goldberg).
Robert Shaplen. 38:49-112
Ap7'62; 38:49-105 Ap14'62.
                                 3693
The peaches. Prose. Ted
Walker. 44:56-9 O12'68.
                                 3694
The peacock. Prose. Edith
Templeton. 36:27-36
S3'60.                           3695
The peacock village. Prose.
Christine Weston. 33:32-46
Jy13'57.                         3696
Peasant. Verse. W.S.
Merwin. 43:44 Je10'67.           3697
The peasant. Verse. Leonard
Wolf. 33:100 Ap20'57. 3698
A pelican in her piety. Verse.
Helen Bevington. 31:202
*N12'55.                         3699
The penny. Prose. Ellen Bay.

The pheasant. Verse. Gene
Baro. 36:92 Je25'60.　　3737
Pheasants. Prose.
L. Woiwode. 43:62-6 N18'67.
　　　　　3738
Philadelphia. Prose. Donald
Barthelme. 44:56-8 N30'68.
　　　　　3739
Philatelic lessons: the German
collection. Verse.
Lawrence P. Spingarn.
42:58 S10'66.　　　3740
Philatelist's prayer at twi-
light. Verse. Frederick
Ebright. 32:115*Ap7'56.
　　　　　3741
Philological. Verse. John
Updike. 33:109 Ag6'57. 3742
The philosopher and the
oyster. FFT. James
Thurber. 32:19*Jy7'56. 3743
Philosopher in a new key.
PR (Langer). Winthrop
Sargeant. 36:67-100
D3'60.　　　　3744
The philosophy lesson. Prose.
Jean Stafford. 44:59-63
N16'68.　　　3745
Philosophy 1. Verse. E.F.
Weisslitz. 44:145 O5'68.
　　　　　3746
Philpot. Prose. Penelope
Mortimer. 38:24-9
Ag25'62.　　　3747
The phone call. Prose. Tom
Mayer. 40:84-94 My30'64.
　　　　　3748
Phone call. Prose. Berton.
Roueché. 41:38-9
Ag28'65.　　　3749
Photograph of a comtesse.
Verse. Derek Parfit.
38:24 Je23'62.　　3750
Photographs of the poets.
Verse. Karl Shapiro. 32:
36*Je2'56.　　　3751
Photography. Verse. Joan
Swift. 38:159 Ap7'62.
　　　　　3752
Pianists. Verse. Barbara
Gibbs. 34:32 Mr1'58.　3753
The piano player. Prose.
Donald Barthelme. 39:24
Ag31'63.　　　3754

Piano practice. Verse.
Howard Moss. 44:46
F24'68.　　　3755
The piano tuner. Verse.
Stephen Mooney. 39:120
F15'64.　　　3756
The picnic. Prose. Shirley
Hazzard. 38:30-3
Je16'62.　　　3757
The picture. Prose.
Nancy Hale. 32:24-36*S1'56.
　　　　　3758
A picture history of the war.
Prose. Donald Barthelme.
40:28-31 Je20'64.　3759
Picture in rain. Verse.
Frances Minturn Howard.
32:54 D8'56.　　3760
Pictures from an exhibition.
Verse. R.P. Lister.
34:27 D20'58.　　3761
Pictures of burning. Verse.
John Ratti. 36:80
Ja14'61.　　　3762
A piece of happiness. Verse.
Adrienne Cecile Rich.
33:50 N9'57.　　3763
The pieces. RL. Daniel Lang.
36:191-211 N5'60.　3764
Pierce's. Prose. Nancy
Hale. 31:46-9*N19'55.　3765
Pierre rumblings. Prose.
Roger Angell. 44:58-9
D14'68.　　　3766
The pigeon. Prose. H.L.
Mountzoures. 42:32-4
Jy16'66.　　　3767
Pigeon feathers. Prose. John
Updike. 37:25-34 Ag19'61.
　　　　　3768
The pigeon loft. Prose. Ida
Treat. 34:95-107
Mr15'58.　　　3769
Pigeon woman. Verse. May
Swenson. 38:54 O13'62. 3770
A pikunikku. Prose. Allan
R. Bosworth. 33:31-6
Ja11'58.　　　3771
A pilgrim son. Prose. Terence
Hanbury White. 35:40-6
My23'59.　　　3772
Pilgrim's progress. PR (Pilgrim
State Hospital). Morton
M. Hunt. 37:51-116

Poem about morning. Verse.
William Meredith. 42:213
D3'66.                          3808
Poem at equinox. Verse.
Hilary Corke. 34:30 Mr22'58.
                                3809
A poem for father's going.
Verse. Robert David
Cohen. 43:111 S30'67.    3810
Poem for you. Verse. Robert
Pack. 33:49 My11'57.     3811
A poem on dancing. Verse.
Mark Strand. 38:122
Mr31'62.                        3812
Poems of North and South
Georgia. Verse. James
Dickey. 38:60-1 D1'62.   3813
Poems to a brown cricket.
Verse. James Wright.
41:31 Jy3'65.                   3814
Poet and pedagogue. RL.
A.J. Liebling. 38:104-17
Mr3'62.                         3815
Poetry, modern. Louise
Bogan. 33:172-4 Ap13'57.
                                3816
Point Pelee in March. Verse.
Will McConnell. 39:130
Mr23'63.                        3817
The police band. Prose.
Donald Barthelme. 40:28
Ag22'64.                        3818
The policemen's ball.
Prose. Donald Barthelme.
44:31 Je8'68.                   3819
A political fiction. Prose.
Bailey Laird. 43:42-6
S16'67.                         3820
The politics of the Presby-
terians. Prose. St. Clair
McKelway. 32:34-8
S29'56.                         3821
Polka with the general.
Prose. Harriet Harvey.
31:74-9 Mr5'55.           3822
Polly Andrews, class of '33.
Prose. Mary McCarthy.
39:23-61 Je29'63.        3823
Polymers everywhere. PR
(Mark). Morton M. Hunt
34:48-72 S13'58; 34:46-83
S20'58.                         3824
The pond. Verse. Anthony

Thwaite. 41:34 Ag14'65.
                                3825
Ponti, Carlo. TT. 45:31-2
Ap5'69.                         3826
The poodle, the supernatural,
Mr. Wilson, Mr. Tatos,
and my mother. Prose.
Sylvia Townsend Warner.
32:20-4*Ag4'56.           3827
Pooem. Verse. John
Updike. 31:34*O1'55.     3828
A pool. Verse. Thomas
Whitbread. 38:35 Ja26'63.
                                3829
Poor Goldie. Prose.
Arthur Kober. 31:28-30
*F18'56.                        3830
The poor man's war between
the states. Prose. Nancy
Hale. 37:34-7 Mr25'61.
                                3831
Poor signora! Prose. Nigel
Dennis. 37:157-65
My13'61.                        3832
Pope, Alexander. W.H.
Auden. 45:128-40 F22'69.
                                3833
The poplar's shadow. Verse.
May Swenson. 34:138
My10'58.                        3834
Porgy and Bess in Russia.
OUWA. Truman Capote.
32:38-105 O20'56; 32:41-
114 O27'56.                     3835
A portable gallery of
pastoral animals. Verse.
Jon Swan. 39:44 My4'63.
                                3836
Porter, Katherine Anne
(Parody). Peter DeVries.
38:28-9 Je16'62.         3837
The "Portland" going out.
Verse. W.S. Merwin.
32:28 Ja19'57.           3838
Portland, Me. NFG.
Philip Hamburger. 36:
177-9 O8'60.             3839
"Portrait de femme," after
Picasso. Verse. Irving
Feldman. 40:188
Ap25'64.                        3840
Portrait of a friend. Verse.
Ben Ray Redman. 31:141
Mr19'55.                        3841

Portrait of a nun. Prose. A.R. von Weidinger. 33:96-104 F23'57. 3842

Portrait of the artist as a young mime. Prose. S.J. Perelman. 36:28-31 Ja28'61. 3843

Portrait of the left hand. Verse. Henri Coulette. 45:140 Je7'69. 3844

Portraits in a village. Prose. Natacha Stewart. 42:32-8 F4'67. 3845

Posies from a second childhood. Verse. Ogden Nash. 32:32*Ap7'56. 3846

Possibilities. Verse. Peter Kane Dufault. 36:48 N12'60. 3847

The possibilities of disaster. Prose. Doris Peel. 31:70-7*Ag20'55. 3848

Post, Emily. TT. 31:35 My14'55. 3849

Post pastoral. Prose. Colleen Brooks. 44:28-9 Je1'68. 3850

Postcards from Soviet cities. Verse. John Updike. 41:34 My29'65. 3851

The postman arrives in a bright-red boat. OFFC. Christopher Rand. 32:25-46 *Jy28'56. 3852

Post-vacation pibroch. Verse. Florence B. Jacobs. 32:115 *S8'56. 3853

The potato gatherers. Prose. Brian Friel. 36:172-81 N19'60. 3854

Potemkin rides again. WP. A.J. Liebling. 37:121-5 Ap29'61. 3855

A potted watch never boils. Verse. Ogden Nash. 34:28 Ag9'58. 3856

Pound, Ezra. S.N. Behrman and Max Beerbohm. 36:80-1 Mr19'60. 3857

Powder River in the old days. Prose. Allan Seager. 33:28-34 Ag17'57. 3858

Powder your face with sunshine. PR (Lombardo). E.J. Kahn, Jr. 32:35-49 Ja5'57; 32:35-57 Ja12'57. 3859

Powell, Anthony. TT. 41:17-18 Jy3'65. 3860

Power and light. Verse. James Dickey. 43:60-1 Mr11'67. 3861

The power of prayer. Prose. Elizabeth Cullinan. 36:28-34 Ja7'61. 3862

A powerful sense of his duty. PR (Carlsen). Thomas Whiteside. 34:49-103 D13'58. 3862a

Powerful sword. PR (Mehta). Winthrop Sargeant. 43:53-92 D16'67. 3863

The powerhouse. Verse. May Swenson. 44:46 My4'68. 3864

Powwow. Verse. W.D. Snodgrass. 38:28 Je2'62. 3865

A practical joke at Trois-Fontaines. OFFC. A.J. Liebling. 32:33-57 *Ag18'56. 3866

The practitioner. Prose. Alexander Frater. 43:42-5 Ap1'67. 3867

Praz, Mario. Edmund Wilson. 41:152-62 F20'65. 3868

Preble's law and other matters. OFFC. Charles Frankel. 39:74-109 My25'63. 3869

Precious stones. Verse. William Dickey. 39:26 Jy20'63. 3870

The predator. Prose. Linda Grace Hoyer. 43:53 My13'67. 3871

A predisposition to enchantment. Prose. Linda Grace Hoyer. 41:40-3 Mr13'65. 3872

Preface to a posthumous opus. Verse. William Walden. 37:85 F3'62. 3873

A prelude. PR (Wilson).
Edmund Wilson. 43:50-131
Ap29'67; 43:52-149 My6'67;
43:54-157 My13'67.　　　3874

Preminger, Otto. PR.
Lillian Ross. 41:42-129
F19'66.　　　3875

The prerogative of love.
Prose. Elizabeth Taylor.
36:22-7 Jy23'60.　　　3876

The Presbyterian call system.
Prose. St. Clair
McKelway. 33:29-33 My18'57.
　　　3877

The Presbyterian captives.
Prose. St. Clair
McKelway. 45:45-52 Ap12'69.
　　　3878

The Presbyterian nomads.
Prose. St. Clair McKelway.
37:48-52 D30'61.　　　3879

The Presbyterian topers.
Prose. St. Clair
McKelway. 32:29-32*Je2'56.
　　　3880

The president. Prose. Donald
Barthelme. 40:26-7 S5'64.
　　　3881

Presidential address to a party
of exiles leaving for the
moon. Verse. Howard
Nemerov. 43:92 Ag12'67.
　　　3882

The pretender. Prose.
Nadine Gordimer. 32:33-8
*Mr24'56.　　　3883

The price of peace is
confusion. RL. Ved Mehta.
41:195-216 D11'65.　　　3884

Priestly fellowship. Prose.
J.F. Powers. 45:36-46
S27'69.　　　3885

Prime minister/premier
ministre. PR (Trudeau).
Edith Iglauer. 45:36-60
Jy5'69.　　　3886

The prime of Miss Jean
Brodie. Prose. Muriel
Spark. 37:52-161 O14'61.
　　　3887

A primer of the daily round.
Verse. Howard Nemerov.
33:46 O12'57.　　　3888

The prince. Prose. Arturo
Vivante. 39:161-8
My11'63.　　　3889

A prince of the city. PR
(Warburg). Joseph
Wechsberg. 42:45-78
Ap9'66.　　　3890

Princeton pond. Prose.
St. Clair McKelway.
41:48-51 Ja1'66.　　　3891

The principal. PR
(Shapiro). Nat Hentoff.
42:52-119 My7'66.　　　3892

The prints. Verse. W.S.
Merwin. 44:61 D28'68.
　　　3893

Prison chronicle. RL. Joan
Colebrook. 41:47-101
Je12'65.　　　3894

Privacy. Verse. Robert
Graves. 37:52 O21'61.　　　3895

A private ghost. Prose.
Joyce Cary. 32:128-38
*N10'56.　　　3896

The private letters of the
president of the B.J.
Roberts Hand Tool Corpora-
tion. Prose. St. Clair
McKelway. 35:38-9
Ap18'59.　　　3897

The private meeting place.
Verse. James Wright.
34:28 Ja3'59.　　　3898

Private prince. Prose.
Charles G. Finney.
37:72-83 Je24'61.　　　3899

A private truce. Verse.
Gerald Jonas. 42:63
Jy30'66.　　　3900

Prizes. Prose. Janet
Frame. 38:44-6 Mr10'62.
　　　3901

The pro. Prose. John
Logan. 42:53-4 S17'66. 3902

Pro senior-signing scramble:
Fulcourt inks Swinburne;
Appledore nabs Bronkowski.
Prose. Thomas Meehan.
42:68-9 N12'66.　　　3903

A problem in history. Verse.
Robert A. Wallace.
33:28*Je1'57.　　　3904

A problem of identity.

RL. William Wertenbaker.
38:68-117 D1'62.          3905

The procession. Verse. Gene
Baro. 42:122 My14'66.     3906

The prodigal parent. Prose.
Mavis Gallant. 45:42-4 Je7'69.
                          3907

Prodigy's progress. PR
(Menuhin). Winthrop
Sargeant. 31:50-85*O8'55;
31:49-68*O15'55.          3908

Progress report. Prose.
Philip Hamburger. 39:38-
40 Mr30'63.               3909

The promise of heat. Prose.
Ethan Ayer. 42:30-5
S3'66.                    3910

The promise of the pencils.
Prose. Ruth Domino.
34:137-44 Ap12'58.        3911

The promontory moment. Verse.
May Swenson. 32:21*Jy28'56.
                          3912

The prophets. Verse.
Richard Shelton. 45:26
Ag30'69.                  3913

Propinquity. Verse. Alastair
Reid. 36:36 Ja14'61.      3914

Protest. Prose. L.D.
Hamilton. 36:133-5 O1'60.
                          3915

Proteus. Verse. Robert
Hillyer. 32:99 F9'57.     3916

Prothalamion. Verse.
Maxine W. Kumin. 38:74
Jy21'62.                  3917

A Proust in Wall Street.
PR(Gutman). John Brooks.
35:41-70 Je20'59.         3918

Proust, Marcel. Janet
Flanner. 38:175-8 Mr17'62;
41:92-4 Je26'65.          3919

Proust, Marcel. Mollie
Panter-Downes. 31:167
*N5'55.                   3920

Providence, R.I. NFG.
Philip Hamburger. 36:60-4
Jy16'60.                  3921

The pruned tree. Verse.
Howard Moss. 39:38
My11'63.                  3922

Pseudonyms, Literary. TT.
32:26-7*Mr24'56.          3923

The psychosemanticist will
see you now, Mr.
Thurber. Prose. James
Thurber. 31:28-31 My
28'55.                    3924

The public be served.
PR (Isaacs). J.M. Flagler.
35:59-96 D12'59; 35:41-
71*D19'59.                3925

The public Dorothy. Prose.
John O'Hara. 38:36-7
D15'62.                   3926

Publisher. PR (Cerf).
Geoffrey T. Hellman.
35:48-92 My9'59; 35:
49-84 My16'59.            3927

Publisher. PR (Schiff).
Geoffrey T. Hellman.
44:37-65 Ag10'68.         3928

Publius Vergilius Maro,
the Madison Avenue hick.
Verse. John Updike.
32:32*Mr31'56.            3929

The Puerto Ricans. RL.
Christopher Rand.
33:57-93*N30'57; 33:105
-37 D7'57; 33:93-131
D14'57; 33:56-78 D21'57.
                          3930

Puerto Rico song. Verse.
William Carlos Williams.
33:94 S14'57.             3931

Pulse rapid, respiration
lean, no mustard.
Prose. S.J. Perelman.
32:48-50 D8'56.           3932

The purchase. Prose.
Elizabeth Hardwick. 35:
28-62 My30'59.            3933

The put-on. OUWA. Jacob
Brackman. 43:34-73
Je24'67.                  3934

Pyes and pasties at the Lizzie.
OUWA. Geoffrey T.
Hellman. 35:112-31 Mr7'59.
                          3935

A pylos before a pylos.
OFFC. Joseph Alsop.
38:59-117 N24'62.         3936

The pythons. Verse. Ted
Walker. 43:99 D9'67.
                          3937

## Q

## R

English childhood--Italy,
1900-1910. Verse. Osbert
Sitwell. 33:34-5 F23'57.
4004

Recollections of an Intourist
tourist. RL. E.J. Kahn,
Jr. 34:35-66 D20'58;
34:26-51 D27'58. 4005

The recorded companions.
RL. Kevin Wallace. 38:
204-22 N3'62. 4006

Recovery. Verse. Kenneth
Scholes. 40:109
Je13'64. 4007

The red alert. Prose.
Thomas Meehan. 34:101-107
F7'59. 4008

The red bicycle. Prose.
Richard Berczeller. 40:
151-66 Mr7'64. 4009

Red gates and water devils.
Prose. David Kidd. 31:86-
97 My28'55. 4010

A red maple leaf. Verse.
Luke Zilles. 33:91
S28'57. 4011

The red rowboat. Verse.
Gene Baro. 43:76 S2'67.
4012

Red trees. Verse. Andrew
Oerke. 36:44 D31'60. 4013

Reel. Verse. John Updike.
34:133 My3'58. 4014

Reflection. Verse. John
Updike. 33:216*N30'57.
4015

Reflections on Vietnam.
Prose. Richard N. Goodwin.
42:57-116 Ap16'66. 4016

Regarding a door. Verse.
David Antin. 41:162 N20'65.
4017

Reincarnation. Verse.
James Dickey. 40:51 Mr7'64.
4018

Reiner, Carl. TT. 45:
47-9 D13'69. 4019

The rejection. Prose. Mavis
Gallant. 45:42-4 Ap12'69.
4020

The remains. Verse. Mark
Strand. 45:34 My31'69.
4021

Remarks from the man on
the stern end at the
second carry. Verse.
W.G. Van Keuren
33:118 S21'57. 4022

Remarks to a depressed
patient. Verse. Ames
Rowe Quentin. 39:110
Je15'63. 4023

Remembering Althea. Verse.
William Stafford. 42:144
O8'66. 4024

The remembering machines
of tomorrow. Prose.
W.S. Merwin. 45:52-3
N29'69. 4025

Remembrance. Prose.
Brendan Gill. 36:39
O29'60. 4026

The renegade. Prose.
Penelope Mortimer. 34:
41-8 Mr15'58. 4027

The renewal. RL. John
Colebrook. 41:35-45
Ja1'66. 4028

The renewal. Verse.
Theodore Roethke. 34:
103*Ap26'58. 4029

Renoir, Jean. Janet
Flanner. 31:142-3
My7'55. 4030

Rent me and I'll come to
you. Prose. S.J.
Perelman. 34:22-4
Jy12'58. 4031

The reply. Verse.
Theodore Roethke. 37:23
Jy1'61. 4032

Reply from a non-colonist.
Prose. H.F. Ellis.
33:28-9 Ap20'57. 4033

Reply to a friend in New
England. Verse. Arthur
Gregor. 40:170
S12'64. 4034

Reply to the provinces.
Verse. Galway Kinnell.
34:44 N1'58. 4035

Report. Prose. Donald
Barthelme. 43:34-5
Je10'67. 4036

A report. Prose. Mavis
Gallant. 42:62-5 D3'66. 4037

The report. Verse. Jon
  Swan. 40:48 Ap4'64.  4038
Report from California.
  Verse. Lois Moyles. 42:30
  Ja14'67.  4039
Report of health. Verse.
  John Updike. 45:40
  F22'69.  4040
A reporter at home. Prose.
  E.J. Kahn, Jr. 33:118-24
  Mr23'57.  4041
A reporter at home. Prose.
  Eli Waldron. 32:66-72
  Jy28'56.  4042
A reporter in Africa. Prose.
  Alan Moorehead. 33:45-81
  My25'57; 33:35-67*Je1'57;
  33:39-85 Je8'57.  4043
A reporter in Egypt. Prose.
  A.J. Liebling. 32:34-53
  *D22'56; 32:31-44 D29'56;
  32:82-9 Ja12'57.  4044
A reporter in the D.D.R.
  Prose. Joseph Wechsberg.
  37:44-64 Jy1'61.  4045
A reporter in Vietnam: Diem.
  Prose. Robert Shaplen.
  38:103-31 S22'62.  4046
A reporter in Vietnam: the
  delta, the plateau, and the
  mountains. Prose. Robert
  Shaplan. 38:48-71 Ag11'62.
  4047
A reporter on wheels: come
  see us again soon. Prose.
  E.J. Kahn, Jr. 36:117-44
  D10'60.  4048
A reporter on wheels: the
  best medicine on the market.
  Prose. Berton Roueché.
  37:37-58 Ja20'62.  4049
A reporter outside looking in.
  Prose. Eli Waldron.
  31:49-74*N5'55.  4050
A reproach to skeptics. RL.
  A.J. Liebling. 35:58-71
  Jy11'59.  4051
Requiem. Prose.
  Frank O'Connor. 33:31-4
  Je29'57.  4052
Requiem for a southpaw.
  Prose. J.M. Flagler.
  35:230-5 D5'59.  4053

Res communis omnium.
  RL. Daniel Lang.
  42:37-44 D24'66.  4054
The rescue. Verse.
  John Logan. 42:54
  S17'66.  4055
Rescue. Verse.
  Dabney Stuart. 41:96
  S4'65.  4056
The rescue. Prose.
  John Updike. 40:28-31
  Ja2'65.  4057
Rescue with Yul Brynner.
  Verse. Marianne Moore.
  37:40 My20'61.  4058
Reservations. Prose.
  Peter Taylor. 37:37-72
  F25'61.  4059
The reservoir. Prose.
  Janet Frame. 38:31-6
  Ja12'63.  4060
Resolution. Verse.
  W.S. Merwin. 39:34
  F1'64.  4061
Resources and responsibilities.
  PR (Rockefeller). E.J.
  Kahn, Jr. 40:37-83 Ja9'65;
  40:40-73 Ja16'65.  4062
Respect. Prose. Joseph
  Slate. 40:140-8 D19'64.
  4063
Resting place. Prose.
  Joseph Papaleo. 32:122-7
  *Mr17'56.  4064
The restless baker. PR
  (Arnold). Robert Lewis
  Taylor. 33:49-80
  D14'57.  4065
The restored. Verse.
  Theodore Roethke. 36:58
  D10'60.  4066
Retreat from the sea. Prose.
  Taylor Morris. 41:45-53
  My22'65.  4067
Retrospect. Verse. Peter
  Kane Dufault. 42:220
  S24'66.  4068
Return. Prose. Robert M.
  Coates. 32:29-35
  *My26'56.  4069
The return. Verse. George
  MacBeth. 41:26
  Ja1'66.  4070

Rhinoceros. Verse. Adrien
  Stoutenburg. 38:159 Ap21'62.
                              4102
Rhythm in my mind. PR
  (Hines). Whitney Balliett.
  40:39-57 Ja2'65.           4103
Rice, rice, rice. OFFC.
  E.J. Kahn, Jr. 41:154-83
  O23'65.                    4104
Rich in Russia. Prose. John
  Updike. 45:31-6 Ja31'70.
                              4105
Rich people. Prose. Nancy
  Hale. 36:32-54 Jy9'60.
                              4106
Ricing. RL. Berton
  Roueché. 43:34-42 D23'67.
                              4107
A ride into town. Prose.
  Berton Roueché. 40:96-100
  Ag22'64.                   4108
A ride on the milky way.
  Prose. Marguerite Dorian.
  37:30-6 F25'61.            4109
A ride with Mrs. Padgett.
  Prose. John Powell. 33:
  34-8 Ap27'57.              4110
The right light. PR (Feder).
  Joseph Wechsberg. 36:49-
  84 O22'60.                 4111
Rillons, rillettes. Verse.
  Richard Wilbur. 41:28
  Ja29'66.                   4112
The ring. Prose. Nathaniel
  Benchley. 32:97-105
  Ja19'57.                   4113
Ring out the old, ring in the
  new, but don't get caught
  in between. Verse. Ogden
  Nash. 32:28 D29'56.        4114
Rise and shine. Verse.
  Richmond Lattimore. 33:29
  Ap6'57.                    4115
The rites. Verse. Maxine
  W. Kumin. 33:67 My18'57.
                              4116
The river. Verse. Dabney
  Stuart. 41:50 O9'65.       4117
River daughter. Verse.
  Paul Engle. 32:103
  *My19'56.                  4118
The riverman. Verse.
  Elizabeth Bishop.

36:40 Ap2'60.                4119
The rivermen. PR (Lyons).
  Joseph Mitchell.
  35:42-111 Ap4'59.          4120
The road. Prose. Arturo
  Vivante. 38:32-6 S8'62.    4121
The road and the meadow.
  OFFC. Anthony Bailey.
  41:129-64 My8'65.          4122
The road back. Verse.
  Anne Sexton. 35:30
  Ag29'59.                   4123
The road through granite and
  darkness. RL. Joseph
  Wechsberg. 39:140-68
  My18'63.                   4124
The road to Barcelona. Prose.
  Frederick L. Keefe.
  32:94-101*My5'56.          4125
The roadway. Verse.
  Adrienne Cecile Rich.
  31:101 Mr26'55.            4126
Robbe-Grillet, Alain. TT.
  40:24-5 Ja9'65.            4127
Robbins, Harold. TT.
  45:45-8 N29'69.            4128
Robbins, Jerome. TT.
  35:32-3 Ap4'59.            4129
Robert. Prose. Berry
  Morgan. 45:22-5 Jy19'69.4130
Robinson. Verse. Howard
  Moss. 41:42 Mr13'65.       4131
Rochefort, Christiane. Edmund
  Wilson. 42:79-91 My21'66.
                             4131a
Rochester, N.Y. NFG.
  Philip Hamburger.
  35:179-82 S19'59.          4132
Rock Creek. Prose. Julian
  Mazor. 42:53-7
  D17'66.                    4133
Rodgers, Richard. PR.
  Winthrop Sargeant. 37:
  58-95 N18'61.              4134
Rodgers, Richard. TT.
  35:21 My30'59.             4135
Rod-Island is real, but I'll
  never believe in Wisconsin.
  Prose. Noel Perrin.
  38:48-51 N24'62.           4136
Roland Magruder, freelance
  writer. Prose. Calvin
  Trillin. 41:26-7 Ag14'65.4137

A role in Manila. Prose.
Eugene Burdick.
32:108-16 S29'56.          4138

The Roman forum. Verse.
Elizabeth Jennings. 34:36
My3'58.                    4139

The roof garden. Verse.
Howard Moss. 40:32
Ag8'64.                    4140

The roof of the world. Verse.
Michael Dennis Browne.
44:40 Jy20'68.            4141

Rook pie. Prose. Samuel
B. Griffith. 34:80-5
Je21'58.                   4142

The room. Prose. Arturo
Vivante. 42:24-5 Jy30'66.
                           4143

A room in the villa. Verse.
William Jay Smith. 31:20
*Ja7'56.                   4144

Room 28. Verse. John
Updike. 33:40 N2'57.      4145

The room under Pascal's.
Prose. Francis Steegmuller.
37:94-6 Ja27'62.           4146

A roomful of Hovings. PR
(Hoving). John McPhee.
43:49-137 My20'67.        4147

Root-light, or the lawyer's
daughter. Verse. James
Dickey. 45:52 N8'69.      4148

Rose. Prose. Mavis
Gallant. 36:34-7
D17'60.                   4149

The rose. Verse. Theodore
Roethke. 39:26-7
Jy6'63.                    4150

The rose and the weed. FFT.
James Thurber. 32:39
*My12'56.                  4151

The rose garden. Prose.
Maeve Brennan. 35:31-8
Mr28'59.                   4152

A rose is a rose is a
business. RL. Katharine
T. Kinkead. 34:37-72
Jy19'58.                   4153

The Rose of Sharon.
Prose. Calvin Kentfield.
35:30-51 Je27'59.          4154

The rose, the fountain, and
the dove. FFT. James
Thurber.   32:24*Je23'56.
                           4155

The rose, the mauve, the
white. Prose. Elizabeth
Taylor. 33:20-6*Je22'57.
                           4156

Rosenthal, Jean. PR.
Winthrop Sargeant. 31:33-53
*F4'56.                    4157

Roses. Verse. George
Johnston. 31:96 Je18'55.
                           4158

The roses of Mazar. Prose.
Christine Weston. 36:44-
50 My14'60.               4159

Rossetti circle. S.N.
Behrman and Max Beer-
bohm. 36:74-7
Mr19'60.                   4160

Rough shoot. Prose.
Robert B. Asprey. 33:209-
19 N16'57.                 4161

Rough winds do shake the
darling buds of May.
Verse. Robert Hillyer.
33:146 My11'57.            4162

Roulette. Prose. Wallace
White. 39:42-5 N2'63. 4163

Roussel, Raymond.
George Steiner. 43:206-
12 O28'67.                 4164

Route. Verse. Peter Kane
Dufault. 33:138 N16'57.
                           4165

Row. Verse. Ralph
Pomeroy. 32:156 S22'56.
                           4166

The royal diversion. Prose.
John D. Stewart. 34:47-
51 D6'58.                  4167

Rueful lines by two-fifths of
a centenarian. Verse.
William Walden. 31:119
My21'55.                   4168

Rufus. Prose. James
Agee. 33:36-41
N2'57.                     4169

The rug. Prose. Edna
O'Brien. 39:55-7
Mr16'63.                   4170

Rummage sale. Prose.
Sally Benson. 32:33-8
*Mr3'56.                   4171

Rogin. 41:28-34 Ja1'66. 4377
A short walk from the station. Prose. John O'Hara. 38:32-4 F24'62. 4378
The shortest way home. Prose. Benedict Kiely. 38:38-45 Mr17'62. 4379
Should (or would) you like some vegetables? Prose. A.J. Liebling. 34:86-103*Ap26'58. 4380
Should Wizard hit Mommy? Prose. John Updike. 35:38-40 Je13'59. 4381
A shower of gold. Prose. Donald Barthelme. 39:33-7 D28'63. 4382
The shudder. Verse. Donald Hall. 34:44 My3'58. 4383
.Sic semper Mr. Sherman's temper. Verse. Ogden Nash. 32:34 D15'56. 4384
The sick fox. Prose. Paul Brodeur. 33:90-108 Je15'57. 4385
The sickness of friends. Verse. Henri Coulette. 40:63 N21'64. 4386
Sidlesham Harbor. Verse. Paddy Webb. 40:234 N14'64. 4387
The sign in Sidney Brustein's window (Play). TT. 40:49-51 D5'64. 4388
The significance of saffron. OFFC. Christopher Rand. 32:96-115*Mr24'56. 4389
The silent lover. Verse. Louis Simpson. 38:34 Ag25'62. 4390
The silent sphinx. Prose. St. Clair McKelway. 38:90-8 Je9'62. 4391
Silent Spring. RL. Rachel Carson. 38:35-99 Je16'62; 38:31-89 Je23'62; 38:35-67 Je30'62. 4392
Silver pins and blood-red skirts. Prose. David Kidd. 32:120-33 O6'56. 4393
Sim ines. Verse. Jane Stubbs 33:184 O5'57. 4394

The simple life. Verse. John Updike. 33:108 Ja18'58. 4395
The sin of pride. Prose. Natacha Stewart. 40:53-60 S19'64. 4396
Sing a song of symmetry. Verse. David Daiches. 32:53 D29'56. 4397
The sinus viridis packers and the neo-eboraci giants. Prose. Noel Perrin. 39:213-20 N9'63. 4398
Sire. Verse. W.S. Merwin. 38:54 N24'62. 4399
The sirens of the Potomac. Prose. St. Clair McKelway. 33:28-30 S7'57. 4400
Siskins under the skin. Prose. H.F. Ellis. 41:40-1 Ap24'65. 4401
Sisters. Prose. Elizabeth Taylor. 45:38-41 Je21'69. 4402
Sister's on the other line. Prose. Noel Perrin. 43:150-3 N18'67. 4403
Sisyphus. Verse. Josephine Miles. 34:30 My31'58. 4404
The sitter. Prose. Andy Logan. 31:60-3*Ja28'56. 4405
Sitting in the woods: a contemplation. Verse. W.R. Moses. 37:154 N18'61. 4406
Six daggers east. Prose. S.J. Perelman. 41:28-31 F27'65. 4407
Six poems. Verse. Jorge Luis Borges. Norman Thomas di Giovanni, trans. 45:52-3 D13'69. 4408
Six poems. Verse. Robert Graves. 43:32 Jy8'67. 4409
Six poems. Verse. Kathleen Raine. 40:32-3 Ja16'65. 4410
Six poems. Verse. Theodore Roethke. 39:50-1 O19'63. 4411
Six poets in search of a lawyer. Verse. Donald Hall. 31:40 Mr19'55. 4412
Sixth child. Prose. R. Prawer

Jhabvala. 34:39-60
Ap5'58.                                      4413
The skaters' waltz. Verse.
Howard Moss. 42:26 Ja21'67.
                                             4414
The skeleton. Prose. V.S.
Pritchett. 42:44-78
Mr5'66.                                      4415
The skeleton in the closet.
Verse. Richmond Lattimore.
40:36 Mr28'64.                               4416
The skelper. Prose. Brian
Friel. 35:20-3 Ag1'59.                       4417
The skier's progress. Prose.
Thomas Williams. 38:34-66
F2'63.                                       4418
Skimmers. Verse. Ted
Walker. 39:28 Ja11'64.                       4419
The skin divers. Verse.
George Starbuck. 38:36 Ag18
'62.                                         4420
Skin diving in the Virgins.
Verse. John Malcolm Brinnin.
39:30 Ja4'64.                                4421
The skin game. RL. Jane
Kramer. 42:138-61 Ap2'66.
                                             4422
The skull. Verse. Gene Baro.
38:160 N17'62.                               4423
Sky blue. OFFC. Christopher
Rand. 35:112-39 My9'59. 4424
The slaughterer. Prose.
Isaac Bashevis Singer. Mirra
Ginsburg, trans. 43:60-5
N25'67.                                      4425
The slave of Hebrew. PR
(Persky). Dwight Macdonald.
35:57-105 N28'59.                            4426
Slave quarters. Verse. James
Dickey. 41:28-9
Ag14'65.                                     4427
Sleep. Prose. Sharon Moore.
44:30-7 Je1'68.                              4428
The Sleeping Giant. Verse.
Donald Hall. 31:43*Ag6'55.
                                             4429
Sleeping with one eye open. Verse.
Mark Strand. 38:188 N3'62.
                                             4430
The slicker the vet, the slicker
the pet. Prose. S.J.
Perelman. 36:23-6 D24'60.
                                             4431

Slides. Prose. Jane Richmond.
42:188-90 N26'66.                            4432
A slight case of obscenity.
OUWA. Frederic J. Warburg.
33:106-33 Ap20'57.                           4433
Slim-shin's monument.
RL. Kevin Wallace. 36:
104-46 N19'60.                               4434
The small. Verse. Theodore
Roethke. 32:32*S8'56.              4435
A small boy, dreaming.
Verse. Albert Herzing.
36:46 My7'60.                                4436
Small change. WP. E.J.
Kahn, Jr. 33:145-54
Ap6'57.                                      4437
Small colored boy in the sub-
way. Verse. Babette
Deutsch. 33:36 Mr30'57.
                                             4438
Small elegy. Verse. Howard
Moss. 32:32*Je16'56.              4439
Small is my cinema, deep
my doze. Prose. S.J.
Perelman. 34:36-8 S20'58.
                                             4440
Small sad song. Verse.
Alastair Reid. 34:92
Ja10'59.                                     4441
A small thing. Verse.
Dorothy Donnelly. 38:152
My26'62.                                     4442
Smiling William. Prose.
Nigel Dennis. 36:115-21
My14'60.                                     4443
Smoke. Verse. Charles
Wright. 45:42 My31'69.
                                             4444
Snake. Verse. Theodore
Roethke. 31:48*S17'55.            4445
Snakebite. Verse. James
Dickey. 43:44 F25'67.              4446
Snap snap. Prose. Donald
Barthelme. 41:108-11 Ag
28'65.                                       4447
The snapshots. Prose. Uli
Beigel. 32:54-8
N24'56.                                      4448
Snatches for Charles Ives.
Verse. Daniel Hoffman.
45:32 Ja17'70.                               4449
Snow. Verse. Whitney
Balliett. 32:222 D1'56.           4450

Sound and echo. Verse. Katinka Loeser. 32:122*N10'56. 4523
The sound of morning in New Mexico. Verse. Reeve Spencer Kelley. 31:100 F26'55. 4524
The sound of my own voice. Prose. John Ferris. 37:100-109 Je10'61. 4525
Sources of the public unhappiness. REF. Richard N. Goodwin. 44:38-58 Ja4'69. 4526
South Africa. RL. E.J. Kahn, Jr. 43:38-83 Ja27'68; 43:32-74 F3'68; 43:36-85 F10'68. 4527
South of Ajo. RL. Berton Roueché. 43:76-92 Ag12 '67. 4528
South Sea diary. RL. Hamilton Basso. 35:41-83 Je13'59. 4529
Southbound on the freeway. Verse. May Swenson. 38:32 F16'63. 4530
A southern landscape. Prose. Elizabeth Spencer. 36:28-34 Mr26'60. 4531
Sowing asphodel. Prose. Ivy Litvinov. 42:50-6 Ap23'66. 4532
A space filled in. RL. A.J. Liebling. 37:147-60 Mr25'61. 4533
The space race. Prose. Michael J. Arlen. 38:37 S22'62. 4534
Space-age maestro. PR (von Karajan). Winthrop Sargeant. 36:35-62 Ja7'61. 4535
Spanish blue. Verse. Herbert Morris. 31:44 Mr19'55. 4536
The Spanish lions. Verse. Phyllis McGinley. 34:30 S6'58. 4537
The Spanish steps. Verse. Hawley Truax. 43:44 Ap29'67. 4538
The sparrow shall fall. Prose. Suyin Han. 35:43-50 O10'59. 4539
Sparrows. Verse. Hayden Carruth. 32:218 D8'56. 4540

A sparrow's feather. Verse. George Barker. 39:42 Je8'63. 4541
Sparrows in the leafless willows. Verse. Andrew Oerke. 45:52 O11'69. 4542
Speak. Verse. James Wright. 44:122 Ap6'68. 4543
Speaking a foreign language. Verse. Alastair Reid. 36:105 S3'60. 4544
Speaking of television. Verse. Phyllis McGinley. 33:35 My25'57. 4545
Spectator's guide to contemporary art. Verse. Phyllis McGinley. 31:114 My21'55. 4546
The spectre of the fir tree. Prose. Robert Henderson. 33:38-41 S21'57. 4547
Speech in an orchard. Verse. Hilary Corke. 35:106 My16'59. 4548
Speed cleen. Prose. James Stevenson. 44:165-70 O19'68. 4549
A spell before Winter. Verse. Howard Nemerov. 38:52 N3'62. 4550
The sphinx and the pyramid. Prose. Hannah Green. 42:130-7 Ap2'66. 4551
The spikers. Prose. Ted Walker. 44:56-8 N16'68. 4552
Spindrift. Verse. Galway Kinnell. 39:36 F15'64. 4553
The spinning Earth. Verse. R.P. Lister 34:116 O11'58. 4554
The spiral. Verse. Alastair Reid. 39:40 Ap6'63. 4555
The spirit of the road. Prose. Elizabeth Tingom. 45:32-9 Ag16'69. 4556
A spirit rises. Prose. Sylvia Townsend Warner. 37:20-1 Jy8'61. 4557
Spirits, dancing. Verse. Arthur Gregor. 40:148 N21'64. 4558
Split-level. Prose. Peter De Vries. 32:102-109 *Je9'56. 4559

Split-level living. Prose.
Faith McNulty. 31:102-106
*O1'55.      4560
The spoiler. Prose. Paul
Brodeur. 41:28-34 Ja8'66.
     4561
Spokane, Wash. NFG. Philip
Hamburger. 39:198-204
O26'63.      4562
The spoon ran away with the
dish? Verse. Ogden Nash.
36:40 F20'60.      4563
Spouse leak. Prose. Norman
Kotker. 34:36-7 Mr8'58.
     4564
A spray gun for the varnish. RL.
Joseph Wechsberg. 31:88-109
*F18'56.      4565
The spreading "you know".
Prose. James Thurber. 36:23
D31'60.      4566
Spring. Verse. Eleanor Munro.
45:40 My24'69.      4567
Spring bulletin. Prose. Woody
Allen. 43:38-9 Ap29'67.   4568
Spring changes. Verse. Jon
Swan. 41:42 My1'65.    4569
Spring eclogue. Verse. Anne
Hyde Greet. 32:48*Mr17'56.
     4570
Spring gray. Verse. John
Moffitt. 34:125 My10'58.
     4571
Spring in Korea. OFFC. E.J.
Kahn, Jr. 37:43-71 My27'61.
     4572
Spring interest. Verse.
William Stafford. 34:119 My17
'58.      4573
Spring song. Verse. Donald
Finkel. 41:127 My22'65.
     4574
Springfield, Mass. NFG.
Philip Hamburger. 36:158-63
Mr19'60.      4575
The spy-ban pact. Prose.
H.F. Ellis. 39:48-9 S28'63.
     4576
Squaring the circle. Verse.
Louis O. Coxe. 40:26 Ag15'64.
     4577
Squatter's children. Verse.
Elizabeth Bishop. 33:36 Mr23
'57.      4578

The squinch owl. Prose.
Montgomery Newman. 36:51-
60 N5'60.      4579
The stag. Verse. Otis Kid-
well Burger. 33:178 S21'57.
     4580
Stand back for Walford W.
Oglethorpe, Jr! Prose.
Thomas Meehan. 40:37-8
Ap11'64.      4581
Standing still. Verse. Mark
Strand. 40:163 S19'64.   4582
Stanwoods's Andromeda. Prose.
Samuel Cabot, Jr. 34:62-9
Ag9'58.      4583
A star. Verse. George Mac-
beth. 42:56 O15'66.    4584
Star. PR (Leitzel). Robert
Lewis Taylor. 32:45-66
*Ap21'56; 32:47-69*Ap28'56.
     4585
Star Lake. Prose. Arturo
Vivante. 34:44-7 My17'58.
     4586
The stare. Prose. John Up-
dike. 41:41-3 Ap3'65.   4587
The star-nosed mole. Verse.
Robert A. Wallace. 35:96
F13'60.      4588
The starry night. Verse. George
Starbuck. 39:42 My11'63.
     4589
A state of well-being. Prose.
Robin White. 33:59-62
Jy6'57.      4590
The statues taken down. Prose.
Mavis Gallant. 41:53-6
O9'65.      4591
The status of Canadian geology.
Verse. Nathan Fast. 33:85
D14'57.      4592
Staying alive. Verse. David
Wagoner. 41:66 D4'65.   4593
Stealing trout. Verse. Ted
Hughes. 40:44 Mr21'64.
     4594
Step by step. Verse. Arthur
Kramer. 33:92 Ja25'58.
     4595
Step by step with Mr. Raskin.
WP. A.J. Liebling. 39:143-
52 Ap13'63.      4596
Sterling silver. Prose. John
O'Hara. 37:38-42 Mr11'61.
     4597

Mexico. Verse. Reeve
Spencer Kelley. 33:52 D7'57.
    4636
The stranger. OFFC.
Anthony West. 35:109-29
My16'59. 4637
A stranger in New York.
Prose. A.J. Liebling. 32:165-
75 D8'56. 4638
Stranger on the beach. Prose.
Patricia Collinge. 39:76-84
Je22'63. 4639
The strangers. Prose.
Maurice Shadbolt. 35:38-45
O3'59. 4640
Straw boss. Prose. Grover
Amen. 37:209-21 N18'61.
    4641
The stream. Prose. Arturo
Vivante. 34:23-6 Ag23'58.
    4642
The street. Verse. Gene
Baro. 41:130 Je5'65. 4643
The street of named houses.
Verse. Robert David Cohen.
42:231 O29'66. 4644
A stroll in the garden. OFFC.
Daniel Lang. 33:30-53*Jy20'57.
    4645
Student of the spontaneous. PR
(Funt). J.M. Flagler. 36:59-
92 D10'60. 4646
The study of history. Prose.
Frank O'Connor. 33:32-6
Mr9'57. 4647
The study of something new in
history. RL. Eugene Kinkead.
33:114-69 O26'57. 4648
The stunt flier. Verse. John
Updike. 37:59 Ja6'62. 4649
Stutterer. Verse. Alan Dugan.
36:220 N19'60. 4650
Subdivider. Verse. Adrien
Stoutenburg. 44:32 Jy6'68.
    4651
Subduing of the waters. RL.
Christopher Rand. 35:134-62
My16'59. 4652
The subtle storm. RL. John
Brooks. 34:39-77 F7'59. 4653
Suburb hilltop. Verse. Richard
Moore. 39:34 Ja18'64. 4654

Suburban madrigal. Verse.
John Updike. 35:100 Ap25'59.
    4655
Sue. Prose. Frank O'Connor.
34:34-8 S27'58. 4656
The suicide. Verse. Mark
Strand. 42:158 Mr12'66.
    4657
A suite of children. Verse.
Paul Petrie. 43:32 Je17'67.
    4658
Sullen moods. Verse. Robert
Graves. 37:44 S9'61. 4659
Sulzberger, Arthur Ochs. PR.
Geoffrey T. Hellman. 44:40-
71 Ja18'69. 4660
Summer afternoon, Summer
afternoon. Prose. Hannah
Green. 45:30-49 Ja17'70.
    4661
Summer at Strandhill. Prose.
John McGahern. 39:43-8
S21'63. 4662
Summer camp brochures.
(parody). Roger Angell.
41:40-1 Mr27'65. 4663
A Summer dusk. Prose.
Mary Cable. 31:50-7
*Jy23'55. 4664
A Summer gone. Verse.
Howard Moss. 31:51*S17'55.
    4665
A Summer morning. Verse.
Richard Wilbur. 36:32 Ag6
'60. 4666
Summer: New York. Verse.
Gerald Jonas. 39:52 Jy6'63.
    4667
A Summer on the Dales. Prose.
Edmund Ward. 39:78-91 Je1'63.
    4668
Summer schools. Prose.
Elizabeth Taylor. 34:26-35
S6'58. 4669
Summer storms come and go,
Sidney old kid. Prose.
David Girae. 37:148-60
S16'61. 4670
Summer: West Side. Verse.
John Updike. 36:26 Jy30
'60. 4671
Summer's early end at Hudson

Bay. Verse. Hayden
Carruth. 31:38*O1'55.    4672
A Summer's long dream.
Prose. Nancy Hale. 32:22-8
*Jy14'56.    4673
A Summer's reading. Prose.
Bernard Malamud. 32:149-
56 S22'56.    4674
A summit diary. Prose. Richard
H. Rovere. 37:95-115 Je17'61.
    4675
Summoned by bells. PR
(Betjeman). John Betjeman.
36:31-42 Ag27'60.    4676
Sun. Verse. James Dickey.
42:32 Ja28'67.    4677
The sun. Verse. Anne
Sexton. 38:44 My12'62.    4678
The sun shower. Verse.
George Amabile. 42:38
Jy23'66.    4679
Sunbathers. Verse. Anne
Sexton. 35:93 Je13'59.    4680
The sunbird settles to its
nest. Verse. May Swenson.
45:133 My10'69.    4681
The Sunday after Christmas.
Prose. Mavis Gallant. 43:35-6
D30'67.    4682
Sunday afternoon. Prose.
Mavis Gallant. 38:52-8
N24'62.    4683
Sunday afternoon. Verse.
R.P. Lister. 41:26 Ja8'66.
    4684
Sunday drive to the beach.
Verse. Ted Walker. 45:34
Ja31'70.    4685
Sunday evening. Verse.
Dannie Abse. 36:42
D17'60.    4686
Sunday evenings. Verse.
John Hollander. 41:42 Mr20'65.
    4687
Sunday fishing. Verse. Lisel
Mueller. 37:44 My20'61.
    4688
Sunday, 4 a.m. Verse.
Elizabeth Bishop. 34:42
S20'58.    4689
A Sunday like the others.
Prose. Elizabeth Cullinan.
43:26-33 Ag26'67.    4690

Sunday lunch. Prose.
Nancy Hale. 41:44-9 My8
'65.    4691
Sunday morning. Prose.
John O'Hara. 37:24-6
Ja13'62.    4692
Sunday morning, Watkins Glen.
Verse. L.E. Sissman.
43:100 O28'67.    4693
The Sunday pigeons. Prose.
Robert Henderson. 37:30-3
My27'61.    4694
Sunday teasing. Prose. John
Updike. 32:46-8 O13'56.
    4695
Sunflower. Verse. John
Updike. 31:124*S10'55. 4696
Sunglasses. Verse. John
Updike. 31:65 Jy16'55. 4697
Sunken forest. Verse.
Edward Weismiller.
42:48 Ap30'66.    4698
A super new thing. RL.
Thomas Whiteside. 43:64-161
N4'67.    4699
The Super-American state. PR
(Texas). John Bainbridge.
37:47-111 Mr11'61; 37:51-120
Mr18'61; 37:40-99 Ap1'61;
37:62-131 Ap8'61; 37:48-115
Ap22'61; 37:49-120 My6'61;
37:49-117 My20'61.    4700
The super-express of dreams.
OFFC. E.J. Kahn, Jr.
40:155-62 N21'64.    4701
Superman. Verse. John
Updike. 31:56*N12'55. 4702
The supermarket. Prose.
James Stevenson. 38:102-
106 Je23'62.    4703
The surprise of the century.
PR (Picasso). Janet Flanner.
33:37-63 Mr9'57; 33:39-74
Mr16'57.    4704
Surprised by me. Verse.
Walter Darring. 41:32 Jy24'65.
    4705
The surrounding hills. Prose.
Emily Hahn. 40:184-96
D5'64.    4706
The surveyor. Prose. Henry
Roth. 42:22-30 Ag6'66.
    4707

The tall wild grasses. Verse.
Barbara Gibbs. 31:137
Je11'55. 4742
Tangled web. Prose. Robert
Henderson. 37:38-9 S9'61.
4743
Tank town. Verse. John
Atherton. 33:57*Jy27'57. 4744
Tao in the Yankee Stadium
bleachers. Verse. John
Updike. 32:28*Ag18'56. 4745
Target. Verse. R.P. Lister.
35:180 N28'59. 4746
Tarsaïdzé, Alexandre. TT.
33:24-5 My4'57. 4747
The taste of metal. Prose.
John Updike. 43:49-51
Mr11'67. 4748
The tax. PR (Income Tax).
John Brooks. 41:52-84
Ap3'65; 41:51-83 Ap10'65.
4749
Taxi! Prose. Sara Blackburn.
44:102-104 F8'69. 4750
Tea on the rocks. Prose.
Patrick Kinross. 32:217-22
D1'56. 4751
Tea with the duke. Prose.
Samuel B. Griffith. 31:72-5
*Ag27'55. 4752
The teacher. Verse. Helen
Bevington. 35:87
Je20'59. 4753
The teacher's mass. Prose.
Frank O'Connor. 31:30-3
Ap30'55. 4754
Tebic. Prose. Sylvia Town-
send Warner. 34:28-31
Mr1'58. 4755
Technologies. Verse. George
Starbuck. 35:42 O3'59. 4756
Technology. Lewis Mumford.
36:180-97 O8'60. 4757
The teeming Presbyterians.
Prose. St. Clair McKelway.
32:28-33 F16'57. 4758
Telephone poles. Verse. John
Updike. 36:36 Ja21'61. 4759
Tell it to the Marines. Prose.
Geoffrey T. Hellman. 31:110-
14*F18'56. 4760
Tell me clear, parachutist
dear, are you man or mouse?

Prose. S.J. Perelman.
41:22-4 D25'65. 4761
Tell me, pretty billboard.
Prose. Noel Perrin. 43:
163-72 Ap22'67. 4762
Tell me, tell me. Verse.
Marianne Moore. 36:44
Ap30'60. 4763
Temperature. Verse. Gerard
Malanga. 40:71 Ag1'64.
4764
Tempest in a kitchen. PR
(Dumaine). Joseph Wechs-
berg. 31:32-64 Je18'55.
4765
The temples of the Nile. RL.
Alan Moorehead. 37:106-37
S23'61. 4766
Templex. PR (Fielding).
John McPhee. 43:32-67
Ja6'68. 4767
10-1/2. PR (Fellini).
Lillian Ross. 41:63-107
O30'65. 4768
Ten feet tall. AM. Berton
Roueché. 31:47-75
*S10'55. 4769
Ten haiku. Verse. James
Kirkup. 35:30 Ja9'60. 4770
Ten p.m. Verse. Walter
Stone. 33:44 N2'57. 4771
Ten poems. Verse. E.E.
Cummings. 39:22-3
Ag24'63. 4772
Ten poems. Verse. Nelly
Sachs. 43:30-1 Ag5'67.
4773
10:30, and all quiet on West
Forty-fifth Street. Prose.
S.J. Perelman. 43:24-6
D23'67. 4774
The tenants. Verse. Robert
Graves. 31:28*S3'55. 4775
Tenants and friends. Prose.
Louise Field Cooper.
37:78-85 Ag19'61. 4776
Tenants' harbor. Verse.
Philip Booth. 41:48
S11'65. 4777
The tender age. Prose. John
Collier. 32:34-5
*Mr10'56. 4778

Tenents of the last tree house.
Prose. Nadine Gordimer.
38:39-46 D15'62.                    4779
The tennis. Verse. E.B.
White. 32:46 O6'56.                 4780
Tennis club. Verse. C.A.
Trypanis. 31:108
Je4'55.                             4781
Tennysonian reflections at Barnes
Bridge, London. Verse.
Gavin Ewart. 31:49 Jy2'55.
                                    4782
Tent guest. OFFC. Emily
Hahn. 33:32-51 F1'58.               4783
The tenth man. (play) TT.
36:26-7 Je11'60.                    4784
Terni. Verse. David Posner.
44:199 O26'68.                      4785
Terra incognita. Prose.
Vladimir Nabokov. Dmitri
Nabokov, trans. 39:34-7
My18'63.                            4786
The terrible joys. PR (Ferrari).
Winthrop Sargeant. 41:40-66
Ja15'66.                            4787
Terror and grief. Prose.
Niccolò Tucci. 34:56-98
N15'58.                             4788
Terror in the Grove. Prose.
Burton Bernstein. 35:83-94
Ag29'59.                            4789
The Thames spread out.
Prose. Elizabeth Taylor.
35:34-40*D19'59.                    4790
Thank you for the lovely tea.
Prose. Mavis Gallant.
32:36-48*Je9'56.                    4791
Thank you, Madame President.
Prose. E.J. Kahn, Jr.
40:103-107 My2'64.                  4792
Thanks, possibly, to whatever
powers may be. Verse.
Ogden Nash. 39:40 Mr23'63.
                                    4793
Thanks to Saint Jude. Prose.
Hamilton Basso. 31:92-9
My7'55.                             4794
Thanksgiving for a habitat.
Verse. W.H. Auden.
39:30 Ag17'63.                      4795
A thank-you note for imaginary
gifts. Verse. Howard Moss.
33:104 Ag17'57.                     4796

That dying. Verse. Alastair
Reid. 40:46 Ap25'64.                4797
That great big New York up
there. RL. Philip Ham-
burger. 33:47-88 S28'57.
                                    4798
That was a reporter at wit's
end. Prose. St. Clair
McKelway. 34:38-95
Je14'58.                            4799
That was baseball. Prose.
John Lardner. 32:124-45
*My12'56.                           4800
Thaumas. Verse. Kathleen
Raine. 38:44 Ap14'62.               4801
Thaw on Threadneedle Street.
RL. John Brooks.
36:31-9 D31'60.                     4802
The theatre in Central Park.
Verse. Mary Phelps. 44:34
Ag24'68.                            4803
Théâtre International. Janet
Flanner. 36:145-6
Ap23'60.                            4804
Théâtre National Populaire.
TT. 34:34 O25'58.                   4805
Theatre Season, New York,
1961-62. TT. 37:33-4
S30'61.                             4806
Their party, our house.
Verse. Jon Swan. 37:68
D2'61.                              4807
Their quiet lives. Prose.
Sylvia Townsend Warner.
39:40-8 My11'63.                    4808
Them apples. Prose.
Gilbert Rogin. 40:40 D19'64.
                                    4809
Them, crying. Verse. James
Dickey. 40:42 My9'64.               4810
Theme song. Prose. Robert
M. Coates. 35:120-32
N28'59.                             4811
A theory of waves. Verse.
John Hollander. 32:38
*Mr31'56.                           4812
"There is a host approaching
nigh." Prose. Nancy Hale.
33:52-6*N30'57.                     4813
There is indeed but one Ronda.
OFFC. Hamilton Basso.
32:116-32*S8'56.                    4814
There'll be nobody for lunch

Thou Mets. Verse. Donald
Stewart. 38:36 Mr24'62.
4850
Though tribe and tongue may
differ. OFFC. Emily
Hahn. 36:202-28
D10'60. 4851
A thought for Tristan. Verse.
John Frederick Nims.
43:148 Mr11'67. 4852
The thought-fox. Verse.
Ted Hughes. 33:28
Ag31'57. 4853
Thoughts on living in a Shaker
house. Verse. Janet
Malcolm. 39:170 N2'63.
4854
Thoughts on my head. Verse.
William Meredith. 31:38
*D17'55. 4855
Thoughts on rereading "Don
Juan." Verse. Morris
Bishop. 33:108 Je15'57.
4856
Thoughts while driving home.
Verse. John Updike. 35:180
S26'59. 4857
Thoughts while splitting
wood. Verse. Peter Kane
Dufault. 40:60 N14'64. 4858
The thousand and second night.
Verse. James Merrill.
40:36-8 Je13'64. 4859
The thread remains very thin.
RL. Faith McNulty.
42:31-83 Ag6'66. 4860
The three. PR (DC-3).
E.J. Kahn, Jr. 36:49-75
S10'60. 4861
3 a.m. Verse. John Updike.
34:168 N29'58. 4862
Three birds. Verse. Gene
Baro. 37:66 Jy15'61. 4863
Three Cambridge poems.
Verse. L.E. Sissman.
40:60 O24'64. 4864
The three cats. Prose. Sylvia
Townsend Warner. 40:36-40
My30'64. 4865
Three Christmas days. OFFC.
Christopher Rand. 35:29-47
D26'59; 35:50-9 Ja2'60;
35:84-102 Ja9'60. 4866

Three evenly spaced cheers
for the compulsives.
Prose. Hayes B. Jacobs.
36:28-30 D31'60. 4867
Three green windows. Verse.
Anne Sexton. 40:44 Je6'64.
4868
Three is company. Prose.
Padma Perera. 45:34-44
Mr29'69. 4869
Three loves had I, in assorted
flavors. Prose. S.J.
Perelman. 45:34-7 Mr22'69.
4870
Three more hats. Prose.
Roger Angell. 40:29-31
F29'64. 4871
Three poems. Verse.
Kathleen Raine. 41:50-1
D18'65. 4872
Three poems. Verse. E.N.
Sargent. 41:33 Ja22'66.
4873
Three sick babies. AM.
Berton Roueché. 44:116-
38 O5'68. 4874
Three songs. Verse. Louise
Bogan. 43:45 Ap1'67. 4875
Three stages of Spring. Verse.
Alastair Reid. 33:83
Mr30'57. 4876
Three stories. Prose.
Jorge Luis Borges.
Anthony Kerrigan, trans.
42:23-33 Ja7'67. 4877
Three stories. Prose. Jordan
Crittenden. 42:177-83
Mr19'66. 4878
Threes. Verse. John
Atherton. 33:103 Mr2'57.
4879
A threnody. Verse. Phyllis
McGinley. 34:39 N1'58.
4880
The thrifty elephant.
Verse. John Holmes.
36:87 Ja28'61. 4881
Through the great city. PR
(Northeast Corridor).
Anthony Bailey. 43:35-69
Jy22'67; 43:35-69 Jy29'67;
43:32-63 Ag5'67. 4882
Through the tunnel. Prose.

Verse. John Updike. 32:111
*F25'56.                           5027
The Tsotsis and the Pondos.
Prose. Anthony Delius. 39:26-30
F1'64.                             5028
Tubman bids us toil.   OFFC.
Norman Lewis. 33:80-101
Ja11'58.                           5029
Tuckertee Ridge. Prose.
St. Clair McKelway. 37:36-7
My13'61.                           5030
Tulips. Verse. Sylvia Plath.
38:40 Ap7'62.                      5031
Tulips and addresses.
Verse. Edward Field.
39:47 Ap27'63.                     5032
The tunnel in the chalk. RL.
Thomas Whiteside. 37:105-50
N18'61; 37:102-44 N25'61.
                                   5033
Turgenev, Ivan.   Edmund
Wilson. 33:163-216 O19'57.
                                   5034
The turkey. Verse. Gene
Baro. 39:194 N30'63.      5035
Turn of Spring. Verse. Mary
Phelps. 37:156 My6'61.    5036
Turner, Reginald. S. N.
Behrman and Max Beerbohm.
36:69-80 Mr12'60.         5037
Turpentine. Verse. R. P.
Lister. 32:30 O20'56.     5038
The turtle who conquered
time. FFT. James Thurber.
32:22-3*S1'56.            5039
Twain, Mark. Dwight Mac-
donald. 36:160-96
Ap9'60.                   5040
Twain, Mark. (Parody).
Katherine Hoskins. 34:28
Ag16'58.                  5041
Twelfth night, or what's your
bill?  Verse. Rosalind
Constable. 37:171 D9'61.
                          5042
The twelfth wedding anniversary.
Prose. Maeve Brennan.
42:60-6 S24'66.           5043
Twelve chases on West Ninety-
ninth Street. Prose. Roy
Bongartz. 38:36-41 Ap21'62.
                          5044

The Twenties: American
writers in Paris and their
friends. (Exhibition)
Janet Flanner. 35:154-6
Mr21'59.                  5045
The 20th armored: a recurrent
dream. Verse. L E. Siss-
man. 45:40 Ap5'69.        5046
Twenty to forty. Verse.
Carl O. Denham. 31:116
My28'55.                  5047
Twice of the same fever.
Verse. Robert Graves.
35:32 Ja16'60.            5048
Twigs. Prose. H. L.
Mountzoures.   44:48-51
My4'68.                   5049
Twin beds in Rome. Prose.
John Updike. 39:32-5
F8'64.                    5050
The twin of sleep. Verse.
Robert Graves. 34:107
S27'58.                   5051
Twink drives back, in a bad
mood, from a party in
Massachusetts. Verse.
George Amabile. 41:36
Mr6'65.                   5052
Two. Verse. Winfield
Townley Scott. 32:79
Ja12'57.                  5053
Two against the prepacks.
Prose. Edward B. Marks.
34:192-6 N15'58.          5054
Two at the fair. Verse.
David Morton. 32:154
*My12'56.                 5055
Two dogs. FFT. James
Thurber. 32:22*S1'56.     5056
Two encounters. Verse.
L. E. Sissman. 43:56
Ap15'67.                  5057
Two happenings in Boston.
Verse. L. E. Sissman.
42:58 O8'66.              5058
Two kitchens in Provence.
Prose. M. F. K. Fisher.
42:29-36 Ag27'66.         5059
Two men of affairs. Prose.
Gilbert Rogin. 44:33-5
My25'68.                  5060
Two old tales about men and

women. Prose. William
Maxwell. 34:26-8 Je21'58.
                                    5061
Two old tales about women.
Prose. William Maxwell.
34:36-9 Mr15'58.            5062
2 p.m. going westward on the
Chicago, Burlington &
Quincy. Verse. Ralph
Pomeroy. 43:92 Ja27'68.
                                    5063
Two people and a clock on the
wall. Prose. Anne Tyler.
42:207-17 N19'66.          5064
Two pilgrims. Prose. Peter
Taylor. 39:36-42 S7'63.
                                    5065
Two quatrains for first frost.
Verse. Richard Wilbur.
35:41 O31'59.              5066
Two questions. Prose. Mavis
Gallant. 37:30-6 Je10'61.
                                    5067
The two societies. Verse. John
Hall Wheelock. 31:25
*F4'56.                    5068
Two sonnets from the Encyclo-
paedia Britannica. Verse.
Richmond Lattimore. 31:48
My7'55.                    5069
Two translations of a private
poem awaiting further
translation. Verse. Gerald
Jonas. 44:48 Mr16'68.  5070
Two turtledoves. Prose. John
O'Hara. 37:22-3 D23'61.  5071
Two voices in a meadow. Verse.
Richard Wilbur. 33:26
Ag17'57.                   5072
The tyranny of trivia. Prose.
James Thurber. 31:30-5
*D17'55.                   5073

U

U.N. letter. Richard H.
Rovere. 37:157-64
O7'61.                     5074
U.S. Journal: Atlantic City.
Prose. Calvin Trillin. 45:
104-10  Je14'69.          5075
U.S. journal: Brainerd, Minn.
Prose. Calvin Trillin. 45:68-
73 Ja24'70.               5076

U.S. journal: Clovis. Prose.
Calvin Trillin. 44:106-13
Mr30'68.                   5077
U.S. journal: Denver. Prose.
Calvin Trillin. 45:85-9
My31'69.                   5078
U.S. journal: Eureka Springs,
Ark. Prose. Calvin
Trillin. 45:69-79  Jy26'69.
                                    5079
U.S. journal: Gees Bend, Ala.
Prose. Calvin Trillin. 45:
102-108 Mr22'69.          5080
U.S. journal: Honolulu. Prose.
Calvin Trillin. 44:157-62
O26'68.                    5081
U.S. journal: Iowa. Prose.
Calvin Trillin. 44:170-8
Ap20'68.                   5082
U.S. journal: Jeremiah, Ky.
Prose. Calvin Trillin.
45:178-83 Ap12'69.       5083
U.S. journal: Kansas City.
Prose. Calvin Trillin.
44:107-14 My11'68.       5084
U.S. journal: Kentucky. Prose.
Calvin Trillin. 45:33-6 D27
'69.                       5085
U.S. journal: Lake County, Ill.
Prose. Calvin Trillin. 44:
100-106 F15'69.          5086
U.S. journal: Lower Bucks
County, Pa. Prose. Calvin
Trillin. 45:169-75 N15'69.
                                    5087
U.S. journal: Monroe, N.C.
Prose. Calvin Trillin. 45:144-
54 O11'69.                 5088
U.S. journal: Nassau County.
Prose. Calvin Trillin. 44:
226-35 N16'68.            5089
U.S. journal: New Orleans.
Prose. Calvin Trillin.
44:138-44 Mr9'68; 45:112-18
My3'69.                    5090
U.S. journal: on the circuit.
Prose. Calvin Trillin. 44:38-
43 F1'69.                  5091
U.S. journal: Oshkosh. Prose.
Calvin Trillin. 44:62-6
Ja4'69.                    5092
U.S. journal: Pass Christian,
Miss. Prose. Calvin Trillin.
45:175-84 N29'69.         5093

A victim of noblesse oblige.
PR (Cousy). Robert Rice.
36:38-60 F4'61.                 5199
Victor meets Pnin. Prose.
Vladimir Nabokov. 31:38-45
*O15'55.                        5200
Victory no. 743 at sea. Prose.
Gordon Cotler. 43:128-32
Ap1'67.                         5201
Vidal, Gore. TT. 36:38-9
Ap23'60.                        5202
The view. Verse. Howard
Nemerov. 42:64 O29'66.          5203
A view. Verse. Beverly
Quint. 40:73 Jy25'64.           5204
View from the gorge. Verse.
Ben Belitt. 41:26 Jy3'65.
                                5205
The view from the middle.
Prose. Norman Hankinson.
40:45-51 S12'64.                5206
A view from the treetop.
Prose. Benedict Kiely. 37:24-
32 Ag26'61.                     5207
A view of a trap. OFFC.
Anthony West. 33:128-42
*N30'57.                        5208
View of Earth from a space
station. Verse. Jackson
Morris. 32:175 D8'56.           5209
The view of Rome. Prose.
Sylvia Townsend Warner.
38:62-7 D1'62.                  5210
A view of the river. Prose.
Nadine Gordimer. 35:40-50
Ap11'59.                        5211
Viewer from the 14th floor.
PR (Sulzberger). Geoffrey T.
Hellman. 44:40-71 Ja18'69.
                                5212
Views of my father weeping.
Prose. Donald Barthelme.
45:56-60 D6'69.                 5213
Villa Adriana. Prose. Shirley
Hazzard. 37:28-30 Ag5'61.
                                5214
The village. Prose. Arturo
Vivante. 35:107-11 Mr21
'59.                            5215
The village explainer. Prose.
Calvin Tomkins. 42:53-5
D3'66.                          5216

The village of Ben Suc. RL.
Jonathan Schell. 43:28-93
Jy15'67.                        5217
Village wedding. Verse. John
Betjeman. 35:30 Jy11'59.
                                5218
Violence on Riverside Drive.
Prose. Benedict Thielen.
32:81-95*Mr24'56.               5219
Violent storm. Verse. Mark
Strand. 40:66 O10'64.           5220
Viper's bugloss. Verse. Ruth
Fox. 42:138 Ap16'66.            5221
Virus X. Prose. Mavis
Gallant. 40:29-61 Ja30'65.
                                5222
A vision. Verse. Gray Burr.
35:114 Ja23'60.                 5223
Vision. Verse. Richard
Eberhart. 39:54 O5'63.
                                5224
A vision. Verse. John
Updike. 36:77 Ja7'61.           5225
A vision of the world. Prose.
John Cheever. 38:42-6
S29'62.                         5226
A visionary gleam. Prose.
Sylvia Townsend Warner.
43:36-41 Je3'67.                5227
The visit. Prose. Arturo
Vivante. 41:29-31 Jy3'65.
                                5228
Visit the sick. Prose. Fred
S. Licht. 38:100-19 Ap28
'62.                            5229
A visit to Armenia. Prose.
Sonia Shiragian. 39:44-8
Ap27'63.                        5230
A visit to the château. Verse.
David Posner. 36:22 Jy30
'60.                            5231
The visitation. Prose. L.
Woiwode. 42:56-61
S10'66.                         5232
Visiting chaos. Verse. L. E.
Sissman. 45:44 Mr15'69.
                                5233
Visiting lecturer. Verse.
Alastair Reid. 44:68
Je15'68.                        5234
The visitor. Verse. Michael
Goldman. 43:54 S23'67. 5235

A visitor from Porlock, but,
alas, no Xanadu. Verse.
Ogden Nash. 42:60 N12'66.
5236
Visual welfare state. Prose.
H.F. Ellis. 45:103-106
Ap19'69.                          5237
Vittorio. Prose. Shirley
Hazzard. 37:32-8
Je17'61.                          5238
Vivaldi. Verse. Delmore
Schwartz. 34:50 D6'58.
5239
The vocal mission. PR (London)
Joseph Wechsberg. 33:49-92
O26'57; 33:47-81 N2'57.
5240
Vogue (magazine). Geoffrey T.
Hellman. 38:121-4 F16'63.
5241
Vogue's in its heaven. Prose.
Geoffrey T. Hellman.
38:121-4 F16'63.                  5242
The voice. Verse. Theodore
Roethke. 31:28
Jy9'55.                           5243
The voice from the privet
hedge. Verse. Morris
Bishop. 31:24*Ag13'55.            5244
Voices. RL. William Murray.
44:46-80 My11'68.                 5245
The voices. Prose. Elizabeth
Taylor. 39:28-31 Jy20'63.
5246
Voices from the other world.
Verse. James Merrill. 33:26
Je29'57.                          5247
The voices of the dead. Prose.
Elizabeth Cullinan. 36:40-8
Ap16'60.                          5248
Voltaire. TT. 38:26-7
Mr3'62.                           5249
Vow. Verse. John Updike.
40:48 My23'64.                    5250
Voznessenski, Andrei. Janet
Flanner. 38:102-104 Ja26
'63.                              5251
Vron and Willie. Prose.
Elizabeth Taylor. 40:34-9
Ja16'65.                          5252

W

W + D x .4 + 15 = Ugh!
Prose. John Sack. 35:126-31
S26'59.                           5253
W.R., Jr., in the U.S.S.R.
WP. A.J. Liebling.
31:64-75 F26'55.                  5154
W.S. Landor. Verse.
Marianne Moore.
40:26 F22'64.                     5255
Wah-who-eeee. Prose.
Chester Goolrick. 32:59-63
*Je16'56.                         5256
The wait. Prose. John
Updike. 43:34-96 F17'68.
5257
The waiting. Prose. James
Agee. 33:41-62 O5'57.  5258
Waiting. WP. E.J. Kahn, Jr.
33:156-63*N30'57.                 5259
Waiting for Christmas.
Prose. Faith McNulty. 34:77-
80 D20'58.                        5260
The waiting room. Prose.
Arturo Vivante. 41:40-5
Mr20'65.                          5261
Wake me up for the hoedown.
Prose. Noel Perrin. 35:
46-7 N28'59.                      5262
Wake up and live. RL.
Calvin Trillin. 40:120-77
Ap4'64.                           5263
Waking dream about a lost
child. Verse. William
Meredith. 45:32 Jy12'69.
5264
Waking to sleep. Verse. Gene
Baro. 41:191 O30'65.   5265
Walden in July. Verse. Donalc
Junkins. 38:75 Jy14'62.
Wales visitation. Verse.
Allen Ginsberg. 44:44-5
My11'68.                          5267
Walk from the nearest police-
man. Prose. Hildegarde
Dolson.33:78-85*Je22'57.5268
A walk in late Summer. Verse.
Theodore Roethke. 33:36
S7'57.                            5269

A walk in Massachusetts. Prose.
H. F. Ellis. 36:22-4
Jy2'60.                          5270

A walk in the country, or how
to keep fit to be tied.
Prose. Peter DeVries. 35:
38-40 Je6'59.                    5271

A walk in Würzberg. Verse.
William Plomer. 42:26 Je
25'66.                           5272

A walk on the sweet side.
Prose. S. J. Perelman.
38:20-3 Ag11'62.                 5273

A walk on the towpath. RL.
Berton Roueché. 38:89-99
Je2'62.                          5274

A walk through the tunnel.
OFFC. Joseph Wechsberg.
32:94-117*My12'56.               5275

A walk to the park. PR
(Jones). Whitney Balliett.
44:45-70 My18'68.                5276

A walk with Vinoba. RL.
Christopher Rand. 31:119-37
*O22'55.                         5277

The walkers. RL. J. M.
Flagler. 34:33-47 Ag2'58.
                                 5278

Walking in Naples. OFFC.
Robert M. Coates.
39:176-92 N2'63.                 5279

Walking in the wet. Verse.
Gene Baro. 38:126 N3'62.
                                 5280

Walking on water. Verse.
James Dickey. 36:44 Je18
'60.                             5281

Walking to sleep. Verse. Richard
Wilbur. 43:32-3 D23'67.  5282

Walking with Lulu in the wood.
Verse. Naomi Lazard. 44:
36 Ja18'69.                      5283

Walter Benjamin. REF.
Hannah Arendt. Harry Zohn,
trans. 44:65-156 O19'68.
                                 5284

Walter Jenks' bath. Verse.
William Meredith. 44:38
Je8'68.                          5285

The waltz. Verse. Hilary
Corke. 39:40 My4'63.     5286

Wanda Hawley and the flight
of time. Prose. Frederick L.

Keefe. 36:97-100 F11'61.
                                 5287

The waning oomph of Mrs.
Toplofty. OUWA. Geoffrey T.
Hellman. 31:80-8 Je18'55.
                                 5288

The war canoes. Verse. Beth
Bentley. 34:136 N29'58.
                                 5289

The war in Kansas. RL.
Calvin Trillin. 43:56-145
Ap22'67.                         5290

A war on Salamis. Prose.
Alfred Chester. 35:46-81
Ap25'59.                         5291

A war requiem. Verse. L. E.
Sissman. 45:37-43 My3'69.
                                 5292

War stories. Prose. Howard
Webber. 39:41-5 Je8'63.
                                 5293

A war story. Prose. Paul
Brodeur. 35:177-87
N7'59.                           5294

War with Connecticut. Prose.
Sally Benson. 31:38-43
Ap2'55.                          5295

The war wound. Verse. James
Dickey. 40:54 S12'64.    5296

The ward. Verse. George
Macbeth. 42:42 Ap30'66.
                                 5297

The warlock. Prose. Jean
Stafford. 31:25-45*D24'55.
                                 5298

Warning: new century ahead.
Prose. Hayes B. Jacobs.
39:138-42 Ap27'63.       5299

Warning to haberdashers.
Verse. Phyllis McGinley.
33:30 My18'57.           5300

The wars. Verse. Howard
Moss. 43:60 N18'67.      5301

Was escoffier a false isolate?
Prose. Geoffrey T. Hellman.
37:60-5 Jy8'61.          5302

Was I asleep? Prose.
Penelope Gilliatt. 44:46-55
Ap20'68.                 5303

Was lifted by ears as a boy,
no harm done. Prose. E. B.
White. 40:38 My9'64.
                                 5304

Wash. Verse. John Updike.
36:161 D3'60. 5305
Washington. Prose. Julian
Mazor. 38:29-38 Ja19'63.
5306
The wasp. Verse. Daryl Hine.
39:48 S14'63. 5307
The watcher. Verse. Ruth
Stone. 32:87 Ja19'57. 5308
The watchers. Verse. Paul
Blackburn. 42:56-7 D10'66.
5309
The watchers of the night. Prose.
James Thurber. 35:18-21
D26'59. 5310
Water. Verse. Josephine
Jacobsen. 41:54 O2'65. 5311
Water. Prose. R. Bruce
Moody. 41:24-31 Je26'65.
5312
Water color. Verse. Stephen
Mooney. 33:34 Ja11'58. 5313
Water color of Grantchester
Meadows. Verse. Sylvia
Plath. 36:30 My28'60. 5314
Water Island. Verse. Howard
Moss. 36:28 Ag6'60. 5315
Water lilies. Verse. Luke E.
Zilles. 33:69*Je1'57. 5316
The water moccasin. Verse.
Freda Quenneville. 44:179
D14'68. 5317
Water picture. Verse. May
Swenson. 32:101*Ap14'56.
5318
Watering trough. Verse. Maxine
W. Kumin. 44:116 Mr30'68.
5319
The watermelons. Prose. Alice
Marriott. 32:54-60 Ja5'57.
5320
The waters around Salisbury.
OFFC. Christopher Rand.
43:152-86 S16'67. 5321
Watson, James D. (Parody).
Philip Hamburger. 44:24-6
Je22'68. 5322
Waugh, Alec. TT. 31:17-18
*F4'56; 32:23-4*F25'56. 5323
The wave. Verse. W.S.
Merwin. 41:176 N27'65. 5324
The wave and the dune. Verse.
May Swenson. 41:79 Ag7'65.
5325

The way I figure it. Prose.
Hayes B. Jacobs. 37:148-
55 O7'61. 5326
The way to the river.
Verse. W.S. Merwin.
38:33 D29'62. 5327
The ways of the avalanche.
RL. Joseph Wechsberg.
33:113-38 Ap13'57. 5328
We and they in Rhodesia. Prose.
Mary Cable. 41:36-41
F19'66. 5329
We darned near killed Luella.
RL. Katharine T. Kinkead:
32:106-33*My5'56. 5330
We gather together. Prose.
Pearl Kazin. 31:51-6*N26
'55. 5331
We have met the Sassenachs
and they are ours; even the
year is now MCMLXIX.
Verse. Ogden Nash. 45:36
F22'69. 5332
We have to live here, too.
Prose. Kenneth Lamott.
36:142-55 Mr12'60. 5333
We know that your hearts are
heavy. Prose. Merrill Joan
Gerber. 39:42-52 Ap20'63.
5334
We landed our passengers.
OFFC. A.J. Liebling. 32:
210-16 D1'56. 5335
We settled by the lake. Verse.
F.D. Reeve. 40:48 S26'64.
5336
The weakness. Prose. John
O'Hara. 37:23-9 Jy8'61.
5337
The weary Titans. Prose.
H.F. Ellis. 42:52-3 O15'66.
5338
Weather. Verse. William
Meredith. 41:115 F12'66.
5339
The weather of six mornings.
Verse. Jane Cooper. 43:
42 S9'67. 5340
The weaver and the worm.
FFT. James Thurber.
32:19*Ag11'56. 5341
The wedding gift. Prose. Dan
Evans. 42:219-28 O15'66.
5342

Barbara Gibbs. 42:40
Je18'66. 5378
Whatever the maples meant.
Verse. Peter Kane Dufault.
34:148 N1'58. 5379
What's a girl supposed to do--
sit aroun' and twill her
thumbs? Prose. Arthur
Kober. 33:45-7 S14'57. 5380
What's being worn at Le Pavillon.
Prose. Geoffrey T. Hellman.
39:140-4 Mr9'63. 5381
What's in a name? Here's what's
in a name. Verse. Ogden
Nash. 31:56*N19'55. 5382
What's it like out? Prose.
Penelope Gilliatt. 44:52-61
O26'68. 5383
What's it like outside? Verse.
Ogden Nash. 45:36 Ap5'69.
5384
What's sauce pour l'oie is sauce
pour l'état c'est moi.
Verse. Ogden Nash. 44:28 Ag
17'68. 5385
What's what. Verse. Alastair
Reid. 33:48 D7'57. 5386
What's your problem? Prose.
Robert Boles. 40:55-8
O17'64. 5387
The wheelbarrow. Prose.
V.S. Pritchett. 36:30-40
Jy16'60. 5388
The wheelchair on the grass.
Prose. Lillian Ross. 37:27-
32 Je24'61. 5389
Wheels. Verse. Dorothy
Donnelly. 33:58 N23'57. 5390
Wheep no more. Verse.
R.A.L. 33:123 Je8'57. 5391
When news isn't. WP. A.J.
Liebling. 36:182-6 N5'60.
5392
When shad are running. Verse.
Charles Burgess. 34:86 Ap
12'58. 5393
When the Rockies burned.
Prose. Max Miller. 33:169-78
N9'57. 5394
When the vacation is over for
good. Verse. Mark Strand.
38:26 Ag18'62. 5395

When we looked back. Verse.
William Stafford. 35:150
Je6'59. 5396
When we were nearly young.
Prose. Mavis Gallant. 36:
38-42 O15'60. 5397
When your honey's on the
telephone. Prose. George S.
Kaufman. 34:29 F22'58.
5398
Where do you work-a, John?
Prose. S.J. Perelman.
34:29-31 Je7'58. 5399
Where is the voice coming
from? Prose. Eudora
Welty. 39:24-5 Jy6'63. 5400
Where memories begin. Prose.
Naomi Bliven. 37:135-42
N4'61. 5401
Where nothing is long ago.
Prose. Virginia Sorensen.
31:108-17*O15'55. 5402
Where the castle is. Verse.
Howard Moss. 45:54
N22'69. 5403
Where the curve begins.
Verse. Donald Stewart.
38:127 Ap14'62. 5404
Where the slow fig. Verse.
Robert Penn Warren.
43:145 Je10'67. 5405
Where to catch a wahoo.
Prose. H.F. Ellis.
38:74-6 Jy28'62. 5406
Whereas, the former premises
being kaput--. Prose.
S.J. Perelman. 31:28-31
Mr5'55. 5407
Which came first, obeisance
or obesity? Verse. Ogden
Nash. 35:42 Mr21'59. 5408
Which new era would that be?
Prose. Nadine Gordimer.
31:25-30 Jy9'55. 5409
Which of those two ladies is
he married to? Prose. Edna
O'Brien. 40:49-54 Ap25'64.
5410
While watching the movie
"Trapeze." Verse. Preston
Newman. 32:65*Ag4'56.
5411

The whippet. Verse. Evelyn
Ames. 39:34 Ja11'64.     5412

Whistling in the darkroom. PR
(Godowsky). Joseph
Wechsberg. 32:61-109
*N10'56.     5413

White dwarf. Verse. John
Updike. 38:67 S1'62.     5414

White nights. Verse. Hawley
Truax. 44:64 O12'68.     5415

The white rabbit. Prose.
Penelope Mortimer. 35:52-8
D12'59.     5416

White, Robert M., II. TT.
35:24-6 Ja16'60.     5417

The white wild bronco. Prose.
Benedict Kiely. 34:24-6
D20'58.     5418

Whither Nepostiltskin? Prose.
Calvin Tompkins. 36:26-7
Ag20'60.     5419

Who called that pied-billed
grebe a podilymbus podiceps
podiceps? Verse. Ogden
Nash. 44:40 F24'68.     5420

Who made yellow roses
yellow? Prose. John
Updike. 32:28-34*Ap7'56. 5421

Who wants to travel all over
Europe and see nothing but
a lot of American tourists?
I do. Verse. Ogden Nash.
31:28*Jy30'55.     5422

Who you are and what you think
you're doing. PR (Johnson).
Robert Rice. 37:32-56
D23'61.     5423

Who'll buy my lingual? Verse.
Ogden Nash. 31:30 F19'55.
5424

Who's afraid of Virginia
Woolf? (Play). TT.
39:41-3 O26'63.     5425

Who's who in the cast. Prose.
Bernard Taper. 32:133-4
*Ap28'56.     5426

Whose little girl are you? Prose.
Katinka Loeser. 38:26-31
Jy7'62.     5427

Why cash the club when you
can't get to dummy with a
crowbar? RL. John Brooks.

32:66-92*S8'56.     5428

Why don't we just hum for a
while? PR (Miller).
William Whitworth.
45:38-66 Mr1'69.     5429

Why don't you go home? Prose.
Cecile Lamalle Cuming. 40:
180-93 O3'64.     5430

Why fight it? PR (Janis).
John Brooks. 36:59-101
N12'60.     5431

Wichita, Kan. NFG. Philip
Hamburger. 37:144-9
S23'61.     5432

The widow. Verse. W.S.
Merwin. 42:174 My21'66.
5433

The widow. Prose. R. Prawer
Jhabvala. 39:22-30
Ag10'63.     5434

The widowhood system. Prose.
Brian Friel. 40:29-36
S5'64.     5435

A wife talks to herself.
Verse. Stephen Berg. 40:111
Ja30'65.     5436

Wife-wooing. Prose. John
Updike. 36:49-51 Mr12'60.
5437

Wild asters. Verse. Ruth
Stone. 43:187 N11'67.     5438

The wild bird. Verse. Donald
Lawder, Jr. 31:111*O8'55.
5439

The wild boy. Prose. Benedict
Kiely. 35:29-33 Ja30'60.
5440

The wild heifers. Prose.
Donald Hall. 37:28-34 S2'61.
5441

Wild music. Prose. H.F.
Ellis. 39:58-60 Jy6'63. 5442

Wild, original Spring. Verse.
Howard Moss. 40:40 Je20'64.
5443

Wild Wales. Prose. Sylvia
Townsend Warner. 33:22-6
D28'57.     5444

Wilde, Oscar. S.N. Behrman
and Max Beerbohm. 36:52-
7 F20'60.     5445

Wilder, Thornton. TT. 35:
34-5 My23'59.     5446

Willi. Prose. Mavis Gallant.
  38:29-31 Ja5'63.        5447
Williams, William Carlos. TT.
  34:32-3 S27'58.        5448
Williamsburg, Va. NFG.
  Philip Hamburger. 36:182-5
  S10'60.        5449
Wilmington, Del. NFG.
  Philip Hamburger.
  35:88-92 Je20'59.        5450
Wilson, Edmund. Edmund
  Wilson. 38:118-28 Je2'62.
          5451
Wilson, Edmund. Edmund
  Wilson. PR. 43:50-131 Ap
  29'67; 43:52-149 My6'67.
  43:54-157 My13'67.        5452
Wilson, Mitchell. TT. 37:19-20
  Ja6'62.        5453
Wind. Prose. Anthony Bailey.
  38:22-4 Je23'62.        5454
The wind birds. RL. Peter
  Matthiessen. 43:40-102
  My27'67; 43:42-105 Je3'67.
          5455
Wind WSW 12. Verse. May
  Swenson. 37:60 O14'61.   5456
A winding stair, a fox hunt,
  a fulfilling situation, some
  sycamores, and the church at
  Henning. Prose. Sylvia
  Townsend Warner. 42:38-41
  F26'66.        5457
The window. Verse. Elizabeth
  Hawes. 40:94 S12'64.     5458
A windowful of London. Verse.
  Helen Bevington. 32:147
  O6'56.        5459
The wings of defeat. Prose.
  Csikszentmihalyi Mihaly.
  38:157-67 S15'62.        5460
The wings of Henry James.
  OUWA. James Thurber.
  35:188-201 N7'59.        5461
Winston-Salem, N.C. NFG.
  Philip Hamburger. 36:178-81
  N26'60.        5462
Winter. Verse. Harold Brodkey.
  40:110 F22'64.        5463
Winter. Verse. Joseph
  Langland. 33:79 Ja11'58. 5464
A Winter come. Verse. Howard
  Moss. 32:27 Ja5'57.     5465

Winter dance. Prose. John
  O'Hara. 38:34-6 S22'62.
          5466
Winter dawn. Verse. R.P.
  Lister. 35:62 Ja30'60.
          5467
Winter garden. Prose. Janet
  Frame. 45:37-9 Ja31'70.
          5468
Winter in Etienburgh. Verse.
  Stephen Parker. 41:40
  F5'66.        5469
Winter in the spare-parts yard.
  Prose. Perdita Buchan.
  45:38-44 Mr22'69.     5470
A Winter morning. Verse.
  Grover Amen. 31:30*F4'56.
          5471
Winter morning. Verse. William
  Jay Smith. 43:46 D16'67.
          5472
Winter ocean. Verse. John
  Updike. 36:139 F20'60. 5473
Winter pond. Verse. Ben
  Belitt. 41:38 F19'66.  5474
Winter scene. Verse. Paul
  Carroll. 33:105 Ja25'58.
          5475
Winter skate. Prose. Parke
  Cummings. 33:77-9 F1'58.
          5476
Winter: the city: a ballad.
  Verse. Gerald Jonas. 40:
  92 F13'65.        5477
Winter tourists: London. Verse.
  R.P. Lister. 37:95
  F3'62.        5478
Winter tryst. Verse. Ormonde
  deKay, Jr. 34:85 Mr1'58.
          5479
Winter verse for my sister.
  Verse. William Meredith.
  42:38 Ja28'67.        5480
A Winter's tale. Verse.
  Robert Patrick Dana. 39:28
  F1'64.        5481
A Winter's tale. Verse.
  Sylvia Plath. 35:116
  D12'59.        5482
Wintersong. Verse. Peter
  Kane Dufault. 41:104
  Ja29'66.        5483
The wire forests. Verse.

You must know everything. Prose.
Isaac Babel. Max Hayward,
trans. 42:36-8 Ap9'66. 5553
You never learn to say goodbye.
PR (M. S. Sagafjord)
Lillian Ross. 42:65-177
N19'66. 5554
You read me and I'll read you.
OFFC. Alastair Reid. 38:35-
49 Ag4'62. 5555
You say what I feel. Prose.
Gilbert Rogin. 45:29-33
Jy12'69. 5556
You'll drink your orange
juice and like it, Comrade.
Verse. Ogden Nash. 37:28
Jy8'61. 5557
You'll enjoy it when you get
there. Prose. Elizabeth
Taylor. 33:49-53 N23'57.
5558
You'll never know, dear, how
much I love you. Prose.
John Updike. 36:39-40
Je18'60. 5559
A young girl can spoil her
chances. Prose. Maeve
Brennan. 38:38-79 S8'62.
5560
Young girl in a pool. Verse.
Peter Kane Dufault. 36:24
Jy2'60. 5561
The young goddess. Verse.
Robert Graves. 35:58
D26'59. 5562
Young men remember. Prose.
H.F. Ellis. 44:40-1 S28'68.
5563
Young Mr. Know-it-all. Prose.
Glen Haley. 32:146-54
*My12'56. 5564
Your face on the dog's neck.
Verse. Anne Sexton. 42:40
S3'66. 5565
Your horoscope. Prose. Roger
Angell. 45:33 Mr29'69. 5566
Yrs. truly, A. Lincoln. PR
(Cosey). John Kobler. 32:38-
85*F25'56. 5567
Youth and the lady. Prose.
Sylvia Townsend Warner.
36:38-9 Ap16'60. 5568

Youth's progress. Verse.
John Updike. 31:28 F26'55.
5569

Z

Zen in the art of tennis. Prose.
Calvin Tomkins. 35:24-6
Ag8'59. 5570
Zero. Prose. John O'Hara.
39:28-32 D28'63. 5571
The zinkist and the shawmist.
Prose. Hayes B. Jacobs.
36:38-9 My7'60. 5572
Zola, Emile. Janet Flanner.
43:139-40 Je10'67. 5573
Zooey. Prose. J.D.
Salinger. 33:32-139
My4'57. 5574
Zoological footnote. Verse.
by Paul Preger, Jr.
31:119 Ap5'55. 5575
Zulli, Floyd, Jr. John
Lardner. 33:210-12 D14'57.
5576
Zulli, Floyd, Jr. TT.
34:26-7 Ap5'58. 5577
Zulu, watch the snakes.
Prose. Wolcott Gibbs. 32:
22-3*Je30'56. 5578
The Zulus. RL. Calvin
Trillin. 40:41-119 Je20'64.
5579

List of Reviewers

| | |
|---|---|
| ADLER | Renata Adler |
| ALSOP | Joseph Alsop |
| ANGELL | Roger Angell |
| ARLEN | Michael J. Arlen |
| AUDEN | W. H. Auden |
| BALLIETT | Whitney Balliett |
| BEHRMAN | S. N. Behrman |
| BERNSTEIN | Jeremy Bernstein |
| BETJEMAN | John Betjeman |
| B. BLIVEN | Bruce Bliven, Jr. |
| N. BLIVEN | Naomi Bliven |
| BOGAN | Louise Bogan |
| BRACKMAN | Jacob Brackman |
| BRENNAN | Maeve Brennan |
| COLES | Robert Coles |
| CONNOLLY | Cyril Connolly |
| FISHER | M. F. K. Fisher |
| FLAGLER | J. M. Flagler |
| FLANNER | Janet Flanner |
| FRASER | Kennedy Fraser |
| GALBRAITH | John Kenneth Galbraith |
| GAY | Peter Gay |
| GIBBS | Wolcott Gibbs |
| GILL | Brendan Gill |
| GILLIATT | Penelope Gilliatt |
| GOODWIN | Richard N. Goodwin |
| HAMBURGER | Philip Hamburger |
| HENTOFF | Nat Hentoff |
| HUBBELL | Albert Hubbell |
| HYMAN | Stanley Edgar Hyman |

165

| | |
|---|---|
| KAEL | Pauline Kael |
| KAHN | E. J. Kahn, Jr. |
| KAZIN | Alfred Kazin |
| J. LARDNER | John Lardner |
| S. LARDNER | Susan Lardner |
| LIEBLING | A. J. Liebling |
| McCARTEN | John McCarten |
| McCARTHY | Mary McCarthy |
| MacDONALD | Dwight Macdonald |
| McKELWAY | St. Clair McKelway |
| MALCOLM | Donald Malcolm |
| E. MAXWELL | Emily Maxwell |
| W. MAXWELL | William Maxwell |
| MEHTA | Ved Mehta |
| MILLER | Jonathan Miller |
| MOSS | Howard Moss |
| MUMFORD | Lewis Mumford |
| OLIVER | Edith Oliver |
| PANTER-DOWNES | Mollie Panter-Downes |
| PODHORETZ | Norman Podhoretz |
| PRITCHETT | V. S. Pritchett |
| RAND | Christopher Rand |
| ROSENBERG | Harold Rosenberg |
| ROSS | Lillian Ross |
| ROVERE | Richard H. Rovere |
| RYNNE | Xavier Rynne |
| SARGEANT | Winthrop Sargeant |
| SHEED | Wilfrid Sheed |
| SISSMAN | L. E. Sissman |
| STAFFORD | Jean Stafford |
| STEEGMULLER | Francis Steegmuller |
| STEINER | George Steiner |
| TRILLIN | Calvin Trillin |
| TYNAN | Kenneth Tynan |
| UPDIKE | John Updike |
| URQUHART | Brian Urquhart |

| | |
|---|---|
| WAIN | John Wain |
| WATT | Douglas Watt |
| WEST | Anthony West |
| WILSON | Edmund Wilson |
| WOODCOCK | George Woodcock |

## Symbols Used in Part 2

| | | |
|---|---|---|
| B | = | Book Review |
| CC | = | Current Cinema |
| T | = | Theatre |
| TV | = | Television |

A. E. Housman: a divided life.
by George L. Watson.
(Anon.) 34:67 D27'58.B 5580

A. E. Housman: selected prose.
by A. E. Housman, John
Carter, ed. (Anon.) 37:
242 N25'61. B          5581

A tout prendre. (Gill) 42:182
My7'66. CC             5582

Abandon ship! by Richard F.
Newcomb. (Anon.) 34:173
S20'58. B              5583

Abandoned. by A. L. Todd.
(Anon.) 37:131-2 Ap1'61.
B                      5584

The abdication of King Edward
VIII. by William Maxwell
Aitken Beaverbrook. (Anon.)
42:104 Ag6'66. B       5585

Abdication. by Brian Inglis.
(Anon.) 42:237 S24'66. B
                       5586

Abe Lincoln in Illinois. by
Robert E. Sherwood. (Oliver)
38:69-70 F2'63. T      5587

Abode of snow. by Kenneth
Mason. (Anon.) 31:151
*O29'55. B             5588

The abominable snowman. by
Ralph Izzard. (Anon.)
31:71-2*S3'55. B       5589

About the house. by W. H.
Auden. (Anon.) 41:108
S4'65. B               5590

Above ground. by Jack Ludwig.
(Anon.) 44:64 Jy6'68. B
                       5591

Absence of a cello. by Ira
Wallach. (McCarten) 40:96
O3'64. T               5592

The absent-minded professor.
(Oliver) 37:125 Ap1'61. CC
                       5593

Abundance for what? and other
essays. by David Riesman.

(N. Bliven) 40:202-205
S26'64. B              5594

The academic revolution.
by Christopher Jencks
and David Riesman. (Anon.)
44:96 Ag10'68. B       5595

The acceptance world. by
Anthony Powell. (Anon.)
32:167*Mr17'56. B      5596

Accident. by Elizabeth Janeway. (Anon.) 40:205
My16'64. B             5597

The accident. by Dexter
Masters. (Gill) 31:168
My14'55. B             5598

Accident. (Gill) 43:150-1
Ap22'67. CC            5599

The accidental century. by
Michael Harrington. (Anon.)
41:247 O30'65. B       5600

The achievement of William
Faulkner. by Michael
Millgate. (Anon.) 42:84
Jy30'66. B             5601

Acrobat admits. by Alfred
Grossman. (West) 35:162-
5 Ap4'59. B            5602

No entry                5603

Acropolis. by Stanislaw
Wyspianski. (Flanner)
44:152-3 O5'68 (Oliver)
45:164-5 N15'69. T     5604

Across a red world. by
Geoffrey Blainey. (Anon.)
44:238 N9'68. B        5605

Across Paris and other stories.
by Marcel Aymé. Norman
Denny, trans. (Anon.)
35:118-19 F28'59. B    5606

Across the bridge. (McCarten)
33:109-10 N9'57. CC    5607

Across the common. by
Elizabeth Berridge. (Anon.)
41:238 N27'65. B       5608

Across the river. (Gill)

41:122 My1'65. CC    5609
Act of God. by Margaret
  Kennedy. (Anon.) 31:131
  F19'55. B    5610
Act one. by Moss Hart.
  (Tynan) 35:229-36 N2'59. B
    5611
Ada. by Vladimir Nabokov.
  (Updike) 45:67-75 Ag2'69.
  B    5612
Ada Dallas. by Wirt Williams.
  (Anon.) 35:242-3 N7'59. B
    5613
Adalen 31. (Kael) 45:164-5
  N8'69. CC    5614
The Adams papers: Adams
  family correspondence.
  L. H. Butterfield, ed.
  (Anon.) 39:89-90 Ag10'63.
  B    5615
The adaptable man. by Janet
  Frame. (Anon.) 41:233
  O9'65. B    5616
Adaptation. by Elaine May.
  (Oliver) 45:90-2 F22'69. T
    5617
Addington. by Philip Zeigler.
  (Anon.) 42:190-1 Mr26'66.
  B    5618
Admiral Hornblower in the
  West Indies. by C. S.
  Forester. (Anon.) 34:176
  S27'58. B    5619
The Admiral Horthy memoirs.
  by Nicholas Horthy. (Anon.)
  33:146 Ap27'57. B    5620
Admirals in collision. by
  Richard Hough. (Anon.)
  35:237 D12'59. B    5621
Adult westerns. (J. Lardner)
  33:86-9 Ja18'58; 33:64-8
  Ja25'58. TV    5622
An adventure. by C. A. E.
  Moberly and E. F. Jourdain.
  Joan Evans, ed. (Anon.)
  31:161*S17'55. B    5623
Adventures in Caucasia. by
  Alexandre Dumas. Alma
  Elizabeth Murch, trans.
  (Anon.) 38:135 Ja26'63. B
    5624
Adventures in paradise.

(J. Lardner) 35:167-9
  O24'59. TV    5625
Adventures in Spain. by
  Alexandre Dumas. Alma
  Elizabeth Murch, trans.
  (Pritchett) 35:158-62 My2'59.
  B    5626
Adventures in the skin trade.
  by Dylan Thomas. (Anon.)
  31:138 Je11'55. B    5627
Adventures of a young man.
  (Oliver) 38:46 Ag11'62.
  CC    5628
The adventures of Sadie.
  (McCarten) 31:78 My28'55.
  CC    5629
Adventuring with Beebe.
  by William Beebe. (Anon.)
  31:163*S17'55. B    5630
Adventures with the missing
  link. by Raymond A. Dart
  and Dennis Craig. (Anon.)
  35:203-204 O31'59. B    5631
Adventurous alliance. by
  Louise Hall Tharp. (Anon.)
  35:103-104 Ja9'60. B    5632
Advertisements of myself. by
  Norman Mailer. (Anon.)
  35:245-6 N14'59. B    5633
Advice to a young critic and
  other letters. by George
  Bernard Shaw. E. J. West,
  ed. (Anon.) 31:108*Ja21'56.
  B    5634
Advise and consent. by Loring
  Mandel. (McCarten) 36:104-
  106 N26'60. T    5635
Advise and consent. (Gill)
  38:116-17 Je9'62. CC    5636
The advocate. by Robert
  Noah. (McCarten) 39:113
  O26'63. T    5637
Advocate of the isle. by
  Loys Mason. Antonia White,
  trans. (Anon.) 39:158-9
  S7'63. B    5638
Affable savages. by Francis
  Huxley. (Anon.) 32:143
  F16'57. B    5639
The affair. by C. P. Snow.
  (Anon.) 36:141-2 My28'60. B
    5640

The affair. by Ronald Millar.
(McCarten) 38:98 S29'62.
T                                    5641
Affair at Quala. by Thomas
Helmore. (Anon.) 40:218-
20 Ap18'64. B            5642
An affair in Arcady. by James
Wellard. (Anon.) 35:167-8
O3'59. B                 5643
Affair of honor. by Bill
Hoffman. (Gibbs) 32:72
Ap14'56. T               5644
The affair of the poisons.
by Frances Massiker. (Anon.)
45:92 Ja24'70. B         5645
An affair of the skin. (Gill)
39:236 N23'63. CC        5646
An affair to remember. (Mc-
Carten) 33:48 Ag3'57. CC
                         5647
Affinities. by Vernon Watkins.
(Bogan) 40:180-1 Ap11'64.
B̂                        5648
The affluent society. by John
Kenneth Galbraith. (Anon.)
34:93-4 Je28'58. B       5649
Africa and Africans. by Paul
Bohannan. (Anon.) 40:223-4
Ap18'64. B               5650
The African giant. by Stuart
Cloete. (Anon.) 31:161-2
*S24'55. B               5651
The African lion.
(Hamburger) 31:104*S24'55.
CC                       5652
An African treasury. Langston
Hughes, ed. (Anon.) 36:227-8
N5'60. B                 5653
After experience. by W.D.
Snodgrass. (Bogan) 44:62-3
D28'68. B                5654
After Julius. by Elizabeth
Jane Howard. (Anon.)
42:199 Ap16'66. B        5655
After the assassination: a
positive appraisal of the War-
ren report. by John Sparrow.
(Anon.) 44:186-7 My4'68. B
                         5656
After the banquet. by Yukio
Mishima. (West) 38:153-4
F16'63. B                5657

After the fall. by Arthur
Miller. (McCarten) 39:59
F1'64. T                 5658
After the festival. by March
Cost. (Anon.) 42:122
Ja14'67. B               5659
After the fine weather. by
Michael Gilbert. (Anon.)
39:123-4 Je22'63. B      5660
After the fox. (Gill) 42:89-
90 Ja7'67. CC            5661
After the rain. by John
Bowen. (McCarten) 43:81
O21'67. T                5662
Against all reason. by
Geoffrey Moorhouse.
(Anon.) 45:76 Jy5'69. B
                         5663
Against the wind. by
Geoffrey Household. (Anon.)
34:139 F14'59. B         5664
Agatha Sue, I love you. by
Abe Einhorn. (McCarten)
42:45 D24'66. T          5665
The age of Churchill: heritage
and adventure, 1874-1911.
by Peter de Mendelssohn.
(Anon.) 37:206 D16'61. B
                         5666
An age of enormity: life and
writing in the forties and
fifties. Theodore Solotaroff,
ed. (Anon.) 38:100 Ag18'62.
B                        5667
The age of fighting sail.
by C.S. Forester. (Anon.)
32:71*Ag4'56. B          5668
Age of illusions. (Gill)
43:145 Ap8'67. CC        5669
Age of infidelity. (McCarten)
34:67-8 Ag30'58. CC      5670
The age of Louis XIV: 1618-
1715. by Will Durant and
Ariel Durant. (Anon.) 39:
190-1 S21'63. B          5671
The age of malaise. by Dacia
Maraini. Francis Frenaye,
trans. (Anon.) 39:119-20
Je1'63. B                5672
The age of Napoleon. by J.
Christopher Herold. (Anon.)
39:244 D7'63. B          5673

The Age of reason begins. by
Will Durant and Ariel Durant.
(Anon.) 37:178-9 S16'61.
B                            5674
The age of reconnaissance.
by J.H. Parry. (Anon.)
39:95 Ag17'63. B        5675
The age of Roosevelt: the crisis
of the old order, 1919-1933.
by Arthur M. Schlesinger,
Jr. (Anon.) 33:149 Mr16'57.
B                            5676
The age of the democratic
revolution. by R.R. Palmer.
(Anon.) 35:195-6 S26'59. B
                             5677
The age of the grand tour.
Anon. (Anon.) 43:246-8
D9'67. B                    5678
Agee on film. by James Agee.
(Anon.) 34:215-16 D13'58. B
                             5679
Ages of man. by George
Ryland. (Tynan) 34:68-70
Ja10'59. T                  5680
The aging boy. by Julian
Claman. (Anon.) 39:212-13
O12'63. B                   5681
The agony and the ecstasy.
(Gill) 41:228-9 O16'65. CC
                             5682
Airlift: Vietnam. (Arlen)
43:60-1 D30'67. TV       5683
The airtight cage. by Joseph P.
Lyford. (Hentoff) 42:237-46
N19'66. B                   5684
Aissa saved. by Joyce Cary.
(Anon.) 38:141-2 F9'63. B
                             5685
Akenfield: portrait of an
English village. by Ronald
Blythe. (Anon.) 45:159 O4'69.
B                            5686
Al Capone. (McCarten) 35:97
Ap18'59. CC                 5687
Al Smith and his America.
by Oscar Handlin. (Anon.)
34:152*Ap26'58. B        5688
Al Smith: hero of the cities--
a political portrait drawing on
the papers of Frances
Perkins. by Matthew

Josephson and Hannah
Josephson. (Anon.) 45:209-
10 N8'69. B                 5689
The Alamo. (Gill) 36:187-8
N5'60. CC                   5690
Alas, Babylon. by Pat Frank.
(Anon.) 35:166-7 Ap4'59.
B                            5691
Alban Berg: the man and his
music. by H.F. Redlich.
(Anon.) 33:203-204 O5'57.
B                            5692
Albert Schweitzer. (McCarten)
32:99-100 F2'57. CC        5693
The alchemist. by Ben
Jonson. (Oliver) 40:160-3
S26'64 (McCarten) 42:83
O22'66. T                   5694
The alchemist's voyage. by
Calvin Kentfield. (West)
31:210*D3'55. B            5695
Alcools: poems 1898-1913.
by Guillaume Apollinaire.
William Meredith, trans.
(Anon.) 40:224 Ap18'64. B
                             5696
Aldous Huxley: 1894-1963.
Julian Huxley, ed. (Anon.)
42:211 Mr19'66. B        5697
Alexander Hamilton and the
founding of a nation. by
Alexander Hamilton. Richard
B. Morris, ed. (Anon.)
33:137 Mr9'57. B         5698
Alexander Hamilton: portrait
in paradox. by John C.
Miller. (Anon.) 35:170
O3'59. B                    5699
Alexander Hamilton: youth to
maturity. by Broadus
Mitchell. (Anon.) 33:144-5
Ap27'57. B                  5700
The Alexander memoirs: 1940-
1945. by Harold R.L. Alex-
ander. (Anon.) 39:115 Je22'63.
B                            5701
Alexander Pope: the education
of genius 1688-1728. by
Peter Quennell. (Auden)
45:128-40 F22'69. B  5702
Alexander the great. (McCarten)
32:104*Ap7'56. CC        5703

Alexander the great: power as destiny. by Peter Bamm. J. Maxwell Brownjohn, trans. (Anon.) 44:106 D21'68. B            5704

Alexander Woollcott: the man who came to dinner. by Edwin P. Hoyt. (Anon.) 44:252 N23'68. B       5705

Alexandre Dumas. by André Maurois. (Anon.) 31:133-4 Ap9'55. B            5706

Alexandre Dumas' dictionary of cuisine. by Alexandre Dumas. Louis Colman, trans. (Anon.) 34:179-80 S27'58. B            5707

Alexandria: a history and a guide. by E. M. Forster. (W. Maxwell) 37:129-36 F18'61. B            5708

The Alexandria quartet. by Lawrence Durrell. (N. Bliven) 36:97-103 Ag13'60. B            5709

Alfie! by Bill Naughton. (McCarten) 40:58 Ja2'65. T            5710

Alfie. (Adler) 42:90 Ag27'66. CC            5711

Alfred the great. (Kael) 45:175 D13'69 CC       5712

Alice in wonderland. (Panter-Downes) 42:103-104 Ja14'67. CC            5713

Alice's restaurant. (Gilliatt) 45:96 S6'69. CC       5714

All about ants. by Peggy Pickering Larson and Mervin W. Larson. (Anon.) 41:160 F19'66. B            5715

All American. by Mel Brooks and Charles Strouse and Lee Adams. (Oliver) 38:104-106 Mr31'62. T       5716

All fall down. (Gill) 38:170-1 Ap21'62. CC       5717

All honorable men. by Walter Goodman. (Anon.) 39:111 Ja25'64. B            5718

All honorable men. by David Karp. (Anon.) 31:130-1 *F18'56. B            5719

All in a night's work. (Oliver) 37:138 Mr25'61. CC       5720

All in good time. by Bill Naughton. (McCarten) 41:96 F27'65. T       5721

All in love. by Richard Brinsley Sheridan, Bruce Geller, and Jacques Urbont. (Oliver) 37:96-8 N18'61. T            5722

All in the family. by Edwin O'Connor. (Oliver) 42:241-2 O15'66. B            5723

All kinds of giants. by Tom Whedon and Sam Pottle. (Oliver) 37:58-9 Ja6'62. T            5724

All my pretty ones. by Anne Sexton. (Bogan) 39:175 Ap27'63. B            5725

All the best years. by Desmond Young. (Anon.) 37:66-7 D30'61. B       5726

All the day long. by Howard Spring. (Anon.) 36:196 Mr12'60. B       5727

All the happy endings. by Helen Waite Papashvily. (Anon.) 32:200 O20'56. B       5728

All the loving couples. (Kael) 45:162-3 N29'69. CC       5729

All the Summer days. by Ned Calmer. (Anon.) 37:74-7 Jy15'61. B       5730

All the way home. by Tad Mosel. (McCarten) 36:97-8 D10'60. T       5731

All the way home. (Gill) 39:210 N9'63. CC       5732

All the young men. (Balliett) 36:78-80 S10'60. CC       5733

All these women. (Gill) 40:187 O17'64. CC       5734

All told. by Frédéric O'Brady. (Anon.) 40:190 Mr14'64. B            5735

Allenby of Arabia, Lawrence's general. by Brian Gardner. (Anon.) 41:159 F19'66. B            5736

The alliance of necessity. by Lionel Gelber. (Anon.) 42:167-8 F18'67. B            5737

The alligators. by Molly
Kazan. (Balliett) 36:108
N26'60. T                     5738
Almost paradise. by Luis
Spota. Ray Morrison, trans.
and Renate Morrison, trans.
(Anon.) 39:70-1 Jy6'63. B
                              5939
Along came a spider. by Joe
Sauter. (Oliver) 39:128
Je8'63. T                     5740
Along the clipper way. by
Francis Chichester. (Anon.)
43:103-104 Ag12'67. B
                              5741
Alphabets and birthdays. by
Gertrude Stein. (Anon.)
33:242-3*N30'57. B            5742
Alphaville. (Flanner) 41:116-18
Je12'65 (Gill) 41:203-204
O30'65. CC                    5743
The alternate case. by Joseph
F. Dinneen. (Anon.) 35:169
O3'59. B                      5744
Altgeld's America. by Ray
Ginger. (Anon.) 34:72-4
Ja3'59. B                     5745
The Amazon. by Robin
Furneaux. (Anon.) 45:82
Ja17'70. B                    5746
The ambassador's daughter.
(McCarten) 32:64*S8'56.
CC                            5747
Ambassador's journal. by John
Kenneth Galbraith. (Rovere)
45:185-9 O25'69. B            5748
Ambrosia and small beer: the
record of a correspondence
between Edward Marsh and
Christopher Hassall. by
Christopher Hassall and
Edward Marsh. Christopher
Hassall, ed. (Anon.) 41:183-4
My8'65. B                     5749
Amelie in love. by Henri
Troyat. (Anon.) 32:199
O13'56. B                     5750
The amen corner. by James
Baldwin. (McCarten) 41:85
Ap24'65. T                    5751
America, America. (Gill)
39:74 Ja4'64. CC              5752

America as a civilization. by
Max Lerner. (Sargeant)
34:152-4 Mr22'58. B           5753
America at last: the American
journal of T.H. White. by
Terence Hanbury White.
(Anon.) 41:80 Jy31'65. B
                              5754
America hurrah. by Jean-
Claude van Itallie. (Oliver)
42:69-70 Ja21'67. T           5755
America, I like you. by
P.G. Wodehouse. (Anon.)
32:130*My26'56. B             5756
America in the market place.
by Paul H. Douglas. (Anon.)
42:224 O1'66. B               5757
America pauses for the merry
month of May. (J. Lardner)
35:101-102 My30'59. TV
                              5758
America the raped. by Gene
Marine. (Anon.) 45:166-7
My10'69. B                    5759
American album. American
Heritage, eds. (Anon.)
44:248 N30'68. B              5760
American ambassador: Joseph
C. Grew and the develop-
ment of the United States
diplomatic tradition. by
Waldo H. Heinrichs, Jr.
(Anon.) 43:160 F25'67. B
                              5761
An American architecture. by
Frank Lloyd Wright. Edgar
Kaufmann, ed. (Mumford)
31:80*F4'56. B                5762
The American challenge. by
Jean-Jacques Servan-
Schreiber. Ronald Steel,
trans. (N. Bliven) 44:240-8
N23'68. B                     5763
American commissar. by
Sandor Voros. (Anon.) 37:
96 Je24'61. B                 5764
An American dilemma: the
Negro problem and modern
democracy. by Gunnar
Myrdal and Richard Sterner
and Arnold M. Rose. (N.
Bliven) 40:195-210 Ap18'64.
B                             5765

The American dream. by
Edward Albee. (Balliett)
36:62-6 F4'61. T          5766

An American dream. (Gill)
42:103-104 S10'66. CC     5767

The American earthquake. by
Edmund Wilson. (Anon.)
34:62-3 Jy5'58. B         5768

American education: a national
failure. by H.G. Rickover.
(Anon.) 39:245 N16'63. B
                          5769

American English. by Albert
H. Marckwardt. (Macdonald)
34:153-4 My17'58. B       5770

An American epic, vol. I: the
relief of Belgium and
northern France, 1914-1930.
by Herbert Hoover. (Anon.)
35:71 Ja2'60. B           5771

American foreign policy: three
essays. by Henry A.
Kissinger. (Anon.) 45:92
Jy12'69. B                5772

The American health scandal.
by Roul Tunley. (Anon.)
42:134-5 F26'66. B        5773

The American Henry James.
by Quentin Anderson. (Anon.)
33:168 Ap6'57. B          5774

American in Italy. by Herbert
Kubly. (Anon.) 31:152 Mr19'55.
B                         5775

American in Russia. by Harrison
E. Salisbury. (Anon.)
31:132 F19'55. B          5776

The American journalism of
Marx and Engels. Henry
M. Christman, ed. (Anon.)
42:246-7 N26'66. B        5777

The American jury. by Harry
Kalven, Jr., Hans Zeisel,
and Thomas Callahan and
Philip Ennis. (Anon.) 42:
245 O8'66. B              5778

American painting: from the
Armory Show to the
Depression. by Milton W.
Brown. (Anon.) 31:208
*D10'55. B                5779

American poetry. by Gay
Wilson Allen, W.B. Rideout,

and J.K. Robinson. (Bogan)
42:221-3 O1'66. B         5780

The American Revolution. by
George Otto Trevelyan.
Richard B. Morris, ed.
(Anon.) 40:112 Je27'64.
B                         5781

American skyline. by
Christopher Tunnard and
Henry Hope Reed. (Mumford)
32:108-12*Mr3'56. B       5782

The American treasury.
Clifton Fadiman, ed.
(Anon.) 31:154*D17'55.
B                         5783

An American visitor. by
Joyce Cary. (West) 37:202-
203 O7'61. B              5784

The American way of death.
by Jessica Mitford.
(Anon.) 39:159 S7'63. B
                          5785

The American writer and the
great depression. Harvey
Swados, ed. (Anon.) 42:
128 Ag27'66. B            5786

The Americanization of Emily.
(Gill) 40:203 N7'64. CC
                          5787

Americans by choice. by
Angelo M. Pellegrini. (Anon.)
32:155*Ap14'56. B         5788

Americans on Everest. by
James Ramsey Ullman.
(Anon.) 40:78-9 Ag1'64
B                         5789

America's new policy makers. by
Donald W. Cox. (Anon.)
40:143 Je13'64. B         5790

America's next twenty years.
by Peter F. Drucker.
(Anon.) 33:166 Ap6'57. B
                          5791

America's stake in Asia. by
Drew Middleton. (Anon.)
44:193 Ap20'68. B         5792

Amerigo and the New World.
by Germán Arciniegas.
(Anon.) 31:144*S10'55. B
                          5793

The amorous adventures of
Moll Flanders. (Gill) 41:68-
71 My29'65. CC            5794

The amorous flea. by Bruce
Montgomery and Jerry
Devine. (Oliver) 40:108-109
F29'64. T                       5795
The anarchy of love. by
Colin Spencer. (Anon.)
43:189 O7'67. B              5796
Anastasia. (McCarten) 32:65
*D22'56. CC                   5797
The anathemata. by David
Jones. (Anon.) 39:95-6
Ag17'63. B                     5798
Anatomy of a marriage.
(Gill) 40:200-202 N7'64. CC
                                5799
Anatomy of a moral: the political
essays of Milovan Djilas.
by Milovan Djilas. Abraham
Rothberg, ed. (Anon.) 35:
67-8 Ag1'59. B               5800
Anatomy of a murder.
(McCarten) 35:55-6 Jy11'59.
CC                              5801
Anatomy of Britain. by
Anthony Sampson. (Liebling)
39:169-77 My11'63. B      5802
The anatomy of courage.
by Charles McMoran Wilson
Moran. (Anon.) 43:179 My
20'67. B                       5803
Anatomy of Europe. by Anthony
Sampson. (Anon.) 45:140
Mr22'69. B                    5804
An ancient enemy. by Pierre
Moinot. Francis Price,
trans. (Anon.) 41:222-3
S25'65. B                      5805
The ancient Greeks. by M.I.
Finley. (Anon.) 39:74-6
Jy6'63. B                      5806
And not to yield: an auto-
biography. by Ella Winter.
(Anon.) 39:243 N16'63. B
                                5807
... And suddenly it's murder!
(Gill) 39:108 F8'64. CC
                                5808
And the bridge is love. by
Alma Mahler Werfel and E.B.
Ashton. (Anon.) 34:130
S6'58. B                       5809
And the wind blows. by Edgard
da Rocha Miranda. (Malcolm)
35:95 My9'59. T             5810

And things that go bump in the
night. by Terrence
McNally. (McCarten) 41:
120-2 My1'65. T            5811
And Tyler too: a biography
of John and Julia Gardiner
Tyler. by Robert Seager, II.
(Anon.) 39:118-19 Ja18'64.
B                               5812
The Andersonville trial. by
Saul Levitt. (Tynan)
35:69-73 Ja9'60. T         5813
Andorra. by Max Frisch.
George Tavori, adapt.
(McCarten) 38:114 F16'63. T
                                5814
Andrei Rublev. (Flanner)
45:179-81 D13'69. CC    5815
Andrew Johnson: president on
trial. by Milton Lomask.
(Anon.) 36:118-19 Ja14'61.
B                               5816
Androcles and the lion. by
George Bernard Shaw. (Oliver)
37:119-20 D2'61. T         5817
Andromaque. by Jean Baptiste
Racine. (Oliver) 40:112-
14 Mr14'64. T               5818
Aneurin Bevan: a biography. by
Michael Foot. (Anon.)
39:214-15 O12'63. B       5819
Angel. by Elizabeth Taylor.
(Balliett) 33:193-4 O5'57.
B                               5820
Angell, Pearl and little God.
by Winston Graham. (Anon.)
45:91-2 Ja24'70. B         5821
Angels falling. by Janice
Elliott. (Anon.) 45:242-4
D6'69. B                       5822
Angels in the snow. by Derek
Lambert. (Anon.) 45:117-
18  Mr1'69. B               5823
Angels of Anadarko. by
Samuel Birnkrant. (Oliver)
38:88 O20'62. T             5824
Anglo-Saxon attitudes. by Angus
Wilson. (Gill) 32:176-8
O6'56. B                       5825
The angry silence. (Angell)
36:51 D24'60. CC           5826
Animals of East Africa. by
C.A. Spinage. (Anon.) 39:
123-4 Je1'63. B             5827

Ankles aweigh. by Guy
Bolton and Eddie Davis.
(Gibbs) 31:71-2 Ap30'55. T
5828
Anna Lucasta. (McCarten)
34:111-12 Ja24'59. CC  5829
Anne Frank: a portrait in
courage. by Ernst
Schnabel.  Richard Winston,
trans. and Clara Winston,
trans. (Anon.) 34:202-203
O11'58. B               5830
Anne of the thousand days.
(Kael) 45:77-8 Ja24'70.
CC                      5831
Anno domini. by George
Steiner. (West) 40:120-2
Ja30'65. B              5832
The annotated Mother Goose.
William S. Baring-
Gould and Ceil Baring-
Gould, eds. (Anon.)
38:99-100 Ja5'63. B     5833
Another country. by James
Baldwin. (Balliett) 38:69-70
Ag4'62. B               5834
Another evening with Harry
Stoones. by Jeff Harris.
(Oliver) 37:132 N4'61. T
5835
Another sky. (Gill) 36:188
N5'60. CC               5536
Another time, another place.
(McCarten) 34:141-2 My10'58.
CC                      5837
Anselm: fides quarens intellectum.
by Karl Barth. Ian W.
Robertson, trans. (Updike)
39:203-10 O12'63. B     5538
An answer from limbo. by
Brian Moore. (Anon.)
38:215 O27'62. B        5839
Antarctic crossing. (McCarten)
35:86 My23'59. CC       5840
Antarctica. by Emil
Schulthess. (Anon.)
36:88 Ja7'61. B         5841
The ante-room. by Lovat
Dickson. (Anon.) 36:205-206
S10'60. B               5842
The anthill: the human
condition in Communist
China. by Suzanne Labin.

Edward Fitzgerald, trans.
(Anon.) 37:127 Mr4'61. B
5843
Anthology of Chinese literature
from early times to the
fourteenth century.
Cyril Birch and Donald
Keene, eds. (Anon.)
41:144 F12'66. B        5844
Anthology of Japanese
literature. Donald Keene,
ed. (Anon.) 31:148
*O29'55. B              5845
An anthology of Scandinavian
literature. Hallberg
Hallmundsson, ed. (Anon.)
42:168 Ap30'66. B       5846
Antigone. by Jean Anouilh.
(Malcolm) 35:96-101
S26'59. T               5847
Antigone. by Jean Cocteau.
(Oliver) 38:77 Ja12'63.
T                       5848
Antigone. by The Living Theatre.
(Oliver) 44:161 O19'68.
T                       5849
Anti-intellectualism in American
life. by Richard Hofstadter.
(Malcolm) 39:102-10 Ja25'64.
B                       5850
Anti mémoires. by André
Malraux. (Flanner) 43:188-
94 N11'67. B            5851
Anti-slavery: the crusade for
freedom in America. by Dwight
Lowell Dumond. (Anon.)
37:211 O21'61. B        5852
Antiworlds. by Andrei
Voznesensky. Patricia
Blake and Max Hayward, eds.
(Anon.) 42:240 S24'66. B
5853
Antonello da Messina. by
Stefano Bottari. Gustina
Scaglia, trans. (Anon.)
33:148 Ap27'57. B       5854
Any God will do. by Richard
Condon. (Brennan) 42:126-
30 F4'67. B             5855
Any number can win. (Gill)
39:146-8 O19'63. CC     5856
Any Wednesday. by Muriel
Resnik. (McCarten) 40:106
F29'64. T               5857

Any Wednesday. (Gill) 42:
164 O22'66. CC          5858

Anya. by George Abbott, Guy
Bolton, Robert Wright and
George Forrest. (McCarten)
41:142-4 D11'65. T      5959

Anybody's Spring. by A. A.
Murray. (Anon.) 36:138-9
Je18'60. B              5860

Anyone can whistle, by Arthur
Laurents and Stephen
Sondheim. (McCarten) 40:95
Ap11'64. T              5861

Anything goes. by P. G. Wodehouse, Guy Bolton, Howard
Lindsay, Russel Crouse, and
Cole Porter. (Oliver)
38:92-3 My26'62. T      5862

Anything goes. (McCarten)
32:92*Mr31'56. CC       5863

Anzio. by Wynford Vaughan-
Thomas. (Anon.) 37:179-80
S16'61. B               5864

The apartment. (McCarten)
36:71 Je25'60. CC       5865

The ape woman. (Gill) 40:
194-5 S26'64. CC        5866

Apes, angels, and Victorians.
by William Irvine. (West)
31:137-44 Ap23'55. B
                        5867

Apocalypsis cum figuris.
by Jerzy Grotowski, et al.
(Oliver). 45:85-6 N29'69.
T                       5868

Apollinaire. by Margaret
Davies. (Anon.) 41:184
Mr27'65. B              5869

Apollinaire: poet among the
painters. by Francis
Steegmuller. (Anon.) 41:107
Ja22'66. B              5870

Apollo's Summer look. by Kathleen Conlon. (Anon.) 44:103-
104 Ja25'69. B          5871

The appaloosa. (Gill) 42:111
S17'66. CC              5872

The apparition theatre of
Prague. Anon. (McCarten)
42:155 D3'66. T         5873

Appeasement: a study in decline.
by A. L. Rowse. (Anon.) 37:
117 Ja20'62. B          5874

The appeasers. by Martin
Gilbert and Richard Gott.
(Anon.) 39:246 N9'63. B
                        5875

Appendix A. by Hayden
Carruth. (Balliett)
39:75-6 Ja4'64. B       5876

The apple. by Jack Gelber.
(Oliver) 37:97-8 D16'61.
T                       5877

The apple cart. by George
Bernard Shaw.
(Gibbs) 32:117-18 O27'56.
T                       5878

The apple tree. by Mark
Twain, Frank R. Stockton,
Jules Feiffer, Jerry Bock
and Sheldon Harnick.
(McCarten) 42:95 O29'66.
T                       5879

The April fools. (Gilliatt)
45:83 Je14'69. CC       5880

Arabesque. (Gill) 42:120
My14'66. CC             5881

Arabia felix: the Danish expe-
dition of 1761-67. by
Thorkild Hansen. James
McFarlane and Kathleen
McFarlane, trans. (Anon.)
40:246 N21'64. B        5882

Arabian sands. by Wilfred
Thesiger. (Anon.) 35:236-7
D12'59. B               5883

The Archie Moore story.
by Archie Moore and Bob
Condon. (Anon.) 36:207
S10'60. B               5884

Architecture, an introduction
to the history and theory of the
art of building. by W. R.
Lethaby. (Mumford) 31:78-9
*F4'56. B               5885

The arctic year. by Peter
Freuchen and Finn Salomon-
sen. (Anon.) 34:126-7
Mr29'58. B              5886

Aren't we wonderful? (Mc-
Carten) 35:186 O24'59. CC
                        5887

Arf. by Dan Greenburg.
(Oliver) 45:112 Je7'69. T
                        5888

The aristocrats. by Michel de Saint Pierre. (Gill) 32:233 N17'56. B 5889

Arms and influence. by Thomas C. Schelling. (Goodwin) 43:127-34 F17'68. B 5890

Arms and the man. by George Bernard Shaw. (Oliver) 40:143-4 My9'64. T 5891

Arms and the woman. by Boris Uxkull. Detlev von Uexküll, ed. Joel Carmichael, trans. (Anon.) 42:244-5 O15'66. B 5892

Arms control, disarmament, and national security. by Donald G. Brennan. (Anon.) 37:82-3 S2'61. B 5893

The arms debate. by Robert A. Levine. (Anon.) 39:190-1 O5'63. B 5894

The arms of Krupp, 1587-1968. by William Manchester. (Anon.) 44:244 N30'68. B 5895

Armstrong's last goodnight. by John Arden. (Panter-Downes.) 41:102-103 Ag14'65. T 5896

The army game. (Gill) 39: 167 Ap27'63. CC 5897

Arnold Bennett and H. G. Wells. by Arnold Bennett and H. G. Wells. Harris Wilson, ed. (Anon.) 36:62-4 D24'60. B 5898

Around the world in 80 days. (McCarten) 32:158-9 O27'56. CC 5899

The arrangement. (Kael) 45:211-17 N22'69. CC 5900

The arrogance of power. by J. William Fulbright. (Anon.) 43:192-3 Mr11'67. B 5901

Arshile Gorky: the man, the time, the idea. by Harold Rosenberg. (Anon.) 38:179 My12'62. B 5902

Art and argyrol. by William Shack. (Anon.) 36:139 Je18'60. B 5903

Art and illusion: a study in the psychology of pictorial representation. by E. H. Gombrich. (Anon.) 36: 183-4 O1'60. B 5904

Art and reality: ways of the creative process. by Joyce Cary. (Anon.) 34:95 Ag16'58. B 5905

The art of Egypt. by Irmgard Woldering. Ann E. Keep, trans. (Anon.) 40:128 F22'64. B 5906

The art of fiction. by W. Somerset Maugham. (Anon.) 31:142-3 My21'55. B 5907

The art of French fiction. by Martin Turnell. (Anon.) 35:201 S12'59. B 5908

The art of India. by Stella Kramrisch. (Anon.) 31: 139-40 Mr12'55. B 5909

The art of Indian Asia. by Heinrich Zimmer. Joseph Campbell, ed. (Anon.) 31:147-8*S10'55. B 5910

The art of jazz: essays on the nature and development of jazz. Martin Williams, ed. (Anon.) 35:122 Ja16'60. B 5911

The art of Llewellyn Jones. by Paul Hyde Bonner. (Anon.) 35:95 Ag8'59. B 5912

The art of poetry. by Paul Valéry. (Anon.) 34:214-15 N8'58. B 5913

The art of politics as practiced by three great Americans. by Rexford Guy Tugwell. (Anon.) 34:66 D27'58. B 5914

The art of seduction. by John Barton. (Panter-Downes) 38:132 Ap7'62. T 5915

The art of the essay. Leslie A. Fiedler, ed. (Anon.) 34:139-40 F14'59. B 5916

The art of victory: the life and achievements of Generalissimo Suvorov, 1729-1800. by Philip Longworth. (Anon.) 42:144 My28'66. B 5917

The artist as critic. by
Oscar Wilde. Richard
Ellmann, ed. (Auden) 45:
205-10 N29'69. B        5918
The artist in his studio. by
Alexander Liberman. (Sargeant)
36:177-83 O29'60. B.     5919
The artists' & writers' cook-
book. Beryl Barr and
Barbara Turner Sachs, eds.
(Malcolm) 38:134-40 Mr31'62.
B                        5920
The arts and civilization of
Angkor. by Bernard-Philippe
Groslier. (Anon.) 33:199
N2'57. B                 5921
Arts and ideas. by William
Fleming. (Anon.) 31:133-4
*O1'55. B                5922
The arts in America: the
colonial period. by Louis B.
Wright, George B. Tatum,
John W. McCoubrey and Robert
C. Smith. (Anon.) 42:247-8
N26'66. B                5923
The arts of the beautiful. by
Étienne Gilson. (Anon.)
41:135-6 F5'66. B        5924
Artur Schnabel. by César
Saerchinger. (Anon.) 34:
147-8 Mr8'58. B          5925
Arturo Ui. by Bertolt Brecht.
(McCarten) 39:143 N23'63.
T                        5926
Arturo's island. (Gill) 38:68
Ja5'63. CC               5927
As France goes. by David
Schoenbrun. (Hubbell) 33:
133-6 My25'57. B         5928
As I remember it: some
epilogues in recollection. by
James Branch Cabell. (Wilson)
32:129-56*Ap21'56. B    5929
As music and splendour. by
Kate O'Brien. (Anon.) 34:73-4
Jy26'58. B               5930
As you like it. by William
Shakespeare. (Tynan) 44:154-9
N9'68. T                 5931
Ashes and diamonds. (Gilliatt)
44:66-8 Ag10'68. CC     5932
Asian drama: an inquiry into
the poverty of nations.

by Gunnar Myrdal. (N.
Bliven) 44:116-22 F15'69.
B                        5933
Asian psychology. Gardner
Murphy and Lois B.
Murphy, eds. (Anon.) 44:99
Ja18'69. B               5934
Ask any girl. (McCarten) 35:
90-1 My30'59. CC         5935
Ask me no more. by Pamela
Frankau. (Anon.) 34:234-6
N29'58. B                5936
Aspects of E. M. Forster. Oliver
Stallybrass, ed. (Anon.)
44:123-4 F15'69. B       5937
Aspects of love. by David
Garnett. (West) 31:88
*F4'56. B                5938
Aspects of modern art. Georges
Bernier and Rosamond
Bernier, eds. (Anon.) 33:
100 D21'57. B            5939
Aspects of revolt. by Max
Nomad. (Wilson) 36:192-204
O15'60. B                5940
The Aspern papers. by Michael
Redgrave. (Panter-Downes)
35:163-4 S12'59 (McCarten)
37:92-4 F17'62. T        5941
The asphalt campus. by
Geoffrey Wagner. (Anon.)
39:204-205 Mr16'63. B   5942
Assassination of Kennedy.
(Miller) 39:63-4 D28'63.
TV                       5943
The assassins: a radical sect
in Islam. by Bernard Lewis.
(Anon.) 44:158-60 Mr23'68.
B                        5944
Assault on a queen. by Jack
Finney. (Anon.) 35:192-3
S26'59. B                5945
Assault on a queen. (S.
Lardner) 42:66 Jy30'66. CC
                         5946
Assault on Olumpus: the rise
of the House of Gramont.
By W. H. Lewis. (Anon.)
34:94-5 Je28'58. B       5947
The assistant. by Bernard
Malamud. (Anon.) 33:94-5
Jy13'57. B               5948

The associate professor. by
Robert Pease. (Anon.)
43:148-9 Je10'67. B      5949

The Astors: a family chronicle
of pomp and power. by
Lucy Kavaler. (Anon.) 42:
207 My21'66. B      5950

Astragal. by Albertine
Sarrazin. (Updike) 45:178-
80 Mr15'69. B      5951

The astrakhan coat. by Pauline
Macaulay. (McCarten) 42:69
Ja21'67. T      5952

At home. by William Plomer.
(Anon.) 34:234 N22'58. B
5953

At Lady Molly's. by Anthony
Powell. (Anon.) 34:176 S27
'58. B      5954

At the court of Versailles:
eyewitness reports from the
reign of Louis XIV. Gilette
Ziegler, ed. Simon Watson
Taylor, trans. (Anon.) 42:
104 Jy16'66. B      5955

At the drop of a hat. by
Donald Swann and Michael
Flanders. (Tynan) 35:133-4
O17'59. T      5956

At the drop of another hat.
by Michael Flanders and
Donald Swann. (McCarten) 42:
78 Ja7'67. T      5957

At the Hemingways. by
Marcelline Hemingway Sanford.
(Anon.) 38:98 Ag18'62. B
5958

At twelve Mr. Byng was shot.
by Dudley Pope. (Anon.)
38:139-40 Je9'62. B      5959

At war as children. by Kit
Reed. (Anon.) 40:126-7
F22'64. B      5960

At whatever cost: the story of
the Dieppe raid. by R.W.
Thompson. (Anon.) 33:166-7
My4'57. B      5961

Athalie. by Jean Baptiste
Racine. (Flanner) 31:122-3 My
21'55. T      5962

The Atlantic book of British
and American poetry. Edith
Sitwell, ed. (Anon.) 35:179
Mr21'59. B      5963

The Atlantic community: a study
in unity and disunity. by
Drew Middleton. (Anon.) 41:
203 D18'65. B      5964

The Atlantic salmon: a vanishing species? by Anthony
Netboy. (Anon.) 44:214 O12
'68. B      5965

Atlas of the Bible. by L.H.
Grollenberg. Joyce M.H.
Reid, trans. & ed. and
H.H. Rowley, trans. & ed.
(Anon.) 33:139 Mr9'57. B
5966

Atlas shrugged. by Ayn Rand.
(Malcolm) 33:194-8 O26'57.
B      5967

The atomic age. Morton Grodzins and Eugene Rabino-
witch, eds. (Bernstein) 40:
136-41 Je13'64. B      5968

Atomic weapons and East-West
relations. by P.M.S.
Blackett. (Anon.) 32:73-4
Ja5'57. B      5969

Atoms for the world. by Laura
Fermi. (Anon.) 33:168 My18
'57. B      5970

Atoms in the family. by Laura
Fermi. (Bernstein) 45:141
My10'69. B      5971

Attack! (McCarten) 32:88 S29
'56. CC      5972

Attorney for the damned.
Arthur Weinberg, ed. (Anon.)
33:222 D14'57. B      5973

Aubrey Beardsley. by Brian
Reade. (Anon.) 43:72 D23'67.
B      5974

Auction! by James Brough.
(Anon.) 39:196 S14'63. B
5975

Auntie Mame. by Jerome
Lawrence and Robert E. Lee.
(Gibbs) 32:110-12*N10'56.
(Panter-Downes) 34:169 N1'58.
T      5976

Aura. by Carlos Fuentes.
Lysander Kemp, trans. (West)
41:62-3 D25'65. B      5977

Austerlitz. by Claude Manceron.
George Unwin, trans. (Anon.)
42:174 Ap2'66. B      5978

Australia: aboriginal paintings--
Arnhem Land UNESCO
(Anon.) 31:140 Mr12'55. B
5979
Author! Author! by P. G.
Wodehouse. (Anon.) 38:108
Ag25'62. B 5980
An autobiography. by Edwin
Muir. (Anon.) 31:162-3
My7'55. B 5981
The autobiography of Bertrand
Russell. by Bertrand Rus-
sell. (Steiner) 43:101-10
Ag19'67. B 5982
The autobiography of Malcolm
X. by Malcolm Little and
Alex Haley. (Anon.) 41:
246-7 N13'65. B 5983
The autobiography of Mark
Twain. by Charles Neider.
(Macdonald) 36:160-96
Ap9'60. B 5984
The autobiography of Thomas
Whythorne. by Thomas
Whythorne. James M. Os-
born, ed. (Anon.) 38:135-6
Ja26'63. B 5985
The autobiography of Upton
Sinclair. by Upton Sinclair.
(Anon.) 38:113 Ja12'63. B
5986
The autobiography of W. E. B.
DuBois. by W. E. B. Du-
Bois. (Anon.) 44:174
Ap6'68. B 5987
Auto-da-fé. by Elias Canetti.
(West) 40:172-4 Ap1'64.
B 5988
The automobile graveyard. by
Fernando Arrabal. Richard
Howard, trans. (Oliver) 37:95
N25'61. T 5989
Autumn across America. by
Edwin Way Teale. (Anon.)
32:225-6*N10'56. B 5990
Autumn leaves. (McCarten)
32:50*Ag11'56. CC 5991
Avalanche! by Joseph Wechsberg.
(Anon.) 34:129 S6'58. B 5992
Avanti! by Samuel Taylor.
(Gill) 43:86-8 F10'68. T
5993
The avenue of the presidents.

by Mary Cable. (Anon.)
45:239 N15'69. B 5994
Avignon in flower: 1309-1403.
by Marzieh Gail. (Anon.)
41:121-2 Ag28'65. B 5995
The awakened eye. by Ross
Parmenter. (Anon.) 44:
146 Je8'68. B 5996
The awakening. (McCarten)
34:113-14 Mr8'58. CC 5997
The awakening of Spring. by
Frank Wedekind. (Oliver)
40:134 My23'64. T 5998
Azala1. by John Skolle.
(Anon.) 32:142-3*S8'56. B
5999

B

B. B. C. (Arlen) 43:182-8
My13'67. TV 6000
Baa baa black sheep. by Gregory
Boyington. (Anon.) 34:83
Ag9'58. B 6001
Baal. by Bertolt Brecht.
(Oliver) 41:158-60 My15'65.
T 6002
Babes in the wood. by Rick
Besoyan. (Oliver) 40:84
Ja9'65. T 6003
Babo 73. (Gill) 40:187 O17
'64. CC 6004
The Baby Dodds story. by
Baby Dodds and Larry Gara.
(Balliett) 36:176-7 Mr19'60.
B 6005
Baby doll. (McCarten) 32:59-60
D29'56. CC 6006
Baby the rain must fall. (Gill)
40:104 Ja23'65. CC 6007
Baby want a kiss. by James
Costigan. (McCarten) 40:143
My9'64. T 6008
Bachelor in paradise. (Gill)
37:235-6 D9'61. CC 6009
The bachelor party. (McCarten)
33:135 Ap20'57. CC 6010
The bachelors. by Muriel
Spark. (Updike) 37:161-7
S30'61. B 6011
Back from eternity. (McCarten)
32:76*S15'56. CC 6012
Back to Methuselah. by George

conflict, 1941-45. by
Alan Clark. (Anon.) 41:157-8
Je12'65. B                6051
The Barbary light. by P.H.
Newby. (West) 40:119-20
Ja30'65. B                6052
Barefoot in the park. by Neil
Simon. (McCarten) 39:93
N2'63. T                  6053
Barefoot in the park. (Gill)
43:72 Je10'67. CC         6054
The baron in the trees. by
Italo Calvino and Archibald
Colquhoun. (Anon.) 35:243
D5'59. B                  6055
Barren victories: Versailles to
Suez. by Basil Collier. (Anon.)
40:206-207 My16'64. B 6056
The Barretts of Wimpole
Street. (McCarten) 32:95
Ja26'57. CC               6057
The barroom monks. by Joseph
Carroll. (Oliver) 38:83
Je9'62. T                 6058
Bartleby. by James Hinton, Jr.,
Edward Albee and William
Flanagan. (Balliett) 36:66
F4'61. T                  6059
Baruch: my own story. by
Bernard M. Baruch. (Anon.)
33:176-7 S14'57. B        6060
The basement. by Harold
Pinter. (Oliver) 44:140-1
O26'68. T                 6061
The bathtub hoax, and other
blasts and bravos. by H.L.
Mencken. Robert McHugh,
ed. (Anon.) 34:180 N1'58. B
                          6062
Battle hymn. (McCarten)
33:75-6 F23'57. CC        6063
The battle of Algiers. (Gill)
43:93 S23'67. CC          6064
The battle of Cassino. by Fred
Majdalany. (Anon.) 33:177
S14'57. B                 6065
The battle of Dienbienphu. by
Jules Roy. Robert Baldick,
trans. (Anon.) 41:170-1 Mr6
'65. B                    6066
The battle of El Alamein. by
Fred Majdalany. (Anon.) 41:
80 Jy31'65. B             6067

The battle of Plassey. by
Michael Edwardes. (Anon.)
39:211-12 N2'63.B         6068
The battle of silence. by Jean
Bruller. Rita Barisse, trans.
(N. Bliven) 45:203-206
N8'69. B                  6069
The battle of the sexes. (Mc-
Carten) 36:168-9 Ap30'60.
CC                        6070
The battle of the Villa Fiorita.
by Rumer Godden. (Anon.) 39:
187-8 O5'63. B            6071
Battle: the story of the Bulge.
by John Toland. (Anon.) 35:
205-206 O10'59. B         6072
Battles of the English civil war.
by Austin Woolrych. (Anon.)
37:143 F17'62. B          6073
Baudelaire. by Enid Starkie.
(West) 34:149-58 Ap12'58.
B                         6074
Baudelaire as a literary critic.
by Charles Baudelaire. Lois
Boe Hyslop and Francis E.
Hyslop, trans. (Anon.) 40:
247 N7'64. B              6075
Bay of the angels. (Gill) 40:
156-8 D5'64. CC           6076
Be not angry. by William
Michelfelder. (Anon.) 36:202-
203 S10'60. B             6077
The beast in me. by Haila
Stoddard. (McCarten) 39:57
My25'63. T                6078
The beast in the jungle. by
James Lord and Marguerite
Duras. (Flanner) 38:104
Ja12'63. T                6079
Beasts and men. by Pierre
Gascar. (West) 32:76-7*Je
30'56. B                  6080
The beat of life. by Barbara
Probst Solomon. (Anon.)
36:204-205 O15'60. B   6081
Beau Brummel: his life and
times. by Carlo Maria
Franzero. (Anon.) 34:214-15
D13'58. B                 6082
Beau James. (McCarten) 33:58
Jy6'57. CC                6083
Beautiful dreamer. by William
Engvick. (Balliett) 36:74
Ja14'61. T              6084

The beautiful people. by
Marylin Bender. (Anon.) 43:
223-4 O21'67.  B          6085
The beauty part. by S. J.
Perelman. (McCarten) 38:75
Ja12'63.  T               6086
The beaux' stratagem. by
George Farquhar. (Malcolm)
35:82-7 Mr7'59.  T        6087
Bebo's girl. (Gill) 40:150
N21'64.  CC               6088
Becket.  by Jean Anouilh.
(McCarten) 36:73-4 O15'60.
T                         6089
Becket. (Gill) 40:155-6
Mr14'64.  CC              6090
The bed. (McCarten) 31:43
*Jy2'55.  CC              6091
The bed sitting room. by John
Antrobus and Spike Milligan.
(Panter-Downes) 39:151-2
My25'63.  T               6092
The bed sitting room. (Kael)
45:158-9 O11'69.  CC      6093
Bedazzled. (Gill) 43:108-10
D16'67.  CC               6094
The Bedford incident. (Gill)
41:122 N6'65.  CC         6095
Bedtime story. by Sean O'Casey.
(Tynan) 35:84-5 Ap25'59.
T                         6096
Bedtime story. (McCarten) 40:
123 Je20'64.  CC          6097
Beekman Place. by Samuel
Taylor. (McCarten) 40:108
O17'64.  T                6098
Beer in the Snooker Club. by
Waguih Ghali. (West) 40:
203 S12'64.  B            6099
Beerbohm Tree: his life and
laughter.  by Hesketh
Pearson. (Anon.) 33:136-7
Mr9'57.  B                6100
Beethoven and his nephew. by
Editha Sterba and Richard
Sterba. (Sargeant) 31:118-23
Ap30'55.  B               6101
Before my time. by Niccolò
Tucci. (N. Bliven) 39:180-2
Ap6'63.  B                6102
Before noon.  by Ramón J.
Sender. (West) 34:147-8
Ap19'58.  B               6103

Before the colors fade. by Fred
Ayer, Jr. (Anon.) 40:91
Jy25'64.  B               6104
Before the revolution. (Gill)
41:66 Ag7'65.  CC         6105
Before you go.  by Lawrence
Holofaner. (Gill) 43:85
Ja20'68.  T               6106
Beg, borrow or steal. by Bud
Freeman and Leon Pober.
(Tynan) 36:101-102 F20'60.
T                         6107
Beginning again.  by Leonard
Woolf. (Auden) 41:159-92
Ap3'65.  B                6108
Behind closed doors: politics
in the public interest. by
Edward N. Costikyan. (Anon.)
42:186-7 My7'66.  B       6109
Behind the golden curtain:
a view of the U.S.A. by
Susan Cooper. (Anon.)
42:248 O22'66.  B         6110
Behind the great wall.
(McCarten) 35:119-20*D19'59.
CC                        6111
Behold a pale horse. (Gill)
40:78-9 Ag29'64.  CC      6112
Being and nothingness. by
Jean-Paul Sartre. (Adler)
39:237-43 N9'63.  B       6113
Being busted.  by Leslie A.
Fiedler. (Anon.) 45:131-2
F14'70.  B                6114
The believers.  by Josephine
Jackson and Joseph A.
Walker. (Oliver) 44:75-6
My18'68.  T               6115
Bell'Antonio.  (Gill) 38:148-9
Ap7'62.  CC               6116
Bell, book and candle.
(McCarten) 34:84 Ja17'59.  CC
                          6117
Belle de jour. (Gilliatt) 44:
165-6 Ap20'68.  CC        6118
Bellini and Titian at Ferrara:
a study of styles and taste.
by John Walker. (Anon.)
33:143-4 Je8'57.  B       6119
Bells are ringing. by Betty
Comden and Adolph Green.
(Gibbs) 32:88-90 D8'56.
T                         6120

Bells are ringing. (McCarten)
36:55 Jy9'60. CC          6121
Bell's Landing. by Gerald
Warner Brace. (Anon.)
31:94*Ag27'55. B          6122
The bells of Bicêtre. by
Georges Simenon. Jean
Stewart, trans. (N. Bliven)
40:113-15 Ja9'65. B       6123
Belmarch: a legend of the first
crusade. by Christopher
Davis. (Anon.) 39:96 F1'64.
B                         6124
Beloved infidel. by Sheilah
Graham and Gerold Frank.
(Wilson) 34:115-24 Ja24'59.
B                         6125
Below the tide. by Penelope
Tremayne. (Anon.) 35:171-2
Ap4'59. B                 6126
Ben Butler. by Hans Louis
Trefousse. (Anon.) 33:107
*Je1'57. B                6127
Ben Franklin in Paris. by
Mark Sandrich, Jr. and Sidney
Michaels. (McCarten) 40:99
N7'64. T                  6128
The bench. by N.R. Teitel.
(Oliver) 44:135 Mr16'68.
T                         6129
Beneath the wheel. by
Hermann Hesse. (Steiner) 44:
89-90 Ja18'69. B          6130
Ben-Hur. (Flanner) 34:96-8
S27'58 (McCarten) 35:153-4
D5'59. CC                 6131
Benjamin. (Flanner) 43:80
F3'68 (Kael) 44:114 Mr30
'68. CC                   6132
Benny, Jack. (J. Lardner)
34:112-13 Ap19'58. TV     6133
The Bernal Díaz chronicles. by
Bernal Díaz del Castillo.
Albert Idell, trans. & ed.
(Anon.) 32:74 Ja5'57. B
                          6134
The Bernard Berenson
treasury. by Bernard
Berenson. Hanna Kiel, ed.
(Anon.) 38:232 O13'62.
B                         6135
Bernard Shaw. by St. John
Ervine. (West) 33:126-9

F23'57. B                 6136
Bernard Shaw: a reassessment.
by Colin Wilson. (Anon.)
45:212 N29'69. B          6137
Bernard Shaw: collected letters,
1874-1897. by George Ber-
nard Shaw. Dan H.
Laurence, ed. (N. Bliven)
42:173-5 Mr12'66. B       6138
Bernard Shaw's letters to
Granville Barker. by
George Bernard Shaw. C.B.
Purdom, ed. (Anon.) 33:167-8
Ap6'57. B                 6139
Bertha. by Kenneth Koch.
(Oliver) 38:104 F24'62. T
                          6140
Bertrand Russell speaks his
mind. by Bertrand Russell.
(Anon.) 36:246 N26'60. B
                          6141
Bertrand Russell: the passionate
skeptic. by Alan Wood.
(Anon.) 33:118-19 Ja25'58.
B                         6142
Best foot forward. by John
Cecil Holm, Hugh Martin and
Ralph Blane. (Oliver)
39:140 Ap13'63. T         6143
The best house in London.
(Gilliatt) 45:48 Ag2'69.
CC                        6144
The best house in Naples.
by F. Hugh Herbert. (Gibbs)
32:73-4 N3'56. T          6145
The best laid plans. by
Gwen Davis. (McCarten)
42:122-4 Ap2'66. T        6146
The best man. by Gore
Vidal. (Tynan) 36:88-91
Ap9'60. T                 6147
The best man. (Gill) 40:118-
20 Ap18'64. CC            6148
The best of enemies. (Balliett)
38:69 Ag18'62. CC         6149
The best of Redouté's roses.
Eva Mannering, ed.
(Anon.) 36:179-80 Ap30'60.
B                         6150
Best regards to Aida. by
Hans W. Heinsheimer. (Anon.)
44:244-6 N30'68. B
                          6151

Best short stories from the
Paris Review.   Paris Review.
(Anon.) 35:203 O31'59.   B
                                    6152
The best short stories of
Edith Wharton.   by Edith
Wharton.   Wayne Andrews,
ed. (Anon.) 34:242 N15'58.
B                              6153
The best things in life are
free.   (McCarten) 32:182
O13'56.   CC              6154
The best-kept secret.   by
John Francis Purcell.
(Anon.) 39:119 Ja18'64.
B                              6155
Bethnal Green.   by Michael
Fisher. (Anon.) 37:205-206
O28'61.   B               6156
The better song. by Luc Estang.
(West) 40:161-2 Mr28'64.
B                              6157
Bettina.   by Arthur Helps and
Elizabeth Jane Howard.
(Anon.) 33:202-203 O12'57.
B                              6158
Between friends: letters of
James Branch Cabell and
others.   by James Branch
Cabell.   Padraic Colum and
Margaret Freeman Cabell,
eds.   (Anon.) 38:183-4
Ap21'62. B               6159
Between life and death.   by
Nathalie Sarraute.   Maria
Tolas, trans. (N. Bliven)
45:222 N22'69.   B       6160
Between the wars.   by James
Laver.   (Anon.) 38:180
Mr24'62.   B              6161
Between then and now.   by
Alba de Céspedes. (Anon.)
36:177-8 Ap23'60.   B   6162
Between two seas: the creation
of the Suez Canal.   by John
Patrick Kinross. (Anon.)
45:184 Ap12'69. B       6163
Beware of Caesar.   by
Vincent Sheean. (Anon.)
41:74 Jy3'65. B         6164
Beyond the Alps: a Summer in
the Italian hill towns.   by
Robert M. Coates. (Anon.)

37:246 D2'61. B          6165
Beyond the dreams of avarice.
by Russell Kirk. (Anon.)
32:71-2*Ag4'56. B        6166
Beyond the fringe. by
Alexander H. Cohen.
(McCarten) 38:111 N3'62.
T                              6167
Beyond the fringe '65.   by
Alexander Cohen, et al.
(McCarten) 40:50 D26'64.
T                              6168
Beyond the melting pot: the
Negroes, Puerto Ricans,
Jews, Italians, and Irish
of New York City.   by
Nathan Glazer and Daniel P.
Moynihan.   (N. Bliven)
40:198-202 S26'64.   B  6169
Beyond the welfare state. by
Gunnar Myrdal. (Anon.)
36:70 Jy2'60. B          6170
Bhowani junction.   (McCarten)
32:118*Je2'56.   CC     6171
The Bible.   (Gill) 42:184-5
O1'66.   CC              6172
Biffen's millions.   by P. G.
Wodehouse. (Anon.) 40:90
Ag8'64.   B              6173
The big blue line: police
power versus human rights.
by Ed   Cray. (Anon.)
42:127 Ja28'67.   B     6174
The big boxcar. by Alfred
Maund. (Anon.) 33:197-8
O12'57.   B              6175
The big circus.   (McCarten)
35:46 Jy25'59. CC       6176
The big city.   (Gilliatt) 43:52-5
Jy8'67.   CC             6177
The big city; or, the new
Mayhew.   by Alex Atkinson
and Ronald Searle. (Anon.)
35:180 Ap25'59.   B     6178
The big country. (McCarten)
34:93 O11'58. CC        6179
The big deal.   (Gill) 36:108-
109 D3'60.   CC          6180
Big fish, little fish.   by Hugh
Wheeler.   (McCarten) 37:
113 Mr25'61. T          6181
The big gamble. (Gill)
37:112-13 S9'61.   CC   6182

A big hand for the little lady.
(Oliver) 42:110 Je18'66.
CC                            6183
The big knife. (McCarten)
31:184*N19'55. CC      6184
The big land. (McCarten)
33:76-8 Mr9'57. CC      6185
Big Mac. by Erih Kos. Lovett
F. Edwards, trans. (Anon.)
38:176-7 S22'62. B      6186
The big machine. by Robert
Jungk. (Bernstein) 45:154-8
O4'69. B                 6187
Big man. by Lawrence
Weinberg. (Oliver) 42:79-80
My28'66. T               6188
The big party. (J. Lardner)
35:122-8 N21'59. TV      6189
Big Sur and the oranges of
Hieronymus Bosch. by
Henry Miller. (Anon.) 33:127-
8 Je15'57. B             6190
The big thaw. by C.L.
Sulzberger. (Anon.) 32:234-5
D8'56. B                 6191
Big time buck white.
by Joseph Dolan Tuotti.
(Oliver) 44:65 D21'68. T
                          6192
The big war. by Anton Myrer.
(Anon.) 33:139 My25'57. B
                          6193
Big woods. by William
Faulkner. (Anon.) 31:224
*N19'55. B               6194
Bigger than life. (McCarten)
32:50*Ag11'56. CC       6195
Billion dollar brain. (Gill)
43:50 D30'67. CC        6196
Billy. by Stephen Glassman,
and Gene Allan and Ron
Dante. (Gill) 45:99 Mr29'69.
T                         6197
Billy Budd. (Gill) 38:116-17
N3'62. CC                6198
Billy Liar. by Keith Water-
house and Willis Hall.
(Oliver) 41:144-6 Mr27'65.
T                         6199
Billy Liar. (Gill) 39:88-9
D21'63. CC               6200
A biography of Edward Marsh.
by Christopher Hassall.

(Anon.) 35:194 S19'59. B
                          6201
The biological time bomb.
by Gordon Rattray Taylor.
(Steiner) 44:237-46 N16'68.
B                         6202
Birdbath. by Leonard
Melfi. (Oliver) 42:126-7 Ap
23'66. T                 6203
Birdman of Alcatraz. by
Thomas E. Gaddis. (Anon.)
31:160-1*S17'55. B      6204
The birds. (Gill) 39:177
Ap6'63. CC               6205
The birds fall down. by
Rebecca West. (Pritchett)
42:225-33 D3'66. B      6206
Birds of the world. by
Oliver L. Austin, Jr.
(Anon.) 37:246 N11'61.
B                         6207
The birth of a grandfather.
by May Sarton. (Balliett)
33:194-7 O5'57. B       6208
The birth of Europe. by
Robert Lopez. (Gay)
43:100-106 Je24'67. B   6209
The birth of the missle. by
Ernest Klee and Otto Merk.
T. Schoeters, trans. (Anon.)
41:109-10 Ja22'66. B    6210
The birth of Western civiliza-
tion: Greece and Rome.
Michael Grant, ed. (Anon.)
40:248 O10'64. B        6211
The birthday boy. by Al
Hine. (Anon.) 35:170-1
Ap11'59. B               6212
The birthday king. by Gabriel
Fielding. (Balliett) 39:174-5
My18'63. B               6213
The birthday party. by Harold
Pinter. (McCarten) 43:151
O14'67. T                6214
The birthday party. (Kael)
44:90-1 D21'68. CC      6215
Biscuit. by Maxime
Furlaud. (Oliver)
42:82 My28'66. T        6216
Bismarck. by Werner Richter.
Brian Battershaw, trans.
(Anon.) 41:179 My22'65.
B                         6217

Bitter lemons. by Lawrence
Durrell. (Anon.) 34:146
Mr8'58. B                     6218
Bitter victory. by René
Hardy. Galway Kinnell,
trans. (Anon.) 32:100-101
Ja12'57. B                     6219
Bizet and his world. by Mina
Curtiss. (West) 35:108-
17 F28'59. B                   6220
Black and conservative. by
George S. Schuyler. (Anon.)
42:247-8 O29'66. B             6221
The black book. by Lawrence
Durrell. (Anon.) 36:205
O15'60. B                      6222
Black comedy. by Peter
Shaffer. (Panter-Downes)
41:104 Ag14'65 (McCarten)
43:91 F25'67. T                6223
Black grapes. by Livia
de Stefani. (Anon.) 34:150-1
*Ap26'58. B                    6224
Black like me. by John Howard
Griffin. (Anon.) 37:209-10
O7'61. B                       6225
Black like me. (Gill) 40:151-2
My23'64. CC                    6226
Black Monday. by Reginald
Rose. (Oliver) 38:118 Mr17
'62. T                         6227
Black mother: the years of
the African slave trade. by
Basil Davidson. (Anon.)
37:118 Ja20'62. B              6228
Black nativity. by Langston
Hughes. (Oliver)37:57 D23'61.
T                              6229
The black obelisk. by Erich
Maria Remarque. Denver
Lindley, trans. (Anon.)
33:174-5 Ap13'57. B            6230
Black Orpheus. (McCarten) 35:
47 Ja2'60. CC                  6231
Black rage. by William H.
Grier and Price M. Cobbs.
(Anon.) 44:181 S28'68.
B                              6232
Blackboard jungle. (McCarten)
31:120-1 Mr26'55. CC    6233
The blacking factory &
Pennsylvania gothic. by Wil-
frid Sheed. (S. Lardner)

44:234-42 N30'68. B     6234
The blacks. by Jean Genet.
(Balliett) 37:93-4 My13'61.
T                              6235
The blanket. by A. A.
Murray. (Anon.) 34:73 Jy26
'58. B                         6236
The blast of war: 1939-1945.
by Harold Macmillan. (N.
Bliven) 44:90-5 Ag10'68. B
                               6237
The blind cave. by Leo
Katcher. (Anon.) 42:248
O8'66. B                       6238
No entry                       6239
Blindfold. (Oliver)
42:112 Je11'66. CC             6240
Blitz! by Lionel Bart.
(Panter-Downes) 38:85-6
Je2'62. T                      6241
The block. by Ralph
Schoenstein. (Anon.)
36:183 O1'60. B                6242
Blockade runners of the Con-
federacy. by Hamilton
Cochran. (Anon.) 34:213
N8'58. B                       6243
Blood and roses. (Gill)
37:179 O14'61. CC              6244
Blood from the sky. by
Piotr Rawicz. (West)
40:160-1 Mr28'64. B     6245
The blood knot. by Athol
Fugard. (Oliver) 40:110-12
Mr14'64. T                     6246
The blood of the lamb. by
Peter DeVries. (Balliett)
38:180-2 Ap7'62. B      6247
Blood on the balcony. (Balliett)
40:74 Jy11'64. CC              6248
Blood, sweat and Stanley
Poole. by James Goldman
and William Goldman.
(Oliver) 37:165 O14'61. T
                               6249
Blood-and-thunder. by Dwight
Taylor. (N. Bliven) 38:
213-14 O27'62. B               6250
Blow-up. (Gill) 42:60-2 D31'66.
CC                             6251
The blue book. by Robert
H. W. Welch, Jr. (Liebling)
37:156-65 My20'61. B    6252

The blue boy in black. by
Edmund White. (Oliver)
39:88 My11'63. T        6253
Blue denim. by James Leo
Herlihy and William Noble.
(J. Lardner) 34:88-9
Mr15'58. T        6254
Blue denim. (McCarten)
35:86-9 Ag8'59. CC        6255
The blue hen's chick. by A. B.
Guthrie, Jr. (Anon.)
41:109-10 Je26'65. B        6256
The blue lantern. by Sidonie
Gabrielle Colette. Roger
Senhouse, trans. (Anon.)
39:246-7 O19'63. B        6257
The blue max. (Oliver) 42:55
Je25'66. CC        6258
Blueprints for leviathan,
American style. by Roy F.
Nichols (Anon.) 39:83-4
Je29'63. B        6259
Blues for Mister Charlie.
by James Baldwin. (McCarten)
40:143 My9'64. T        6260
Bob & Carol & Ted & Alice.
(Kael) 45:144-9 O4'69. CC
        6261
The bobo. (Gill) 43:148 O7'67.
CC        6262
Boccaccio '70. (Gill) 38:64
Jy7'62. CC        6263
Body and soul. (J. Lardner)
35:164-6 O17'59. TV        6264
The body beautiful. by Will
Glickman, Joseph Stein, Jerry
Bock and Sheldon Harnick.
(Gibbs) 33:54-6 F1'58. T
        6265
The body of a young man. by
Mildred Walker. (Anon.)
36:201-202 O8'60. B        6266
Boeing-boeing. by Marc
Camoletti (McCarten)
40:76 F13'65. T        6267
Boeing, boeing. (Gill) 41:71
Ja15'66. CC        6268
Bohemian versus bourgeois:
French society and the French
man of letters in the nine-
teenth century. by César
Graña. (Anon.) 40:142-3 Je13
'64. B        6269

Bohikee Creek. by Robert
Ungar. (Oliver) 42:120-2
My7'66. T        6270
The bolsheviks. by Adam
B. Ulam. (Anon.) 41:244
N20'65. B        6271
Bombers B-52. (McCarten)
33:100 D7'57. CC        6272
Bon voyage! (Gill) 38:133-4
My26'62. CC        6273
The Bonapartes. by David
Stacton. (Anon.) 42:165-6
Je4'66. B        6274
Bondu saved from drowning.
(Gilliatt) 45:96-8 S6'69.
CC        6275
The bone pickers. by Al Dewlen.
(Anon.) 34:72 Ja3'59. B
        6276
Bone thoughts. by George
Starbuck. (Bogan) 36:157-8
Mr26'60. B        6277
Bones, bodies, and disease.
by Calvin Wells. (Anon.)
40:178-9 Je6'64. B        6278
Bongo. by Arnold E. Grisman.
(N. Bliven) 37:168-9 Mr11
'61. B        6279
Bonheur, impair et passe. by
Françoise Sagan. (Flanner)
39:80-2 Ja25'64. T        6280
Bonjour Tristesse. by
Françoise Sagan. (Gill)
31:114-15 Mr5'55. B        6281
Bonjour Tristesse. (McCarten)
33:106 Ja25'58. CC        6282
Bonnie and Clyde. (Gilliatt)
43:77-9 Ag19'67 (Kael) 43:
147-71 O21'67. CC        6283
A book of Australia. T. Inglis
Moore, ed. (Anon.) 38:
187 Ap14'62. B        6284
A book of French quotations.
by Norbert Guterman.
(Steegmuller) 39:114-16
Ja18'64. B        6285
The book of little knowledge. by
Goodman Ace. (Anon.)
31:166-7*O22'55. B        6286
The book of the dance. by
Agnes deMille. (Anon.) 39:
237 D14'63. B
        6287

Book of the Eskimos. by Peter
Freuchen. Dagmar
Freuchen, ed. (Anon.)
37:155-6 S9'61. B      6288
Boom! (Gilliatt) 44:117-19
Je8'68. CC             6289
Borak. by Robert D. Hock.
(Balliett) 36:40-1 D24'60.
T                      6290
Border country. by Raymond
Williams. (Anon.) 38:136-7
Je9'62. B              6291
Borderline ballads. by
William Plomer. (Bogan) 31:94
*F4'56. B              6292
The Borgias. by Anny Latour.
Neil Mann, trans. (Anon.)
43:194 Mr11'67. B      6293
The Borgias. by J. Lucas-
Dubreton. Philip John
Stead, trans. (Anon.)
31:145-6 Ap2'55. B     6294
Born free. by Joy Adamson.
(Anon.) 36:158-9 Je4'60. B
                       6295
Born free. (S. Lardner)
42:78 Jy9'66. CC       6296
Born in a book shop. by
Vincent Starrett. (Anon.)
41:143 F12'66. B       6297
Born losers. (Gilliatt) 43:110-
12 S9'67. CC           6298
Borneo people. by Malcolm
MacDonald. (Anon.) 34:
209-10 O18'58. B       6299
Borstal boy. by Brendan
Behan. (Malcolm) 35:69-
72 Jy4'59. B           6300
The Borzoi book of French folk
tales. Paul Delarue, ed.
(Auden) 33:139-47 Mr16'57.
B                      6301
Boston and return. by Gladys
Brooks. (Anon.) 38:90 Je
30'62. B               6302
The Boston strangler. by Gerold
Frank. (Anon.) 42:246-7
N12'66. B              6303
The Boston strangler. (Kael)
44:209-10 O26'68. CC   6304
Boswell for the defense. by
James Boswell. Frederick
A. Pottle and William K.

Wimsatt, eds. (Connolly)
35:99-105 Ja30'60. B   6305
Boswell in search of a wife: 1766-
1769. by James Boswell.
Frank Brady and Frederick
A. Pottle, eds. (Anon.)
32:210-11 N3'56. B     6306
Boswell on the grand tour: Italy,
Corsica, and France, 1765-
1766. by James Boswell.
Frank Brady and Frederick
A. Pottle, eds. (Anon.)
31:138 Je11'55. B      6307
Boswell: the ominous years,
1774-76. by James Boswell.
Charles Ryscamp and
Frederick A. Pottle, eds.
(Balliett) 39:78-82 Je29'63.
B                      6308
Bottoms up! by Cornelia Otis
Skinner. (Anon.) 31:136 Ap9
'55. B                 6309
Boudu saved from drowning.
(Gill) 43:132-5 F25'67. CC
                       6310
The bourgeois poet. by Karl
Shapiro. (Bogan) 40:238-42
N7'64. B               6311
A bowl of red. by Frank X.
Tolbert. (Anon.) 42:231
S17'66. B              6312
Box. by Edward Albee. (Gill)
44:103-106 O12'68. T   6313
The boy in the Model-T. by
Stephen Longstreet. (Anon.)
32:171*Mr17'56. B      6314
A boy named Charlie Brown.
(Kael) 45:72-3 Ja17'70. CC
                       6315
Boyhood with Gurdjieff. by
Fritz Peters. (Anon.) 40:
246 O10'64. B          6316
Boys and girls together.
by William Goldman.
(Anon.) 40:118 S5'64. B
                       6317
The boys from Syracuse. by
Richard Rodgers and Lorenz
Hart and George Abbott
(Oliver) 39:84-5 Ap27'63. T
                       6318
The boys in the band. by Mart
Crowley. (Oliver) 44:84-6

Ap27'68. T 6319

Boys' night out. (Gill)
38:68 Je30'62. CC 6320

The brains trust. by Rexford
Guy Tugwell. (Anon.)
44:180-1 S28'68. B 6321

Brand. by Henrik Ibsen.
(Panter-Downes.) 35:79 My30
'59. T 6322

Branwell Brontë. by Winifred
Gérin. (Anon.) 37:206-207
O28'61. B 6323

Brave day, hideous night:
the Tate Gallery years, 1939-
65. by John Rothenstein.
(Anon.) 43:177-8 My20'67.
B 6324

The brave one. (McCarten)
33:128 Mr30'57. CC 6325

Bravo Giovanni. by A.J.
Russell, Ronny Graham,
and Milton Schafer. (Mc-
Carten) 38:91-2 My26'62. T
6326

Breakfast at Tiffany's. by
Truman Capote. (Anon.)
34:241-2 N15'58. B 6327

Breakfast at Tiffany's. (Gill)
37:198-9 O7'61. CC 6328

The breaking wall. by Louis
A. Lippa. (Malcolm) 35:90-
|2 F6'60. T 6329

The breaking wave. by Nevil
Shute. (Anon.) 31:156-7
Ap16'55. B 6330

Break-up: the core of modern
art. by Katherine Kuh.
(Anon.) 41:244-5 N27'65.
B 6331

Breathless. (Flanner) 36:92-3
Ag13'60. (Angell) 36:102-
104 F11'61. CC 6332

Brecht on Brecht. by Bertolt
Brecht. (Oliver) 37:62-6 Ja
13'62. T 6333

The bride that got away.
by George Selmark. (Anon.)
43:180 S23'67. B 6334

The bride wore black. (Gilliatt)
44:46-7 Jy6'68. CC 6335

The bridge. (Oliver) 37:
167 My13'61. CC 6336

The bridge and the abyss.
by Bertram D. Wolfe.
(Anon.) 43:111-12 F3'68.
B 6337

The bridge at Andau. by
James A. Michener. (Anon.)
33:149-50 Mr16'57. B 6338

The bridge on the River Kwai.
(McCarten) 33:48 D28'57.
CC 6339

Brief lives. by John Aubrey.
Oliver Lawson Dick, ed.
(Auden) 33:129-39 F15'58.
B 6340

Brief lives. by Patrick Garland. (Oliver) 43:46 D30'67.
T 6341

The brig. by Kenneth H.
Brown. (Oliver) 39:57-9
My25'63. T 6342

The brig. (Gill) 42:131-2
Ap23'66. CC 6343

Bright day, dark runner.
by George Cuomo. (Anon.)
40:122-3 Ag22'64. B 6344

The bright lights. by Frank
Swinnerton. (Anon.) 44:236-7
N9'68. B 6345

The bright prison. by Penelope
Mortimer. (Balliett) 33:130-
4 Mr30'57. B 6346

Brighter than 1,000 suns. by
Robert Jungk. (Bernstein) 45:
154 O4'69. B 6347

Brightower. by Dore Schary.
(Gill) 45:72-3 F7'70. T
6348

Bring me a warm body. by
Robert Dale Martin. (Oliver)
38:97 Ap28'62. T 6349

Brink of life. (McCarten) 35:
172-3 N21'59. CC 6350

British art since 1900. by
John Rothenstein. (Anon.) 38:
248 D1'62. B 6351

The British soldier. by H. de
Watteville. (Anon.) 31:148
*O29'55. B 6352

Broadway, U.S.S.R. by
Faubion Bowers. (Tynan)
35:185-90 My16'59. B 6353

Brokenburn: the journal of

Kate Stone, 1861-1868. by
Kate Stone. John Q. Ander-
son, ed. (Wilson) 31:173-6
*N5'55. B                    6354
Broken-hearted clowns. by Butch
Reynolds. (Anon.) 31:118
*F11'56. B                   6355
The Brontës. Margaret Webster,
adapt. (Oliver) 39:61-2 Ja4
'64. T                       6356
The Brontës and their world.
by Phyllis Bentley. (Anon.)
45:211 N8'69. B              6357
Broth of a boy. (McCarten)
35:74 Ja9'60. CC             6358
Brother animal: the story of
Freud and Tausk. by Paul
Roazen. (Anon.) 45:178-9
N1'69. B                     6359
The brotherhood. (Kael)
44:95-8 Ja25'69. CC          6360
Brotherly love. by Gabriel
Fielding. (Balliett)
37:174-9 S23'61. B           6361
Brothers and sisters. by Ivy
Compton-Burnett. (Anon.)
32:106-107 Ja19'57. B    6362
The brothers Karamazov. (Mc-
Carten) 34:104-107 Mr1'58.
CC                           6363
Brown girl, brownstones. by
Paule Marshall. (Anon.)
35:191-2 S19'59. B           6364
Bruno Santini. by Vasco
Pratolini. Raymond
Rosenthal, trans. (West)
41:179-81 My8'65. B      6365
Bruno's dream. by Iris
Murdoch. (Anon.) 44:90
F1'69. B                     6366
The brutal friendship: Mussolini,
Hitler, and the fall of Italian
facism. by F.W. Deakin.
(Anon.) 38:142-4 F9'63.
B                            6367
Brutus's orchard. by Roy
Fuller. (Bogan) 34:162-3
S13'58. B                    6368
Buck white. by Oscar Brown,
Jr. (Gill) 45:116 D13'69.
T                            6369
The buffalo head. by R.M.
Patterson. (Anon.) 37:241-2

N25'61. B                    6370
Bugles and a tiger. by John
Masters. (Anon.) 31:96-7
*F4'56. B                    6371
Bull fever. by Kenneth
Tynan. (Anon.) 31:175-6
*O15'55. B                   6372
Bullitt. (Kael) 44:209 O26'68.
CC                           6373
Bundle of joy. (McCarten)
32:60 D29'56. CC             6374
A bundle of sensations.
by Goronwy Rees. (Anon.)
37:166-7 Ap15'61. B      6375
Bunny Lake is missing.
(Gill) 41:229-30 O16'65.
CC                           6376
Buoyant billions. by George
Bernard Shaw. (Malcolm)
35:120-2 Je6'59. T       6377
The burden of proof. by James
Barlow. (Anon.) 44:211-12
O12'68. B                    6378
Burghley: Tudor statesman,
1520-98. by B.W. Beckingsale.
(Anon.) 44:158 Mr23'68. B
                             6379
The buried city: excavations at
Leptis Magna. by Giacomo
Caputo and Ernesto Vergara
Caffarelli. (Anon.) 43:180
S9'67. B                     6380
The buried Day. by C. Day
Lewis. (Anon.) 36:226 N5'60.
B                            6381
The buried people. by Sibylle
Cles-Reden. C. M. Woodhouse
trans. (Anon.) 31:135*F18'56.
B                            6382
Burn me to ashes! by Nikos
Kazantzakis. (Oliver) 39:112
N30'63. T                    6383
The burning. by Wallace
Hamilton. (Oliver) 39:80 D14'63.
T                            6384
The burning brand: diaries
1935-50. by Cesare Pavese.
A. E. Murch and Jeanne
Molli, trans. (Anon.) 45:
83-4 Ja17'70. B              6385
The burning glass. by S.N.
Behrman. (N. Bliven) 44:
240-5 D7'68. B               6386

A burnt-out case. by Graham
Greene. (Anon.) 37:169-70
Mr11'61. B                 6387
Bus stop. by William Inge.
(Gibbs) 31:62-4 Mr12'55.
T                          6388
Bus stop. (McCarten) 32:76
*S15'56. CC                6389
Bushido. (Gill) 40:128 S19'64.
CC                         6390
The buskers. by Kenneth
Jupp. (Oliver) 37:121
N11'61. T                  6391
But for whom Charlie. by
S. N. Behrman. (McCarten)
40:64 Mr21'64. T           6392
But not for me. (McCarten)
35:172-3 O10'59. CC        6393
But, seriously .... by Julius
J. Epstein. (Gill) 45:94
Mr8'69. T                  6394
Butch Cassidy and the Sundance
Kid. (Kael) 45:128-9 S27'69.
CC                         6395
The butler did it. by P.G.
Wodehouse. (Anon.) 33:164
Ap6'57. B                  6396
The butter and egg man. by
George S. Kaufman. (Oliver)
42:98-9 O29'66. T          6397
Butterfield 8. (Gill) 36:152
N19'60. CC                 6398
Butterflies are free. by
Leonard Gershe. (Gill)
45:127-8 N1'69. T          6399
The butterfly dream. Anon.
(Oliver) 42:80-2 My28'66.
T                          6400
By George. by Michael Voysey.
(McCarten) 43:82 O21'67. T
                           6401
By Jupiter. by Richard Rodgers
and Lorenz Hart. (Oliver)
42:46-9 Ja28'67. T         6402
By love possessed. by James
Gould Cozzens. (Gill)
33:106-109 Ag24'57. B
                           6403
By love possessed. (Gill)
37:54-5 Jy22'61. CC        6404
By Quentin Reynolds. by
Quentin Reynolds. (Anon.)
39:114-15 Je22'63. B       6405

By rocking chair across
Russia. by Alex Atkinson
and Ronald Searle. (Anon.)
36:247-8 N26'60. B         6406
Bye bye Birdie. by Michael
Stewart, Charles Strouse,
and Lee Adams. (Tynan)
36:116-18 Ap23'60. T    6407
Bye bye Braverman. (Kael)
44:125-6 Mr2'68. CC     6408
By-line: Ernest Hemingway.
by Ernest Hemingway.
William White, ed. (Anon.)
43:145-6 Je3'67. B         6409
Byron: a biography. by Leslie
A. Marchand. (Auden)
34:133-50*Ap26'58. B  6410
Byzantine empresses. by
Charles Diehl. Harold Bell,
and de Theresa de Kerpely.
trans. (Anon.) 39:71
Ag3'63. B                  6411
Byzantium: the imperial cen-
turies A. D. 610-1071. by
Romilly Jenkins. (Anon.)
43:154-5 Ap1'67. B         6412

-C-

A cab at the door. by V. S.
Pritchett. (Gilliatt) 44:206-11
O12'68. B                  6413
Cabaret. by Joe Masteroff,
John Kander and Fred Ebb.
(McCarten) 42:155-6
D3'66. T                   6414
Cabiria. (McCarten) 33:109
N9'57. CC                  6415
Cactus flower. by Abe
Burrows. (McCarten) 41:152
D18'65. T                  6416
Cadmus: the poet and the
world. by Victor Purcell.
(Wilson) 34:119-50 My24'58.
B                          6417
Caesars and saints: the
evolution of the Christian
state, 180-313 A. D. by
Stewart Perowne. (Anon.)
38:145-6 F9'63. B          6418
The Caesars: might and mad-
ness. by Ivar Lissner. J.
Maxwell Brownjohn, trans.
(Anon.) 34:66-7 D27'58.
B                          6419

Café Crown. by Hy Kraft,
Albert Hague and Marty Brill.
(McCarten) 40:130 Ap25'64.
T                                6420
A cage of spines. by May
Swenson. (Bogan) 34:237-8
D6'58. B                         6421
Calculated risk. by Joseph
Hayes. (McCarten) 38:146
N10'62. T                        6422
California Street. by
Niven Busch. (Anon.) 35:89
Je27'59. B                       6423
Caligula. by Albert Camus.
(Tynan) 36:100-104 F27'60.
T                                6424
Call me by my rightful name.
by Michael Shurtleff.
(Balliett) 36:78 F11'61. T
                                 6425
A call on Kuprin. by Jerome
Lawrence and Robert E.
Lee. (McCarten) 37:94 Je10
'61. T                           6426
Calling in crazy. by Henry
Bloomstein. (Oliver) 45:151
O18'69. T                        6427
Calvin Coolidge: the quiet
president. by Donald R.
McCoy. (Anon.) 43:150-1
Je10'67. B                       6428
Cambridge circus. by Bill
Oddie, et al. (McCarten)
40:108 O17'64. T                 6429
Camelot. by Alan Jay Lerner
and Frederick Loewe. (Mc-
Carten) 36:95-6 D10'60.
T                                6430
Camelot. (Gill) 43:168 N4'67.
CC                               6431
Camera three. (J. Lardner)
35:144-8 Mr7'59. TV     6432
Camino real. by Tennessee
Williams. (Gill) 45:50-2
Ja17'70. T                       6433
The campaigns of Napoleon. by
David Chandler. (Anon.)
42:244-6 D3'66. B       6434
The Camperlea girls. by
Olivia Manning. (Anon.)
45:84 Jy19'69. B        6435
Can-can. (McCarten) 36:170-3
Mr19'60. CC             6436

Candid camera. (J. Lardner)
35:54-60 Jy4'59. TV     6437
Candidates 1960. Eric
Sevareid, ed. (Anon.)
35:206 O10'59. B        6438
Candide. by Voltaire. (Gibbs)
32:52-4 D15'56. T       6439
Candide. (Gill) 38:205
N24'62. CC              6440
A candle in the sun. by
Marguerite Steen. (Anon.)
39:116-17 Ja18'64. B    6441
Candles in the sun. by Emily
Lutyens. (Anon.) 33:241-2
N23'57. B               6442
Candy. (Kael) 44:69-70 Ja4'69.
CC                      6443
The cannibals. by George
Tabori. (Oliver) 44:118-23
N9'68. T                6444
Canterbury tales. by Nevill
Coghill and Martin Starkie.
(Gill) 44:90 F15'69. T
                        6445
A canticle for Leibowitz. by
Walter M. Miller, Jr. (Bal-
liett) 36:159-60 Ap2'60. B
                        6446
The cantilevered terrace. by
William Archibald. (Oliver)
37:73-6 Ja27'62. T      6447
The canvas dagger. by Helen
Reilly. (Anon.) 32:75-6
Ja5'57. B               6448
The Cape Fear. by Malcolm
Ross. (Anon.) 41:135 F5'66.
B                       6449
Capital punishment. by James
Avery Joyce. (Anon.) 37:
143-4 F17'62. B         6450
The Capri letters. by Mario
Soldati. (Anon.) 32:130-1
*F25'56. B              6451
Captain Cook and the South
Pacific. by John Gwyther.
(Anon.) 31:86-7*Ag20'55. B
                        6452
Captain Dreyfus. by Nicholas
Halasz. (Hubbell) 31:82-4
*Ag20'55. B             6453
Captain Newman, M. D. (Gill)
40:122-3 F29'64. CC     6454

The captain with the whiskers.
by Benedict Kiely. (Anon.)
38:137 Je9'62. B        6455
The captains and the kings. by
Leo Lieberman. (McCarten)
37:61-2 Ja13'62. T      6456
Caravans. by James A.
Michener. (Anon.) 39:89
Ag10'63. B              6457
A card from Morocco. by
Robert Shaw. (Anon.) 45:
178 Ap19'69. B          6458
The cardinal. (Gill) 39:198
D14'63. CC              6459
Cards of identity. by Nigel
Dennis. (West) 31:206-208*
D3'55. B                6460
Career. (McCarten) 35:197 O17
'59. CC                 6461
The career of philosophy: Vol-
ume II. by John Herman
Randall, Jr. (Anon.) 41:235-6
O9'65. B                6462
The carefree tree. by Aldyth
Morris. (Gibbs) 31:86-8
*O22'55. T              6463
Careful, he might hear you.
by Sumner Locke Elliott.
(Anon.) 39:238-41 N16'63.
B                       6464
The caretaker. by Harold
Pinter. (Panter-Downes) 36:
60-1 Jy9'60 (Oliver) 37:162
O14'61. T               6465
Carlos: the king who would
not die. by John Langdon-
Davies. (Anon.) 39:189-90
O5'63. B                6466
Carnets intimes de G. Braque.
by Georges Braque. (Flanner)
31:115*D3'55. B         6467
A carnival of buncombe. by
H.L. Mencken. Malcolm
Moos, ed. (Anon.) 32:189-
90 D15'56. B            6468
Carnival! by Michael Stewart
and Bob Merrill. (McCarten)
37:116-18 Ap22'61. T    6469
Carousel. (McCarten) 32:63
*Mr3'56. CC             6470
The carpentered hen and other
tame creatures. by John

Updike. (Bogan) 35:170
Ap18'59. B              6471
The carpetbaggers. (Balliett)
40:76 Jy11'64. CC       6472
Carricknabauna. by Padraic
Colum and Basil Burwell.
(Oliver) 43:138-40 Ap8'67.
T                       6473
Carry me back to Morning-
side Heights. by Robert Alan
Aurthur. (Gill) 44:132-3 Mr
9'68. T                 6474
Carry on nurse. (Gill)
36:168 S24'60. CC       6475
Cartouche. (Oliver) 40:74
Ag8'64. CC              6476
Carving a statue. by Graham
Greene. (Oliver) 44:92 My11
'68. T                  6477
Casanova. by Hermann
Kesten. James Stern and
Robert Pick, trans. (Anon.)
31:136 Mr26'55. B       6478
Casanova. by John Masters.
(Anon.) 45:76 Ja10'70. B
                        6479
Casanova '70. (Gill) 41:56-8
Jy31'65. CC             6480
Casanova's Chinese restaurant.
by Anthony Powell. (N.
Bliven) 36:53-4 D31'60. B
                        6481
The case against Congress.
by Drew Pearson and Jack
Anderson. (Anon.) 44:182-3
S28'68. B               6482
The case of Colonel Petrov.
by Michael Bialoguski. (Anon.
32:149-50*Ap7'56. B     6483
The case of Dr. Laurent.
(McCarten) 34:60 Jy5'58. CC
                        6484
A case of libel. by Henry
Denker. (McCarten) 39:99
O19'63. T               6485
The case of Richard Sorge.
by F.W. Deakin and G.R.
Storry. (Anon.) 42:167
Je4'66. B               6486
A case of samples: poems
1946-1956. by Kingsley
Amis. (Bogan) 34:161-2 S13
'58. B                  6487

Casebook of the curious and
true. by Francis X. Busch.
(Anon.) 33:96*Je22'57. B
6488
Casino Royale. (Gill) 43:172
My6'67. CC 6489
Cassandra at the wedding. by
Dorothy Baker. (Anon.)
38:130 F24'62. B 6490
Cast a dark shadow. (Mc-
Carten) 33:99 D7'57. CC
6491
Cast a giant shadow. (Gill)
42:88-91 Ap9'66. CC 6492
Castle in Italy: an autobiography.
by Lina Waterfield. (Anon.)
38:178 S22'62. B 6493
Castle keep. (Gilliatt) 45:67
Jy26'69. CC 6494
Castle to castle. by Louis-
Ferdinand Céline. Ralph Man-
heim, trans. (N. Bliven)
45:222-6 N22'69. B 6495
The castles and the crown. by
Townsend Miller. (Anon.)
39:207 Mr16'63. B 6496
Castles in the air. by Irene
Castle. (Anon.) 34:72 Ja
3'59. B 6497
Castro, Fidel. (J. Lardner)
35:121-5 F21'59. TV 6498
A casual past. by Francis
Biddle. (Anon.) 37:181
S23'61. B 6499
The cat. (McCarten) 35:97-8
Ap18'59. CC 6500
Cat and mouse. by Günter
Grass. Ralph Manheim,
trans. (Anon.) 39:88-9
Ag10'63. B 6501
The cat and the canary. by
John Willard. (Oliver) 40:94-5
Ja23'65. T 6502
The cat and the mice. by
Leonard Mosley. (Anon.)
35:195 S26'59. B 6503
Cat Ballou. (Oliver) 41:78-80
Je26'65. CC 6504
Cat on a hot tin roof. by
Tennessee Williams. (Gibbs)
31:68-70 Ap2'55. T 6505
Cat on a hot tin roof. (Mc-
Carten) 34:163-4 S27'58.
CC 6506

The cat with two faces. by
Gordon Young. (Anon.)
34:154*Ap26'58. B 6507
The catafalque. by Robert
C. Goldston. (Anon.)
33:117 Ja25'58. B 6508
Catch a star! by Paul Webster.
and Ray Golden. (Gibbs)
31:68-70*S17'55. T 6509
Catch me if you can. by Jack
Weinstock and Willie
Gilbert. (McCarten) 41:83-4
Mr20'65. T 6510
Catch-22. by Joseph Heller.
(Balliett) 37:247-8
D9'61. B 6511
The catered affair. (McCarten)
32:64-5*Je23'56. CC 6512
Catherine Chailey. by
Humphrey Pakington. (Anon.)
36:189-90 O22'60. B 6513
Cat's cradle. by Kurt Vonnegut,
Jr. (Balliett) 39:117-18
Je15'63. B 6514
The cat's pajamas & witch's
milk. by Peter DeVries.
(Anon.) 44:246-7 N16'68.
B 6515
The Caucasian chalk circle.
by Bertolt Brecht. (Flanner)
31:61-3 Jy16'55 (Panter-
Downes) 38:159-60 My12'62
(McCarten) 42:122 Ap2'66.
T 6516
The cause of Japan. by Togo
Shigenori. (Anon.) 32:239-
40 N17'56. B 6517
Caution: a love story. Anon.
(Oliver) 45:132 Ap12'69.
T 6518
Cavalier and Yankee: the old
South and the American
national character. by William
R. Taylor. (Wilson) 37:197-
205 O28'61. B 6519
The cave. by Robert Penn
Warren. (Malcolm) 35:198-
202 O31'59. B 6520
The cave dwellers. by William
Saroyan. (Gibbs) 33:84-7 N2
'57 (Oliver) 37:138 O28'61.
T 6521

Cave of ice. by Penelope
Mortimer. (Balliett) 35:
167-70 Mr21'59. B        6522
Cecil Rhodes: the colossus of
southern Africa. by J.G.
Lockhart and C.M. Wood-
house. (Anon.) 39:113-14 Je
22'63. B                 6523
Celebration. by Harvey
Schmidt and Tom Jones.
(Gill) 44:49 F1'69. T    6524
Céline and his vision. by
Erika Ostrovsky. (Steiner)
43:106-15 Ja20'68. B     6525
The centaur. by John Updike.
(Adler) 39:182-8 Ap13'63.
B                        6526
Centenary at Jalna. by Mazo
de la Roche. (Anon.) 34:
92 Je 28'58. B           6527
The center of the action. by
Jerome Weidman. (Anon.)
45:213-14 O18'69. B      6528
The center of the green. by
John Bowen. (Anon.) 36:158
Mr26'60. B               6529
The central blue. by John
Slessor. (Anon.) 33:165 My
11'57. B                 6530
Central Park: a history and
a guide. by Henry Hope
Reed and Sophia Duckworth.
(Anon.) 43:99-100 Ag26'67.
B                        6531
Centuries of childhood: a social
history of family life. by
Philippe Ariès. Robert
Baldick, trans. (Anon.)
38:247 D1'62. B          6532
Ceremonies in dark old
men. by Lonne Elder, III.
(Oliver) 44:90-3 F15'69. T
                         6533
Ceremony of innocence. by
Ronald Ribman. (Oliver)
43:68-70 Ja6'68. T       6534
A certain evil. by David
Kraslow and Robert Boyd.
(N. Bliven) 41:89-94 Ag7'65.
B                        6535
A certain smile. by Françoise
Sagan. (Flanner) 32:76
*Mr31'56. B              6536

A certain smile. (Hamburger)
34:60 Ag9'58. CC         6537
Cervantes. by Sebastian
Juan Arbó. (Anon.) 31:
133*F18'56. B            6538
Chafed elbows. (Gill) 42:105
Ja14'67. CC              6539
Chagall. by Jean Cassou. Alisa
Jaffa, trans. (Anon.) 42:
178 Mr12'66. B           6540
Chaim Weizmann: a biography
by several hands. Meyer
W. Weisgal and Joel
Carmichael, eds. (Anon.)
39:179 Mr30'63. B        6541
The chairman. (Gilliatt) 45:74-5
Jy5'69. CC               6542
The chairs. by Eugène Ionesco.
(Flanner) 32:127-8*Mr10
'56 (Gibbs) 33:68 Ja18'58.
T                        6543
Chaliapin: an autobiography
as told to Maxim Gorky.
By Maxim Gorky. Nina
Froud and James Hanley,
eds. and trans. (Anon.)
44:127-8 Je1'68. B       6544
The chalk garden. by Enid
Bagnold. (Gibbs) 31:77-8
*N5'55. T                6545
The chalk garden. (Gill)
40:112-14 My30'64. CC 6546
Champagne complex. by Leslie
Stevens. (Gibbs) 31:68
Ap23'55. T               6547
Chance meeting. (McCarten)
31:117 Ap30'55. CC       6548
Chance or destiny. by Giorgio
de Santillana. (Anon.)
31:128-9 My28'55. B      6549
Chancellor Robert R. Livingston
of New York: 1746-1813.
by George Dangerfield.
(Anon.) 36:244-5 D10'60.
B                        6550
A change of skin. by Carlos
Fuentes. Sam Hileman,
trans. (West) 44:143-5 Je8'68.
B                        6551
The changeling. by Thomas
Middleton and William Row-
ley. (McCarten) 40:99
N7'64. T                 6552

The changing face of beauty.
by Madge Garland. (Anon.)
33:243-4*N30'57. B        6553
The changing world of Soviet
Russia. by David J.
Dallin. (Anon.) 32:86-7*Jy
14'56. B                  6554
Channel dash. by Terence
Robertson. (Anon.) 34:76
Jy26'58. B                6555
Chaos and night. by Henry
de Montherlant. Terrence
Kilmartin, trans. (West)
40:117-18 Ja30'65. B   6556
Chaparral. by Valgene Massey.
(Malcolm) 34:74-8 S27'58.
T                         6557
The Chapman report. (Gill)
38:205 O27'62. CC         6558
Chappaqua. (Gill) 43:195-6
N11'67. CC                6559
Charade. (Gill) 39:196-7
D14'63. CC                6560
The charge of the light brigade.
(Kael) 44:166-8 O12'68. CC
                          6561
Charlatans. by Claude
Fredericks. (Oliver) 38:124-6
My5'62. T                 6562
Charles Darwin and his world.
by Julian Huxley and
H.B.D. Kettlewell. (Anon.)
41:95-6 Ag7'65. B         6563
Charles Dickens: a pictorial
biography. by J.B.
Priestley. (Anon.) 37:140
F10'62. B                 6564
Charles Evans Hughes and
American democratic states-
manship. by Dexter Perkins.
(Anon.) 32:154*S15'56.B 6565
Charles Francis Adams, Jr.,
1835-1915: the patrician at
bay. by Edward Chase
Kirkland. (Anon.) 42:190
Mr26'66. B                6566
Charles Péguy: a study in
integrity. by Marjorie
Villiers. (Anon.) 42:207-208
My21'66. B                6567
Charles Sumner and the coming
of the Civil War. by David
Donald. (Anon.) 36:184-5
O29'60. B                 6568

Charles Townshend. by Lewis
Namier and John Brooke.
(Anon.) 41:187-8 Mr20'65.
B                         6569
Charley is my darling. by
Joyce Cary. (West) 36:170-
6 Ap30'60. B              6570
Charlie Bubbles. (Kael) 44:
106-107 F24'68. CC        6571
Charlie Pocock and the princess.
by George Beardmore.
(Gilliatt) 45:113-15  Mr1'69.
B                         6572
Charly. (Kael) 44:170-2
O12'68. CC                6573
The charm of politics. by
R.H.S. Crossman. (Anon.)
35:170-1 Ap4'59. B        6574
The chase. (Gill) 42:108
F26'66. CC                6575
The château. by William Max-
well. (N. Bliven) 37:161-3
Mr25'61. B                6576
Château en suède. by Françoise
Sagan. (Flanner) 36:184-5
My7'60. T                 6577
Che! (Gilliatt) 45:83-4
Je14'69. CC               6578
The cheaters. (Oliver) 37:58-
61 Je24'61. CC            6579
Checkpoint. (McCarten) 33:90-1
S28'57. CC                6580
Cheers, Major Barlow. by Wil-
liam Fain. (Anon.) 34:143-4
Ap5'58. B                 6581
Chekhov. by Ernest J.
Simmons. (Moss) 39:138-50
Mr2'63. B                 6582
A Chekhov sketchbook. by
Luba Kadison and Helen Waren.
(Oliver) 38:94-5 Mr3'62.
T                         6583
Cher Antoine. by Jean Anouilh.
(Flanner) 45:196-200 N29'69.
T                         6584
Chéri. by Sidonie Gabrielle
Colette. (Tynan) 35:91-4
O24'59. T                 6585
The cherry orchard. by Anton
Chekhov. (Panter-Downes) 34:
80 Jy12'58 (Oliver) 38:118-20
N24'62; 41:54-6 F20'65 (Gill)
44:104 Mr30'68. T         6586

The chestnut tree. by Evelyn
Page. (Anon.) 40:204-205
My16'64. B                    6587
Chevalier, Maurice. (Gibbs)
31:91-2*O8'55. T              6588
Cheyenne Autumn. (Gill)
40:65 Ja2'65. CC             6589

Chez Pavan. by Richard
Llewellen. (Anon.) 34:64
Ag2'58. B                     6590
Chickamauga. (Gill) 43:94-6
Ap1'67. CC                    6591
The chief thing. by Nikolai
Evreinov. (Oliver) 39:88-
90 My11'63. T                6592
Chiefs. (Gilliatt) 45:121-5
Mr22'69. CC                  6593
The child buyer. by Paul Shyre.
(Oliver) 40:58-9 Ja2'65. T 6594
A child is waiting. (Gill)
39:146-7 F23'63. CC          6495
Child of fortune. by Guy
Bolton. (Gibbs) 32:124-5
N24'56. T                     6596
The child of Montmartre. by
Paul Léautaud. Humphrey
Hare, trans. (N. Bliven)
35:165-7 O3'59. B            6597
Child of our times. by Michel
del Castillo. (West) 34:
172-5 N1'58. B               6598
Child of the Revolution. by
Wolfgang Leonhard. C.M.
Woodhouse, trans. (Anon.)
34:153-4*Ap26'58. B          6599
The children at the gate. by
Edward Lewis Wallant.
(Balliett) 40:210-13 S19'64.
B                             6600
Children from their games.
by Irwin Shaw. (McCarten)
39:96 Ap20'63. T             6601
Children of Lucifer. by Dana
Faralla. (Anon.) 39:244-5
N9'63. B                      6602
Children of the mist: a true
and informal account of an
eighteenth-century scandal.
by Elizabeth Foster. (Anon.)
36:92 Ja28'61. B             6603
Children of violence: Volume I,
Martha Quest; Volume II, a

proper marriage. by Doris
Lessing. (Anon.) 40:122-3
Ja30'65. B                    6604
The children's hour. (Gill)
38:123-4 Mr17'62. CC   6605
China! (Gill) 41:119 Je5'65.
CC                            6606
China: empire of the 700
million. by Harry Hamm.
Victor Andersen, trans.
(Anon.) 42:223-4 S10'66. B
6607
China is near. (Kael) 43:90-5
Ja13'68. CC                  6608
China only yesterday: 1850-
1950, a century of change.
by Emily Hahn. (Anon.)
39:178-80 My11'63. B
6609
China under Communism.
By Richard L. Walker.
(Anon.) 31:87-8 Jy16'55.
B                             6610
The Chinese prime minister.
by Enid Bagnold. (McCarten)
39:69 Ja11'64. T             6611
Chinoiserie: the vision of
Cathay. by Hugh Honour.
(Anon.) 38:143-4 Mr31'62.
B                             6612
Chips with everything. by
Arnold Wesker. (McCarten)
39:89 O12'63. T              6613
Chips with everything. by
Arnold Wesker. (Panter-
Downes) 38:160-3 My12'62.
T                             6614
Chitty chitty bang bang. (Kael)
44:70-1 Ja4'69. CC          6615
Chocolates. by Ian Bernard.
(Oliver) 43:148-9 Ap22'67.
T                             6616
A choice of weapons. by Gordon
Parks. (Anon.) 41:159
F19'66. B                     6617
The christening party. by
Francis Steegmuller. (Anon.)
36:181 O1'60. B              6618
Christine. by Pearl S. Buck,
Charles K. Peck, Jr., Paul
Webster and Samuel Fain.
(Tynan) 36:114-16 My7'60.
T                             6619

Christophe: King of Haiti. by
Hubert Cole. (Anon.) 43:246-7
N11'67. B                6620
Christopher Marlow: his life
and work. by A.L. Rowse.
(Anon.) 40:124 Ja30'65. B
                          6621
Chronicle of a Summer. (Gill)
41:167 My8'65. CC      6622
Chronicle of Anna Magdalena
Bach. (Gilliatt) 44:145-7
S21'68. CC             6623
Churchill, taken from the
diaries of Lord Moran: the
struggle for survival, 1940-
1965. by Charles McMoran
Wilson Moran. (Anon.)
42:144 Je18'66 (Panter-
Downes) 42:73-4 Jy23'66. B
                          6624
Chushingura. Anon. (Gill) 45:90
S20'69. T              6625
Chushingura. (Gill) 39:170-1
O12'63; 42:152-3 O29'66.
CC                     6626
Cicero. by Upton Sinclair.
(Balliett) 37:94-5 F18'61.
T                      6627
Cimarron. (Angell) 37:126-9
F25'61. CC             6628
The Cincinnati kid. (Gill)
41:235 N13'65. CC      6629
Cindy. by Johnny Brandon,
Joe Sauter, and Mike Sawyer.
(Oliver) 40:136 Mr28'64.
T                      6630
Cinerama holiday. (McCarten)
31:125 F19'55. CC      6631
Cinerama's Russian adventure.
(Gill) 42:121-2 Ap16'66. CC
                          6632
Circle of love. (Gill) 41:104-
106 Ap3'65. CC         6633
Ciske, the rat. (Miller)
39:60 Ag10'63. CC      6634
Cities in Bezique. by Adrienne
Kennedy. (Oliver) 44:77
Ja25'69. T             6635
Cities in revolt. by Carl
Bridenbaugh. (Mumford)
32:102-106 Mr3'56. B   6636
Citizen Hearst. by W.A. Swan-
berg. (Anon.) 37:153 S9'61.
B                      6637

A citizen looks at Congress.
by Dean Acheson. (Anon.)
33:152-3 Ap20'57. B    6638
The city in history. by Lewis
Mumford. (Gill) 37:84-7
Ag12'61. B             6639
The city is the frontier.
by Charles Abrams. (Anon.)
41:246 N20'65. B       6640
City politics. by James Q.
Wilson and Edward C. Ban-
field. (Anon.) 39:78-9 Ja4'64.
B                      6641
The Civil War in pictures. by
Fletcher Pratt. (Anon.)
31:219-20*N12'55. B    6642
Civil War on the western border,
1854-65. by Jay Monaghan.
(Anon.) 31:87 Je25'55. B
                          6643
A claim in the hills. by James
Wickenden. (Anon.) 33:131
F23'57. B              6644
Clandestine on the morning
line. by Josh Greenfeld.
(Oliver) 37:118-21 N11'61.
T                      6645
The clap of silent thunder.
by Peter de Polnay. (Anon.)
33:89 F1'58. B         6646
Clarence King: a biography.
by Thurman Wilkins. (Anon.)
34:174-5 S20'58. B     6647
A clash of destinies: the Arab-
Jewish war and the founding
of the state of Israel. by
Jon Kimche and David Kimche.
(Anon.) 36:242 N26'60. B
                          6648
Clean young Englishman. by
John Gale. (Anon.) 42:165
Je4'66. B              6649
Clear skies. (Gill) 39:205-
206 D7'63. CC          6650
A clearing in the woods. by
Arthur Laurents. (Gibbs)
32:57-8 Ja19'57. T     6651
Clem Anderson. by R.V.
Cassill. (Balliett) 37:70 Jy
8'61. B                6652
Cleo from 5 to 7. (McCarten)
38:95-6 S15'62. CC     6653
A clergyman's daughter. by
George Orwell. (Anon.)

36:106 S3'60. B          6654

The climax. (Gill) 43:187-8
S16'67. CC               6655

Clochemerle les bains. by
Gabriel Chevallier. Xan
Fielding, trans. (Anon.) 41:74
Jy3'65. B                6656

The clock with four hands.
by James Leasor. (Anon.)
35:202 S12'59. B         6657

Clock without hands. by
Carson McCullers. (Balliett)
37:179 S23'61. B         6658

Cloportes. (Gill) 42:155-6
Ap30'66. CC              6659

Close to Colette. by Maurice
Goudeket. (Flanner) 32:119-
20 S29'56 (W. Maxwell) 33:
116-25 Je15'57. B        6660

Cloud 7. by Max Wilk. (Gibbs)
34:64-5 F22'58. T        6661

The coach with six insides.
by James Joyce and Teiji
Ito. (Oliver) 38:150-1 D8'62.
T                        6662

A coat of many colours. by Herbert
Read. (Anon.) 32:147-8*Ap28
'56. B                   6663

Coat upon a stick. by Norman
Fruchter. (Anon.) 38:133
Ja26'63. B               6664

Cock-a-doodle dandy. by Sean
O'Casey. (Gill) 44:44-9
F1'69. T                 6665

Cock-a-doodle dandy. by Sean
O'Casey. (Malcolm) 34:100-
102 N22'58. T            6666

Cockatrice. by Wolf
Mankowitz. (Anon.) 39:175-6
Ap27'63. B               6667

Cockerell. by Wilfrid Blunt.
(Anon.) 41:109 Je26'65. B
                         6668

The cocktail party. by T.S.
Eliot. (Gill) 44:159-60
O19'68. T                6669

Coco. by Alan Jay Lerner and
André Previn. (Gill) 45:38
D27'69. T                6670

A coffin for King Charles: the
trial and execution of King
Charles I. by C.V. Wedgwood.
(Anon.) 40:226-7 O3'64. B
                         6671

The coin of Carthage. by
Winifred Bryher. (Balliett)
39:69 Jy6'63. B          6672

The cold wind and the warm. by
S.N. Behrman. (Tynan)
34:69-70 D20'58. T       6673

A cold wind in August. (Gill)
37:37-8 Ag5'61. CC       6674

Collages. by Anaïs Nin. (Anon.)
40:244 D12'64. B         6675

The collapse of the third Republic: an inquiry into the
fall of France in 1940. by
William L. Shirer. (Anon.)
45:211 N29'69. B         6676

The collected essays, journalism
and letters. by George
Orwell. (Steiner) 45:139-51
Mr29'69. B               6677

Collected poems. by John
Betjeman. (Bogan) 35:169-70
Ap18'59. B               6678

Collected poems. by Lawrence
Durrell. (Anon.) 37:172 Mr11
'61. B                   6679

Collected Poems 1955. by
Robert Graves. (Bogan)
31:63-4*Jy30'55. B       6680

Collected poems. by Rolfe
Humphries. (Bogan) 43:161
Mr4'67. B                6681

Collected poems. by Patrick
Kavanagh. (Bogan)
41:194-6 Ap10'65. B      6682

Collected poems. 1925-48. by
Louis MacNeice. (Bogan)
40:180 Ap11'64. B        6683

Collected poems. by Stephen
Spender. (Bogan) 31:124
Ap30'55. B               6684

The collected poems of Edith
Sitwell. by Edith Sitwell.
(Anon.) 31:120 Mr5'55. B
                         6685

The collected poems of Hugh
MacDiarmid.  by Hugh
MacDiarmid. (Bogan) 38:238-
41·N17'62. B             6686

The collected poems of Theodore
Roethke. by Theodore Roethke.
(Anon.) 42:239-40 S24'66.
B                        6687

The collected poems of Wilfred
Owen. by Wilfred Owen.

C. Day Lewis, ed. (Anon.)
40:188 My23'64. B          6688

Collected short fiction 1892-
1912. by Willa Cather. (Anon.)
41:244 O23'65. B          6689

The collected works of Jane
Bowles. by Jane Bowles.
(S. Lardner) 43:174-6
My20'67. B          6690

The collection. by Harold
Pinter. (Oliver) 38:149-50
D8'62. T          6691

The collector. by John Fowles.
(Balliett) 39:192-3 S28'63.
B          6692

The collector. (Oliver) 41:80
Je26'65. CC          6693

The collectors: Dr. Claribel
and Miss Etta Cone. by Barbara Pollack and Gertrude
Stein. (Anon.) 38:161-2
F16'63. B          6694

College bowl. (J. Lardner)
35:62-7 Ja2'60. TV     6695

A collier's Friday night. by
D. H. Lawrence. (Panter-
Downes) 44:101 My11'68. T
6696

Collision course. by Jules
Feiffer, et al. (Oliver)
44:74-5 My18'68. T     6697

The color curtain: a report
on the Bandung Conference. by
Richard Wright. (Anon.) 32:
102-103*Mr31'56. B     6698

Color of darkness. by James
Purdy. (Oliver) 39:91-2
O12'63. T          6699

The comancheros. (Gill)
37:235 D9'61. CC     6700

Come back, Africa. (McCarten)
36:149 Ap16'60. CC     6701

Come back, Dr. Caligari. by
Donald Barthelme. (Anon.)
40:141-2 Je13'64. B     6702

Come blow your horn. by Neil
Simon. (McCarten) 37:93-4
Mr4'61. T          6703

Come blow your horn. (Gill)
39:54-6 Je15'63. CC     6704

Come dance with me. by
Ninette de Valois. (Anon.)
34:156 Mr15'58. B     6705

Come dance with me. (Gill)
36:205-206 N12'60. CC     6706

Come fill the cup. by Rosalind
Wade. (Anon.) 32:142
*S8'56. B          6707

Come live with me. by Lee
Minoff and Stanley Price.
(Oliver) 42:93 F4'67. T
6708

Come on strong. by Garson
Kanin. (McCarten) 38:180-2
O13'62. T          6709

Come Summer. by Will Holt
and David Baker. (Gill)
45:99 Mr29'69. T     6710

Come September. (Gill)
37:88 S16'61. CC     6711

The comedians. (Gill) 43:
197 N11'67. CC     6712

The comedy man. by Douglas
Hayes. (N. Bliven) 37:167-8
Mr11'61. B          6713

Comes a day. by Speed
Lamkin. (J. Lardner) 34:
103-104 N15'58. T     6714

Comfort me with apples. by
Peter DeVries. (Balliett)
32:157-61*My12'56. B  6715

The comforters. by Muriel
Spark. (Balliett) 33:101 Ja18
'58; 35:127-9 Je13'59. B
6716

The comic. (Kael) 45:190-5
D6'69. CC          6717

Coming apart. (Kael) 45:142
N1'69. CC          6718

The coming explosion in
Latin America. by Gerald
Clark. (Anon.) 39:120-1
Je1'63. B          6719

The coming fury. by Bruce
Catton. (Anon.) 37:223
N4'61. B          6720

Coming of age. by Babette
Deutsch. (Bogan) 35:236
N28'59. B          6721

Coming of age in America:
growth and acquiescence. by
Edgar Z. Friedenberg.
(Anon.) 41:80 Jy31'65. B
6722

The coming of the New Deal. by
Arthur M. Schlesinger, Jr.

(Anon.) 35:173-4 Ap18'59.
B                           6723
The coming of war. by Albert
Z. Carr. (Anon.) 36:118 Ja
14'61. B                    6724
A coming-out party. (Balliett)
38:69 Ag18'62. CC          6725
Commander-1. by Peter
George. (N. Bliven) 41:89-94
Ag7'65. B                   6726
Commando extraordinary. by
Charles Foley. (Anon.) 31:
168*O22'55. B               6727
Comment c'est. by Samuel
Beckett. (Flanner) 37:100
Mr4'61. B                   6728
Comment s'en débarrasser.
by Eugène Ionesco. (Flanner)
33:56 Ja4'58. T             6729
The commissioner. by Richard
Dougherty. (Anon.) 38:243
D8'62. B                    6730
Commitment. by Willard Uphaus.
(Anon.) 39:72-3 Jy6'63. B
                            6731
The Committee. Anon. (McCarten)
40:160 S26'64. T            6732
A commodity of dreams. by
Howard Nemerov. (Anon.)
35:174 Mr14'59. B           6733
The common muse: an anthology
of popular British ballad
poetry, XVth-XXth century.
Vivian de Sola Pinto and
Edwin Allan Rodway, eds.
(Anon.) 33:199-200 N2'57.
B                           6734
Common sense and the fifth
amendment. by Sidney Hook.
(Anon.) 33:163-4 My11'57. B
                            6735
Common sense and world affairs.
by Dorothy Fosdick. (Anon.)
31:143-4 Ap2'55. B          6736
The Communist world and ours.
by Walter Lippmann. (Anon.)
35:147 F21'59. B            6737
The compact history of the
United States Navy. by
Fletcher Pratt. (Anon.) 33:
95-6 Jy13'57. B             6738
Companions of the holiday. by
Donald Richie. (Anon.) 45:

177-8 Ap19'69. B            6739
Company of strangers. by
Anthony Heckstall-Smith.
(Anon.) 36:207-208 O15'60. B
                            6740
The competitor. by Thomas Bont-
ly. (Anon.) 42:189 Mr26
'66. B                      6741
The complaisant lover. by
Graham Greene. (Panter-
Downes) 35:80 Ag29'59.
(McCarten) 37:117-18 N11'61.
T                           6742
The compleat imbiber. Cyril
Ray, ed. (Anon.) 33:203
O12'57. B                   6743
The complete Bolivian diaries
of Ché Guevara and other
captured documents, by
Ernesto Ché Guevara. Daniel
James, ed. (Anon.) 44:139
S7'68. B                    6744
The complete poems of D. H.
Lawrence. by D. H. Lawrence.
Vivian de Sola Pinto and
F. Warren Roberts, eds.
(Anon.) 41:204 Mr13'65. B
                            6745
The complete poetical works of
Amy Lowell. by Amy Lowell.
(Anon.) 32:104*Mr31'56. B
                            6746
A complete state of death. by
John Gardner. (Anon.) 45:204
O11'69. B                   6747
The complete walker. by Colin
Fletcher. (Anon.) 44:250
D7'68. B                    6748
The complete works of Nathanael
West. by Nathanael West.
(Podhoretz) 33:156-65 My18'57.
B                           6749
Compulsion. by Robert Thom.
(Gibbs) 33:83-4 N2'57. T
                            6750
Compulsion. (McCarten) 35:163
Ap11'59. CC                 6751
The concept. by Lawrence
Sacharow. (Oliver) 44:76
My18'68. T                  6752
Conciousness in Concord: the
text of Thoreau's hitherto
"Lost Journal," 1840-41.

by Henry David Thoreau.
Perry Miller, ed. (Anon.)
34:83-4 Ag9'58. B      6753
The concise encyclopedia of
crime and criminals. Harold
Scott, ed. (Anon.) 37:246
N25'61. B              6754
The concubine. by Norah Lofts.
(Anon.) 39:91 Jy20'63. B
                       6755
The condemned of Altona. by
Jean-Paul Sartre. (McCarten)
41:110-12 F12'66. T    6756
Conerico was here to stay.
by Frank Gagliano. (Oliver)
41:108 Mr13'65. T      6757
A confederate girl's diary.
by Sarah Morgan. (Wilson)
31:176-80*N5'55. B     6758
Confess, Dr. Corda! (Gill)
36:103-104 O29'60. CC
                       6759
The confession. by Mario Soldati.
(Anon.) 34:138-9 F22'58.
B                      6760
The confessions of Nat Turner.
by William Styron. (Steiner)
43:236-44 N25'67. B    6761
The confessions of Zeno. by
Italo Svevo. (Steiner) 43:141-3
Je3'67. B              6762
Confrontation: the student re-
bellion and the universities.
Daniel Bell and Irving
Kristol, eds. (Anon.) 45:139-40
My24'69. B             6763
Congressman from Mississippi.
by Frank E. Smith. (Anon.)
40:167-8 D19'64. B     6764
The conjugal bed. (Gill) 39:
112 S21'63. CC         6765
The connection. by Jack
Gelber. (Malcolm) 35:126-
9 O10'59. T            6766
The connection. (Gill) 38:210
N17'62. CC             6767
The conquering hero. by Larry
Gelbart. (McCarten) 36:64
Ja28'61. T             6768
The conqueror. (McCarten)
32:104*Ap7'56. CC      6769
Conquest by man. by Paul
Herrmann. Michael Bullock,

trans. (Anon.) 31:144-5
Ap2'55. B              6770
The conquest of Peru. by
William H. Prescott. (Anon.)
33:83-4 Ag31'57. B     6771
The conscience of the rich.
by C.P. Snow. (Podhoretz)
34:143-6 My10'58. B    6772
Conservatism in America. by
Clinton Rossiter. (Anon.)
31:157-8 Ap16'55. B    6773
The conservative enemy. by
C.A.R. Crosland. (Anon.)
39:178 Ap27'63. B      6774
Conservatives in power: a
study in frustration. by Edwin
L. Dale, Jr. (Anon.) 36:143-4
F27'60. B              6775
Conspiracy among generals. by
Wilhelm von Schramm.
R.T. Clark, trans. & ed.
(Anon.) 33:131-2 F23'57.
B                      6776
The conspirators: a study of
the coup d'état. by D.J.
Goodspeed. (Anon.) 38:179
Mr24'62. B             6777
The constant circle: H.L.
Mencken and his friends. by
Sara Mayfield. (Wilson)
45:110-14 My31'69. B   6778
The constant image. by Marcia
Davenport. (Anon.) 35:122-3
Ja23'60. B             6779
The constant prince. by
Alfredo Puigvert Calderón de
la Barca. (Oliver) 45:139-41
O25'69. T              6780
Contact on Gorky Street, by
Greville Wynne. (Anon.)
43:136 F17'68. B       6781
Contemporary writers. by
Virginia Woolf. (Anon.)
42:229-30 S17'66. B    6782
Contempt. (Gill) 40:73-4 D26
'64. CC                6783
The contenders. by John Wain.
(Balliett) 34:103-104 My31'58.
B                      6784
Contexts of criticism. by Harry
Levin. (Anon.) 33:75-6*Jy27
'57. B                 6785

The contrary experience. by
Herbert Read. (Anon.) 39:72
Jy6'63. B                    6786
Contribution. by Ted Shine.
(Oliver) 45:131 Ap12'69. T
                             6787
Conversations with André Gide.
by Claude Mauriac. Michael
Lebeck, trans. (Anon.)
41:111-12 Ja8'66. B          6788
Conversations with Stalin. by
Milovan Djilas. Michael B.
Petrovich, trans. (Anon.)
38:163 My26'62. B            6789
Conversations with Toscanini. by
B. H. Haggin. (Anon.) 35:
173-4 Ap11'59. B             6790
A cook for Mr. General. by
Steven Gethers. (McCarten)
37:135-7 O28'61. T           6791
Cool hand Luke. (Gill)
43:196-7 N11'67. CC          6792
The cool world. (Gill) 40:
171-2 Ap25'64. CC            6793
Cooper's Creek. by Alan
Moorehead. (Anon.) 40:182-3
Mr7'64. B                    6794
"Cop" as a word. (J. Lardner)
35:55-61 Jy18'59. TV         6795
Cop-out. by John Guare. (Gill)
45:98 Ap19'69. T             6796
Copper and brass. by Ellen
Violett, David Craig, and
David Baker. (Gibbs) 33:98-
100 O26'57. T                6797
Copper beech. by Ariadne
Thompson. (Anon.) 36:96
Jy16'60. B                   6798
Copper town: changing Africa.
by Hortense Powdermaker.
(Anon.) 38:99 Ja5'63. B
                             6799
Coppermine journey. by
Samuel Hearne. Farley
Mowat, ed. (Anon.) 34:100
Jy12'58. B                   6800
Cora Crane. by Lillian Gilkes.
(Liebling) 37:48-72 Ag5'61.
B                            6801
The coral barrier. by Pierre
Gascar. (West) 37:94
Ag26'61. B                   6802
Corbie. by Robert Newman.

(Anon.) 42:192 Ap23'66. B
                             6803
Cork Street, next to the
hatter's. by Pamela Hansford
Johnson. (Anon.) 41:246
D11'65. B                    6804
A corner of the bed. by Allen
Jack Lewis. (Oliver) 45:97
Mr8'69. T                    6805
A Cornish waif's story. by
Emma Smith. (Anon.) 32:
83-4*Je23'56. B              6806
Coronation Everest. by James
Morris. (Anon.) 34:208-209
O18'58. B                    6807
The corridor. by Edmund
Fuller. (Anon.) 39:165-6
My25'63. B                   6808
Corridors of power. by C. P.
Snow. (Anon.) 40:243-4
N7'64. B                     6809
The corrupted land: the social
morality of modern America.
by Fred J. Cook. (Anon.)
42:144 Je18'66. B            6810
Corruption in the palace of
justice. by Ugo Betti.
(Oliver) 39:100-102 O19'63.
T                            6811
Corunna. by Christopher Hib-
bert. (Anon.) 37:168 S30'61.
B                            6812
The council of Egypt. by
Leonardo Sciascia. Adrienne
Foulke, trans. (West) 42:206-
208 Mr19'66. B               6813
Count roller skates. by
Thomas Sancton. (Anon.)
32:73 Ja5'57. B              6814
Count your blessings.
(McCarten) 35:154-7 My2'59.
CC                           6815
Countdown for decision. by John
B. Medaris and Arthur
Gordon. (Anon.) 36:193
O22'60. B                    6816
Counterfeit. by Sonia Cole.
(Anon.) 33:179-80 Ap13'57.
B                            6817
The counterfeit constable. (Gill)
42:161 D3'66. CC             6818
The counterfeit traitor. by
Alexander Klein. (Anon.) 34:
150 Ap19'58. B               6819

The counterfeit traitor. (Gill)
38:142 Ap28'62. CC          6820
The countess. by Hans Habe.
Catherine Hutter, trans.
(Anon.) 39:234 D14'63. B
6821
A countess from Hong Kong.
(Gill) 43:153 Mr25'67. CC
6822
Counting my steps: an auto-
biography. by Jakov Lind.
(Anon.) 45:214-15 O18'69. B
6823
The country blues. by Samuel
B. Charters. (Anon.)
35:244-5 N28'59. B          6824
The country girls. by Edna
O'Brien. (Anon.) 36:178
Ap30'60. B          6825
The country house. by Desmond
Greig. (Anon.) 44:123 F15'69.
B          6826
A country scandal. by Anton
Chekhov. Alex Szogyi, adapt.
(Malcolm) 36:94-6 My14'60.
T          6827
The country wife. by William
Wycherley. (Gibbs) 33:95-6
D7'57 (McCarten) 41:154 D
18'65. T          6828
The countrywoman. by Paul
Smith. (Anon.) 37:177 S16'61.
B          6829
Coup d'etat: a practical hand-
book. by Edward Luttwak.
(Anon.) 45:84 Jy19'69. B
6830
Courage for every day. (Gilliatt)
43:57-8 Jy1'67. CC          6831
The courage of his convictions.
by Tony Parker and
Robert Allerton. (Anon.)
38:183 S15'62. B          6832
The courage to be happy. by
Dorothy Thompson. (Anon.)
33:224 D14'57. B          6833
The court and the castle. by
Rebecca West. (Anon.) 34:
140 F22'58. B          6834
The court jester. (McCarten)
31:93*F11'56. CC          6835
The court-martial of Billy
Mitchell. (McCarten) 31:36

*D31'55. CC          6836
The courtship of Mr. Lincoln.
by Ruth Painter Randall.
(Anon.) 33:137 Mr9'57.
B          6837
The cousins. (McCarten)
35:120*D19'59. CC          6838
Cowboy. (McCarten) 34:107
Mr1'58. CC          6839
Cow-boys and colonels. by
Edmond Mandat-Grancy.
William Conn, trans. (Anon.)
39:191-2 Ap6'63. B          6840
A crackling of thorns. by
John Hollander. (Bogan) 34:
236-7 D6'58. B          6841
The cradle of Neptune. by
John Lodwick. (Anon.)
31:116-17 Mr5'55. B          6842
The craft of intelligence. by
Allen Dulles. (Anon.)
39:215 O12'63. B          6843
The cranes are flying.
(McCarten) 36:88-90 Ap2
'60. CC          6844
Cranks. by John Cranko and
John Addison. (Gibbs) 32:90-
1 D8'56. T          6845
Crazy desire. (Balliett)
40:93 Jy18'64. CC          6846
The crazy quilt. (Gill)
42:203-204 O15'66. CC 6847
Creezy. by Félicien Marceau.
(Flanner) 45:202 N29'69.
B          6848
Creditors. by August Strind-
berg. (Oliver) 37:72-3
F 3'62. T          6849
The crime. by Stephen
Longstreet. (Anon.) 36:
199-200 Mr12'60. B          6850
Crime and the committee. (J.
Lardner) 34:85-7 Mr8'58.
TV          6851
The crime of Monsieur Lange.
(Gilliatt) 44:54-5 Ag31'68.
CC          6852
The crime of punishment. by
Karl Menninger. (Coles) 45:
63-7 Ja3'70. B          6853
The crippled tree. by Suyin
Han. (Anon.) 41:233 O9'65.
B          6854

The crisis of the Negro intellectual. by Harold Cruse. (Anon.) 43:112 F3'68. B 6855

Criss-crossing. by Philip Magdalany. (Gill) 45:56 Ja31'70. T 6856

The Criterion book of modern American verse. W. H. Auden, ed. (Bogan) 33:111 Mr2'57. B 6857

A critical history of English literature. by David Daiches. (Anon.) 36:245 N26'60. B 6858

Critic's choice. by Ira Levin. (McCarten) 36:38-40 D24'60. T 6859

The cross of iron. by Willi Heinrich. (West) 32:113 *Je16'56. B 6860

Cross of the living. (Gill) 38:149 F16'63. CC 6861

The crossing. by Jean Reverzy. Edward Hyams, trans. (West) 32:173-4 O27'56. B 6862

Crossroads of power: essays on eighteenth century England. by Lewis Namier. (Anon.) 39:183 Mr23'63. B 6863

Crow. by Donald Stewart. (Balliett) 35:170-3 Mr21'59. B 6864

A crowd of voices. by Richard Lortz. (Anon.) 34:209-10 N8'58. B 6865

The crowning privilege: collected essays on poetry. by Robert Graves. (Anon.) 32:72*Ag11 '56. B 6866

The crucial decade. by Eric F. Goldman. (Anon.) 32:173-4 S22'56. B 6867

Crusade in Asia. by Carlos P. Romulo. (Anon.) 31: 173-4 My14'55. B 6868

Crusader in crinoline. by Forrest Wilson. (Wilson) 31:125-41*S10'55. B 6869

Cry for happy. (Angell) 37: 166 Mr11'61. CC 6870

A cry from the streets. (McCarten) 35:92-4 Mr7'59. CC 6871

The cry of jazz. by Warren Miller and Robert Rossen. (Tynan) 36:120-2 Mr5'60. T 6872

A cry of players. by William Gibson. (Gill) 44:122-4 N23'68. T 6873

Cry terror! (McCarten) 34:74 My24'58. CC 6874

The crystal heart. by William Archibald and Baldwin Bergersen. (Malcolm) 36:104-106 F27'60. T 6875

The Cuban thing. by Jack Gelber. (Gill) 44:95-6 O5 '68. T 6876

Cue for passion. by Elmer Rice. (Tynan) 34:116-17 D6'58. T 6877

Cul-de-sac. (Gill) 42:115 N12'66. CC 6878

Culture and commitment: a study of the generation gap. by Margaret Mead. (Anon.) 45:131 F14'70. B 6879

Culture under canvas: the story of tent Chautauqua. by Harry P. Harrison and Karl Detzer. (Anon.) 34:159-60 My17'58. B 6880

Curiosities from Parliament. by Stanley Hyland. (Anon.) 32:153-4*S15'56. B 6881

Curiosities of medicine: an assembly of medical diversions, 1552-1962. Berton Roueché, ed. (Anon.) 39:160 S7'63. B 6882

A curious evening with Gypsy Rose Lee. by Gypsy Rose Lee. (Balliett) 37:118-20 My20'61. T 6883

Currahee! by Donald R. Burgett. (Anon.) 43:151 Je10'67. B 6884

The curse of the misbegotten: a tale of the House of O'Neill. by Croswell Bowen. (Anon.) 35:93-4 Je27'59. B 6885

The curtain falls. by Maurice
Druon. Humphrey Hare,
trans. (Anon.) 36:178-9 Mr
19'60. B                    6886
The Custer wolf. by Roger
Caras. (Anon.) 42:174-5
Ap2'66. B                   6887
Custer's fall. by David
Humphreys Miller. (Anon.)
33:201 O12'57. B            6888
Cut of the axe. by Sheppard
Kerman. (Tynan) 35:92-4
F13'60. T                   6889
Cypress and acacia. by Vernon
Watkins. (Bogan) 36:154
Mr26'60. B                  6890
The cypresses believe in God.
by José María Gironella.
(West) 31:120-2 My28'55. B
                            6891
Cyrano de Bergerac. by Edmond
Rostand. (Gill) 44:129-30
My4'68. T                   6892

-D-

The D.A.R. by Margaret Gibbs.
(Anon.) 45:116 Je14'69. B
                            6893
D.H. Lawrence. by Edward
Nehls. (Anon.) 34:150 Ap19'58.
B                           6894
D.H. Lawrence: a composite
biography. Edward Nehls, ed.
(Anon.) 33:198-200 O5'57 (West)
35:157-66 Mr7'59. B         6895
D.H. Lawrence: a personal
record. by Jessie Chambers.
(Anon.) 41:74-6 Jy3'65. B
                            6896
D.H. Lawrence: an unprofessional
study. by Anaïs Nin. (Anon.)
40:136 My30'64. B           6897
D.H. Lawrence: novelist. by F.R.
Leavis. (Anon.) 32:132
*My26'56. B                 6898
D.H. Lawrence: selected literary
criticism. by D.H. Lawrence.
Anthony Beal, ed. (Anon.)
32:211-12 N3'56. B          6899
Daddy goodness. by Richard
Wright and Louis Sapin.
(Oliver) 44:65 Je15'68. T

Daddy long legs. (McCarten)    6900
31:145 My14'55. CC          6901
The daffodil sky. by H.E.
Bates. (Anon.) 32:74*
Jy21'56. B                  6902
Daily life of the Etruscans.
by Jacques Heurgon. James
Kirkup, trans. (Anon.)
40:91-2 Ag8'64. B           6903
The daisies. (Gilliatt) 43:56-7
Jy1'67. CC                  6904
Dames at sea. by George
Haimsohn and Robin Miller.
(Oliver) 44:60-1 Ja4'69.
T                           6905
Damn the defiant! (Gill)
38:141 S29'62. CC           6906
Damn Yankees. by George
Abbott and Douglass Wallop.
(Gibbs) 31:132-4 My14'55. T
                            6907
Damn Yankees. (McCarten)
34:158-9 O4'58. CC          6908
The damned. (Kael) 45:61-2
Ja3'70. CC                  6909
A dance in the sun. by Dan
Jacobson. (West) 32:77-8
*Je30'56. B                 6910
Dance little lady. (McCarten)
31:48*Ja7'56. CC            6911
The dance of death. by
Jeremy Potter. (Anon.)
45:152 Je7'69. B            6912
The dance of death. by
August Strindberg. (Panter-
Downes) 43:158-63 Ap15'67
(Tynan) 44:150-2 N9'68.
T                           6913
A dancer in darkness. by David
Stacton. (Anon.) 38:215-16
O27'62. B                   6914
The dandy: Brummell to Beer-
bohm. by Ellen Moers. (Anon.)
36:195-6 My7'60. B          6915
A dandy in aspic. by Derek
Marlowe. (N. Bliven) 42:
160-1 F11'67. B             6916
Danger my ally. by F.A. Mit-
chell-Hedges. (Anon.) 31:
94-5*Ag27'55. B             6917
Dangerfield. by Barnaby Conrad.
(Anon.) 37:206 O28'61. B
                            6918

A dangerous innocence. by
Victoria Lincoln. (Anon.)
34:150*Ap26'58. B          6919
Daninoscope. by Pierre
Daninos. (Flanner) 39:133
O12'63. B          6920
Dans un mois, dans un an.
see In a month, in a year.
6921
Danton's death. by Georg
Buechner. Herbert Blau,
adapt. (McCarten) 41:108-10
O30'65. T          6922
Daphne in cottage D. by
Stephen Levi. (McCarten)
43:105-106 O28'67. T     6923
The dark and the light. by
Elio Vittorini. (West)
37:96 Ag26'61. B          6924
The dark at the top of the
stairs. By William Inge.
(Gibbs) 33:83-4 D14'57. T
6925
The dark at the top of the
stairs. (Gill) 36:167-8
O1'60. CC          6926
Dark corners. by Stanley
Koven. (Oliver) 40:165
My16'64. T          6927
Dark ghetto: dilemmas of social
power. by Kenneth Clark
(Hentoff) 41:71-4 Jy31'65.
B          6928
The dark glasses. by Francis
King. (Anon ) 32:135*Mr24'56.
B          6929
The dark is light enough. by
Christopher Fry. (Gibbs)
31:67-8 Mr5'55. T     6930
A darker flower. by Tim
Kelly. (Oliver) 39:138-9
Mr16'63. T          6931
Darling. (Gill) 41:66 Ag7'65.
CC          6932
The darling Daisy affair.
by Theo Lang. (Anon.)
42:67-8 D24'66. B     6933
Darling of the day. by
Jule Styne and E.Y.
Harburg. (Gill) 43:77-8 F3
'68. T          6934
Darwin and the Darwinian
revolution. by Gertrude

Himmelfarb. (West) 35:188-
201 O10'59. B          6935
The Darwin reader. by
Charles Darwin. Marston
Bates and Philips Humphrey,
eds.(Anon.) 32:128 F9'57.
B          6936
Dateline-Peking. by Frederick
Nossal. (Anon.) 38:122-3
F2'63. B          6937
The daughter in law. by
D.H. Lawrence. (Panter-
Downes) 44:101-102 My11'68.
T          6938
Daughter of silence. by
Morris L. West. (Anon.)
37:205 D16'61. B          6939
Daughter of silence. by
Morris L. West (McCarten)
37:160-2 D9'61. T     6940
Daughters and rebels. by
Jessica Mitford. (Panter-
Downes) 36:89-96 Jy16'60.
B          6941
The daughters of Jasper Clay.
by Lucille Fletcher. (Anon.)
34:124-5 Mr29'58. B     6942
The daughters of necessity. by
Peter S. Feibleman. (Bal-
liett) 35:203-204 O10'59. B
6943
David and Lisa. (Gill) 38:
100-101 Ja12'63. CC     6944
The David show. by A.R.
Gurney, Jr. (Oliver) 44:115-
16 N9'68; 45:63 Jy5'69. T
6945
Davy Crockett, king of the wild
frontier. (McCarten) 31:
102 Je4'55. CC          6946
Dawn like thunder: the Barbary
wars and the birth of the U.S.
Navy. by Glenn Tucker.
(Anon.) 39:214 O12'63. B
6947
The day and the hour. (Gill)
40:123 F29'64. CC     6948
A day by the sea. by N.C.
Hunter. (Gibbs) 31:89-91
*O8'55. T          6949
A day in late September. by
Merle Miller. (Balliett) 39:
76-7 Ja4'64. B          6950

A day in the death of Joe Egg.
by Peter Nichols. (Panter-
Downes) 43:84-5 Ag19'67
(Gill) 43:86 F10'68 (Tynan)
44:130-2 N9'68. T        6951
Day of absence. by Douglas
Turner Ward. (McCarten)
41:50 D25'65. T          6952
Day of infamy. by Walter
Lord. (Anon.) 33:165 Ap6'57.
B                        6953
The day of the tortoise. by
Pietro Garinei and Sandro
Giovannini. (Flanner)
41:220-1 O16'65. T       6953a
Day of trinity. by Lansing
Lamont. (Anon.) 41:245-6
O23'65. B                6954
The day on fire. by James
Ramsey Ullman. (Anon.)
34:201 O11'58. B         6955
The day the Earth caught fire.
(Gill) 38:149 Mr24'62. CC
                         6956
The day the fish came out.
(Gill) 43:160 O14'67. CC
                         6957
The day the money stopped.
by Brendan Gill. (Behrman)
32:103-105 Ja26'57. B    6958
The day the money stopped.
by Maxwell Anderson and
Brendan Gill. (Gibbs) 34:
56-8 Mr1'58. T           6959
The day the whores came out
to play tennis. by Arthur
Kopit. (Oliver) 41:146-7
Mr27'65. T               6960
The day they killed the king.
by Hugh Ross Williamson.
(Anon.) 33:149 S7'57. B
                         6961
The day they shook the plum
tree. by Arthur H. Lewis.
(Anon.) 39:178-9 Ap27'63.
B                        6962
Daybreak in Iran. by Schulze-
Holthus. Mervyn Savill,
trans. (Anon.) 32:81-2*
Je23'56. B               6963
Daylight and dark. by Agnes
Adams Fisher. (Anon.) 31:
146*O29'55. B            6964

The days and nights of Beebee
Fenstermaker. by William
Snyder. (Oliver) 38:101-102
S29'62. T                6965
The days of Henry Thoreau.
by Walter Harding. (Anon.)
41:118-19 Ja15'66. B     6966
Days of the phoenix: the nine-
teen-twenties I remember. by
Van Wyck Brooks. (Anon.)
33:178-9 Ap13'57. B      6967
Days of thrills and laughter.
(Oliver) 37:165 Ap8'61. CC
                         6968
Days of wine and roses. (Gill)
38:121-2 Ja26'63. CC     6969
De Gaulle. by François Mauriac.
Richard Howard, trans.
(Anon.) 42:191 Mr26'66. B
                         6970
de Sade. (Kael) 45:160-1 O11'69.
CC                       6971
de Sade illustrated. by Josef
Bush. (Oliver) 45:114 My24'69.
T                        6972
The dead are mine. by James
E. Ross. (Anon.) 39:242 D7
'63. B                   6973
Dead heat on a merry-go-round.
(Gill) 42:164 O22'66. CC
                         6974
The Dead Sea scriptures.
Theodor H. Gaster, trans.
(Anon.) 33:138-9 Mr9'57. B
                         6975
The Dead Sea scrolls. by J. M.
Allegro. (Anon.) 33:137-8
Mr9'57. B                6976
The Dead Sea scrolls. by
Millar Burrows. (Anon.)
32:145-6*Ap28'56. B      6977
Dead souls. by Mikhail
Bulgakov. (Oliver) 40:76-80
F13'65. T                6978
Deadfall. by Leonard Lee.
(Gibbs) 31:82-4*N5'55. T
                         6979
Deadlier than the male.
(McCarten) 33:88 O19'57.
CC                       6980
The deadlock of democracy:
four-party politics in America.
by James MacGregor Burns.

(Anon.) 39:150-1 F23'63.
B                    6981
The deadly affair. (Gill)
42:98 F4'67. CC       6982
The deadly game. by James
Yaffe. (Tynan) 35:89-90
F13'60 (Oliver) 42:72 F26
'66. T               6983
Dear beast. by Nancy Hale.
(N. Bliven) 35:241-4 N14'59.
B                    6984
Dear Bertrand Russell...
by Barry Feinberg and Ronald
Kasrils, ed. (Anon.) 45:178
N1'69. B             6985
Dear John. (Gill) 42:114
Mr12'66. CC          6986
Dear liar. by Jerome
Kilty. (Tynan) 36:80-1 Mr
26'60. T             6987
Dear me, the sky is falling.
by Leonard Spigelgass.
(McCarten) 39:132 Mr2'63.
T                    6988
Dear preceptor: the life and
times of Thomas Wentworth
Higginson. by Anna Mary
Wells. (Anon.) 39:112 Je22'63.
B                    6989
Dear world. by Jerome
Lawrence, Robert E. Lee
and Jerry Herman. (Gill)
44:90 F15'69. T      6990
Dearest child: letters between
Queen Victoria and the
Princess Royal, 1858-61. by
Victoria, Queen of Great
Britain and Victoria Adelaide
Mary Louisa. Roger Fulford,
ed. (N. Bliven) 41:82-4
Jy10'65. B           6991
"Dearest Emmie": Thomas
Hardy's letters to his first
wife. by Thomas Hardy.
Carl J. Weber, ed. (Anon.)
39:117-18 Ja18'64. B  6992
Dearest mama: letters between
Queen Victoria and the
Crown Princess of Prussia,
1861-64. by Victoria, Queen
of Great Britain and Victoria
Adelaide Mary Louisa. Roger
Fulford, ed. (Anon.) 45:96
Ag9'69. B            6993

Death and the Supreme Court.
by Barrett Prettyman, Jr.
(Anon.) 37:212 O21'61. B
                     6994
Death at an early age. by
Jonathan Kozol. (Hentoff)
44:166 Mr16'68. B     6995
Death, grief, and mourning.
by Geoffrey Gorer. (Anon.)
41:246-7 O23'65. B    6996
Death in life. by Robert Jay
Lifton. (Steiner) 44:76-80
Ag3'68. B            6997
A death in the family. by
James Agee. (Macdonald)
33:224-41 N16'57. B   6998
Death of a fool. by Ngaio
Marsh. (Anon.) 32:75
Ja5'57. B            6999
Death of a highbrow. by
Frank Swinnerton. (Anon.)
38:186 My19'62. B     7000
The death of a president. by
William Manchester. (Rovere0
43:172-6 Ap8'67. B    7001
The death of Achilles. by
Victor Price. (Anon.)
39:70 Ag3'63. B       7002
The death of Adolf Hitler.
by Lev Bezymenski. (Anon.)
44:214-15 O12'68. B   7003
The death of Adam. by John
C. Greene. (Anon.) 35:71-2
Ja2'60. B            7004
The death of Africa. by
Peter Ritner. (Anon.) 36:
156-7 Je4'60. B       7005
The death of Artemio Cruz.
by Carlos Fuentes. Sam
Hileman, trans. (West)
40:88-9 Ag8'64. B     7006
The death of Bessie Smith.
by Edward Albee. (Balliett)
37:114 Mr11'61. T     7007
The death of Satan. by Ronald
Duncan. (Malcolm) 36:137-8
Ap16'60. T           7008
Death of the battleship. by
Richard Hough. (Anon.)
39:96 D21'63. B       7009
The death of William Posters.
by Alan Sillitoe. (Anon.) 41:
242-4 N20'65. B       7010

Death watch. by Jean Genet. (Anon.) 31:88 Je25'55. B 7011

Debut. by Mary Drayton. (Gibbs) 32:59*Mr3'56. T 7012

Decade in Europe. by Barrett McGurn. (Anon.) 35:151 My23'59. B 7013

The decameron. by Edward Earle and Yvonne Tarr. (Balliett)37:119-20 Ap22'61. T 7014

The decision to drop the bomb. by Len Giovannitti and Fred Freed. (Anon.) 41:247-8 N6'65. B 7015

The decision to intervene. by George F. Kennan. (Anon.) 34:155 Mr15'58. B 7016

The decline and fall of Lloyd George. by William Maxwell Aitken Beaverbrook. (Anon.) 39:166-7 My25'63. B 7017

The decline of pleasure. by Walter Kerr. (Anon.) 38:163-4 My26'62. B 7018

Declaration. Tom Maschler, ed. (Malcolm) 34:96-102 Je21'58. B 7019

The decorative twenties. by Martin Battersby. (Anon.) 45:68 Ja3'70. B 7020

The deed. by Gerold Frank. (Anon.) 39:121-2 Je1'63. B 7021

The deer cry pavilion: a story of westerners in Japan 1868-1905. by Pat Barr. (Anon.) 45:152 Je7'69. B 7022

The deer park. by Norman Mailer. (Gill) 31:161-5*O22'55. B 7023

The deer park. by Norman Mailer. (Oliver) 42:116 F11'67. T 7024

The defector. (Gill) 42:184 N19'66. CC 7025

The defiant ones. (McCarten) 34:159 O4'58. CC 7026

Deirdre of the sorrows. by John Millington Synge. (Malcolm) 35:95-6 O24'59. T 7027

Delacroix. by Lee Johnson. (Anon.) 39:140 F8'64. B 7028

A delicate balance. by Edward Albee. (McCarten) 42:121 O1'66. T 7029

Deliver us from evil. by Thomas A. Dooley. (Anon.) 32:155-6*My5'56. B 7030

Deliverance to the captives. by Karl Barth. Marguerite Wieser, trans. (Anon.) 37:155 S9'61. B 7031

Delmonico's: a century of splendor. by Lately Thomas. (Anon.) 43:244-6 D9'67. B 7032

The deluge: British society and the first world war. by Arthur Marwick. (Anon.) 42:158 Mr5'66. B 7033

A Democrat looks at his party. by Dean Acheson. (Anon.) 31:212*D3'55. B 7034

Democratic national convention. (Arlen) 44:109-13 S7'68. TV 7035

The demon of progress in the arts. by Wyndham Lewis. (Anon.) 31:175*O15'55. B 7036

Demon of the North. by Peter Krott. Edward Fitzgerald, trans. (Anon.) 35:155-6 Mr28'59. B 7037

Démoniaque. (McCarten) 34:94 Mr15'58. CC 7038

The demons. by Heimito von Doderer. Richard Winston and Clara Winston, trans. (West) 37:221-2 N4'61. B 7039

The deputy. by Rolf Hochhuth. (Flanner) 39:54-6 D28'63 (McCarten) 40:118 Mr7'64.T 7040

The descent. by Gina Berriault. (Anon.) 36:181-2 O1'60. B 7041

The descent of Pierre Saint-Martin. by Norbert Casteret. John Warrington, trans. (Anon.) 32:82-4*Je30'56. B 7042

The desegregated heart: a Virginian's stand in time of transition. by Sarah Patton Boyle. (Anon.) 38:230-1 O 20'62. B 7043

A desert incident. by Pearl S. Buck. (Tynan) 35:112-16 Ap4'59. T 7044

The desert king: Ibn Saud and his Arabia. by David Howarth. (Anon.) 40:118 S5'64. B 7045

Desert solitaire: a season in the wilderness. by Edward Abbey. (Anon.) 44:174-7 Ap6'68. B 7046

The deserted house. by Lydia Chukovskaya. (Wilson) 43:231-2 D9'67. B 7047

Designing woman. (McCarten) 33:129 My25'57. CC 7048

Desire under the elms. by Eugene O'Neill. (Oliver) 38:62-4 Ja19'63. T 7049

Desire under the elms. (McCarten) 34:95-6 Mr22'58. CC 7050

The desk set. by William Marchant. (Gibbs) 31:78-81 *N5'55. T 7051

Desk set. (McCarten) 33:129-30 My25'57. CC 7052

The desolate South: 1865-66. by John T. Trowbridge. Gordon Carroll, ed. (Wilson) 32:120*Je9'56. B 7053

Desperate characters. by Paula Fox. (Anon.) 45:99-100 F7'70. B 7054

The desperate hours. by Joseph Hayes. (Gibbs) 31:76-7 F19'55. T 7055

The desperate hours. (McCarten) 31:150*O15'55. CC 7056

Destinations. by Georges Simenon. (Anon.) 31:86 Ag20'55. B 7057

Destiny and glory. by Edward S. Wallace. (Anon.) 33:154 Ap20'57. B 7058

Destruction and reconstruction: personal experiences of the late war. by Richard Taylor.

Richard B. Harwell, ed. (Wilson) 32:120-6*Je9'56. B 7059

The destruction of California. by Raymond F. Dasmann. (Anon.) 41:234-5 O9'65. B 7060

The destruction of Dresden. by David Irving. (Anon.) 40:207 Ap25'64. B 7061

The destruction of Lord Raglan. by Christopher Hibbert. (West) 38:244-8 N10'62. B 7062

Destry rides again. by Harold Rome and Leonard Gershe. (Tynan) 35:95-6 My2'59. T 7063

Deuces wild. by Holly Beye. (Oliver) 38:124 My5'62. T 7064

The development of academic freedom in the United States. by Richard Hofstadter and Walter P. Metzger. (Anon.) 31:218-19*N12'55. B 7065

The devil and the ten commandments. (Gill) 39:150 O19'63. CC 7066

The devil at 4 o'clock. (Gill) 37:196 O28'61. CC 7067

Devil by the sea. by Nina Bawden. (Anon.) 35:176 Ap11'59. B 7068

The devil by the tail. (Gilliatt) 45:75 Jy5'69. CC 7069

The devil in Bucks County. by Edmund Schiddel. (Anon.) 35:168 Ap4'59. B 7070

The devil strikes at night. (McCarten) 34:121 F7'59. CC 7071

The devils. by John Whiting. (Panter-Downes) 37:168-9 Ap22'61. (McCarten) 41:170-2 N27'65. T 7072

The devil's advocate. by Morris L. West. (Anon.) 35:190-1 S26'59. B 7073

The devil's advocate. by Dore Schary. (McCarten) 37:126 Mr18'61. T 7074

The devil's brigade. (Gilliatt) 44:115-17 Je1'68. CC 7075

Devil's diary. John L. Stipp,
ed. (Anon.) 31:142 My21'55.
B                          7076
The devil's disciple. (Balliett)
35:68 Ag29'59. CC      7077
The devil's eye. (Gill)
37:207-208 N4'61. CC   7078
The devil's wanton. (Gill)
38:60-1 Jy14'62. CC    7079
The Dharma bums. by Jack
Kerouac. (Anon.) 34:175-7
N1'58. B                   7080
Diabolique. (McCarten) 31:90
*N26'55. CC            7081
Dialogue. (Gill) 43:138-9
O21'67. CC             7082
Diamond. by Brian Glanville.
(Anon.) 38:108 Ag25'62. B
7083
Diamond Head. (Gill) 39:146-7
Mr9'63. CC             7084
Diana. by R. F. Delderfield.
(Anon.) 36:197 S17'60.
B                          7085
Diaries and letters, 1930-39.
by Harold Nicolson. Nigel
Nicolson, ed. (Anon.) 42:
247-8 N19'66. B        7086
Diaries, 1915-18. by Cynthia
Asquith. E. M. Horsley, ed.
(Anon.) 45:140-1 Ap5'69.
B                          7087
Diary and autobiography of
John Adams. by John Adams.
L. H. Butterfield, ed. (N.
Bliven) 38:225-32 N3'62. B
7088
A diary from Dixie. by Mary
Chestnut. (Wilson) 31:180-93
*N5'55. B              7089
Diary, 1928-57. by Julian
Green. Anne Green, trans.
(Anon.) 40:246 N14'64. B
7090
Diary of a chambermaid. (Gill)
41:153-4 Mr20'65. CC   7091
Diary of a dying empire. by
Hans Peter Hanssen. (Anon.)
31:131-2*F18'56. B     7092
Diary of a mad housewife. by
Sue Kaufman. (Anon.) 43:107
Je24'67. B                 7093

Diary of a mad old man. by
Junichirō. Tanizaki. (West)
41:237-8 N27'65. B     7094
Diary of a madman. by
Nikolai Gogol. (Oliver)
40:130-2 Ap25'64. T    7095
Diary of a nightmare: Berlin,
1942-1945. by Ursula von
Kardorff. Ewan Butler,
trans. (Anon.) 42:205 My21
'66. B                     7096
Diary of a sit-in. by Merrill
Proudfoot. (Anon.) 38:174-5
Ap28'62. B                 7097
Diary of a union lady, 1861-5.
by Maria Daly. Harold Earl
Hammond, ed. (Anon.)
38:71-2 Ag4'62. B      7098
The diary of Alice James.
by Alice James. Leon Edel,
ed. (Anon.) 40:224-5 O3'64.
B                          7099
Diary of an art dealer. by
René Gimpel. John Rosenberg,
trans. (Flanner) 39:136-8
O12'63 (Rosenberg) 43:182-90
Ap22'67. B                 7100
The diary of Anaïs Nin: 1931-34.
by Anaïs Nin. Gunther
Stuhlmann, ed. (Anon.) 42:
166 Je4'66. B          7101
The diary of Anne Frank. by
Frances Goodrich and
Albert Hackett. (Gibbs) 31:
71-2*O15'55. T         7102
The diary of Anne Frank.
(McCarten) 35:95 Mr28'59.
CC                     7103
Diary of Charles Francis
Adams. by Charles Francis
Adams. Aida Di Pace Donald
and David Donald, eds. (Anon.)
40:206-207 S26'64. B   7104
The diary of "Helena Morley."
by Helena Morley. Elizabeth
Bishop, trans. (Anon.) 33:
105 Ja18'58. B         7105
Diary of the Sinai campaign. by
Moshe Dayan. (Anon.) 42:88
Jy23'66. B             7106
The (Diblos) notebook.   by James
Merrill. (N. Bliven) 41:221-4
S11'65. B              7107

Dickens and crime. by Philip
Collins. (Anon.) 39:152
Mr2-63. B                    7108
A dictionary of American-
English usage. by H.W.
Fowler. Margaret Nicholson,
adapt. (Macdonald) 34:136-53
My17'58. B                    7109
Dictionary of American slang.
Harold Wentworth and
Stuart Berg Flexner, eds.
(Wilson) 37:136-8 F18'61. B
7110
Die ratten. by Gerhart Haupt-
mann. (Oliver) 42:127 Ap
20'66.                        7111
Dieu est né en exil. by
Vintila Horia. (Flanner) 36:
147 D10'60. B                 7112
A difficult love. (Gilliatt)
43:54-6 Jy1'67. CC            7113
Diff'rent. by Eugene O'Neill.
(Oliver) 37:137-8 O28'61.
T                             7114
The dignity of man. by Russell
W. Davenport. (Anon.) 31:
174 My14'55. B                7115
Digs and diggers: a book of
world archaeology. by
Leonard Cottrell. (Anon.)
40:247-8 D12'64. B            7116
The Dillinger days. by John
Toland. (Anon.) 39:121 Je15
'63. B                        7117
Dimka. (Gill) 40:191-2
My16'64. CC                   7118
Dingo. by Charles Wood.
(Tynan) 44:138-40 N9'68. T
7119
Dinner at eight. by George S.
Kaufman and Edna Ferber.
(McCarten) 42:116 O8'66.
T                             7120
The dinner party. by Claude
Mauriac. Merloyd Lawrence,
trans. (Flanner) 35:63-5
Jy25'59 (Balliett) 36:194-9
My14'60. B                    7121
Dinny and the witches. by
William Gibson. (Malcolm)
35:78-80*D19'59. T            7122
Diplomat. by Charles W.
Thayer. (Anon.) 35:246 D5'59.
B                             7123

Diplomatic bags. by Pietro
Quaroni. (Anon.) 42:246
O15'66. B                     7124
The dirty dozen. (Gilliatt) 43:
70-3 Jy22'67. CC              7125
Disaster at Dundee. by
John Prebble. (Anon.) 32:
106 Ja26'57. B                7126
A discord of trumpets. by
Claud Cockburn. (West)
32:163-70 S22'56. B           7127
Discourse on thinking. by
Martin Heidegger. John M.
Anderson and E. Hans Freund,
trans. (Anon.) 42:135-6 Ag
20'66. B                      7128
The discovery and conquest of
Mexico. by Bernal Diaz del
Castillo.  A. P. Maudslay,
trans. (Anon.) 32:148
*Ap7'56. B                    7129
Discovery of a genius: William
Dean Howells and Henry
James. by William Dean
Howells. Albert Mordell, ed.
(Anon.) 37:170-1 S30'61.
B                             7130
The discovery of Neptune. by
Morton Grosser. (Bernstein)
39:158-64 My25'63. B          7131
The discovery of the Great West:
La Salle. by Francis Park-
man. William R. Taylor, ed.
(Anon.) 32:129-30*Je9'56.
B                             7132
The discovery of the world.
by Albert Bettex. (Anon.)
36:228 N5'60. B               7133
The discovery of time. by Stephen
Toulmin and June Goodfield.
(Bernstein) 41:231-43
N6'65. B                      7134
The discriminating thief.
by David Leitch. (Anon.)
45:248 D6'69. B               7135
The disenchanted. by Budd
Schulberg and Harvey Breit.
(Tynan) 34:107-109 D13'58.
T                             7136
The disintegration of James
Cherry. by Jeff Wanshel.
(Oliver) 45:76-7 F7'70.
T                             7137

The Disney version. by Richard
Schickel. (Anon.) 44:159-60
My25'68. B                7138
The disorderly knights. by
Dorothy Dunnett. (Anon.)
42:246-7 N19'66. B        7139
Disraeli. by Robert Blake.
(Steiner) 43:142-9 Ap1'67.
B                         7140
The dissent of Dominick Shapiro.
by Bernard Kops. (Anon.)
43:162-3 Mr4'67. B        7141
A distant bell. by Katherine
Morrill. (Tynan) 35:70-2
Ja23'60. T                7142
A distant drum. by Charles
Bracelen Flood. (Anon.)
33:134 Mr9'57. B          7143
Disturbance on Berry Hill. by
Elizabeth Fenwick. (Anon.)
44:180 Ap6'68. B          7144
Disturber of the peace. by
William Manchester. (Mc-
Kelway) 31:219-21 N19'55.
B                         7145
Diversions. by Steven Vinaver.
(Malcolm) 34:104-106
N15'58. T                 7146
Divide by seven. by Robert
Chambers. (Anon.) 45:
239-40 N15'69. B          7147
The divided heart. (McCarten)
31:62*Ag20'55. CC         7148
Divided loyalties. by Janet Teis-
sier du Cros. (Anon.) 40:126-7
Ag22'64. B                7149
Division Street: America. by
Studs Terkel. (Anon.)
43:154 Ap1'67. B          7150
Divorce American style.
(Gilliatt) 43:73 Jy22'67. CC
                          7151
Divorce--Italian style. (Gill)
38:139-40 S29'62. CC      7152
Do I hear a waltz? by Richard
Rodgers and Stephen Sond-
heim. (McCarten) 41:144
Mr27'65. T                7153
Do not go gentle. by David
MacCuish. (Anon.) 36:243
D10'60. B                 7154
Do not pass go. by Charles
Nolte. (Oliver) 41:122-3
My8'65. T                 7155

Do re mi. by Garson Kanin,
Jule Styne, Betty Comden,
and Adolph Green. (Mc-
Carten) 36:68 Ja14'61. T
                          7156
Do you know the Milky Way?
by Karl Wittlinger. (Mc-
Carten) 37:137 O28'61. T
                          7157
The dock brief. by John
Mortimer. (Oliver) 37:120-1
D2'61. T                  7158
Doctor at sea. (McCarten)
32:66*Mr10'56. CC         7159
Dr. Bowdler's legacy. by
Noel Perrin. (Anon.) 45:192
O25'69. B                 7160
Dr. Burney's musical tours in
Europe. by Percy A.
Scholes. (Sargeant) 36:193-
202 S10'60. B             7161
Dr. Cook's garden. by Ira
Levin. (McCarten) 43:131
O7'67. T                  7162
Doctor Darwin. by Hesketh
Pearson. (Anon.) 40:205-206
Ap25'64. B                7163
Doctor Faustus. by Christopher
Marlowe. (Oliver) 40:108
O17'64. T                 7164
Doctor Faustus. (Kael) 43:110-
11 F17'68. CC             7165
Doctor Glas. by Hjalmar Söder-
berg. Paul Britten Austin,
trans. (Anon.) 40:90 Ag8'64.
B                         7166
Doctor in the house. (McCarten)
31:89 F26'55. CC          7167
Dr. Johnson: his life in letters.
by Samuel Johnson. David
Littlejohn, ed. (Anon.) 43:
195-6 Mr18'67. B          7168
Dr. Joyce Brothers. (J. Lardner)
34:131-5 S13'58. TV       7169
Dr. No. (Gill) 39:65-6 Je1'63.
CC                        7170
Dr. Strangelove or: how I
learned to stop worrying and
love the bomb. (Gill) 39:75-6
F1'64. CC                 7171
Doctor Zhivago. by Boris
Pasternak. Max Hayward and
Manya Harari, trans. (Wilson)
34:213-38 N15'58. B       7172

Doctor Zhivago. (Gill) 41:46-7
Ja1'66. CC 7173
The doctors. (McCarten) 32:58
*Ag18'56. CC 7174
The doctor's dilemma. (Mc-
Carten) 34:60 D27'58. CC
7175
Does a tiger wear a necktie?
by Don Peterson. (Gill)
45:94 Mr8'69. T 7176
The dog at Clambercrown. by
Jocelyn Brooke. (Anon.)
33:151 Mr23'57. B 7177
Dog of Flanders. (McCarten)
36:108 Ap9'60. CC 7178
Dog years. by Günter Grass.
(West) 41:236-41 N20'65. B
7179
Doings and undoings. by Norman
Podhoretz. (Adler) 40:62-80
Jy4'64. B 7180
The doll. (Gill) 39:40-2 Ja25
'64. CC 7181
A doll's house. by Henrik
Ibsen. (Oliver) 38:68-72
F9'63. T 7182
A doll's house. (J. Lardner)
35:208 D5'59. TV 7183
Don Juan, or the feast of the
statue. by Molière. (Flanner)
43:149-51 Mr11'67 (Gill) 45:
58-60 F14'70. T 7184
Dome of many-coloured glass.
by Post Wheeler and Hallie
Erminie Rives. (Anon.)
31:217-18*N12'55. B 7185
The domesticated Americans.
by Russell Lynes. (Anon.)
39:248 O19'63. B 7186
The dominant fifth. by Audrey
Laski. (Anon.) 45:213 O18'69.
B 7187
Don Carlos. by Johann
Christoph Schiller. (Oliver)
38:85-6 Mr10'62. T 7188
Don Juan (McCarten) 32:76
*Mr17'56. CC 7189
Don Quixote. (Angell) 36:88-9
Ja21'61. CC 7190
Donizetti. by Herbert Wein-
stock. (Anon.) 39:246-7
D7'63. B 7191
Donnybrook! by Robert E.

McEnroe and Johnny Burke.
(McCarten) 37:72-4 My27'61.
T 7192
Donogoo. by Jules Romains.
Gilbert Seldes and James B.
Gidney, trans. (Balliett)
36:64-6 Ja28'61. T 7193
Donovan's reef. (Balliett) 39:
50 Ag3'63. CC 7194
Don't drink the water. by
Woody Allen. (McCarten)
42:155 D3'66. T 7195
Don't let them scare you: the
life and times of Elmer
Davis. by Roger Burlingame.
(Anon.) 37:119-20 Je17'61.
B 7196
Don't look back. (Gilliatt)
43:116 S9'67. CC 7197
Don't raise the bridge, lower
the river. (Gilliatt) 44:78-80
Jy20'68. CC 7198
Don't tempt the devil. (Gill)
40:86-8 My2'64. CC 7199
The doomed oasis. by Hammond
Innes. (Anon.) 36:238
N26'60. B 7200
Dorothy and Red. by Vincent
Sheean. (Anon.) 39:241-2
N16'63. B 7201
Dorothy Richardson: an ad-
venture in self-discovery. by
Horace Gregory. (N. Bliven)
44:181-6 My4'68. B 7202
Dostoevsky: a self-portrait.
by Fyodor Dostoevsky.
Jessie Coulson, ed. (Anon.)
39:149-50 F23'63. B 7203
Double entry. by Jay Thompson.
(Balliett) 37:115-16 Mr11'61.
T 7204
The double helix. by James D.
Watson. (Bernstein) 44:172-
82 Ap13'68. B 7205
Double in hearts. by Paul
Nathan. (Gibbs) 32:118-19
O27'56. T 7206
Double lives: an autobiography.
by William Plomer. (Anon.)
32:186-8 D15'56. B 7207
Double talk. by Lewis John
Carlino. (Oliver) 40:165
My16'64. T 7208

The doubtful guest. by Edward
Gorey. (Wilson) 35:62-5
D26'59. B              7209
The doughboys. by Laurence
Stallings. (Anon.) 39:73-4
Jy6'63. B              7210
Doulos--the finger man. (Gill)
40:170 Mr7'64. CC     7211
The doves of Venus. by Olivia
Manning. (Anon.) 32:185
D15'56. B             7212
Down there on a visit. by
Christopher Isherwood. (N.
Bliven) 38:77-80 S1'62. B
                      7213
The downfall of the liberal
party, 1914-35. by Trevor
Wilson. (Anon.) 42:130-1
F4'67. B              7214
Downhill all the way. by
Leonard Woolf. (W. Max-
well) 43:63-71 D23'67. B
                      7215
Downhill racer. (Kael)
45:179-81 N15'69. CC  7216
The dozens. by Laird Koenig.
(Gill) 45:87 Mr22'69. T
                      7217
The dragon. by Eugene
Schwarz. (Oliver) 39:96-9
Ap20'63. T            7218
Dragon sky. (Gill) 40:108
S5'64. CC             7219
The dragon's seed. by Robert
S. Elegant. (Anon.) 35:92
Jy25'59. B            7220
Drat! the cat! by Ira Levin
and Milton Schafer. (Mc-
Carten) 41:96 O23'65. T
                      7221
Drawn in color: African
contrasts. by Noni Javabu.
(Anon.) 38:181-2 S15'62. B
                      7222
Dream castles. by Mary
Cable. (Anon.) 42:68 D24'66.
B                     7223
The dream of Arcadia; Amer-
ican writers and artists in
Italy, 1760-1915. by Van
Wyck Brooks. (Anon.) 34:
191-2 O4'58. B        7224
The dream of success. by

Kenneth S. Lynn. (Anon.)
31:129 My28'55. B     7225
The dream of the red chamber.
by Tsao Hsueh Chin.
Chi-Chen Wang, trans.
(West) 34:223-32 N22'58.
B                     7226
A dream play. by August
Strindberg. (Balliett)
36:103-104 D3'60. T   7227
Dreams. (McCarten) 36:66-8
Je11'60. CC           7228
The Dreyfus case: a reassess-
ment. by Guy Chapman.
(Anon.) 31:117*F11'56. B
                      7229
The drifter. (Gill) 43:119
Je3'67. CC            7230
Drink to me only. by Abram
S. Ginnes and Ira Wallach.
(J. Lardner) 34:56-8 O18
'58. T                7231
Drinkers of darkness. by Gerald
Hanley. (Anon.) 31:165-6
*O22'55. B            7232
Drive. by Charles R. Codman.
(Anon.) 33:223 D14'57. B
                      7233
A drop of patience. by William
Melvin Kelley. (Balliett)
41:177-8 My22'65. B   7234
Drugs and the mind. by
Robert S. de Ropp. (Anon.)
33:200-201 O5'57. B   7235
Drum. by Anthony Sampson.
(Anon.) 33:169-70 My18'57.
B                     7236
Drums in the night. by
Bertolt Brecht. (Oliver)
43:106 Je3'67. T      7237
Drums under the windows. by
Paul Shyre. (Balliett)
36:90-2 O22'60. T     7238
Du rififi chez les hommes.
See Rififi.            7239
The Duchess of Dino. by
Philip Ziegler. (Anon.)
39:151 Mr2'63. B      7240
The duchess of Jermyn Street:
the life and good times of
Rosa Lewis of the Cavendish
Hotel. by Daphne Fielding.
(Anon.) 40:126 Ag22'64. B
                      7241

Due to circumstances beyond
our control. by Fred W.
Friendly. (Anon.) 43:178
My20'67. B          7242
The duel. by Robert Baldick.
(Anon.) 42:211 Mr19'66.
B                   7243
Duel of angels. by Jean
Giraudoux. (Tynan) 36:83-4
Ap30'60. T          7244
Duet for cannibals. (Kael)
45:141-2 N1'69. CC  7245
Duffy. (Kael) 44:170
O12'68. CC          7246
Duke Ellington: his life and
music. Peter Gammond, ed.
(Anon.) 36:162 Mr26'60. B
                    7247
Dumbell people in a barbell
world. by Dan Blue. (Oliver)
38:102-103 F24'62. T 7248
The dumbwaiter. by Harold
Pinter. (Oliver) 38:148-9
D8'62. T            7249
Dunkirk. (McCarten) 34:84-6
S20'58. CC          7250
Dürer: his life and work. by
Marcel Brion. James Cleugh,
trans. (Anon.) 36:64
D24'60. B           7251
Dust in the lion's paw: auto-
biography, 1939-1946, by Freya
Stark. (Anon.) 37:107-108
Ja27'62. B          7252
Dust on the paw. by Robin
Jenkins. (Anon.) 37:140-1
F17'62. B           7253
The Dutch seaborne empire:
1600-1800. by Charles R.
Boxer. (Anon.) 41:247 N6'65.
B                   7254
Dutchman. by LeRoi Jones.
(Oliver) 40:78-9 Ap4'64. T
                    7255
Dutchman. (Gill) 43:140-2
Mr4'67. CC          7256
The dyer's hand. by W.H.
Auden. (Malcolm) 39:185-90
My4'63. B           7257
Dylan. by Sidney Michaels.
(McCarten) 39:72 Ja25'64.
T                   7258
Dynamite tonite. by Arnold Wein-
stein and William Bolcom. (Oliver)

43:140 Ap8'67. T          7259

-E-

E. Nesbit. by Doris Langley
Moore. (W. Maxwell)
43:156-9 F25'67. B  7260
Earliest civilizations of the
Near East. by James
Mellaart. (Anon.) 42:192
Mr26'66. B          7261
The early Churchills. by A.L.
Rowse. (West) 32:232-3 D
8'56. B             7262
The early Joyce: the book
reviews. by James Joyce.
Stanislaus Joyce and
Ellsworth Mason, eds.
(Anon.) 32:143*Mr10'56. B
                    7263
The early life of Stephen Hind.
by Storm Jameson. (Anon.)
42:135 Ag20'66. B   7264
Early to rise. by Arnold E.
Grisman. (Anon.) 34:146-7
My10'58. B          7265
The early years of Alec
Waugh. by Alec Waugh.
(Anon.) 39:211 N2'63. B
                    7266
The Earth shook, the sky
burned. by William Bronson.
(Anon.) 35:207 O31'59. B
                    7267
The earthly paradise. by
Robert Thom. (Anon.) 41:
110 Ja8'66. B       7268
Earthshaker. by Robert W.
Krepps. (Anon.) 34:199-
200 O25'58. B       7269
The easiest profession. (Mc-
Carten) 36:90 Ap2'60. CC
                    7270
East and West. by C. North-
cote Parkinson. (Anon.)
39:244-5 D7'63. B   7271
East of Eden. (McCarten)
31:140-1 Mr19'55. CC 7272
East side, West side. (Miller)
39:120-2 N16'63. TV 7273
East to West: a journey round
the world. by Arnold J.
Toynbee. (Anon.) 34:201-202
O25'58. B           7274

The East wind. by Leo
Lehman. (McCarten) 42:132
F18'67. T 7275
Easter in Sicily. by Herbert
Kubly. (Anon.) 32:179 O27'56.
B 7276
Eastern exposure. by Marvin
L. Kalb. (Anon.) 34:66
D27'58. B 7277
The easy chair. by Bernard
DeVoto. (Anon.) 31:219
*N12'55. B 7278
The easy life. (Gill) 39:73
Ja4'64. CC 7279
Easy rider. (Gilliatt) 45:70-2
Jy19'69. CC 7280
The eater of darkness. by
Robert M. Coates. (Anon.)
35:66-7 D26'59. B 7281
Eating people is wrong. by
Malcolm Bradbury. (Anon.)
36:96-7 Jy16'60. B 7282
The eating valley. by
Augusta Walker. (Anon.)
32:182-5 D15'56. B 7283
The eavesdropper. by Tai-yi
Lin. (Anon.) 35:166 Mr7'59.
B 7284
The eavesdroppers. by Samuel
Dash, Robert E. Knowlton
and Richard F. Schwartz.
(Anon.) 35:246-7 N14'59.
B 7285
Ecce homo. by George Grosz.
(Anon.) 42:120 Ja21'67. B
7286
Echoes of revolt: the masses.
1911-17. William L.
O'Neill, ed. (Anon.) 43:156
Ap1'67. B 7287
Echoes of silence. (Gill)
43:148 Ap15'67. CC 7288
Eclipse. (Gill) 38:60-2
D29'62. CC 7289
Economic development in
perspective. by John
Kenneth Galbraith. (Anon.)
38:132 Je16'62. B 7290
The ecstasy business. by
Richard Condon. (Anon.)
43:89 Ja6'68. B 7291
The Ed Sullivan show. (J.
Lardner) 34:52-5 Jy5'58.

TV 7292
Eden: the making of a states-
man. by Alan Campbell-
Johnson. (Anon.) 31:169-70
*O22'55. B 7293
The Eddy Duchin story.
(McCarten) 32:49*Je30'56.
CC 7294
The edge of day. by Laurie
Lee. (W. Maxwell) 36:
172-8 Ap16'60. B 7295
The edge of sadness. by
Edwin O'Connor. (Galbraith)
37:87-94 Je24'61. B 7296
Edge of the city. (McCarten)
32:107 F9'57. CC 7297
Edmond Halley. by Colin A.
Ronan. (Anon.) 45:182
S20'69. B 7298
Education and freedom. by
H.G. Rickover. (Anon.)
34:137-8 F14'59. B 7299
Education by uncles. by
Abigail Adams Homans.
(Anon.) 42:223-4 O1'66.
B 7300
The education of H*y*m*a*n
K*a*p*l*a*n. by Benjamin
Bernard Zavin, Paul
Nassau and Oscar Brand.
(Gill) 44:114 Ap13'68. T
7301
Edward Durell Stone. by
Edward Durell Stone. (Anon.)
43:90-2 Ja6'68. B 7302
Edward Gibbon the historian.
by Joseph Ward Swain. (Anon.)
43:195-6 Mr11'67. B 7303
Edwardian promenade. James
Laver, ed. (Anon.) 34:66
D27'58. B 7304
An Edwardian youth. by L.E.
Jones. (Anon.) 32:108 Ja19
'57. B 7305
The Edwardians. by Charles
Petrie. (Anon.) 41:119-20
Ja15'66. B 7306
Edwin Booth. by Milton Geiger.
(Tynan) 34:113-16 D6'58.
T 7307
The egg. by Félicien Marceau.
(Flanner) 33:66-7 Je29'57.
T 7308

The egg. by Félicien Marceau.
Robert Schlitt, trans.
(McCarten) 37:63-4 Ja20'62.
T                                 7309
The egg and I. by Hal
Pockriss. (Malcolm) 34:78-80
S27'58. T                        7310
Egypt in transition. by Jean
Lacouture and Simonne
Lacouture. Francis Scarfe,
trans. (Anon.) 34:243 N15'58.
B                                7311
Egypt's destiny. by Mohammed
Naguib. (Anon.) 31:127
Ap30'55. B                      7312
Egypt's liberation. by Gamal
Abdul Nasser. (Anon.) 31:
127-8 Ap30'55. B                7313
Eh? by Henry Livings. (Oliver)
42:96-8 O29'66. T                7314
Ehrengard. by Isak Dinesen.
(Anon.) 39:111-12 Je22'63.
B                               7315
8-1/2. (Gill) 39:62 Je29'63.
CC                               7316
Eight men out: the Black Sox
and the 1919 world series.
by Eliot Asinof. (Anon.)
39:191 S21'63. B                7317
Eight o'clock walk. (McCarten)
31:131-2 My7'55. CC             7318
1815: an end and a beginning.
by John Fisher. (Anon.)
39:167-8 My25'63. B             7319
The 1826 journal of John James
Audubon. by John James Audu-
bon. Alice Ford, ed. (Anon.)
43:108 Je24'67. B               7320
The eighth day. by Thornton
Wilder. (Oliver) 42:146-8
My27'67. B                      7321
Einen jux will er sich machen.
by Johann Nestroy. (Gill)
44:114-16 Ap13'68. T            7322
Einstein: his life and times.
by Philipp Frank. (Bernstein)
42:174-7 Ap16'66. B             7323
Eisenhower: captive hero. by
Marquis Childs. (Anon.)
34:129-30 S6'58. B              7324
El Greco. by Antonina Vallentin.
Andrew Révai and Robin
Chancellor, trans. (Anon.)

31:72*S3'55. B                  7325
El Greco. (Gill) 43:119 Je3'67.
CC                               7326
El señor presidente. by Miguel
Angel Asturias. (West)
40:158-60 Mr28'64. B            7327
The elder statesman. by T.S.
Eliot. (Panter-Downes)
34:168 N1'58. T                 7328
The elder statesman: a play.
by T.S. Eliot. (Anon.)
35:96 Je27'59. B                7329
The Eleanor Roosevelt story.
(Gill) 41:231-3 N20'65. CC
                                 7330
The election of Andrew Jack-
son. by Robert V. Remini.
(Anon.) 40:195-6 My9'64.
B                               7331
Electra. by Sophocles. (Mal-
colm) 35:101-102 F21'59. T
                                 7332
Electra. (Gill) 38:78 D22'62.
CC                               7333
The electronic nigger. by
Ed Bullins. (Oliver) 44:
133-4 Mr9'68. T                 7334
Elementary particles. by
Chen Ning Yang. (Anon.)
37:140 F10'62. B                7335
Elena et les hommes. (Flanner)
32:118-19 S29'56. CC            7336
Elephants and ivory. by
John Alfred Jordan. (Anon.)
32:137*Mr24'56. B               7337
Elise or the real life. by
Claire Etcherelli. June P.
Wilson and Walter Benn
Michaels, trans. (Anon.)
43:95 Ag9'69. B                 7338
Elizabeth and Leicester. by
Elizabeth Jenkins. (Anon.)
37:104 F3'62. B                 7339
Elizabeth I. by Donald Barr
Chidsey. (Anon.) 31:106-107
Je18'55. B                      7340
Elizabeth the great. by
Elizabeth Jenkins. (Anon.)
35:174 Mr14'59. B               7341
Elizabethan taste. by John
Buxton. (Anon.) 40:138-9
Je20'64. B                      7342
Elmer Gantry. (McCarten)

36:57-8 Jy16'60. CC    7343
Eloise. by Kay Thompson.
(Anon.) 31:55-6*D31'55. B
                       7344
The elusive corporal. (Gill)
39:135 Mr2'63. CC    7345
Elvira Madigan. (Gill)
43:164-7 N4'67. CC    7346
Embezzled heaven. (McCarten)
35:106 My16'59. CC    7347
The emergence of the new
South, 1913-45. by George
B. Tindall. (Anon.) 44:158
Mr23'68. B             7348
Emergent Americans: a report
on "crossroads Africa".
by Harold R. Isaacs. (Anon.)
38:185 Ap14'62. B    7349
The emigrants. by George
Lamming. (West) 31:122-5
My28'55. B             7350
Emily Dickinson: a revelation.
by Millicent Todd Bingham.
(Anon.) 31:120 Mr5'55.
B                      7351
Emily Dickinson: an interpretive
biography. by Thomas H.
Johnson. (Anon.) 32:103-104
*Mr31'56. B            7352
Emily Dickinson's home: letters
of Edward Dickinson and his
family. by Edward Dickin-
son. Millicent Todd
Bingham, ed. (Anon.)
31:147*S10'55. B       7353
Eminent domain: Yeats among
Wilde, Joyce, Pound, Eliot,
and Auden. by Richard
Ellmann. (Bogan) 44:134-5
Mr30'68. B             7354
Eminent Victorians. by Lytton
Strachey. (Steiner) 45:150
S13'69. B              7355
Emma in blue. by Gerald
Hamilton and Desmond
Stewart. (Anon.) 34:174
S20'58. B              7356
Emmanuel. by James Forsyth.
(Balliett) 36:98 D17'60.
T                      7357
The emperor. by George
White. (Oliver) 39:85-6
Ap27'63. T             7358

The empire builders. by Boris
Vian. (Oliver) 44:112
O12'68. T              7359
The empire city: a treasury
of New York. Alexander
Klein, ed. (Anon.) 31:88
Jy16'55. B             7360
Empire of fear. by Vladimir
Petrov and Evdokia Petrov.
(Anon.) 33:114-15 Mr2'57.
B                      7361
The empire of the Arabs.
by John Bagot Glubb.
(Anon.) 41:202 D18'65. B
                       7362
The Empress Brown: the true
story of a Victorian scandal.
by Tom A. Cullen. (Anon.)
45:96 Ag16'69. B       7363
The empty canvas. by Alberto
Moravia. Angus Davidson,
trans. (Anon.) 37:222-3
N4'61. B               7364
The empty canvas. (Gill)
40:114-16 My30'64. CC 7365
The empty fortress. by Bruno
Bettelheim. (Gay) 44:160-73
My18'68. B             7366
En cas de malheur. (Flanner)
34:190-2 O11'58. CC    7367
The enchantress. by H.E.
Bates. (Anon.) 37:222
O14'61. B              7368
The encounter. by Henri
Troyat. (Anon.) 38:186-7
Mr17'62. B             7369
Encounter with the future. by
Fred Hoyle. (Anon.) 42:177
Mr12'66. B             7370
Encounters with Lenin. by Niko-
lay Valentinov. (Anon.)
44:246-8 D7'68. B      7371
The end of all things natural.
by G. Zoffer. (Oliver) 45:
92 S20'69. T           7372
End of desire. (Gill) 38:60
Jy14'62. CC            7373
End of innocence. (Balliett)
36:80 S10'60. CC       7374
The end of it. by Mitchell
Goodman. (Balliett) 37:248
D9'61. B               7375
The end of something nice.

by Angus Wolfe Murray.
(Anon.) 43:177-8 S9'67. B
                              7376
The end of the affair.
(McCarten) 31:131 My7'55.
CC                           7377
The end of the House of
Lancaster. by R. L. Storey.
(Anon.) 43:150 My27'67.
B                            7378
End of the road. (Kael)
45:117-18 F14'70. CC  7379
The end of the Romanovs. by
Victor Alexandrov. William
Sutcliffe, trans. (Anon.) 43:
193 Ap22'67. B        7380
An end of valor: the last days
of the Civil War. by Philip
Van Doren Stern. (Anon.)
34:151-2*Ap26'58. B   7381
An end to dying. by Sam
Astrachan. (Anon.) 32:138
*My19'56. B           7382
An end to innocence. by Leslie
A. Fiedler. (Rovere) 31:137-8
My21'55. B            7383
The enemy joy. by Ben Belitt.
(Bogan) 40:243 N7'64. B
                              7384
Endecott and the red cross.
by Robert Lowell. (Oliver)
44:85-91 My11'68. T   7385
Enderby. by Anthony Burgess.
(Anon.) 44:87 Je29'68. B
                              7386
Endgame. by Samuel Beckett.
(Oliver) 38:103-104 F24'62.
T                     7387
The endless hours. by Wallace
L. Brown. (Anon.) 37:171-2
Mr11'61. B            7388
The endless Summer. (S.
Lardner) 42:78 Jy9'66. CC
                              7389
Endurance: Shackleton's in-
credible voyage. by Alfred
Lansing. (Anon.) 35:174-5
My9'59. B             7390
The enemy below. (McCarten)
33:95-6 Ja18'58. CC   7391
The enemy camp. by Jerome
Weidman. (Balliett) 34:
124-7 S6'58. B        7392

An enemy of the people.
by Henrik Ibsen. Arthur
Miller, adapt. (Malcolm)
34:68-70 F14'59. T    7393
Engaged and disengaged. by
Douglas Bush. (Anon.) 42:
239 S24'66. B         7394
Engagement Italiano. (Oliver)
42:55 Je25'66. CC     7395
England, half English. by
Colin MacInnes. (Anon.)
38:180 My12'62. B     7396
England without Richard: 1189-
1199. by John T. Appleby.
(Anon.) 42:194-5 Ap23'66.
B                     7397
English hours. by Henry
James. Alma Louise Lowe,
ed. (Anon.) 37:172 Mr11'61.
B                     7398
English literature of the early
eighteenth century: 1700-1740.
by Bonamy Dobrée. (Anon.)
36:182-3 Ap16'60. B   7399
The English novel. by Walter
Allen. (Anon.) 31:88*Ag20'55.
B                     7400
The English woman in history.
by Doris Mary Stenton.
(Anon.) 33:165-6 My11'57. B
                              7401
Enough rope. (S. Lardner)
42:64-6 Jy30'66. CC   7402
Enter laughing. by Joseph
Stein. (McCarten) 39:74
Mr23'63. T            7403
Enter laughing. (Gilliatt) 43:
64-7 Ag5'67. CC       7404
The enterprising Americans: a
business history of the United
States. by John Chamberlain.
(Anon.) 38:146-7 F9'63. B
                              7405
The entertainer. (Gill) 36:134
O15'60. CC            7406
The entertainer. by John
Osborne. (Panter-Downes)
33:153-4 S28'57 (Gibbs) 34:
63-4 F22'58. T        7407
Entertaining Mr. Sloane. by
Joe Orton. (McCarten) 41:94
O23'65. T             7408
Episode in the Transvaal.

by Harry Bloom. (Anon.) 31:
198*N5'55. B          7409
Epitaph for George Dillon. by
John Osborne and Anthony
Creighton. (J. Lardner) 34:
101-103 N15'58 (Balliett) 36:
68-72 Ja14'61. T          7410
Epitaph for kings. by Sanche
de Gramont. (Anon.) 44:183
Ap13'68. B          7411
Epoch and artist. by David
Jones. (Rosenberg) 40:114-
22 Ag22'64. B          7412
Epstein: an autobiography. by
Jacob Epstein. (Anon.)
31:164*S24'55. B          7413
The era of reconstruction:
1865-77. by Kenneth M.
Stampp. (Anon.) 41:197-8
Ap24'65. B          7414
Ergo. by Jakov Lind. (Oliver)
44:134-5 Mr16'68. T          7415
Ernest Hemingway. by Carlos
Baker. (Steiner) 45:147-50
S13'69. B          7416
Ernest in love. by Anne
Croswell and Lee Pockriss.
(Malcolm) 36:117 My21'60.
T          7417
Eroica. (Gill) 41:125 F5'66.
CC          7418
Eros denied: sex in Western
society. by Wayland Young.
(Anon.) 40:143-4 Je13'64.
B          7419
Erotic poetry: the lyrics, ballads,
idyls and epics of love--
classical to contemporary.
William Cole, ed. (Anon.)
39:248 N23'63. B          7420
The Erpingham cramp. by
Joe Orton. (Oliver) 45:156
N8'69. T          7421
An error of judgement. by
Pamela Hansford Johnson.
(Anon.) 38:171 S29'62. B
7422
Esau and Jacob. by Machado
de Assis. (West) 41:218-21
S25'65. B          7423
The escape of Charles II. by
Richard Ollard. (Anon.) 43:
112 F3'68. B          7424

Escape of the Amethyst. by
C. E. Lucas Phillips and
J. S. Kerans. (Anon.) 33:
139-40 F15'58. B          7425
Esmond in India. by R.
Prawer Jhabvala. (Balliett)
34:229-30 N29'58. B          7426
Essays in appreciation. by
Bernard Berenson. (Anon.)
34:130-1 S6'58. B          7427
The essays of A. J. Muste. by
A. J. Muste. Nat Hentoff,
ed. (Anon.) 43:194 Mr18'67.
B          7428
Essays on music. by Alfred
Einstein. (Anon.) 33:151-2
Mr16'57. B          7429
The estate. by Isaac Bashevis
Singer. (Sissman) 45:97-9
F7'70. B          7430
Eternal fire. by Calder
Willingham. (Balliett) 39:
174-7 Mr30'63. B          7431
The eternal present. by
Siegfried Giedion. (Mumford)
41:158-70 Mr6'65. B          7432
Ethel Waters. (Malcolm)
35:81-2 Ap18'59. T          7433
Eugenia. by Randolph Carter.
(J. Lardner) 32:72-5 F9'57.
T          7434
Europe: a natural history.
by Kai Curry-Lindahl. (Anon.)
40:248 N14'64. B          7435
Europe views America. by
Edward W. Chester. (Anon.)
38:175-6 Ap28'62. B          7436
European brasses. by A. C.
Bouquet. (Anon.) 44:176
My18'68. B          7437
A European education. by
Romain Gary. (Anon.)
36:88 Jy23'60. B          7438
Eva. (S. Lardner) 41:102-104
Je12'65. CC          7439
Eva Braun: Hitler's mistress.
by Nerin E. Gun. (Anon.)
45:120 Mr1'69. B          7440
Evelyn Waugh: portrait of an
artist. by Frederick J.
Stopp. (Anon.) 34:97 Ja17
'59. B          7441
An evening for Merlin Finch.

by Charles Dizenzo. (Oliver)
44:56-8 Ja11'69. T      7442
An evening with Max Morath.
by Max Morath. (Oliver)
45:96-7 Mr8'69. T       7443
An evening with Mike Nichols
and Elaine May. by Mike
Nichols and Elaine May. (Mc-
Carten) 36:74-5 O15'60. T
                        7444
An evening with the Times
Square two. Anon. (Oliver)
43:106 Je3'67. T        7445
An evening with Yves Montand.
by Yves Montand. (Tynan)
35:94-6 O3'59. T        7446
An evening's Frost. by
Robert Frost. Donald Hall,
arr. (Oliver) 41:96-8
O23'65. T               7447
Evenings with Chekhov. by
Anton Chekhov. (Balliett)
37:123 My6'61. T        7448
Evenings with the orchestra.
by Hector Berlioz. Jacques
Barzun, trans. (Anon.)
32:160 *My5'56. B       7449
Events leading up to the
comedy. by Elliot Nugent.
(Anon.) 41:118 Ja15'66.
B                       7450
Everest: the west ridge. by
Thomas F. Hornbein. (Anon.)
42:179 Mr12'66. B       7451
Everybody go home! (Gill)
38:204-205 N24'62. CC
                        7452
Everybody loves Opal. by
John Patrick. (McCarten)
37:131-2 O21'61. T      7453
Everything in the garden. by
Giles Cooper. (Panter-Downes)
38:132-3 Ap7'62. T      7454
Everything in the garden. by
Edward Albee and Giles
Cooper. (McCarten) 43:93
D9'67. T                7455
Everything must go. by Keith
Waterhouse. (Anon.) 45:
140 Mr22'69. B          7456
Everything that rises must
converge. by Flannery
O'Connor. (N. Bliven) 41:
220-1 S11'65. B         7457

Evidence of love. by Dan
Jacobson. (Balliett) 36:199-
200 My14'60. B          7458
The evolution of political
thought. by C. Northcote
Parkinson. (Anon.) 34:192
O4'58. B                7459
The exchange of joy. by Isabel
Quigly. (Anon.) 31:71
*Ag6'55. B              7460
Ex-communist witnesses: four
studies in fact finding. by
Herbert L. Packer. (Anon.)
38:90-1 Je30'62. B      7461
Execution. by Colin McDougall.
(Balliett) 34:232-4 N29'58.
B                       7462
The exercise. by Lewis John
Carlino. (Gill) 44:130-1
My4'68. T               7463
Exercise hoodwink. by
Maurice Proctor. (Anon.)
43:68 D30'67. B         7464
The exhaustion of our son's
love. by Jerome Max.
(Oliver) 41:110-11 O30'65.
T                       7465
Exile and the kingdom. by
Albert Camus. (Podhoretz)
34:115-22 Mr29'58. B    7466
The exiles. by Albert J. Guerard.
(Anon.) 39:176 Ap27'63.
B                       7467
Exit. by George Deaux. (Anon.)
42:104 Jy16'66. B       7468
Exit the king. by Eugène
Ionesco. (Gill) 43:82-5
Ja20'68. T              7469
Exodus. (Angell) 36:136-7
D17'60. CC              7470
Expansion and coexistence: the
history of Soviet foreign
policy, 1917-67. by Adam
B. Ulam. (Anon.) 44:249-50
N23'68. B               7471
The expansion of Elizabethan
England. by A. L. Rowse
(Anon.) 31:214-15*N12'55.
B                       7472
The experiment. by David
Halliwell. and David Calderisi.
(Oliver) 43:138 My20'67. T
                        7473

The fair game. by Constantine
FitzGibbon. (Gill) 32:233-4
N17'56. B                    7508
Fair game. by Sam Locke.
(Gibbs) 33:103-104 N16'57.
T                            7509
Fair game for lovers. by
Richard Dougherty. (Mc-
Carten) 40:92 F22'64. T
                             7510
The fair sister. by William
Goyen. (Anon.) 39:217-18
O26'63. B                    7511
A fair trial. by Jean Laborde.
David Hughes, trans.
(Anon.) 38:173 Ap28'62.
B                            7512
Faithful are the wounds.
by May Sarton. (Anon.)
31:150-1 Mr19'55. B          7513
The falcon's story. by William
Du Bois. (Anon.) 34:190
O4'58. B                     7514
The fall. by Albert Camus.
(Flanner) 32:75-6*Jy14'56.
B                            7515
A fall from aloft. by Brian
Burland. (Anon.) 45:87-8
Ja31'70. B                   7516
The fall of Constantinople,
1453. by Steven Runciman.
(Anon.) 41:95 Ag7'65. B
                             7517
The fall of eagles: precursors
of Peter the Great. by
Zinaïda Schakovskoy. J.
Maxwell Brownjohn, trans.
(Anon.) 40:244 N14'64. B
                             7518
The fall of the British
empire, 1918-68. by Colin
Cross. (Anon.) 44:90-1
F1'69. B                     7519
The fall of the dynasties.
by Edmond Taylor. (Anon.)
39:151-2 F23'63. B           7520
The fall of the Roman empire.
(Gill) 40:178 Ap4'64. CC
                             7521
Fallen angels. by Noël Coward.
(Gibbs) 31:52-4*Ja28'56. T
                             7522

Fallout. by John M. Fowler.
(Malcolm) 35:71 My30'59.
T                            7523
False coin. by Harvey Swados.
(Balliett) 36:138-9 F27'60.
B                            7524
Falstaff. (Flanner) 42:116
Ag13'66 (Gill) 43:152 Mr25
'67. CC                      7525
Familiar garden birds of
America. by Henry Hill
Collins, Jr. and Ned R.
Boyajian. (Anon.) 41:247-8
D11'65. B                    7526
A family affair. by James
Goldman, John Kander, and
William Goldman. (McCarten)
37:94-6 F10'62. T            7527
Family diary. (Gill) 39:235-6
N23'63. CC                   7528
Family favorites. by Alfred
Duggan. (Anon.) 37:138
F18'61. B                    7529
A family lawsuit. by S.
Mitchell. (Anon.) 34:163
Ap12'58. B                   7530
The family letters of Samuel
Butler. by Samuel Butler.
Arnold Silver, ed. (W. Max-
well) 38:225-31 O13'62.
                             7531
The family of man. Edward
Steichen, ed. (Anon.)
31:163-4*S17'55. B           7532
The family of Pascual Duarte.
by Camilo José Cela.
Anthony Kerrigan, trans.
(West) 40:118-19 Ja30'65.
B                            7533
Family portrait. by Lenore
Coffee and William Joyce
Cowen. (Malcolm) 35:87-8
My16'59. T                   7534
The family reunion. by T.S.
Eliot. (Malcolm) 34:99-101
N1'58. T                     7535
The family way. (Gilliatt)
43:100-101 Jy15'67. CC
                             7536
Fandango Rock. by John
Masters. (Anon.) 35:173-4
Mr21'59. B                   7537

Fanny. (Gill) 37:58 Jy8'61. CC
7538
Fantastic stories. by Abram
Tertz. (West) 39:186-8
S21'63. B              7539
Fantastic voyage. (Gill) 42:
225 S17'66. CC        7540
The fantasticks. by Tom Jones
and Harvey Schmidt. (Mal-
colm) 36:96-7 My14'60. T
7541
Fantasy and fugue. by Roy
Fuller. (Anon.) 32:175-6
S22'56. B             7542
Fantomas. (Gill) 42:122
Ap16'66. CC           7543
A far country. by Henry Denker.
(McCarten) 37:76 Ap15'61.
T                     7544
Far, far the mountain peak.
by John Masters. (Anon.)
33:165 My18'57. B     7545
Far from the madding crowd.
(Gill) 43:165-6 O28'67. CC
7546
Farewell, farewell Eugene.
by John Vari and Rodney
Ackland. (McCarten) 36:95
O8'60. T              7547
A farewell to arms.
(McCarten) 33:65-6 F1'58
CC                    7548
Farewell to Eden. by Matthew
Huxley. (Anon.) 41:110-11
Jy17'65. B            7549
Farewell Victoria. by Terence
Hanbury White. (Anon.)
36:206 O15'60. B      7550
The farther shore. by Robert
M. Coates. (Anon.) 31:145
*O29'55. B            7551
Fashion, or life in New York.
by Anna Cora Mowatt.
(Malcolm) 34:64-9 Ja31'59. T
7552
The fastest gun alive.
(McCarten) 32:41 *Jy21'56. CC
7553
The fatal decisions. Seymour
Freidin and William
Richardson, eds. (Anon.)
32:129*Je2'56. B      7554

Fatal fascination. by Nigel
Balchin, C.S. Forester,
Eric Linklater and Chris-
topher Sykes. (Anon.) 41:
171 Mr6'65. B         7555
The fatal impact: an account
of the invasion of the South
Pacific, 1767-1840. by
Alan Moorehead. (Anon.)
42:193-4 Ap23'66. B   7556
The fatal inheritance: Philip II
and the Spanish Netherlands.
by Edward Grierson. (Anon.)
45:152 My17'69. B     7557
Fate is the hunter. by Ernest
K. Gann. (Anon.) 36:125-6
F11'61. B             7558
Fate of a man. (Gill) 37:51
Jy29'61. CC           7559
The fate of Admiral Kolchak.
by Peter Fleming. (Anon.)
39:159-60 S7'63. B    7560
Father. (Gill) 43:147 O7'67.
CC                    7561
Father Goose. (Gill) 40:151
D19'64. CC            7562
Father sets the pace. by
Gontran de Montaigne Poncins.
Bernard Frechtman, trans.
(Anon.) 31:145-6*S10'55.
B                     7563
Father Uxbridge wants to
marry. by Frank Gagliano.
(Oliver) 43:163 N4'67. T
7564
Father Vikenty. by Paul
Chavchavadze. (West) 31:
104-105 Je18'55. B    7565
Faulkner at West Point. by
William Faulkner. Joseph
L. Fant, III and Robert
Ashley, eds. (Anon.) 40:
186-7 My2'64. B       7566
The Faulkner-Cowley file:
letters and memories, 1944-
1962. by William Faulkner.
Malcom Cowley, ed. (Anon.)
42:127 Ag27'66. B     7567
Faulkner's county: Yoknapatawpha.
by Martin J. Dain. (Anon.)
40:248 N7'64. B       7568
Fausto's keyhole. by Jean

Arnaldi. (Anon.) 38:191 My5
'62. B                          7569
The favourite. by Françoise
Mallet-Joris. Herma
Briffault, trans. (Anon.)
38:79 Jy28'62. B                7570
Fear strikes out. (McCarten)
33:128-9 Mr30'57. CC            7571
The fearless vampire killers.
(Gill) 43:154 N25'67. CC
                                7572
A feast of freedom. by Leonard
Wibberly. (Anon.) 40:185-6
My2'64. B                       7573
Felix Frankfurter reminisces.
by Felix Frankfurter. Harlan
B. Phillips, ed. (Anon.)
36:155-6 Je4'60. B              7574
Felix walking. by Hilary Ford.
(Anon.) 34:154-5 My17'58.
B                               7575
Fénelon: letters of love and
counsel. by Francois de
Salignac Fénelon. John Mc-
Ewen, ed. and trans. (Anon.)
40:207 S12'64. B                7576
Fenollosa and his circle. by
Van Wyck Brooks. (Anon.)
38:183-4 S15'62. B              7577
Ferdinand Magellan, circum-
navigator: his life and ex-
plorations. by Charles Mc-
Kew Parr. (Anon.)
40:214 S19'64. B                7578
Ferdydurke. by Witold
Gombrowicz. Eric Mas-
bacher, trans. (Updike)
43:169-76 S23'67. B             7579
Fertig. by Sol Yurick. (Anon.)
42:89-90 Jy9'66. B              7580
Fête. by Roger Vailland. (N.
Bliven) 37:172-4 Ap8'61.
B                               7581
Fever. by J.M.G. Le Clézio.
Daphne Woodward, trans.
(West) 42:226-8 S17'66.
B                               7582
The few and the many. by
Hans Sahl. (Anon.) 38:97-8
Ja5'63. B                       7583
The fiancés. (Gill) 39:76-7
F1'64. CC                       7584
Fiasco in Milan. (Gill) 39:114
Ap20'63. CC                     7585

Ficciones. by Jorge Luis
Borges. (N. Bliven) 38:95-7
Ag18'62. B                      7586
The fiction factory. by Quentin
Reynolds. (Anon.) 31:120
*F11'56. B                      7587
Fiddle Hill. by James Mc-
Cague. (Anon.) 36:116-17
Ja14'61. B                      7588
Fiddler on the roof. by
Joseph Stein, Jerry Bock and
Sheldon Harnick. (McCarten)
40:96 O3'64. T                  7589
The field of vision. by Wright
Morris. (Gill) 32:236
N17'56. B                       7590
The fierce pawns. by Patrick
A. Macrory. (Anon.) 42:
231 S17'66. B                   7591
The fifteen weeks. by Joseph
M. Jones. (Anon.) 31:160
*S24'55. B                      7592
The fifteenth century: the
prospect of Europe.
by Margaret Aston. (Anon.)
44:175 Ap27'68. B               7593
The fifth queen. by Ford
Madox Ford. (Anon.) 39:77-8
Ja4'64. B                       7594
Fifty grand. (J. Lardner) 34:
125-6 My17'58. TV              7595
50 years of modern art. by
Emile Langui. Geoffrey
Sainsbury and James Oliver,
trans. (Anon.) 35:245-6
N28'59. B                       7596
Fifty-five days at Peking.
(Gill) 39:68 Je1'63. CC
                                7597
A fig leaf in her bonnet. by
Jesse Torn. (Balliett) 37:52
Je24'61. T                      7598
The fig leaves are falling. by
Allan Sherman. (Gill)
44:56 Ja11'69. T                7599
The fighting cock. by Jean
Anouilh. (Tynan) 35:72-7
*D19'59. T                      7600
Fighting Warsaw. by Stefan
Korbonski. (Anon.) 32:142-3
F16'57. B                       7601
Figures in the foreground:
literary reminiscences, 1917-
40. by Frank Swinnerton.

(Anon.) 40:205-206 My16'64.
B                          7602
Film as art. by Rudolf Arn-
heim. (Macdonald) 34:133-6
Mr15'58. B                 7603
Film form. by Sergei Eisen-
stein. Jay Leyda, trans. &
ed. (Macdonald) 34:147-54
Mr15'58. B                 7604
The film sense. by Sergei
Eisenstein. Jay Leyda, trans.
& ed. (Macdonald) 34:147-54
Mr15'58. B                 7605
Final solutions. by Frederick
Seidel. (Bogan) 39:211-12
O12'63. B                  7606
The fine and the wicked: the
life and times of Ouida. by
Monica Stirling. (Anon.)
34:122 Mr1'58. B           7607
The fine art of literary mayhem.
by Myrick Land. (Anon.)
38:123 F2'63. B            7608
A fine madness. (S. Lardner)
42:78-80 Jy9'66. CC        7609
The finest hours. (Gill)
40:149 N21'64. CC          7610
Finian's rainbow. (Kael) 44:
212-15 O19'68. CC          7611
The finishing touch. by Brigid
Brophy. (N. Bliven) 40:75-7
D26'64. B                  7612
Fiorello! by George Abbott,
Jerome Weidman, Jerry
Bock and Sheldon Harnick.
(Tynan) 35:95-7 D5'59. T   7613
Fire! by John Roc. (Gill) 44:
96 F8'69. T                7614
The fire and the rose. by Arthur
Bryant. (Anon.) 42:88 Jy23'66.
B                          7615
Fire at sea: the story of the
Morro Castle. by Thomas
Gallagher. (Anon.) 35:95
Ag8'59. B                  7616
Fire from heaven. by Mary
Renault. (Anon.) 45:59
D27'69. B                  7617
The fire within. by Pierre
Drieu La Rochelle. Richard
Howard, trans. (Updike)
41:216-21 O2'65. B         7618

The fire within. (Gill) 40:112-
14 F22'64. CC              7619
The firebugs. by Max Frisch.
(Oliver) 39:114 F23'63. T
                           7620
The fires of Autumn. by Helen
Howe. (Anon.) 35:199 S12
'59. B                     7621
Fireworks. by Jon Swan.
(Gill) 45:75 Je28'69. T
                           7622
The firmament of time.
by Loren Eiseley. (Anon.)
36:105-106 Ag13'60. B  7623
First and last love. by
Vincent Sheean. (Anon.)
32:242-3 N17'56. B         7624
First blood: the story of
Fort Sumter. by W.A.
Swanberg. (Anon.) 33:90
F1'58. B                   7625
The first day of Friday. by
Honor Tracy. (Balliett) 39:
233-4 D14'63. B            7626
The first four Georges. by
J.H. Plumb. (Anon.) 32:
125-6 F9'57. B             7627
The first gentleman. by
Norman Ginsbury. (Gibbs)
33:140-2 My4'57. T         7628
First gentleman of the bed-
chamber: the life of Louis-
François-Armand, Maréchal
duc de Richelieu. by Hubert
Cole. (Anon.) 41:112 Je26
'65. B                     7629
First love. by Samuel Taylor.
(McCarten) 37:56-7 Ja6'62.
T                          7630
The first New Deal. by Raymond
Moley and Elliot A. Rosen.
(Anon.) 42:118-19 Ja21'67. B
                           7631
First one asleep, whistle. by
Oliver Hailey. (McCarten)
42:84-6 Mr5'66. T          7632
The first born. by Christopher
Fry. (Gibbs) 34:83-4
My10'58. T                 7633
Firsthand report. by Sherman
Adams. (Rovere) 37:72-7
Jy22'61. B                 7634
Fitz. by Maxime Furlaud.

(Oliver) 42:82 My28'66. T
                                7635
Five a.m. by Jean Dutourd.
(West) 32:174-7 O27'56. B
                                7636
5 a.m. jazz. by Will Holt.
(Oliver) 40:129-30 O31'64.
T                               7637
5 against the house. (Mc-
Carten) 31:65 Je18'55. CC
                                7638
Five boyhoods. Martin Levin,
ed. (Anon.) 38:174 Ap28'62.
B                               7639
The five day lover. (Gill) 37:
111-12 D16'61. CC       7640
Five evenings. by Alexander
Volodin. (Oliver) 39:82-4
My18'63. T              7641
Five families: Mexican case
studies in the culture of
poverty. by Oscar Lewis.
(Anon.) 35:202-203 S12'59.
B                               7642
Five finger exercise. by
Peter Shaffer. (Panter-Downes)
34:121 S6'58 (Tynan) 35:100-
102 D12'59. T           7643
Five finger exercise. (Gill)
38:141-2 Ap28'62. CC   7644
Five journeys from Jakarta. by
Maslyn Williams. (Anon.)
41:143 F12'66. B       7645
Five on the black hand side. by
Charlie L. Russell (Oliver)
45:65-6 Ja10'70. T     7646
The five pennies. (McCarten)
35:54 Je27'59. CC      7647
Five sea captains: their own
accounts of voyages under
sail. Walter Teller, ed.
(Anon.) 36:162 D17'60. B
                                7648
The fixer. by Bernard Mala-
mud. (Balliett) 42:234-5
D10'66. B              7649
The fixer. (Kael) 44:86-9
D21'68. CC             7650
A flag full of stars. by Don
Robertson. (Anon.) 40:108
Ag29'64. B             7651
Flame and the fire. (Gill)
42:163-4 Ap2'66. CC    7562

The flame trees of Thika. by
Elspeth Huxley. (N. Bliven)
35:160-2 O3'59. B      7653
Flattop. by Barrett Gallagher.
(Anon.) 35:202 S12'59. B
                                7654
Flaubert. by Benjamin F. Bart.
(N. Bliven) 44:88-92 Je22'68.
B                               7655
Flaubert: the making of the
master. by Enid Starkie.
(N. Bliven) 44:88-92 Je22'68.
B                               7656
A flea in her ear. by Georges
Feydeau. (Gill) 45:86-8
O11'69. T              7657
Flee seven ways. by James
Burke. (Anon.) 40:166-7
D19'64. B              7658
Flemish music and society in
the fifteenth and sixteenth
centuries. by Robert
Wangermée. Robert Erich
Wolf, trans. (Anon.) 45:175
Ap26'69. B             7659
Flesh. by Brigid Brophy.
(Anon.) 39:177 My18'63. B
                                7660
Flight. by Jacques F. Ormond.
(Anon.) 39:99-100 D21'63. B
                                7661
The flight. by Ruth Stephan.
(Anon.) 32:82*D22'56. B
                                7662
The flight from the enchanter.
by Iris Murdoch. (Anon.)
32:161*My12'56. B      7663
The flight into Egypt. by Jean
Bloch-Michel. (Anon.) 31:
70*S3'55. B            7664
The flight of the Nez Percé: a
history of the Nez Percé war.
by Mark H. Brown. (Anon.)
43:193-4 Mr11'67. B    7665
The flight of the Phoenix. (Gill)
41:140 F12'66. CC      7666
The flim-flam man. (Gilliatt)
43:77-8 Ag26'67. CC    7667
Flood, a romance of our time.
by Robert Penn Warren.
(West) 40:204-205 S12'64.
B                               7668
Flora: a biography. by

by Elizabeth Gray Vining.
(Anon.) 42:165-6 Ap30'66.
B                    7669
Flora, the red menace. by George
Abbott, Robert Russell, John
Kander and Fred Ebb. (Mc-
Carten) 41:114 My22'65. T
                     7670
Flower chronicles. by Buckner
Hollingsworth. (Anon.)
34:167-8 S13'58. B      7671
Flower drum song. by Richard
Rodgers and Oscar Hammer-
stein, II. (Tynan) 34:104-106
D13'58. T               7672
Flower drum song. (Gill)
37:207-208 N18'61. CC  7673
Flowering cherry. by Robert
Bolt. (Tynan) 35:136 O31'59.
T                       7674
The flowering of the Renais-
sance. by Vincent Cronin.
(Anon.) 45:104 F7'70. B
                     7675
The flowers of evil. by Charles
Baudelaire. Jackson Mathews
and Marthiel Mathews, eds.
(Anon.) 31:180*O15'55. B
                     7676
The flowers of the forest. by
David Garnett. (Anon.)
32:143-4*S8'56. B       7677
Flush times. by Warren Miller.
(Anon.) 38:229-30 O20'62.
B                    7678
Fly blackbird. by C. Jackson
and James Hatch. (Oliver)
37:94-5 F17'62. T       7679
Foenix in choir. by Frank
Merlin. (Malcolm) 34:93-4
N8'58. T                7680
Folk songs of the world.
Charles Haywood, ed. (Anon.)
42:248 D10'66. B        7681
Follow a star. (Oliver) 37:159-
60 My6'61. CC           7682
Fontamara. by Ignazio Silone.
(West) 36:180-1 O1'60. B
                     7683
Food for the rich. by Paul
Reboux. Margaret Costa,
trans. (Anon.) 36:127-8 F
11'61. B                7684

For a new novel: essays on
fiction. by Alain Robbe-
Grillet. Richard Howard,
trans. (N. Bliven) 42:165-7
Ap9'66. B               7685
For love of a king. by
Alexandra, Queen of Yugo-
slavia. (Anon.) 32:179-80 O
27'56. B                7686
For love of Ivy. (Gilliatt)
44:81-2 Jy27'68. CC     7687
For love of some islands.
by Floyd Schmoe. (Anon.)
40:144 Je13'64. B       7688
For love or money. by Tim
Jeal. (Anon.) 43:148-9
My27'67. B              7689
For the life of me. by
Robert Briscoe and Alden
Hatch. (Anon.) 34:178-9
N1'58. B                7690
For the Union dead. by Robert
Lowell. (Bogan) 41:194
Ap10'65. B              7691
Forbidden childhood. by Ruth
Slenczynska. (Sargeant)
34:193-4 O11'58. B      7692
Forbidden colors. by Yukio
Mishima. (West) 44:105-109
Je15'68. B              7693
Forbidden fruit. (McCarten)
35:92 Mr7'59. CC        7694
Forbidden planet. (McCarten)
32:92*My12'56. CC       7695
Forbush and the penguins. by
Graham Billing. (Anon.)
42:186 My7'66. B        7696
Force of circumstance. by
Simone de Beauvoir. Richard
Howard, trans. (N. Bliven)
41:104-106 Ja8'66. B    7697
Ford: decline and rebirth, 1933-
62. by Allan Nevins and
Frank Ernest Hill. (Anon.)
39:92-3 Ag17'63. B      7698
Ford: expansion and challenge.
1915-33. by Allan Nevins
and Frank Ernest Hill. (Anon.)
33:239-40*N30'57. B     7699
Foreign intrigue. (McCarten)
32:41*Jy21'56. CC       7700
The foreigner. by Ralph Blum.
(West) 37:203-204 O7'61. B
                     7701

The forest people. by Colin M.
Turnbull. (Anon.) 37:170
S30'61. B          7702
Forever darling. (McCarten)
31:116*F18'56. CC          7703
Forge of democracy: the House
of Representatives. by
Neil MacNeil. (Anon.) 39:
112-13 Je22'63. B          7704
The forger. by Jay Williams.
(Balliett). 37:69-70 Jy8'61.
B          7705
Forgers, dealers, experts:
strange chapters in the
history of art. by Sepp
Schüller. James Cleugh,
trans. (Anon.) 36:241-2
N26'60. B          7706
The forgotten people. by
Seymour Freidin. (Anon.)
38:231-2 O20'62. B          7707
Fortuna. by Arnold Weinstein.
(Oliver) 37:67 Ja13'62. T
7708
Fortune and men's eyes. by
John Herbert. (Oliver) 43:
134 Mr4'67. T          7709
The fortune cookie. (Gill)
42:150-2 O29'66. CC          7710
Forty carats. by Jay Allen.
(Gill) 44:59 Ja4'69. T          7711
40 pounds of trouble. (Gill)
38:102 F2'63. CC          7712
Forty years on. by Alan Bennett.
(Panter-Downes) 44:206-207
D14'68. T          7713
Forty years with Berenson. by
Nicky Mariano. (Anon.)
42:246 N12'66. B          7714
The 49th cousin. by Menasha
Skulnik. (McCarten) 36:116-
18 N5'60. T          7715
41 in a sack. by Shai K. Ophir.
(Malcolm) 36:91-2 Ap9'60. T
7716
The founding father: the story
of Joseph P. Kennedy.
by Richard J. Whalen. (Anon.)
40:78-9 D26'64. B          7717
Fountain of the elephants. by
Desmond Young . (Anon.)
36:183 Ap16'60. B          7718
The fountain overflows. by

Rebecca West. (Gill) 32:66-9
Ja5'57. B          7719
Fountains in the sand. by
Norman Douglas. (West)
33:112-16 Ja11'58. B          7720
Four against Everest. by
Woodrow Wilson Sayre.
(Anon.) 40:195 My9'64. B
7721
Four bags full. (McCarten)
33:94 S14'57. CC          7722
The four days of Naples. (Gill)
39:169-70 Mr23'63. CC
7723
The four horsemen of the
apocalypse. (Gill) 38:127-8
Mr31'62. CC          7724
The 400 blows. (McCarten)
35:227-8 N28'59. CC          7725
The 480. by Eugene Burdick.
(Anon.) 40:92 Jy11'64. B
7726
The four seasons. by Arnold
Wesker. (Oliver) 44:102
Mr23'68. T          7727
**** (Gill) 43:74 Ja6'68.
CC          7728
Four winds. by Thomas W.
Phipps. (Gibbs) 33:64-6
O5'57. T          7729
The four-gated city. by Doris
Lessing. (Anon.) 45:114
Je14'69. B          7730
1492. (Miller) 39:116-18 N16'63.
TV          7731
The fourteenth century, 1307-
1399. by May McKisack.
(Anon.) 36:161-2 Mr26'60.
B          7732
The fourth horseman of Miami
Beach. by Albert Halper.
(Anon.) 42:223 O1'66. B
7733
The fourth of June. by David
Benedictus. (West) 38:154-7
F16'63. B          7734
The fourth session. by Xavier
Rynne. (Anon.) 42:104 Ag6
'66. B          7735
The fourth wall. (Oliver) 44:
129 S14'68. T          7736
Fowlers end. by Gerald Kersh.
(Anon.) 33:139 Je8'57. B
7737

The fox. (Kael) 43:100-105
F10'68. CC          7738
The fox and the camellias. by
Ignazio Silone. (West)
37:94-6 Ag26'61. B     7739
The fox in the attic. by Richard
Hughes. (Anon.) 38:176
Mr24'62. B            7740
The foxglove saga. by Auberon
Waugh. (Panter-Downes)
37:75-7 S2'61. B      7741
Foxy. by Ian McLellan Hunter
and Ring Lardner, Jr.
(McCarten) 40:106 F29'64.
T                     7742
Fractions. by Andrew Field.
(Anon.) 45:156-7 S13'69. B
                      7743
Fragebogen. by Ernst von
Salomon. (Liebling) 31:122-4
Mr26'55. B            7744
Fragments. by Murray Schisgal.
(Oliver) 43:151-2 O14'67. T
                      7745
France against herself. by
Herbert Luethy. (Flanner)
31:152-7*S24'55. B    7746
France and Algeria: comple-
mentary enemies. by Ger-
maine Tillion. Richard How-
ard, trans. (Anon.) 37:91
Ag19'61. B            7747
France, steadfast and changing:
the Fourth to the Fifth
Republic. by Raymond Aron.
(Anon.) 36:205 S10'60. B
                      7748
Francis Bacon: the temper
of a man. by Catherine
Drinker Bowen. (Anon.)
39:70 Ag3'63. B       7749
Francis of Assisi. (Gill)
37:38-9 Ag5'61. CC    7750
Frank Harris: the life and
loves of a scoundrel. by
Vincent Brome. (Anon.)
36:179-80 Ap23'60. B  7751
Frank V. by Friedrich
Dürrenmatt. (Flanner)
38:103 Ja12'63. T     7752
Frankenstein. by the Living
Theatre. (Oliver) 44:106-
12 O12'68. T          7753

Franklin D. Roosevelt: the
triumph. by Frank Freidel.
(Anon.) 32:155 S29'56. B
                      7754
Frantic. (Gill) 37:42 Jy1'61.
CC                    7755
The fratricides. by Maurice
Edelman. (Anon.) 39:83
Je29'63. B            7756
Frédéric Joliot-Curie. by
Pierre Biquard. (Anon.)
42:196 Ap23'66. B     7757
The free enterprisers: Kennedy,
Johnson, and the business
establishment. by Hobart
Rowen. (Anon.) 40:227 O3'64.
B                     7758
Free fall. by William Golding.
(West) 36:176-8 Ap30'60.
B                     7759
Freedom in the ancient world.
by Herbert J. Muller. (N.
Bliven) 37:86-90 Ja6'62. B
                      7760
Freedom in the modern world.
by Herbert J. Muller.
(Anon.) 42:143 My28'66. B
                      7761
Freedom or death. by Nikos
Kazantzakis. (West) 31:88-90
*F4'56. B             7762
Freedom under Lincoln. by
Dean Sprague. (Anon.)
41:182-3 Mr27'65. B   7763
The French. by François
Nourissier. Adrienne Foulke,
trans. (Anon.) 44:120 Ag24
'68. B                7764
French-cancan (McCarten)
32:82*Ap28'56. CC     7765
French cathedrals. by Jean
Bony and Martin Hürlimann.
(Anon.) 37:172 S30'61. B
                      7766
A French mistress. (Angell)
36:50 D31'60. CC      7767
The French nation: from
Napoleon to Pétain. by D.W.
Brogan. (Anon.) 34:152-3
*Ap26'58. B           7768
The French: portrait of a peo-
ple. by Sanche de Gramont.
(Anon.) 45:157 S13'69. B
                      7769

The French Revolution from its
origins to 1793. by Georges
Lefebvre. Elizabeth Moss
Evanson, trans. (Anon.) 38:
194-5 My5'62. B          7770
The French they are a funny
race. (McCarten) 33:95
*Je1'57. CC              7771
Freud. (Gill) 38:77-8 D22'62.
CC                       7772
Friday. by Michel Tournier.
Norman Denny, trans. (Anon.)
45:115 Je14'69. B        7773
Friday night. by James
Elward. (Oliver) 41:58 F20
'65. T                   7774
Friday, or the Pacific limbo.
by Michel Tournier. (Flanner)
44:151-5 Ap27'68. B      7775
A friend in power. by Carlos
Baker. (Anon.) 34:91-2
Je28'58. B               7776
Friendly persuasion. (McCarten)
32:125-6*N10'56. CC      7777
Friends and enemies. by
Adlai E. Stevenson. (Anon.)
35:175-6 Mr21'59. B      7778
Friends and lovers. by Oscar
Pinkus. (West) 39:186
S21'63. B                7779
A frieze of girls: memoirs as
fiction. by Allan Seager.
(Anon.) 40:135 F29'64. B
                         7780
The Frisbies of the South
Seas. by Johnny Frisbie.
(Anon.) 35:104 Ja9'60. B
                         7781
From a Roman balcony. (Gill)
37:194-5 O28'61. CC      7782
From beginning to end. by
Jozsef Lengyel. (West)
45:102-104 Je21'69. B
                         7783
From every zenith. by John
Collier. (Anon.) 39:195-6
S28'63. B                7784
From Galileo to Newton: 1630-
1720. by A. Rupert Hall.
(Anon.) 39:90-1 Ag10'63.
B                        7785
From merciless invaders.
by Alexander McKee. (Anon.)

40:245 N7'64. B          7786
From Russia with love. (Gill)
40:120-2 Ap18'64. CC     7787
From Sarajevo to Potsdam. by
A. J. P. Taylor. (Anon.)
42:126-7 Ja28'67. B      7788
From the hand of the hunter.
by John Braine. (Anon.)
36:178-9 Ap23'60. B      7789
From the N. R. F. Justin
O'Brien. (Anon.) 34:63-4
Jy5'58. B                7790
From the second city. by
Fred Kaz. (Oliver) 45:141-2
O25'69. T                7791
From the second city. by
William Mathieu, et al.
(Oliver) 37:129-30 O7'61.
T                        7792
From the terrace. by John
O'Hara. (Wain) 34:112-13
Ja10'59. B               7793
From the terrace. (McCarten)
36:72-3 Jy23'60. CC      7794
From Vienna to Versailles.
by L. C. B. Seaman. (Anon.)
32:75*Jy21'56. B         7795
The front page. by Ben
Hecht and Charles Mac-
Arthur. (Oliver) 44:160-1
O19'68 (Gill) 45:112 My17'69.
T                        7796
The Frontenacs. by François
Mauriac. Gerard Hopkins,
trans. (West) 37:219-21
N4'61. B                 7797
Frontiers of astronomy. by
Fred Hoyle. (Anon.) 31:182
*O8'55. B                7798
Fuel for the flame. by Alec
Waugh. (Anon.) 35:120
Ja16'60. B               7799
The fugitive kind. (McCarten)
36:147-8 Ap23'60. CC     7800
Full circle: the memoirs of
Anthony Eden. by Anthony
Eden. (Anon.) 36:179 Mr19
'60. B                   7801
Full of life. (McCarten) 33:75
F23'57. CC               7802
Fullness of days. by Edward
Frederick Halifax. (Anon.)
33:200-201 O12'57. B     7803

The fume of poppies. by Jonathan Kozol. (Anon.) 34: 205-206 O18'58. B            7804

Fun in a Chinese laundry. by Josef von Sternberg. (Anon.) 41:198-9 Ap24'65. B            7805

Funeral in Berlin. (Gill) 42:60-1 D24'66. CC            7806

Funny face. (McCarten) 33:76 Ap6'57. CC            7807

Funny girl. by Jule Styne and Bob Merrill. (McCarten) 40:76 Ap4'64. T            7808

Funny girl. (Kael) 44:167-70 S28'68. CC            7809

A funny thing happened on the way to the Forum. By Burt Shevelove and Larry Gelbart and Stephen Sondheim. (McCarten) 38:103 My19'62. T            7810

A funny thing happened on the way to the Forum. (Gill) 42:164-5 O22'66. CC            7811

Funnyhouse of a Negro. by Adrienne Kennedy. (Oliver) 39:76-8 Ja25'64. T            7812

Further letters of Gerard Manley Hopkins. by Gerard Manley Hopkins. Claude Colleer Abbott, ed. (Anon.) 33:96 Jy13'57. B            7813

The future of man. by P.B. Medawar. (Anon.) 36:59 D31'60. B            7814

The future of religions. by Paul Tillich. (Anon.) 42:91-2 Jy9'66. B            7815

The future of the Republican Party. by Robert Donovan. (Anon.) 40:124 Ja30'65. B            7816

Future to let. by Jerzy Peterkiewicz. (Anon.) 35: 176 Ap25'59. B            7817

Futz. by Rochelle Owens. (Oliver) 43:88-90 F10'68; 44:51 D28'68. T            7818

Futz. (Kael) 45:158-62 N29'69. CC            7819

G

Gabriela, clove and cinnamon. by Jorge Amado. James L. Taylor and William L. Grossman, trans. (Anon.) 38:175-6 S22'62. B            7820

Gaily, gaily. (Kael) 45:70 D20'69. CC            7821

Galaxies, nuclei, and quasars. by Fred Hoyle. (Anon.) 41:144 F12'66. B            7822

A galaxy of fathers. by Frank Swinnerton. (Anon.) 42:244 O15'66. B            7823

Galia. (Gill) 42:60 D24'66. CC            7824

Galileo. by Bertolt Brecht. (McCarten) 43:146 Ap22'67. T            7825

Galileo Galilei. by Ludovico Geymonat. Stillman Drake, trans. (Anon.) 41:217-18 My15'65. B            7826

Gallipoli. by Alan Moorehead. (Podhoretz) 32:191-7 O20'56. B            7827

Gallows humor. by Jack Richardson. (Balliett) 37: 93-4 Ap29'61. T            7828

Gambit. (Gill) 42:89 Ja7'67. CC            7829

Gamblers' money. by Wallace Turner. (Anon.) 41:217 My15'65. B            7830

The game is over. (Gill) 42:105 Ja14'67. CC            7831

The game of hearts. by Harriette Wilson. Lesley Blanch, ed. (West) 31:78-86 Jy16'55. B            7832

Game without rules. by Michael Gilbert. (Anon.) 43:76 Jy1'67. B            7833

Games. (Gill) 43:95 S23'67. CC            7834

The gang's all here. by Jerome Lawrence and Robert E. Lee. (Tynan) 35:125-6 O10'59. T            7835

A gap in the wall. by Gabrielle Estivals. (West) 38:157-8 F16'63. B            7836

Garbo. by John Bainbridge. (Anon.) 31:143 Ap2'55. B 7837

The gardener and other poems. by John Hall Wheelock. (Anon.) 38:188 Ap14'62. B 7838

The Garnett family. by Carolyn G. Heilbrun. (Anon.) 37:242 N25'61. B 7839

The Garrick year. by Margaret Drabble. (Anon.) 41:197 Ap24'65. B 7840

Gates of Paris. (McCarten) 33:106-107 Ja25'58. CC 7841

The gates of the forest. by Elie Wiesel. (Anon.) 42:135 Ag20'66. B 7842

The gates of the sea. by Philippe Diolé. (Anon.) 31: 140 My21'55. B 7843

Gauguin. by Henri Perruchot. Humphrey Hare, trans. (Anon.) 40:208 My16'64. B 7844

A gay and melancholy sound. by Merle Miller. (Anon.) 37:165-6 My20'61. B 7845

The gay divorce. by Dwight Taylor, Kenneth Webb, Samuel Hoffenstein and Cole Porter. (Malcolm) 36:136-7 Ap16'60. T 7846

The gay life. by Fay Kanin, Michael Kanin, Arthur Schwartz and Howard Dietz. (McCarten) 37:118 D2'61. T 7847

Gay monarch. by Virginia Cowles. (West) 32:224-32 D8'56. B 7848

The gazebo. by Alec Coppel (Tynan) 34:72 D20'58. T 7849

The gazebo. (McCarten) 35: 121 Ja23'60. CC 7850

Gazella. by Stuart Cloete. (Anon.) 34:200 O25'58. B 7851

A gazelle on the lawn. by Douglas Fairbairn. (Anon.) 40:194 My9'64. B 7852

General della Rovere. (Gill) 36:206-207 N26'60. CC 7853

General George B. McClellan: shield of the Union. by Warren W. Hassler, Jr. (Anon.) 33:178 Ap13'57. B 7854

General Gordon's Khartoum journal. by Charles George Gordon. Godfrey Elton, ed. (Anon.) 39:91-2 Ag10'63. B 7855

General Graham, Lord Lynedoch. by Antony Brett-James. (Anon.) 35:91-2 Jy25'59. B 7856

General Grant by Matthew Arnold, with a rejoinder by Mark Twain. by Matthew Arnold and Mark Twain. John Y. Simon, ed. (Anon.) 42:206-207 My21'66. B 7857

The general says no: Britain's exclusion from Europe. by Nora Beloff. (Anon.) 39:191-2 S21'63. B 7858

General Seeger. by Ira Levin. (McCarten) 38:83 Mr10'62. T 7859

Generation. by William Goodhart. (McCarten) 41:195-6 O16'65. T 7860

The Genesee. by Henry W. Clune. (Anon.) 39:121-2 Je15 '63. B 7861

The genius and the goddess. by Aldous Huxley. (West) 31:168-70*O15'55. B 7862

The genius and the doddess. by Aldous Huxley. (Gibbs) 33:42-3 D21'57. T 7863

The genteel murderer. by Charles Norman. (Anon.) 32:187 O6'56. B 7864

The gentleman and the tiger. by George B. McClellan, Jr. Harold C. Syrett, ed. (Anon.) 32:136-7*Mr24'56. B 7865

Gentlemen in their season. by Gabriel Fielding. (Anon.) 42:117 S3'66. B 7866

Gentlemen, scholars and scoundrels, a treasury of

the best of Harper's magazine
from 1850 to the present.
Horace Knowles, ed. (Anon.)
35:247-8 N14'59. B    7867
Gentlemen, start your engines.
by Wilbur Shaw. (Anon.)
31:107-08 Je18'55. B    7868
George: an early autobiography. by
Emlyn Williams. (N. Bliven)
38:210-13 O27'62. B    7869
George Bernard Shaw. by
Archibald Henderson. (West)
33:119-26 F23'57. B    7870
George C. Marshall: education
of a general, 1880-1939. by
Forrest C. Pogue. (Anon.)
39:244-5 N16'63. B    7871
George Canning. by P.J.V.
Rolo. (Anon.) 41:245 N6'65.
B    7872
George Eliot. by Gordon S.
Haight. (Anon.) 44:237-8
N9'68. B    7873
The George Eliot letters:
volumes 4 through 7. by
George Eliot. Gordon S.
Haight, ed. (Anon.) 31:134
*F18'56. B    7874
George Frideric Handel. by
Paul Henry Lang. (Sargeant)
43:146-8 Je10'67. B    7875
George M! by Michael
Stewart, John Pascal and
Fran Pascal. (Gill) 44:156
Ap20'68. T    7876
George Orwell. by John Atkins.
(Anon.) 31:182-3*O8'55.
B    7877
George Orwell: fugitive from
the camp of victory. by Richard
Rees. (Anon.) 38:184 Ap7'62.
B    7878
George Sandys: poet-
adventurer. by Richard
Beale Davis. (Anon.) 31:
176-7 O15'55. B    7879
George W. Cable: a biography.
by Arlin Turner. (Wilson)
33:180-228 N9'57. B    7880
George Washington: first in
peace. by John Alexander
Carroll and Mary Wells
Ashworth. (Anon.) 33:71-2

Ja4'58. B    7881
George Washington: the forge
of experience (1732-75).
by James Thomas Flexner.
(Anon.)41:106 Ja22'66.B 7882
Georgian afternoon. by L.E.
Jones. (Anon.) 34:162 Ap
12'58. B    7883
Georgy girl. (Gill) 42:150
O29'66. CC    7884
The geranium hat. by Bernard
Evslin. (Malcolm) 35:92-4
Mr28'59. T    7885
Germaine: a portrait of
Mme. de Staël. by Wayne
Andrews. (Anon.) 39:245-6
N16'63. B    7886
The German atomic bomb.
by David Irving. (Anon.)
44:114-15 Je15'68. B    7887
Germans against Hitler. by
Terence Prittie. (Anon.)
40:207-208 S26'64. B    7888
The Germans: an indictment of
my people. by Gudrun Tem-
pel. Sophie Wilkins, trans.
(Anon.)39:122 Je1'63. B 7889
Germany divided: the legacy
of the Nazi era. by Terence
Prittie. (Anon.) 36:242-3
N26'60. B    7890
Gertrude Stein: her life and
work. by Elizabeth Sprigge.
(Anon.) 33:150-1 Mr16'57.
B    7891
Gertrude Stein's America. by
Gertrude Stein and Gilbert
A. Harrison. (Anon.) 42:
176 Mr12'66. B    7892
Gertrude Stein's first reader.
by Gertrude Stein. (Oliver)
45:39 D27'69. T    7893
Gervaise. (McCarten) 33:83-4
N23'57. CC    7894
Gestapo. by Edward Crankshaw.
(West) 32:134-41*S8'56.B7895
Getting married. by George
Bernard Shaw. (Malcolm)
35:84-6 Je13'59. T    7896
Ghana. by Kwame Nkrumah.
(Anon.) 33:151-2 Mr23'57. B
7897
Ghost ship of the Confederacy.

by Edward Boykin. (Anon.)
33:74*Jy27'57. B    7898
Ghost ship of the Pole. by
Wilbur Cross. (Anon.)
36:206 S10'60. B    7899
The ghost sonata. by August
Strindberg. (Flanner) 38:
96 Je23'62. T    7900
Ghosts. by Henrik Ibsen. (Oliver)
37:120-2 S30'61. T    7901
Giacomo Joyce. by James
Joyce. Richard Ellmann, ed.
(Updike) 44:167-74 Ap6'68. B
    7902
Giant. (McCarten) 32:178-9
O20'56. CC    7903
The giant dwarfs. by Gisela
Elsner. Joel Carmichael,
trans. (Anon.) 41:244 N6'65.
B    7904
Giant's arrow. by Samuel
Youd. (Anon.) 36:195-6
Mr12'60. B    7905
The giant's dance by Otis
Bigelow. (Oliver) 40:131
N28'64. T.    7906
Giants, sons of giants. by
Joseph Kramm. (McCarten)
37:64 Ja20'62. T    7907
Gideon. by Paddy Chayefsky.
(McCarten) 37:96 N18'61. T
    7908
The gift. by Vladimir Nabokov.
(Malcolm) 40:198-205 Ap25'64.
B    7909
Gift from the sea. by Anne
Morrow Lindbergh. (Anon.)
31:152 Mr19'55. B    7910
The gift of love. (McCarten)
34:76 F22'58. CC    7911
Gift of time. by Andrew
Varna. (Anon.) 32:188 O6'56.
B    7912
A gift of time. by Garson
Kanin. (McCarten) 38:93
Mr3'62. T    7913
Gigi. (Flanner) 33:76-8 S7'57
(McCarten) 34:73-4 My24'58.
CC    7914
Gigot. (Gill) 38:158
O6'62. CC    7915
Gilbert: his life and strife. by
Hesketh Pearson. (Anon.)

33:134-5 F8'58. B    7916
Giles goat-boy. by John
Barth. (Balliett) 42:234
D10'66. B    7917
Gilligan's last elephant by
Gerald Hanley. (Anon.)
38:152 S8'62. B    7918
The ginger man. by J. P.
Donleavy. (Malcolm) 34:194-8
O25'58 (Adler) 40:203-204
My16'64. B    7919
The ginger man. by J. P.
Donleavy. (Oliver) 39:131
D7'63. T    7920
The gingerbread age. by
John Maass. (Betjeman) 33:
66-9 D28'57. B    7921
The gingham dog. by Lanford
Wilson. (Gill) 45:107
My3'69. T    7922
Giovanni's room. by James
Baldwin. (West) 32:220-2
*N10'56. B    7923
A girl could get lucky. by
Don Appell. (McCarten)
40:96 O3'64. T    7924
The girl he left behind. (Mc-
Carten) 32:126*N10'56. CC
    7925
A girl in black. (McCarten)
33:91 S28'57. CC    7926
The girl in the red velvet
swing. (McCarten) 31:84
*O29'55. CC    7927
A girl like I. by Anita Loos.
(Anon.) 42:243-4 O15'66. B
    7928
A girl named Tamiko. (Gill)
39:144-5 Mr30'63. CC    7929
The girl on a motorcycle.
(Kael) 44:89-90 D21'68.
CC    7930
The girl who came to supper.
by Terence Rattigan.
(McCarten) 39:62 D21'63.
T    7931
Girl with a suitcase. (Gill)
37:86-8 S16'61. CC    7932
Girl with a zebra. by Perdita
Buchan. (Anon.) 42:245-6
N5'66. B    7933
A girl with class. by Dave
Wallis. (Anon.) 35:122 Ja23
'60. B    7934

Girl with green eyes. (Gill)
40:87-8 Ag22'64. CC    7935
The girl with the golden eyes.
(Balliett)38:56 S1'62. CC
                              7936
The girl-getters. (Gill) 42:
156 Ap30'66. CC    7937
The girls against the boys. by
Arnold B. Horwitt and
Richard Lewine. (Tynan)
35:121-2 N14'59. T    7938
The girls are willing. (Mc-
Carten) 35:86 My23'59. CC
                              7939
The girls in 509. by Howard
Teichmann. (J. Lardner)
34:90-2 O25'58. T    7940
The girls of slender means.
by Muriel Spark. (Updike)
39:192-4 S14'63. B    7941
Girls of Summer. by N. Richard
Nash. (Gibbs) 32:117-18 D1'56.
T                              7942
Give us this day. by Sidney
Stewart. (Anon.) 32:107-108
Ja19'57. B    7943
The given word. (Gill) 40:179
Ap4'64. CC    7944
The glass bees. by Ernest
Juenger.  Louise Bogan and
Elizabeth Mayer, trans.
(Anon.) 37:178 My13'61. B
                              7945
The glass bottom boat. (Oliver)
42:110 Je18'66. CC    7946
The glass menagerie. by
Tennessee Williams. (Mc-
Carten) 41:158 My15'65. T
                              7947
The glass slipper. (McCarten)
31:117-18 Ap2'55. CC    7948
The glass tower. (McCarten)
35:123-4 S12'59. CC    7949
The glass-blowers. by Daphne
du Maurier. (Anon.) 39:181-2
Mr23'63. B    7950
The gleam of bayonets: the
battle of Antietam and Robert
E. Lee's Maryland campaign,
September, 1862. by James
V. Murfin. (Anon.) 41:122-3
Ag28'65. B    7951
Glenport, Illinois. by Paul

Darcy Boles. (Anon.) 31:101
*Ja14'56. B    7952
Glide path. by Arthur C.
Clarke. (Anon.) 39:188-9
O5'63. B    7953
Gloria and Esperanza. by Julie
Bovasso. (Gill) 45:57 F14'70.
T                              7954
The glorious fault: the life
of Lord Curzon. by Leonard
Mosley. (Anon.) 36:156
Je4'60. B    7955
The glorious oyster. by Hector
Bolitho and Maurice Burton
and W. A. Bentley. (Anon.)
37:171-2 S30'61. B    7956
Glückel of Hameln 1646-1724,
written by herself. by Frau
Glückel Segal. Beth-Zion
Abrahams, ed. and trans.
(Anon.) 39:179 Ap27'63. B
                              7957
The gnostic religion. by Hans
Jonas. (Anon.) 35:171-2 O3
'59. B    7958
Go ask the river. by Evelyn
Eaton. (Anon.) 45:114-15
Je14'69. B    7959
Go in beauty. by William
Eastlake. (Anon.) 32:177-8
O27'56. B    7960
Go naked in the world. (Oliver)
37:137-8 Mr25'61. CC    7961
Go South to sorrow. by Carl
T. Rowan. (Anon.) 33:140
Je8'57. B    7962
Goa. by Asif Currimbhoy.
(Oliver) 44:84 Mr2'68. T
                              7963
The goal. by Phyllis Bottome.
(Anon.) 39:84 Je29'63. B
                              7964
Goal! (Gill) 42:77 Ja28'67.
CC    7965
God, Allah, and Ju Ju. by
Jack Mendelsohn. (Anon.)
38:195-6 My5'62. B    7966
A god and his gifts. by Ivy
Compton-Burnett. (Adler)
40:183-5 My2'64. B    7967
God and Kate Murphy. by Kieran
Tunney and John Synge.
(Tynan) 35:80-2 Mr7'59. T
                              7968

God bless you, Mr. Rosewater.
by Kurt Vonnegut, Jr.
(Anon.) 41:216 My15'65. B
7969
God is a (guess what?). by Ray
McIver. (Oliver) 44:50-1 D
28'68. T 7970
The goddess. (McCarten) 34:60
Jy5'58. CC 7971
The godmother. by Janice
Elliott. (Anon.) 43:106-107
Je24'67. B 7972
Gods and men: the origins of
Western culture. by Henry
Bamford Parkes. (Anon.)
35:175-6 Ap18'59. B 7973
God's country and my people.
by Wright Morris. (Coles)
45:205-213 O18'69. B 7974
Gods, demons, and others.
by R.K. Narayan. (Mehta)
41:193-201 Mr13'65. B
7975
The gods were kind. by William
Willis. (Anon.) 31:215-16*
N12'55. B 7976
Gogol: a life. by David
Magarshack. (Auden) 33:221-
37*N30'57. B 7977
Going away. by Clancy Sigal.
(Balliett) 38:181-5 Mr17'62.
B 7978
Going to the river. by Constantine
FitzGibbon. (West) 39:233-6
D7'63. B 7979
The gold of Naples. (McCarten)
32:123-4 F16'57. CC 7980
The golden age. by Richard
Johnson. (McCarten) 39:110
N30'63. T 7981
The golden age of Burgundy:
the magnificent dukes and
their courts. by Joseph
Calamette. Doreen Weightman,
trans. (Anon.) 39:205-206
Mr16'63. B 7982
The golden age of Greece.
(Miller) 39:118-19 N16'63.
TV 7983
The golden age of Indian art.
by Pierre Rambach and
Vitold de Golish. (Anon.) 32:
148*Ap28'56. B 7984

The golden bees. by Theo
Aronson. (Anon.) 40:226
O3'64. B 7985
Golden boy. by William Gibson,
Charles Strouse and Lee
Adams. (McCarten) 40:129
O31'64. T 7986
Golden demon. (McCarten)
31:93*F11'56. CC 7987
The golden fleece. by A.R.
Gurney, Jr. (Oliver) 45:63-4
Jy5'69. T 7988
Golden fleecing. by Lorenzo
Semple, Jr. (Tynan) 35:94-5
O24'59. T 7989
The golden fruits. by Nathalie
Sarraute. Maria Jolas, trans.
(Adler) 40:181-3 My2'64.
B 7990
Golden interlude: the Edens in
India. by Janet Dunbar.
(Anon.) 32:173 S22'56. B
7991
The golden notebook. by Doris
Lessing. (N. Bliven) 39:114-
19 Je1'63. B 7992
Golden rainbow. by Ernest
Kinoy and Walter Marks.
(Gill) 43:88 F10'68. T 7993
The golden screw. by Tom
Sankey. (Oliver) 42:116-18
F11'67. T 7994
The golden six. by Maxwell
Anderson. (Malcolm) 34:
91-3 N8'58. T 7995
The golden spur. by Dawn
Powell. (Wilson) 38:233-8
N17'62. B 7996
The golden trade of the Moors.
by E.W. Bovill. (Anon.)
34:75-6 Jy26'58. B 7997
Goldfinger. (Gill) 40:73 D26'64.
(Flanner) 41:165-7 Mr20'65.
CC 7998
Goldilocks. by Walter Kerr
and Jean Kerr. (J. Lardner)
34:55-6 O18'58. T 7999
The gold-rimmed spectacles.
by Giorgio Bassani. Isabel
Quigley, trans. (Anon.) 36:61-
2 D24'60. B 8000
Goldstein. (Gill) 41:214-15 My
15'65. CC 8000a

The golem. by H. Leivick.
(Malcolm) 35:87-8 Mr7'59.
T                        8001
Golk. by Richard G. Stern.
(Balliett) 36:200-201 My14'60.
B                        8002
The gondoliers. by William S.
Gilbert and Arthur Sullivan.
(Malcolm) 35:94-5 F13'60.
T                        8003
Gone are the days. (Gill)
39:178-9 O5'63. CC      8004
Good as gold. by Cheryl
Crawford and John Patrick.
(Gibbs) 33:79-80 Mr16'57.
T                        8005
Good behaviour. by Harold
Nicolson. (Anon.) 32:144-5
*Ap28'56. B              8006
The good cause. by David
Stone. (Anon.) 39:69-70
Ag31'63. B               8007
Good children don't kill. by
Louis Thomas. Graham
Snell, trans. (Anon.) 44:147
Je8'68. B                8008
The good light. by Karl Bjarnhof.
(Balliett) 36:174-6 Mr19'60.
B                        8009
A good man is hard to find.
by Flannery O'Connor. (Anon.)
31:105 Je18'55. B        8010
Good morning, Miss Dove.
(McCarten) 31:178*D3'55.
CC                       8011
Good neighbor Sam. (Oliver)
40:74-6 Ag8'64. CC       8012
The good soldier Schweik. by
Jaroslav Hasek. (Oliver)
39:99 Ap20'63. T         8013
The good soup. by Félicien
Marceau. Garson Kanin,
adapt. (Tynan) 36:113-14
Mr12'60. T               8014
The good, the bad and the
ugly. (Kael) 44:127-8 Mr2'68.
CC                       8015
Good times, wonderful times.
(S. Lardner) 42:64 Jy30'66.
CC                       8016
The good woman of Setzuan. by
Bertolt Brecht. Eric Bentley,
trans. (Gibbs) 32:45-6 D29
'56. T                   8017

Goodbye. by William Sansom.
(Anon.) 43:149-50 Ap1'67.
B                        8018
Goodbye again. (Gill) 37:54-5
Jy15'61. CC              8019
Goodbye Charlie. by George
Axelrod. (Tynan) 35:48-50
D26'59. T                8020
Goodbye, Columbus. by Philip
Roth. (Anon.) 35:118-19
Je20'59. B               8021
Goodbye, Columbus. (Gilliatt)
45:171-3 Ap12'69.
CC                       8022
Good-bye Dolly Gray: the
story of the Boer War.
by Rayne Kruger. (Anon.)
36:227 N5'60. B          8023
Goodbye, Mr. Chips. (Kael)
45:161-4 N8'69. CC       8024
The goodbye people. by Herb
Gardner. (Gill) 44:180
D14'68. T                8025
Goodbye to Uncle Tom. by
J.C. Furnas. (Anon.) 32:76
*Jy21'56. B              8026
Goodnight pelican. by
Diana Marr-Johnston. (Anon.)
34:93 Ag16'58. B         8027
The goose. by J.I. Rodale.
(Malcolm) 36:81-3 Mr26'60.
T                        8028
Gorilla queen. by Ronald
Tavel. (Oliver) 43:152-5
My6'67. 45:102-105 Mr29'69.
T                        8029
The gospel according to St.
Matthew. (Gill) 42:157 Mr5'66.
CC                       8030
Gothic sculpture. Harald
Busch and Bernd Lohse, eds.
Peter Gorge, trans. (Anon.)
40:190-1 Mr14'64. B      8031
Goya. by Xavière Desparmet
FitzGerald. (Anon.) 33:172
My18'57. B               8032
Grace and favour: the memoirs
of Loelia, Duchess of West-
minster. by Loelia Grosvenor
Westminster. (Anon.) 38:138-
9 Je9'62. B              8033
The Grace divorce. by Frank
Swinnerton. (Anon.) 36:243-4
D10'60. B                8034

The graduate. (Gill) 43:48-50
D30'67 (Brackman) 44:34-66
Jy27'68. CC          8035
Graf Spee: the life and death
of a raider. by Dudley
Pope. (Anon.) 32:106-107
Ja26'57. B           8036
The grain race. by Eric
Newby. (Anon.) 32:188
O6'56. B             8037
The grand mademoiselle.
by Francis Steegmuller.
(W. Maxwell) 31:68-74*Ja7'56.
B                    8038
Grand maneuver. (McCarten)
32:181-2 O13'56. CC   8039
The grand Olympics. (Gill)
40:152 My23'64. CC    8040
Grand prix. (Gill) 42:60 D31'66.
CC                    8041
The grand tour. by Christopher
Hibbert. (Anon.) 45:179-
80 N1'69. B          8042
The grand tour. by Geoffrey
Trease. (Anon.) 43:223
O21'67. B            8043
The grandeur that was Rome.
by Giuseppe Gatteschi.
(Anon.) 31:147-8 Ap2'55. B
                     8044
Grandmother's house. by Carl
Erik Soya.  Agnes Camilla
Hansen, trans. (Anon.)
42:243 O15'66. B     8045
Granite and rainbow. by
Virginia Woolf. B.L. Kirk-
patrick and Mary Lyon, eds.
(Wm. Maxwell) 34:198-200
O11'58. B            8046
Grant moves South. by Bruce
Catton. (Anon.) 36:161-2 Ap2
'60. B               8047
The grapes of paradise. by
H.E. Bates. (Anon.) 36:224-5
N5'60. B             8048
The grass is greener. (Angell)
36:63 Ja7'61. CC     8049
The graveyard. by Marek
Hlasko. Norbert Guterman,
trans. (Anon.) 35:192 S26'59.
B                    8050
Gray fox: Robert E. Lee and
the Civil War. by Burke Davis.

(Anon.) 32:164-5*My12'56. B
                     8051
Gray ghosts and rebel raiders.
by Virgil Carrington Jones.
(Anon.) 32:226*N10'56. B
                     8052
The great adventure. (Mc-
Carten) 31:123 Je11'55. CC
                     8053
The great airplane snatch. by
Dan Greenburg. (Oliver)
45:112 Je7'69. T     8054
The great American desert. by
W. Eugene Hollon. (Anon.)
42:203 My14'66. B    8055
The great Arab conquests. by
John Bagot Glubb. (Anon.)
40:135-6 F29'64. B   8056
The great auk. by Allan W.
Eckert. (Anon.) 39:234-6
D14'63. B            8057
The great British train robbery.
(Gill) 43:144-5 Ap8'67. CC
                     8058
The great challenge. (J.
Lardner) 34:87-8 Mr8'58.
TV                   8059
The great chase. (Gill)
38:60 D29'62. CC     8060
The great circle. by Frank
Rooney. (Balliett) 38:111-12
Ja12'63. B           8061
Great cities of the world,
their government, politics,
and planning.  William A.
Robson, ed. (Mumford) 32:
106-108*Mr3'56. B    8062
Great companions. by Max
Eastman. (Anon.) 35:178-9
Ap25'59. B           8063
Great day in the morning. by
Alice Cannon. (McCarten)
38:115 Ap7'62. T     8064
The great days. by John Dos
Passos. (Anon.) 34:102-103
Je21'58. B           8065
The great escape. (Miller)
39:64 Ag24'63. CC    8066
Great family collections. by
Douglas Cooper. (Anon.) 41:
203-204 D18'65. B    8067
The great fear. by John Gerassi.
(Anon.) 39:121 Je1'63. B 8068

Great folktales of wit and humor. James R. Foster, ed. (Anon.) 31:170 O22'55. B 8069

The great forgery. by Edith Simon. (Anon.) 37:238 N25'61. B 8070

The great Gatsby. (J. Lardner) 34:70-2 Jy12'58. TV 8071

The great god Brown. by Eugene O'Neill. (Tynan) 35:131-3 O17'59. T 8072

Great house. by Kate Thompson. (Anon.) 31:116-17 Mr5'55. B 8073

The great indoors. by Irene Kamp. (McCarten) 41:112 F12'66. T 8074

The great infidel. by Joseph Jay Deiss. (Balliett) 39:69-70 Jy6'63. B 8075

The great locomotive chase. (McCarten) 32:59*Jy7'56. CC 8076

The great man. (McCarten) 32:80-1 Ja12'57. CC 8077

The great philosophers. by Karl Jaspers. Hannah Arendt, ed. Ralph Mannheim, trans. (Anon.) 38:193 My5'62; 42: 206 My21'66. B 8078

The great pianists from Mozart to the present. by Harold C. Schonberg. (Sargeant) 40:122-6 F22'64. B 8079

The great race. (Gill) 41:126 S18'65. CC 8080

The great rapprochement: England and the United States, 1895-1914. by Bradford Perkins. (Anon.) 44:183 S28'68. B 8081

The great rebel: Ché Guevara in Bolivia. by Luis J. González and Gustavo A. Sánchez Salazar. Helen R. Lane, trans. (Anon.) 45:116 Je14'69. B 8082

The great red island. by Arthur Stratton. (Anon.) 40: 246-7 O10'64. B 8083

The great Sahara. by James Wellard. (Anon.) 41:198 Ap24'65. B 8084

The great Sebastians. by Howard Lindsay and Russel Crouse. (Gibbs) 31:56-8 *Ja14'56. T 8085

The great Shakespeare jubilee. by Christian Deelman. (Anon.) 40:111 Je27'64. B 8086

The great tea venture. by J. M. Scott. (Anon.) 41:188 Mr20'65. B 8087

The great terror. by Robert Conquest. (Wilson) 45:148 S27'69. B 8088

The great travelers. Milton Rugoff, ed. (Anon.) 36:242-3 N12'60. B 8089

The Great War. by Cyril Falls. (Anon.) 35:195-6 S19'59. B 8090

The Great War. (Gill) 37: 60-2 S2'61. CC 8091

The great white fleet. by Robert A. Hart. (Anon.) 42:209 Mr19'66. B 8092

The great white hope. by Howard Sackler. (Gill) 44:103 O12'68. T 8093

The great world and Timothy Colt. by Louis Auchincloss. (West) 32:219-20*N10'56. B 8094

The great world: portraits and scenes from Greville's memoirs 1814-60. by Charles Cavedish Fulke Greville. Louis Kronenberger, ed. (Anon.) 38:123 F2'63. B 8095

The greatest man alive! by Tony Webster. (Gibbs) 33:68-70 My18'57. T 8096

The greatest problem, and other essays. by F. L. Lucas. (Anon.) 37:167-8 My20'61. B 8097

The greatest story ever told. (Gill) 41:137 F20'65. CC 8098

Greek lyrics. by Richmond Lattimore. (Bogan) 31:90-3 *F4'56. B 8099

The Greek myths. by Robert Graves. (West) 31:58-64 *Jy23'55. B 8100

Greek painting. by Pierre Devambez. Jean Stewart, trans. (Anon.) 39:179-80 Mr30'63. B 8101

Greek painting. by Martin Robertson. (Anon.) 35:239-40 D12'59. B 8102

The green berets. (Gilliatt) 44:44-6 Jy6'68. CC 8103

Green holly. by Sue Kaufman. (Anon.) 38:186 Mr17'62. B 8104

The green kingdom. by Rachel Maddux. (Anon.) 32:105-106 Ja26'57. B 8105

Green lights are blue. by Ursule Molinaro. (Anon.) 43:106 Je24'67. B 8106

Green magic. (McCarten) 31:78 My28'55. CC 8107

The green man. (McCarten) 33:95*Je1'57. CC 8108

Green mansions. (McCarten) 35:95-6 Mr28'59. CC 8109

The green mare. by Marcel Aymé. (West) 32:94-7 *Mr31'56. B 8110

The green mare. (Gill) 37:195-6 O28'61. CC 8111

The green wall. by James Wright. (Bogan) 33:173-4 S14'57. B 8112

The greengage Summer. by Rumer Godden. (Anon.) 34:148-9 Ap19'58. B 8113

Greenland journal. by Rockwell Kent. (Anon.) 38:162 F16'63. B 8114

Greenwich Village story. (Balliett) 39:96 Jy27'63. CC 8115

Greenwich Village, U.S.A. by Jeanne Bargy, Frank Gehrecke and Herb Corey. (Balliett) 36:97-8 O8'60. T 8116

Greenwillow. by Frank Loesser and Lesser Samuels. (Tynan) 36:117-18 Mr19'60. T 8117

The Greer case. by David W. Peck. (Anon.) 31:130-2*O1'55. B 8118

Greetings. (Kael) 44:91 D21'68. CC 8119

Grenfell, Joyce. (Gibbs) 31:84-6*O22'55. T 8120

Grisbi. (McCarten) 35:50 Jy18'59. CC 8121

The ground I walked on. by George N. Shuster. (Anon.) 37:242-4 N25'61. B 8122

The group. (Gill) 42:173-4 Mr19'66. CC 8123

Growing up absurd: problems of youth in the organized system. by Paul Goodman. (Anon.) 36:239-40 N26'60. B 8124

The guardians. by J.I.M. Stewart. (Gill) 32:140-1 F16'57. B 8125

Guerrilla. by Charles W. Thayer. (Anon.) 39:244 N16'63. B 8126

Guess who's coming to dinner. (Gill) 43:108 D16'67. CC 8127

The guest. (Gill) 39:77 F1'64. CC 8128

The guide. by R.K. Narayan. (West) 34:145-7 Ap19'58. B 8129

The guide. by Harvey Breit and Patricia Rinehart. (Gill) 44:130 Mr16'68. T 8130

A guide for the married man. (Gill) 43:72 Je10'67. CC 8131

A guide to Communist jargon. by R.N. Carew Hunt. (Anon.) 33:242 N23'57. B 8132

Guide to the art treasure. by Françoise Olivier-Michel and Claude Gisler. Raymond Rudorff, trans. (Anon.) 42:246-7 O8'66. B 8133

Guilt. (Gill) 43:153-4 N25'67. CC 8134

Guns at Batasi. (Gill) 40:202-203 N28'64. CC 8135

The guns of August. by Barbara W. Tuchman. (B. Bliven) 38:178-82 Ap14'62. B 8136

The guns of August. (Gill) 40:74
Ja16'65. CC                     8137
The guns of Navarone. (Gill)
37:41-2 Jy1'61. CC              8138
Gunsmoke. (J. Lardner) 35:
98-9 F28'59. TV                8139
The guru. (Gilliatt) 45:135-8
My10'69. CC                     8140
Guys and dolls. (McCarten)
31:119*N5'55. CC               8141
Gypsy. by Arthur Laurents,
Jule Styne and Stephen Sond-
heim. (Tynan) 35:65-7
My20'59. T                      8142
Gypsy. (Gill) 38:234-5 N10'62.
CC                              8143
The gypsy moths. (Gilliatt) 45:
73-4 Ag30'69. CC               8144

H

H. L. Mencken--l'homme, l'oeuvre,
l'influence. by Guy Jean
Forgue. (Wilson) 45:110 My31
'69. B                          8145
H. L. Mencken on music. by
H. L. Mencken, Louis Cheslock
ed. (Anon.) 37:245 N11'61.
B                               8146
H. L. Mencken's 'Smart Set'
criticism. by H. L. Mencken.
William H. Nolte, ed.
(Wilson) 45:107-108 My31'69.
B                               8147
H. M. S. Pinafore. by William S.
Gilbert and Arthur Sullivan.
(Malcolm) 35:94-5 F13'60.
(Balliett) 36:137-8 S17'60.
T                               8148
The hack. by Wilfrid Sheed.
(Balliett) 39:94-5 D21'63.
B                               8149
Hadrian. by Stewart Perowne.
(Anon.) 37:139 F10'62. B
8150
Hadrian VII. by Peter Luke.
(Gill) 44:72 Ja18'69. T 8151
Hadrian the seventh. by
Frederick Rolfe. (Panter-
Downes) 44:66-8Ag3'68. T
8152
Hail, hero! (Kael) 45:165-6
N8'69. CC                      8153

Hail Scrawdyke! by David
Halliwell. (McCarten) 42:118
D17'66. T                      8154
Hair. by Gerome Ragni, James
Rado and Galt MacDermot.
(Oliver) 43:128-30 N11'67
(Gill) 44:84-5 My11'68
(Flanner) 45:102 Je14'69.
T                               8155
Hal Holbrook as Mark Twain.
(Malcolm) 35:80-1 Ap18'59.
T                               8156
Half a sixpence. by David
Heneker and Beverley Cross.
(McCarten) 41:120 My1'65.
T                               8157
Half a sixpence. (Kael) 44:126-
7 Mr2'68. CC                   8158
Half-way to the moon: new
writing from Russia. by
Patricia Blake and Max
Hayward ed. (Anon.) 40:77
D26'64. B                      8159
Halfway up the tree. by Peter
Ustinov. (McCarten) 43:131
N18'67. T                      8160
Hallelujah, Baby! by Arthur
Laurents, Jule Styne, Betty
Comden and Adolph Green.
(McCarten) 43:150 My6'67.
T                               8161
Hallelujah the hills. (Gill)
39:90 D21'63. CC               8162
Hamlet. by William Shakespeare.
(Panter-Downes) 31:49*D31'55
(Tynan) 34:52-5 D27'58
(Balliett) 37:114 Mr25'61
(McCarten) 40:108 Ap11'64
(McCarten) 43:91-2 F25'67
(Oliver) 43:68 Ja6'68
(Gill) 45:131-2 Mr15'69 (Gill)
45:121-2 My10'69. T    8163
Hamlet. (Gill) 42:125-6 Mr26'66
(Kael) 45:66-72Ja17'70. CC
8164
Hamlet. (J. Lardner) 35:144-6
Mr7'59. TV                     8165
Hamlet of Stepney Green. by
Bernard Kops. (Malcolm)
34:102-103 N22'58. T    8166
Hamp. by John Wilson. (Oliver)
43:123 Mr18'67. T      8167
Hand in hand. (Angell) 37:99
F18'61. CC                     8168

Hand in the trap. (Oliver) 39:68
Jy13'63. CC                    8169
A hand is on the gate. (Mc-
Carten) 42:121-2 O1'66. T
                               8170
Handful of fire. by N.
Richard Nash. (J. Lardner)
34:87-9 O11'58. T              8171
Hang down your head and
die. by David Wright.
(Oliver) 40:130 O31'64. T
                               8172
The hanging tree. (McCarten)
35:137-8 F21'59. CC            8173
Hannibal: enemy of Rome. by
Leonard Cottrell. (Anon.)
37:82 S2'61. B                 8174
The happening. (Gill) 43:104
My27'67. CC                    8175
The happiest girl in the world.
by Fred Saidy, Henry Myers,
E.Y. Harburg and Jacques
Offenbach. (McCarten)
37:76 Ap15'61. T               8176
The happiest millionaire. by
Kyle Crichton. (Gibbs)
32:112-14 D1'56. T             8177
The happiest millionaire. (Gill)
43:100 D9'67. CC               8178
Happily never after. by J.A.
Ross. (McCarten) 42:160-2
Mr19'66. T                     8179
Happiness. by Mayo Simon.
(Oliver) 43:149 D2'67. T
                               8180
Happiness is just a little
thing called a Rolls-Royce.
by Arthur Alsberg and
Robert Fisher. (Gill) 44:73
My18'68. T                     8181
Happiness of us alone. (Gill)
39:166-7 Ap27'63. CC    8182
Happy anniversary. (McCarten)
35:196 D12'59. CC              8183
Happy as Larry. by Thomas
Hinde. (Balliett) 34:146-7
My3'58. B                      8184
Happy as Larry. by Donagh
MacDonagh. (Balliett) 37:124
My6'61. T                      8185
Happy days. by Samuel
Beckett. (Oliver) 37:119
S30'61. T                      8186

Happy ending. by Douglas
Turner Ward. (McCarten)
41:50 D25'65. T                8187
Happy hunting. by Howard
Lindsay and Russel Crouse.
(Gibbs) 32:54-6*D22'56.
T                              8188
Happy hunting ground: an ex-
Marine's odyssey in
Vietnam. by Martin Russ.
(Anon.) 44:182-3 Ap13'68.
B                              8189
The happy hypocrite. by
Edward Eager and James
Bredt. (Oliver) 44:129-30
S14'68. T                      8190
The happy journey to Trenton
and Camden. by Thornton
Wilder. (Oliver) 42:129
S17'66. T                      8191
The happy road. (McCarten)
33:72-3 Je29'57. CC            8192
The happy Summer days. by
Sue Kaufman. (Anon.) 34:
136 F14'59. B                  8193
The happy time. by N.
Richard Nash, John Kander
and Fred Ebb. (Gill) 43:84-6
Ja27'68. T                     8194
Happy town. by Max Hampton,
Gordon Duffy and Harry M.
Haldane. (Tynan) 35:134-5
O17'59. T                      8195
Harakiri. (Flanner) 39:161-2
S28'63 (Gill) 40:88-9 Ag22'64.
CC                             8196
The harangues. by Joseph A.
Walker. (Oliver) 45:58 Ja
24'70. T                       8197
Harbor lights. by Norman
Vane. (Gibbs) 32:100-101
O13'56. T                      8198
Hard contract. (Gilliatt) 45:
114-16 Je7'69. CC              8199
A hard day's night. (Gill)
40:89 Ag22'64. CC             8200
Hard travellin': the hobo and
his history. by Kenneth
Allsop. (Anon.) 44:194-6
Ap20'68. B                     8201
The hard way to Haparanda. by
R.P. Lister (Anon.) 42:167-8
Ap30'66. B                     8202

The hard winners. by John
Quirk. (Anon.) 41:182
Mr27'65. B          8203
The harder they fall. (Mc-
Carten) 32:126*My19'56.
CC                  8204
Harlem: the making of a
ghetto. by Gilbert Osofsky.
(Anon.) 42:176-7 Mr12'66. B
                    8205
Harlequinade. by Terence
Rattigan. (Malcolm) 35:102
F21'59. T          8206
Harlow. (Gill) 41:71 My29'65;
41:58 Jy31'65. CC   8207
The harmful effects of tobacco.
by Anton Chekhov. (Tynan)
35:84 Ap25'59. T    8208
The harmless people. by
Elizabeth Marshall Thomas.
(Rovere) 35:97-100*Ag15'59.
B                   8209
Harold. by Frederick Feirstein.
(Oliver) 43:138-40 My20'67.
T                   8210
The Harold Arlen songbook.
by Harold Arlen. (Oliver)
43:130 Mr11'67. T   8211
Harold Lloyd's world of
comedy. (Gill) 38:117
Je9'62. CC          8212
Harper. (Gill) 42:162-3 Ap2'66.
CC                  8213
The Harper encyclopedia of
science. by James R.
Newman, ed. (Anon.) 39:74
Jy6'63. B          8214
Harriet Shelley: five long
years. by Louise Schutz
Boas. (Anon.) 38:182-3
Ap21'62. B          8215
Harry, noon and night. by
Ronald Ribman. (Oliver)
41:160-1 My15'65. T  8216
Harry, the rat with women.
by Jules Feiffer. (Anon.)
39:71-2 Jy6'63. B   8217
Harvard: through change
and through storm. by E.J.
Kahn, Jr. (Anon.) 45:119-
20 D20'69. B        8218
Harvest on the Don. by Mikhail
Sholokhov. (West) 37:143-9
Ap29'61. B          8219

Harvey Middleman, fireman.
(Arlen) 41:87-8 Jy24'65.
CC                  8220
Hatari! (Oliver) 38:39 Jy21'62.
CC                  8221
A hatful of rain. by Michael
V. Gazzo. (Gibbs) 31:115-17
*N19'55. T          8222
A hatful of rain. (McCarten)
33:67-8*Jy27'57. CC  8223
The haunting. (Gill) 39:108
S28'63. CC          8224
The haunting of Hill House.
by Shirley Jackson. (Anon.)
35:197 O24'59. B    8225
Haute cour. by Alfred
Fabre-Luce. (Flanner)
38:106-109 Ja12'63. B 8226
Have gun, will travel. (J.
Lardner) 35:97-8 F28'59. TV
                    8227
Have I got a girl for you!
by Irving Cooper. (Mc-
Carten) 39:80 D14'63. T
                    8228
Hawaii. (Gill) 42:152 O29'66.
CC                  8229
The hawk. by Murray Mednick
and Tony Barsha. (Oliver)
44:91-2 Ap27'68. T   8230
Hay fever. by Noël Coward.
(Panter-Downes) 40:200-201
N21'64. T           8231
Hayes: the diary of a president,
1875-81. by Rutherford B.
Hayes. T. Harry Williams,
ed. (Anon.) 40:138 Je20'64.
B                   8232
He who must die. (McCarten)
34:110-11 Ja10'59. CC
                    8233
Head. (Kael) 44:201-202 N23'68.
CC                  8234
Headlines all my life. by
Arthur Christiansen. (Anon.)
37:143 F17'62. B    8235
Headquarters. by Quentin
Reynolds. (Anon.) 31:175
My14'55. B          8236
Heads, figures and ideas. by
Henry Moore. (Anon.) 34:
247-8 N15'58. B     8237
Hear me talkin' to ya. Nat
Shapiro and Nat Hentoff, eds.

(Anon.) 31:106 Je18'55. B
8238
Heard round the world: the
impact abroad of the Civil
War. Harold M. Hyman,
ed. (Anon.) 44:127 F8'69.
B                    8239
Heart flights. by Félicien
Marceau. David Hughes
and Marie-Jacqueline Mason,
trans. (Anon.) 34:198-9 O25
'58. B                    8240
The heart is a lonely hunter.
(Gilliatt) 44:72-4 Ag3'68.
CC                    8241
The heart prepared: grace
and conversion in Puritan
spiritual life. by Norman
Pettit. (Anon.) 42:246-7
D10'66. B                    8242
Heartbreak House. by George
Bernard Shaw. (Tynan)
35:131-2 O31'59. T    8243
The heart-keeper. by Françoise
Sagan. Robert Westhoff,
trans. (Anon.) 44:201-202
N2'68. B                    8244
Hearts and heads. by Christopher
Veiel. (Gill) 31:168-70
My14'55. B                    8245
Heart's needle. by W.D.
Snodgrass. (Bogan) 35:196
O24'59. B                    8246
The heat of the sun. by Sean
O'Faolain. (Anon.) 42:243-4
O8'66. B                    8247
Heaven and hell. by Aldous
Huxley. (Anon.) 32:101-102
*Mr31'56. B                    8248
Heaven knows, Mr. Allison.
(McCarten) 33:103 Mr23'57.
CC                    8249
The heavenly twins. by Albert
Husson. (Gibbs) 31:86
*N12'55. T                    8250
Heavens above! (Gill) 39:153-4
My25'63. CC                    8251
Heaven's my destination.
by Thornton Wilder. (Anon.)
33:139-40 My25'57. B    8252
Hecht, Ben. (J. Lardner) 34:
110-13 O4'58. TV    8253

Hedda Gabler. by Henrik
Ibsen. (Balliett) 36:94-7
N19'60. (Flanner) 38:175-6
D15'62. T                    8254
The Heike story. by Eiji
Yoshikawa. (Anon.) 32:70-2
Ja5'57. B                    8255
Heine: poet in exile. by Anto-
nina Vallentin (Bogan)
32:142-6*Ap7'56. B    8256
The heir of starvelings. by
Evelyn Berckman. (Anon.)
43:84-5 S2'67. B    8257
Heiresses and coronets. by
Elizabeth Eliot. (Anon.)
36:198-9 Mr12'60. B    8258
Helen Keller: sketch for a
portrait. by Van Wyck
Brooks. (Anon.) 32:149
*Ap7'56. B                    8259
Helen of Troy. (McCarten)
31:81 *F4'56. CC    8260
Hell in a very small place:
the siege of Dien Bien Phu. by
Bernard B. Fall. (Anon.)
43:190 Mr25'67. B    8261
Hell in the Pacific. (Kael)
45:74 Mr1'69. CC    8262
Heller in pink tights.
(McCarten) 36:149 Mr26'60.
CC                    8263
Hello and goodbye. by Athol
Fugard. (Oliver) 45:97
S27'69. T                    8264
Hello, Dolly! by Michael
Stewart and Jerry Herman.
(McCarten) 43:149 N25'67.
T                    8265
Hello, Dolly! (Kael) 45:57-61
Ja3'70. CC                    8266
Hell's angels. by Hunter S.
Thompson. (Anon.) 43:163-4
Mr4'67. B                    8267
Hell's kitchen. by Richard
O'Connor. (Anon.) 34:92 Ag
23'58. B                    8268
Héloïse. by James Forsyth.
(Malcolm) 34:82-4 O4'58.
T                    8269
Help! (Gill) 41:101-102 Ag28
'65. CC                    8270
Help stamp out marriage!

by Keith Waterhouse and
Willis Hall. (McCarten)
42:116-18 O8'66. T      8271
Henderson the rain king. by
Saul Bellow. (Malcolm)
35:171-3 Mr14'59. B    8272
A Henry Adams reader. by
Henry Adams. Elizabeth
Stevenson, ed. (Anon.)
34:148 Mr8'58. B       8273
Henry Adams: the major phase.
by Ernest Samuels. (Anon.)
40:128 Ja16'65. B      8274
Henry Adams: the middle
years. by Ernest Samuels.
(Anon.) 34:240 D6'58. B
                       8275
Henry V. by William Shakespeare.
(Tynan) 34:72 Ja10'59
(Gill) 45:178 N22'69. T
                       8276
Henry Ford. by Roger
Burlingame. (Anon.) 31:134
Ap9'55. B              8277
Henry IV, part I. by William
Shakespeare. (Malcolm)
36:119-20 Mr12'60. T   8278
Henry IV, part II. by William
Shakespeare. (Malcolm)
36:86-9 Ap30'60. T     8279
Henry Garnet and the gunpowder
plot. by Philip Caraman.
(Anon.) 41:76 Jy3'65. B
                       8280
Henry James and H.G. Wells.
by Henry James, and H.G.
Wells. Leon Edel and
Gordon N. Ray, eds. (Anon.)
34:154-5*Ap26'58. B    8281
Henry James and the Jacobites.
by Maxwell Geismar. (Anon.)
39:219-20 O26'63. B    8282
Henry James: the conquest of
London: 1870-1881. by
Leon Edel. (N. Bliven)
39:151-7 S7'63. B      8283
Henry James: the treacherous
years, 1895-1901. by Leon
Edel. (Anon.) 45:95-6
Je28'69. B             8284
Henry Miller letters to
Anaïs Nin. by Henry Miller.
Gunther Stuhlmann, ed.

(Anon.) 41:245 N27'65. B
                       8285
Henry of Navarre. by Hesketh
Pearson. (Anon.) 39:96-7
F1'64. B               8286
Henry, sweet Henry. by
Nunnally Johnson and Bob
Merrill. (McCarten) 43:162
N4'67. T               8287
Her first Roman. by George
Bernard Shaw and Ervin
Drake. (Gill) 44:139-40
O26'68. T              8288
Her master's voice. by Clare
Kummer. (Oliver) 40:84-6
Ja9'65. T              8289
Herbal. by Joseph Wood
Krutch. (Fisher) 42:226-8
S24'66. B              8290
Herbert Hoover and the great
depression. by Harris
Gaylord Warren. (Anon.)
35:154-5 My28'59. B    8291
Herblock's here and now. by
Herbert Block. (Anon.) 32:
103*Mr31'56. B         8292
Here before Kilroy. by Su
Walton. (Anon.) 45:115 My31
'69. B                 8293
Here come the clowns. by
Philip Barry. (Balliett)
36:128-32 O1'60. T     8294
Here comes there goes you
know who. by William
Saroyan. (Anon.) 37:104
F3'62. B               8295
Here is your enemy. by
James Cameron. (Anon.)
42:205-206 My21'66. B
                       8296
Here, of all places. by
Osbert Lancaster. (Betjeman)
34:211-14 D13'58. B    8297
Here we go round the mulberry
bush. (Kael) 44:157-8 Mr16
'68. CC                8298
Heredity and human life. by
Hampton L. Carson. (Anon.)
39:72 Ag3'63. B        8299
Heredity and the nature of man.
by Theodosius Dobzhansky.
(Anon.) 41:164 F20'65. B
                       8300

Here's a villain! See the lady is waiting. 8301
Here's love. by Meredith Willson. (McCarten) 39:89-90 O12'63. T 8302
Here's where I belong. by Robert Waldman and Alfred Uhry. (Gill) 44:132 Mr9'68. T 8303
The Heresiarch and Co. by Guillaume Apollinaire. Rémy Inglis Hall, trans. (Anon.) 41:107 Ja22'66. B 8304
The heretic. by Fitzroy Maclean. (Anon.) 33:193-4 N2'57. B 8305
Heritage. by Anthony West. (Behrman) 31:138-45*O29'55. B 8306
A heritage and its history. by Julian Mitchell. (Panter-Downes) 41:139-40 Je5'65. T 8307
A hermit disclosed. by Raleigh Trevelyan. (Anon.) 37:139-40 F18'61. B 8308
The hero. by Derek Monsey. (Anon.) 37:172-3 Mr18'61. B 8309
The hero in eclipse in Victorian fiction. by Mario Praz. Angus Davidson, trans. (Anon.) 33:151 Mr16'57. B 8310
Herod and Mariamne. by Pär Lagerkvist. Naomi Walford, trans. (Anon.) 45:170-3 Ap26'69. B 8311
Heroes and orators. by Robert Phelps. (Anon.) 34:200-201 O11'58. B 8312
The heroine. by Frank Tarloff. (McCarten) 39:93 Mr2'63. T 8313
Heroines of Dixie: Confederate women tell their story of the war. Katherine M. Jones, ed. (Wilson) 31:173 *N5'55. B 8314
Herzog. by Saul Bellow. (Gill) 40:218-22 O3'64. B 8315
Hesketh Pearson, by himself. by Hesketh Pearson. (Anon.)

42:203 My14'66. B 8316
Hey you, light man. by Oliver Hailey. (Oliver) 39:134 Mr9'63. T 8317
Hi, paisano! by Ernest Chambers, Robert Holton and June Carroll. (Oliver) 37:131-2 O7'61. T 8318
The hidden image. (J. Lardner) 35:207 D5'59. TV 8319
A hidden life. by Autran Dourado. Edgar H. Miller, Jr., trans. (Anon.) 45:118-19 Mr1'69. B 8320
The hidden persuaders. by Vance Packard. (Anon.) 33:167-8 My18'57. B 8321
The hidden river. by Storm Jameson. (Anon.) 31:142-3 Ap2'55. B 8322
The hidden river. by Ruth Goetz and Augustus Goetz. (Gibbs) 32:70-2 F2'57. T 8323
Hidden strangers. by Maxwell Maltz. (McCarten) 38:60-2 Ja19'63. T 8324
Hide and seek. by Stanley Mann and Roger MacDougall. (Gibbs) 33:72-4 Ap13'57. T 8325
The hiding place. by Robert Shaw. (Anon.) 36:179-80 Ap16'60. B 8326
High and low. by John Betjeman. (Anon.) 43:87-8 S2'67. B 8327
High and low. (Gill) 39:197-8 D14'63. CC 8328
The high commissioner. by Jon Cleary. (N. Bliven) 42:161-2 F11'67. B 8329
High dam at Aswan. by Tom Little. (Anon.) 41:245-6 N6'65. B 8330
High dam over Nubia. by Leslie Greener. (Anon.) 38:131-2 F24'62. B 8331
High on foggy bottom: an outsider's inside view of the government. by Charles Frankel. (Anon.) 45:75 Ja 10'70. B 8332

High school. (Kael) 45:199-204
O18'69. TV 8333
High Sierra country. by Oscar
Lewis. (Anon.) 31:133
*O1'55. B 8334
High society. (McCarten)
32:58*Ag18'56. CC 8335
High spirits. by Hugh Martin
and Timothy Gray.
(McCarten) 40:108 Ap18'64.
T 8336
High time. (Gill) 36:168
O1'60. CC 8337
The high valley. by Kenneth E.
Read. (Anon.) 42:211-12 Mr19
'66. B 8338
High, wide, and lonesome.
by Hal Borland. (Anon.)
32:172-3 S22'56. B 8339
A high wind in Jamaica.
(S. Lardner) 41:114 Je19'65.
CC 8340
The highest tree. by Dore Schary.
(Tynan) 35:117-18 N14'59.
T 8341
Highland welcome. by A. A.
Thompson. (Anon.) 32:189
O6'56. B 8342
Hilaire Belloc. by J. B.
Morton. (Anon.) 31:217*N12'55.
B 8343
Hilda Crane. (McCarten) 32:92
My12'56. CC 8344
The hill. (Gill) 41:189-90
O9'65. CC 8345
The hills of Adonis. by Colin
Thubron. (Anon.) 45:95
Ag9'69. B 8346
Himalayan circuit. by G. D.
Khosla. (Anon.) 32:199 O20'56.
B 8347
Himmler. by Roger Manvell
and Heinrich Fraenkel. (Anon.)
41:128 Ag21'65. B 8348
The hireling. by L. P. Hartley.
(Anon.) 34:155-6 My17'58.
B 8349
Hiroshima. (McCarten)
31:76-7 My28'55. CC 8350
Hiroshima, mon amour.
(Flanner) 35:78-80 Jy11'59
(McCarten) 36:133-4 My28'60.
CC 8351

His brother, the bear. by
Jack Ansell. (Anon.) 36:197-
8 S17'60. B 8352
Histoire de Vasco. by Georges
Schéhadé. (Flanner) 33:54
Ja4'58. T 8353
Histoire parallèle. by Louis
Aragon and André Maurois.
(Flanner) 38:106-107 Ja26'63.
B 8354
A history of art, from pre-
historic times to the
present. by Germain Bazin.
Francis Scarfe, trans.
(Anon.) 35:246-7 N28'59.
B 8355
The history of baseball. by
Allison Danzig and Joe
Reichler. (Anon.) 35:135-6
*D19'59. B 8356
History of cartography. by Leo
Bagrow. D. L. Paisey,
trans. R. A. Skelton, ed.
(Anon.) 40:247-8 N7'64.
B 8357
History of color in painting. by
Faber Birren. (Anon.) 42:
175-6 Ap2'66. B 8358
A history of French civilization.
by Georges Duby and Robert
Mandrou. James
Blakely Atkinson, trans.
(Anon.) 40:246 N14'64. B
8359
History of Germany. by Minna
R. Falk. (Anon.) 33:196-7
N2'57. B 8360
The history of impressionism.
by John Rewald. (Anon.)
37:208 D16'61. B 8361
The history of Italy. by
Francesco Guicciardini.
Sidney Alexander, trans & ed.
(Anon.) 45:142 Ap5'69. B
8362
A history of militarism,
civilian and military. by
Alfred Vagts. (Anon.) 35:
84 Jy11'59. B 8363
A history of modern criticism:
1750-1950. by René Wellek.
(Anon.) 31:146*S10'55. B
8364

The history of photography. by
Helmut Gernsheim. (Anon.)
32:147*Ap28'56. B       8365
A history of Sicily. by M.I.
Finley and Denis Mack Smith.
(Sargeant) 45:113-14 Je14'69.
B                       8366
A history of Soviet Russia.
by Georg von Rauch. Peter
Jacobsohn and Annette
Jacobsohn, trans. (Anon.)
33:180 Ap13'57. B       8367
The history of surrealism. by
Maurice Nadeau. Richard
Howard, trans. (Anon.)
41:247-8 O30'65. B      8368
A history of technology. Charles
Singer, ed. (Mumford) 31:91-
101*Ja14'56; 34:165-76 S27
'58. B                  8369
History of the cold war. by
Kenneth Ingram. (Anon.)
32:146*Ap28'56. B       8370
A history of the cold war.
by John Lukacs. (Anon.)
37:164 Mr25'61. B       8371
History of the cold war: from
the Korean War to the present.
by André Fontaine. Renaud
Bruce, trans. (Anon.) 45:158
S13'69. B               8372
A history of the dollar. by
Arthur Nussbaum. (Anon.)
33:119-20 Ja25'58. B    8373
A history of the English-
speaking peoples: the age of
revolution. by Winston S.
Churchill. (Anon.) 33:198-9
O12'57. B               8374
A history of the English-speak-
ing peoples: the birth of
Britain. by Winston S.
Churchill. (Anon.) 32:162-4
*My12'56. B             8375
A history of the English-speak-
ing peoples: the great
democracies. by Winston
S. Churchill. (Anon.) 34:
126 Mr29'58. B          8376
A history of the English-speak-
ing peoples: the new world.
by Winston S. Churchill.
(Anon.) 32:234 D8'56. B 8377

The history of the Jews. by
Poul Borchaenius. (Anon.)
41:234 O9'65. B         8378
A history of toys. by
Antonia Fraser. (N. Bliven)
42:233-41 D3'66. B      8379
A history of Western
morals. by Crane Brinton.
(Sargeant) 35:169-73 My9'59.
B                       8380
Hit the deck. (McCarten)
31:76-7 Mr12'55. CC     8381
Hitler. by Otto Dietrich.
(Anon.) 31:176*O15'55.B 8382
Hitler confronts England.
by Walter Ansel. (Anon.)
36:62 D24'60. B         8383
Ho Chi Minh on revolution.
by Ho Chi Minh. Bernard
B. Fall, ed. (Anon.) 43:147-
8 Je3'67. B             8384
Hobo. by John Dooley. (Balliett)
37:118-19 Ap22'61. T    8385
Hogan's goat. by William
Alfred. (Oliver) 41:150-2 N
20'65. T                8386
Hokusai. by J. Hillier. (Anon.)
31:171-2*O22'55. B      8387
The hole. by N. F. Simpson.
(Balliett) 37:80 Ap15'61.
T                       8388
A hole in the head. by Arnold
Shulman. (Gibbs) 33:64-8
Mr9'57. T               8389
A hole in the head. (McCarten)
35:61 Ag1'59. CC        8390
A holiday by the sea. by
Gerald Brenan. (N. Bliven)
37:134-7 F17'62. B      8291
Holiday for lovers. by
Ronald Alexander. (Gibbs)
33:69-70 F23'57. T      8392
The hollow crown. by John
Barton. (McCarten) 38:66
F9'63. T                8393
Hollywood in transition. by
Richard Dyer. (Anon.) 38:
247-8 N17'62. B         8394
Holocaust at sea. by Fritz-Otto
Busch. Eleanor Brockett and
Anton Ehrenzweig, trans.
(Anon.) 33:105-106*Je1'57.
B                       8395

The Holstein papers. Norman Rich and M.H. Fisher, eds. (Anon.) 33:165-6 S28'57. B 8396

Holy week. by Louis Aragon. Haakon Chevalier, trans. (Anon.) 37:179-80 S23'61. B 8397

Homage to Clio. by W.H. Auden. (Bogan) 36:197-9 O8'60. B 8398

Homage to Galileo. by Morton F. Kaplan. (Anon.) 42:194 Ap23'66. B 8399

A home away from. by Glenn Allen Smith. (Oliver) 45:123 My10'69. T 8400

Home before dark. (McCarten) 34:147 N15'58. CC 8401

Home fires. by John Guare. (Gill) 45:98 Ap19'69. T 8402

Home free! by Lanford Wilson. (Oliver) 41:58 F20 '65. T 8403

Home from the hill. by William Humphrey. (Anon.) 33:133 F8'58. B 8404

Home from the hill. (McCarten) 36:184-5 Mr12'60. CC 8405

Home is the place. by Stefanie Lauer. (Anon.) 33:72 Ja4'58. B 8406

Home is the sailor. by Jorge Amado. (West) 40:89-90 Ag8'64. B 8407

Home movies. by Rosalyn Drexler. (Oliver) 40:134 My23'64. T 8408

Home to Texas. by Stanley Walker. (McKelway) 32:66-70*Ag4'56. B 8409

The homecoming. by Harold Pinter. (Panter-Downes) 41:59 Jy31'65 (McCarten) 42:48 Ja14'67. T 8410

Homecoming. by C.P. Snow. (Anon.) 32:208-209 N3'56. B 8411

Homer: the Odyssey. by Homer. Robert Fitzgerald, trans. (Anon.) 37:168 My20'61. B 8412

The honest-to-God Schnozzola. by Israel Horovitz. (Oliver) 45:108-109 My3'69. T 8413

The honey pot. (Gill) 43:119 Je3'67. CC 8414

Honeybuzzard. by Angela Carter. (Anon.) 43:163 Mr4'67. B 8415

Honeymoon hotel. (McCarten) 40:90 Je13'64. CC 8416

The honeymoon killers. (Kael) 45:93-4 F7'70. CC 8417

The honeys. by Roald Dahl. (Gibbs) 31:88-90 My7'55. T 8418

An honorable estate. by Lane Kauffman. (Anon.) 40:137 Je20'64. B 8419

The hook. (Gill) 39:145-6 Mr9'63. CC 8420

Hooray!! It's a glorious day ... and all that. by Arthur Gordon, Ethel Beiber, Maurice Teitelbaum and Charles Grodin. (Oliver) 42:163-4 Mr19'66. T 8421

Hop, Signor! by Michel de Ghelderode. (Oliver) 38: 104-106 My19'62. T 8422

The Hopkins manuscript. by R.C. Sherriff. (Anon.) 39:95-6 D21'63. B 8423

Horace Walpole. by Wilmarth Sheldon Lewis. (Anon.) 37:78 Jy15'61. B 8424

The horrors of love. by Jean Dutourd. (West) 43:220-2 O14'67. B 8425

Horse and buggy West: a boyhood on the last frontier. by Jack O'Connor. (Anon.) 45: 152 My17'69. B 8426

Horse under water. by Len Deighton. (Anon.) 43:112 F 3'68. B 8427

Horseman, pass by. by Rocco Bufano and John Duffy. (Oliver) 44:77-8 Ja25'69. T 8428

The horse's mouth. (McCarten) 34:137-8 N22'58. CC 8429

Hospital. (Kael) 45:75-6 Ja31 '70. CC 8430

The hostage. by Brendan
Behan. (Flanner) 35:156 Ap18
'59. (McCarten) 36:128 O1'60
(Oliver) 37:57-8 D23'61. T
                                        8431
Hostile allies: FDR and Charles
de Gaulle. by Milton Viorst.
(Anon.) 41:195-6 Ap17'65.
B                                       8432
Hostile witness. by Jack Rof-
fey. (McCarten) 42:71 F26'66.
T                                       8433
The hot corner. by Allen
Boretz and Ruby Sully. (Gibbs)
31:55-6 *F4'56. T            8434
Hot millions. (Gilliatt) 44:147
S21'68. CC                              8435
Hot spell. (McCarten) 34:164
S27'58. CC                              8436
Hot spot. by Jack Weinstock,
Willie Gilbert and Martin
Charnin. (McCarten) 39:82
Ap27'63. T                              8437
Hotel. (Gill) 42:77-8 Ja28'67.
CC                                      8438
Hotel Paradiso. by Georges
Feydeau. Peter Glenville,
adapt. (Gibbs) 33:81-2
Ap20'57. T                              8439
Hotel Paradiso. (Gill) 42:
153 O29'66. CC               8440
Hotel Passionato. by Jerome J.
Schwartz, Philip Springer
and Joan Javits. (Oliver)
41:116 N6'65. T              8441
Hour of the wolf. (Gilliatt)
44:163-5 Ap20'68. CC         8442
The hourglass. by Edwin
Gilbert. (Anon.) 35:166 Ap4
'59. B                                  8443
The hours of Catherine of
Cleves. by Catherine of
Cleves. (Anon.) 42:247-8
D10'66. B                               8444
The hours of love. (Gill)
41:100-102 S11'65. CC        8445
The house at sunset. by Norah
Lofts. (Anon.) 38:244 N17'62.
B                                       8446
A house for Mr. Biswas.
by V.S. Naipaul. (Balliett)
38:70-1 Ag4'62. B            8447
The house in the country. by

Nan Fairbrother. (Anon.)
41:179-80 My22'65. B         8448
The house in the mulberry
tree. by Zena Garrett.
(Anon.) 35:173 Mr21'59.
B                                       8449
The house in Vienna. by
Edith de Born. (Anon.)
35:118-20 Ja16'60. B         8450
A house is not a home. (Gill)
40:106-108 S5'64. CC         8451
The house of Atreus. by
John Lewin. (Gill) 44:48-50
D28'68. T                               8452
House of bondage. by Ernest
Cole. (Anon.) 43:242-4
D2'67. B                                8453
A house of children. by
Joyce Cary. (West) 32:
137-8*Mr10'56. B             8454
The house of Elrig. by
Gavin Maxwell. (Anon.)
41:241 N27'65. B             8455
The house of five talents. by
Louis Auchincloss. (Anon.)
36:237-8 N26'60. B           8456
House of flowers. by Truman
Capote and Harold Arlen.
(Oliver) 43:91 F10'68. T
                                        8457
House of gold. by Elizabeth
Cullinan. (Brennan) 45:
130-1 F14'70. B              8458
The house of Morgan. by
Edwin P. Hoyt. (Anon.) 42:
130 F4'67. B                            8459
The house of words. by Lovat
Dickson. (Anon.) 39:205
Mr16'63. B                              8460
House out of order. by Richard
Bolling. (Anon.) 41:187 Mr20
'65. B                                  8461
House without a roof. by
Maurice Hindus. (Anon.)
37:181 S23'61. B             8462
Houseboat. (McCarten)
34:138 N22'58. CC            8463
The householder. by R.
Prawer Jhabvala. (Balliett)
36:83-4 Ja7'61. B            8464
The householder. (Gill) 39:
206-207 O26'63. CC
                                        8465

How far the promised land?
by Walter White. (Anon.)
31:215*N12'55. B     8466
How I changed my mind. by
Karl Barth. (Anon.) 42:247
N26'66. B     8467
How I won the war. (Gill)
43:137 N18'67. CC     8468
How it is. by Samuel Beckett.
(Updike) 40:165-6 D19'64.
B     8469
How not to rob a department
store. (Gill) 41:103 Ja8'66.
CC     8470
How not to write a play. by
Walter Kerr. (Anon.) 31:138-
9 Je11'55. B     8471
How now, Dow Jones. by
Max Shulman, Elmer Bern-
stein, and Carolyn Leigh.
(McCarten) 43:97 D16'67.
T     8472
How the West was won. (Gill)
39:175-6 Ap6'63. CC     8473
How to be a Jewish mother.
by Seymour Vall, Michael
Leonard and Herbert Martin.
(Gill) 43:57 Ja13'68. T 8474
How to be very, very popular.
(McCarten) 31:42*Jy30'55.
CC     8475
How to become a musical
critic. by George Bernard
Shaw, Dan H. Laurence, ed.
(Sargeant) 37:132-2 My27'61.
B     8476
How to make a man. by William
Welch. (McCarten) 36:75
F11'61. T     8477
How to murder your wife.
(Gill) 40:114 Ja30'65. CC
8478
How to save a marriage--and
ruin your life. (Kael)
43:106-108 Ja27'68. CC
8479
How to steal a million.
(S. Lardner) 42:92 Jy16'66.
CC     8480
How to steal an election. by
William F. Brown and
Oscar Brand. (Oliver) 44:142
O26'68. T     8481

How to succeed in business
without really trying. by
Abe Burrows, Jack Wein-
stock, Willie Gilbert and
Frank Loesser. (McCarten)
37:129 O21'61. T     8482
Howie. by Phoebe Ephron.
(J. Lardner) 34:74 S27'58.
T     8483
How's the world treating you?
by Roger Milner. (McCarten)
42:128 N5'66. T     8484
Hubert and Jan van Eyck. by
Léo Van Puyvelde. (Anon.)
33:116 Mr2'57. B     8485
Hud. (Gill) 39:166 Je8'63.
CC     8486
Hughie. by Eugene O'Neill.
(McCarten) 40:58 Ja2'65.
T     8487
Hugo Wolf: a biography. by
Frank Walker. (Anon.)
44:248-50 D7'68. B     8488
Hugs and kisses. (Gilliatt)
44:92-4 Ag24'68. CC     8489
The human condition. by
Hannah Arendt. (McCarthy)
34:198-205 O18'58. B     8490
The humbler creation. by Pamela
Hansford Johnson. (Anon.)
36:141 F27'60. B     8491
The hundred days. by Edith
Saunders. (Anon.) 40:244-6
N14'64. B     8492
The hundred flowers campaign
and the Chinese intellectuals.
by Roderick MacFarquhar.
(Anon.) 36:245-6 N26'60.
B     8493
A hundred hours to Suez. by
Robert Henriques. (Anon.)
33:176-7 Ap13'57. B     8494
Hunger. by Knut Hamsun.
Robert Bly, trans. (Updike)
43:223-32 D2'67. B     8495
Hunger. (Gilliatt) 44:74-7 Ag
17'68. CC     8496
The hungry future. by René
Dumont and Bernard Rosier.
Rosamund Linell and R.B.
Sutcliffe, trans. (Anon.)
45:202-203 O11'69. B     8496a
The hunt. by Maurice Sachs.
Richard Howard, trans.

(Anon.) 41:107 S4'65. B
8497
The hunt. (Gill) 43:132 Ap29'67
CC                          8498
The hunted children. by
Donald A. Lowrie. (Anon.)
39:115-16 Je22'63. B    8499
The hunting and exploring ad-
ventures of Theodore
Roosevelt. by Theodore
Roosevelt. Donald Day, ed.
(Anon.) 31:160 My7'55. B
8500
Hurry sundown. (Gill) 43:145
Ap8'67. CC                8501
Hush ... hush, sweet
Charlotte. (Gill) 41:168-9
Mr13'65. CC              8502
The hustler. (Gill) 37:140-1
S30'61. CC              8503
Huui, huui. by Anne Burr.
(Oliver) 44:142 D7'68. T
8504
The hyphenated family. by
Hermann Hagedorn. (Anon.)
36:240 N26'60. B        8505
Hypnos waking. by René
Char. (Bogan) 32:180-1 O6
'56. B                    8506

I

I, a man. (Gilliatt) 43:112-16
S9'67. CC                8507
I accuse! (McCarten) 34:93-4
Mr15'58. CC              8508
I am a camera. (McCarten)
31:62 Ag20'55. CC        8509
I am a composer. by Arthur
Honegger. Wilson O. Clough
and Allan Willman, trans.
(Anon.) 42:224 S10'66.B 8510
I am a mathematician. by
Norbert Weiner. (Anon.)
32:170-1*Mr17'56. B      8511
I am curious (yellow).
(Gilliatt) 45:97-8 Ap5'69. CC
8512
I can get it for you wholesale.
by Jerome Weidman and
Harold Rome. (Oliver) 38:
102-104 Mr31'62. T      8513
I come from the stone age. by

Heinrich Harrer. Edward
Fitzgerald, trans. (Anon.)
41:203 Mr13'65. B       8514
I do! I do! by Tom Jones and
Harvey Schmidt. (McCarten)
42:117 D17'66. T        8515
I, Don Quixote. (J. Lardner)
35:206-207 D5'59. TV    8516
I got shoes. by Frank
Merlin. (Oliver) 38:72-5
F2'63. T                8517
I had a ball. by Jerome
Chodorov, Jack Lawrence
and Stan Freeman. (Mc-
Carten) 40:50 D26'64. T
8518
I have fought the good fight.
by Carter Wilson. (Anon.)
43:212-13 O28'67. B     8519
I hear thunder. by Samuel
Selvon. (West) 39:238-42
D7'63. B                8520
I, John Mordaunt. by Virgil
Scott. (Anon.) 40:220 Ap
18'64. B                8521
I knock at the door. by Paul
Shyre. (Oliver) 40:88-90
D5'64. T                8522
I know my love. by
Catherine Gaskin. (Anon.)
38:176-8 Mr24'62. B     8523
I like it here. by Kingsley
Amis. (Anon.) 34:150-1
My24'58. B              8524
I like money. (Gill)
My26'62. CC             8525
I lost it at the movies. by
Pauline Kael. (Anon.) 41:
196 Ap17'65. B          8526
I love you, Alice B. Toklas!
(Kael) 44:212 O19'68. CC
8527
I must be talking to my
friends. by Micheál Mac-
Liammóir. (Oliver) 43:147-9
D2'67. T                8528
I never sang for my father.
by Robert Anderson. (Gill)
43:77 F3'68. T          8529
I only want an answer. by
Fred Denger. (Oliver) 43:
101 F17'68. T           8530
I remember! I remember!
by Sean O'Faolain. (Anon.)

37:110-11 Ja13'62. B    8531
I saw my mortal sight. by
  Evelyn Eaton. (Anon.) 35:204-
  205 O10'59. B          8532
I thank a fool. (McCarten)
  38:86-7 S22'62. CC     8533
I want it now. by Kingsley
  Amis. (Sissman) 45:167-70
  Ap26'69. B             8534
I want to live! (McCarten)
  34:108-10 N29'58. CC   8535
I was Cicero. by Elyesa Bazna
  and Hans Nogly. Eric Mos-
  bacher, trans. (Anon.)
  38:146 F9'63. B        8536
I was dancing. by Edwin
  O'Connor. (Anon.) 40:192
  Ap4'64. B              8537
I was dancing. by Edwin
  O'Connor. (McCarten)
  40:143 N21'64. T       8538
I wonder as I wander. by
  Langston Hughes. (Anon.)
  32:103-104 Ja12'57. B  8539
Ice palace. (McCarten)
  36:55-6 Jy9'60. CC     8540
Ice station zebra. (Kael)
  44:69 Ja4'69. CC       8541
The iceman cometh. by
  Eugene O'Neill. (Gibbs)
  32:66-8*My26'56. T     8542
The icon and the axe: an
  interpretive history of
  Russian culture. by James
  H. Billington. (Anon.)
  42: 127-8 Ag27'66. B   8543
I'd do it again. by James
  Michael Curley. (Anon.)
  33:126-7 Je15'57. B    8544
I'd rather be rich. (Gill)
  40:96-8 S12'64. CC     8545
The idea of a party system:
  the rise of legitimate op-
  position in the United
  States, 1780-1840. by
  Richard Hofstadter. (Anon.)
  45:103-104 F7'70. B    8546
The ideas of biology. by
  John Tyler Bonner. (Anon.)
  38:178-9 S22'62. B     8547
The ides of August. by
  William Converse Haygood.

(Anon.) 32:70*Ag11'56.
  B                      8548
The idiot. by Fyodor
  Dosteovski. (Rosenberg)
  44:159-81 O5'68. B     8549
The idiot. by Boris Tumarin
  and Jack Sydow. (Balliett)
  36: 95-7 O8'60. T      8550
The idiot. (Flanner) 35:93
  Ag8'59. (McCarten) 36:54
  Jy30'60. CC            8551
If ... (Kael) 45:152-60
  My15'69. CC            8552
If all the guys in the world.
  (McCarten) 33:162-3
  My4'57. CC             8553
If five years pass. by
  Federico García Lorca.
  (Oliver) 38:103-104 My
  19'62. T               8554
If the sun dies. by Oriana
  Fallaci. Pamela Swingle-
  hurst, trans. (Anon.) 42:
  246 D3'66. B           8555
Ikiru. (McCarten) 35:125-6
  F13'60. CC
                         8556
Il duce. by Christopher
  Hibbert. (N. Bliven)
  38:153-9 My26'62. B    8557
Il faut passer par les nuages.
  by François Billetdoux.
  (Flanner) 40:108 Ja23'65. T
                         8558
Il giornale dell'anima. by John
  XXIII. Don Loris Capo-
  villa. ed. (Rynne) 40:173 S19'64.
  B                      8559
Il successo. (Gill) 41:168 My8
  '65. CC                8560
I'll cry tomorrow. (McCarten)
  31:83*Ja21'56. CC      8561
I'll never forget what's 'is name.
  (Gilliatt) 44:144-6 Ap27'68.
  CC                     8562
I'll sing you the death of Bill
  Brown. by Bruce Dexter.
  (Anon.) 39:82-3 Je29'63. B
                         8563
Ill-stared general: Braddock of
  the Coldstream Guards. by Lee
  McCardell. (N. Bliven) 34:
  166-72 S20'58. B       8564

An illustrated history of England. by André Maurois. Hamish Miles, trans. (Anon.) 40: 248 D12'64. B          8565
The illustrated man. (Gilliatt) 45:98-9 Ap5'69. CC     8566
Illya darling. by Jules Dassin, Manos Hadjidakis and Joe Darion. (McCarten) 43:146 Ap 22'67. T            8567
Ilona. by Hans Habe. Michael Bullock, trans. (Anon.) 37:242 N11'61. B        8568
I'm all right, Jack. (Panter-Downes) 35:204-206 N21'59. (McCarten) 36:190-1 My7'60. CC               8569
I'm Solomon. by Anne Croswell and Dan Almagor and Ernest Gold. (Gill) 44:129 My4'68. T          8570
The image men. by J.B. Priestley. (Anon.) 45:147-8 My3'69. B           8571
The image merchants. by Irwin Ross. (Anon.) 35:70-1 Ja2 '60. B               8572
The image, or what happened to the American dream. by Daniel J. Boorstin. (Anon.) 38:142-3 Mr31'62. B     8573
Images of the universe--Leonardo da Vinci: the artist as scientist. by Richard Mc-Lanathan. (Anon.) 43:194-5 Mr18'67. B          8574
Images of truth. by Glenway Wescott. (Anon.) 38:172 S29 '62. B               8575
Images of war. by Robert Capa. (Anon.) 40:80 Ag1'64. B          8576
The imaginary invalid. by Molière. (McCarten) 43:158 My13'67. T               8577
Imitation general. (McCarten) 34:68 Ag30'58. CC       8578
Imitation of life. (McCarten) 35:167-8 Ap25'59. CC    8579
Imitations. by Robert Lowell. (Anon.) 37:120 Ja20'62. B          8580
The imminent rains: a visit

among the last pioneers of Africa. by Jonn Hylan, Hemingway, Jr. (Anon.) 44:139-40 S7'68. B         8581
The immortal story. (Gilliatt) 44:143-5 S21'68. CC    8582
Impact: essays on ignorance and the decline of American civilization. by Ezra Pound. (Anon.) 36:106-107 Je25'60. B               8583
The impartial knife. by Peter Paris. (Anon.) 38:186 Ap14'62. B          8584
The importance of being earnest. by Oscar Wilde. (Oliver) 39:132-4 Mr9'63. T               8585
The important man. (Gill) 38:64 Jy7'62. CC     8586
Impossible object. by Nicholas Mosley. (Steiner) 45:89-91 Jy12'69. B     8587
Impossible on Saturday. (Gill) 42:108-109 F26'66. CC    8588
The impossible years. by Robert Fisher and Arthur Marx. (McCarten) 41:94-6 O23'65. T               8589
Impressions of Lenin. by Angelica Balabanoff. Isotta Cesari, trans. (Anon.) 40:137-8 Je20'64. B     8590
Impromptu at Versailles. by Molière. (McCarten) 37:93 Mr 4'61 (Oliver) 40:66-7 Mr21'64. T               8591
In a Corsican village. by Shirley Deane. (Anon.) 42:164 F11'67. B          8592
In a farther country. by William Goyen. (Anon.) 31:71*Ag6'55. B               8593
In a month, in a year. by Françoise Sagan. (Flanner) 33:111-12 S21'57. B     8594
In a Summer season. by Elizabeth Taylor. (Anon.) 36: 124 F11'61. B          8595
In an iridescent time. by Ruth Stone. (Bogan) 35:238-40 N 28'59. B          8596
In another country. by John

Bayley. (Anon.) 31:150-1
*D17'55. B                    8597
In any case. by Richard G.
Stern. (Anon.) 38:230 O20'62.
B                             8598
In brief authority. by Francis
Biddle. (Anon.) 38:246 N17'62.
B                             8599
In circles. by Gertrude Stein.
and Al Carmines. (Oliver)
43:131-3 N18'67. T            8600
In cold blood. (Gill) 43:47
D23'67. CC                    8601
In Flanders fields. by Leon
Wolff. (Anon.) 34:208 O18'58.
B                             8602
In God we trust/all others pay
cash. by Jean Shepherd.
(Anon.) 42:94 Ja7'67. B
                              8603
In harm's way. (Gill) 41:158
Ap17'65. CC                   8604
In like Flint. (Gill) 43:175
Mr18'67. CC                   8605
In love and war. (McCarten)
34:182-3 N8'58. CC            8606
In my fashion. by Bettina
Ballard. (Anon.) 36:180
Ap23'60. B                    8607
In my time. by Robert Strausz-
Hupé. (Anon.) 41:248 O30'65.
B                             8608
In pious memory. by Margery
Sharp. (Anon.) 43:87 Jy22'67.
B                             8609
In pursuit of the English. by
Doris Lessing. (N. Bliven)
37:234-8 D2'61. B             8610
In pursuit of the mous, the snaile,
and the clamm. by Mary
Durant. (Anon.) 45:96 Ag23
'69. B                        8611
In retrospect: the history of a
historian. by Arthur M.
Schlesinger. (Anon.) 39:97
D21'63. B                     8612
In search of Bisco. by Erskine
Caldwell. (Balliett) 41:174-7
My22'65. B                    8613
In search of Swift. by Denis
Johnston.(Anon.) 36:159
Mr26'60. B                    8614
In the absence of Mrs. Petersen.

by Nigel Balchin. (Anon.)
42:244-5 N12'66. B            8615
In the bar of a Tokyo hotel. by
Tennessee Williams. (Oliver)
45:114 My24'69. T             8616
In the clearing. by Robert
Frost. (Bogan) 38:242-4
N17'62. B                     8617
In the company of eagles. by
Ernest K. Gann. (Anon.)
42:245 O29'66. B              8618
In the counting house. by
Leslie Weiner. (McCarten)
38:66 D22'62. T               8619
In the court of public opinion.
by Alger Hiss. (Anon.)
33:141 My 25'57. B            8620
In the fist of the revolution: life
in a Cuban country town. by
Jose Yglesias. (Anon.) 44:
110-11 Je15'68. B             8621
In the French style. (Gill)
39:106-108 S28'63. CC         8622
In the heat of the night. (Gilliatt)
43:64 Ag5'67. CC              8623
In the jungle of cities. by Bertolt
Brecht. (Balliett) 36:42-3
D31'60. T                     8624
In the labyrinth. by Alain
Robbe-Grillet. Richard
Howard, trans. (Anon.) 36:244
D10'60. B                     8625
In the matter of J. Robert Op-
penheimer. by Heinar Kipphardt.
(Gill) 45:131 Mr15'69. T
                              8626
In the name of humanity. by
Alexander Thomsen. Maurice
Michael, trans. (Anon.) 39:
246-7 N9'63. B                8627
In the thick of the fight. by
Paul Reynaud. (Anon.) 31:98
*F4'56. B                     8628
In the time of Greenbloom.    by
Gabriel Fielding. (Anon.) 33:
85 Je29'57. (Balliett) 37:174-7
S23'61. B                     8629
In the world. by George P.
Elliott. (West) 41:105-106
Ja29'66. B                    8630
In the year of the pig. (Kael)
45:177-9 N15'69. CC
                              8631

In this house of Brede. by
Rumer Godden. (Anon.) 45:178
N1'69. B                   8632
In White America. by Martin B.
Duberman. (Oliver) 39:98-9
N9'63 (Flanner) 41:118-20 Je12
'65. T                     8633
Inadmissible evidence. by John
Osborne. (Panter-Downes) 41:
176-9 Ap17'65 (McCarten) 41:
142 D11'65. T              8634
Inadmissible evidence. (Gill)
44:62-4 Je29'68. CC        8635
The Incas: the royal commen-
taries of the Inca Garcilaso de
la Vega. by Garcilaso de la
Vega. Alain Gheerbrant, ed.
Maria Jolas, trans. (Anon.)
37:117 Ja20'62. B          8636
Incense to idols. by Sylvia
Ashton-Warner. (Anon.) 36:61
D24'60. B                  8637
The incident. (Gill) 43:138
N18'67. CC                 8638
Incident at Vichy. by Arthur
Miller. (McCarten) 40:152
D12'64. T                  8639
Income and welfare in the
United States. by James N.
Morgan. (Macdonald) 38:86-91
Ja19'63. B                 8640
The increased difficulty of
concentration. by Václav
Havel. (Oliver) 45:116-18
O13'69. T                  8641
The incredible Krupps. by
Norbert Muhlen. (Anon.) 35:
244-5 D5'59. B             8642
Incubus. by Guiseppe Berto.
William Weaver, trans.
(West) 42:171-2 Ap2'66.
B                          8643
An index to literature in the
New Yorker. by Robert
Owen Johnson. (Anon.) 45:60
D27'69. B                  8644
India and the West. by Barbara
Ward. (Anon.) 37:134 My27
'61. B                     8645
India today. by Frank Moraes.
(Anon.) 36:160-1 Mr26'60.
B                          8646

India wins freedom. by Maulana
Abul Kalam Azad. (Anon.)
36:88 Jy23'60. B           8647
Indian painting: the scene,
themes, and legends. by Mo-
hinder Singh Randhawa and John
Kenneth Galbraith. (Anon.)
44:106-107 D21'68. B       8648
The Indian wants the Bronx. by
Israel Horovitz. (Oliver)
43:86-7 Ja27'68. T         8649
The Indian war of 1864. by
Eugene F. Ware. (Anon.)
36:126-7 F11'61. B         8650
Indians. by Arthur Kopit. (Gill)
45:149-150 O18'69. T       8651
Indiscreet. (McCarten) 34:99
Jy12'58. CC                8652
Indonesian upheaval. by John
Hughes. (Anon.) 43:237-40
D2'67. B                   8653
The infernal machine. by
Jean Cocteau. Albert Bermel,
trans. (Gibbs) 33:60-1 F15'58.
T                          8654
The infernal world of Branwell
Brontë. by Daphne Du
Maurier. (Anon.) 37:163-4
Mr25'61. B                 8655
An infinity of mirrors. by
Richard Condon. (Anon.)
40:227-8 O17'64. B         8656
The inflexible prince. by Pedro
Calderón. (Flanner) 42:103
Jy16'66. T                 8657
Inherit the wind. by Jerome
Lawrence and Robert E. Lee.
(Gibbs) 31:67 Ap30'55. T
                           8658
Inherit the wind. (Gill) 36:98-
100 O22'60. CC             8659
The inn of the sixth happiness.
(Panter-Downes) 34:124-5 D13
'58. (McCarten) 34:98-9 D20
'58. CC                    8660
The inner journey. by James
Hanley. (Oliver) 45:105 Mr29
'69. T                     8661
The inner presence: recollections
of my spiritual life. by
François Mauriac. Herma Brif-
fault, trans. (Anon.) 44:92 F1
'69. B                     8662

The innkeepers. by Theodore Apstein. (Gibbs) 31:64-6 *F11'56. T 8663

The innocent ambassadors. by Philip Wylie. (Anon.) 33:166 My11'57. B 8664

The innocents. by William Archibald. (Malcolm) 35:97-9 My2'59. T 8665

The inquisitory. by Robert Pinget. Donald Watson, trans. (Updike) 43:234-8 N4'67. B 8666

The insect woman. (Balliett) 40:74-6 Jy11'64. CC 8667

Inside Africa. by John Gunther. (Rovere) 31:212-13*N12'55. B 8668

Inside Daisy Clover. (Gill) 42:109 F26'66. CC 8669

Inside Europe today. by John Gunther. (Anon.) 37:88-9 Ag12'61. B 8670

Inside Hitler's headquarters. by Walter Warlimont. R.H. Barry, trans. (Anon.) 41: 163-4 F20'65. B 8671

Inside Lincoln's army. by Marsena Rudolph Patrick. David S. Sparks, ed. (Anon.) 40:182-3 Ap11'64. B 8672

Inside Lincoln's cabinet: the Civil War diaries of Salmon P. Chase. by Salmon P. Chase. David Donald, ed. (Anon.) 31:174*O15'55. B 8673

The inside passage. by Anthony Bailey. (Anon.) 41:183 Mr27'65. B 8674

Inside Russia today. by John Gunther. (Anon.) 34:147-8 My 10'58. B 8675

Inside South America. by John Gunther. (Anon.) 43:190-2 Mr25'67. B 8676

The insolent breed. by Borden Deal. (Anon.) 35:193-4 S26'59. B 8677

Inspector Clouseau. (Gilliatt) 44:80-1 Jy27'68. CC 8678

Inspector Maigret. (McCarten) 34:156 O18'58. CC 8679

Instead of a letter. by Diana Athill. (Anon.) 38:232 O20'62. B 8680

Instructions for the running of trains, etc. on the Erie Railway, to go into effect January 1, 1862. Anon. (Oliver) 45:52-3 Ja17'70. T 8681

The intelligent woman's guide to conservatism. by Russell Kirk. (Anon.) 33:139-40 Je8'57. B 8682

Interlock. by Ira Levin. (Gibbs) 33:58-60 F15'58. T 8683

International conflict for beginners. by Roger Fisher. (Anon.) 45:160 S27'69. B 8684

International soirée. Anon. (Gibbs) 34:90 Mr22'58. T 8685

The interplay of East and West. by Barbara Ward. (Anon.) 33:79-80*Jy20'57. B 8686

The interpreter. by March Cost. (Anon.) 36:183-4 O29'60. B 8687

Interrupted melody. (McCarten) 31:145-6 My14'55. CC 8688

The interurban era. by William D. Middleton. (Anon.) 37:154 S9'61. B 8689

An intimate journal of the Dreyfus case. by Maurice Paléologue. (Anon.) 33:150 Mr16'57. B 8690

Intimate relations. by Jean Cocteau. (Oliver) 38:148 N10'62. T 8691

Intolerance. (Kael) 44:102-106 F24'68. CC 8692

An introduction to the French poets. by Geoffrey Brereton. (Anon.) 33:146 My25'57. B 8693

The intruder. (Gill) 38:134 My26 '62. CC 8694

The invasion of France and Germany. by Samuel Eliot Morison. (Anon.) 33:73-4*Jy 27'57. B 8695

Invasion: 1066. by Rupert
Furneaux. (Anon.) 42:167
Je11'66. B                    8696
The investigation. by Peter  ]
Weeks. (McCarten) 42:118
O15'66. T                     8697
The invincible Monet. by C.P.
Weekes. (Anon.) 36:206-207
S10'60. B                     8698
The invisible presidency. by
Louis W. Koenig. (Anon.)
36:162 Ap2'60. B              8699
Invitation to a beheading. by
Vladimir Nabokov. (Anon.)
35:240-1 N28'59. B            8700
Invitation to a beheading.
by Russell McGrath. (Oliver)
45:100-102 Mr29'69.
T                             8701
Invitation to a march. by
Arthur Laurents. (McCarten)
36:116 N5'60. T               8702
Invitation to the dance. (McCarten)
32:118*Je2'56. CC            8703
The Ipcress file. (Gill) 41:92
Ag14'65. CC                   8704
Iphigenia in Aulis. by Euripides.
(Oliver) 43:147 D2'67. T
                              8705
Iphigenia in Tauris. by Johann
Wolfgang von Goethe. (Malcolm)
35:136-8 O17'59. T            8706
Iran: the new imperialism
in action. by Bahman
Nirumand. Leonard Mins,
trans. (Anon.) 45:95-6 Ag9
'69. B                        8707
The Irish answer. by Tony Gray.
(Anon.) 42:223 S10'66. B
                              8708
Irma la douce. by Julian More,
David Heneker and Monty
Norman. (McCarten) 36:95
O8'60. T                      8709
Irma la douce. (Gill) 39:54
Je15'63. CC                   8710
The iron petticoat. (McCarten)
32:107-108 F9'56.             8711
Ironies of history: essays on
contemporary Communism. by
Isaac Deutscher. (Anon.)
42:123 Ja14'67. B             8712
The irrational journey. by

Pauline de Rothschild. (Flan-
ner) 44:103-104 Mr2'68. B
                              8713
Irrational man: a study in
existential philosophy. by
William Barrett. (Anon.) 34:
211 O18'58. B                 8714
The irregular verb to love. by
Hugh Williams and Margaret
Williams. (McCarten) 39:94
S28'63. T                     8715
Is Paris burning? by Larry
Collins and Dominique Lapierre.
(Anon.) 41:74 Jy3'65. B
                              8716
Is Paris burning? (Gill)
42:183 N19'66. CC             8717
Isaac Newton's papers & letters
on natural philosophy. by
Isaac Newton. I. Bernard
Cohen, ed. (Anon.) 34:211-12
O18'58. B                     8718
Ishi in two worlds. by Theodora
Kroeber. (Anon.) 37:244-5
N11'61. B                     8719
Islam inflamed. by James
Morris. (Anon.) 33:162-4 S
28'57. B                      8720
The island. (McCarten) 38:86
S22'62. CC                    8721
The island: a journey to Sakhalin.
by Anton Chekhov. Luba
Terpak and Michael Terpak
trans. (Hyman) 43:113-16
F10'68. B                     8722
Island in the sun. (McCarten)
33:68*Je22'57. CC             8723
Island of goats. by Ugo Betti.
Henry Reed, trans. (Gibbs)
31:77-8*O15'55. T             8724
Isle of children. by Robert L.
Joseph. (Oliver) 38:106 Mr31
'62. T                        8725
Israel. Nicolas Lazar, ed. and
Izis, ed. (Anon.) 34:180
S27'58. B                     8726
Issues of freedom. by Herbert
J. Muller. (Anon.) 36:144
F27'60. B                     8727
It happened here. (Adler) 42:
98 Ag13'66. CC               8728
It happened in broad daylight. (Gill)
36:106 O8'60. CC             8729

It happened in the park. (Hamburger) 33:73 Ag24'57. CC
8730
It isn't all mink. by Ginette Spanier. (Anon.) 36:186 O29'60. B                8731
It started in Naples. (Gill) 36:169-70 S17'60. CC        8732
It started with a kiss. (Balliett) 35:68 Ag29'59. CC        8733
Italian bouquet. by Samuel Chamberlain. (Anon.) 35:168 Mr7'59. B                8734
The Italian girl. by Iris Murdoch. (Anon.) 40:167 D19'64. B                8735
Italian high renaissance and baroque sculpture. by John Pope-Hennessy. (Anon.) 39: 124 Je1'63. B                8736
Italian journey. by Johann Wolfgang von Goethe. W. H. Auden and Elizabeth Mayer, trans. (Anon.) 38:162-3 F16 '63. B                8737
The Italian lakes. by Gabriel Faure. George Millard, trans. (Anon.) 34:104 Je21'58. B                8738
The Italian story. by Geoffrey Trease. (Anon.) 41:183 Mr27 '65. B                8739
Italiano brava gente. (Gill) 41:140-2 F12'66. CC        8740
The Italians. by Luigi Barzini. (Anon.) 40:206-207 S12'64. B                8741
The Italians: face of a nation. by John Phillips. (Anon.) 41:248 N6'65. B                8742
The italics are mine. by Nina Berberova. (Anon.) 45:96 Ag16'69. B                8743
Italo Svevo, the man and the writer. by P.N. Furbank (Steiner) 43:137-43 Je3'67. B                8744
Italy builds. by G.E. Kidder Smith. (Mumford) 31:78 *F4'56. B                8745
It's a bird ... it's a plane ... its Superman. by David Newman,

Robert Benton, Charles Strouse and Lee Adams. (McCarten) 42:81 Ap9'66. T        8746
It's a dog's life. (McCarten) 31:84*Ja14'56. CC        8747
It's a free country. by Leonard Brain. (Anon.) 42:229 S17'66. B                8748
It's a gift. (Gilliatt) 45:86-90 Je21'69. CC        8749
It's a mad, mad, mad, mad world. (Gill) 39:137-8 N30'63. CC        8750
It's always fair weather. (Hamburger) 31:104*S24'55. CC
8751
It's an old country. by J.B. Priestley. (Anon.) 43:108 Jy 15'67. B                8752
It's me, O Lord. by Rockwell Kent. (Anon.) 31:127 My28'55. B                8753
Ivanov. by Anton Chekhov. (Malcolm) 34:58-62 O18'58 (McCarten) 42:114 My14'66. T                8754

-J-

J.B.: a play in verse. by Archibald MacLeish. (Anon.) 34:96 Ag16'58. B                8755
J.B. by Archibald MacLeish. (Tynan) 34:70-2 D20'58. T
8756
Jackknife. by Rock Anthony. (Malcolm) 34:84-6 O4'58. T
8757
Jacob. by Jean Cabriès. Gerard Hopkins, trans. (Anon.) 34:200 O25'58. B        8758
Jacobean pageant or the court of King James I. by G.P.V. Akrigg. (Anon.) 38:181 S15'62. B                8759
J'ai tué Raspoutine. (Flanner) 43:128 My27'67. CC        8760
The jail diary of Albie Sachs. by Albert Louis Sachs. (Anon.) 43:74 Jy1'67. B
8761
Jamaica. by E.Y. Harburg, Fred Saidy and Harold Arlen.

(Gibbs) 33:103 N9'57. T
                                    8762
Jamaican blood and Victorian
  conscience. by Bernard
  Semmel. (Anon.) 39:243-4
  N16'63. B              8763
Jambo means hello. by Olle
  Strandberg. (Anon.) 32:155-6
  S29'56. B              8764
James Forrestal: a study of
  personality, politics, and
  policy. by Arnold A. Rogow.
  (Anon.) 39:139-40 F15'64.
  B                      8765
James Gibbons Huneker: critic
  of the seven arts. by Arnold
  T. Schwab. (Sargeant) 39:208-
  17 O26'63. B           8766
James Joyce. by Richard
  Ellmann. (Macdonald) 35:213-
  34 D12'59. B           8767
A James Joyce miscellany: second
  series. Marvin Magalaner, ed.
  (Anon.) 35:228 O17'59. B
                                    8768
James Madison: commander in
  chief, 1812-1836. by Irving
  Brant. (Anon.) 37:91 Ja6'62.
  B                      8769
James Madison: the president.
  by Irving Brant. (Anon.)
  32:102 Ja12'57. B      8770
Jamie. by Jack Bennett.
  (West) 39:236-7 D7'63. B
                                    8771
Jane Eyre. by Huntington
  Hartford. (Gibbs) 34:84-6
  My10'58. T             8772
Janus. by Carolyn Green. (Gibbs)
  31:104-106*D3'55. T    8773
Japan: portrait of a paradox.
  by Quentin Crewe. (Anon.)
  38:193-4 My5'62. B     8774
Japan subdued. by Herbert Feis.
  (N. Bliven) 37:205-209
  O21'61. B              8775
Japanese literature. by Donald
  Keene. (Anon.) 31:136
  Mr26'55. B             8776
The jar. by Luigi Pirandello.
  (Oliver) 45:108 My3'69. T
                                    8777
Jason and the argonauts.

(Miller) 39:65 Ag24'63. CC
                                    8778
Javelin. by Owen Rachleff.
  (McCarten) 42:180 N19'66.
  T                      8779
Jazz: its evolution and essence.
  by André Hodeir. David
  Noakes, trans. (Anon.) 32:156
  *S15'56. B             8780
Jazz Street. by Dennis Stock.
  (Anon.) 36:208 O15'60. B
                                    8781
The jazz world. Dom Cerulli,
  Burt Korall, and Mort
  Nasatir, eds. (Anon.)
  36:183-4 Ap16'60. B    8782
The jealous god. by John
  Braine. (Anon.) 41:188-9
  My1'65. B              8783
Jeanne Eagels. (Hamburger)
  33:74 S7'57. CC         8784
Jefferson and his time, Vol.III:
  Jefferson and the ordeal of
  liberty. by Dumas Malone.
  (Anon.) 38:134 Ja26'63. B
                                    8785
Jefferson Davis: American
  patriot. by Hudson Strode.
  (Anon.) 31:158*S24'55. B
                                    8786
Jefferson Davis: private letters,
  1823-1889. by Jefferson
  Davis. Hudson Strode, ed.
  (Anon.) 42:246-8 D3'66. B
                                    8787
The Jefferson image in the
  American mind. by Merrill
  D. Peterson. (Anon.) 36:107
  S3'60. B               8788
A Jefferson profile. by Thomas
  Jefferson. Saul K. Padover,
  ed. (Anon.) 32:164*My12'56.
  B                      8789
Jennie. by Arnold Schulman,
  Howard Dietz and Arthur
  Schwartz. (McCarten) 39:113
  O26'63. T              8790
Jenny Lind, the Swedish nightin-
  gale. by Gladys Denny
  Schultz. (Anon.) 38:164 My
  26'62. B               8791
Jennie: the life of Lady
  Randolph Churchill, Volume I:

the romantic years, 1854-95.
by Ralph G. Martin. (Anon.)
45:140 F22'69. B 8792
Jerusalem the golden. by
Margaret Drabble. (Anon.)
43:74-5 Jy8'67. B 8793
Jessica. (Gill) 38:182 My19'62.
CC 8794
Jesting apostle: the private
life of Bernard Shaw. by Stephen
Winsten. (Anon.) 33:127 Je15
'57. B 8795
The jet set. by Burton Wohl.
(Anon.) 40:181-2 Mr7'64.
B 8796
Jeu de massacre. (Flanner)
43:127-8 My27'67. CC 8797
A jewel in the crown. by Paul
Scott. (N. Bliven) 42:66 Jy2
'66. B 8798
The Jews of silence. by Elie
Wiesel. Neal Kozodoy, trans.
(Anon.) 42:168 F18'67. B
8799
Jimmy. by Bill Jacob and
Patti Jacob. (Gill) 45:128 N1
'69. T 8800
Jimmy Shine. by Murray
Schisgal. (Gill) 44:180-1
D14'68. T 8801
Jo. by William Dyer. (Oliver)
40:92-4 F22'64. T 8802
No entry. 8803
Joan of the angels? (Gill)
38:181-2 My19'62. CC 8804
Joanna. (Kael) 44:200-201
D7'68. CC 8805
Joanna and Ulysses. by May
Sarton. (Anon.) 39:95 D21'63.
B 8806
John and Mary. (Kael) 45:
68-70 D20'69. CC 8807
John Buchan. by Janet Adam
Smith. (Anon.) 41:108-109
Ja22'66. B 8808
John D. Rockefeller's secret
weapon. by Albert Z. Carr.
(Anon.) 38:171-2 S29'62. B
8809
John Dewey. by Irwin Edman.
(Anon.) 31:96 Ag27'55. B 8810

John F. Kennedy: years of
lightning. days of drums.
(Gill) 42:121 Ap16'66. CC
8811
John Goldfarb, please come
home. (Gill) 41:103-104
Ap3'65. CC 8812
John Gunther's high road.
(J. Lardner) 35:166-7 O
24'59. TV 8813
John Keats. by Walter Jackson
Bate. (Anon.) 39:245 D7'63.
B 8814
John Keats. by Robert Gittings.
(Bogan) 44:62 D28'68. B
8815
John Locke. by Maurice Cran-
ston. (Anon.) 33:149-50
S7'57. B 8816
John Maynard Keynes. by
Seymour Harris. (Anon.)
31:153 Mr19'55. B 8817
John Quincy Adams and the Union.
by Samuel Flagg Bemis.
(Anon.) 32:126 F9'57. B
8818
John Singer Sargent. by Charles
Merrill Mount. (Anon.)
31:216-17*N12'55. B 8819
John Sloan. by Van Wyck
Brooks. (Anon.) 31:139 Mr
12'55. B 8820
John Sloan's New York scene.
Bruce St. John, ed. (Anon.)
41:110-11 Ja22'66. B 8821
Johnny nobody. (Gill) 41:112
D4'65. CC 8822
Johnny No-trump. by Mary
Mercier. (McCarten) 43:81-2
O21'67. T 8823
The Johnstown flood. by David
G. McCullough. (Anon.)
44:174-5 My11'68. B 8824
Johnstown: the day the dam
broke. by Richard O'Connor.
(Anon.) 33:199-200 O12'57. B
8825
The joker. (Gill) 37:68-70
Ag12'61. CC 8826
The joker is wild. (McCarten)
33:146 O5'57. CC 8827
The jokers. (Gill) 43:169
My20'67. CC 8828

Jolly's progress. by Lonnie Coleman. (Tynan) 35:78*D19'59. T 8829

Jomo Kenyatta. by George Delf. (Anon.) 37:90 Ag12'61. B 8830

Jonah. by Paul Goodman. (Oliver) 42:71-2 F26'66. T 8831

Jonah! by T.J. Spencer. (Oliver) 43:136-8 O7'67. T 8832

Jonathan Swift. by John Middleton Murry. (Anon.) 31:105-106 *Ja21'56. B 8833

Joseph Conrad. by Jocelyn Baines. (West) 36:137-41 My28'60. B 8834

Joseph Conrad: letters to William Blackwood and David S. Meldrum. by Joseph Conrad. William Blackburn, ed. (Anon.) 35:67 Ag1'59. B 8835

Joseph Conrad's letters to R.B. Cunninghame Graham. by Joseph Conrad. C.T. Watts, ed. (Anon.) 45:159-60 O4'69. B 8836

Joseph Kilian. (S. Lardner) 42:75 Jy23'66. CC 8837

Joséphine. by Hubert Cole. (Anon.) 38:144-5 F9'63. B 8838

Journal d'un collectionneur; Marchand de tableaux. See Diary of an art dealer. B 8839

Journal littéraire. by Paul Léautaud. (Flanner) 31:80-2 *S10'55. B 8840

The journal of Jules Renard. by Jules Renard. Louise Bogan and Elizabeth Roget, trans. (N. Bliven) 41:153-5 Je12'65. B 8841

The journals of David E. Lilienthal, Volumes I and II. by David E. Lilienthal. (Anon.) 40:246-7 N21'64. B 8842

The journey. by Jiro Osaragi. (West) 36:178-9 O1'60. B 8843

The journey. (McCarten) 35:106-107 F28'59. CC 8844

Journey among brave men. by Dana Adams Schmidt. (Anon.) 40:111-12 Je27'64. B 8845

Journey behind the iron curtain. by Robert Westbrook. (Anon.) 39:123 Je1'63. B 8846

Journey down a rainbow. by J.B. Priestley and Jacquetta Hawkes. (Anon.) 31:97*F4'56. B 8847

Journey into the whirlwind. by Eugenia Semyonovna Ginzburg. Paul Stevenson and Max Hayward, trans. (Wilson) 45:149-53 S27'69. B 8848

Journey of an American. by Albion Ross. (Anon.) 33:143-4 Ap27'57. B 8849

The journey of the fifth horse. by Ronald Ribman. (Oliver) 42:79-80 Ap30'66. T 8850

Journey through China. by Jules Roy. Francis Price, trans. (Anon.) 43:178-9 My20'67. B 8851

Journey through dread. by Arland Ussher. (Anon.) 31:179 *O15'55. B 8852

Journey to Italy. (Flanner) 31:89*Ag27'55. CC 8853

A journey to Matecumbe. by Robert Lewis Taylor. (Malcolm) 37:74-6 Jy1'61. B 8854

Journey to the day. by Roger O. Hirson. (Oliver) 39:144 N23'63. T 8855

Journey to the East. by Herman Hesse. (Steiner) 44:87-9 Ja18'69. B 8856

Journey to the ends of time, vol. I: lost in the dark wood. by Sacheverell Sitwell. (Anon.) 35:245 D5'59. B 8857

Journey to the jade sea. by John Hillaby. (Anon.) 41:190 My1'65. B 8858

The journey's echo: selections from Freya Stark. by Freya Stark. (Anon.) 40:207-208 Ap25'64. B 8859

Jowett. by Geoffrey Faber.
(Anon.) 33:91 F1'58. B      8860
Joy house. (Gill) 41:114
F27'65. CC                  8861
Joy in the morning. by Betty
Smith. (Anon.) 39:70 Ag31'63.
B                           8862
Joy in the morning. (S. Lard-
ner) 41:114 Je19'65. CC
                            8863
Joy to Levine! by Norma
Stahl Rosen. (Balliett) 38:177-
8 Ap7'62. B                 8864
A joyful noise. by Edward
Padula, Oscar Brand and
Paul Nassau. (McCarten) 42:
45 D24'66. T                8865
Jubal. (McCarten) 32:139*My5
'56. CC                     8866
Jubb. by Keith Waterhouse.
(Malcolm) 40:234-8 N7'64.
B                           8867
Jubilee, one hundred years
of the "Atlantic." Edward
Weeks and Emily Flint, eds.
(Anon.) 33:243-4 N23'57.
B                           8868
The Judas tree. by A.J.
Cronin. (Anon.) 37:208-209
O7'61. B                    8869
Judex. (Gill) 42:182 My7'66.
CC                          8870
Judgment at Nuremberg. (Gill)
37:68 D23'61; 39:209-210
N9'63. CC                   8871
The judgment of Eve. by
Edgar Pangborn. (Anon.)
42:244 O8'66. B             8872
Judith. by Jean Giraudoux.
(Oliver) 41:86 Ap3'65. T
                            8873
Judith. (Gill) 41:99 Ja22'66.
CC                          8874
Judy Garland. (Tynan) 35:79-80
My23'59. T                  8875
Juice. by Stephen Becker.
(Anon.) 34:114-15 Ja10'59.
B                           8876
Jules and Jim. (Gill) 38:184-5
My5'62. CC                  8877
Julia, Jake, and Uncle Joe.
by Howard Teichmann.
(McCarten) 36:62 F4'61. T 8878

Julie. (McCarten)
32:130 D1'56. CC            8879
Julie the redhead. (Gill)
39:207 O26'63. CC           8880
Juliet of the spirits. (Gill)
41:120-2 N6'65. CC          8881
Julius Caesar. by William
Shakespeare. (Panter-
Downes) 31:114*O8'55.
T                           8882
The jumbie bird. by Ismith
Khan. (West) 39:237-8
D7'63. B                    8883
Jumbo. (Gill) 38:135-6
D15'62. CC                  8884
Jungle cat. (Balliett) 36:56
Ag27'60. CC                 8885
Jungle Child. by Norah Burke.
(Anon.) 31:132*F18'56.
B                           8886
Jungle quest. by Edward
Weyer, Jr. (Anon.) 31:
135 Ap9'55. B               8887
Juno. by Marc Blitzstein
and Joseph Stein. (Tynan)
35:97-8 Mr21'59. T          8888
Jusep Torres Campalans. by
Max Aub. Herbert Weinstock,
trans. (Anon.) 39:210
N2'63. B                    8889
Just for love. by Daisy Ashford
et al. and Michael Valenti.
(Oliver) 44:142 O26'68. T
                            8890
Just off Fifth. by Edith P.
Begner. (Anon.) 35: 168-9
Je6'59. B                   8891
Justice in Moscow. by George
Feifer. (Anon.) 40:91 Jy25
'64. B                      8892
Justice of the heart. by E.
Arnot Robertson. (Anon.)
34:238-41 N15'58. B         8893
Justine. (Gilliatt) 45:67-9 Ag9
'69. CC                     8894

K

Kagami jishi. (Gill) 45:90
S20'69. T                   8895
The Kaiser. by Virginia
Cowles. (Anon.) 40:163-4
Mr28'64. B                  8896

The Kaiser. by Joachim von
Kürenberg. (Anon.) 31:94*Ag
27'55. B　　　　　　8897
The Kaiser and his court: the dia-
ries, note books, and letters of
Admiral Georg Alexander von
Müller. by Georg Alexander von
Müller. WalterGörlitz, ed. Mer-
vyn Sevill, trans. (Anon.) 40:187
My2'64. B　　　　　　8898
Kaleidoscope. (Gill) 42:185-6
O1'66. CC　　　　　　8899
Kampoon Street. by Lin Tai-yi.
(Anon.) 40:134 F29'64. B
　　　　　　　　　　　8900
Kapo. (McCarten) 40:90 Je13
'64. CC　　　　　　8901
Karakoram: the ascent of
Gasherbrum IV. by Fosco
Maraini. James Cadell,
trans. (Anon.) 37:212 O7'61.
B　　　　　　　　　　8902
Kataki. by Shimon Wincelberg.
(Tynan) 35:79-80 Ap18'59.
T　　　　　　　　　　8903
Kean. by Robert Wright, George
Forrest and Peter Stone.
(McCarten) 37:117 N11'61.
T　　　　　　　　　　8904
Keep it in the family. by Bill
Naughton. (McCarten) 43:131
O7'67. T　　　　　　8905
Keep the aspidistra flying. by
George Orwell. (West) 31:86-
92 *Ja28'56. B　　　　8906
Kelly. by Eddie Lawrence and
Moose Charlap. (McCarten)
40:76 F13'65. T　　　8907
Ken Murray's Hollywood. by
Ken Murray. (McCarten)
41:114-16 My22'65. T　8908
Kennedy. by Theodore C.
Sorensen. (Rovere) 41:238-
44 D11'65. B　　　　8909
Kennedy, John F. (J. Lardner)
35:110-12 Ja16'60. TV　8910
Kenneth Grahame. by Peter
Green. (Anon.) 35:151-2
My23'59. B　　　　　8911
The Kentuckian. (Hamburger)
31:115 S10'55. CC　　8912
Kepler's dream. by Johannes
Kepler. Patricia Frueh Kirk-

wood, trans. (Anon.) 41:
107-108 S4'65. B　　　8913
The Kersten memoirs. by Felix
Kersten. Constantine Fitz-
Gibbon and James Oliver,
trans. (Anon.) 33:153-4
Ap20'57. B.　　　　　8914
Kesselring--a soldier's record.
by Alfred Kesselring.
(Liebling) 31:124-32 Mr26
'55. B　　　　　　　8915
The Kessler legacy. by Richard
Martin Stern. (Anon.)
43:104 Ag12'67. B　　8916
The key. (McCarten) 34:99
Jy12'58. CC　　　　　8917
Key to the door. by Alan
Sillitoe. (Anon.) 38:176
S22'62. B　　　　　　8918
The keyhole. by Jean Tardieu.
George Wellwarth, trans.
(Oliver) 37:96-8 F10'62.
T　　　　　　　　　　8919
Khartoum. (S. Lardner) 42:75
Jy23'66. CC　　　　　8920
Krushchev: a career. by Ed-
ward Crankshaw. (Anon.)
42:117-18 S3'66. B　　8921
Krushchev, Nikita. (J. Lardner)
35:156-9 O3'59. TV　8922
Krushchev: the making of a
dictator. by George Paloczi-
Horvath. (Anon.) 36:241
N26'60. B　　　　　　8923
Kicking canvas. by A.A.
Bestic. (Anon.) 34:145-6
Mr8'58. B　　　　　　8924
A kid for two farthings. (Mc-
Carten) 32:82*Ap28'56. CC
　　　　　　　　　　　8925
Kidnap: the story of the Lind-
bergh case. by George
Waller. (Anon.) 37:81-2 S2'61.
B　　　　　　　　　　8926
Kill and overkill. by Ralph E.
Lapp. (Anon.) 38:80 D29'62.
B　　　　　　　　　　8927
The killer. by Eugène Ionesco.
(Malcolm) 36:82-4 Ap2'60.
T　　　　　　　　　　8928
The killing of Sister George.
by Frank Marcus. (McCarten)
42:120 O15'66. T　　8929

The killing of Sister George.
(Kael) 44:86 D21'68. CC
8930
Killing time. by Thomas
Berger. (Anon.) 43:221-2
O21'67. B          8931
Kilvert's diary. by Francis
Kilvert. (W. Maxwell) 37:168-
78 My13'61. B      8932
The kimono mind. by Bernard
Rudofsky. (Anon.) 41:158
Je12'65. B         8933
A kind of loving. (Gill) 38:158
O6'62. CC          8934
The kindly ones. by Anthony
Powell. (N. Bliven) 39:182-8
Ap6'63. B          8935
The king. by Charles Samuels.
(Anon.) 38:132 F24'62. B
8936
King: a critical biography.
by David L. Lewis. (Anon.)
45:92 Ja24'70. B   8937
King and country. (Gill) 41:
124 F5'66. CC      8938
The king and I. (McCarten) 32:
71*Jy14'56. CC     8939
King Cohn. by Bob Thomas.
(Anon.) 43:155 Ap1'67. B
8940
The king dies. by Eugène
Ionesco. (Flanner) 38:102-3
Ja12'63. T         8941
King George VI: his life and
reign. By John W. Wheeler-
Bennett. (Anon.) 34:72 Ja3
'59. B             8942
King Henry V. by Harold F.
Hutchison. (Anon.) 43:116
Ja20'68. B         8943
King James VI and I. by D.
Harris Willson. (Anon.) 32:
129*My26'56. B     8944
King Kong. by Todd Matshikiza,
Harry Bloom and Pat Wil-
liams. (Panter-Downes) 37:
125-6 Mr11'61. T   8945
King Lear. by William Shakes-
peare. (Gibbs) 31:75-6*Ja21
'56 (Malcolm) 34:72-4 Ja10'59
(McCarten) 40:78 My30'64
(Gill) 44:115 N16'68. T
8946

King mob. by Christopher Hib-
bert. (Anon.) 34:167 S13'58.
B                  8947
King, Murray. (Gilliatt)
45:134-5 My10'69. CC  8948
The king of a rainy country.
by Brigid Brophy. (Anon.)
33:112-14 Mr2'57.
B                  8949
King of hearts. (McCarten) 32:
49 Je30'56. (Gilliatt) 43:76-7
Je24'67. CC        8950
King of kings. (Gill) 37:196
O21'61. CC         8951
King of Rome. by André
Castelot. (West) 36:186-9
O22'60. B          8952
The king of the dark chamber.
by Rabindranath Tagore.
(Balliett) 37:93 F18'61. T
8953
King of the whole damn world.
by George Panetta and Robert
Larimer. (Oliver) 38:97
Ap28'62. T         8954
King, queen, knave, by
Vladimir Nabokov. (Anon.)
44:173 My18'68. B  8955
The King ranch. by Tom Lea.
(Anon.) 33:167-8 S28'57. B
8956
King rat. by James Clavell.
(Anon.) 38:152 S8'62. B
8957
King rat. (Gill) 41:203
O30'65. CC         8958
Kingdom of illusion. by
Edward R.F. Sheehan.
(Anon.) 40:213-14 S19'64. B
8959
Kings go forth. (McCarten) 34:
98-9 Jy12'58. CC   8960
Kings, lords, and commons: an
anthology from the Irish.
Frank O'Connor, trans.
(Anon.) 35:196 S19'59. B
8961
Kings of fashion. by Anny
Latour. Mervyn Savill, trans.
(Anon.) 34:243-4 D6'58. B
8962
The king's peace: 1637-1641. by
C.V. Wedgwood (Anon.) 31:163
*S24'55. B         8963

A king's story. (Gill) 43:72-4
Je10'67. CC          8964
The king's war: 1641-47. by
C.V. Wedgwood. (Anon.)
35:169 Ap4'59. B        8965
Kings without thrones. by
Geoffrey Bocca. (Anon.)
35:120 Je20'59. B       8966
Kira Georgievna. by Viktor
Nekrasov. Walter N.
Vickery, trans. (Anon.) 38:
137-8 Je9'62. B         8967
Kismet. (McCarten) 31:134
*D17'55. CC             8968
Kiss Mama. (Oliver) 40:95-6
O10'64. T               8969
Kiss me, stupid. (Gill) 40:74
D26'64. CC              8970
Kiss them for me. (McCarten)
33:109-10 N16'57. CC    8971
Kissed the girls and made
them cry. by John Hale.
(Anon.) 42:228-9 S17'66.
B                       8972
Kissing cousins. by Emily
Hahn. (Anon.) 34:146-7 Ap5
'58. B                  8973
The kitchen. (Gill) 37:208-209
N4'61. CC               8974
Kitchener: portrait of an
imperialist. by Philip Magnus.
(Anon.) 35:119-20 F28'59.
B                       8975
Kittiwake Island. by Arnold
Sundgaard and Alec Wilder.
(Balliett) 36:93 O22'60. T
                        8976
The knack. by Ann Jellicoe.
(Oliver) 40:86-8 Je6'64. T
                        8977
The knack. (Panter-Downes) 41:
82-4 Je26'65 (Oliver) 41:54
Jy10'65. CC             8978
Knaves and fools. by Neville
Williams. (Anon.) 36:163
Mr26'60. B              8979
Knife in the water. (Gill) 39:
195-6 N2'63. CC         8980
Kokoro. by Natsume Soseki.
(West) 33:221 D14'57. B
                        8981
Kongi's harvest. by Wole
Soyinka. (Oliver) 44:86-91 Ap
27'68. T                8982

The koumiko mystery. (Gill)
43:148 Ap15'67. CC      8983
Krakatoa, east of Java.
(Gilliatt) 45:67 Jy26'69. CC
                        8984
Krapp's last tape. by Samuel
Beckett. (Malcolm) 35:75
Ja23'60. T              8985
The Kremlin. by David
Douglas Duncan. (Sargeant)
36:192-3 My7'60. B      8986
Kremlin chimes. by Nikolai
Pogodin. (Oliver) 41:80-2
Mr6'65. T               8987
The Kremlin letter. (Kael)
45:91-3 F7'70. CC       8988
The Kreutzer sonata. by
Roderick Lovell and Hannah
Watt. (Balliett) 37:77-8
F25'61. T               8989
Kwaidan. (Gill) 41:233 N27'65.
CC                      8990
Kwamina. by Robert Alan
Aurthur and Richard Adler.
(McCarten) 37:126 N4'61.
T                       8991
Kyra. by Kyra Petrovskaya.
(Anon.) 35:179 Ap25'59. B
                        8992

L

LBJ: a foreign observer's view-
point. by Michael Davie.
(Anon.) 42:186 My7'66. B
                        8993
La bâtarde. by Violette Leduc.
(Flanner) 40:108-14 Ja23'65.
B                       8994
La belle Américaine. (Gill)
37:45 D30'61. CC        8995
La bonne soupe. (Gill) 40:147
Mr28'64. CC             8996
La chamade. by Françoise
Sagan. Robert Westhoff,
trans. (Flanner) 41:200-202
O2'65. (Brennan) 42:66-7
D24'66. B               8997
La chinoise. (Kael) 44:156-66
Ap6'68. CC              8998
La chute. See The fall. B 8999
La communiante. by Fernando Ar-
rabal. (Flanner) 42:146-8
S10'66. T               9000

La dolce vita. (Flanner) 36:93-4
Ag13'60 (Oliver) 37:126-8
Ap29'61. CC                    9001
La femme infidèle. (Kael)
45:158 N29'69. CC             9002
La force des choses. by Simone
de Beauvoir. (Flanner) 39:
88-91 Ja11'64. B             9003
La fuga. (Gill) 42:163
Ap2ᵗ66. CC                   9004
La gangrène. Anon. (Flanner)
35:65-6 Jy25'59. B           9005
La grande vadrouille. (Flanner)
42:83-4 Ja28'67. CC          9006
La grosse valise. by Robert
Dhéry. (McCarten) 41:50 D25
'65. T                       9007
LaGuardia: a fighter against
his times, 1882-1933. by
Arthur Mann. (Anon.) 35:246
N14'59. B                    9008
La guerre d'Algérie. by Jules
Roy. (Flanner) 36:138-41 N12
'60. B                       9009
La guerre de troi n'aura
pas lieu. See Tiger at the
gates. T                     9010
La guerre est finie. (Gill) 42:
134 F11'67. CC               9011
La jeune fille à marier. by
Eugène Ionesco. (Flanner)
42:148 S10'66. T             9012
La journée d'une rêveuse. by
Copi. (Flanner) 43:79-80
F3'68. T                     9013
La loi. by Roger Vailland.
(Flanner) 33:135-6 D14'57.
B                            9014
La maison de rendez-vous.
by Alain Robbe-Grillet. Richard
Howard, trans. (Updike) 43:223-
30 N4'67. B                  9015
La métamorphose des dieux.
by André Malraux. (Flanner)
33:80-3 Ja18'58. B           9016
La modification. by Michel
Butor. (Flanner) 33:136-7 D
14'57. B                     9017
La mouche bleue. by Marcel
Aymé. (Flanner) 33:55-6 Ja4
'58. T                       9018
La notte brava. (Gill) 37:78
F3'62. CC                    9019

La Parisienne. (Hamburger)
34:58-60 Ag9'58. CC          9020
La périchole. by Jacques
Offenbach. (Flanner) 45:131
N1'69. T                     9021
La plume de ma tante. by
Robert Dhéry. (Tynan) 34:99-
100 N22'58. T                9022
La porte retombée. by Marie-
Louise Badaut. (Flanner)
36:147-8 D10'60. B           9023
La poupée. (McCarten) 39:
147 S7'63. CC                9024
La princesse. by Fernando
Arrabal. (Flanner) 42:146
S10'66. T                    9025
La prisonnière. (Gilliatt) 45:
173 Ap12'69. CC              9026
La promesse de l'aube. See
Promise at dawn. B           9027
La punaise. by Vladimir
Mayakovsky. (Flanner) 34:
129-31 F7'59. T              9028
La reine de Césarée. by Robert
Brasillach. (Flanner) 33:55
Ja4'58. T                    9029
La révolution et les fétiches. by
Pierre Hervé. (Flanner) 31:
103-105*F11'56. B            9030
La robe mauve de Valentine.
by Françoise Sagan. (Flanner)
38:107-109 Ja26'63. T        9031
La ronde. by Arthur Schnitzler.
(Malcolm) 36:117-18 My21'60.
T                            9032
La semaine sainte. by Louis
Aragon. (Flanner) 35:156-61
Ap18'59. B                   9033
La soif et la faim. by Eugène
Ionesco. (Flanner) 42:101-102
Jy16'66. T                   9034
La sonate des spectres. See
The ghost sonata. T          9035
La sorcière. (McCarten) 32:81
Ja12'57. CC                  9036
La strada. by Charles K. Peck,
Jr. and Lionel Bart. (Gill)
45:57 D20'69. T              9037
La strada. (Flanner) 31:115-16 Mr
26'55 (McCarten) 32:48-9
*Jy28'56. CC                 9038
La terra trema. (Gill) 41:198-9
O23'65. CC                   9039

La troupe du roi: homage to Molière. by Molière. (Gill) 45:57-8 F14'70. T 9040
La vérité. (Flanner) 36:148-50 D10'60. CC 9041
La viaccia. (Gill) 38:140-1 S29'62. CC 9042
La vida. by Oscar Lewis. (Hentoff) 43:154-60 Mr4'67. B 9043
La vie de chateau. (Gill) 43:152-3 Mr25'67. CC 9044
La vie Parisienne. by Jacques Offenbach. (Flanner) 34:108-109 D20'58 (Oliver) 40:67 Mr21'64. T 9045
La vieille dame indigne. (Flanner) 41:185-6 Ap17'65. CC 9046
La ville natale. by Viktor Nekrasov. (Flanner) 33:86-8 Ag24'57. B 9047
La visita. (Adler) 42:108 Ag20'66. CC 9048
La voie lactée. (Flanner) 45:119-20 Ap5'69. CC 9049
Ladies' delight. by Emile Zola. (Anon.) 34:172-3 S20'58. B 9050
Ladies who do. (Gill) 39:204-205 D7'63. CC 9051
Lady and the tramp. (McCarten) 31:43*Jy2'55. CC 9052
Lady Chatterley's lover. by D.H. Lawrence. (Malcolm) 35:193-8 S12'59. B 9053
Lady Chatterley's lover. (McCarten) 35:48-50 Jy18'59. CC 9054
Lady Gregory. by Elizabeth Coxhead. (Anon.) 37:210 O7 '61. B 9055
Lady in a cage. (McCarten) 40:123-4 Je20'64. CC 9056
The lady is waiting. by James Mitchell. (Balliett) 34:141-2 F7'59. B 9057
Lady L. by Romain Gary. (West) 35:161-2 Ap4'59. B 9058
Lady L. (Gill) 42:98-101 My21'66. CC 9059
The lady of the camellais.

by Giles Cooper and Terrence McNally. (McCarten) 39:110 Mr30'63. T 9060
The lady with the dog. (Gill) 38:235 N10'62. CC 9061
The ladykillers. (McCarten) 32:62*Mr3'56. CC 9062
The lake lovers. by Geoffrey Wagner. (Anon.) 39:242-4 D7'63. B 9063
L'amante anglaise. by Marguerite Duras. Barbara Bray, trans. (Anon.) 44:237 N9'68. B 9064
The lamb. by François Mauriac. (Anon.) 31:116*F11'56. B 9065
L'Amérique. by Jean-Louis Barrault. (Flanner) 41:146-8 Ap3'65. T 9066
L'amour profane. by Alfred Kern. Vincent Cronin, trans. (Anon.) 37:244 D2'61. B 9067
The land and people of South Africa. by Alan Paton. (Anon.) 31:87 Je25'55. B 9068
Land of fury. (McCarten) 31: 146 My14'55. CC 9069
Land of tempest: travels in Patagonia 1958-62. by Eric Shipton. (Anon.) 39:237-8 D14'63. B 9070
Land of the high flags. by Rosanne Klass. (Anon.) 40:79 D26'64. B 9071
Land of the living. by John Hearne. (Anon.) 38:179-80 S15'62. B 9072
Land of the Pharaohs. (McCarten) 31:44*Ag6'55. CC 9073
Land to the west. by Geoffrey Ashe. (Anon.) 38:186 My19'62. B 9074
Land under the pole star. by Helge Ingstad. Naomi Walford, trans. (Anon.) 42:119 S3'66. B 9075
Land without justice. by Milovan Djilas. (Anon.) 34:151-2 My 24'58. B 9076
The landlord. by Kristin Hunter.

(Anon.) 42:222 S10'66. B
                                    9077
Landru. (Gill) 39:113-14
Ap20'63. CC                         9078
Langrishe, go down. by Aidan
Higgins. (Anon.) 43:160 F25
'67. B                              9079
The Langston Hughes reader.
by Langston Hughes. (Anon.)
34:155*Ap26'58. B                   9080
Language and mind. by Noam
Chomsky. (Steiner) 45:217-
36 N15'69. B                        9081
The language of life. by George
Beadle and Muriel Beadle.
(Bernstein) 42:132-42 My28'66.
B                                   9082
Language, thought, and
reality. by Benjamin Lee
Whorf. (Anon.) 32:131-2*My
26'56. B                            9083
L'architecte et l'Empereur
d'Assyrie. by Fernando
Arrabal. (Flanner) 43:176-8
Ap15'67. T                          9084
Larger than life. by Dino
Buzzati. Henry Reed, trans.
(Hyman) 44:122-5 Je1'68. B
                                    9085
The lark. by Jean Anouilh.
Lillian Hellman, adapt. (Gibbs)
31:106-12*D3'55. B                  9086
Larousse encyclopedia of
mythology. Felix Guirand,
ed. Richard Aldington and
Delano Ames, trans. (Bogan)
35:131-6 F6'60. B                   9087
The last analysis. by Saul
Bellow. (McCarten) 40:95
O10'64. T                           9088
The last angry man. by Gerald
Green. (Anon.) 33:147-8 Mr16
'57. B                              9089
The last angry man. (McCarten)
35:173 O31'59. CC                   9090
The last battle. by Cornelius
Ryan. (N. Bliven) 42:122-4
Ag27'66. B                          9091
The last blitzkrieg. (McCarten)
34:114 F14'59. CC                   9092
The last Bourbons of Naples.
by Harold Acton. (N. Bliven)
38:159-62 My26'62. B                9093

The last Confucian. by Denis
Warner. (Anon.) 39:247
O19'63. B                           9094
The last days of the British Raj.
by Leonard Mosley. (Anon.)
38:182 Ap21'62 B                    9095
The last eagle. by Dan Mannix.
(Anon.) 42:189-90 Mr26'66.
B                                   9096
The last grand duchess: Her
Imperial Highness Olga
Alexandrovna. by Ian Vorres.
(Anon.) 41:111 Jy17'65.
B                                   9097
The last hundred days. by John
Toland. (N. Bliven)
42:124-6 Ag27'66. B                 9098
The last hunt. (McCarten) 32:
66*Mr10'56. CC                      9099
The last hurrah. by Edwin
O'Connor. (West) 31:113-16
*F11'56 (Galbraith) 37:87-94
Je24'61. B                          9100
The last hurrah. (McCarten)
34:170 N1'58. CC                    9101
Last letters from Stalingrad.
by Franz Schneider and Charles
Gullans, trans. (Anon.) 38:
182-3 S15'62. B                     9102
Last letters to a friend: 1952-
58. by Rose Macaulay.
Constance Babington-Smith,
ed. (Anon.) 39:151-2 Mr2'63.
B                                   9103
The last minute. by Lorees
Yerby. (Oliver) 39:82 My18
'63. T                              9104
The last of Lazarus. by Robert
C. Goldston. (Anon.)
42:126 Ag27'66. B                   9105
The last of the Greeks. by
Olivia Davis. (Anon.) 44:
211 O26'68. B                       9106
The last of the Incas: the rise
and fall of an American
empire. by Edward Hyams
and George Ordish. (Anon.)
39:91 Jy20'63. B                    9107
Last of the red hot lovers. by
Neil Simon. (Gill) 45:64
Ja10'70. T                          9108
The last paradise. (McCarten)
34:114 Mr8'58. CC                   9109

The last parallel. by Martin
Russ. (Anon.) 32:107 Ja26'57.
B                              9110
The last poor man. by Edward
Hyams. (Anon.) 42:142-3
My28'66. B                     9111
The last Summer. by Elizabeth
Gunn. (N. Bliven)
37:133-4 F17'62. B             9112
Last Summer. (Gilliatt) 45:
87-8 Je28'69. CC               9113
The last sweet days of Isaac.
by Gretchen Cryer and
Nancy Ford. (Oliver) 45:73-6
F7'70. T                       9114
Last tales. by Isak Dinesen.
(Anon.) 33:99 D21'57. B
                               9115
The last temptation. by Joseph
Viertel. (Anon.) 31:139-40
My21'55. B                     9116
Last train from Gun Hill.
(McCarten) 35:86 Ag8'59. CC
                               9117
The last voyage. (McCarten)
36:168 Mr5'60. CC              9118
The last voyage of the
Lusitania. by A.A. Hoehling
and Mary Hoehling. (Anon.)
32:128*Je2'56. B               9119
The last word. (J. Lardner)
34:74-8*Ap26'58; 35:55-61
Jy18'59. TV                    9120
The last works of Henri
Matisse. by Pierre Reverdy and
Georges Duthuit. (Anon.)
34:242 N29'58. B               9121
Last year at Marienbad.
(Flanner) 37:153-4 N25'61
(Gill) 38:89-90 Mr10'62. CC
                               9122
The last years: journals, 1853-
1855. by Søren Kierkegaard.
Ronald Gregor Smith, ed.
and trans. (Updike) 42:115-34
F26'66. B                      9123
The last years of a rebel. by
Elizabeth Salter. (Bogan)
44:133 Mr30'68. B              9124
Late call. by Angus Wilson.
(Anon.) 40:128 Ja16'65. B
                               9125

The later Roman Empire. by
A.H.M. Jones (Alsop)
41:114-21 Ag28'65. B           9126
Laughter in the dark. (Gilliatt)
45:121-2 My24'69. CC           9127
The laundry. by Howard
Richardson. (Oliver) 39:114-
16 F23'63. T                   9128
Laurel and Hardy's laughing
20's. (Gill) 41:234 N27'65.
CC                             9129
Laurence, John. (Arlen)
43:161-76 S30'67. TV           9130
Laurette. by Marguerite
Courtney (Anon.) 31:72*Ag
6'55. B                        9131
L'auventura. (Oliver) 37:
144-5 Ap22'61. CC              9132
Law and disorder. (Hamburger)
34:70 Ag16'58. CC              9133
The law and Jake Wade.
(McCarten) 34:112 Je14'58.
CC                             9134
Law and order. (Kael)
45:199 O18'69. TV              9135
The law is the law. (McCarten)
35:165 Mr21'59. CC             9136
The law of primitive man. by
E. Adamson Hoebel. (Anon.)
31:137-8 Mr12'55.
B                              9137
A law unto themselves. by
C. Northcote Parkinson.
(Anon.) 42:247-8 O22'66.
B                              9138
Law west of Fort Smith. by
Glenn Shirley. (Anon.)
33:166-7 My11'57. B            9139
The lawless decade. by Paul
Sann. (Anon.) 33:152-3
S7'57. B                       9140
Lawrence and Oppenheimer. by
Nuel Pharr Davis. (Bern-
stein) 45:141-65 My10'69.
B                              9141
Lawrence Durrell and Henry
Miller: a private correspon-
dence. by Lawrence Durrell and
Henry Miller. George Wickes,
ed. (Anon.) 39:92 Jy20'63.
B                              9142
Lawrence in love: letters to

Louie Burrows. by D.H.
Lawrence. James T.
Boulton, ed. (Anon.) 45:167
My10'69. B                    9143
Lawrence of Arabia. by Richard
Aldington. (West) 31:199-204
*D10'55. B                    9144
Lawrence of Arabia. (Gill)
38:77 D22'62. CC              9145
Layard of Ninevah. by
Gordon Waterfield. (Anon.)
44:176 Ap27'68. B            9146
Lazarillo. (Gill) 39:156-7
Ap13'63. CC                   9147
Le amiche. (Gill) 39:171
Mr23'63. CC                   9148
Le bonheur. (Gill)
42:113-14 My28'66. CC
                              9149
Le bourgeois gentilhomme. by
Molière. (Gibbs) 31:81-2
*N5'55. T                     9150
Le cardinal d'Espagne. by
Henry de Montherlant. (Flan-
ner) 36:94 Ja21'61. T        9151
Le chateau. by Franz Kafka.
(Flanner) 33:56 Ja4'58. T
                              9152
Le cheval évanoui. by
Françoise Sagan. (Flanner)
42:179-80 O1'66. T           9153
Le cimetière des voitures.
by Fernando Arrabal. (Flan-
ner) 43:97-8 Ja20'68. T
                              9154
Le concile d'amour. by
Oscar Panizza. (Flanner) 45:
127-31 Mr22'69. T            9155
Le Corbusier: 1910-65.
by W. Boesiger and H. Girs-
berger. (Anon.) 43:65-6 D30
'67. B                       9156
Le défi Americain. by Jean-
Jacques Servan-Schreiber.
(Flanner) 43:99-100 Ja20'68.
B                            9157
Le démon de onze heures.
(Gill) 41:99-100 Ag21'65. CC
                              9158
Le départ. (Gilliatt) 44:146-9
Ap27'68. CC                   9159
Le détour. (Gilliatt) 45:76-8
Ag16'69. CC                   9160

Le dindon. by Georges Feydeau.
(McCarten) 37:124-6 Mr18
'61. T                        9161
Le dîner en ville. See The
dinner party.                 9162
Le dossier Oppenheimer. by
Jean Vilar. (Flanner) 40:
67 D26'64. T                  9163
Le feu follet. (Flanner) 39:
148-50 N16'63. CC            9164
Le gardien. by Harold Pinter.
(Flanner) 37:107-108 F18
'61. T                        9165
Le goûter des Généraux.
by Boris Vian. (Flanner)
41:222-3 O16'65. T           9166
Le grand jamais. by Elsa
Triolet. (Flanner) 41:155-6
Mr6'65. B                     9167
Le jardin des délices. by
Fernando Arrabal. (Flanner)
45:200-202 N29'69. T         9168
Le jour de la tortue. See
The day of the tortoise. T
                              9169
Le journal d'une femme de
chambre. (Flanner) 40:186-7
Ap4'64. CC                   9170
Le mariage de Figaro. by
Pierre Augustin Beaumarchais.
(Oliver) 40:120-2 Mr7'64.
T                            9171
Le mensonge. by Nathalie
Sarraute. (Flanner) 42:124
F11'67. T                     9172
Le monde du silence. See
The silent world. CC          9173
Le mystère Picasso. (Flanner)
32:112-15*Je9'56. CC         9174
Le personnage combattant. by
Jean Vauthier. (Flanner)
32:127*Mr10'56. T            9175
Le piéton de l'air. by
Eugène Ionesco. (Oliver)
40:112-14 Mr14'64. T         9176
Le planétarium . by Nathalie
Sarraute. (Flanner) 35:60-3
Jy25'59. B                    9177
Le ravissement de Lol V. Stein.
by Marguerite Duras. (Flan-
ner) 40:92-7 My2'64. B
                              9178

Le repos du guerrier. by
Christiane Rochefort. (Flanner)
34:105-106 D20'58. B      9179
Le roi se meurt. See
Exit the king. T           9180
Le silence. by Nathalie
Sarraute. (Flanner) 42:124
F11'67. T                  9181
Le songe d'une nuit d'été.
by Jacques Fabbri. (Flanner)
41:174-7 N13'65. T         9182
Le square. by Marguerite
Duras. (Flanner) 32:136-7
*My5'56. B                 9183
Le sud. by Yves Berger.
(Flanner) 39:134 O12'63.
B                          9184
Le temps de soupir. by Anne
Philipe. (Flanner) 39:144-7
N16'63. B                  9185
Le vampire de Düsseldorf.
(Flanner) 41:171-2 My15'65.
CC                         9186
Le vicaire. See The deputy.
T                          9187
Le vray mystère de la
passion. by Arnoul Gréban.
(Flanner) 32:71-2*Jy21'56.
T                          9188
The league of gentlemen.
(Angell) 36:70-1 Ja28'61.
CC                         9189
Leah. by Seymour Epstein.
(Balliett) 40:120 Ja23'65. B
                           9190
Leap through the curtain.
by Nora Kovach and Istvan
Rabovsky. (Anon.) 32:141
*Mr10'56. B                9191
The learning tree. by Gordon
Parks. (Balliett) 39:209
N2'63. B                   9192
Lease of life. (McCarten) 31:116
*F18'56. CC                9193
The leather boys. (Gill)
41:233-4 N13'65. CC        9194
Leave it to Jane. by P.G.
Wodehouse, Guy Bolton and
Jerome Kern. (Malcolm)
35:120 Je6'59. T           9195
Leave me alone. by David
Karp. (Anon.) 33:193
N2'57. B                   9196

Leaves from a journal. by
Victoria, Queen of Great
Britain. (Anon.) 37:111
Ja13'62. B                 9197
Leaves of grass: one hundred
years after. by Milton Hundus,
ed. (Bogan) 31:106-108
F26'55. B                  9198
Lectures in America. by F.R.
Leavis and Q.D. Leavis.
(Anon.) 45:96 Je28'69.
B                          9199
Leda. (Gill) 37:55 Jy22'61.
CC                         9200
Lee: a portrait of Lee Harvey
Oswald. by Robert L.
Oswald, Barbara Land and
Myrick Land. (Anon.) 43:
242 D2'67. B               9201
The left hand of God. (McCarten)
31:74*O1'55. CC            9202
Leftover life to kill. by
Caitlin Thomas. (Panter-
Downes) 33:56 Jy13'57.
(Bogan) 33:193-7 O12'57.
B                          9203
A legacy. by Sybille Bedford.
(Flanner) 33:136-41 Ap27
'57. B                     9204
The legacy of China. Raymond
Dawson, ed. (Anon.) 40:207-
208 S12'64. B              9205
The legacy of Hiroshima. by
Edward Teller and Allen
Brown. (Anon.) 38:183
Ap7'62. B                  9206
The legacy of the Civil War. by
Robert Penn Warren. (Anon.)
37:150 Ap29'61. B          9207
The legend of Lizzie. by
Reginald Lawrence. (Tynan)
35:100-101 F21'59. T       9208
Legend of lovers. by Jean
Anouilh. (Malcolm) 35:88-92
N7'59. T                   9209
The legend of Lylah Clare.
(Gilliatt) 44:198-200 S14'68.
CC                         9210
Leigh Hunt's literary criticism.
Lawrence Huston Houtchens
and Carolyn Washburn Hout-
chens, eds. (Anon.) 33:
155-6 Ap20'57. B           9211

Leigh Hunt's political and
occasional essays. by Leigh
Hunt. Lawrence Huston
Houtchens and Carolyn
Washburn Houtchens, eds.
(Anon.) 38:146 F9'63. B
                                  9212
Lemonade Joe. (Gill) 43:154
D2'67. CC                         9213
Leningrad. by Nigel Gosling.
(Anon.) 41:248 D11'65. B
                                  9214
Léon Blum: humanist in
politics. by Joel Colton. (Anon.)
42:165 Je4'66. B                  9215
Leonard Sillman's new faces of
1968. by Leonard Sillman.
(Anon.) 44:85 My11'68. T
                                  9216
Leonardo da Vinci. Anon.
(Anon.) 32:236 D8'56. B
                                  9217
Leonardo da Vinci. by Ludwig
H. Heydenreich. (Anon.)
31:179 My14'55. B                 9218
The leopard. by Giuseppe di
Lampedusa. Archibald
Colquhoun, trans. (N. Bliven)
36:98-103 Je25'60. B              9219
The leopard. (Flanner) 39:70-3
Jy13'63 (Miller) 39:54-6 Ag17
'63. CC                           9220
Leopard in my lap. by Michela
Denis. (Anon.) 31:178*O15'55.
B                                 9221
Les abysses. (Gill) 40:203-204
N28'64. CC                        9222
Les amants. See The lovers.
CC                                9223
Les anneaux de bicêtre. by
Georges Simenon. (Flanner)
39:133-4 O12'63. B                9224
Les biches. (Kael) 44:168-9
O12'68. CC                        9225
Les carabiniers. (Gilliatt)
44:157-60 My11'68. CC   9226
Les chaises. See the chairs.
T                                 9227
Les champs magnétiques. by
André Breton and Philippe
Soupault. (Flanner) 42:202-
204 O22'66. B                     9228
Les choses: a story of the

sixties. by Georges Perec.
Helen R. Lane, trans. (Anon.)
44:158 My25'68. B       9229
Les clés de Saint Pierre. by
Roger Peyrefitte. (Flanner)
31:75 Je25'55. B        9230
Les Fourberies de scapin. See
Scapin. T               9231
Les fruits d'or. by Nathalie
Sarraute. (Flanner) 39:138-9
O12'63. B               9232
Les Gaullistes: rituel et
annuaire. by Pierre Viansson-
Ponté. (Flanner) 39:60-4
Ag17'63. B              9233
Les gauloises bleues. (Gilliatt)
45:122-5 My24'69. CC    9234
Les girls. (McCarten) 33:108-
109 O12'57. CC          9235
Les glorieuses. by André
Roussin. (Flanner) 36:213
N26'60. T               9326
Les grandes manoeuvres. (Flan-
ner) 31:146-7*N19'55. CC
                        9237
Les jouets. by Georges Michel.
(Flanner) 40:97-8 My2'64.
T                       9238
Les liaisons dangereuses.
(Gill) 37:68 D23'61. CC
                        9239
Les mots. by Jean-Paul Sartre.
(Flanner) 39:242-4 N16'63.
B                       9240
Les nonnes. by Eduardo Manet.
(Flanner) 45:101-102 Je14'69.
T                       9241
Les oiseaux de lune. See
Moonbirds. T            9242
Les parapluies de Cherbourg.
See The umbrellas of
Cherbourg. CC           9243
Les paravents. by Jean Genet.
(Flanner) 42:180-1 O1'66;
42:223-5 N19'66. T      9244
Les pavillons: French pavilions of
the eighteenth century. by
Cyril Connolly and Jerome
Zerbe. (Anon.) 39:183-4 Mr23
'63. B                  9245
Les possédés. by Albert Camus.
(Flanner) 35:106-107 Mr
7'59. T                 9246

Les quatre cents coups.
(Flanner) 35:80-2 Jy11'59.
CC                    9247
Les racines du ciel. See
The roots of heaven. B  9248
Les régates de San Francisco.
(Flanner) 36:88-92 Ag13'60.
CC                    9249
Les séquestrés d'Altona.
by Jean-Paul Sartre.
(Flanner) 41:206-208 O2'65. T
                      9250
Les taxis de la Marne. by Jean
Dutourd. (Flanner) 32:146-8
O20'56. B             9251
Les troyennes. by Euripides.
(Flanner) 37:104 D16'61. T
                      9252
Les yeux crevés. by Jean Cau.
(Flanner) 44:165-6 My11'68.
T                     9253
The less deceived. by Philip
Larkin. (Bogan) 34:162 S13'58;
41:193-4 Ap10'65. B   9254
The lesson. by Eugène
Ionesco. (Gibbs) 33:68 Ja18'58;
(Oliver) 39:96 S28'63. T
                      9255
Lesson in love. by Margaret
Creal. (Anon.) 33:189-90
N2'57. B              9256
A lesson in love. (McCarten)
36:148 Mr26'60. CC    9257
Let it ride. by Abram S.
Ginnes and Ronny Graham.
(McCarten) 37:129-30 O21'61.
T                     9258
Let me be awake. by Stuart
Mitchner. (Anon.) 35:244
D5'59. B              9259
Let no man write my epitaph.
by Willard Motley. (Anon.)
34:92 Ag23'58. B      9260
Let no man write my epitaph.
(Gill) 36:154 D10'60. CC
                      9261
L'été. by Romain Weingarten.
(Flanner) 42:112-13 Ja14'67.
T                     9262
L'etouffe-chrétien. by Félicien
Marceau. (Flanner) 36:213-14
N26'60. T             9263
Let's make love. (Gill) 36:169
S17'60. CC            9264

Let's talk about women. (Gill)
40:201-202 O10'64. CC
                      9265
Letter from a distant land.
by Philip Booth. (Bogan)
33:173-4 S14'57. B    9266
The letter that was never sent.
(Gill) 38:132-3 D1'62. CC
                      9267
The letters and journals of
James Fenimore Cooper,
Volumes III and IV, 1833-44.
by James Fenimore Cooper.
James Franklin Beard, ed.
(Anon.) 41:202-203 Mr13'65.
B                     9268
Letters from my windmill.
(McCarten) 31:51-2*D24'55.
CC                    9269
Letters of a Russian traveler.
by N.M. Karamzin. Florence
Jonas, trans. (Anon.) 33:
241-2*N30'57. B       9270
Letters of C.S. Lewis. by
C.S. Lewis. W.H. Lewis, ed.
(Anon.) 42:127-8 Ja28'67.
B                     9271
Letters of Edward FitzGerald
by Edward FitzGerald. J.M.
Cohen, ed. (Anon.) 36:246-7
N26'60. B             9272
Letters of Ellen Glasgow. by
Ellen Glasgow. Blair
Rouse, ed. (Anon.) 33:91-2
F1'58. B              9273
The letters of Emily Dickinson.
by Emily Dickinson. Thomas H.
Johnson and Theodora Ward, eds.
(Anon.)34:242-3D6'58.B 9274
The letters of F. Scott Fitzgerald.
by F. Scott Fitzgerald. Andrew
Turnbull, ed. (Anon.) 39:
245-6 N9'63. B        9275
The letters of George Santayana.
by George Santayana. Daniel
Cory, ed. (Anon.) 31:207-
208*D10'55. B         9276
Letters of James Joyce. by
James Joyce. Stuart Gilbert,
ed. (Gill) 33:76-8*Jy20'57. B
                      9277
Letters of James Joyce, volumes
II and III.    by James Joyce.
Richard Ellmann, ed. (Anon.)

42:67 D24'66. B          9278
The letters of John Ruskin to
Lord and Lady Mount-
Temple. by John Ruskin.
John Lewis Bradley, ed.
(Anon.) 41:172 Mr6'65. B
                         9279
The letters of Joseph Burckhardt.
by Joseph Burckhardt. Alex-
ander Dru, ed. and trans.
(Anon.) 31:179 My14'55. B
                         9280
The letters of Oscar Wilde.
by Oscar Wilde. Rupert
Hart-Davis, ed. (Auden)
39:155-77 Mr9'63. B      9281
The letters of Peter Paul Rubens.
by Peter Paul Rubens. Ruth
Saunders Magurn, trans. & ed.
(Anon.) 31:147-8*O29'55. B
                         9282
The letters of Rainer Maria
Rilke and Princess Marie
von Thurn und Taxis. by
Rainer Maria Rilke and
Marie von Thurn. Nora Wy-
denbruck. (Anon.) 34:127-8
Ja24'59. B               9283
The letters of Robert Frost to
Louis Untermeyer. by
Robert Frost. (Anon.) 39:219
O26'63. B                9284
Letters of Sigmund Freud. by
Sigmund Freud. Ernst L.
Freud, ed. Tania Stern and
James Stern, trans. (Anon.)
36:119 Ja14'61. B        9285
Letters of the Lewis and Clark
expedition, with related docu-
ments, 1783-1854. by Meri-
wether Lewis and William
Clark. Donald Jackson, ed.
(Anon.) 38:89 Je30'62. B
                         9286
Letters of Theodore Dreiser. by
Theodore Dreiser. Robert H.
Elias, ed. (West) 35:169-74
Ap25'59. B               9287
The letters of Thomas Wolfe.
by Thomas Wolfe. Elizabeth
Nowell, ed. (Anon.) 32:198
O20'56. B                9288

The letters of W.B. Yeats. by
William Butler Yeats. Allan
Wade, ed. (Auden) 31:142-50
Mr19'55. B               9289
The letters of Wyndham Lewis.
by Wyndham Lewis. W.K.
Rose, ed. (Anon.) 40:125
Ag22'64. B               9290
Letters on wave mechanics.
by K. Przibram. Martin J.
Klein, trans. (Anon.) 44:178
Ap6'68. B                9291
Letters to a friend, 1950-1952.
by Rose Macaulay. Constance
Babington-Smith, ed. (Anon.)
37:142-3 F17'62. B       9292
Letters to Georgian friends.
by Boris Pasternak. David
Magarshack, ed. & trans.
(Anon.) 44:109-10 Je15'68.
B                        9293
Letters to Vernon Watkins.
by Dylan Thomas. Vernon
Watkins, ed. (Anon.) 34:163-4
Ap12'58. B               9294
Letters: Virginia Woolf and
Lytton Strachey. by Virginia
Woolf, Lytton Strachey,
Leonard Woolf and James
Strachey, eds. (W. Maxwell)
32:116-24. F9'57. B      9295
Letting go. by Philip Roth.
(Anon.) 38:176 S22'62. B
                         9296
Level 7. by Mordecai
Roshwald. (Anon.) 36:179
Ap16'60. B               9297
Levenson, Sam. (J. Lardner)
35:54-60 Jy4'59. TV      9298
Lewis Carroll. by Derek
Hudson. (Anon.) 31:111 F26
'55. B                   9299
L'hurluberlu, ou le réactionnaire
amoureux. by Jean Anouilh.
(Flanner) 35:111-12 F21'59.
T                        9300
Libel. (McCarten) 35:174-5
O31'59. CC               9301
The liberal hour. by John
Kenneth Galbraith. (Malcolm)
36:110-16 Ja14'61. B     9302
The liberal mind. by Kenneth R.

Minogue. (Anon.) 40:125-6
Ag22'64. B　　　　9303
The libertine librettist. by
April Fitzlyon. (Anon.)
33:137-8 Mr30'57. B　　9304
The license. by Luigi
Pirandello. (Oliver) 45:108
My3'69. T　　　　9305
The Liddell Hart memoirs.
1895-1938. by B.H. Liddell Hart. (Anon.) 41:135 F5'66.
B　　　　　9306
The Liddell Hart memoirs: the
later years. B.H. Liddell Hart.
(Anon.) 42:83 Jy30'66. B
9307
Lies like truth. by Harold
Clurman. (Tynan) 34:98-100
Ja31'59. B　　　　9308
Lieutenant in Algeria. by
Jean-Jacques Servan-
Schreiber. (Liebling) 34:134-9
Mr8'58. B　　　　9309
Life. by Zeno (pseudo.) (Fraser)
45:134-40 Ap5'69. B　　9310
The life and death of Dietrich
Bonhoeffer. by Mary
Basanquet. (Anon.) 45:179
Ap19'69. B　　　　9311
The life and death of Lenin. by
Robert Payne. (Anon.) 40:111
Je27'64. B　　　　9312
Life and labor in ancient
Mexico. by Alonso de Zorita.
Benjamin Keen, ed. and
trans. (Anon.) 40:183-4
Ap11'64. B　　　　9313
The life and times of Cleopatra.
by Carlo Maria Franzero.
(Anon.) 34:155-6 Mr15'58.
B　　　　　9314
The life and work of Sigmund
Freud, 1901-1919. by
Ernest Jones. (Anon.)
31:211-12*D3'55. B　　9315
Life at the top. (Gill) 41:162-3
D18'65. CC　　　　9316
Life in the Crystal Palace. by
Alan Harrington. (Anon.)
35:204 O31'59. B　　　9317
Life in the universe. by A.
Oparin and V. Fesenkov. (Bern-
stein. 38:134-6 Je9'62. B
9318

Life is a dream. by Roy
Campbell. (Oliver) 40:136-8
Mr28'64. T　　　　9319
Life, love, death. (S. Lardner)
45:82-3 My31'69. CC　　9320
Life of Beethoven. by Alexander
Wheelock Thayer. Elliot
Forbes, ed. (Sargeant)
41:192-4 Ap17'65. B　　9321
The life of David Hume. by
Ernest Campbell Mossner.
(Anon.) 31:138-9 Mr12'55.
B　　　　　9322
The life of Dylan Thomas. by
Constantine FitzGibbon.
(N. Bliven) 41:100-102
Ja22'66. B　　　　9323
The life of Girolamo Savonarola.
by Roberto Ridolfi. Cecil
Grayson, trans. (Anon.)
35:243-4 N28'59. B　　9324
The life of Hilaire Belloc. by
Robert Speaight. (Anon.)
33:145-6 Ap27'57. B　　9325
Life of Lady Mary Wortley
Montagu. by Robert Halsband.
(West) 33:127-9 Mr9'57. B
9326
The life of Lenin. by Louis
Fischer. (Anon.) 40:111 Je27'64.
B　　　　　9327
The life of Ludwig von
Beethoven. by Alexander
Wheelock Thayer. (Anon.)
36:243-4 N26'60. B　　9328
A life of one's own. by Gerald
Brenan. (Anon.) 39:90 Ag10
'63. B　　　　9329
The life of politics. by Henry
Fairlie. (Anon.) 44:140 S7'68.
B　　　　　9330
Life of Rossini. by Marie Henri
Beyle. Richard N. Coe, trans.
(Sargeant) 33:90-3 Jy13'57. B
9331
The life of Rudyard Kipling.
by C.E. Carrington.
(Anon.) 31:153*D17'55.
B　　　　　9332
The life of Samuel Johnson, LL.D.
by John Hawkins. Bertram
H. Davis, ed. (Balliett) 37:
134-8 F10'62. B　　　9333

The life of Sir Alexander Fleming.
by André Maurois. (Anon.)
35:130-1 Je13'59. B    9334
The life of the Admiral Chris-
topher Columbus by his son
Ferdinand. by Ferdinand
Columbus. Benjamin Keen,
trans. (N. Bliven) 35:141-6
F21'59. B    9335
Life plus 99 years. by Nathan F.
Leopold, Jr. (Anon.) 34:144-5
Mr8'58. B    9336
Life studies. by Robert Lowell.
(Bogan) 35:195 O24'59. B
    9337
The life that late he led: a
biography of the late Cole
Porter. by George Eells.
(Anon.) 43:74 Jy1'67. B
    9338
Life upside down. (Gill)
41:100 Ag21'65. CC    9339
Life with Fiorello. by Ernest
Cuneo. (Anon.) 31:224*N19'55.
B    9340
Life with Picasso. by Françoise
Gilot and Carlton Lake. (Anon.)
40:244-6 D12'64. B    9341
Life with Queen Victoria: Marie
Mallet's letters from court,
1887-1901. by Marie Mallet.
Victor Mallet, ed. (Anon.)
44:98-9 Ja18'69. B    9342
The light across the street.
(McCarten) 33:71*Ag10'57. CC
    9343
The light in the piazza. (Gill)
37:130 F10'62. CC    9344
The light of common day.
by Diana Cooper. (Anon.)
35:246-7 N7'59. B    9345
Like a bulwark. by Marianne
Moore. (Bogan) 33:111-12
Mr2'57. B    9346
Like a conquered province: the
moral ambiguity of America.
by Paul Goodman. (Anon.)
43:85-6 S2'67. B    9347
Li'l Abner. by Norman
Panama, Melvin Frank,
Johnny Mercer, and Jean de
Paul. (Gibbs) 32:114-17 D1'56.
T    9348

The lilac's overgrow. by Lin
Tai-yi.(Anon.) 36:158-60
D17'60. B    9349
L'ile nue. (Flanner)
37:75-6 Ja6'62. CC    9350
Lilith. (Gill) 40:202 O10'64. CC
    9351
Limited war in the nuclear age.
by Morton H. Halperin.
(Anon.) 39:196 S14'63. B
    9352
The limits of defense. by
Arthur I. Waskow. (Anon.)
38:178-9 My12'62. B    9353
The limits of intervention.
by Townsend Hoopes. (Anon.)
45:59-60 D27'69. B    9354
The limits of love. by Frederic
Raphael. (Anon.) 37:164-6
Ap15'61. B    9355
L'impromptu de Versailles.
See Impromptu at Versailles.
T    9356
Lincoln and the Negro. by
Benjamin Quarles. (Anon.)
38:139 Je9'62. B    9357
Lincoln as they saw him.
Herbert Mitgang, ed. (Anon.)
32:189 D15'56. B    9358
Lincoln finds a general. by
Kenneth P. Williams. (Anon.)
32:240 N17'56. B    9359
The Lincoln Lords. by Cameron
Hawley. (Anon.) 36:142-3 F
27'60. B    9360
Lincoln the president: last full
measure. by J.G. Randall
and Richard N. Current.
(Anon.) 31:173-4*O15'55.
B    9361
Lincoln's commando. by Ralph
J. Roske and Charles Van
Doren. (Anon.) 33:142 My25
'57. B    9362
The linden trees. by Carlo Levi.
Joseph M. Bernstein, trans.
(Anon.) 38:187-8 My19'62.
B    9363
Lindsay's campaign: a behind-
the-scenes diary. by Oliver
Pilat. (Anon.) 44:177 Ap6'68.
B    9364
Lines /of /life. by François Mauriac.

Gerard Hopkins, trans.
(Anon.) 33:240-1 N23'57.
B                    9365
The lion. by Joseph Kessel.
Peter Green, trans. (Anon.)
35:118 Je20'59. B        9366
The lion. (Gill) 38:68 Ja5'63.
CC                    9367
The lion and the throne. by
Catherine Drinker Bowen.
(Anon.) 33:149-50 Mr23'57.
B                    9368
The lion in love. by Shelagh
Delaney. (Oliver) 39:90-3
My4'63. T            9369
Lion in the garden: interviews
with William Faulkner, 1926-
1962. by William Faulkner.
James B. Meriwether and
Michael Millgate, eds. (Anon.)
44:116 Je15'68. B        9370
The lion in Winter. by James
Goldman. (McCarten) 42:110
Mr12'66. T            9371
The lion in Winter. (Kael)
44:189-92 N9'68. CC      9372
Lions love. (Kael) 45:179-80
O25'69. CC            9373
The lion's share. by Bosley
Crowther. (Anon.) 33:145
Ap27'57 (Macdonald) 34:142-3
Mr15'58. B            9374
Lions three: Christians nothing.
by Ann Borowik. (Anon.)
41:181-2 Mr27'65. B      9375
Lisa. (Gill) 38:100-102 Je16'62.
CC                    9376
Lisbon. (McCarten) 32:64
*S8'56. CC            9377
The Lisbon earthquake. by
T.D. Kendrick. (Anon.) 33:
148-9 Mr16'57. B        9378
The list of Adrian Messenger.
(Gill) 39:166-8 Je8'63. CC
                      9379
The listener's musical companion.
by B.H. Haggin. (Anon.)
32:159-60*My5'56. B      9380
The listing attic. by Edward
Gorey. (Wilson) 35:60-2 D26
'59. B                9381
Literary and philosophical essays.
by Jean-Paul Sartre. (Anon.)

32:157-8*Ap14'56. B      9382
Literary biography. by Leon
Edel. (Anon.) 35:238 D12'59.
B                    9383
The literary life: a scrapbook
almanac of the Anglo-American
literary scene from 1900-
1950. by Robert Phelps and
Peter Deane. (Anon.) 44:248
N16'68. B            9384
Literary reminiscences and
autobiographical fragments.
by Ivan Turgenev. David
Magarshack, trans. (Anon.)
34:175 S20'58. B        9385
Literature and science. by
Aldous Huxley. (Anon.)
39:189-90 S21'63. B      9386
Literature and Western man.
by J.B. Priestley. (Anon.)
36:194-5 My7'60. B      9387
Little boxes. by John Bowen.
(Oliver) 45:116 D13'69. T
                      9388
The little conquerors. by Ann
Abelson. (Anon.) 36:184
O29'60. B            9389
Little Eyolf. by Henrik Ibsen.(Oliver)
40:138 Mr28'64. T       9390
The little foxes. by Lillian
Hellman. (McCarten) 43:162-3
N4'67. T             9391
Little glass clock. by Hugh
Mills. (Gibbs) 32:52-3*Ap7'56.
T                    9392
The little hut. (McCarten) 33:152-3
My11'57. CC          9393
The Little Karoo. by Pauline
Smith. (Anon.) 35:66 Ag1'59.
B                    9394
A little learning. by Evelyn
Waugh. (Auden) 41:159-92
Ap3'65. B            9395
Little Mary Sunshine. by Rick
Besoyan. (Malcolm) 35:110-12
N28'59. T            9396
Little me. by Neil Simon,
Carolyn Leigh and Cy Cole-
man. (McCarten) 38:118-20
D1'62. T             9397
The little men. by Luis Harss.
(West) 40:177-8 Ap11'64. B
                      9398

Little moon of Alban. by James Costigan. (McCarten) 36:98-9 D10'60. T 9399

Little murders. by Jules Feiffer. (McCarten) 43:150-2 My6'67 (Oliver) 44:100 F8'69. T 9400

The little Ottleys. by Ada Leverson. (N. Bliven) 39:111-14 Je1'63. B 9401

The little people. by John Christopher. (Anon.) 43:191 Mr11'67. B 9402

The little saint. by Georges Simenon. Bernard Frechtman, trans. (Anon.) 41:200 D18'65. B 9403

The little war of Private Post. by Charles Johnson Post. (Anon.) 36:178-9 Ap30'60. B 9404

The littlest review. by Ben Bagley, Ogden Nash and Vernon Duke. (Gibbs) 32:54 *Je2'56. T 9405

The littlest outlaw. (McCarten) 31:48 *Ja7'56. CC 9406

Live for life. (Gill) 43:47-8 D23'67. CC 9407

The liveliest art. by Arthur Knight. (Macdonald) 34:138-42 Mr15'58. B 9408

Lives of the wits. by Hesketh Pearson. (Anon.) 38:134-5 Ja26'63. B 9409

Livin' the life. by Dale Wasserman, Bruce Geller and Jacques Urbont. (Gibbs) 33:142-3 My4'57. T 9410

Living free: the story of Elsa and her cubs. by Joy Adamson. (Anon.) 37:244 N25 '61. B 9411

The living house. by George Ordish. (Anon.) 36:198 S17'60. B 9412

Living in the present. by John Wain. (Anon.) 36:178-9 Ap16'60. B 9413

The living Lincoln. by Abraham Lincoln. Paul M. Angle and Earl Schenck Miers, eds. (Anon.) 31:119*F11'56. B 9414

Living mammals of the world. by Ivan T. Sanderson. (Anon.) 31:148-9*O29'55. B 9415

The living North. (McCarten) 35:91 S19'59. CC 9416

The living novel and later appreciations. by V.S. Pritchett. (Anon.) 40:100 Jy18'64. B 9417

The living sea. by Jacques-Yves Cousteau and James Dugan. (Anon.) 39:181-2 My11'63. B 9418

The living sea. by John Crompton. (Anon.) 33:144 Ap27'57. B 9419

Living theatre. by Donald Malcolm. 34:74-6 Ja24'59. T 9420

Living with ballads. by Willa Muir. (Anon.) 42:191-2 Mr26'66. B 9421

Lizzie. (McCarten) 33:165-6 Ap13'57. CC 9422

Lizzie Borden: the untold story. by Edward D.Radin. (Anon.) 37:118-19 Je17'61. B 9423

L'obsédé. by France Roche. (Flanner) 42:162-5 N5'66. T 9424

The local stigmatic. by Heathcote Williams. (Oliver) 45:165-6 N15'69. T 9425

Lock up your daughters. by Bernard Miles, Lionel Bart, and Laurie Johnson. (Panter-Downes) 35:81-2 Ag29'59. T 9426

Lockout. by Leon Wolff. (Anon.) 41:159-60 Je12'65. B 9427

L'oeuf. See The egg. T 9428

The logic of scientific discovery. by Karl R. Popper. (N. Bliven) 35:189-91 S19'59. B 9429

Lola Montès. (Gilliatt) 45:137-43 My3'69. CC 9430

Lolita. by Vladimir Nabokov. (Malcolm) 34:195-201 N8'58 (Panter-Downes) 34:56-7 Ja3'59. B 9431

Lolita. (Gill) 38:90 Je23'62. CC
                                    9432
A London childhood. by John
  Holloway. (Anon.) 44:87
  Je29'68. B              9433
London labour and the London
  poor. by Henry Mayhew.
  (Auden) 44:121-33 F24'68.
  B                       9434
London perceived. by V.S.
  Pritchett. (Liebling)
  38:131-41 F9'63. B      9435
Lone voyager. by Joseph E.
  Garland. (Anon.) 39:190
  O5'63. B                9436
The loneliness of the long
  distance runner. by Alan
  Sillitoe. (West) 36:145-6 Je
  11'60. B                9437
The loneliness of the long dis-
  tance runner. (Gill) 38:190-1
  O13'62. CC              9438
Lonely are the brave. (Gill)
  38:61 Jy14'62. CC       9439
Lonely command. by A.A.
  Hoehling. (Anon.) 34:153*
  Ap26'58. B              9440
The lonely empress: a biography
  of Elizabeth of Austria
  by Joan Haslip. (Anon.)
  41:96 Ag7'65. B         9441
The lonely Londoners. by
  Samuel Selvon. (Balliett)
  33:99-100 Ja18'58. B    9442
Lonelyhearts. (McCarten)
  35:164-5 Mr14'59. CC    9443
Lonesome cowboys. (Gilliatt)
  45:124 My17'69. CC      9444
Lonesome traveler. by Jack
  Kerouac. (Anon.) 36:59
  D31'60. B               9445
The long absence. (Gill) 38:
  134 D1'62. CC           9446
A long and happy life. by
  Reynolds Price. (Balliett) 38:
  178-80 Ap7'62. B        9447
The long and the short and the
  tall. by Willis Hall. (Oliver)
  38:116-18 Ap7'62. T     9448
Long before forty. by C.S.
  Forester. (Anon.) 44:181-2
  S28'68. B               9449

The long Christmas dinner.
  by Thornton Wilder. (Oliver)
  42:126 S17'66. T        9450
The long day's dying. (Gilliatt)
  44:112-15 Je1'68. CC    9451
Long day's journey into night.
  by Eugene O'Neill. (Gibbs)
  32:120-2 N24'56. T      9452
Long day's journey into night.
  (Gill) 38:215-16 O20'62.
  CC                      9453
The long dream. by Ketti
  Frings. (Tynan) 36:120
  Mr5'60. T               9454
The long fuse: an interpretation
  of the origins of World War
  I. by Laurence Lafore. (Anon.)
  41:107 S4'65. B         9455
The long gray line. (McCarten)
  31:122-5 F19'55. CC     9456
The long pursuit. by Richard
  Hough. (Anon.) 45:75-6
  Ag2'69. B               9457
The long season. by Jim
  Brosnan. (Anon.) 36:98 Jy
  16'60. B                9458
The long view. by Elizabeth
  Jane Howard. (Anon.) 32:85
  *Jy14'56. B             9459
The long voyage. by Jorge
  Semprun. (West) 40:87-8
  Ag8'64. B               9460
The long walk. by Slavomir
  Rawicz and Ronald Downing.
  (Anon.) 32:139*My19'56. B
                          9461
The longest day. by Cornelius
  Ryan. (Anon.) 35:67 D26'59.
  B                       9462
The longest day. (Gill) 38:188-
  90 O13'62. CC           9463
Longfellow: his life and work.
  by Newton Arvin. (Wilson)
  39:174-80 Mr23'63. B    9464
Look after Lulu. Noël Coward.
  (Tynan) 35:80-3 Mr14'59.
  T                       9465
Look at the U.S.A. Editors of
  Look. (Anon.) 31:171*O22'55.
  B                       9466
Look back in anger. by John
  Osborne. (Gibbs) 33:93-4
  O12'57. T               9467

Look back in anger. (McCarten) 35:179-80 S26'59. CC    9468
Look homeward, angel. by Ketti Frings. (Gibbs) 33:93-5 D7'57. T    9469
Look: we've come through. by Hugh Wheeler. (McCarten) 37:128-9 N4'61. T    9470
The looking glass heart. by Myron Brinig. (Anon.) 34: 142-3 Ap5'58. B    9471
The loom of history. by Herbert J. Muller. (Sargeant) 34:77-81 Ag9'58. B    9472
Loot. by Joe Orton. (Gill) 44:103-104 Mr30'68. T    9473
Lord Burghley and Queen Elizabeth. by Conyers Read. (Anon.) 36:142-3 My28'60. B    9474
Lord Byron's wife. by Malcolm Elwin. (Anon.) 39:180-1 My11'63. B    9475
Lord Jim. (Gill) 41:94-6 Mr6'65. CC    9476
Lord love a duck. (Gill) 42:106-108 F26'66. CC    9477
Lord of the flies. (Miller) 39:56-60 Ag31'63. CC    9478
Lord Pengo. by S.N. Behrman. (McCarten) 38:118 D1'62. T    9479
Lord Randolph Churchill Winston Churchill's father. by Robert Rhodes James. (Anon.) 36:226-7 N5'60. B    9480
Lords of the atlas. by Gavin Maxwell. (Anon.) 42:119 Ja21 '67. B    9481
The lore and language of schoolchildren. by Iona Opie and Peter Opie. (N. Bliven) 36:132-8 Je18'60. B    9482
Lorenzo. by Jack Richardson. (McCarten) 39:112-14 F23'63. T    9483
Lorenzo Lotto. by Bernard Berenson. (Anon.) 32:191-2 O6'56. B    9484
Los tarantos. (Balliett) 40:76 Jy11'64. CC    9485

The loser. by William S. Hoffman, Jr. (Anon.) 44:146 Je8'68. B    9486
Loss of innocence. (Gill) 37:126 D2'61. CC    9487
A loss of roses. by William Inge. (Tynan) 35:99-100 D12'59. T    9488
The lost centuries: from the Muslim empires to the renaissance of Europe, 1145-1453. by John Bagot Glubb. (Anon.) 44:138-9 Mr30'68. B    9489
The lost city. by John Gunther. (Anon.) 40:205-206 S26'64. B    9490
Lost command. (Gill) 42:111-12 S24'66. CC    9491
The lost flight. by H.F.M. Prescott. (Anon.) 35:168 Ap4'59. B    9492
Lost languages. by P.E. Cleator. (Anon.) 37:91 Ag12'61. B    9493
A lost paradise. by Samuel Chotzinoff. (Anon.) 31:110-11 F26'55. B    9494
The lost pyramid. by M. Zakaria Goneim. (Anon.) 32:240-1 N17'56. B    9495
The lost revolutionary. by Richard O'Connor and Dale L. Walker. (Anon.) 43:215-16 O28'67. B    9496
The lost sheep. by Henry Bordeaux. Frances Frenaye, trans. (Anon.) 31:213-14*N 12'55. B    9497
The lost ships. by Peter Throckmorton. (Anon.) 40: 215 S19'64. B    9498
The lost shore. by Anna Langfus. (West) 40:160-1 Mr28'64. B    9499
The lost steps. by Alejo Carpentier. (Anon.) 32:224 *N10'56. B    9500
The lost towns and roads of America. by J.R. Humphreys. (Anon.) 37:166-7 My20'61. B    9501
The lost world of the Caucasus. by Negley Farson. (Anon.)

34:160-1 Ap12'58. B 9502
The lost world of the Kalahari.
by Laurens van der Post.
(Anon.) 34:242-3 N15'58. B
9503
The lotus and the robot. by
Arthur Koestler. (Anon.) 37:
174-5 Mr18'61. B 9504
The loud red Patrick. by John
Boruff. (Gibbs) 32:98-100 O
13'56. T 9505
Louis XIV. by Vincent Cronin.
(Anon.)41:202 Mr13'65.
B 9506
Louis XIV: an informal portrait.
by W.H. Lewis. (Anon.)
35:206-207 O10'59. B 9507
Louis XIV and Marie Mancini.
by Monica Sutherland. (Anon.)
33:164-5 S28'57. B 9508
Love à la carte. (Gill)
40:107 Ja23'65. CC 9509
Love affair. by Robert Carson.
(Anon.) 34:199 O22'58. B
9510
Love and be silent. by Curtis
Harnack. (Anon.) 37:104
F3'62. B 9511
Love and death in the American
novel. by Leslie A. Fiedler.
(Anon.) 36:161 Ap2'60. B
9512
Love and larceny. (Gill) 38:82
F9'63. CC 9513
Love and let love. by Stanley
Jay Gelber. (Oliver) 43:58-9
Ja13'68. T 9514
Love and libel. by Robertson
Davies. (McCarten) 36:96 D
17'60. T 9515
Love and maple syrup. by
Louis Negin, et al. (Oliver)
45:52 Ja17'70. T 9516
Love and marriage. (Adler)
42:108 Ag20'66. CC 9517
Love and money. by Noel
Clad. (West) 35:99-102 Jy18
'59. B 9518
Love and the Caribbean. by
Alec Waugh. (Anon.) 35:172
Ap4'59. B 9519
Love and the English. by Nina
Epton. (N. Bliven) 37:233-4
D2'61. B 9520

Love and the Frenchwoman.
(Angell) 37:165-6 Mr11'61.
CC 9521
Love at twenty. (Gill) 38:147-8
F16'63. CC 9522
The love chase. by James
Barlow. (Anon.) 44:64 Jy6
'68. B 9523
Love declared: essays on the
myths of love. by Denis de
Rougemont. Richard Howard,
trans. (Updike) 39:97-104
Ag24'63. B 9524
The love game.(Gill) 36:109
-10 D3'60. CC 9525
The love goddesses. (Gill)
41:167-8 Mr13'65. CC 9526
Love in E-flat. by Norman
Krasna. (McCarten) 43:92
F25'67. T 9527
Love in four dimensions. (Gill)
41:212 O2'65. CC 9528
Love in the afternoon.
(Hamburger) 33:54 Ag31'57.
CC 9529
Love in the western world.
by Denis de Rougement.
(Updike) 39:90-7 Ag24'63. B
9530
Love is a many-splendored thing.
(Hamburger) 31:77*Ag27'55.
CC 9531
Love is a time of day. by John
Patrick. (Gill) 45:43 Ja3'70.
T 9532
Love is my profession.
(McCarten) 35:160 My9'59.
CC 9533
The love letters. by Madeleine
L'Engle. (Anon.) 42:246
N5'66. B 9534
Love me little. by Amanda
Vail. (Anon.) 33:166 My4'57.
B 9535
Love me or leave me. (Mc-
Carten) 31:101-102 Je4'55.
CC 9536
Love me tender. (McCarten)
32:196-7 N24'56. CC 9537
The love nest. by Deric Wash-
burn. (Oliver) 38:70-2
F2'63. T 9538
Love on a pillow. (Gill) 39:52
D28'63. CC 9539

Love poems of ancient Egypt.
Ezra Pound and Noel
Stock, trans. (Anon.) 38:136
Ja26'63. B                    9540
Love with the proper stranger.
(Gill) 39:85-6 Ja11'64. CC
9541
Love your crooked neighbor.
by Harold J. Chapler. (Oliver)
45:66 Ja10'70. T          9542
The loved and the lost. by Mor-
ley Callaghan. (Wilson)
36:224-37 N26'60. B       9543
The loved one. (Gill) 41:198
O23'65. CC                9544
A lovely light. by Edna St.
Vincent Millay. (Tynan)
36:102-104 F20'60. T      9545
The lovemaker. (McCarten) 34:
96 Mr22'58. CC            9546
The lover. by Harold Pinter.
(Oliver) 39:69-70 Ja11'64. T
9547
Lover come back. (Gill) 38:110-
11 F24'62. CC             9548
Lovers. by Brian Friel. (Gill)
44:65 Ag3'68. T           9549
The lovers. by Leslie Stevens.
(Gibbs) 32:84-6*My19'56.
T                         9550
The lovers. (Flanner) 34:94-5
Ja24'59 (McCarten) 35:204-
205 N7'59. CC             9551
Lovers and lollipops. (McCarten)
32:82*Ap28'56 CC          9552
Lovers and other strangers. by
Renée Taylor and Joseph
Bologna. (Gill) 44:89 S28' 68.
T                         9553
The lovers in the métro. by
Jean Tardieu. George Well-
warth, trans. (Oliver) 37:96
F 10'62. T                9554
Lovers' net. (McCarten)
33:48 Ag3'57. CC          9555
Loves of a blonde. (Gill) 42:
197-8 N5'66. CC           9556
The loves of Cass McGuire.
by Brian Friel. (McCarten)
42:118-20 O15'66.T        9557
The loves of Isadora. (Gilliatt)
45:85-91 Ap26'69. CC      9558
The loves of Krishna. by W.G.

Archer. (Anon.) 33:171-2
My18'57. B                9559
Lovey. by Joseph Morgenstern.
(Oliver) 41:86-8 Ap3'65. T
9560
Loving couples. (Gill) 42:186
O1'66. CC                 9561
The loving cup. by Allan Prior.
(Anon.)  45:151-2 Mr29'69.
B                         9562
The lower depths. by Maxim
Gorky. (Oliver) 40:95-7 Ag
11'64. T                  9563
The lower depths. (Gill) 37:117-
19 F17'62 (Gilliatt) 45:99-
101 S6'69. CC             9564
Low's autobiography. by David
Low. (Pritchett) 33:167-72
Ap13'57. B                9565
Loyalty is my honour. by
Ewan Butler. (Anon.) 40:205
S12'64. B                 9566
The L-shaped room. (Gill)
39:66-8 Je1'63. CC        9567
The Lucifer cell. by William
Fennerton. (Anon.) 44:159 My
25'68. B                  9568
Lucifer falling. by Thomas de
Vere White. (Anon.) 43:176
S23'67. B                 9569
The luck of Ginger Coffey.
(Gill) 40:193-4 S26'64. CC
9570
Lucky Jim. by Kingsley Amis.
(Sissman) 45:163-4 Ap26'69.
B                         9571
Lucky Jim. (McCarten) 34:78
S13'58. CC                9572
Ludlow Fair. by Lanford Wilson.
(Oliver) 42:124 Ap2'66. T
9573
Ludwig von Beethoven, his life
and his work in pictures.
Robert Bory, ed. (Anon.)
40:118-19 S5'64. B        9574
Lulu. by Frank Wedekind.
(Malcolm) 34:89-90 O11'58.
T                         9575
A lume spento and other early
poems. by Ezra Pound. (Anon.)
42:159 Mr5'66. B          9576
The lunatic fringe. by Gerald W.
Johnson. (Anon.) 33:85-6 Je29
'57. B                    9577

Lust for life. (McCarten)
32:86-8 S29'56. CC        9578
Luther. by John Osborne.
(Panter-Downes) 37:200-
201 O14'61 (McCarten)
39:133 O5'63. T           9579
Luv. by Murray Schisgal.
(McCarten) 40:143 N21'64.
T                         9580
Luv. (Gilliatt) 43:72-5
Jy29'67. CC               9581
Lyonel Feininger: city at the
edge of the world. by T.
Lux Feininger. (Anon.)
42:158 Mr5'66. B          9582
Lyrical and critical essays.
by Albert Camus. Philip
Thody, ed. Ellen Conroy
Kennedy, trans. (Anon.)
44:64 D28'68. B           9583
Lysistrata. by Aristophanes.
(Malcolm) 35:67-71 My30
'59; 35:98-9 D5'59. T 9584
Lytton Strachey. by Michael
Holroyd. (Steiner) 45:150-6
S13'69. B                 9585

M

M*A*S*H. (Kael) 45:74-7
Ja24'70. CC               9586
M-GM's big parade of
comedy. (Gill) 40:126-8
S19'64. CC                9587
Macbeth. by William Shake-
speare. (Gibbs) 32:120-2
*N10'56 (McCarten) 37:92
F17'62 (Tynan) 44:149-50
N9'68. T                  9588
Macbeth. (Gill) 37:126-7
D2'61. CC                 9589
MacBird. by Barbara Garson.
(Oliver) 43:127 Mr11'67.
T                         9590
McGinnis speaks. by Frank
Rooney. (Anon.) 36:146-8
Je11'60. B                9591
Machinal. by Sophie Treadwell.
(Malcolm) 36:134-6 Ap16'60.
T                         9592
The mackerel plaza. by Peter
DeVries. (Balliett) 34:147-8
My3'58. B                 9593

McLuhan, Marshall.
(Arlen) 43:
135-8 Ap1'67. TV          9594
Mad little island. (McCarten)
34:83-4 Ja17'59. CC       9595
The mad show. by Larry
Siegel, Stan Hart, Marshall
Barer, Steven Vinaver and
Mary Rodgers. (McCarten)
41:74-6 Ja22'66. T        9596
Madame. by John Selby.
(Anon.) 37:221-2 O14'61.
B                         9597
Madame Aphrodite. by Tad
Mosel and Jerry Herman.
(Oliver) 37:66-7 Ja13'62.
T                         9598
Madame Bovary. by Gustave
Flaubert. Francis Steeg-
muller, trans. (W. Maxwell)
33:116-17 Ja25'58. B      9599
Madame Letizia: a portrait of
Napoleon's mother. by
Monica Stirling. (Anon.)
38:130-1 F24'62. B        9600
Madame Solario. Anon. (Anon.)
32:152-3 S29'56. B        9601
Made in Italy. (Gill) 43:178
My13'67. CC               9602
Mademoiselle. (Flanner)
42:72 Jy30'66. (Adler)
42:84-6 Ag6'66. CC        9603
Madison Avenue, U.S.A. by
Martin Mayer. (Anon.)
34:155 Mr22'58. B         9604
Madman's diary. by Nikolai
Gogol. (Flanner) 38:103-104
Ja12'63. T                9605
The madness of Lady Bright.
by Lanford Wilson. (Oliver)
42:124 Ap2'66. T          9606
The madwoman of Chaillot.
(Kael) 45:196-9 O18'69. CC
                          9607
Mafioso. (Balliett) 40:74
Jy11'64. CC               9608
Maggie Flynn. by Hugo Peretti,
Luigi Creatore, and George
David Weiss. (Gill) 44:125
N2'68. T                  9609
Magic and mystery in Tibet.
by Alexandra David-Neel.
(Anon.) 34:95 Je28'58. B
                          9610

The magic toyshop. by Angela
Carter. (Anon.) 44:133-4
F24'68. B                    9611
The magician. (Balliett)
35:76-7 S5'59. CC           9612
The magician's wife. by James
M. Cain. (Anon.) 41:111
Ja8'66. B                    9613
The magic-maker: E.E.
Cummings. by Charles Norman.
(Anon.) 34:128 Ja24'59.
B                            9614
The magnificent cuckold. (Gill)
41:120-2 My1'65. CC        9615
The magnificient seven. (Mc-
Carten) 32:129 D1'56. CC
                             9616
Magnificent sinner. (Gill)
39:104 My4'63. CC          9617
The magnolia jungle: the life,
times, and education of a
Southern editor. by P.D.
East. (Anon.) 36:106-107
Ag13'60. B                   9618
The magus. by John Fowles.
(Anon.) 42:198-9 Ap16'66.
B                            9619
Mahatma Gandhi. by B.R.
Nanda. (Anon.) 35:176 Mr21
'59. B                       9620
Maidens and mistresses at
home in the zoo. by Meade
Roberts. (Malcolm) 34:
63-4 Ja31'59. T            9621
The maids. by Jean Genet.
(Oliver) 39:143-6 N23'63.
T                            9622
The maids and death watch.
by Jean Genet. (Anon.)
31:88 Je25'55. B           9623
A Maine hamlet. by Lura
Beam. (Anon.) 33:135 F8'58.
B                            9624
Major Barbara. by George
Bernard Shaw. (Gibbs)
32:114-20*N10'56. T        9625
A majority of one. by Leonard
Spigelgass. (Tynan) 35:66-8
F28'59. T                    9626
A majority of one. (Gill)
37:113 Ja20'62. CC         9627
Makbeth. by Richard Schechner.
(Oliver) 45:166-8 D6'69. T
                             9628

Make a million. by Norman
Barasch and Carroll Moore.
(J. Lardner) 34:99 N1'58.
T                            9629
Make mine mink. (Angell)
36:105 Ja14'61. CC         9630
Making do. by Paul Good-
man. (Malcolm) 40:238-45
N28'64. B                    9631
The making of a quagmire.
by David Halberstam.
(Anon.) 41:126 Je19'65.
B                            9632
The making of modern Ireland,
1603-1923. by J.C. Beckett.
(Anon.) 42:230-1 S17'66. B
                             9633
The making of South East
Asia. by Georges Coedès.
H.M. Wright, trans. (Alsop)
42:112-16 Ja28'67. B       9634
The making of the English
working class. by E.P.
Thompson. (Anon.) 40:177-8
Je6'64. B                    9635
The making of the king: 1066.
by Alan Lloyd. (Anon.) 42:
167 Ap30'66. B             9636
The making of the President
1960. by Theodore H.
White. (Rovere) 37:77-8 Jy
22'61 (Anon.) 41:94 Ag7'65.
B                            9637
The Makioka sisters. by
Junichirō Tanizaki. (West)
33:218-21 D14'57. B        9638
The Makropoulos secret. by
Karel Capek. (Gibbs) 33:84-5
D14'57. T                    9639
Malamondo. (Gill) 40:198
D12'64. CC                  9640
Malcochon. by Derek Walcott.
(Oliver) 45:131 Ap12'69.
T                            9641
Malcolm. by James Purdy.
(Balliett) 35:130-1*D19'59.
B                            9642
Malcolm. by Edward Albee.
(McCarten) 41:74 Ja22'66.
T                            9643
Male companion. (Gill) 41:
145 F19'66. CC             9644
Male hunt. (Gill) 41:120 My
1'65. CC                     9645

The malediction. by Julian
Claman. (Anon.) 45:140
Ap5'69. B          9646
The malefactors. by Caroline
Gordon. (Anon.) 32:168-70
*Mr17'56. B          9647
The Maltese bippy. (Gilliatt)
45:86 Je21'69. CC   9648
Mambo. (McCarten) 31:111
Ap9'55. CC          9649
Mame. by Jerome Lawrence,
Robert E. Lee and Jerry
Herman. (McCarten) 42:75
Je4'66. T           9650
Mam'zelle Pigalle. (McCarten)
34:131*Ap26'58. CC  9651
A man and a woman. (S.
Lardner) 42:75 Jy23'66. CC
                    9652
Man and boy. by Terence
Rattigan. (McCarten) 39:143
N23'63. T           9653
Man and crisis. by José
Ortega y Gasset. (Anon.)
34:234-5 N22'58. B  9654
Man and dolphin. by John C.
Lilly. (Anon.) 37:178
S16'61. B           9655
A man and his master. by
François Billetdoux. Ralph
Manheim, trans. (West)
40:174-7 Ap11'64. B 9656
Man and stone. by Andreas
Feininger. (Anon.) 37:207
D16'61. B           9657
Man and superman. by George
Bernard Shaw. (Oliver) 40:
66-8 D19'64. T      9658
Man and the living world. by
Karl von Frisch. Elsa B.
Lowenstein, trans. (Anon.)
39:191 O5'63. B     9659
Man and time. by J.B. Priest-
ley. (Anon.) 40:244-5
N7'64. B            9660
Man as an end: a defense of
humanism. Literary, social,
and political essays. by
Alberto Moravia. Bernard
Wall, trans. (N. Bliven)
42:165-8 Ap9'66. B  9661
Man better man. by Coleridge-
Taylor Perkinson and Errol

Hill. (Oliver) 45:58 Jy12'69.
T                   9662
A man called Lucy. by Pierre
Accoce and Pierre Quet. A.
M. Sheridan Smith, trans.
(Anon.) 43:75-6 Jy8'67. B
                    9663
A man could get killed.
(Gill) 42:102 My21'66. CC
                    9664
A man for all seasons. by
Robert Bolt. (McCarten)
37:117-18 D2'61. T  9665
A man for all seasons. (Gill)
42:124 D17'66. CC   9666
The man from Laramie.
(Hamburger) 31:115*S10'55.
CC                  9667
The man from New York:
John Quinn and his friends.
by B.L. Reid. (Anon.)
45:76 Jy5'69. B     9668
Man hunt in Kenya. by Ian
Henderson and Philip
Goodhart. (Anon.) 34:191
O4'58. B            9669
Man in a cocked hat.
(McCarten) 36:71 Je25'60. CC
                    9670
The man in the dog suit. by Al-
bert Beich and William H.
Wright. (J. Lardner) 34:
88-91 N8'58. T      9671
The man in the glass booth.
by Robert Shaw. (Gill)
44:95 O5'68 (Tynan) 44:130
N9'68. T            9672
The man in the gray flannel
suit. (McCarten) 32:69
*Ap21'56. CC        9673
Man in the moon. (Oliver)
37:80 Je17'61. CC   9674
The man in the net. (McCarten)
35:72-4 Je20'59. CC 9675
The man in the raincoat.
(Hamburger) 34:49 Ag2'58.
CC                  9676
Man in the universe. by Fred
Hoyle. (Anon.) 42:187-8
My7'66. B           9677
Man into space. by Hermann
Oberth. (Anon.) 33:140 Je8
'57. B              9678

Man is man. by Bertolt
Brecht. Eric Bentley,
adapt. (Oliver) 38:98-101
S29'62. T                9679
A man must choose. by Eric
Chou. (Anon.) 39:93-4
Ag17'63. B               9680
Man of a thousand faces.
(Hamburger) 33:70-3 Ag24'57.
CC                       9681
A man of his time. by
Phyllis Bentley. (Anon.)
42:242-3 O15'66. B       9682
Man of La Mancha. by Dale
Wasserman, Mitch Leigh
and Joe Darion. (McCarten)
41:106-108 D4'65. T      9683
A man of means. by Luís de
Sttau Monteiro. Ann Stevens,
trans. (Anon.) 41:170 Mr6'65.
B                        9684
The man of principle: a
biography of John Galsworthy.
by Dudley Barker. (Anon.)
45:173-4 Ap26'69. B      9685
The man of sensibility. by Jean
Dutourd. Robin Chancellor,
trans. (N. Bliven) 37:72-4
Jy15'61. B               9686
Man on fire. (Hamburger)
33:54 Ag31'57. CC        9687
The man on the rock. by Francis
King. (Anon.) 33:101-102 Ja18
'58. B                   9688
Man out loud, girl quiet. by
William Herman. (Oliver)
38:109-10 Ap14'62. T     9689
A man survives. by Vladimir
Maximov. Anselm Hollo,
trans. (Anon.) 39:70
Ag3'63. B                9690
Man--the reluctant brother.
by Matthew Ies Spetter.
(Anon.) 43:100 Ag26'67. B
                         9691
Man under the sea. by
James Dugan. (Anon.)
32:130*My26'56. B        9692
The man upstairs. (Balliett)
35:96 Ap22'59. CC        9693
The man Verdi. by Frank
Walker. (Anon.) 39:208
Mr16'63. B               9694

The man who broke things.
by John Brooks. (Anon.)
34:149 Ap19'58. B        9695
The man who knew Kennedy.
by Vance Bourjaily.
(Anon.) 43:149-50 My27'67.
B                        9696
The man who knew too much.
(McCarten) 32:109*My26'56.
CC                       9697
The man who loved redheads.
(McCarten) 31:44*Ag6'55.
CC                       9698
The man who never died.
by Barrie Stavis. (Malcolm)
34:118-19 D6'58. T       9699
The man who never was.
(McCarten) 32:78*Ap14'56.
CC                       9700
The man who plays alone. by
Danilo Dolci. (Anon.) 45:76
Ag2'69. B                9701
The man who rediscovered
America: a biography of
John Wesley Powell. by John
Upton Terrell. (Anon.) 45:
157-8 S13'69. B          9702
The man who rocked the boat.
by William J. Keating and
Richard Carter. (Anon.) 32:
156*Ap14'56. B           9703
The man who rode the tiger.
by Herbert Mitgang. (Anon.)
39:178-9 My18'63. B      9704
The man who saved London.
by George Martelli. (Anon.)
37:89-90 Ag12'61. B      9705
The man who shot Liberty
Valance. (Gill) 38:102 Je16
'62. CC                  9706
The man who understood
women. (McCarten) 35:172
O10'59. CC               9707
The man who wagged his tail.
(Gill) 37:171 S23'61. CC
                         9708
The man who walked through
time. by Colin Fletcher.
(Anon.) 44:135-6 F24'68.
B                        9709
The man who was not with it.
by Herbert Gold. (West) 32:
134-7*Mr10'56. B         9710

Man with a load of mischief. by
Ben Tarver and John Clifton.
(McCarten) 42:178-80 N19'66.
T                         9711
Man with a racket. by
Pancho Gonzáles. (Anon.)
35:172 Ap11'59. B        9712
The man with the flower in his
mouth. by Luigi Pirandello.
(Oliver) 45:107-108 My3'69.
T                         9713
The man with the golden arm.
(McCarten) 31:52-3*D24'55.
CC                        9714
The man with the golden gun.
by Ian Fleming. (Anon.)
41:124 Ag28'65. B        9715
Man with the gun. (McCarten)
31:84*Ja14'56. CC        9716
The man with three faces.
by Hans-Otto Meissner.
(Anon.) 31:103*Ja14'56. B
                          9717
The man with two shadows.
by Robin Maugham. (Anon.)
35:103 Jy18'59. B        9718
Man without a star. (McCarten)
31:118 Ap2'55. CC        9719
Manchild in the promised
land. by Claude Brown.
(Balliett) 41:242-6
N13'65. B                9720
The Manchurian candidate. by
Richard Condon. (Balliett)
35:105-107 My30'59. B 9721
The Manchurian candidate.
(Gill) 38:115-16 N3'62. CC
                          9722
Mandarin red. by James
Cameron. (Rovere) 31:211-12
*N12'55. B               9723
The mandarins. by Simone
de Beauvoir. (Podhoretz)
32:145-50*S15'56. B      9724
Mandate for change. by
Dwight D. Eisenhower.
(Rovere) 39:235-8 N16'63.
B                         9725
Mandingo. by Jack Kirkland.
(McCarten) 37:90 Je3'61.
T                         9726
Mandragola. (Oliver) 42:112
Je11'66. CC              9727

The man-eater of Malgudi.
by R.K. Narayan. (West)
37:123 Mr4'61. B         9728
Manhattan pastures. by
Sandra Hochman. (Bogan)
39:173-4 Ap27'63. B      9729
Manhattan project: the untold
story of the making of the
atom bomb. by Stephane
Groueff. (Anon.) 43:107-108
Je24'67. B               9730
Manhood: a journey from
childhood into the fierce
order of virility. by Michel
Lieris. Richard Howard,
trans. (Anon.) 39:247-8
O19'63. B                9731
Manifest destiny and mission
in American history: a
reinterpretation. by Frederick
Merk. (Anon.) 39:120
Je1'63. B                9732
Manifestoes of surrealism. by
André Breton. Richard
Seaver and Helen R. Lane,
trans. (Anon.) 45:95-6
Ag16'69. B               9733
Manjiro, the man who dis-
covered America. by Hisakazu
Kaneko. (Anon.) 32:155
*S15'56. B               9734
Mankind evolving. by Theodosius
Dobzhansky. (Anon.) 38:113-
14 Ja12'63. B            9735
Manners and morals in the age
of optimism, 1848-1914. by
James Laver. (Anon.) 43:
193-4 Mr18'67. B         9736
Mano Majra. by Khushwant
Singh. (Anon.) 32:167*Mr17
'56. B                   9737
The manor. by Isaac Bashevis
Singer. (Sissman) 45:97-9
F7'70. B                 9738
A man's blessing. by Leonardo
Sciascia. Adrienne Foulke,
trans. (West) 45:144-5 My3
'69. B                   9739
Man's western quest. by Denis
de Rougemont. Montgomery
Belgion, trans. (Anon.) 33:
203-204 O26'57. B        9740
The mansion. by William

Faulkner. (West) 35:246-43
D5'59. B                    9741
The many colored coat. by
Morley Callaghan. (Wilson)
36:224-37 N26'60. B    9742
The many lives of Otto Kahn.
by Mary Jane Matz. (Anon.)
40:183 Mr7'64. B        9743
Many loves. by William Carlos
Williams. (Malcolm) 34:74-6
Ja24'59. T                  9744
Many slippery errors. by
Alfred Grossman. (Anon.)
40:111 Je27'64. B        9745
Mao Tse-Tung: emperor of the
blue ants. by George Paloczi-
Horvath. (Anon.) 39:190 S21'63.
B                            9746
Map of another town. by M. F. K.
Fisher. (Anon.) 40:92 Jy11'64.
B                            9747
Marat /Sade. by Peter Weiss.
Geoffrey Skelton and Adrian
Mitchell, trans. (Panter-
Downes) 40:204-206 S19'64
(McCarten) 41:98-100 Ja8'66.
T                            9748
Marat/Sade. (Gill) 43:140
Mr4'67. CC                9749
Marathon '33. by June Havoc.
(McCarten) 39:58-60 Ja4'64.
T                            9750
The marauders. by Charlton
Ogburn, Jr. (Anon.) 35:191-2
My16'59. B                9751
Marc Chagall: the Jerusalem
windows. by Jean Leymarie.
Elaine Desautels, trans.
(Anon.) 39:184 Mr23'63.
B                            9752
Marceau, Marcel. (Gibbs)
31:71-3*O1'55. T          9753
Marcel Proust: a biography. by
Richard H. Barker. (Anon.)
34:98 Ja17'59. B          9754
Marcel Proust on art and litera-
ture 1896-1919. by Marcel
Proust. Sylvia Townsend
Warner, trans. (Anon.) 34:
110-11 My31'58. B        9755
Marcelino. (Flanner) 32:59
*Ag4'56 (McCarten) 32:175
N3'56. CC                9756

Marcellin, pain, et vin. See
Marcelino. CC            9757
The march of archaeology.
by C. W. Ceram. Richard
Winston and Clara Winston,
trans. (Anon.) 34:245-6
N15'58. B                9758
The march of conquest: the
German victories in Western
Europe, 1940. by Telford
Taylor. (Anon.) 34:100 Jy12
'58. B                    9759
March the ninth. by R. C.
Hutchinson. (Anon.) 33:239-40
N23'57. B                9760
The marches of El Dorado.
by Michael Swan. (Anon.)
34:241 N29'58. B        9761
Marco millions. by Eugene
O'Neill. (McCarten) 40:
106-108 F29'64. T        9762
The Marconi scandal. by
Frances Donaldson. (Anon.)
39:182-3 Mr23'63. B    9763
Marcus Aurelius. by Anthony
Birley. (Anon.) 42:247
N12'66. B                9764
Marcus in the high grass. by
Bill Gunn. (Balliett) 36:104
D3'60. T                  9765
Margaret of Cortona.
(McCarten) 32:100 F2'57. CC
                          9766
The margin. by André Pieyre
de Mandiargues. Richard
Howard, trans. (Anon.) 45:
226 N22'69. B            9767
Margin released. by J. B.
Priestley. (Anon.) 38:160-1
F16'63. B                9768
Maria Light. by Lester Goran.
(Anon.) 38:107 Je23'62. B
                          9769
A Marianne Moore reader.
by Marianne Moore. (Anon.)
37:207 D16'61. B        9770
Marianne Thornton. by E. M.
Forster. (Anon.) 32:238-9
D1'56. B                9771
Marie and the Duke of H.
by Doris Langley Moore.
(Anon.) 42:245-6 O8'66. B
                          9772

Marie Avinov: pilgrimage through hell. by Paul Chavchavadze. (Wilson) 45:148-9 S27'69. B 9773

Marie Bonnard. by Alice Ekert-Rotholz. Michael Bullock, trans. (Anon.) 38: 180 S15'62. B 9774

Marie Fedorovna, empress of Russia. by E.E.P. Tisdall. (Anon.) 33:90-1 F1'58. B 9775

Marilyn. (Balliett) 39:96 Jy27'63. CC 9776

Mariners' prison. by Michel Mohrt. Xan Fielding, trans. (Anon.) 39:177 Mr30'63. B 9777

Marjorie Morningstar. (Mc-Carten) 34:60-2 My3'58. CC 9778

The mark. (Gill) 37:197-8 O7'61. CC 9779

Mark the glove boy. by Mark Harris. (Anon.) 40:194-5 My9'64. B 9780

Markings. by Dag Hammarskjöld. (Urquhart) 40:232-44 O31'64. B 9781

Marnie. (Oliver) 40:65 Ag1'64. CC 9782

Marooned. (Kael) 45:61 Ja3'70. CC 9783

The marquis. by Joan Sanders. (Anon.) 39:188-9 S21'63. B 9784

The marquise went out at five. by Claude Mauriac. Richard Howard, trans. (Balliett) 38:174-8 S15'62. B 9785

The marriage-go-round. (Angell) 36:104-105 Ja14'61. CC 9786

Marriage--Italian style. (Gill) 40:64-5 Ja2'65. CC 9787

Marriage on the rocks. (Gill) 41:212 O2'65. CC 9788

The marriage-go-round. by Leslie Stevens. (J. Lardner) 34:87-8 N8'58. T 9789

A married couple. (Kael) 45:114-17 F14'70. CC 9790

Married to Tolstoy. by Cynthia Asquith. (Anon.) 37:211 O7'61. B 9791

Marry me! Marry me! (Gilliatt) 45:75 Jy12'69. CC 9792

Mars in Capricorn. by Beverley Cross. (Anon.) 31:70*S3'55. B 9793

The marsh Arabs. by Wilfred Thesiger. (N. Bliven) 41:126-8 My29'65. B 9794

Martereau. by Nathalie Sarraute. (N. Bliven) 36:150-4 Mr26'60. B 9795

Martha, Eric and George. by Margery Sharp. (Anon.) 40:163 Mr28'64. B 9796

Marty. (McCarten 31:133-4 Ap23'55. CC 9797

The martyred. by Richard E. Kim. (Anon.) 40:220-1 Ap18 '64. B 9798

Mary, Mary. by Jean Kerr. (McCarten) 37:124 Mr18'61. T 9799

Mary, Mary. (Gill) 39:196-7 N2'63. CC 9800

Mary Poppins. (Gill) 40:132-4 O3'64. CC 9801

Mary Queen of Scots. by Antonia Fraser. (Anon.) 45:191 O25'69. B 9802

Mary Shelly. by Eileen Bigland. (Anon.) 35:206-207 O31'59. B 9803

Masaccio: frescoes in Florence. Peter Bellew and Anton Schutz, eds. (Anon.) 33:107-108*Je1'57. B 9804

Masculine feminine. (Gill) 42:112 S24'66. CC 9805

The mask of Apollo. by Mary Renault. (Anon.) 42:241-4 D3'66. B 9806

The masks of God: creative mythology. by Joseph Campbell. (Anon.) 44:92 F1'69. B 9807

Masquerade. by Sigmund Miller. (Tynan) 35:90-2 Mr28'59. T 9808

Masquerade. (Gill) 41:168 My22'65. CC 9809

Massacre at Tangini. by Robert
Lait. (Anon.) 39:177-8
My11'63. B                    9810
The master builder. by Henrik
Ibsen. (Gibbs) 31:64-7 Mr12'55.
T                    9811
The master of Badger's Hall.
by Henry Treece. (Anon.)
35:234 D12'59. B                    9812
Master Prim. by James
Whitfield Ellison. (Steiner)
44:134-5 S7'68. B                    9813
Mastering the art of French
cooking. by Simone Beck,
Louisette Bertholle and Julia
Child. (Anon.) 37:207-8
O28'61. B                    9814
Masterpieces of European sculp-
ture. Martin Hürliman,
ed. (Anon.) 35:94-5 Je27'59.
B                    9815
Masters of photography. by
Beaumont Newhall and Nancy
Newhall. (Anon.) 34:247-8
N15'58. B                    9816
The masters of power. by
Brian Crozier. (Anon.) 45:
100-102 F7'70. B                    9817
Masters of the Congo jungle.
(McCarten) 36:189-90 My14'60.
CC                    9818
Masters of the Japanese print.
by Richard Lane. (Anon.)
38:247-8 D8'62. B                    9819
Mata Hari. by Sam Waagenaar.
(Anon.) 41:247 O23'65. B
                    9820
The matchmaker. by Thornton
Wilder. (Gibbs) 31:70-2
*D17'55. T                    9821
The matchmaker. (McCarten)
34:66 Ag23'58. CC                    9822
Match-play. by Lee Kalcheim.
(Oliver) 42:83-5 O22'66. T
                    9823
The mathematical sciences.
Anon. (Anon.) 45:174-5
Ap26'69. B                    9824
A mathematician's apology.
by G. H. Hardy. (Bernstein)
44:80-90 F1'69. B                    9825
Mating dance. by Eleanor
Harris Howard and Helen Mc-

Avity. (McCarten) 41:156
N13'65. T                    9826
Matisse: a portrait of the
artist and the man. by
Raymond Escholier. Geraldine
Colvile and like. M. Colvile,
trans. (Anon.) 36:163-4 D
17'60. B                    9827
A matter of days. (Gilliatt)
45:125-6 My24'69. CC                    9828
A matter of innocence. (Kael)
44:128 Mr2'68. CC                    9829
A matter of like life and
death. by John Cromwell.
(Oliver) 39:90-1 O12'63. T
                    9830
A matter of WHO. (Oliver)
38:50 Ag4'62. CC                    9831
Matty and the moron and
madonna. by Herbert Lieber-
man. (Oliver) 41:84 Ap10'65.
T                    9832
Maverick. (J. Lardner) 35:99-
100 F28'59. TV                    9833
Max. by David Cecil. (Auden)
41:227-44 O23'65. B                    9834
Max in verse. by Max Beerbohm.
(Updike) 40:176-81 Mr7'64.
B                    9835
Maximum feasible misunderstand-
ing: community action in the
war on poverty. by Daniel P.
Moynihan. (N. Bliven) 45:
143-51 Je7'69. B                    9836
Mayakovsky. by Vladimir
Mayakovsky. Herbert
Marshall, ed. and trans.
(Anon.) 41:245 N27'65. B
                    9837
Maybe Tuesday. by Mel Tonkin
and Lucille Kallen. (Gibbs)
33:95-6 F8'58. T                    9838
Mayerling. (Kael) 45:71-4
Mr1'69. CC                    9839
The mayor who mastered New
York: the life and opinions
of William J. Gaynor. by
Lately Thomas. (Anon.)
45:246-8 D6'69. B                    9840
The Mazarine legacy: the life
of Hortense Mancini, Duchess
Mazarin. by Toivo David Ros-
vall. (Anon.) 45:81-2 Ja17'70.
B                    9841

Me and the colonel. (McCarten)
34:92-3 S6'58. CC    9842
The meaning of the Dead Sea
scrolls. by A. Powell
Davies. (Anon.) 32:202-203
O20'56. B    9843
The meanings of architecture:
buildings and writings by John
Wellborn Root. by John Well-
born Root. Donald Hoffmann,
ed. (Anon.) 44:128 Je1'68.
B    9844
Measure for measure. by
William Shakespeare. (Gibbs)
32:72-3 F2'57 (McCarten)
43:91-2 F25'67. T    9845
Medical research: a mid-
century survey. by Esther
Everett Lape, ed. (Anon.)
31:152-3*D17'55. B    9846
The medieval world: Europe
1100-1350. by Friedrich
Heer. Janet Sondheimer,
trans. (Anon.) 38:88 Ag11'62.
B    9847
Meditations on a hobby horse,
and other essays on the
theory of art. by E.H.
Gombrich. (Anon.) 39:140
F15'64. B    9848
Medium cool. (Gilliatt) 45:143-4
S13'69. CC    9849
Meet me in Las Vegas. (Mc-
Carten) 32:116*Mr24'56. CC
9850
Meet me in Moscow. (Gill)
42:120-2 My14'66. CC 9851
Meet Peter Grant. by Elliot
Arluck and Ted Harris.
(Balliett) 37:120
My20'61. T    9852
Meet the press. (J. Lardner)
33:199-201 N23'57. TV
9853
Meeting at the last judgment.
by Petru Dumitriu. Richard
Howard, trans. (Anon.) 38:79
Jy28'62. B    9854
A meeting by the river. by
Christopher Isherwood.
(Anon.) 43:193-4Ap15'67.
B    9855

Meeting with Japan. by Fosco
Maraini. Eric
Mosbacher, trans. (Anon.)
35:123 Ja23'60. B    9856
The megilla of Itzik Manger.
by Hugh Williams and
Margaret Williams. (Gill)
44:160 O19'68. T    9857
Mein kampf. (Oliver) 37:166-7
My13'61. CC    9858
Melba. by John Hetherington.
(Anon.) 44:111 Je15'68.B
9859
Melbourne. by David Cecil.
(Macdonald) 31:127-36 Mr12
'55. B    9860
Memed, my hawk. by Yashar
Kemal. Edouard Roditi,
trans. (Anon.) 37:77 Jy15'61.
B    9861
Memoir of an aged child. by
Alfred Duhrssen. (Anon.)
43:232-4 D2'67. B    9862
Mémoires de guerre. by
Charles de Gaulle. (Flanner)
32:68-9*Jy21'56. B    9863
Mémoires d'une jeune fille
rangée. See Memoirs of a
dutiful daughter.    9864
Memoirs. by Clara Malraux.
Patrick O'Brian, trans.
(Anon.) 43:75 Jy8'67. B
9865
Memoirs: 1925-1950. by
George F. Kennan. (Rovere)
43:238-45 N11'67. B    9866
Memoirs of a dutiful daughter.
by Simone de Beauvoir.
(Flanner) 34:190-3 N8'58
(Sargeant) 35:186-90 S26'59.
B    9867
Memoirs of a medieval woman.
by Louise Collis. (Anon.)
40:246-7 D12'64. B    9868
Memoirs of a renaissance
Pope: the commentaries of
Pius II. by Pius II. Florence
A. Gragg, trans. Leona C.
Gabel, ed. (Anon.) 35:177-8
Ap25'59. B    9869
Memoirs of a revolutionary. by
Victor Serge. Peter Sedgwick,

ed. and trans. (Anon.) 39:
195-6 S14'63. B        9870
Memoirs of a revolutionist.
by Peter Kropotkin. (Anon.)
45:96 Je28'69. B        9871
Memoirs of a revolutionist. by
Dwight Macdonald. (Anon.)
33:164 S28'57. B        9872
Memoirs of a Soviet ambassador.
by Ivan Maisky. Andrew Roth-
stein, trans. (Anon.) 44:
177-8 Ap6'68. B        9873
Memoirs of a special case. by
Chaim Raphael. (Anon.) 38:
99 Ag18'62. B        9874
The memoirs of Anthony Eden,
Earl of Avon: facing the
dictators, 1923-38. by
Anthony Eden. (Anon.)
38:244 D1'62. B        9875
The memoirs of Catharine the
Great. by Catharine II.
Dominique Maroger, ed.
(Anon.) 31:107 Je18'55.
B        9875a
The memoirs of Colonel John
S. Mosby. by John
Singleton Mosby. (Wilson)
34:117-36 F14'59. B        9876
The memoirs of Field-Marshall
Montgomery. by Bernard Law
Montgomery. (Anon.) 34:
210-11 N8'58. B        9877
The memoirs of General Lord
Ismay. by Hastings Lionel
Ismay. (Anon.) 36:240-1
N26'60. B        9878
Memoirs of General William
T. Sherman. by William T.
Sherman. (Wilson) 34:114-44
Je7'58. B        9879
The memoirs of Lord Chandos.
by Oliver Lyttelton Chandos.
(Anon.) 39:246 N23'63. B
        9880
Memoirs of Lorenzo Da Ponte.
by Lorenzo Da Ponte.
Elizabeth Abbott, trans.
(Anon.) 35:242 N28'59. B
        9881
Memoirs of Michael Károlyi.
by Michael Károlyi. (Anon.)
32:126-7 F9'57. B        9882

Memoirs of World War I. by
William Mitchell. (Anon.)
36:98-9 Jy16'60. B        9883
Memoirs: ten years and
twenty days. by Karl
Doenitz. (Anon.) 35:197-8
O24'59. B        9884
The memorandum. by Václav
Havel. Vera Blackwell,
trans. (Oliver) 44:73-4
My18'68. T        9885
Memories, dreams, reflec-
tions. by Carl Gustav Jung.
(Mumford) 40:155-85
My23'64. B        9886
Memories: 1898-1939. by C. M.
Bowra. (Anon.) 43:115-16
Ja20'68. B        9887
The memory bank. by Martin
Duberman. (Oliver) 45:58
Ja24'70. T        9888
Men and atoms: the discovery,
the uses, and the future of
atomic energy. by William
L. Laurence. (Anon.) 35:
226-7 O17'59. B        9889
Men and decisions. by Lewis L.
Strauss. (Anon.) 38:79 Jy28
'62. B        9890
Men and power: 1917-1918.
by William Maxwell Aitken
Beaverbrook. (Anon.) 33:95
Jy13'57. B        9891
The men and the mountain. by
William Brandon. (Anon.)
31:159 Ap16'55. B        9892
Men die. by H. L. Humes.
(Balliett) 35:130-2*D19'59.
B        9893
Men in prison. by Victor
Serge. Richard Greeman,
trans. (Anon.) 45:68
Ja3'70. B        9894
Men in war. (McCarten) 33:
76-8 Ap6'57. CC        9895
Men into space. (J. Lardner)
36:155-9 F20'60. TV        9896
Men of ideas. by Lewis A.
Coser. (Rosenberg) 41:98-
105 Je26'65. B        9897
Men, rockets and space rats.
by Lloyd Mallan. (Anon.)
31:118*F11'56. B        9898

The men who made the nation. by
John Dos Passos. (Anon.)
33:130-1 F23'57. B 9899
Men who play god. by Norman
Moss. (Anon.) 45:180 Ap19
'69. B 9900
The men who tread on the
tiger's tail. (McCarten)
35:97-8 Ja16'60. CC 9901
Mencken. by Carl Bode.
(Anon.) 45:119 D20'69. B
9902
The merchant of Prato. by
Iris Origo. (Anon.) 33:140-1
My25'57. B 9903
The merchant of Venice. by
William Shakespeare. (Oliver)
37:98-100 F10'62. T 9904
Merchants of art: eighty years
of professional collecting.
by Germain Seligman. (Anon.)
38:187-8 Ap14'62. B 9905
Mercury presides. by Daphne
Fielding. (Anon.) 31:145
Ap2'55. B 9906
The mercy of God. by Jean
Cau. Richard Howard,
trans. (West) 39:186-7 O5'63.
B 9907
Meriwether Lewis. by
Richard Dillon. (Anon.)
41:187 Mr20'65. B 9908
Merry Andrew. (McCarten)
34:105-106 Mr29'58. CC
9909
Message from Moscow. An
observer. (Anon.) 45:82-3
Ja17'70. B 9910
Message from the interior.
by Walker Evans. (Anon.)
42:95-6 Ja7'67. B 9911
Messages of love. by Samuel
Youd. (Anon.) 37:126 Mr4'61.
B 9912
The messenger. by Charles
Wright. (Balliett) 39:206-
209 N2'63. B 9913
The metamorphosis of the
gods. by André Malraux.
Stuart Gilbert, trans. (Anon.)
36:185 O29'60. B 9914
Method--or madness? by Robert
Lewis. (Tynan) 34:100-101
Ja31'59. B 9915

Meyer Berger's New York. by
Meyer Berger. (Anon.)
36:180 Mr19'60. B 9916
Meyer Meyer. by Helen
Hudson. (Anon.) 43:176-7
S9'67. B 9917
Mickey one. (Gill) 41:211-12
O2'65. CC 9918
Midcentury. by John Dos
Passos. (Anon.) 37:173-4
Mr18'61. B 9919
The middle age of Mrs. Eliot.
by Angus Wilson. (Wain)
35:164-6 Ap11'59. B 9920
A middle class education. by
Wilfrid Sheed. (N. Bliven)
37:170-2 Ap8'61. B 9921
Middle of the night. by Paddy
Chayefsky. (Gibbs) 31:56-8
*F18'56; 32:122-3 N24'56.
T 9922
Middle of the night. (McCarten)
35:54 Je27'59. CC 9923
The middle passage. by V.S.
Naipaul. (Anon.) 39:213-14
O12'63. B 9924
Midgie Purvis. by Mary
Chase. (McCarten) 36:75
F11'61. T 9925
Midnight cowboy. (S. Lardner)
45:80 My31'69. CC 9926
Midnight lace. (Gill) 36:103
O29'60. CC 9927
Midsummer night's dream. by
William Shakespeare.
(Flanner) 44:136 Mr16'68. T
9928
Midsummer night's dream.
(Kael) 44:142-5 Mr23'68. CC
9929
Midway: the battle that
doomed Japan. by Mitsuo
Fuchida and Masatake
Okumiya. (Anon.) 31:145
*S10'55. B 9930
A Midwest story. by Augusta
Walker. (Anon.) 35:241-2
N7'59. B 9931
The mighty and their fall. by
Ivy Compton-Burnett.
(N. Bliven) 38:190-1 My5'62.
B 9932
A mighty man is he. by George
Oppenheimer and Arthur

Kober. (Tynan) 35:86-90
Ja16'60. T                9933
Miguel Street. by V. S.
Naipaul. (Balliett) 36:98-
100 Ag27'60. B            9934
Mike downstairs. by George
Panetta. (Gill) 44:84
Ap27'68. T                9935
Military histories. (Liebling)
39:216-45 O19'63. B       9936
A military history of the
Western world, volume II.
by J. F. C. Fuller. (Anon.)
31:126-7 My28'55. B       9937
A military history of the
western world, volume III.
by J. F. C. Fuller. (Anon.)
32:185 O6'56. B           9938
The military philosophers. by
Anthony Powell. (Anon.)
45:76 Jy5'69. B           9939
Milk and honey. by Don Appell
and Jerry Herman. (McCarten)
37:130-1 O21'61. T        9940
The milk train doesn't stop
here anymore. by Tennessee
Williams. (McCarten) 38:72
Ja26'63; 39:69 Ja11'64. T
                          9941
The milky way. (Kael) 45:91
F7'70. CC                 9942
The millionairess. by
George Bernard Shaw.
(Oliver) 45:133-4 Mr15'69.
T                         9943
The millionairess. (Angell)
37:129 F25'61. CC         9944
The millionth chance. by
James Leasor. (Anon.)
34:111 My31'58. B         9945
The millstone. by Margaret
Drabble. (Anon.) 42:204-205
My21'66. B                9946
Mind: an essay on human
feeling, vol. I. by Susanne
K. Langer. (Sargeant) 43:98
102 Ag12'67. B            9947
The mind and art of Henry
Adams. by J. C. Levenson.
(Anon.) 33:141-2 Je8'57.
B                         9948
The mind benders. (Gill) 39:
100-101 My11'63. CC       9949

The mind of an assassin. by
Isaac Don Levine. (Anon.)
35:198 O24'59. B          9950
The minister and the choir
singer: the Hall-Mills
murder case. by William M.
Kunstler. (Anon.) 39:139
F8'64. B                  9951
A minor adjustment. by Eric
Nicol. (McCarten) 43:151
O14'67. T                 9952
Minor miracle. by Al Morgan.
(McCarten) 41:196 O16'65.
T                         9953
Minority reports: H. L.
Mencken's notebooks. by
H. L. Mencken. (Wilson)
45:114-15 My31'69. B      9954
Miracle of the rose. by Jean
Genet. Bernard Frechtman,
trans. (Updike) 43:230-4 N4'67.
B                         9955
The miracle worker. by
William Gibson. (Tynan)
35:132-4 O31'59. T        9956
The miracle worker. (Gill)
38:79 Je2'62. CC          9957
Miraclejack. by Michael
Baldwin. (S. Lardner) 44:
170-3 My11'68. B          9958
Mirage. by Andrea Newman.
(Anon.) 42:192 Ap23'66.
B                         9959
Mirage. (Gill) 41:118-19 Je5
'65. CC                   9960
A mirror for Narcissus. by
Negley Farson. (Hubbell)
33:142-7 Mr23'57. B       9961
The mirror in the roadway.
by Frank O'Connor. (Anon.)
32:186 D15'56. B          9962
The mirror of art: critical
studies. by Charles
Baudelaire. (Anon.) 31:155
*D17'55. B                9963
Misalliance. by George
Bernard Shaw. (Oliver) 37:
132-3 O21'61. T           9964
Misalliance. (J. Lardner) 35:
204-205 D5'59. TV         9965
The misanthrope. by Molière.
Richard Wilbur, trans.
(Bogan) 31:93-4*F4'56. B
                          9966

The misanthrope. by Molière.
(Gill) 44:159 O19'68. T
9967
The miscreant. by Lawrence
O'Sullivan. (Anon.) 45:184
Ap12'69. B 9968
The miser. by Molière. (Gill)
45:110-12 My17'69. T
9969
The misfits. (Angell) 36:86-8
F4'61. CC 9970
Miss Alcott of Concord. by
Marjorie Worthington. (Anon.)
34:210 O18'58. B 9971
Miss Elizabeth: a memoir. by
Elizabeth Anderson and Gerald
R. Kelly. (Anon.) 45:104 Je
21'69. B 9972
Miss Isobel. by Michael
Plant and Denis Webb.
(Gibbs) 33:64-6 Ja11'58. T
9973
Miss Julie. by August Strind-
berg. (Gibbs) 32:59-60
*Mr3'56. (Panter-Downes)
41:103-104 Ag14'65. T
9974
Miss Lonelyhearts. by Howard
Teichmann. (Gibbs) 33:94-5
O12'57. T 9975
Miss Mary Cassatt: impres-
sionist from Pennsylvania.
by Frederick A. Sweet.
(Anon.) 42:118-19 S3'66.
B 9976
Miss Owen-Owen. by Margaret
Forster. (Anon.) 45:95 Je
28'69. B 9977
The missile crisis. by Elie
Abel. (Anon.) 42:199-200
Ap16'66. B 9978
The missing Macleans. by
Geoffrey Hoare. (Anon.)
31:119 Mr5'55. B 9979
Mission in torment: an intimate
account of the U.S. role in
Vietnam. by John Mecklin.
(Anon.) 41:79-80 Jy31'65.
B 9980
Mississippi: the closed society.
by James W. Silver. (Trillin)
40:107-12 Ag15'64. B 9981

Mist over Talla. by Audrey
Erskine Lindop. (Anon.)
33:69-70 D28'57. B 9982
Mr. Arkadin. (Gill) 38:204-205
O27'62. CC 9983
Mr. Balfour's poodle: peers v.
people. by Roy Jenkins.
(Anon.) 44:126 Je1'68. B
9984
Mister Buddwing. (Gill) 42:
165 O22'66. CC 9985
Mr. Chairman, ladies and
gentlemen ... by Norman
Thomas. (Anon.) 31:163
My7'55. B 9986
Mr. Churchill's secretary.
by Elizabeth Nel. (Anon.)
34:203 O25'58. B 9987
Mr. Clemens and Mark
Twain. by Justin Kaplan.
(Gill) 42:114-17 S3'66. B
9988
Mr. Five per cent. by Ralph
Hewins. (Anon.) 34:122-3
Mr1'58. B 9989
Mr. Grossman. by Stanley
Koven. (Oliver) 40:165-6
My16'64. T 9990
Mr. Johnson. by Norman
Rosten. (Gibbs) 32:50-2
*Ap7'56. T 9991
Mr. Lyward's answer. by
Michael Burn. (Anon.)
33:167 Ap6'57. B 9992
Mister Margolies. by James
Yaffe. (Anon.) 38:108
Ag25'62. B 9993
Mr. Novak. (Miller) 39:119-20
N16'63. TV 9994
Mr. President. by Howard
Lindsay, Russel Crouse and
Irving Berlin. (McCarten)
38:147 O27'62. T 9995
Mr. Sammler's planet. by
Saul Bellow. (Sissman) 45:
82-7 Ja31'70. B 9996
Mr. Secretary Cecil and Queen
Elizabeth. by Conyers Read.
(Anon.) 31:143*S10'55. B
9997
Mr. Simian. by Sheppard
Kerman. (Oliver) 39:95-6
N2'63. T 9998

Mr. Wonderful. by Joseph Stein and Will Glickman. (Gibbs) 32:60-1*Mr31'56. T    9999
The mistress. (McCarten) 34:113-14 F14'59. CC 10000
Mrs. 'Arris goes to Paris. by Paul Gallico. (Anon.) 34:233 N22'58. B      10001
Mrs. Dally has a lover. by William Hanley. (Oliver) 38:183 O13'62 (McCarten) 41:176 O2'65. T      10002
Mrs. Fitzherbert. by Anita Leslie. (Anon.) 36:103 Ag27'60. B      10003
A mistress for the Summer. (Gill) 40:168-9 Ap11'64. CC      10004
Mrs. Satan: the incredible saga of Victoria C. Woodhull. by Johanna Johnston. (Anon.) 43:195 Ap15'67. B     10005
Mistress to an age. by J. Christopher Herold. (West) 34:222-36 D6'58. B    10006
Mrs. Warren's profession. by George Bernard Shaw. (Oliver) 39:93-4 My4'63. T      10007
Mrs. Wilson's diary. by Richard Ingrams and John Wells. (Panter-Downes) 43:228-31 N11'67. T      10008
Misty. (Gill) 37:51 Jy29'61. CC      10009
Mitsou. (McCarten) 34:131-2 *Ap26'58. CC      10010
A mixture of frailties. by Robertson Davies. (Anon.) 34:127 S6'58. B     10011
Mobile. by Michel Butor. (Flanner) 38:96-100 Je23'62. B      10012
Moby Dick. by Philip Hanson. (Balliett) 37:118 Ap22'61. T      10013
Moby Dick. by Orson Welles. (McCarten) 38:148 D8'62. T      10014
Moby Dick. (McCarten) 32:71 *Jy14'56. CC      10015
Model shop. (Kael) 45:122-7 F22'69. CC      10016

Moderato cantabile. by Marguerite Duras. Richard Seaver, trans. (Anon.) 36: 224 N5'60. B      10017
Moderato contabile. (Gill) 39:72 Ja18'64. CC      10018
Modern art USA: men, rebellion, conquest, 1900-1956. by Rudi Blesh. (Anon.) 33:147-8 Ap27'57. B      10019
A modern French republic. by Pierre Mendès France. Anne Carter, trans. (Anon.) 39: 98-9 D21'63. B      10020
The modern poets: an American-British anthology. John Malcolm Brinnin and Bill Read, eds. (Anon.) 40:208 Ap25'64. B     10021
Modesty Blaise. (Adler) 42:96-8 Ag13'66. CC      10022
Modesty in dress: an inquiry into the fundamentals of fashion. by James Laver. (Anon.) 45:160 S27'69. B      10023
Modigliani. by André Salmon. Dorothy Weaver and Randolph Weaver, trans. (Anon.) 37:175-6 Ap8'61. B      10024
Modigliani of Montparnasse. (Angell) 37:102 Mr4'61. CC      10025
The Moffat papers. by Jay Pierrepont Moffat. Nancy Harvison Hooker, ed. (Anon.) 32:152-3*S15'56. B     10026
Mohawk baronet. by James Thomas Flexner. (Anon.) 35:237-8 D12'59. B     10027
The Molly Maguires. (Kael) 45:91 F7'70. CC      10028
Moment in the sun: a report on the deteriorating quality of the American environment. by Robert Rienow and Leona Train Rienow. (Anon.) 43:76 Jy8'67. B      10029
The moment of truth. (Gill) 41:92 Ag14'65. CC      10030
A moment of warmth. by

Francis Irby Gwaltney. (Anon.)
32:124 F9'57. B    10031
Moments preserved. by Irving
Penn. (Anon.) 36:248 D10
'60. B    10032
Mon cher papa: Franklin and
the ladies of Paris. by
Claude-Anne Lopez. (Anon.)
42:246 N26'66. B    10033
Mona Lisa, Part I: the Prince
of Taranto. by Tiffany
Thayer. (Anon.) 32:74*Jy21
'56. B    10034
Monckton Milnes. by James
Pope-Hennessy. (West) 31:
51-5*D31'55. B    10035
Mondo cane. (Gill) 39:158
Ap13'63. CC    10036
Mondo pazzo. (Gill) 41:160 Ap
10'65. CC    10037
Money, money, money. (Oliver)
38:70-3 Jy28'62. CC    10038
Money talks! by Charles
Sopkin. (Anon.) 40:91 Ag8
'64. B    10039
The money that money can't
buy. by James Munro.
(Anon.) 44:80 Ag31'68. B
10040
Monique. by Dorothy Blank-
fort and Michael Blankfort.
(Gibbs) 33:87-8 N2'57. T
10041
A monkey in Winter. by
Antoine Blondin. Robert
Baldick, trans. (Anon.)
36:91 Ja28'61. B    10042
Monkey in Winter. (Gill)
38:148-9 F16'63. CC    10043
The monkey watcher. by
Robert Towers. (Anon.) 40:
227 O17'64. B    10044
Monopoly. by Jerome Kass.
(Oliver) 42:120-2 Mr26'66. T
10045
Monsignor Ronald Knox. by
Evelyn Waugh. (Betjeman)
36:174-7 Ap23'60. B
10046
Montaigne: a biography. by
Donald M. Frame. (Anon.)
41:244-5 O23'65. B    10047

The Monte Carlo story. (Mc-
Carten) 34:76-7 F22'58.
CC    10048
Monterey pop. (Gilliatt) 45:
120-1 Mr22'69. CC    10049
A month in the country. by
Ivan Turgenev. (Oliver)
39:126 Je8'63. T    10050
A month in the country. by
Ivan Turgenev. (Gibbs)
32:72-4*Ap14'56. T    10051
Month of Sundays. by Romeo
Muller, Maury Laws and
Jules Bass. (Oliver) 44:89-
90 S28'68. T    10052
A month soon goes. by Storm
Jameson. (Anon.) 39:148-9
F23'63. B    10053
Montserrat. by Lillian Hell-
man. (Balliett) 36:68-70
Ja21'61. T    10054
The moon and sixpence.
(J. Lardner) 35:205-206
D5'59. TV    10055
The moon beseiged. by Seyril
Schochen. (McCarten)
38:130 D15'62. T    10056
The moon dreamers. by
Julie Bovasso. (Oliver)
45:58 D20'69. T    10057
A moon for the misbegotten.
by Eugene O'Neill. (Gibbs)
33:84-6 My11'57. T    10058
The moon in the Yellow River.
by Denis Johnston. (Balliett)
37:93-4 F18'61. T    10059
Moon on a rainbow shawl. by
Errol John. (Oliver) 37:73
Ja27'62. T    10060
Moon pilot. (Gill) 38:172 Ap
14'62. CC    10061
Moonbirds. by Marcel Aymé.
(Flanner) 32:128*Mr10'56
(Tynan) 35:135-6 O17'59. T
10062
Morality and beyond. by Paul
Tillich. (Anon.) 39:97-8
F1'64. B    10063
More lives than one. by
Charles Bracelen Flood.
(Anon.) 43:190 Mr25'67. B
10064

More stately mansions. by
Eugene O'Neill. (Oliver) 43:
127-8 N11'67. T          10065
Morgan! (Gill) 42:86-8 Ap9'66.
CC                       10066
Morley Safer's Vietnam.
(Arlen) 43:184-8 Ap15'67. TV
                         10067
Morning. by Israel Horovitz.
(Gill) 44:139-40 D7'68. T
                         10068
Morning and noon: a memoir.
by Dean Acheson. (Anon.)
41:200-202 D18'65. B
                         10069
Morning noon and night. by James
Gould Cozzens. (Updike)
44:197-201 N2'68. B   10070
Morning sun. by Fred Ebb
and Paul Klein. (Oliver)
39:102 O19'63. T         10071
Mosby's memoirs and other
stories. by Saul Bellow.
(Anon.) 44:247 N16'68. B
                         10072
Mosby's war reminiscences and
Stuart's cavalry campaigns.
by John Singleton Mosby.
(Wilson) 34:117-36 F14'59. B
                         10073
Moscow journal: the end of
Stalin. by Harrison E.
Salisbury. (Anon.) 37:67
D30'61. B                10074
A most contagious game. by
Catherine Aird. (Anon.)
43:247-8 N25'67. B    10075
A most contagious game. by
Samuel Grafton. (Anon.)
31:134 Mr26'55. B     10076
"The most English minister ...":
the policies and politics of
Palmerton. by Donald
Southgate. (Anon.) 42:187
My7'66. B                10077
The most happy fella. by
Frank Loesser. (Gibbs) 32:
75-6*My12'56. T          10078
Mostly murder. by Sydney
Smith. (Anon.) 36:199 S17
'60. B                   10079
The moth and the star: a
biography of Virginia Woolf.

by Aileen Pippett. (Anon.)
31:167*O22'55. B         10080
Mother and son. by Ivy
Compton-Burnett. (West)
31:123-9 Ap9'55. B       10081
Mother Courage and her
children. by Bertolt Brecht.
(McCarten) 39:71 Ap6'63.
T                        10082
Mother isn't dead she's only
sleeping. by Kit Reed.
(Anon.) 37:176 S16'61. B
                         10083
The mother lover. by
Jerome Weidman. (Gill)
44:96-8 F8'69. T         10084
A mother's kisses. by Bruce
Jay Friedman. (Anon.)
40:213 S19'64. B         10085
Mouchette. by Georges
Bernanos. J.C. Whitehouse,
trans. (Updike) 42:91-2 Ja7
'67. B                   10086
Mount Hope: a New England
chronicle. by George Howe.
(Anon.) 35:167 Mr7'59. B
                         10087
The mountain. (McCarten)
32:197-8 N24'56. CC  10088
The mountain and the feather.
by John Ashmead. (Anon.)
37:81 S2'61. B           10089
The mountain is young. by
Suyin Han. (Anon.) 34:236
N29'58. B                10090
The Mountbattens: the last
royal success story. by
Alden Hatch. (Anon.) 41:122
Ag28'65. B               10091
The mouse on the moon. (Gill)
39:62-4 Je29'63. CC   10092
The mouse that roared.
(McCarten) 35:205 N7'59. CC
                         10093
The mousetrap. by Agatha
Christie. (Balliett) 36:97
N19'60. T                10094
Move over, darling. (Gill)
39:86 Ja11'64. CC     10095
The movies. by Richard
Griffith and Arthur Mayer.
(Macdonald) 34:136-8 Mr15
'58. B                   10096

Mozart the dramatist. by Brigid
Brophy. (N. Bliven) 40:75-7
D26'64. B          10097
Mr. Nyedly. by Eleanor L.
Glaze. Prose. 36:132-42
Je4'60.          10097a
Much ado about me. by Fred Allen.
(Anon.)32:239 D1'56. B 10098
Much ado about nothing. by
William Shakespeare. (Tynan)
35:92-5 S26'59. T     10099
Muffs and morals. by Pearl
Binder. (Anon.) 31:178-9
My14'55. B          10100
The multimillionaires. by
Goronwy Rees. (Anon.) 37:71
Jy8'61. B          10101
A multitude of sins. by J.A.
Cuddon. (Anon.) 39:150
Mr2'63. B          10102
The Muqaddimah, an introduc-
tion to history. by Ibn
Khaldun. (Liebling) 35:213-41
N7'59. B          10103
Murder and the android. (J.
Lardner) 35:206 D5'59. TV
          10104
Murder at the gallop. (Gill)
39:64 Je29'63. CC     10105
Murder fantastical. by Patricia
Moyes. (Anon.) 43:66-8 D30
'67. B          10106
Murder, she said. (Gill)
37:110-13 Ja20'62. CC 10107
A murderer among us. by
Yves Jamiaque. George
White, adapt. (McCarten)
40:76-8 Ap4'64. T     10108
The murderers among us:
the Simon Wiesenthal memoirs.
by Simon Wiesenthal.
Joseph Wechsberg, ed.
(Anon.) 43:190-3 Ap22'67. B
          10109
Muriel. (Flanner) 39:160-1
S28'63 (Gill) 39:196 N2'63.
CC          10110
Museum piece. by James
Laver. (Anon.) 40:121-2
Ap18'64. B          10111
The mushroom hunter's field
guide. by Alexander H.
Smith. (Malcolm) 34:86-91
Je28'58. B          10112

Music and ceremonies. by
Edith Sitwell. (Bogan) 40:
181 Ap11'64. B     10113
Music in American life. by
Jacques Barzun. (Anon.)
32:83*Je23'56. B     10114
Music in the twentieth century.
by William W. Austin.
(Anon.) 42:88 Jy23'66. B
          10115
The music man. by
Meredith Willson. (Gibbs)
33:48-51 Ja4'58. T     10116
The music man. (McCarten)
38:80-2 S8'62. CC     10117
Music of the spheres. by Guy
Murchie. (Anon.) 37:179
S16'61. B          10118
The music room. (Gill)
39:148-50 O19'63. CC
          10119
Music U.S.A. (J. Lardner)
34:162-5 S20'58. TV 10120
Music-study in Germany in the
nineteenth century. by Amy
Fay. (Anon.) 42:191 Mr26
'66. B          10121
Mussolini: a study in power.
by Irone Kirkpatrick.
(Anon.) 40:178 Je6'64. B
          10122
Must you conform? by Robert
Lindner. (Anon.) 32:131
*F25'56. B          10123
Mustang: the forbidden
kingdom. by Michel Peissel.
(Anon.) 43:84 Ag5'67. B
          10124
The mute stones speak. by
Paul MacKendrick. (Anon.)
36:243 N26'60. B     10125
Mutiny on the Bounty. (Gill)
38:208-209 N17'62. CC
          10126
Muzeeka. by John Guare.
(Oliver) 44:91-2 My11'68. T
          10127
My Aunt Maxine: the story
of Maxine Elliott. by
Diana Forbes-Robertson.
(Anon.) 40:136 My30'64. B
          10128
My autobiography. by Charles
Chaplin. (Gill) 40:235-44

D12'64. B                10129
My brother Bill: an affectionate
reminiscence. by John
Faulkner. (Anon.) 39:216
O12'63. B                10130
My brother's keeper: James
Joyce's early years. by
Stanislaus Joyce. Richard
Ellmann, ed. (Anon.) 34:
123-4 Mr1'58. B          10131
My confession. by Samuel E.
Chamberlain. (Anon.) 32:
225*N10'56. B            10132
My dear Dorothea. by George
Bernard Shaw. (Auden)
33:142-6 S7'57. B        10133
My diary North and South.
by William Howard Russell.
(Anon.) 31:127-8 Je4'55.
B                        10134
My fair lady. by Alan Jay
Lerner and Frederick Loewe.
(Gibbs) 32:74-6*Mr24'56
(Panter-Downes) 32:80
F16'57; 34:81 Jy5'58. T
                         10135
My fair lady. (Gill) 40:134-5
O31'64. CC               10136
My fellow devils. by L.P.
Hartley. (Anon.) 35:174
Mr21'59. B               10137
My foe outstretch'd beneath
the tree. by V.C. Clinton-
Baddeley. (Anon.) 44:183-4
O5'68. B                 10138
My friend Ché. by Ricardo
Rojo. Julian Casart, trans.
(Anon.) 44:83-4 Ja4'69. B
                         10139
My friend Degas. by Daniel
Halévy. Mina Curtiss,
trans. and ed. (Anon.) 41:
218-19 My15'65. B        10140
My friends the Miss Boyds. by
Jane Duncan. (Anon.) 35:
202-203 O31'59. B        10141
My god died young. by Sasthi
Brata. (Anon.) 44:250
N23'68. B                10142
My grandmothers and I. by
Diana Holman-Hunt. (Anon.)
36:117-18 Ja14'61. B
                         10143

My hobo. (Balliett) 39:50 Ag3'63.
CC                       10144
My life. by Leon Trotsky.
(Macdonald) 35:135-50 Mr
28'59. B                 10145
My life and loves. by Frank
Harris. John F. Gallagher,
ed. (Anon.) 39:79-80 Ja4
'64. B                   10146
My life in jazz. by Max
Kaminsky and V.E. Hughes.
(Anon.) 39:91 Ag10'63. B
                         10147
My life to live. (Gill) 39:179
O5'63. CC                10148
My life with the big cats.
by Alfred Court. (Anon.)
31:169*O22'55. B         10149
My lord of Canterbury. by
Godfrey Turton. (Anon.)
43:190 Mr25'67. B        10150
My Lord, what a morning. by
Marian Anderson. (Anon.)
32:239 N17'56. B         10151
My man Godfrey. (McCarten)
33:87-8 O19'57. CC       10152
My mother, my father and
me. by Lillian Hellman.
(McCarten) 39:108 Mr30'63.
T                        10153
My name is Ivan. (Oliver)
39:42 Jy6'63. CC         10154
My nine lives in the Red
Army. by Mikhail Soloviev.
(Anon.) 31:218*N12'55. B
                         10155
My past and thoughts. by
Alexander Herzen. Constance
Garnett, trans. (Steiner)
44:114-26 F8'69. B       10156
My people is the enemy: an
autobiographical polemic.
by William Stringfellow.
(Anon.) 40:179 Je6'64. B
                         10157
My ship is so small. by Ann
Davison. (Anon.) 32:158
*My5'56. B               10158
My sister, my love. (Gill)
43:132 F25'67. CC        10159
My Stephen Crane. by Corwin
K. Linson. Edwin H. Cady,
ed. (Anon.) 35:153-4 Mr28
'59. B                   10160

My sweet Charlie. by David
Westheimer. (McCarten)
42:117-18 D17'66.  T  10161
My ten years as a counterspy. by
Boris Morros. (Anon.)
34:97 Ja17'59.  B  10162
My troubles began. by Paolo
Volponi. Belén Sevareid,
trans. (West) 41:178-9 My8
'65.  B  10163
My uncle. (McCarten) 34:147-8
N15'58.  CC  10164
My Uncle Harry. by Geoffrey
Willans. (Anon.) 34:143
F7'59.  B  10165
My view of the world. by Erwin
Schrödinger. (Bernstein)
41:180-8 My1'65.  B  10166
My wife and I. by Bill
Mahoney. (Oliver) 42:86
O22'66.  T  10167
My wife's husband. (Gill)
40:120 F6'65.  CC  10168
My wilderness: east to Katahdin.
by William O Douglas. (Anon.)
37:245-6 N11'61.  B  10169
My years and seasons. by Pierre
Balmain. Edward Lanchberry
and Gordon Young, trans.(Anon.)
41:241-4 N27'65.  B  10170
Mysteries of the sea. by Robert
de la Croix. James Cleugh,
trans. (Anon.) 33:177-8
Ap13'57.  B  10171
Mystery and manners. by
Flannery O'Connor. (Anon.)
45:84 Jy19'69.  B  10172
The mystic mandrake. by
C. J. S. Thompson. (Anon.)
44:80 Ag10'68.  B  10173
The mystic masseur. by V. S.
Naipaul. (Balliett) 35:107-
108 My30'59.  B  10174
The myth of Rome's fall. by
Richard Mansfield Haywood.
(Anon.) 34:115-16 Ja10'59.
B  10175
The myth of Sisyphus. by
Albert Camus. Justin O'Brien,
trans. (Anon.) 32:158*Ap
14'56. B  10176
The mythmakers. by Mary
Barnard. (Anon.) 43:195-6
Ap15'67. B  10177

N

The naked and the dead.
(Hamburger) 34:68-70 Ag
16'58. CC  10178
Naked Autumn. (Gill)
39:232 N16'63. CC  10179
Naked earth. (McCarten)
34:76-8 S13'58. CC  10180
The naked edge. (Gill)
37:55 Jy15'61. CC  10181
The naked god: the writer
and the Communist Party.
by Howard Fast. (Anon.)
33:222 D14'57. B  10182
Naked lunch. by William
Burroughs. (Malcolm)
38:114-21 F2'63. B  10183
The naked maja. (McCarten)
35:72 Je20'59. CC  10184
The naked martini. by John
Leonard. (Anon.) 40:123
Ag22'64. B  10185
The naked prey. (S. Lardner)
42:92 Jy16'66. CC  10186
The naked runner. (Gilliatt)
43:75 Jy29'67. CC  10187
Naked we came. by J. Donald
Adams. (Anon.) 43:90
Ja6'68. B  10188
The Nan Patterson case. by
Newman Levy. (Anon.) 35:66-7
Ag1'59. B  10189
Nancy Astor: an informal
biography. by Maurice
Collis. (Anon.) 36:148
Je11'60. B  10190
Naples gold. (Flanner) 31:86-9
*Ag27'55. CC  10191
Napoleon. by Felix Markham.
(Anon.) 40:183 Ap11'64.
B  10192
Napoleon. (Flanner) 31:113-14
Ap9'55. CC  10193
Napoleon after Waterloo. by
Michael John Thornton.
(Anon.) 45:141-2 Ap5'69.
B  10194
Napoleon and Mademoiselle
George. by Edith Saunders.
(Anon.) 35:169-70 Ap4'59.
B  10195
Narcissus and Goldmund. by
Herman Hesse. (Steiner)

44:90-7 Ja18'69. B    10196
The narrowest circle. by
  Katharine Shattuck.
  (Anon.) 34:143 Ap5'58.
  B                         10197
Nathan Weinstein, Mystic,
  Connecticut. by David
  Rayfiel. (McCarten) 42:84
  Mr5'66. T                 10198
Nationalism and ideology. by
  Barbara Ward. (Anon.) 42:
  104 Jy16'66. B            10199
The nation's safety and arms
  control. by Arthur T.
  Hadley. (B. Bliven) 37:210-21
  O14'61. B                 10200
Natural affection. by William
  Inge. (McCarten) 38:66-8
  F9'63. T                  10201
Natural histories. by Jules
  Renard. Richard Howard,
  trans. (Anon.) 42:131 F4'67.
  B                         10202
The natural history of
  aggression. J.D. Carthy and
  F.J.G. Ebling, eds. (Alsop)
  42:209-22 S10'66. B   10203
A natural history of New
  York City. by John Kieran.
  (Anon.) 35:169-70 O3'59. B
                            10204
The natural look. by Lee
  Thuna. (McCarten) 43:121
  Mr18'67. T                10205
A naturalist in Trinidad. by
  C. Brooke Worth. (Anon.)
  43:179 S9'67. B           10206
The nature of art. John
  Gassner and Sydney Thomas,
  eds. (Anon.) 40:187 My23
  '64. B                    10207
The nature of passion. by
  R. Prawer Jhabvala. (Balliett)
  33:93-4*Je22'57. B    10208
Nature's way. by Herman
  Wouk. (Gibbs) 33:96-8 O26
  '57. T                    10209
Naught for your comfort.
  by Trevor Huddleston.
  (Anon.) 32:129-30*Je2'56.
  B                         10210
Nazarin. (Gilliatt) 44:66 Je22
  '68. CC                   10211

Near the ocean. by Robert
  Lowell. (Anon.) 43:179-80
  My20'67. B                10212
Necessary end. by Anita Rowe
  Block. (Anon.) 36:196-7
  Mr12'60. B                10213
The necklace of Kali. by
  Robert Towers. (Anon.)
  36:225 N5'60. B           10214
The negotiators. by Francis
  Walder. Denise Folliot,
  trans. (Flanner) 34:106 D20
  '58 (Anon.) 35:243-4 N7'59.
  B                         10215
The Negro revolt. by Louis
  E. Lomax. (Anon.) 38:79-
  80 Jy28'62. B             10216
Nehru, a political biography.
  by Michael Brecher. (Anon.)
  35:90-1 Jy25'59. B    10217
Nehru: the years of power.
  by Vincent Sheean. (Anon.)
  36:175 F20'60. B          10218
Nekrassov. by Jean-Paul
  Sartre. (Flanner) 31:58
  *Jy2'55. T                10219
Nepal. by Giuseppe Tucci.
  Lovett F. Edwards, trans.
  (Anon.) 38:91-2 Je30'62.
  B                         10220
The nervous set. by Jay
  Landesman, Theodore J.
  Flicker, Tommy Wolf and Fran
  Landesman. (Tynan) 35:72-9
  My23'59. T                10221
The net that covers the world.
  by E.H. Cookridge. (Anon.)
  31:144-5*S10'55. B    10222
Nevada Smith. (S. Lardner)
  42:80 Jy9'66. CC          10223
Never a dull moment. by
  Marguerite Cassini. (Anon.)
  32:165-6*My12'56. B   10224
Never live over a pretzel
  factory. by Jerry Devine.
  (McCarten) 40:76 Ap4'64.
  T                         10225
Never on Sunday. (Gill) 36:
  102-103 O29'60. CC    10226
Never steal anything small.
  (McCarton) 35:137 F21'59.
  CC                        10227
Never too late. by Sumner

Arthur Long. (McCarten)
38:148 D8'62. T          10228
Never too late. (Gill) 41:234-5
N13'65. CC          10229
Neville Chamberlain. by Iain
Macleod. (Anon.) 38:178
My12'62. B          10230
The new American poetry
1945-1960. Donald M.
Allen, ed. (Bogan) 36:199-200
O8'60. B          10231
The new American Right.
Daniel Bell, ed. (Anon.)
31:214*D3'55. B          10232
New and selected poems. by
Howard Nemerov. (Bogan)
37:129-30 Ap1'61. B 10233
New art in America. John I. H.
Baur, ed. (Anon.) 33:180
S14'57. B          10234
New bottles for new wine.
by Julian Huxley. (Anon.)
34:146 Ap5'58. B          10235
The new class. by Milovan
Djilas. (Anon.) 33:191-2
S21'57. B          10236
The new dimensions of peace.
by Chester Bowles. (Anon.)
31:222*N19'55. B          10237
New England discovery. Nancy
Hale, ed. (Anon.) 39:247
N16'63. B          10238
The New England story. by
Henry Beetle Hough.
(Anon.) 33:88-9 F1'58. B
          10239
The new face of war. by
Malcolm W. Browne. (Anon.)
41:125-6 Je19'65. B 10240
New faces of '56. by Leonard
Sillman. (Gibbs) 32:58-60
*Je23'56. T          10241
New girl in town. by George
Abbott and Bob Merrill.
(Gibbs) 33:82-4 My25'57. T
          10242
The new industrial state.
by John Kenneth Galbraith.
(N. Bliven) 43:85-9
Ja6'68. B          10243
The new language of politics:
an anecdotal dictionary of
catchwords, slogans, and
political usage. by William

Safire. (Anon.) 44:183 S28'68.
B          10244
A new life. by Bernard
Malamud. (Malcolm) 37:105-
107 Ja27'62. B          10245
The new look: a social history
of the forties and fifties in
Britain. by Harry Hopkins.
(Anon.) 40:187-8 My23'64.
B          10246
The new look of the universe.
by Patrick Moore. (Anon.)
43:194-5 Mr11'67. B 10247
The new moon with the old.
by Dodie Smith. (Anon.)
39:244 N9'63. B          10248
New music hall of Israel.
by Jonathan Karmon. (Gill)
45:88-91 O11'69. T          10249
New paths in biology. by
Adolf Portmann. (Anon.)
41:112 Ja8'66. B          10250
New poems. by Robert
Graves. (Bogan) 40:178-80
Ap11'64. B          10251
New poets of England and
America. Donald Hall,
Robert Pack and Louis
Simpson, eds. (Bogan)
34:122-4 Mr29'58. B 10252
The new politics: America and the
end of the postwar world. by
Edmund Stillman and William
Pfaff. (B. Bliven) 37:210-21
O14'61. B          10253
The new rythum and other pieces.
by Ronald Firbank. (Anon.) 39:
91-2 Jy20'63. B          10253a
A new Russia? by Harrison E.
Salisbury. (Anon.) 38:88
Ag11'62. B          10254
The new scientist--essays on
the methods and values of
modern science. Paul C.
Obler and Herman A. Estrin,
eds. (Bernstein) 39:66-9
Ag31'63. B          10255
The new statesman: the history
of the first fifty years. by
Edward Hyams. (Anon.)
39:247-8 N16'63. B          10256
New statesmanship: an anthology.
Edward Hyams, ed. (Anon.)
39:247-8 N16'63. B          10257

A new year's tale. by Vladimir
Dudintsev. Gabriella
Azrael, trans. (Anon.)
36:224 N5'60. B          10258
The New York diary of Ned
Rorem. by Ned Rorem.
(Anon.) 43:216 O28'67.
B                        10259
New York film festival, 1968.
(Gilliatt) 44:140-3 S21'68.
CC                       10260
The New York I know. by
Marya Mannes. (Anon.)
37:210-11 O7'61. B       10261
New York landmarks. Alan
Burnham, ed. (Anon.) 39:
245-6 D7'63. B           10262
New York proclaimed. by V.S.
Pritchett. (Anon.) 41:190-
2 My1'65. B              10263
Newman: light in Winter. by
Meriol Trevor. (Anon.) 39:
178 My18'63. B           10264
Next. by Terrence McNally.
(Oliver) 45:92 F22'69. T
                         10265
The next generation. by Donald
Michael. (Hentoff) 41:78-9
Jy31'65. B               10266
Next time I'll sing to you.
by James Saunders. (Panter-
Downes) 39:148-51 My25'63
(Oliver) 39:131-2 D7'63. T
                         10267
Nicholas and Alexandra. by
Robert K. Massie. (N.
Bliven) 44:152-7 Mr23'68.
B                        10268
The niggerlovers. by George
Tabori and Richard Peaslee.
(Oliver) 43:152-3 O14'67. T
                         10269
Night. by Elie Wiesel
and Stella Rodway. (Anon.)
37:175 Mr18'61. B        10270
Night. by Leonard Melfi.
(Gill) 44:140 D7'68. T
                         10271
The night. (Gill) 38:102-103
Mr3'62. CC               10272
Night affair. (Gill) 37:197
O21'61. CC               10273

Night ambush. (McCarten)
34:62 My3'58. CC         10274
Night and silence who is
here: an American comedy.
by Pamela Hansford
Johnson. (Anon.) 39:70 Ag3'63.
B                        10275
Night beat. (J. Lardner)
33:164-8 N9'57; 34:76-9
Je21'58. TV              10276
The night circus. by Michael
V. Gazzo. (Tynan) 34:106-
107 D13'58. T            10277
The night cometh. by Eugene
O'Donnell. (Anon.) 35:
234-5 D12'59. B          10278
Night drop. by S. L. A.
Marshall. (B. Bliven)
38:182-4 Ap14'62. B      10279
Night falls on the city. by
Sarah Gainham. (Anon.)
43:82 Ag5'67. B          10280
Night games. by Mai Zetter-
ling. (Anon.) 42:122
Ja14'67. B               10281
Night games. (Gill) 42:61 D24
'66. CC                  10282
The night is black bottles.
by Sam Soffer. (Oliver)
38:132 D15'62. T         10283
Night life. by Sidney Kingsley.
(McCarten) 38:111-12
N3'62. T                 10284
Night must fall. (Gill) 40:
144 Mr28'64. CC          10285
The night my number came
up. (McCarten) 31:36*D31
'55. CC                  10286
Night of the dunce. by Frank
Gagliano. (McCarten) 42:78
Ja7'67. T                10287
The night of the following day.
(Kael) 45:116-17 Mr8'69.
CC                       10288
The night of the generals. (Gill)
42:98 F4'67. CC          10289
The night of the giraffe and
other stories. by Alfred
Andersch. Christa Arm-
strong, trans. (Anon.)
40:245 N28'64. B         10290
The night of the hammer. by

Ned O'Gorman. (Bogan) 35:196
O24'59. B          10291
The night of the hunter.
(McCarten) 31:94*O8'55.
CC          10292
The night of the iguana.
by Tennessee Williams. (Mc-
Carten) 37:61 Ja13'62. T
          10293
The night of the iguana.
(Oliver) 40:84-5 Ag15'64. CC
          10294
Night/of the quarter moon.
(McCarten) 35:165 Mr14'59.
CC          10295
A night of their own. by
Peter Abrahams. (West)
41:221-2 S25'65. B          10296
The night they raided
Minsky's. (Kael) 44:76-8
Ja18'69. CC          10297
A night to remember. by Walter
Lord. (Anon.) 31:212-13
*D5'55. B          10298
A night to remember.
(McCarten) 34:60 D27'58.
CC          10299
The night visitor and other
stories. by B. Traven.
(West) 43:82-7 Jy22'67.
B          10300
The night watch. (Gill)
40:164-6 Je6'64. CC     10301
The night watchman. by
Simonne Jacquemard. L.D.
Emmet, trans. (N. Bliven)
40:113 Ja9'65. B          10302
Nightmare of the innocents.
by Otto Larsen. (Anon.)
33:167 S28'57. B          10303
Nikos Kazantzakis. by
Helen Kazantzakis. (Anon.)
44:88 Ja11'69. B          10304
Nine coaches waiting. by
Mary Stewart. (Anon.)
34:94 Ja17'59. B          10305
Nine days of one year. (Gill)
40:105 Ja9'65. CC          10306
Nine hours to Rama. (Gill)
39:157-8 Ap13'63. CC
          10307
Nine lives. (McCarten) 34:83
Ja17'59. CC          10308

Nine men. by Fred Rodell.
(Anon.) 31:159-60*S24'55.
B          10309
Nine rivers from Jordan.
by Denis Johnston. (West)
31:150-9*S17'55. B     10310
Nine Soviet portraits. by
Raymond Bauer. (Anon.)
31:177 My14'55. B     10311
1918: the last act. by Barrie
Pitt. (Anon.) 38:161
F16'63. B          10312
1984. (McCarten) 32:91
O6'56. CC          10313
1914. by James Cameron.
(Anon.) 35:96 Ag8'59.
B          10314
1913: an end and a beginning.
by Virginia Cowles. (Anon.)
44:245-6 D7'68. B     10315
1933: characters in crisis.
by Herbert Feis. (Anon.)
42:192 Ap23'66. B     10316
19th century British minor
poets. W.H. Auden, ed.
(Anon.) 42:176 Ap2'66. B
          10317
The nine-tiger man. by
Lesley Blanch. (Anon.)
41:195 Ap17'65. B     10318
The 90 day mistress. by J.J.
Coyle. (McCarten) 43:131
N18'67. T          10319
95 poems. by E.E. Cummings.
(Anon.) 34:120 D20'58. B
          10320
The ninth circle. (Gill) 37:
170-1 S23'61. CC          10321
Nisei: the quiet Americans.
by Bill Hosokawa. (Anon.)
45:67-8 Ja3'70. B     10322
Nixon speech. (Arlen) 44:167-
71 S21'68. TV          10323
Njegoš: poet, prince, bishop.
by Milovan Djilas. Michael
B. Petrovich, trans. (West)
42:76-82 Jy30'66. B     10324
No compromise! by Arnold
Whitridge. (Anon.) 36:225-6
N5'60. B          10325
No easy victories. by John W.
Gardner. Helen Rowan, ed.
(Anon.) 44:119 Ag24'68. B
          10326

No end of a lesson. by
Anthony Nutting. (Anon.)
43:247-8 N11'67. B 10327
No escape from adventure. by
Michael Bruce. (Anon.)
31:83-4 Jy9'55. B 10328
No exit. (Gill) 38:233-4
D8'62. CC 10329
No further West. by Dan
Jacobson. (Malcolm) 37:132-6
Je10'61. B 10330
No laurels for de Gaulle: an
appraisal of the London years.
by Robert Mengin. Jay Allen,
trans. (N. Bliven) 42:242-7
O22'66. B 10331
No love for Jennie. by Wilfred
Feinburgh. (Anon.) 35:192
S19'59. B 10332
No love for Johnnie. (Gill)
37:112 D16'61. CC 10333
No man's time. by V.S.
Yanovsky. (Gilliatt) 43:242-6
N18'67. B 10334
No more excuses. (Gilliatt)
44:87-8 My25'68. CC
10335
No place to be somebody.
by Charles Gordone. (Oliver)
45:112-14 My17'69. (Gill)
45:64-5 Ja10'70. T 10336
No room for bears. by
Frank Dufresne. (Anon.)
41:108 Ja22'66. B 10337
No strings. by Samuel Taylor
and Richard Rodgers.
(Oliver) 38:100-102 Mr31
'62. T 10338
No sun in Venice. (McCarten)
34:69 Je21'58. CC 10339
No third path. by Joseph
Novak. (Anon.) 38:188
Mr17'62. B 10340
No time for sergeants. by
Ira Levin. (Gibbs) 31:80-2
*O29'55. T 10341
No time for sergeants. (Mc-
Carten) 34:64-5 Je7'58. CC
10342
No trifling with love. by
Alfred de Musset. (Malcolm)
35:117-18 N21'59. T 10343

No way to treat a lady.
(Kael) 44:114-16 Mr30'68.
CC 10344
A noble profession. by Pierre
Boulle. (Anon.) 36:183
O29'60. B 10345
Noblesse oblige. Nancy
Mitford, ed. (Anon.) 32:
155-6*S15'56. B 10346
Nobody knows my name.
by James Baldwin.
(Malcolm) 37:233-8 N25'61.
B 10347
Nobody laughs last. (Gilliatt)
43:54-6 Jy1'67. CC 10348
Nobody loves an albatross.
by Ronald Alexander.
(McCarten) 39:58 Ja4'64.
T 10349
Nobody waved goodbye. (Gill)
41:163-4 Ap24'65.
CC 10350
Noël Coward's sweet potato.
by Noël Coward. (Gill)
44:97-8 O5'68. T 10351
Nomads and commissars:
Mongolia revisited. by Owen
Lattimore. (Anon.) 38:246-
7 N17'62. B 10352
Nonviolence in America: a
documentary history. by
Staughton Lynd. (Anon.)
42:167-8 Je4'66. B 10353
Noon. by Terrence McNally.
(Gill) 44:140 D7'68. T
10354
Noontide. by Howard Hart.
(Balliett) 37:94-5 Je10'61.
T 10355
Norman Thomas. by Harry
Fleischman. (Anon.) 39:98-
9 F1'64. B 10356
North African powder keg.
by Edmund Stevens. (Anon.)
31:206-207*D10'55. B
10357
North by northwest. (Balliett)
35:80*Ag15'59. CC 10358
The North reports the Civil
War. by J. Cutler Andrews.
(Anon.) 31:70-1* S3'55.
B 10359

North toward home. by Willie Morris. (S. Lardner) 43: 106-11 F3'68. B    10360

Not a way of life. by James Rush. (Oliver) 43:140-1 Ap8'67. T    10361

Not a word about nightingales. by Maureen Howard. (Anon.) 38:140-1 Mr31'62. B    10362

Not as a stranger. (McCarten) 31:66-7 Jy9'55. CC    10363

Not by bread alone. by Vladimir Dudintsev. (Podhoretz) 33:224-33 D7'57. B    10364

Not in the calendar. by Margaret Kennedy. (Anon.) 40:136-7 Je20'64. B    10365

Not of this time, not of this place. by Yehuda Amichai. Shlomo Katz, trans. (West) 45:146-7 My3'69. B    10366

Not on your life. (Gill) 41:158 Ap17'65. CC    10367

Not under oath. by John Kieran. (Anon.) 40:228 O17'64. B    10368

A note of grace. by Betty Singleton. (Anon.) 34:154-5 Mr22'58. B    10369

Notebooks. by Albert Camus. Philip Thody, trans. (Liebling) 39:128-38 F8'64. B    10370

The notebooks for "The Idiot." by Fyodor Dostoevski. Edward Wasiolek, ed. (Rosenberg) 44:159-81 O5'68. B    10371

The notebooks of Major Thompson. by Pierre Daninos. Robin Farn, trans. (Anon.) 31:213-14 *D3'55. B    10372

The notebooks of Samuel Taylor Coleridge, Volume I (1794-1804). by Samuel Taylor Coleridge. Kathleen Coburn, ed. (Anon.) 33:246-7 D7'57. B    10373

Notes from a dark street. by Edward Adler. (Anon.) 38:132 Je16'62. B    10374

Notes from a sea diary: Hemingway all the way. by Nelson Algren. (Anon.) 41: 107 S4'65. B    10375

Notes from the Warsaw ghetto: the journal of Emmanuel Ringelbaum. by Emmanuel Ringelbaum. Jacob Sloan, trans & ed. (Anon.) 34:165-6 S13'58. B    10376

Notes of a native son. by James Baldwin. (Anon.) 32:150*Ap7'56. B    10377

Notes of a pianist. by Louis Moreau Gottschalk. Jeanne Behrend, ed. (Sargeant) 41:189-92 Ap17'65. B    10378

Notes on a cowardly lion: the biography of Bert Lahr. by John Lahr. (Anon.) 45: 244 D6'69. B    10379

Nothing but a man. (Gill) 40:104 Ja9'65. CC    10380

Nothing but the best. (Balliett) 40:56 Jy25'64. CC    10381

Nothing new under the sun. by Riccardo Bacchelli. (Anon.) 31:146*O29'55. B    10382

The notion of sin. by Robert McLaughlin. (Anon.) 35:171-2 Ap18'59. B    10383

The notorious Lady Essex. by Edward Le Comte. (Anon.) 45:116 My31'69. B    10384

The notorious landlady. (Oliver) 38:46 Ag11'62. CC    10385

Nova express. by William Burroughs. (Anon.) 40:245-8 N28'64. B    10386

Novels into film. by George Bluestone. (Macdonald) 34: 146-7 Mr15'58. B    10387

Now comes Theodora. by Daniel Ford. (Anon.) 41:105-106 Je26'65. B    10388

Now is the time for all good men. by Gretchen Cryer and Nancy Ford. (Oliver) 43:133-4 O7'67. T    10389

Now it can be told. by Leslie R. Groves. (Anon.) 38:186-7 Ap14'62. B    10390

Nowhere to go but up. by James Lipton and Sol Berkowitz. (McCarten) 38:147-8 N17'62. T    10391

Nuclear weapons and the conflict of conscience. John C. Bennett, ed. (Anon.) 38:187 My19'62. B     10392

The nude: a study in ideal form. by Kenneth Clark. (Anon.) 33:155 Ap20'57. B     10393

Nude descending a staircase. by X. J. Kennedy. (Bogan) 38:175 Mr24'62. B     10394

Nude with violin. by Noël Coward. (Gibbs) 33:78-80 N23'57. T     10395

Number one. (Gilliatt) 45:152-3 S20'69. CC     10396

No. 10 Downing Street: a house in history. by R. J. Minney. (Anon.) 39:122 Je15 '63. B     10397

The nun of Monza. by Mario Mazzucchelli. by Evelyn Gendel, trans. (Anon.) 39:92 Ag17'63. B     10398

The nun's story. by Kathryn Hulme. (Hubbell) 32:146-52 S29'56. B     10399

The nun's story. (McCarten) 35:52-4 Je27'59. CC     10400

Nutty, naughty château. (Gill) 40:150-1 O24'64. CC     10401

The nutty professor. (Miller) 39:61 Ag10'63. CC     10402

O

O marry me! by Oliver Goldsmith, Lola Pergament and Robert Kessler. (Oliver) 37:130-2 N4'61. T     10403

O say can you see! by Bill Conklin and Bob Miller. (Oliver) 38:86-8 O20'62. T     10404

O strange new world--American culture: the formative years. by Howard Mumford Jones. (Anon.) 40:205-206 S12'64. B     10405

The object-lesson. by Edward Gorey. (Wilson) 35:65-6 D 26'59. B     10406

Obstacle course on Capitol Hill. by Robert Bendiner. (Anon.)

40:186-7 My23'64. B     10407

The obstructed path: French social thought in the years of desperation, 1930-60. by H. Stuart Hughes. (Anon.) 43:135 F17'68. B     10408

Occasion for loving. by Nadine Gordimer. (Anon.) 38:132-3 Ja26'63. B     10409

Occupied with crime. by Richard Jackson. (Anon.) 43:71-2 D23'67. B     10410

Ocean road. by Jack Bennett. (Anon.) 42:241-4 N26'66. B     10411

Ocean's 11. (Balliett) 36:72-3 Ag20'60. CC     10412

The octoroon. by Dion Boucicault. (Balliett) 36:75-8 F11'61. T     10413

The odd couple. by Neil Simon. (McCarten) 41:83 Mr20'65. T     10414

Odd obsession. (Gill) 37:98 Ja13'62. CC     10415

Odds against tomorrow. (McCarten) 35:185-6 O24'59. CC     10416

Ode to a young love. by Basil Davidson. (Anon.) 35:90 Jy25'59. B     10417

The odyssey: a modern sequel. by Nikos Kazantzakis. Kimon Friar, trans. (Anon.) 34:144 F7'59. B     10418

The odyssey of Homer. by Homer. Richmond Lattimore, trans. (Bogan) 44:135 Mr30'68. B     10419

Oedipus rex. by Sophocles. (Malcolm) 35:95-6 My9'59. T     10420

Oedipus rex. (McCarten) 32:96 Ja19'57. CC     10421

Of carriages and kings. by Frederick John Gorst and Beth Andrews. (Anon.) 32:185-6 O6'56. B     10422

Of human bondage. (Gill) 40:134 O3'64. CC     10423

Of love remembered. by Arnold Sundgaard. (McCarten) 43:92 F25'67. T     10424

Of men and galaxies. by Fred
Hoyle. (Anon.) 41:223-4
S25'65. B                    10425
Of men and marshes. by
Paul L. Errington. (Anon.)
33:119 Ja25'58. B            10426
Of mice and men. by John
Steinbeck. (Malcolm) 34:
109-11 D13'58. T             10427
Of molecules and men. by
Francis Crick. (Anon.) 42:
123-4 Ja14'67. B             10428
Of stars and men. by Harlow
Shapley. (Anon.) 34:177 S
27'58. B                     10429
Of streets and stars. by Alan
Marcus. (Balliett) 39:176-7
My18'63. B                   10430
Of thee I sing. by George S.
Kaufman, Morrie Ryskind,
George Gershwin, and Ira
Gershwin. (Oliver) 45:135
Mr15'69. T                   10431
Of time and space and other
things. by Isaac Asimov.
(Anon.) 41:247 O30'65. B
                             10432
Of time, work and leisure.
by Sebastian de Grazia.
(Anon.) 38:80 Jy28'62. B
                             10433
Of wayward love. (Gill) 40:
178-9 Ap4'64. CC             10434
The ofay watcher. by Frank
Cucci. (Oliver) 45:97-8 S27
'69. T                       10435
Off the record with F.D.R.:
1942-45. by William D.
Hassett. (Anon.) 34:241-2
D6'58. B                     10436
Offbeat history. Bulkley S.
Griffin, ed. (Anon.) 43:179
S23'67. B                    10437
The "Office": the story of the
British Foreign Office, 1919-
51. by John Connell.
(Anon.) 34:211-12 N8'58. B
                             10438
The officer factory. by Hans
Hellmut Kirst. Robert Kee,
trans. (Anon.) 39:191
My4'63. B                    10439
Officers and gentlemen. by

Evelyn Waugh. (Anon.) 31:83
Jy9'55. B                    10440
The official atlas of the Civil
War. by Calvin D. Cowles.
(Anon.) 34:236 N22'58. B
                             10441
Oh! Calcutta! by Kenneth
Tynan, et al. (Gill) 45:72-5
Je28'69. T                   10442
Oh captain! by Al Morgan,
José Ferrer, Jay Livingston
and Ray Evans. (Gibbs) 33:
55 F15'58. T                 10443
Oh Dad, poor Dad. (Gill)
43:135 F25'67. CC            10444
Oh Dad, poor Dad, Mamma's
hung you in the closet and
I'm feelin' so sad. by
Arthur Kopit. (Oliver) 38:84-5
Mr10'62. T                   10445
Oh, say can you see L.A.
by John Allen. (Oliver) 43:100-
101 F17'68. T                10446
Oh! what a lovely war. by
Charles Chilton, et al.
(Flanner) 39:76-7 Je29'63
(Panter-Downes) 39:98 S7'63
(McCarten) 40:95 O10'64. T
                             10447
Oh! what a lovely war. (Kael)
45:157-8 O11'69. CC          10448
Ohayo. (Gill) 41:125 F5'66.
CC                           10449
Oklahoma! (McCarten) 31:138
*O22'55. CC                  10450
The old blood. by Edgar Mittel-
holzer. (West) 34:90-3
Ag16'58. B                   10451
The old boys. by William
Trevor. (Anon.) 40:181-2
Ap11'64. B                   10452
Old bucks and new wings. by
Harvey Lasker and Eddie
Stuart. (Oliver) 38:148
N17'62. T                    10453
Old friends. by Clive Bell.
(Anon.) 33:115 Mr2'57. B
                             10454
The old glory. by Robert
Lowell. (Oliver) 40:143-4
N14'64. T                    10455
Old house of fear. by Russell
Kirk. (Anon.) 37:92 Ag12'61.
B                            10456

OLD                    -316-                    ON

The old man and the sea.
(McCarten) 34:154-6 O18'58.
CC                        10457
The old man dies. by Georges
Simenon. Bernard Frecht-
man, trans. (Brennan) 43:81-
4 S2'67. B                10458
Old songs. (J. Lardner) 36:
147-50 Mr19'60. TV       10459
The old tune. by Robert Pinget.
Samuel Beckett, trans. &
adapt. (Balliett) 37:100 Ap1
'61. T                    10460
The oldest confession. by
Richard Condon. (Anon.) 34:
103 Je21'58 (Balliett) 35:
105 My30'59. B            10461
Oliver! by Lionel Bart.
(Panter-Downes) 36:144-5
O8'60. (McCarten) 38:60 Ja19
'63. T                    10462
Oliver! (Kael) 44:193-6 D14
'68. CC                   10463
Oliver Cromwell. by C. V.
Wedgwood. (Anon.) 32:186 O
6'56. B                   10464
Oliver Cromwell and the
Puritan revolution. by Maurice
Ashley. (Anon.) 34:102-103
Ja31'59. B                10465
Olympio. by André Maurois.
(West) 32:122-28*My26'56.
B                         10466
Omnibus. (J. Lardner) 33:
145-6 N16'57. TV          10467
On a clear day you can see
forever. by Alan Jay
Lerner and Burton Lane.
(McCarten) 41:108 O30'65. T
                          10468
On fighting poverty. James
L. Sundquist, ed. (Anon.)
45:96 Ag23'69. B          10469
On her majesty's secret
service. (Kael) 45:61 Ja3'70.
CC                        10470
On love. by José Ortega y
Gasset. Toby Talbot, trans.
(Sargeant) 34:151-2 Mr22'58.
B                         10471
On overgrown paths. by Knut
Hamsun. Carl S. Anderson,
trans. (Updike) 43:223-32
D2'67. B                  10472

On poetry and poets. by T. S.
Eliot. (Anon.) 33:247 D7
'57. B                    10473
On revolution. by Hannah
Arendt. (N. Bliven) 40:210-
18 Ap18'64. B             10474
On the beach. (McCarten)
35:47 Ja2'60. CC          10475
On the boundary. by Paul
Tillich. (Anon.) 42:91-2
Jy9'66. B                 10476
On the double. (Oliver) 37:121
Je3'61. CC                10477
On the edge of the rift:
memories of Kenya. by
Elspeth Huxley. (Anon.)
38:244 D8'62. B           10478
On the poetry of Keats. by
E. C. Pettet (Anon.) 33:203
O12'57. B                 10479
On the prevention of war.
by John Strachey. (Anon.)
39:179-80 Ap27'63. B      10480
On the shoulders of giants: a
Shandean postscript. by
Robert K. Merton. (Anon.)
41:224 S25'65. B          10481
On the track of unknown
animals. by Bernard Heuvel-
mans. Richard Garnett,
trans. (Anon.) 35:195 S19
'59. B                    10482
On understanding poverty.
Daniel P. Moynihan, ed.
(Anon.) 45:96 Ag23'69. B
                          10483
Once a Greek . . . by Friedrich
Dürrenmatt. Richard
Winston and Clara Winston,
trans. (Anon.) 41:119 Ag
14'65. B                  10484
Once a thief. (Gill) 41:126
S18'65. CC                10485
Once an eagle. by Anton Myrer.
(Anon.) 44:118-19 Ag24'68.
B                         10486
Once for the asking. by Owen
G. Arno. (McCarten) 39:
110 N30'63. T             10487
Once more, with feeling. by
Harry Kurnitz. (J. Lardner)
34:98-9 N1'58. T          10488
Once there was a Russian. by
Samuel Spewack. (McCarten)

37:94 Mr4'61. T          10489
Once there was a war. by John
Steinbeck. (Anon.) 34:215
N8'58. B                 10490
Once upon a city: New York
from 1890-1910. by Grace
M. Mayer. (Anon.) 34:192
O4'58. B                 10491
Once upon a mattress. by
Jay Thompson, Marshall
Barer and Dean Fuller.
(Malcolm) 35:80-1 My23'59.
T                        10492
Once upon a tailor. by
Baruch Lumet. (Gibbs) 31:
90 Je4'55. T             10493
One by one. by Dore Schary.
(McCarten) 40:156 D12'64.
T                        10494
One day in the life of Ivan
Denisovich. by Alexander
Solzhenitsyn. (West) 39:168-
9 Ap27'63. B             10495
One eyed jacks. (Oliver)
37:153-4 Ap15'61. CC     10496
One fat Englishman. by
Kingsley Amis. (Panter-
Downes) 40:134-6 Je20'64. B
                         10497
One first love: the letters of
Ellen Louisa Tucker to Ralph
Waldo Emerson. by Ellen
Louisa Tucker. Edith W.
Gregg, ed. (Anon.) 38:244-5
D8'62. B                 10498
One flew over the cuckoo's
nest. by Ken Kesey. (Anon.)
38:181-2 Ap21'62. B      10499
One flew over the cuckoo's nest.
by Dale Wasserman.
(McCarten) 39:143 N23'63.
T                        10500
One foot in Eden. by Edwin
Muir. (Bogan) 32:178-9 O6'56.
B                        10501
One hour. by Lillian Smith.
(Anon.) 35:191 S26'59. B
                         10502
One hundred dollar misunder-
standing. by Robert Gover.
(Balliett) 38:76 D29'62. B
                         10503
101 dalmatians. (Oliver) 37:163

Mr18'61. CC              10504
One hundred poems from the
Chinese. Kenneth Rexroth,
trans. (Anon.) 33:168 My4
'57. B                   10505
One hundred poems from the
Japanese. Kenneth Rexroth,
trans. (Bogan) 31:93*F4'56.
B                        10506
110 in the shade. by N. Richard
Nash, Harvey Schmidt and
Tom Jones. (McCarten) 39:
93-4 N2'63. T            10507
110 Livingston Street: politics
and bureaucracy in the New
York City schools. by David
Rogers. (Anon.) 44:104
Ja25'69. B               10508
One man's Africa. by John
Seymour. (Anon.) 32:155
*Ap14'56. B              10509
One man's freedom. by
Edward Bennett Williams.
(Anon.) 38:107 Je23'62.
B                        10510
One man's gold rush. by
Murray Morgan. (Anon.)
43:111-12 Ag19'67. B     10511
One man's Montana. by John K.
Hutchens. (Anon.) 40:247
O10'64. B                10512
One million dead. by José
María Gironella. Joan
MacLean, trans. (West) 40:
130-4 F29'64. B          10513
1,000,000 delinquents. by
Benjamin Fine. (Anon.) 31:
129 My28'55. B           10514
One more river. by Beverley
Cross. (Tynan) 36:78-80
Mr26'60. T               10515
One night stand. (J. Lardner)
35:102-104 My30'59. TV
                         10516
One of the founders. by P.H.
Newby. (West) 41:62 D25
'65. B                   10517
One plus one. (Gill) 37:208
N18'61. CC               10518
One potato, two potato. (Oliver)
40:65-6 Ag1'64. CC       10519
One star general. by Al Morgan.
(Anon.) 35:116-17 Je20'59. B
                         10520

One step to eternity. (McCarten)
31:94*O8'55. CC          10521
The one that got away. by
Kendal Burt and James Leasor.
(Anon.) 33:201-202 O12'57.
B                        10522
One, two, three. (Gill)
37:70-2 Ja6'62. CC       10523
One way pendulum. by N. F.
Simpson. (Panter-Downes)
36:104-105 My28'60 (Oliver)
37:119-20 S30'61. T      10524
One way pendulum. (Gill) 41:169
Mr13'65. CC              10525
The one-eyed man. by Larry L.
King. (Anon.) 42:82-3
Jy30'66. B               10526
O'Neill. by Arthur Gelb and
Barbara Gelb. (N. Bliven)
38:206-10 O27'62. B      10527
O'Neill: son and playwright.
by Louis Sheaffer. (Anon.)
44:127-8 F8'69. B        10528
One-leg: the life and letters of
Henry William Paget, first
marquess of Anglesey, K.G.,
1768-1854. by George
Charles Anglesey. (Anon.)
37:117-18 Ja20'62. B     10529
One-way to New York. by
Claude Roy. (Anon.) 42:245-6
D10'66. B                10530
Onibaba. (Gill) 41:113-14 F27
'65. CC                  10531
Onionhead. (McCarten) 34:93-4
O11'58. CC               10532
Onions in the stew. by Betty
MacDonald. (Anon.) 31:126
Je4'55. B                10533
The only game in town. by
Frank D. Gilroy. (Gill)
44:102 Je1'68. T         10534
Only in America. by Jerome
Lawrence and Robert E. Lee.
(Tynan) 35:97-8 D5'59. T
                         10535
Only one New York. (Gill)
40:185-6 O17'64. CC      10536
Only one year. by Svetlana
Alliluyeva. Paul
Chavchavadze, trans. (Wilson)
45:153-9 S27'69. B       10537
Only to God: the extraordinary
life of Godfrey Lowell.

Cabot. by Leon Harris.
(Anon.) 43:234-7 D2'67. B
                         10538
Only two can play. (Gill)
38:148-9 Mr24'62. CC     10539
Oona O'. by Thomas
Gallagher. (Balliett) 40:118-
20 Ja23'65. B            10540
The open heart. by Nikolai
M. Amosoff. George St.
George, trans. (Anon.) 43:
193 Mr11'67. B           10541
The open mind. by J. Robert
Oppenheimer. (Anon.) 31:
153-4*D17'55. B          10542
Open the door and see all the
people. (Gill) 40:122 Ap18
'64. CC                  10543
Open 24 hours. by Roger
Cornish. (Oliver) 45:92
F22'69. T                10544
Opening night. by John
Cromwell. (Oliver) 39:90
O12'63. T                10545
The opening of a window. by
Gene Radano. (Oliver) 37:
165-6 O14'61. T          10546
Opera as drama. by Joseph
Kerman. (Anon.) 32:190
D15'56. B                10547
The operation. by Leonard
Engel. (Anon.) 34:116 Ja10
'59. B                   10548
Operation crossbow. (Gill)
41:158-9 Ap10'65. CC     10549
Operation mad ball. (McCarten)
33:145-6*N30'57. CC      10550
Operation Noah. by Charles
Lagus. (Anon.) 36:200
S17'60. B                10551
Operation petticoat. (McCarten)
35:196-7 D12'59. CC      10552
Operation sea lion. by Peter
Fleming. (Anon.) 33:79
*Jy20'57. B              10553
An operational necessity. by
Gwyn Griffin. (Anon.) 43:
222 O21'67. B            10554
The opoponax. by Monique
Wittig. Helen Weaver, trans.
(N. Bliven) 42:66-8 Jy2'66.
B                        10555
The Oppenheimer case. by Charles
P. Curtis. (Anon.) 31:160

\*S24'55. B          10556
The opposing self. by Lionel
  Trilling. (Anon.) 31:132
F19'55. B          10557
The opposite sex. (McCarten)
  32:176-9 D15'56. CC   10558
The optimist. by Herbert Gold.
  (Balliett) 35:129-30 Je13'59.
  B                10559
The optimistic tragedy. by
  Vishnevsky. (Flanner) 35:82-3
  Jy11'59. T         10560
Opus posthumous. by Wallace
  Stevens. Samuel French
  Morse, ed. (Anon.) 33:245-6
  D7'57. B           10561
Or I'll dress you in mourning.
  by Larry Collins and
  Dominique Lapierre. (Anon.)
  44:80 Ag31'68. B      10562
Ordeal by ice. Farley Mowat,
  ed. (Anon.) 37:180 Ap22'61.
  B                10563
The ordeal of Major Grigsby.
  by John Sherlock. (Anon.)
  40:188-9 Mr14'64. B    10564
The ordeal of power. by
  Emmet John Hughes. (Rovere)
  39:195-204 Mr16'63. B
                   10565
The ordeal of the captive
  nations. by Hawthorne Daniel
  (Anon.) 34:82-3 Ag9'58. B
                   10566
The ordeal of Woodrow Wilson.
  by Herbert Hoover. (Anon.)
  34:151 My24'58. B     10567
Orders of chivalry. by Peter
  Vansittart. (Wain) 35:166-9
  Ap11'59. B         10568
Orders to kill. (McCarten)
  34:108 N29'58. CC     10569
An ordinary camp. by
  Micheline Maurel. Margaret
  S. Summers, trans. (Anon.)
  34:240-1 N29'58. B    10570
An ordinary lunacy. by Jessica
  Anderson. (West) 40:86-7
  Ag8'64. B          10571
An ordinary man. by Mel
  Arrighi. (Oliver) 44:90
  S28'68. T          10572
The Ordways. by William
  Humphrey. (Anon.) 41:189

My1'65. B          10573
Orfeo in paradise. by Luigi
  Santucci. Joseph Green,
  trans. (Anon.) 45:139-40 Mr22
  '69. B             10574
Orfeu negro. (Flanner) 35:78
  Jy11'59. CC        10575
The organizer. (Gill) 40:191
  My9'64. CC         10576
The Orient express. by Michael
  Barsley. (Anon.) 43:111
  Ag19'67. B         10577
The origin of the solar
  system. Thornton Page, ed.
  (Bernstein) 42:117-32
  My28'66. B         10578
The original water-color
  paintings by John James
  Audubon for "The birds of
  America." Richard
  Ketchum, ed. (Anon.) 42:
  247-8 N12'66. B       10579
The origins of the Second
  World War. by A.J.P.
  Taylor. (Anon.) 37:91-2
  Ja6'62. B          10580
Orlando King. by Isabel
  Colegate. (Anon.) 45:165-6
  My10'69. B         10581
Orphée. by Jean Cocteau.
  (Oliver) 38:77-8 Ja12'63.
  T                10582
Orpheus descending. by
  Tennessee Williams. (Gibbs)
  33:84-6 Mr30'57. (Flanner)
  35:123 Ap4'59. T      10583
Orsini: the story of a con-
  spirator. by Michael St.
  John Packe. (Anon.) 34:109-
  10 My31'58. B      10584
Orvet. by Jean Renoir. (Flanner)
  31:142-3 My7'55. T    10585
Ossian's ride. by Fred Hoyle.
  (Anon.) 35:173 My9'59. B
                   10586
Othello. by William Shakespeare.
  (Panter-Downes) 35:143-4
  Ap25'59 (Panter-Downes) 40:
  98 Je13'64 (Oliver) 40:93-5
  O24'64. T          10587
Othello. (Hamburger) 31:132
  \*S17'55 (Gill) 41:145 F19'66.
  CC               10588

The other America: poverty in
the United States. by
Michael Harrington. (Mac-
donald) 38:82-4 Ja19'63. B
                              10589
Other inquisitions. by Jorge
Luis Borges. Ruth L. C.
Simms, trans. (West) 41:
177-8 My8'65. B        10590
The other kingdom. by Victor
Price. (Anon.) 40:205
Ap25'64. B             10591
The other man. by John Allen.
(Oliver) 43:100-101 F17'68. T
                              10592
The other side of the coin. by
Pierre Boulle. Richard
Howard, trans. (Anon.)
34:236-7 N29'58. B     10593
The other side of the hill.
by Robert Molloy. (Anon.)
38:182 Ap7'62. B       10594
The other side of the river:
Red China today. by Edgar
Snow. (Anon.) 38:77-8
D29'62. B              10595
Other Winters, other Springs.
by Flora Sandstrom.
(Anon.) 39:243-4 N9'63. B
                              10596
The others. by Ann Aikman.
(Anon.) 36:180-1 Ap16'60. B
                              10597
Otto Hahn: a scientific auto-
biography. by Otto Hahn.
Willy Ley, ed. and trans.
(Anon.) 42:68 D31'66. B
                              10598
Our literary heritage. by
Van Wyck Brooks and Otto
L. Bettmann. (Anon.) 32:
180 O27'56. B          10599
Our man Flint. (Gill) 41:124-5
F5'66. CC              10600
Our man in Havana. by Graham
Greene. (Anon.) 34:209
N8'58. B               10601
Our man in Havana. (McCarten)
35:104-105 F6'60. CC   10602
Our mother's house. (Gill)
43:159-60 O14'67. CC   10603
Our Samoan adventure, by
Fanny Stevenson and Robert

Louis Stevenson. Charles
Neider, ed. (Anon.) 31:130
*O1'55. B              10604
Our town. by Thornton Wilder.
(Malcolm) 35:80-2 Ap11'59
(Oliver) 44:98 O5'68 (Gill)
45:166 D6'69. T        10605
Our town. (J. Lardner) 35:207-
208 D5'59. TV          10606
Out in the mid-day sun. by
Boris Gussman. (Anon.)
39:94-5 Ag17'63. B     10607
Out in the open. by Katherine
Hoskins. (Bogan) 35:238
N28'59. B              10608
Out of Noah's ark. by Herbert
Wendt. Michael Bullock, trans.
(Anon.) 36:198 Mr12'60.
B                      10609
Out of the burning. by Ira
Henry Freeman. (Anon.)
36:106 Je25'60. B      10610
Outer dark. by Cormac Mc-
Carthy. (Coles) 45:133-9 Mr
22'69. B               10611
The outrage. (Gill) 40:186-7
O17'64. CC             10612
The outsider. by Colin Wilson.
(Macdonald) 32:187-99
O13'56. B              10613
The outsider. (Gill) 37:119
F17'62. CC             10614
Over the mountains. by
Pamela Frankau. (Anon.)
43:159-60 F25'67. B    10615
The overcoat. (Gill) 41:169
Mr13'65. CC            10616
Overtaken by events. by John
Bartlow Martin. (Rovere)
42:224-41 N26'66. B    10617
The owl and the pussycat. by
Bill Manhoff. (McCarten)
40:131 N28'64. T       10618
The ox cart. by René Marques.
(McCarten) 42:59 D31'66.
T                      10619
The Oxford book of Canadian
verse. A. J. M. Smith, ed.
(Anon.) 37:136 F25'61. B
                              10620
The Oxford book of Irish verse,
XVIIth-XXth century. Donagh
MacDonagh and Lennox

Robinson, eds. (Anon.) 35:178-9
Mr21'59. B            10621
The Oxford book of nineteenth-
century English verse. John
Hayward, ed. (Anon.) 40:227-8
O3'64. B             10622
The Oxford book of Scottish
verse. John MacQueen and
Tom Scott, eds. (Anon.) 43:84
Jy29'67. B            10623
Oyster River: one Summer on an
inland sea. by George
Millar. (Anon.) 40:187 My2'64.
B                    10624

P

P.J. (Kael) 44:158 Mr16'68. CC
                     10625
P.O.W. by Douglas Collins.
(Anon.) 44:98 Ja18'69. B
                     10626
P.S. 193. by David Rayfiel.
(Oliver) 38:146-8 N10'62. T
                     10627
PT 109. (Oliver) 39:68 Jy 13
'63. CC              10628
Paar, Jack. (J. Lardner)
34:114-16 Ap19'58; 34:108-11
S6'58. TV            10629
Pacific ordeal. by Kenneth
Ainslie. (Anon.) 32:127 F9'57.
B                    10630
The pad (and how to use it).
(Adler) 42:88-90 Ag27'66. CC
                     10631
Pagan Spain. by Richard
Wright. (Anon.) 33:150-1 Mr
23'57. B             10632
Paganini, the Genoese.
by G.I.C. de Courcy.
(Sargeant) 34:194-8 O11'58. B
                     10633
The pageant of Stuart England.
by Elizabeth Burton. (Anon.)
38:180 D15'62. B     10634
Pages from the Goncourt
journal. Robert Baldick, ed.
and trans. (West) 38:124-32
Ja26'63. B           10635
Paint your wagon. (Kael) 45:
176-9 O25'69. CC     10636

A pair of briefs. (Gill) 39:123
F15'64. CC           10637
Pairing off. by Julian
Moynahan. (Sissman) 45:180-
2 S20'69. B          10638
The paisley convertible. by
Harry Cauley. (McCarten)
42:132-4 F18'67. T   10639
The pajama game. (Hamburger)
33:72-4 S7'57. CC    10640
Pal Joey. (McCarten) 33:166-7
N2'57. CC            10641
The palace. by Claude Simon.
Richard Howard, trans.(Anon.)
39:245-6 O19'63. B   10642
The palace guard. by Donald
Braider. (Anon.) 34:206
O18'58. B            10643
Palace of ice. by Tayei Vesaas.
Elizabeth Rokkan, trans.
(West) 45:145-6 My3'69. B
                     10644
The palace of money. by W.H.
Manville. (Anon.) 42:104
Ag6'66. B            10645
Pale fire. by Vladimir Nabokov.
(Malcolm) 38:166-75 S22'62.
B                    10646
The pale horse. by Agatha
Christie. (Anon.) 38:115-16
Ja12'63. B           10647
The Panama portrait.
by Stanley Ellin. (Anon.)
38:244-5 N17'62. B   10648
Pandora's last voyage. by
Geoffrey Rawson. (Anon.)
40:206 S12'64. B     10649
Panorama of magic. by
Milbourne Christopher. (Anon.)
40:223 Ap18'64. B    10650
Pantagleize. by Michel de
Ghelderode. (McCarten) 43:93
D9'67. T             10651
Pantaloon. by Philip Toynbee.
(N. Bliven) 38:189-90 My5
'62. B               10652
Papa, Mama, the maid, and I.
(McCarten) 32:64*S8'56. CC
                     10653
Papa's delicate condition. (Gill)
39:143-4 Mr16'63. CC 10654
The paper boats. by Roger

Longrigg. (Anon.) 39:241
N16'63. B                10655
The paper dolls. by Laura
Beheler. (Anon.) 32:181-2
O6'56. B                 10656
Paper lion. by George Plimpton.
(Anon.) 42:245-6 N12'66. B
10657
Paper tiger. by Stanley
Woodward. (Anon.) 40:127-8
F22'64. B                10658
The paper wall. by Ira Morris.
(Anon.) 36:124-5 F11'61. B
10659
Papers of Alexander Hamilton.
by Alexander Hamilton. Harold
C. Syrett, ed. (N. Bliven)
38:232-6 N3'62. B        10660
The papers of Ulysses S. Grant,
1837-61. by Ulysses S. Grant.
John Y. Simon, ed. (Anon.)
43:98-9 Ag26'67. B       10661
Papillon. by Henri Charrière.
(Flanner) 45:200-207 N15'69.
B                        10662
Papirer, Vol. I. by Søren
Kierkegaard. Howard Hong
and Edna Hong, trans. & eds.
(Auden) 44:141-58 My25'68.
B                        10663
Papp. by Kenneth Cameron.
(Oliver) 45:122-3 My10'69. T
10664
Parade. by Jerry Herman.
(Malcolm) 35:46-8 Ja30'60.
T                        10665
The paradise bum. by Andrew
Sinclair. (Anon.) 39:177-8
Mr30'63. B               10666
Paradise now. by Living Theatre.
(Oliver) 44:141-2 O26'68. T
10667
The paradox players. by
Maureen Duffy. (Anon.) 44:
181-2 O5'68. B           10668
Parallax. by Vladimir
Yurasov. Tatiana Balkoff
Drowne, trans. (Anon.) 42:
246 N19'66. B            10669
The paranoid style in American
politics and other essays. by
Richard Hofstadter. (Anon.)
41:119 Ja15'66. B        10670

Parasitism and subversion: the
case of Latin America. by
Stanislav Andreski. (Anon.)
43:150-2 My27'67. B      10671
Paris belongs to us. (Gill)
38:235-6 N10'62. CC      10672
Paris blues. (Gill) 37:130-1
N11'61. CC               10673
Paris fin de siècle. by Jean
Roman. (Anon.) 36:108 S3'60.
B                        10674
Paris holiday. (McCarten) 34:
92 My17'58. CC           10675
Paris is out! by Richard
Seff. (Gill) 45:72 F7'70. T
10676
A Paris surgeon's story. by
Charles F. Bove and Dana Lee
Thomas. (Anon.) 32:131-2*F25
'56. B                   10677
Paris under seige, 1870-71: from
the Goncourt journal. by
Jules de Goncourt. George J.
Becker, ed. & trans. (Anon.)
45:88 Ja31'70. B         10678
Paris when it sizzles. (Gill)
40:167-8 Ap11'64. CC     10679
The Parkman reader. by
Francis Parkman. Samuel
Eliot Morison, ed. (Anon.)
31:144 My21'55. B        10680
Parlez-vous Franglais? by
René Etiemble. (Flanner)
40:104-106 F22'64. B     10681
Parodies: an anthology from
Chaucer to Beerbohm--and
after. Dwight Macdonald, ed.
(Updike) 37:163-76 S16' 61.
B                        10682
Parrish. (Oliver) 37:108
My27'61. CC              10683
Part of a long story. by
Agnes Boulton. (Anon.) 34:
128-9 S6'58. B           10684
Part of our time: some ruins
and monuments of the thirties.
by Murray Kempton. (Rovere)
31:131-7 My21'55. B      10685
The parting of the way: Lao
Tzu and the Taoist movement.
by Holmes Welch. (Anon.)
33:154-5 S7'57. B        10686
Partir avant du jour. by Julien

Green. (Flanner) 39:134-6
O12'63. B          10687
Partisans. by Peter Matthiessen.
(Anon.) 31:179-80*O8'55. B
10688
The party. by Rudolph von
Abele. (Balliett) 39:175-6 My
18'63. B          10689
A party for divorce. by Lee
Kalcheim. (Oliver) 42:85-6
O22'66. T          10690
Party of one. by Clifton
Fadiman. (Anon.) 31:126-7
Ap30'55. B          10691
The party on Greenwich Avenue.
by Grandin Conover. (Oliver)
43:140-1 My20'67. T          10692
A party with Betty Comden and
Adolph Green. by Betty
Comden and Adolph Green.
(Tynan) 34:70 Ja10'59. B
10693
Passage of arms. by Eric
Ambler. (Anon.) 36:158-9 Mr26
'60. B          10694
Passage through the Red Sea.
by Zofia Romanowicz. Virgilia
Peterson, trans. (Anon.)
38:243-4 D8'62. B          10695
A passage to England. by
Nirad C. Chaudhuri. (Anon.)
36:241-2 N12'60. B          10695a
A passage to India. by Santha
Rama Rau. (Panter-Downes)
36:184-7 My14'60 (McCarten)
37:94 F10'62. T          10696
Passages from James Joyce's
Finnegans wake. (Gill) 43:
159 O14'67. CC          10697
Passenger to London. by
Gerard Fay. (Anon.) 37:119
Je17'61. B          10698
Passing through from exotic
places. by Ronald Ribman.
(Oliver) 45:57-8 D20'69. T
10699
Passing time. by Michel Butor.
Jean Stewart, trans. (Anon.)
36:117 Ja14'61. B          10700
A passion for Sicilians: the world
around Danilo Dolci. by Jerre
Mangione. (Anon.) 45:76 Ag2
'69. B          10701

The passion of Josef D. by
Paddy Chayefsky. (McCarten)
40:92 F22'64. T          10702
The passion of slow fire. (Gill)
38:204 O27'62. CC          10703
The passionate exiles: Madame
de Staël and Madame Ré-
camier. by Maurice Levaillant.
Malcolm Barnes, trans.
(Anon.) 34:148 My10'58. B
10704
A passionate prodigality. by
Guy Chapman. (Anon.)
42:144 Je18'66. B          10705
The passionate state of mind.
by Eric Hoffer. (Rovere)
31:138-9 My21'55. B          10706
Passionate Summer. (McCarten)
33:71-2 *Ag10'57. CC          10707
Passport to Paris. by Vernon
Duke. (Anon.) 32:148-9
*Ap7'56. B          10708
The password is courage. by
John Castle. (Anon.) 31:162-3
*S17'55. B          10709
The past we share. by Peter
Quennell and Alan Hodge.
(Anon.) 36:162-3 D17'60.
B          10710
The Pasternak affair: courage
of genius, a documentary
report. by Robert Conquest.
(Anon.) 38:179-80 S22'62. B
10711
Patate. by Marcel Achard.
Irwin Shaw, adapt. (J. Lard-
ner) 34:91 N8'58. T          10712
A patch of blue. (Gill) 41:58-61
D25'65. CC          10713
The Pathans. by Olaf Caroe.
(Anon.) 35:174-5 Ap18'59.
B          10714
Pather panchali. (McCarten)
34:170-1 N1'58. CC          10715
Paths of glory. (McCarten)
33:70 Ja4'58. CC          10716
A patriot for me. by John
Osborne. (Panter-Downes) 41:
59-60 Jy31'65 (Gill) 45:85
O11'69. T          10717
The patriots. by James Barlow.
(Anon.) 36:106 S3'60. B
10718

Patterns. (McCarten) 32:78
*Ap14'56. CC          10719
Patton. (Kael) 45:73-5 Ja31'70.
CC                    10720
Paul Klee. by Felix Klee.
Richard Winston and Clara
Winston, trans. (Anon.) 38:115
Ja12'63. B            10721
Pauline. by Pierson Dixon.
(Anon.) 41:79 Jy31'65. B
                      10722
Pauvre Bitos. by Jean Anouilh.
(Flanner) 32:84-7 N3'56. T
                      10723
Pavannes and divagations. by
Ezra Pound. (Anon.) 35:180
Mr21'59. B            10724
The pawnbroker. by Edward
Lewis. (Anon.) 37:90 Ag19'61.
B                     10725
The pawnbroker. (Gill) 41:164-5
Ap24'65. CC           10726
Paxton Quigley's had the
course. by Stephen H. Yafa.
(S. Lardner) 44:189-90
Ap20'68. B            10727
Peace. by Aristophanes. (Oliver)
44:98-100 F8'69. T    10728
Peace agitator: the story of
A.J. Muste. by Nat
Hentoff. (Anon.) 39:111-12 Ja
25'64. B              10729
Peace and war. by Ramond
Aron. (Steiner) 42:117-22 Ja
14'67. B              10730
Peace in Piccadilly: the story of
Albany. by Sheila Birkenhead.
(Anon.) 34:204 O11'58. B
                      10731
Peaceable lane. by Keith
Wheeler. (Anon.) 36:61 D24'60.
B                     10732
The peacemakers: the great
powers and American
independence. by Richard B.
Morris. (Anon.) 41:246-7
N6'65. B              10733
Peary: the explorer and the man.
by John Edward Weems. (Anon.)
43:153-4 Ap1'67. B    10734
Pebbles from my skull. by Stuart
Hood. (Anon.) 39:70-1 Ag31'63.
B                     10735

The peddler. by William
Stevens. (Anon.) 42:247 O22'66.
B                     10736
Pedlock & Sons. by Stephen
Longstreet. (Anon.) 42:241
D3'66 B               10737
Peer Gynt. by Henrik Ibsen.
(Malcolm) 35:72-5 Ja23'60.
T                     10738
Peking and Moscow. by Klaus
Mehnert. Leila Vennewitz,
trans. (Anon.) 39:236-7 D
14'63. B              10739
The pen and the sword. by
Michael Foot. (Anon.) 38:78-
9 D29'62. B           10740
The penance way. by Merton
Naydler. (Anon.) 45:120 Mr
1'69. B               10741
Penelope. (Gill) 42:183-4
N19'66. CC            10742
The penetrators. by Benjamin
Gwilliam Aston. (N. Bliven)
41:89-94 Ag7'65. B    10743
Pennant race. by Jim Brosnan.
(Anon.) 38:88 Ag11'62. B
                      10744
The penny wars. by Elliott
Baker. (Gill) 45:137-8 O25'69.
T                     10745
The penthouse. (Gill) 43:148 O7
'67. CC               10746
People and life, 1891-1921. by
Ilya Ehrenburg, Anna
Bostock and Yvonne Kapp.
(Anon.) 39:177-8 Mr9'63.
B                     10747
The people and the court:
judicial review in a democracy.
by Charles L. Black, Jr.
(Anon.) 36:160 Mr26'60. B
                      10748
The people and the police. by
Algernon D. Black. (Anon.)
44:215 O12'68. B      10749
People is the thing that the
world is fullest of. by Bil
Baird, et al. (Oliver) 43:132
Mr4'67. T             10750
People kill people, sometimes.
(J. Lardner) 35:163-4 O17'59.
TV                    10751
The people of Moscow. by

Henri Cartier-Bresson. (Anon.)
31:135-6*F18'56. B        10752
People of Providence Street.
by John Gooding. (Gilliatt)
45:115-17 Mr1'69. B        10753
The people of the forest. by
Hans Lidman. (Anon.) 39:195
S28'63. B        10754
People of the reeds. by Gavin
Maxwell. (Anon.) 34:139-40
F22'58. B        10755
The people of the sea. by David
Thomson. (Anon.) 43:193-6
Ap22'67. B        10756
The people one knows. by
Robert Boles. (Anon.) 41:163
F20'65. B        10757
People or personnel: decentra-
lizing and the mixed system.
by Paul Goodman. (N. Bliven)
41:124-7 Ag21'65. B        10758
The people vs. Ranchman. by
Megan Terry. (Oliver) 44:116-
18 N9'68. T        10759
The people's war: Britain--1939-
45. by Angus Calder. (Steiner)
45:74-81 Ja17'70. B        10760
Pepe. (Angell) 36:50
D31'60. CC        10761
Pepote. (McCarten) 34:99
D20'58. CC        10762
The peregrine. by J.A. Baker.
(Anon.) 43:213-14 O28'67. B
        10763
The perennial Philadelphians:
the anatomy of an American
aristocracy. by Nathaniel
Burt. (Anon.) 39:243 N16'63.
B        10764
The perfect party. by Charles H.
Fuller, Jr. (Oliver) 45:105
Mr29'69. T        10765
The perfect setup. by Jack
Sher. (McCarten) 38:112 N3'62.
T        10766
A perfect woman. by L.P.
Hartley. (West) 32:99*Mr31'56.
B        10767
Pericles the Athenian. by Rex
Warner. (Anon.) 38:158-60
F16'63. B        10768
A peril and a hope. by Alice
Kimball Smith. (Anon.) 41:
244 N27'65. B        10769

Period of adjustment. by
Tennessee Williams. (Mc-
Carten) 36:93-4 N19'60. T
        10770
Period of adjustment. (Gill)
38:234 N10'62. CC        10771
Perry Mason. (J. Lardner)
34:60-3 Ap2'58. TV        10772
A person from England and
other travellers to Turkestan.
by Fitzroy Maclean. (Anon.)
35:172-3 Ap18'59. B
        10773
Person to person. (J. Lardner)
33:104-106 Ja11'58; 35
235-8 N14'59. TV        10774
Persona. (Gill) 43:180-1 Mr11
'67. CC        10775
Pete Kelly's blues. (Hamburger)
31:76-7*Ag27'55. CC        10776
Peter Breughel the elder. by
Gustav Glück. (Anon.) 31:215
*D5'55. B        10777
Peter Perry. by Michael
Campbell. (Anon.) 36:205-206
O15'60. B        10778
The pets' cookbook. by Richard
de Rochemont. (Fisher)
42:161-3 Ap30'66. B        10779
Petulia. (Gilliatt) 44:87
Je15'68. CC        10780
Peyton Place. (McCarten) 33:52-4
D21'57. CC        10781
Phaedra. (Gill) 38:203-204
O27'62. CC        10782
The phantom horse. (McCarten)
32:54*Ag4'56. CC        10783
The phantom major. by Virginia
Cowles. (Anon.) 34:242 D6'58.
B        10784
Pharos and Pharillon. by E.M.
Forster. (Anon.) 38:187-8
Mr17'62. B        10785
Phèdre. by Jean Baptiste
Racine. William Packard,
trans. (Oliver) 41:130 F19'66.
T        10786
Phèdre. (Flanner) 44:151-2 O5
'68. CC        10787
The Phenix City story. (Ham-
burger) 31:132 S17'55. CC
        10788
Philadelphia, here I come!
by Brian Friel. (McCarten)

42:71 F26'66. T            10789
The Philadelphian. by Richard
Powell. (Anon.) 32:141-2
F16'57. B            10790
Philoktetes. by George
Maxim Ross. (Balliett)
37:123-4 My6'61. T            10791
Philosophy in the twentieth
century. William Barrett
and Henry D. Aiken, eds.
(Anon.) 38:247-8 D1'62.
B            10792
Philosophy of science today.
Sidney Morgenbesser, ed.
(Anon.) 43:75-6 Jy1'67.
B            10793
Phoenix '55. by David Baker,
David Craig and Ira Wallach.
(Gibbs) 31:67-9 Ap30'55. T
10794
Photo finish. by Peter
Ustinov. (Panter-Downes) 38:
85-6 Je2'62 (McCarten) 39:
112 F23'63. T            10795
The photographer. by Pierre
Boulle. Xan Fielding,
trans. (Anon.) 44:248 N23'68.
B            10796
The photographic history of
the Civil War. by Francis
Trevelyan Miller. (Anon.)
33:70-1 D28'57. B            10797
The physician in spite of him-
self. by Molière. (Malcolm)
35:84 Je13'59. T            10798
The physicists. by James
Kirkup. (McCarten) 40:93
O24'64. T            10799
The picaresque saint. by R.W.B.
Lewis. (Anon.) 35:148 F21'59.
B            10800
Picasso and his friends. by
Fernande Olivier. Jane
Miller, trans. (Anon.) 41:244-6
N20'65. B            10801
Picasso: his life and work. by
Roland Penrose. (Anon.) 35:
94  Je27'59. B            10802
Picasso: variations on Velásquez'
painting "The maids of honor."
by Jaime Sabartés. (Anon.)
35:239 D12'59. B            10803

Picasso's Picassos. by David
Douglas Duncan. (Anon.)
37:246-7 N25'61. B            10804
Pickett's charge. by George R.
Stewart. (Anon.) 35:205
O31'59. B            10805
Pickpocket. (Gill) 39:154
My25'63. CC            10806
Pickwick. by Wolf Mankowitz,
Leslie Bricusse and Cyril
Arnadel. (McCarten) 41:195
O16'65. T            10807
Picnic. (McCarten) 32:121
*F25'56. CC            10808
The picnic at Sakkara. by P.H.
Newby. (Anon.) 31:141-2
*S10'55. B            10809
Picnic on the battlefield. by
Fernando Arrabal. (Oliver)
38:86 Mr10'62. T            10810
Picnic on the grass. (Gill)
36:132-3 O15'60. CC            10811
Pictorial history of America.
Editors of Year, eds. (Anon.)
31:134-5*O1'55. B            10812
A pictorial history of the
American Indian. by Oliver
LaFarge. (Anon.) 32:107-108
Ja26'57. B            10813
A pictorial history of the
talkies. by Daniel Blum.
(Anon.) 34:244 D6'58. B
10814
Pictures in the hallway. by
Paul Shyre. (Oliver) 40:52-3
D26'64. T            10815
Picturesque itinerary of the Hud-
son River and the peripheral
parts of North America. by
J. Milbert. Constance D.
Sherman, trans. & ed. (Anon.)
45:143 Ap5'69. B            10816
The piebald standard. by Edith
Simon. (Anon.) 35:134*D19'59.
B            10817
A piece of my mind. by Edmund
Wilson. (Anon.) 32:242 N17
'56. B            10818
Pigeons. by Lawrence Osgood.
(Oliver) 41:108 Mr13'65. T
10819
Pigtails and pernod. by

Simona Pakenham. (N. Bliven) 37:137-40 F17'62. B 10820
The pilgrim hawk. by Glenway Wescott. (Moss) 43:184-91 Mr11'67. B 10821
Pilgrimage. by Dorothy Richardson. (N. Bliven) 44:181-6 My4'68. B 10822
Pillar of salt. by Seymour Epstein. (Anon.) 35:105-106 Ja30'60. B 10823
The pillar of salt. by Albert Memmi. (West) 39:181-6 S21'63. B 10824
The pillow fight. by Nicholas Monsarrat. (Anon.) 41:187 Mr20'65. B 10825
Pillow talk. (McCarten) 35:197-8 O17'59. CC 10826
The Piltdown forgery. by J.S. Weiner. (Anon.) 31:161 My 7'55. B 10827
The pink panther. (Gill) 40:88 My2'64. CC 10828
Pioneer, go home! by Richard Powell. (Anon.) 34:136-7 F14'59. B 10829
Pipe dream. by Oscar Hammerstein, II and Richard Rodgers. (Gibbs) 31:96-8 *D10'55. T 10830
The pistol. by James Jones. (West) 35:165-6 Ap4'59. B 10831
The pit and the century plant. by Pati Hill. (Anon.) 31:181 *O8'55. B 10832
The pit and the pendulum. (Gill) 37:113 S9'61. CC 10833
The pitcher and the well. Anon. (Anon.) 39:116 Je22'63. B 10834
Pity him afterwards. by Donald E. Westlake. (Anon.) 40:136 My30'64. B 10835
The place for chance. by Winthrop Palmer, Maurice Edwards and Jean Reavey. (Oliver) 40:134-6 My23'64. T 10836
A place in the country. by Sarah Gainham. (Anon.)

45:96 Ag23'69. B 10837
A place of stone. by Jim Hunter. (Anon.) 40:192 Ap4'64. B 10838
The plains of Camdeboo. by Eve Palmer. (N. Bliven) 43:189-93 Mr18'67. B 10839
A planet called Earth. by George Gamow. (Bernstein) 39:241-4 N23'63. B 10840
Planet of the apes. (Kael) 43:108-109 F17'68. CC 10841
A plate of red herrings. by Richard Lockridge. (Anon.) 44:240 N9'68. B 10842
Platero and I. by Juan Ramón Jiménez. Eloise Roach, trans. (Anon.) 33:149 S7 '57. B 10843
Play. by Samuel Beckett. (Oliver) 40:79 Ap4'64. T 10844
Play it again, Sam. by Woody Allen. (Gill) 45:89-90 F22'69. T 10845
The play of the week. (J. Lardner) 35:129-32 F13'60. TV 10846
Play with a tiger. by Doris Lessing. (Oliver) 40:86-7 Ja9'65. T 10847
The playboy of the western world. (Gill) 39:170-1 Mr23'63. CC 10848
The playground. (Gill) 41:191 O9'65. CC 10849
Playhouse 90. (J. Lardner) 34:70-5 Jy12'58. TV 10850
The playroom. by Mary Drayton. (McCarten) 41:152-4 D18'65. T 10851
Plays for Bleeker Street. by Thornton Wilder. (Oliver) 36:64-8 Ja20'62. T 10852
Playtime. (Gill) 38:123 Ja26'63 (Flanner) 43:96-7 Ja20'68. CC 10853
Plaza suite. by Neil Simon. (Gill) 44:75-6 F24'68. T 10854
Please don't eat the daisies. (McCarten) 36:107-108 Ap9'60. CC 10855

Please turn over. (Oliver) 37:107-108 My27'61. CC    10856
The pleasure garden. by Oakley Hall. (Anon.) 42:244-5 O8'66. B    10857
The pleasure of his company. by Samuel Taylor. (J. Lardner) 34:97-8 N1'58. T    10858
The pleasure of his company. (Oliver) 37:78-80 Je17'61. CC    10859
Pleasure of ruins. by Rose Macaulay. (Anon.) 42:119-20 Ja21'67. B    10860
The pledge. by Friedrich Duerrenmatt. (Anon.) 35:172 Ap18'59. B    10861
Ploesti. by James Dugan and Carroll Stewart. (Liebling) 38:221-9 O20'62. B    10862
The plough and the stars. by Sean O'Casey. (Balliett) 36:96-8 D17'60. T    10863
The poacher's daughter. (Mc-Carten) 36:168 Mr5'60. CC    10864
The pocket Venus: a Victorian scandal. by Henry Blyth. (Anon.) 43:147 Je3'67. B    10865
Poème de l'angle droit. by Charles Édouard Jeanneret-Gris. (Flanner) 31:114-15 *D3'55. B    10866
Poèmes et extraits de lettres. by Minou Drouet. (Flanner) 31:115-17*D3'55. B    10867
Poems. by Elizabeth Bishop. (Bogan) 31:179*O8'55. B    10868
Poems. by Alan Dugan. (Bogan) 38:175 Mr24'62. B    10869
Poems 1947-1957. by William Jay Smith. (Bogan) 34:124 Mr29'58. B    10870
The poems of Edward Taylor. by Edward Taylor. Donald E. Stanford, ed. (Anon.) 36:187-8 O29'60. B    10871
The poems of Emily Dickinson. by Emily Dickinson. Thomas H. Johnson, ed. (Bogan)

31:178-9*O8'55. B    10872
Poems written in early youth. By T.S. Eliot. (Anon.) 43:88 S2'67. B    10873
The poet and the donkey. by May Sarton. (Anon.) 45:206-209 N8'69. B    10874
Poet in New York. by Federico García Lorca. Ben Belitt, trans. (Anon.) 31:104*Ja14'56. B    10875
The poetry of W.H. Auden: the disenchanted isle. by Monroe K. Spears. (Anon.) 39:96-7 D21'63. B    10876
Poet's choice. Paul Engle and Joseph Langland, eds. (Anon.) 39:76 Jy6'63. B    10877
Poets of today IV. John Hall Wheelock, ed. (Bogan) 33:174-5 S14'57. B    10878
Point blank. .(Gill) 43:112-14 S30'67. CC    10879
Point of departure: an attempt at autobiography. by James Cameron. (Anon.) 44:134-5 F24'68. B    10880
Point of order! (Gill) 39:72 Ja18'64. CC    10881
The poker session. by Hugh Leonard. (Oliver) 43:134-6 O7'67. T    10882
The polar passion. by Farley Mowat. (Anon.) 44:175-6 My11'68. B    10883
The policemen. by Slawomir Mrozek. (Oliver) 37:118-19 D2'61. T    10884
The political ideas of Harold J. Laski. by Herbert A. Deane. (Anon.) 31:153-4 Mr 19'55. B    10885
Politics and diplomacy of peace-making: containment and counterrevolution at Versailles, 1918-19. by Arno J. Mayer. (Anon.) 44:154-5 Mr9'68. B    10886
The politics of hysteria. by Edmund Stillman and William Pfaff. (Anon.) 40:207-208 My16'64. B    10887

The politics of socialism. by
R. H. S. Crossman. (Anon.)
41:159-60 F19'66. B      10888
The politics of upheaval. by
Arthur M. Schlesinger, Jr.
(Anon.) 36:182-3 O1'60. B
10889
Pomp and circumstance. by
Noël Coward. (Anon.) 36:54-6
D31'60. B                10890
Pompes funèbres. by Jean
Genet. (Adler) 39:234-7 N9
'63. B                   10891
The ponder heart. by Joseph
Fields and Jerome Chodorov.
(Gibbs) 32:86*F25'56. T
10892
The Pooh perplex: a freshman
casebook. by Frederick C.
Crews. (Anon.) 39:78 Ja4'64.
B                        10893
Poor Bitos. by Jean Anouilh.
(McCarten) 40:143 N21'64. T
10894
Poor cow. (Kael) 43:92-3
F3'68. CC                10895
Poor no more. by Robert
Ruark. (Malcolm) 35:68-70
Ja2'60. B                10896
The poor old liberal arts. by
Robert I. Gannon. (Anon.)
37:179 S16'61. B         10897
Poor Richard. by Jean Kerr.
(McCarten) 40:152-4
D12'64. T                10898
The poorhouse fair. by John
Updike. (Balliett) 34:138-40
F7'59. B                 10899
The poorhouse state. by
Richard M. Elman. (Hentoff)
42:237-46 N19'66. B      10900
Popcorn. (Kael) 45:163 N29'69.
CC                       10901
Popi. (S. Lardner) 45:81-2
My31'69. CC              10902
Popular music, an annotated
index of American popular
songs, Volume I, 1950-59.
Nat Shapiro, ed. (Anon.)
40:230 O17'64. B         10903
The population explosion. (J.
Lardner) 36:154-5 F20'60.
TV                       19904

Porgy and Bess. (McCarten) 35:
65-6 Jy4'59. CC          10905
Pork Chop Hill. (McCarten)
35:117-18 Je13'59. CC    10906
Pornografia. by Witold
Gombrowicz. Alastair
Hamilton, trans. (Updike)
43:169-76 S23'67. B      10907
Porte de Lilas. (Flanner)
33:130-1 O19'57. CC      10908
Portnoy's complaint. by Philip
Roth. (Gill) 45:118-20
Mr8'69. B                10909
Portofino. by Louis Bellson,
Will Irwin and Richard
Ney. (Gibbs) 34:58-60 Mr1
'58. T                   10910
Portrait in black. (McCarten)
36:55 Ag6'60. CC         10911
Portrait in brownstone. by
Louis Auchincloss. (Anon.)
38:97-8 Ag18'62. B       10912
Portrait in oil: the autobiography
of Nubar Gulbenkian. by
Nubar Gulbenkian. (Anon.)
41:203 D18'65. B         10913
Portrait of a decade: the
second American revolution.
by Anthony Lewis  and the
New York Times. (Anon.)
40:247 D12'64. B         10914
Portrait of a father. by Joan
Simon. (Anon.) 36:190 O22
'60. B                   10915
Portrait of a general. by
William B. Willcox. (Anon.)
40:196 My9'64. B         10916
Portrait of a madonna. by
Tennessee Williams. (Tynan)
35:82-4 Ap25'59. T       10917
Portrait of a queen. by William
Francis. (Gill) 44:130 Mr9
'68. T                   10918
Portrait of a spy. by Gilbert
Renault-Roulier.
Lancelot C. Sheppard, trans.
(Anon.) 31:177*O15'55. B
10919
Portrait of Barrie. by Cynthia
Asquith. (Anon.) 31:158-9
*S24'55. B               10920
Portrait of Elgar. by Michael
Kennedy. (Anon.) 44:246-8

N30'68. B                 10921
A portrait of Japan. by Laurens
van der Post and Burt
Glinn. (Anon.) 44:107-108
D21'68. B                 10922
Portrait of Jason. (Gill)
43:159 O14'67. CC        10923
Portrait of Manet by himself
and his contemporaries.
by Edouard Manet.  Pierre
Courthion and Pierre Cailler,
eds. Michael Ross, trans.
(Anon.) 38:107-108 Je23
'62. B                    10924
A portrait of the artist as a
young man.  by Frederic
Ewen, Phoebe Brand and
John Randolph. (Oliver) 38:83
Je9'62. T                 10925
Portrait of the assassin.
by Gerald R. Ford and
John R. Stiles. (Anon.) 41:74
Jy3'65. B                 10926
Portraits from memory, and
other essays. by Bertrand
Russell. (Anon.) 32:241-2
N17'56. B                 10927
Portraits of Russian per-
sonalities between reform
and revolution. by Richard
Hare. (West) 35:214-24
O17'59. B                 10928
The positive thinkers. by
Donald Meyer.  (Anon.)
41:120 Ag14'65. B         10929
The possessors. by John
Christopher. (Anon.) 41:162-3
F20'65. B                 10930
The possessors. (McCarten)
35:58-61 Ag1'59. CC       10931
Possibilities. by Arthur
Pittman. (Oliver) 44:182-3
D14'68. T                 10932
Post-impressionism: from van
Gogh to Gauguin. by John
Rewald. (Anon.) 32:235-6
D8'56. B                  10933
Postmark zero. by Robert
Nemiroff. (McCarten)
41:154 N13'65. T          10934
Post-war years: 1945-54. by
Ilya Ehrenburg. Tatiana
Shebunina, trans. (Anon.)

43:244-5 N25'67. B        10935
Pot bouille. (McCarten) 34:183
N8'58. CC                 10936
The potting shed. by Graham
Greene. (J. Lardner)
32:70-2 F9'57. T          10937
Pound/Joyce. by Ezra Pound
and James Joyce. Forrest
Read, ed. (Bogan) 44:133-4
Mr30'68. B                10938
A pound on demand. by Sean
O'Casey. (Tynan) 35:84-5
Ap25'59. T                10939
Pousse-café. by Jerome
Weidman, Duke Ellington,
Marshall Barer and Fred
Tobias. (McCarten) 42:120
Mr26'66. T                10940
Poverty and deprivation. by Con-
ference on Economic Progress.
(Macdonald) 38:94-132
Ja19'63. B                10941
Power and diplomacy. by Dean
Acheson. (Anon.) 34:
145-6 Ap5'58. B           10942
Power and influence. by
William Henry Beveridge.
(Anon.) 31:176 My14'55. B
                          10943
Power and policy in the
U.S.S.R. by Robert Con-
quest. (Anon.) 37:91-2 Ag
19'61. B                  10944
The power and the glory. by
Denis Cannan and Pierre
Bost. (Malcolm) 34:72-4 D20
'58. T                    10945
Power at the Pentagon. by
Jack Raymond. (Anon.) 40:
206 My16'64. B            10946
Power in the Kremlin from
Krushchev to Kosygin. by
Michel Tatu. Helen Katel,
trans. (Anon.) 45:152 Mr
29'69. B                  10947
The power of darkness. by
Leo Tolstoy. (Malcolm)
35:129-30 O10'59. T       10948
The power of life or death. by
Michael V. DiSalle and
Lawrence G. Blochman.
(Anon.) 41:247-8 N13'65. B
                          10949

The power structure: political process in American society. by Arnold M. Rose. (Anon.) 43:83-4 Ag5'67. B 10950

Power without property. by Adolf A. Berle. (Anon.) 35:200 O24'59. B 10951

The Praeger picture encyclopedia of art. Anon. (Anon.) 34:244 N29'58. B 10952

Praise a fine day. by Sigrid de Lima. (Anon.) 35:84 Jy11'59. B 10953

A prayer for my brethren. by Mladen Oljača. Alec Brown, trans. (Anon.) 39: 194 S14'63. B 10954

Predilections. by Marianne Moore. (Bogan) 31:63 *Jy30'55. B 10955

Prefabrications. by Josephine Miles. (Bogan) 32:146*Ap7'56. B 10956

Près de Colette. See Close to Colette. B 10957

Present at the creation. by Dean Acheson. (Anon.) 45:119 D20'69. B 10958

The presidency today. by Edward Corwin and Louis W. Koenig. (Anon.) 32: 155-6*Ap14'56. B 10959

The president's analyst. (Gill) 43:74 Ja6'68. CC 10960

The Presidents' men: White House assistants of Franklin D. Roosevelt, Harry S. Truman, Dwight D. Eisenhower, John F. Kennedy, and Lyndon B. Johnson. by Patrick Anderson. (Anon.) 44:203 N2'68. B 10961

Pretty Leslie. by R. V. Cassill. (Anon.) 39:71 Jy6 '63. B 10962

The pretty penny. by J. D. Scott. (Anon.) 40:223 O3'64. B 10963

Pretty poison. (Kael) 44:180-1 N2'68. CC 10964

The prevalence of people. by Marston Bates. (Anon.) 31:141-2 My21'55. B 10965

The price. by Arthur Miller. (Gill) 43:99 F17'68. T 10966

The price of my soul. by Bernadette Devlin. (Anon.) 45:75-6 Ja10'70. B 10967

The price of power. by Herbert Agar. (Anon.) 33:74-5 *Jy27'57. B 10968

Pride and prejudice. by Abe Burrows, Robert Goldman, Glenn Paxton, George Weiss. (Tynan) 35:89-90 My28'59. T 10969

The pride and the passion. (McCarten) 33:48-9 Jy13'57. CC 10970

The prime of Miss Jean Brodie. by Jay Allen. (Panter-Downes) 42:85-6 Jy9 '66 (Gill) 43:84 Ja27'68. T 10971

The prime of Miss Jean Brodie. (Kael) 45:160-1 Mr15'69. CC 10972

Primitive art. by Douglas Fraser. (Anon.) 38:247-8 D8'62. B 10973

Prince Albert and Victorian taste. by Winslow Ames. (Anon.) 44:175 My18'68. B 10974

The prince and the showgirl. (McCarten) 33:68*Je22'57. CC 10975

Prince of carpetbaggers. by Jonathan Daniels. (Anon.) 34:167 S13'58. B 10976

A prince of Mantua. by Maria Bellonci. (Anon.) 32:202-203 O13'56. B 10977

The prince of pleasure and his regency 1811-20. by J. B. Priestley. (Anon.) 45: 120 D20'69. B 10978

The princes. by Manohar Malgonkar. (Anon.) 39:244-5 N23'63. B 10979

Princess Mathilde. by Joanna Richardson. (Anon.) 45:210 N8'69. B 10980

A prison, a paradise. by Loran
Hurnscot. (Anon.) 34:127
Ja24'59. B                    10981
The prisoner. (McCarten) 31:134
*D17'55. CC                  10982
Privacy and freedom. by
Alan F. Westin. (Anon.)
43:177 S23'67. B              10983
Private. by Lester Atwell.
(Anon.) 34:62 Jy5'58. B
                             10984
Private demons. by Macdonald
Harris. (Anon.) 37:138-9
F10'62. B                    10985
The private ear. by Peter
Shaffer. (McCarten)
39:99-100 O19'63. T          10986
Private lives. by Noël Coward.
(Gill) 45:115-16 D13'69. T
                             10987
Private property. (McCarten)
36:137-8 My21'60. CC  10988
The private world of high
society. by Lucy Kavaler.
(Malcolm) 36:234-8 D10'60.
B                            10989
Private's progress. (McCarten)
32:54*Ag4'56. CC            10990
Privilege. (Gilliatt) 43:70-2
Jy29'67. CC                 10991
A privileged character. by
Jean Laborde. Francis
Price, trans. (Anon.) 39:183
My11'63. B                   10992
Proconsul in politics: a study
of Lord Milner in opposition
and in power. by A.M.
Gollin. (Anon.) 40:123-4
Ag22'64. B                   10993
The prodigal. by Jack
Richardson. (Malcolm)
36:104-107 F20'60. T   10994
The prodigal. (McCarten)
31:129-30 My21'55. CC
                             10995
The prodigal rake: memoirs of
William Hickey. by William
Hickey. Peter Quennell, ed.
(Balliett) 38:178-81 Ap21'62.
B                            10996
The prodigal son. by Langston
Hughes. (Oliver) 41:61-2
My29'65. T                   10997

The producers. (Kael) 44:140-1
Mr23'68. CC                 10998
Products of the perfected
civilization: selected
writings of Chamfort. by
Sebastien Roch Nicholas Cham-
fort. W.S. Merwin, trans.
(Anon.) 45:191-2 O25'69.
B                            10999
The professional soldier.
by Morris Janowitz. (Anon.)
36:242 N12'60. B          11000
The professional writer in
Elizabethan England. by
Edwin Haviland Miller.
(Anon.) 35:68 Ag1'59. B
                             11001
The professionals. (Gill) 42:199
N5'66. CC                  11002
The professor and the commis-
sions. by Bernard Schwartz.
(Anon.) 35:120 F28'59. B
                             11003
The professor and the prime
minister: the official life of
Professor F.A. Lindemann,
Viscount Cherwell. by Freder-
ick Winston Birkenhead.
(Anon.) 38:143 Mr31'62. B
                             11004
Profiles in courage. by John
F. Kennedy. (Anon.) 31:97-8
*F4'56. B                  11005
Promenade. by Al Carmines
and Maria Irene Fornes.
(Oliver) 45:63 Jy5'69. T
                             11006
Prometheus: the life of Balzac.
by André Maurois. Norman
Denny, trans. (West) 42:88-9
Jy9'66. B                  11007
The promise. by Aleksei
Arbuzov. Ariadne Nicolaeff,
trans. (McCarten) 43:149
N25'67. T                  11008
Promise at dawn. by Romain
Gary. (Flanner) 36:85-8
Ag27'60 (Anon.) 37:210-11
O21'61. B                  11009
Promise of greatness: the war
of 1914-18. George A.
Panichas, ed. (Anon.) 44:
99-100 Ja18'69. B         11010

Promises, promises. by Neil Simon, Burt Bacharach and Hal David. (Gill) 44:139 D7'68 (Watt) 44:84-6 Ja18'69. T 11011

Propaganda: the formation of men's attitudes. by Jacques Ellul. Konrad Kellen and Jean Lerner, trans. (Anon.) 41:143-4 F12'66. B 11012

The prophet. by Sholem Asch. (Anon.) 31:197-8*N5'55. B 11013

A prophet in his own country. by Kenneth S. Davis. (Anon.) 33:178 S14'57. B 11014

The prophet outcast. by Isaac Deutscher. (N. Bliven) 40:167-77 Je6'64. B 11015

The prophet unarmed: Trotsky, 1921-1929. by Isaac Deutscher. (Anon.) 35:194-5 S26'59. B 11016

Prospero's cell and reflections on a marine Venus. by Lawrence Durrell. (Anon.) 36: 246-7 D10'60. B 11017

Protective custody. by Howard Richardson and William Berney. (Gibbs) 32:60-2 Ja12'57. T 11018

The proud and profane. (McCarten) 32:65*Je23'56. CC 11019

The proud and the beautiful. (McCarten) 32:52*Je9'56. CC 11020

Proust recaptured: six radio sketches based on the author's characters. by Pamela Hansford Johnson. (Anon.) 34:98-100 Ja17'59. B 11021

Prudence and the pill. (Gilliatt) 44:66-9 Je22'68. CC 11022

Prunier's: the story of a great restaurant. by Simone B. Prunier. (Anon.) 33:178-9 S14'57. B 11023

Psycho. (McCarten) 36:70 Je25 '60. CC 11024

The psychological novel: 1900-1950. by Leon Edel. (Anon.) 31:139 Je11'55. B 11025

Psycosissimo. (McCarten) 38:95 S15'62. CC 11026

Public broadcast laboratory. (Arlen) 43:143-8 N18'67; 43:54-9 D30'67. TV 11027

The public eye. by Peter Shaffer. (McCarten) 39:100 O19'63. T 11028

The public happiness. by August Heckscher. (Anon.) 38:180-1 S15'62. B 11029

The public philosophy. by Walter Lippmann. (Rovere) 31:126-31 F19'55. B 11030

Puccini, a critical biography. by Mosco Carner. (Sargeant) 35:161-7 Je6'59. B 11031

Pulitzer. by W. A. Swanberg. (Anon.) 43:215 O28'67. B 11032

Pullman car Hiawatha. by Thornton Wilder. (Oliver) 38:130-2 D15'62. T 11033

The pumpkin eater. (Gill) 40:148-9 N14'64. CC 11034

Purlie victorious. by Ossie Davis. (Oliver) 37:130-1 O7'61. T 11035

Purple noon. (Gill) 37:62-3 S2'61. CC 11036

The purple plain. (McCarten) 31:145-6 Ap16'55. CC 11037

Pursuit. by Berry Morgan. (Updike) 42:241-5 O29'66. B 11038

A pursuit of furies. by Janet Warnke. (Anon.) 42:90-1 Jy 9'66. B 11039

The pursuit of happiness. by Thomas Rogers. (Anon.) 44:80 Ag31'68. B 11040

Pursuit of the Graf Spee. (McCarten) 33:102-103 Ja11 '58. CC 11041

Pursuit of the prodigal. by Louis Auchincloss. (Anon.) 35:244-6 N7'59. B 11042

Put another nickel in: a history of coin-operated pianos and orchestrions. by Q. David Bowers. (Anon.) 42:231-2 S17'66. B 11043

Putney Swope. (Gilliatt) 45: 46-8 Ag2'69. CC 11044

Puttin' on ole massa. Gilbert
Osofsky, ed. (Anon.) 45:
244-6 D6'69. B            11045
Puzzles and epiphanies. by
Frank Kermode. (Anon.) 39:
178-9 Mr9'63. B           11046
Pygmalion in the classroom. by
Robert Rosenthal and Lenore
Jacobson. (Coles) 45:169-77
Ap19'69. B                11047
The pyramid climbers. by
Vance Packard. (Anon.)
38:79-80 D29'62. B        11048

Q

Quadrille. by Frank Swinner-
ton. (Anon.) 41:178-9 My22'65.
B                         11049
Quantity cooking books.
(Fisher) 43:207'21 O21'67. B
                          11050
Quantrill and the border wars.
by William Elsey Connelley.
(Anon.) 32:202 O13'56. B 11051
The quare fellow. by Brendan
Behan. (Malcolm) 34:119-20
D6'58. T                  11052
The quare fellow. (Gill)
39:132-5 Mr2'63. CC       11053
The quarry. by Friedrich
Duerrenmatt. (Anon.) 38:
141-2 Mr31'62. B          11054
The queen. (Gill) 44:65
Je29'68. CC               11055
Queen Alexandra. by Georgina
Battiscombe. (Anon.) 45:103
F7'70. B                  11056
The queen and the rebels. by
Ugo Betti. (Oliver) 41:80
Mr6'65. T                 11057
Queen Mary. by James Pope-
Hennessy. (Auden) 36:146-
66 My21'60. B             11058
Queen Victoria: born to succeed.
by Elizabeth Pakenham Long-
ford. (N. Bliven) 41:80-2
Jy10'65. B                11059
The queens. (Kael) 44:158
Mr16'68. CC               11060
The queens and the hive. by Edith
Sitwell. (Anon.) 38:114 Ja12
'63. B                    11061

The queen's necklace.
Frances Mossiker, ed.
(Anon.) 37:170-1 Mr11'61.
B                         11062
Queens of France. by
Thornton Wilder. (Oliver)
42:126-9 S17'66. T        11063
Quentin Durward. (McCarten)
31:178*D3'55. CC          11064
The quest for Sumer. by
Leonard Cottrell. (Anon.)
41:244-5 N6'65. B         11065
The quest for Timbuctoo. by
Brian Gardner. (Anon.)
44:242-4 N30'68. B        11066
The quest of three abbots.
by Brendan Lehane. (Anon.)
44:87 Je29'68. B          11067
The question. by Henri Alleg.
John Calder, trans. (Anon.)
34:93 Je28'58. B          11068
The questioners: physicists and
the quantum theory. by
Barbara Lovett Cline.
(Bernstein) 42:174-98
Ap16'66. B                11069
Qui a peur de Virginia Woolf?
See Who's afraid of Virginia
Woolf? T                  11070
Qui etes-vous Polly Maggoo?
(Flanner) 42:225 N19'66. CC
                          11071
The quick rich fox. by Isabella
Taves. (Anon.) 35:193 S19
'59. B                    11072
The quick years. by Jean
Ariss. (Anon.) 34:105-106
My31'58. B                11073
The quicksand war: prelude
to Vietnam. by Lucien
Bodard. Patrick O'Brian,
trans. (Anon.) 43:190 Ap22
'67. B                    11074
The quiet American. by
Graham Greene. (Liebling)
32:136-42*Ap7'56. B       11075
The quiet American. (McCarten)
33:80-1 F15'58. CC        11076
The quiet crisis. by Stewart
L. Udall. (Anon.) 39:245-6
N23'63. B                 11077
Quisling: prophet without honour.
by Ralph Hewins. (Anon.)
42:209-10 Mr19'66. B 11078

The Qumrān Community: its history and scrolls. by Charles T. Fritsch. (Anon.) 32:203 O20'56. B           11079
Quotations from Chairman Mao Tse-Tung. by Edward Albee. (Gill) 44:103-106 O12'68. T           11080

R

Rabbit, run. by John Updike (Balliett) 36:222-4 N5'60. B           11081
Race for the Pole. by John Edward Weems. (Anon.) 36:197-8 Mr12'60. B     11082
Rachel, Rachel. (Gilliatt) 44:85-8 S7'68. CC        11083
Racine and Shakespeare. by Henri Marie Beyle. Guy Daniels, trans. (Anon.) 38:124 F2'63. B            11084
The rack. by A.E. Ellis. (West) 35:113-18 Ja16'60. B           11085
The rack. (McCarten) 32: 102 N17'56. CC        11086
The radical right. Daniel Bell, ed. (Anon.) 39:179-80 My18'63. B           11087
A radical's America. by Harvey Swados. (Anon.) 38:195 My5'62. B        11088
Raditzer. by Peter Matthiessen. (Anon.) 37:178-9 Ap22'61. B           11089
The rag dolls. by Simon Cooper. (Anon.) 45:104 Je 21'69. B            11090
The ragged edge. by John Christopher. (Anon.) 41:134 F5'66. B            11091
The railroad man. (Gill) 41: 204 O30'65. CC        11092
The rainbow comes and goes. by Diana Cooper. (Panter-Downes) 34:220-9 N29'58. B           11093
The rainmaker. (McCarten) 32:64-5*D22'56. CC     11094
Raintree County. (McCarten) 33: 102 Ja11'58. CC        11095

A rainy day in Newark. by Howard Teichmann. (McCarten) 39:94 N2'63. T           11096
A raisin in the sun. by Lorraine Hansberry. (Tynan) 35:100-102 Mr21'59. T           11097
A raisin in the sun. (Oliver) 37:164-5 Ap8'61. CC     11098
Ramakrishna and his disciples. by Christopher Isherwood. (Anon.) 41:110 Jy17'65. B           11099
The Random House dictionary of the English language. Jess Stein and Laurence Urdang, eds. (Anon.) 42: 247-8 O15'66. B        11100
Ransom! (McCarten) 31:81 *F4'56. CC        11101
The rape of the belt. by Benn W. Levy. (McCarten) 36:104-105 N12'60. T     11102
The rape of the fair country. by Alexander Cordell. (Anon.) 35:173-4 My9'59. B     11103
The rape of the mind. by Joost A.M. Meerloo. (Anon.) 32:156 S29'56. B           11104
Rapture. (Gill) 41:86 S4'65. CC           11105
Rashomon. by Fay Kanin and Michael Kanin. (Tynan) 34:81-2 F7'59. T     11106
Rattle of a simple man. by Charles Dyer. (McCarten) 39:82 Ap27'63. T     11107
Rattle of a simple man. (Gill) 40:65 Ja2'65. CC     11108
Ravenna mosaics. by Giuseppe Bovini. Gustina Scaglia, trans. (Anon.) 33:87 Je29 '57. B            11109
Raymond Chandler speaking. by Raymond Chandler. Dorothy Gardiner and Kathrine Sorley Walker, eds. (Anon.) 38:192-3 My5'62. B           11110
Raymond Roussel, a critical study. by Rayner Heppenstall.

(Steiner) 43:206-10
O28'67. B                11111
Re Joyce. by Anthony
Burgess. (Anon.) 41:120 Ja
15'66. B                 11112
Reach for the sky. (McCarten)
33:152 My11'57. CC       11113
Reading the Cantos: the study
of meaning in Ezra Pound.
by Noel Stock. (Bogan)
44:134 Mr30'68. B        11114
Ready when you are, C.B.!
by Susan Slade. (McCarten)
40:66 D19'64. T          11115
The real C.I.A. by Lyman
B. Kirkpatrick, Jr. (Anon.)
44:183-4 Ap13'68. B      11116
The real Figaro: the extra-
ordinary career of Caron de
Beaumarchais. by Cynthia
Cox. (Anon.) 39:246-7
N16'63. B                11117
Real people. by Alison Lurie.
(Sissman) 45:199-200 O11'69.
B                        11118
Reason and chance in scientific
discovery. by R. Taton.
A.J. Pomerans, trans.
(Anon.) 33:71 Ja4'58. B
                         11119
The reawakening. by Primo
Levi. Stuart Woolf, trans.
(Anon.) 41:216 My15'65. B
                         11120
Rebel without a cause. (Mc-
Carten) 31:119*N5'55. CC
                         11121
The reckoning. by Douglas
Turner Ward. (Oliver)
45:105 S13'69. T         11122
The reckoning: the memoirs
of Anthony Eden, Earl of
Avon. by Anthony Eden.
(Anon.) 41:190 My1'65. B
                         11123
The recluse of Herald
Square. by Joseph A. Cox.
(Anon.) 40:225 O3'64. B
                         11124
The recognitions. by William
Gaddis. (Anon.) 31:129 Ap9'55.
B                        11125
Recollections of early Texas:

the memoirs of John Holland
Jenkins. by John Holmes Jenkins
III. (Anon.) 34:177-8
S27'58. B                11126
The rector of Justin. by
Louis Auchincloss. (Balliett)
40:76-8 Ag1'64. B        11127
The red and the white. (Gilliatt)
45:106-108 Mr29'69. CC
                         11128
Red cross. by Sam Shepard.
(Oliver) 44:91 My11'68.
T                        11129
Red desert. (Gill) 40:88-90
F13'65. CC               11130
Red eye of love. by Arnold
Weinstein. (Balliett)
37:52 Je24'61. T         11131
The red fort. by James
Leasor. (Anon.) 33:140
My25'57. B               11132
The red lances. by Arturo
Uslar Pietri. (West) 39:
69-73 D28'63. B          11133
Red lanterns. (Gill) 41:160
Ap10'65. CC              11134
Red roses for me. by Sean
O'Casey. (Gibbs) 31:58-60
*Ja14'56. (Oliver) 37:162-4
D9'61. T                 11135
Red, white, and Maddox.
by Don Tucker and Jay
Broad. (Gill) 44:49-50
F1'69. T                 11136
The redemptor. by James
Dey. (Malcolm) 35:87 My
16'59. T                 11137
Redhead. by Dorothy Fields,
Herbert Fields, Sidney
Sheldon and David Shaw.
(Tynan) 35:98-100 F21'59. T
                         11138
Redoing America: a nationwide
report on how to make our
cities and suburbs livable.
by Edmund K. Faltermayer.
(Anon.) 44:88 Ja11'69. B
                         11139
Reflections from a village.
by Frank Swinnerton. (Anon.)
45:80 Ag30'69. B         11140
Reflections in a golden eye.
(Gill) 43:137-8 O21'67

(Kael) 43:100-105 F10'68.
CC                        11141
Reflections on America. by
Jacques Maritain. (Anon.)
34:146-7 Mr8'58. B      11142
Reflections on hanging. by
Arthur Koestler. (Rovere)
33:164-70 S14'57. B      11143
A regency visitor. by Hermann
von Pückler-Muskan. E. M.
Butler, ed. (Anon.) 34:147
Mr8'58. B              11144
Regional speech habits.
(J. Lardner) 35:181-5 S26'59.
TV                       11145
The rehearsal. by Jean
Anouilh. (McCarten) 39:133-4
O5'63. T              11146
Rehearsal for reconstruction: the
Port Royal experiment.
by Willie Lee Rose. (Anon.)
40:118 S5'64. B        11147
The Reichstag fire. by Fritz
Tobias. A. J. Pomerans,
trans. (Anon.) 40:189-90 Mr14
'64. B               11148
The reivers. (Kael) 45:47
D27'69. CC             11149
Relatively speaking. by Alan
Ayckbourn. (Tynan) 44:124-6
N9'68. T              11150
The reluctant African. by
Louis E. Lomax. (Anon.)
36:245 D10'60. B       11151
The reluctant art. by Benny
Green. (Anon.) 39:94 Ag17'63.
B                     11152
The reluctant débutante. by
William Douglas Home.
(Panter-Downes) 31:56-7*Jy
30'55. (Gibbs) 32:108-10
O20'56. T             11153
The reluctant debutante. (Mc-
Carten) 34:66-8 Ag23'58. CC
                       11154
The reluctant saint. (Gill)
38:234 D8'62. CC       11155
The remains of a father. by
Michael Ramsbotham.
(Fraser) 45:92-5 Ag16'69. B
                       11156
Remember the house. by
Santha Rama Rau. (West)

32:148-53*Ap14'56. B   11157
Remember the wind: a prairie
memoir. by William McK.
Chapman. (Anon.) 41:96
Ag7'65. B             11158
Remembering Mr. Maugham.
by Garson Kanin. (Anon.)
42:247-8 N5'66. B      11159
Reminiscences. by Douglas
MacArthur. (Anon.) 40:225-6
O3'64. B              11160
The reminiscences and recol-
lections of Captain Gronow.
by Rees Howell Gronow.
John Raymond, ed. (Anon.)
40:79-80 D26'64. B     11161
Renaissance and baroque. by
Heinrich Wölfflin. Kathrin
Simon, trans. (Anon.) 42:
247 O15'66. B          11162
Renaissance painting. by
Franco Russoli. Angus
Malcolm, trans. (Anon.)
39:180 Mr30'63. B      11163
Rendezvous at Senlis. by Jean
Anouilh. (Balliett) 37:114-15
Mr11'61. T            11164
The Rennläufer. by Nina
Galen. (Anon.) 43:149-50
Je10'67. B            11165
Report from Malaya. by Vernon
Bartlett. (Anon.) 31:135-6
Ap9'55. B             11166
Report from Palermo. by
Danilo Dolci. P. D. Cummins,
trans. (West) 36:164-73
F20'60. B             11167
Report of the committee on
homosexual offences and
prostitution. by Her Majesty's
Stationery Office. (Panter-
Downes) 33:151-3 S28'57. B
                       11168
Report on Bruno. by Joseph
Breitbach. (West) 40:203-204
S12'64. B             11169
A report on the party and the
guests. (Gilliatt) 44:142-3
S21'68. CC            11170
Report to Greco. by Nikos
Kazantzakis. P. A. Bien,
trans. (Anon.) 41:128 Ag21
'65. B               11171

The reporter's trade. by Joseph
Alsop and Stewart Alsop.
(Liebling) 34:113-18 D20'58.
B                    11172
The Republican establishment:
the present and future of
the G.O.P. by Stephen Hess
and David S. Broder. (Anon.)
43:246 N25'67. B        11173
Republican national convention.
(Arlen) 44:78-84 Ag17'68. TV
                         11174
Repulsion. (Gill) 41:190-1
O9'65. CC               11175
Requiem for a heavyweight.
(Gill) 38:216 O20'62. CC
                         11176
Requiem for a nun. by
William Faulkner and Ruth
Ford. (Tynan) 34:82-7 F7'59.
T                        11177
Resistance. by Georges
Bidault. Marianne Sinclair,
trans. (Anon.) 43:178 S9'67.
B                        11178
Resistance: France 1940-45.
by Blake Ehrlich. (Anon.)
41:123-4 Ag28'65. B     11179
The resistible rise of Arturo
Ui. by Bertolt Brecht.
(Flanner) 36:67-8 Jy2'60
(Gill) 44:59-60 Ja4'69. T
                         11180
The resounding tinkle. by N.F.
Simpson. (Balliett) 37:76-80
Ap15'61. T              11181
Responsibility and response.
by Maxwell D. Taylor.
(Anon.) 42:163-4 F11'67. B
                         11182
Rest for the warrior. (Flanner)
38:142-3 S22'62. CC     11183
The rest is silence. (Balliett)
36:58 Ag13'60. CC       11184
The restless wind. by Peter
Hamilton. (Anon.) 39:122-3
Je1'63. B               11185
The restlessness of Shanti
Andīa. by Anthony Kerrigan.
(West) 36:104-105 Ag20'60.
B                        11186
Return from the ashes. (Gill)
41:234 N27'65. CC       11187

The return of Ansel Gibbs.
by Frederick Buechner.
(Anon.) 34:158-60 Ap12'58.
B                        11188
The return of Don Camillo.
(McCarten) 32:104*Ap7'56.
CC                       11189
The return of Lady Brace.
by Nancy Wilson Ross.
(Anon.) 33:241-2 N16'57.
B                        11190
The return of the snow-white
Puritan. by John Paolotti.
(Anon.) 39:157-8 S7'63.
B                        11191
The return of the vanishing
American. by Leslie A.
Fiedler. (Anon.) 44:126-7
Je1'68. B               11192
Return to the islands. by
Arthur Grimble. (Anon.)
33:194 N2'57. B         11193
Revenge at sea. by Barrie
Pitt. (Anon.) 40:245-6
N7'64. B                11194
A reviewer's ABC: collected
criticism of Conrad Aiken
from 1916 to the present.
by Conrad Aiken. Rufus A.
Blanshard, ed. (Anon.) 35:
175-6 My9'59. B         11195
The revolt in Tibet. by Frank
Moraes. (Anon.) 35:107
Ja30'60. B              11196
The revolt of French Canada,
1800-35. by Helen Taft
Manning. (Anon.) 38:178-9
Mr24'62. B              11197
The revolt of Gunner Asch. by
Hans Hellmut Kirst. (West)
32:138*Mr10'56. B       11198
The revolt of Mamie Stover.
(McCarten) 32:126*My19'56.
CC                       11199
Revolution and roses. by P.H.
Newby. (Podhoretz) 33:69-70
*Jy27'57. B             11200
The revolutionary journal of
Baron Ludwig von Closen,
1780-83. by Ludwig von
Closen. Evelyn M. Acomb,
trans. & ed. (Anon.) 34:119
D20'58. B               11201

Revolutionary road. by
Richard Yates. (Anon.) 37:131
Ap1'61. B          11202
The reward.
by Michael Barrett. (Anon.)
32:100*Mr31'56. B     11203
Rhinoceros. by Eugène
Ionesco. (Panter-Downes)
36:103-104 My28'60 (Mc-
Carten) 36:66-8 Ja21'61. T
                   11204
The rich nations and the
poor nations. by Barbara
Ward. (Anon.) 38:188 Mr17
'62. B             11205
Richard Coeur de Lion. by
Philip Henderson. (Anon.)
35:227 O17'59. B      11206
Richard II. by William
Shakespeare. (Gibbs) 32:70-3
N3'56. T           11207
Richard the third. by Paul
Murray Kendall. (Anon.)
32:86-7*S1'56. B      11208
Richard III. (Panter-Downes)
31:49-50*D31'55 (McCarten)
32:76*Mr17'56. CC     11209
Richard Wagner, the man, his
mind, and his music. by
Robert W. Gutman. (Anon.)
44:174-5 My18'68 (Auden)
44:72-82 Ja4'69. B     11210
The rickshaw man. (McCarten)
36:190 My14'60. CC    11211
Riders in the chariot. by
Patrick White. (Balliett)
37:244-7 D9'61. B     11212
Riding to the Tigris. by
Freya Stark. (Anon.) 36:181-
2 Ap16'60. B         11213
Rififi. (Flanner) 31:85*Ag27'55
(McCarten) 32:64*Je23'56. CC
                   11214
The right honourable gentle-
man. by Michael Dyne. (Mc-
Carten) 41:108 O30'65. T
                   11215
The right to an answer. by
Anthony Burgess. (N. Bliven)
37:169-70 Ap8'61. B    11216
The right to know. by Kent
Cooper. (Anon.) 32:156*My5
'56. B             11217

Right you are if you think you
are. by Luigi Pirandello.
(Oliver) 40:109-10 Mr14'64
(McCarten) 42:156-7 D3'66.
T                  11218
The righteous are bold. by
Frank Carney. (Gibbs)
31:60-2*Ja14'56. T     11219
Right-hand man. by John A.
Garraty. (West) 36:121-4
F11'61. B          11220
The rimers of Eldritch. by
Lanford Wilson. (Oliver)
43:132-4 Mr4'67. T     11221
The ring in Meiji. by
William Butler. (Anon.)
41:106 Je26'65. B     11222
Ring Lardner. by Donald
Elder. (Anon.) 32:102-103
Ja12'57. B         11223
Ring of bright water. by Gavin
Maxwell (Anon.) 37:150-1
Ap29'61. B         11224
The riot act. by Will Greene.
(McCarten) 39:137 Mr16'63.
T                  11225
The ripening. by Edouard
Glissant. Frances Frenaye,
trans. (Anon.) 35:242
N7'59. B           11226
The ripening seed. by
Sidonie Gabrielle Colette.
(Anon.) 32:86*Jy14'56. B
                   11227
The rise and fall of T. D.
Lysenko. by Zhores A.
Medvedev. I. Michael
Lerner, trans. (Bernstein)
45:85-91 Ja24'70. B    11228
The rise of the house of
Duveen. by James Henry
Duveen. (Anon.) 33:86 Je29
'57. B             11229
The rise and fall of the Third
Reich: a history of Nazi
Germany. by William L.
Shirer. (N. Bliven) 36:
174-7 O29'60. B       11230
The rising of the moon.
(McCarten) 33:54*Jy20'57.
CC                 11231
The risk. (Gill) 37:142 S30'61.
CC                 11232

Ritual in the dark. by Colin
Wilson. (West) 36:105-108
Ag20'60. B          11233
The rivalry. by Norman
Corwin. (Tynan) 35:96-8
F21'59. T          11234
Riverside Drive. by John
Donovan. (Oliver) 39:113
F15'64. T          11235
Riverwind. by John Jennings
and Joseph Benjamin.
(Oliver) 38:66-7 D22'62.
T                   11236
The road and the star. by
Berkeley Mather. (Anon.)
41:127-8 Ag21'65. B     11237
The road from the monument.
by Storm Jameson. (Anon.)
38:185-6 Mr17'62. B     11238
The road past Mandalay,
Volume II. by John Masters.
(Anon.) 37:177-8 S16'61. B
                    11239
Road to Ghana. by Alfred
Hutchinson. (Anon.) 36:56-8
D31'60. B           11240
The road to H: narcotics,
delinquency, and social
policy. by Isador Chein,
Donald L. Gerard, Robert
S. Lee, Eva Rosenfeld and
Daniel M. Wilner. (Anon.)
40:100 Jy18'64. B       11241
The road to Hong Kong. (Oliver)
38:39 Jy21'62. CC       11242
Road to Mandalay. by Geoffrey
Rawson. (Anon.) 43:102-103
Ag12'67. B          11243
The road to Mayerling. by
Richard Barkeley. (Anon.)
34:164-5 S13'58. B      11244
The road to Monte Cristo. by
Alexandre Dumas. Jules
Eckert Goodman, ed.
(West) 33:129-33 Mr9'57.
B                   11245
Road to Ninevah. by
Nora Benjamin Kubie.
(Anon.) 40:164 Mr28'64. B
                    11246
The road to number 10. by
Anthony Howard and Richard
West. (Anon.) 41:160 Je12'65.
B                   11247

The road to Sarajevo. by
Vladimir Dedijer. (Anon.)
42:222-3 S10'66. B      11248
The road to Wigan Pier. by
George Orwell. (Macdonald)
35:135-50 Mr28'59. B    11249
Roar like a dove. by Lesley
Storm. (McCarten) 40:80
My30'64. T          11250
The roar of the greasepaint--
the smell of the crowd. by
Anthony Newley and Leslie
Bricusse. (McCarten) 41:56
My29'65. T          11251
Robbery. (Gill) 43:147-8
O7'67. CC           11252
Robert and Elizabeth. by
Ronald Millar and Ron
Grainger. (Panter-Downes)
40:62-3 Ja2'65. T       11253
Robert Frost: the trial by
existence. by Elizabeth
Shepley Sergeant. (Bogan)
36:197 O8'60. B         11254
Rocco and his brothers.
(Gill) 37:41 Jy1'61. CC
                    11255
The rock garden. by Nikos
Kazantzakis. Richard
Howard, trans. (Anon.)
39:194-5 S14'63. B      11256
Rock of exile. by D.M. Booy.
(Anon.) 34:239-40 N29'58.
B                   11257
Rockefeller and the red
Indians. by Ray Galton and
Alan Simpson. (Gill) 44:125
N2'68. T            11258
Rocket. by Philip Bennet
Joubert de la Ferté. (Anon.)
34:145 Mr8'58. B        11259
Rocking the boat. by Gore
Vidal. (Anon.) 38:80 Jy28'62.
B                   11260
Roger Casement: a new judgment.
by René MacColl. (Anon.) 33:
238-9 *N30'57. B        11261
The rogue of publishers' row.
by Edward Uhlan. (Anon.)
32:130*Je2'56. B        11262
Roman candle. by Sidney
Sheldon. (Tynan) 35:90-2
F13'60. T           11263

A Roman journal. by Marie
Henri Beyle. Haakon Chevalier,
trans. (Kazin) 34:201-209
N8'58. B                    11264
The Roman Spring of Mrs.
Stone. (Gill) 37:97-8 Ja13'62.
CC                          11265
Romanoff and Juliet. by Peter
Ustinov. (Gibbs) 33:81-3
O19'57. T                   11266
Romanoff and Juliet. (Oliver)
37:61 Je24'61. CC           11267
Romantic rebels. by Emily
Hahn. (Anon.) 42:126
Ja28'67. B                  11268
The romantic way. by Vincent
Cronin. (Anon.) 42:178-9
Mr12'66. B                  11269
Romantics at school. by
Morris Marples. (Anon) 43:
224 O14'67. B               11270
Rome. by William Klein.
(Anon.) 36:143-4 My28'60.
B                           11271
Rome adventure. (Gill) 38:
127 Mr31'62. CC             11272
Rome beyond the imperial
frontiers. by Mortimer
Wheeler. (Anon.) 31:163-4*S
24'55. B                    11273
The Rome escape line. by Sam
I. Derry. (Anon.) 36:199-
200 S17'60. B               11274
The Rome I love. by Patrice
Molinard, et al. (Anon.)
34:104 Ja31'59. B           11275
Rome, Naples, and Florence.
by Henri Marie Beyle.
Richard N. Coe, trans. (Anon.)
36:247 N26'60. B            11276
Rome on the Euphrates: the
story of a frontier. by Freya
Stark. (Anon.) 43:196 Ap22'67.
B                           11277
Romeo and Juliet. by
William Shakespeare. (Gibbs)
32:70-2 N3'56 (Flagler) 33:
56-70 Ag31'57 (McCarten) 38:
100-102 F24'62. T           11278
Romeo and Juliet. (Panter-
Downes) 44:121-2 Ap6'68
(Kael) 44:209-12 O19'68. CC
                            11279

Romulus. by Gore Vidal.
(McCarten) 37:63 Ja20'62.
T                           11280
Ronald Firbank. by Miriam J.
Benkovitz. (Anon.) 45:76
Ag2'69. B                   11281
Rondelay. by Jerry Douglas
and Hal Jordan. (Oliver) 45:
166 N15'69. T               11282
The roof. (McCarten) 35:85-6
My23'59. CC                 11283
The room. by Harold Pinter.
(Oliver) 40:68-70 D19'64.
T                           11284
Room at the top. by John
Braine. (Balliett) 33:186-9
N2'57. B                    11285
Room at the top. (McCarten)
35:162-3 Ap11'59. CC        11286
A room in Moscow. by Sally
Belfrage. (Anon.) 35:167-8
Mr7'59. B                   11287
A roomful of roses. by
Edith Sommer. (Gibbs)
31:82-3*O29'55. T           11288
Rooms. by Stanley Mann.
(Oliver) 41:84-6 F5'66. T
                            11289
Rooney. (McCarten) 34:111-12
Je14'58. CC                 11290
Roosevelt and Howe. by
Alfred B. Rollins, Jr.
(Anon.) 38:246-7 D1'62.
B                           11291
The Roosevelt leadership: 1933-
1945. by Edgar Eugene
Robinson. (Anon.) 31:117-18
Mr5'55. B                   11292
The Roosevelt revolution. by
Marfo Einaudi. (Anon.) 35:119-
20 Je20'59. B               11293
Roosevelt: the lion and the fox.
by James MacGregor Burns.
(Rovere) 32:89-92*Ag18'56.
B                           11294
Roots. by Arnold Wesker.
(Panter-Downes) 35:80-1
Ag29'59 (Balliett) 37:126-9
Mr18'61. T                  11295
The roots of American Com-
munism. by Theodore Draper.
(Anon.) 33:136-7 Mr30'57.
B                           11296

The roots of capitalism. by
John Chamberlain. (Anon.) 35:
163 My2'59. B            11297
The roots of heaven. by Romain
Gary. Jonathan Griffin,
trans. (Flanner) 32:174-5
D15'56 (Malcolm) 33:86-8
F1'58. B                 11298
The roots of heaven. (McCarten)
34:192-3 O25'58. CC      11299
The rope dancers. by Morton
Wishengrad. (Gibbs) 33:94-6
*N30'57. T               11300
Rosa Luxemburg. by J. P.
Nettl. (Anon.) 42:167
Je11'66. B               11301
A rose for Winter. by
Laurie Lee. (Anon.) 32:138
*Mr24'56. B              11302
The rose tattoo. (McCarten)
31:52*D24'55. CC         11303
Rosebery. by Robert Rhodes
James. (Anon.) 40:222
Ap18'64. B               11304
Rosemarie. by Erich Kuby.
(Anon.) 36:177-8 Mr19'60.
B                        11305
Rosemary. by Molly Kazan.
(Balliett) 36:107-108
N26'60. T                11306
Rosemary. (McCarten) 35:63-4
Ja30'60. CC              11307
Rosemary's baby. (Gilliatt)
44:87-9 Je15'68. CC      11308
Rosenbach: a biography.
by Edwin Wolf, II and John
Fleming. (Anon.) 36:87
Ja7'61. B                11309
Rosencrantz and Guildenstern
are dead. by Tom Stoppard.
(Panter-Downes) 43:179-80
My6'67 (McCarten) 43:105
O28'67. T                11310
Rosmersholm. by Henrik
Ibsen. Carmel Ross,
trans. (Oliver) 38:85-7
Ap21'62. T               11311
Ross. by Terence Rattigan.
(Panter-Downes) 36:59-60
Jy9'60 (McCarten) 37:55-6
Ja6'62. T                11312
Rosy is my relative. by
Gerald Durrell. (Anon.) 44:

125-6 Je1'68. B          11313
The Rothschilds: a family
portrait. by Frederic
Morton. (Anon.) 38:183-4
Ap7'62. B                11314
Rotten to the core. (Arlen)
41:88 Jy24'65. CC        11315
Rouge et noir. (McCarten)
34:72 Ap19'58. CC        11316
The round up. (Gilliatt)
45:124-7 My17'69. CC     11317
Rousseau and revolution.
by Will Durant and Ariel
Durant. (Anon.) 43:223
O14'67. B                11318
Routes of contagion. by
André Siegfried. Jean
Henderson and Mercedes
Clarasó, trans. (Anon.)
41:123 Ag28'65. B        11319
Royal affairs in Versailles.
(McCarten) 33:85-6 Mr16
'57. CC                  11320
Royal gambit. by Hermann
Gressieker. (Malcolm)
35:104 Mr21'59. T        11321
The royal George: 1819-1904:
the life of H. R. H. Prince
George, Duke of Cambridge.
by Giles St. Aubyn. (Anon.)
40:91 Jy25'64. B         11322
The royal hunt. by Pierre
Moinot. (Gill) 31:115-16
Mr5'55. B                11323
The royal hunt of the sun. by
Peter Shaffer. (Panter-
Downes) 40:209 S19'64
(McCarten) 41:115-16 N6'65.
T                        11324
The royal hunt of the sun.
(Kael) 45:196 O18'69. CC
                         11325
Royal Wales. by Cledwyn
Hughes. (Anon.) 33:142
Je8'57. B                11326
Rue de Paris. (Angell) 36:50
D31'60. CC               11327
The ruffian on the stair. by
Joe Orton. (Oliver) 45:156
N8'69. T                 11328
Rugantino. by Pietro Garinei,
Sandro Giovanni, Armando
Trovaiola. (McCarten) 39:113
F15'64. T                11329

The rules of the game. by
William Murray. (Balliett)
36:43-4 D31'60. T        11330
Rules of the game. (Gilliatt)
45:150-2 S20'69. CC      11331
The rules of the game in
Paris. by Nathan Leites.
Derek Coltman, trans.
(Anon.) 45:160 O4'69. B
                          11332
Rum Row. by Robert Carse.
(Anon.) 35:177-8 Mr21'59. B
                          11333
Rumple. by Irving Phillips,
Ernest G. Schweikert and Frank
Reardon. (Gibbs) 33:104-106
N16'57. T                11334
Run for cover. (McCarten)
31:132 My7'55. CC        11335
Run river. by Joan Didion.
(Anon.) 39:178 My11'63. B
                          11336
Run silent, run deep.
(McCarten) 34:127-8 Ap5'58.
CC                       11337
The runaway. by Albertine
Sarrazin. (Updike) 45:174-8
Mr15'69. B               11338
The running man. (Gill)
39:178 O5'63. CC         11339
Rupert Brooke: a biography.
by Christopher Hassall.
(Panter-Downes) 40:233-45
O10'64. B                11340
Rush to judgment. (Gilliatt)
43:95 Je17'67. CC        11341
Ruskin today. Kenneth
Clark, ed. (Anon.) 40:123-4
Ja30'65. B               11342
Russia against the Kremlin.
by Alexandre Metaxas.
(Anon.) 33:150-1 S7'57. B
                          11343
Russia and history's turning
point. by Alexander
Kerensky. (Anon.) 41:246-7
D11'65. B                11344
Russia and the West under
Lenin and Stalin. by George
F. Kennan. (Wilson) 37:
140-52 S9'61. B          11345
Russia in transition. by Isaac
Deutscher. (Anon.) 33:107 Ag
17'57. B                 11346

Russia leaves the war. by
George F. Kennan. (Anon.)
32:154-5 S29'56. B       11347
Russia 1917: the February
Revolution. by George Katkov.
(Anon.) 43:153 Ap1'67.
B                        11348
Russia revisited. by Louis
Fischer. (Anon.) 33:177-8
S14'57. B                11349
Russia, the atom, and the
West. by George F.
Kennan. (Anon.) 34:145
Ap5'58. B                11350
Russia without Stalin: the
emerging pattern. by
Edward Crankshaw. (Anon.)
32:178-9 O27'56. B       11351
Russian journey. by William
O. Douglas. (Anon.) 32:82
*Je23'56. B              11352
Russian philosophy.
James M. Edie, James P.
Scanlan, Mary-Barbara
Zeldin and George L. Kline,
eds. (Anon.) 41:247-8
O23'65. B                11353
The Russian Revolution. by
Alan Moorehead. (Anon.)
34:92 Ag23'58. B         11354
The Russian Revolution 1917.
by N.N. Sukhanov. Joel
Carmichael, trans. and ed.
(Macdonald) 31:119-30
*F18'56. B               11355
The Russians are coming, the
Russians are coming. (Gill)
42:87 Je4'66. CC         11356
Russians as people. by Wright
W. Miller. (Malcolm) 37:
106-10 Ja13'62. B        11357

S

S.O.P.H.I.A. by Pierre
Boulle. (Anon.) 35:133
*D19'59. B               11358
The saboteur. (Gill) 41:102
Ag28'65. CC              11359
The sacrifice. by Adele
Wiseman. (Anon.) 32:153
S29'56. B                11360
The saddest Summer of Samuel
S. by J.P. Donleavy

(Oliver) 42:241 O15'66. B
11361
Saddle the wind. (McCarten)
34:128 Ap5'58. CC    11362
Safari. (McCarten) 32:49
*Je30'56. CC    11363
Sail away. by Noël Coward.
(Oliver) 37:163-5 O14'61. T
11364
Sail ho! by James Bisset and
P.R. Stephensen. (Anon.)
34:64 Ag2'58. B    11365
The sailor from Gibraltar.
(Gill) 43:178-81 My13'67. CC
11366
The sailor, sense of humour,
and other stories. by V.S.
Pritchett. (Anon.) 32:86
*S1'56. B    11367
The sailor who fell from grace
with the sea. by Yukio
Mishima.  John Nathan,
trans. (West) 42:206 Mr19'66.
B    11368
Saint Joan. by George Bernard
Shaw. (Gibbs) 32:96-8 S22'56
(McCarten) 38:93 Mr3'62
(Gill) 43:57 Ja13'68. T 11369
Saint Joan. (McCarten)
33:58 Jy6'57. CC    11370
St. Louis blues. (McCarten)
34:72-4 Ap19'58. CC    11371
St. Peter's Day and other
tales. by Anton Chekhov.
(Anon.) 36:174 F20'60. B
11372
Sainte-Beuve. by Harold
Nicolson. (Auden) 33:221-37
*N30'57. B    11373
Sainte-Beuve: selected essays.
by Charles Augustin Sainte-
Beuve.  Francis Steegmuller
and Norbert Guterman,
eds. and trans. (Anon.)
39:72 Ag3'63. B    11374
Saint-Exupéry. by Marcel
Migeo. (Pritchett) 37:169-72
Mr18'61. B    11375
Saint-Germain, ou la négociation.
See the negotiators. B 11376
The saintliness of Margery
Kempe. by John Wulp. (Mal-
colm) 34:70-1 F14'59. T
11377

Salad days. Anon. (Malcolm)
34:103-104 N22'58. T
11378
Salesman. (Gilliatt) 45:149-52
Ap19'69. CC    11379
Saloon society. by Bill Man-
ville. (Malcolm) 36:238-43
D10'60. B    11380
Salt. by Herbert Gold. (Adler)
39:104-11 Je22'63. B    11381
Salto. (Gill) 42:129-30
O8'66. CC    11382
Salut à Molière. by Jean-
Louis Barrault. (Oliver)
40:112-14 Mr14'64. T  11383
Salvation. by C.C. Courtney
and Peter Link. (Oliver)
45:114 O4'69. T    11384
Salvatore Giuliano. (Gill)
40:136 O31'64. CC    11385
Sam Ward: king of the lobby.
by Lately Thomas. (Anon.)
41:184 My8'65. B    11386
Sambo. by Ron Steward and
Neal Tate. (Oliver) 45:43
Ja3'70. T    11387
Samuel Adams: the fateful
years: 1764-76. by Stewart
Beach. (Anon.) 41:159
F19'66. B    11388
Samurai. (McCarten) 31:75
*Ja28'56. CC    11389
Samurai assassin. (Gill)
41:168-9 Mr27'65. CC  11390
The sanctity of life and the
criminal law. by Glanville
Williams. (Rovere) 33:164-70
S14'57. B    11391
Sanctuary. by Frank Swinnerton.
(Anon.) 43:143-4 Je3'67. B
11392
Sanctuary. (Angell) 37:101-102
Mr4'61. CC    11393
The sand castle. (Gill)
37:68-9 Ag19'61. CC  11394
The sand pebbles. by Richard
McKenna. (Balliett) 38:110-11
Ja12'63. B    11395
The sand pebbles. (Gill)
42:62 D31'66. CC    11396
The sandpiper. (Arlen)
41:87 Jy24'65. CC    11397
Sandra. (Gill) 41:96-9 Ja22
'66. CC    11398

The sands of Dunkirk. by
Richard Collier. (Anon.)
37:222-3 O14'61. B    11399
The sands of Summer. by
David Pryce-Jones. (Anon.)
40:244 N7'64. B    11400
The sands of the Kalahari. by
William Mulvihill. (Anon.)
36:204 S10'60. B    11401
Sanjuro. (Gill) 39:102
My11'63. CC    11402
The sap of life. by
Richard Maltby and David
Shire. (Oliver) 37:166 O14'61.
T    11403
Sapphire. (McCarten) 35:128
N14'59. CC    11404
Sarajevo. by Joachim Remak.
(Anon.) 35:90-3 Je27'59.
B    11405
Saratoga. by Morton DaCosta,
Harold Arlen and Johnny
Mercer. (Tynan) 35:77-8
*D19'59. T    11406
The Sassoons. by Stanley
Jackson. (Anon.) 44:110
Je15'68. B    11407
Satan in high heels. (Gill)
38:128 Mr31'62. CC    11408
Satan never sleeps. (Gill)
38:90 Mr10'62. CC    11409
Saturday night. by Jerome
Kass. (Oliver) 44:134-7
Mr9'68. T    11410
Saturday night and Sunday
morning. (Oliver) 37:154-5
Ap15'61. CC    11411
Saturday the rabbi went
hunting. by Harry Kemelman.
(Anon.) 42:120 S3'66. B
11412
Saturn: an essay on Goya. by
André Malraux. C.W.
Chilton, trans. (Sargeant)
33:155-61 S28'57. B    11413
The savage affair. by Virgil
Scott. (Anon.) 34:154 Mr15
'58. B    11414
The savage country. by Walter
O'Meara. (Anon.) 36:203
O8'60. B    11415
The savage eye. (McCarten)
36:108-10 Je18'60. CC
11416

Saved. by Edward Bond.
(Panter-Downes) 41:228-31
D11'65. T    11417
The saving grace. by Edwin
Harvey Blum. (Oliver)
39:86-8 Ap27'63. T    11418
Say, darling. by Richard
Bissell and George Abbott.
(Gibbs) 34:67-8 Ap12'58. T
11419
Say nothing. by James
Hanley. (Oliver) 40:94-6
F6'65. T    11420
Sayonara. (McCarten) 33:89-
90 D14'57. CC    11421
The scandalous regent. by
W.H. Lewis. (Mehta) 37:
175-8 Ap22'61. B    11422
The scapegoat. by Daphne
du Maurier. (Anon.)
33:129-30 F23'57. B    11423
The scapegoat. (Balliett)
35:80*Ag15'59. CC    11424
Scapin. by Molière. (McCarten)
37:93 Mr4'61 (Oliver) 40:64-6
Mr21'64. T    11425
Scarlet lancer. by James D.
Lunt. (Anon.) 40:186
My23'64. B    11426
Scarlet lullaby. by Elliott
Taubenslag. (Oliver) 44:
102 Mr23'68. T    11427
The scarperer. by Brendan
Behan. (Anon.) 40:78 Ag1'64.
B    11428
The scene. by Clarence L.
Cooper. (Anon.) 35:105
Ja30'60. B    11429
Scenes from life. by William
Cooper. (West) 37:125-6
Mr4'61. B    11430
A scent of flowers. by James
Saunders. (Oliver) 45:128-30
N1'69. T    11431
Scent of mystery. (McCarten)
36:131-2 F27'60. CC    11432
The Schatten affair. by
Frederic Morton. (Anon.) 41:
107 S4'65. B    11433
The school for scandal. by
Richard Brinsley
Sheridan. (Oliver) 38:122-4
Mr24'62 (McCarten) 38:69 F2
'63; 42:156-7 D3'66. T 11434

School for scoundrels. (Gill)
36:170 S17'69. CC 11435
School of Paris the painters
and artistic climate of
Paris since 1910. by
Raymond Nacenta. (Anon.)
36:247 D10'60. B 11436
School of the sun. by Ana Marie
Matute. Elaine Kerrigan,
trans. (West) 39:182-5
O5'63. B 11437
The schoolchildren: growing
up in the slums. by Mary
Francis Greene and
Orletta Ryan. (Anon.)
42:194 Ap23'66. B 11438
Schubert: a critical
biography. by Maurice J.E.
Brown. (Anon.) 34:178-9
S27'58. B 11439
Schumann and the romantic age.
by Marcel Brion. (Anon.)
32:203-204 O20'56. B 11440
Science and government. by
C.P. Snow. (Anon.) 37:179-80
Ap22'61. B 11441
Science and survival. by
Barry Commoner. (Anon.)
42:244-5 N26'66. B 11442
Science and the shabby curate
of poetry: essays about the
two cultures. by Martin
Green. (Anon.) 41:127-8
Je19'65. B 11443
Science: the glorious enter-
tainment. by Jacques
Barzun. (Bernstein) 40:236-
46 N21'64. B 11444
The scientific renaissance. by
Marie Boas. (Bernstein) 38:
167-71 S29'62. B 11445
The scientists. by Eleazar
Lipsky. (Anon.) 34:142-3 F
7'59. B 11446
Scientists and war. by Solly
Zuckerman. (Anon.) 43:151-2
Je10'67. B 11447
Scorpio rising. (Gill) 42:130-1
Ap23'66. CC 11448
Scotland. Eric Linklater, ed.
(Anon.) 44:120 Ag24'68. B
11449
Scott Fitzgerald. by Andrew

W. Turnbull. (Anon.) 38:
178 Mr24'62. B 11450
Scottsboro: a tragedy of the
American South. by Dan T.
Carter. (Anon.) 45:119 Mr1
'69. B 11451
The scourge of the swastika.
by Edward Frederick
Russell. (Liebling) 31:132-4
Mr26'55. B 11452
Scream of fear. (Gill) 37:
76-7 Ag26'61. CC 11453
Scrutiny. (Magazine) F.R.
Leavis, ed. (Rosenberg)
40:169-88 Mr14'64.
B 11454
Scuba duba. by Bruce Jay
Friedman. (Oliver)43:82-6
O21'67. T 11455
The Scythians. by Tamara
Talbot Rice. (Anon.) 33:84
Ag31'57. B 11456
The sea. by W.A. de Salis,
et al. (Anon.) 38:246 D8'62.
B 11457
The sea and the wedding. by
Pamela Hansford Johnson.
(Anon.) 33:147-8 Mr23'57.
B 11458
A sea change. by J.R.
Salamanca. (Anon.) 45:236-8
N15'69. B 11459
The sea chase. (McCarten)
31:65 Je18'55. CC 11460
Sea war. by Felix Riesenberg,
Jr. (Anon.) 32:130-1*Je9
'56. B 11461
The seagull. by Anton
Chekhov. Alex Szogyi, trans.
(Oliver) 38:115-16 Ap7'62
(McCarten) 40:108-10 Ap18
'64. T 11462
The seagull. (Kael) 44:60-5
Ja11'69. CC 11463
The seagull on the step. by
Kay Boyle. (Anon.) 31:159
*S17'55. B 11464
Seamarks. by St.-John Perse.
Wallace Fowlie, trans.
(Anon.) 35:179-80 Mr21'59.
B 11465
Séance on a wet afternoon.
(Gill) 40:149-50 N14'64. CC
11466

The search for Captain Slocum.
by Walter Magnes Teller.
(Anon.) 32:87*S1'56. B
                                11467
The search for good sense: four
eighteenth-century characters.
by F. L. Lucas. (Anon.)
34:211 N8'58. B         11468
The search for the Tassili
frescoes. by Henri Lhote.
Alan Houghton Brodrick, trans.
(Anon.) 35:123-4 Ja16'60.
B                               11469
The Sears, Roebuck & Company
consumers guide: catalog no.
104 for 1897. Fred L. Israel,
ed. (Anon.) 44:108 D21'68.
B                               11470
The season for love. (Gill)
39:170-3 My18'63. CC    11471
Season of choice. by Nathaniel
Banks. (Malcolm) 35:85-7
Ap25'59. T              11472
The seasons of America past. by
Eric Sloane. (Anon.) 34:74-6
Ja3'59. B               11473
The seat of power. by James
D. Horan. (Anon.) 41:127 Ag21
'65. B                  11474
Sebastian. (Kael) 43:106-108
Ja27'68. CC             11475
The second stone. by Leslie
A. Fiedler. (Malcolm) 39:
84-91 Ag17'63. B        11476
A second string. by Lucienne
Hill. (Tynan) 36:118-19
Ap23'60. T              11477
Secondary worlds. by W. H.
Auden. (Anon.) 45:180
Mr15'69. B              11478
A second-hand life. by
Charles Jackson. (Anon.)
43:98 Ag26'67. B        11479
Seconds. (Gill) 42:128-9
O8'66. CC               11480
The secret. by Alba de
Céspedes. Isabel Quigly,
trans. (Anon.) 34:176-7
S27'58. B               11481
The secret battalion. by
Michael J. Bird. (Anon.)
40:91 Ag8'64. B         11482
Secret ceremony. (Kael)

44:181-2 N2'68. CC      11483
The secret islands. by Frank-
lin Russell. (Anon.) 42:195
Ap23'66. B              11484
The secret life of an American
wife. (Gill) 44:64-5 Je29'68.
CC                      11485
The secret life of Walter
Mitty. by Joe Manchester,
Leon Carr and Earl Shuman.
(Oliver) 40:102 N7'64. T
                                11486
The secret of cooking for cats.
by Martin A. Gardner. (Fisher)
42:157-61 Ap30'66. B    11487
The secret of cooking for dogs.
by Martin A. Gardner.
(Fisher) 42:157-61 Ap30'66.
B                               11488
The secret of Luca. by
Ignazio Silone. (West) 34:
153-8 S13'58. B         11489
The secret of Santa Vittoria.
by Robert Crichton.
(Balliett) 42:235-6 D10'66.
B                               11490
The secret of Santa Vittoria.
(Kael) 45:140-1 N1'69. CC
                                11491
The secret of the Hittites.
by C. W. Ceram.
Richard Winston and Clara
Winston, trans. (Anon.)
31:134-5*F18'56. B      11492
The secret search for peace
in Vietnam. by David
Kraslow and Stuart H. Loory.
(Anon.) 44:119-20 Ag24'68.
B                               11493
The secret surrender. by
Allen Dulles. (Anon.) 42:247
O29'66. B               11494
The secret swinger. by Alan
Harrington. (S. Lardner)
42:242-4 N12'66. B      11495
The secret war against Hitler.
by Fabian von Schlabrendorff.
Hilda Simon, trans. (Anon.)
41:233-4 O9'65. B       11496
The secret war of Harry Frigg.
(Kael) 44:150-2 Mr9'68. CC
                                11497
The secret ways. by Alistair

MacLean. (Anon.) 35:175
Ap11'59. B          11498
Secrets of life. (McCarten)
32:129-30 D1'56. CC    11499
Secrets of women. (Gill)
37:54 Jy22'61. CC      11500
Section: Rockdrill 85-95 de
los cantares. by Ezra
Pound. (Bogan) 32:84-5
*S1'56. B          11501
Seduced and abandoned.
(Balliett) 40:56 Jy25'64.
CC                  11502
The seed. by Pierre Gascar.
(West) 35:99 Jy18'59. B
                    11503
Seeds of time: the background
of southern thinking. by
Henry Savage, Jr. (Anon.)
35:131 Je13'59. B      11504
The seersucker whipsaw. by
Ross Thomas. (Anon.) 43:
144-5 Je3'67. B        11505
The seesaw log. by William
Gibson. (Tynan) 35:182-5
My16'59. B          11506
Segregation: the inner conflict
in the South. by Robert
Penn Warren. (Anon.) 32:
200 O13'56. B          11507
Seidman and son. by Elick
Moll. (McCarten) 38:147-8
O27'62. T          11508
Seize the day. by Saul
Bellow. (Gill) 32:69-70
Ja5'57. B          11509
The selected letters of Bernard
Berenson. by Bernard Berenson.
A.K. McComb, ed. (Anon.)
40:222-3 Ap 18'64. B   11510
The selected letters of Charles
Dickens. by Charles
Dickens. Frederick W. Dupee,
ed. (Anon.) 36:162-3 Mr26
'60. B              11511
Selected letters of Dylan
Thomas. by Dylan Thomas.
(Moss) 43:185-9 O7'67. B
                    11512
Selected letters of Friedrich
Nietzsche. by Friedrich
Nietzsche. Christopher Mid-
dleton, ed. and trans. (Anon.)

45:203-204 O11'69. B    11513
The selected letters of Henry
James. by Henry James.
Leon Edel, ed. (Anon.) 31:
106-107*Ja21'56. B      11514
Selected letters of Robert Frost.
by Robert Frost. Lawrance
Thompson, ed. (Anon.)
40:208 S12'64. B        11515
The selected letters of
William Carlos Williams.
by William Carlos Williams.
John C. Thirlwall, ed. (Anon.)
33:246 D7'57. B        11516
The selected letters of William
James. by William James.
Elizabeth Hardwick, ed.
(Anon.) 37:135 My27'61.
B                  11517
Selected poems. by Roy
Campbell. (Anon.) 31:180
My14'55. B          11518
Selected poems. by Randall
Jarrell. (Anon.) 31:180 My14
'55. B              11519
Selected poems. by Pablo
Neruda. (Bogan) 38:241-2
N17'62. B          11520
Selected poems: 1928-1958.
by Stanley Kunitz. (Bogan)
34:237 D6'58. B        11521
Selected works of Alfred Jarry.
by Alfred Jarry. Roger
Shattuck and Simon Watson
Taylor, eds. (Updike)
41:221-8 O2'65. B      11522
The selected works of Cesare
Pavese. by Cesare Pavese.
R.W. Flint, trans. and ed.
(Hyman) 44:114-18 Ag24'68.
B                  11523
Selected works, Volume II:
poetry. by Rainer Maria Rilke.
J.B. Leishman, trans.
(Anon.) 36:120 Ja14'61. B
                    11524
The selected writings of John
Jay Chapman. by John Jay
Chapman. Jacques Barzun, ed.
(Anon.) 33:202 O26'57. B
                    11525
Selected writings of Juan Ramón
Jiménez. by Juan Ramón

Jiménez. Eugenio Florit,
ed. H.R. Hays, trans.
(Bogan) 33:130-3 F8'58.
B                    11526
Selected writings of Jules
Laforgue. by Jules
Laforgue. William Jay
Smith, ed. and trans.
(Anon.) 33:167-8 My4'57. B
                     11527
Selected writings of Sydney
Smith. by Sydney Smith.
W.H. Auden, ed. (Anon.)
32:103 Ja12'57. B     11528
Self condemned. by Wyndham
Lewis. (Woodcock) 31:115-24
Je4'55. B             11529
Self-portrait: U.S.A. by David
Douglas Duncan. (Anon.)
45:68 Ja3'70. B       11530
The selling of the president
1968. by Joe McGinniss.
(Sissman) 45:57-8 D27'69. B
                     11531
Semi-detached. by Patricia
Joudry. (Tynan) 36:120-1
Mr19'60. T            11532
Semi-detached. by David
Turner. (Panter-Downes) 38:
80 D22'62 (McCarten) 39:99
O19'63. T             11533
A Senate journal, 1943-45. by
Allen Drury. (Anon.) 39:212
N2'63. B              11534
Senator Joe McCarthy. by
Richard H. Rovere. (Malcolm)
35:83-9 Je27'59. B    11535
Send me no flowers. by Norman
Barasch and Carroll Moore.
(McCarten) 36:94-6 D17'60.
T                    11536
Sense of humour. by Stephen
Potter. (Anon.) 31:111-12
F26'55. B             11537
A sense of life in the modern
novel. by Arthur Mizener.
(Adler) 40:60 Jy4'64. B
                     11538
A sense of reality. by
Graham Greene. (Anon.)
39:89 Ag10'63. B      11539
Senso. (Flanner) 32:60
*Ag4'56. CC           11540

A separate peace. by John
Knowles. (Balliett) 36:
158-9 Ap2'60. B       11541
Separate tables. by Terence
Rattigan. (Gibbs) 32:68-70
N3'56. T              11542
Separate tables. (McCarten)
34:59 Ja3'59. CC      11543
The seraglio. by James
Merrill. (Balliett) 33:134-5
Mr30'57. B            11544
Serenade. (McCarten) 32:92
*Mr31'56. CC          11545
The sergeant. (Kael) 44:78-80
Ja18'69. CC           11546
Sergeant Rutledge. (McCarten)
36:100 Je4'60. CC     11547
Serjeant Musgrave's dance.
by John Arden. (Oliver)
42:162-3 Mr19'66. T   11548
The serpent's bite. by
Christine Arnothy. Antonia
White, trans. (Anon.) 37:208
O7'61. B              11549
The serpent's coil. by Farley
Mowat. (Anon.) 38:176-8 My
12'62. B              11550
The servant. (Panter-Downes)
39:207-208 N30'63 (Gill)
40:172-3 Mr21'64. CC  11551
The servant of two masters.
by Carlo Goldoni. (Tynan)
36:122-3 Mr5'60. T    11552
Set Europe ablaze. by E.H.
Cookridge. (Anon.) 43:103
Ag12'67. B            11553
Set this house on fire. by
William Styron. (Malcolm)
36:152-4 Je4'60. B    11554
The seven at dawn. by Louis
A. Lippa. (Balliett) 37:94
Ap29'61. T            11555
7 capital sins. (Gill) 38:76
Ja19'63. CC           11556
Seven cities of gold. (McCarten)
31:150*O15'55. CC     11557
Seven days at the Silbersteins.
by Etienne Leroux. (Gilliatt)
43:237-42 N18'67. B   11558
Seven days in May. (Gill) 40:
112 F22'64. CC        11559
Seven days of mourning. by
Seymour Simckes. (Oliver)

36:126 F11'61. B          11594
Shalako. (Kael) 44:127 N16'68. CC
                          11595
Shame. (Kael) 44:56-9
   D28'68. CC             11596
The shameless old lady. (Gill)
   42:127-8 O8'66. CC     11597
The shape of content. by Ben
   Shahn. (Anon.) 33:242
   *N30'57. B             11598
The shaping of the Arabs: a study
   in ethnic identity. by Joel
   Carmichael. (Anon.) 43:
   87-8 Jy22'67. B        11599
The shaping of the modern
   world, 1870-1914. by
   Maurice Bruce. (Anon.)
   34:128 S6'58. B        11600
The shaping years. by Mark
   DeWolfe Howe. (Rovere)
   33:157-63 Ap6'57. B    11601
Shark! by Thomas Helm.
   (Anon.) 37:179-80 My13'61. B
                          11602
Sharon's grave. by John B.
   Keane. (Oliver) 37:98-9
   N18'61. T              11603
Shaw: an autobiography,
   1856-1898. by George
   Bernard Shaw. Stanley
   Weintraub, ed. (Anon.) 45:
   246 D6'69. B           11604
Shaw and Molly Tomkins. by
   Molly Tompkins. Peter
   Tompkins, ed. (Anon.) 38:
   179-80 Mr24'62. B      11605
Shaw on theater. by George
   Bernard Shaw. E.J. West,
   ed. (Anon.) 34:64 Jy5'58.
   B                      11606
She and he. (Gill) 43:151-2
   Ap22'67. CC            11607
She loves me. by Joe Masteroff,
   Jerry Bock and Sheldon Harnick.
   (Oliver) 39:90 My4'63. T
                          11608
She shall have music. by Stuart
   Bishop. (Malcolm) 34:88-90
   F7'59. T               11609
She stoops to conquer. by
   Oliver Goldsmith. (Balliett)
   36:105-107 N12'60. T   11610

The sheep has five legs.
   (McCarten) 31:62*Ag20'55. CC
                          11611
Sheep on the runway. by Art
   Buchwald. (Gill) 45:70-2
   F7'70. T               11612
Shelburne and reform. by
   John Norris. (Anon.) 39:96
   D21'63. B              11613
The sheltering desert. by
   Henno Martin. Edward
   Fitzgerald, trans. (Anon.)
   34:201 O25'58. B       11614
The shepherd's calendar. by
   John Clare. Eric Robinson
   and Geoffrey Summerfield,
   eds. (Anon.) 42:179-80
   Mr12'66. B             11615
The Sheppard murder case.
   by Paul Holmes. (Anon.) 37:
   168-70 S30'61. B       11616
The Sheriff of Fractured Jaw.
   (McCarten) 35:165-6 Mr21'59.
   CC                     11617
Sherry! by James Lipton and
   Laurence Rosenthal. (Mc-
   Carten) 43:138 Ap8'67. T
                          11618
Sherwood Anderson's memoirs:
   a critical edition. by
   Sherwood Anderson. Ray Lewis
   White, ed. (Anon.) 45:215
   O18'69. B              11619
The shewing-up of Blanco
   Posnet. by George Bernard
   Shaw. (Malcolm) 35:95-6
   S26'59. T              11620
The shield of Achilles. by
   W.H. Auden. (Bogan) 31:
   123-4 Ap30'55. B       11621
Shinbone Alley. by Joe
   Darion and Mel Brooks. (Gibbs)
   33:82-4 Ap20'57. T     11622
Shinny on your own side, and
   other memories of growing up.
   by Max Miller. (Anon.) 33:
   140 F15'58. B          11623
Ship ashore! by Jeanette
   Edwards Rattray. (Anon.)
   31:71-2*Ag6'55. B      11624
Ship of fools. by Katherine Anne
   Porter. (Moss) 38:165-73
   Ap28'62. B             11625

Ship of fools. (Gill) 41:56
Jy31'65. CC            11626
The shoemaker and the peddler.
by Armand Aulicino. (Balliett)
36:92-3 O22'60. T       11627
Shoemaker's holiday. by Ted
Berger and Mel Melvin.
(Oliver) 43:127-30 Mr11'67.
T                      11628
The shoes. (Gill) 38:205
N24'62. CC             11629
The shoes of the fisherman.
(Kael) 44:198-9 N23'68. CC
                       11630
Shoestring '57. Anon. (Gibbs)
32:91-2 D8'56. T        11631
Shoestring review. by Ben
Bagley. (Gibbs) 31:67-8
Mr12'55. T             11632
The shook-up generation. by
Harrison E. Salisbury. (Anon.)
34:213 N8'58. B         11633
Shoot anything with hair that
moves. by Donald Ross.
(Oliver) 44:93 F15'69. T
                       11634
Shoot the piano player. (Oliver)
38:50 Ag4'62. CC        11635
Shooting at Sharpsville. by
Ambrose Reeves. (Anon.)
36:127 F11'61. B        11636
The shop on Main Street. (Gill)
41:90 Ja29'66. CC       11637
The shore dimly seen. by
Robert C. Goldston. (Anon.)
39:188-9 Ap6'63. B      11638
A short course in the secret
war. by Christopher
Felix. (Anon.) 39:190 Ap6
'63. B                 11639
A short history of biology. by
Isaac Asimov. (Anon.)
40:91-2 Jy25'64. B      11640
A shot in the dark. by Harry
Kurnitz. (McCarten) 37:135
O28'61. T              11641
A shot in the dark. (McCarten)
40:58-9 Jy4'64. CC      11642
Shout from the rooftops. by Jess
Gregg. (Oliver) 40:100-102
N7'64. T               11643
The show-off. by George Kelly.
(McCarten) 43:97-8 D16'67.
T                      11644

The shrike. (McCarten) 31:58-9
Jy16'55. CC            11645
Shutters west. by Nina Hull
Miller. (Anon.) 39:215-16
O12'63. B              11646
Siberia and the exile system.
by George F. Kennan.
(Balliett) 34:139-43 Mr8'58.
B                      11647
The sibyl. by Pär Lagerkvist.
(West) 34:135-8 F22'58.
B                      11648
The Sicilian vespers. by
Steven Runciman. (Anon.)
34:160 Ap12'58. B       11649
The sick fox. by Paul Brodeur.
(Balliett) 39:118 Je15'63.
B                      11650
Sickles the incredible. by
W.A. Swanberg. (West)
32:135-43*Ap28'56. B   11651
Sid Caesar invites you. (J.
Lardner) 34:67-71 Mr29'58;
34:110-13 Ap19'58. TV
                       11652
The side of the angels. by
Alexander Fedoroff.
(Anon.) 36:61 D24'60. B
                       11653
The siege of Paris. by Robert
Baldick. (Anon.) 40:215-16
S19'64. B              11654
The siege of the Alcázar. by
Cecil D. Eby. (Anon.)
41:107 Ja22'66. B       11655
The siege of Vienna. by John
Stoye. (Anon.) 42:209 Mr
19'66. B               11656
The sign in Sidney Brustein's
window. by Lorraine
Hansberry. (McCarten) 40:
93 O24'64. T           11657
The sign of Jonah. by Guenter
Rutenborn. (Balliett) 36:97-
100 S24'60. T          11658
Sign on for Tokyo. by Alec
Haig. (Anon.) 44:92 F1'69.
B                      11659
A significant experience. by
Gwyn Griffin. (Anon.) 39:188
O5'63. B               11660
Signore e signori. (Gilliatt) 43:
74-5 Ag12'67. CC       11661

Signs along the cynic route. by Will Holt and Dolly Jonah. (Oliver) 37:68-9 Ja20'62. T 11662

Sigrid and the sergeant. by Robert Buckner. (Malcolm) 33:236-40 D7'57. B 11663

The silence. (Gill) 39:106-108 F8'64. CC 11664

A silence of desire. by Kamala Markandaya. (Anon.) 36:106 S3'60. B 11665

The silence of history. by James T. Farrell. (Anon.) 39:149 F23'63. B 11666

The silencers.(Gill) 42:128 Mr 26'66. CC 11667

The silent explosion. by Philip Appleman. (Anon.) 41:110 Je26'65. B 11668

Silent night, lonely night. by Robert Anderson. (Tynan) 35:102-103 D12'59. T 11669

The silent sky. by Allan W. Eckert. (Anon.) 41:238-41 N27'65. B 11670

Silent voices. by Josephine Carson. (Anon.)45:178 N1'69. B 11671

The silent world. (Flanner) 32:76-8*Mr31'56 (McCarten) 32:181 O13'56. CC 11672

Silhouette in diamonds. by Ishbel Ross. (West) 36:117-21 F11'61. B 11673

Silhouettes. by Ted Harris. (Oliver) 45:90-2 S20'69. T 11674

The silk road. by Luce Boulnois. Dennis Chamberlain, trans. (Anon.) 42:167-8 Je11'66. B 11675

Silk stockings. by Cole Porter, George S. Kaufman, Leueen MacGrath,and Abe Burrows. (Gibbs) 31:68-9 Mr5'55. T 11676

Silk stockings. (McCarten) 33:48 Ag3'57. CC 11677

Silver spoon. by Edwin Gilbert. (Anon.) 33:136-9 My25'57. B 11678

Simon and Laura. (McCarten) 32:41*Jy21'56. CC 11679

Simon of the desert. (Kael) 44:109-15 F15'69. CC 11680

Simon says. by Margaret Ritter. (Anon.) 42:236 S24'66. B 11681

Simone Weil: a fellowship in love. by Jacques Cabaud. (N. Bliven) 41:106-10 Ja8'66. B 11682

Simple stakes a claim. by Langston Hughes. (Anon.) 33:195-6 N2'57. B 11683

The simple truth. by Elizabeth Hardwick. (Anon.) 31:159-60 My7'55. B 11684

The sin of Pat Muldoon. by John McLiam. (Gibbs) 33:98-100 Mr23'57. T 11685

Sinai victory. by S.L.A. Marshall. (Anon.) 34:239-40 D6'58. B 11686

Sinatra, Frank. (J. Lardner) 33:114-18 N2'57. TV 11687

Sincerely, Willis Wayde. by John P. Marquand. (Anon.) 31:109 F26'55. B 11688

Sing muse! by Erich Segal and Joseph Raposo. (Oliver) 37:100-102 D16'61. T 11689

The singing nun. (Gill) 42:125 Mr26'66. CC 11690

The singing wilderness. by Sigurd F. Olson. (Anon.) 32:156-8*My5'56. B 11691

Single man at a party. by Richard Kayne. (Malcolm) 35:99 My2'59. T 11692

A single pebble. by John Hersey. (Anon.) 32:74*Jy21'56. B 11693

A singular man. by J. P. Donleavy. (Adler) 40:203-204 My16'64. B 11694

A sinister twilight: the fall of Singapore, 1942. Noel Barber. (Anon.) 44:211-12 O26'68. B 11695

Sink the Bismarck! (McCarten) 36:162-3 F20'60. CC 11696

The sins of Rose Bernd. (Mc-
Carten) 34:97 Ja31'59. CC
                              11697
Sir Michael and Sir George.
by J. B. Priestley. (Anon.)
41:143 F12'66. B        11698
Sir Robert Walpole, the king's
minister. by J. H. Plumb.
(Anon.) 37:83 S2'61. B
                              11699
Sir Walter Ralegh: his family
and private life. by A. L.
Rowse. (Anon.) 38:89-90 Je
30'62. B                11700
Sir Walter Scott: his life and
personality. by Hesketh Pear-
son. (Anon.) 31:119-20 Mr
5'55. B                 11701
Sir William Hamilton: envoy
extraordinary. by Brian
Fothergill. (Anon.) 45:84
Ja17'70. B              11702
Siren land. by Norman Douglas.
(West) 33:112-16 Ja11'58. B
                              11703
The sitzkrieg of Private Stefan.
by Erich Kuby. Theodore H.
Lustig, trans. (Anon.) 38:121
F2'63. B                11704
Six characters in search of
an author. by Luigi Pirandello.
(Gibbs) 31:46-7*D24'55
(Oliver) 39:74-5 Mr23'63. T
                              11705
600 million Chinese. by
Robert Guillain. Mervyn Savill,
trans. (Anon.) 33:201 O26'57.
B                       11706
The sixteenth century: from
Leonardo to El Greco. by
Lionello Venturi. (Anon.)
32:239-40 D1'56. B      11707
The $64,000 challenge. (J.
Lardner) 34:70-3 Ag9'58.
TV                      11708
Skaterdater. (Adler) 42:108-10
Ag20'66. CC             11709
The skin of our teeth. by
Thornton Wilder. (Gibbs)
31:68-70*Ag27'55. T     11710
The sky above--the mud below.
(Gill) 38:68 Je30'62.
CC                      11711

The sky falls. by Lorenza
Mazzetti. Marguerite
Waldman, trans. (West) 39:
185-6 O5'63. B          11712
The sky suspended. by Drew
Middleton. (Anon.) 36:245-6
D10'60. B               11713
Skyscraper. by Peter Stone,
James Van Heusen, and
Sammy Cahn. (McCarten)
41:149 N20'65. T        11714
A slanting light. by Gerda
Charles. (Balliett) 39:229-33
D14'63. B               11715
Slapstick tragedy. by Tennessee
Williams. (McCarten) 42:83-4
Mr5'66. T               11716
Slaughterhouse five. by Kurt
Vonnegut, Jr. (S. Lardner)
45:145-6 My17'69. B     11717
The slave. by LeRoi Jones.
(Oliver) 40:50-2 D26'64.
T                       11718
Slave ship. by LeRoi Jones.
(Oliver) 45:168 D6'69. T
                              11719
Slave trade in the world today.
(Gill) 40:198-200 D12'64.
CC                      11720
The sleep of reason. by
Warren Miller. (Anon.)
36:56 D31'60. B         11721
The sleep of reason. by
C. P. Snow. (Steiner)
45:85-9 Jy12'69. B      11722
The sleeping car murder.
(Gill) 42:113-14 Mr12'66.
CC                      11723
The sleeping prince. by
Terence Rattigan. (Gibbs)
32:112-14*N10'56. T     11724
The sleepless moon. by H. E.
Bates. (Anon.) 32:153
*Ap14'56. B             11725
The sleepwalkers: a history of
man's changing vision of the
universe. by Arthur Koestler.
(N. Bliven) 35:183-9
S19'59. B               11726
The slender thread. (Gill)
41:71 Ja15'66. CC       11727
A slight ache. by Harold
Pinter. (Oliver) 40:70-1
D19'64. T               11728

Slightly scarlet. (McCarten)
32:116*Mr24'56. CC          11729
Slow dance on the killing
ground. by William Hanley.
(McCarten) 40:154-6 D12
'64. T          11730
The slow natives. by Thea
Astley. (Anon.) 43:246-7
N18'67. B          11731
The small hours. (Balliett)
38:67 Ag25'62. CC          11732
The small room. by May
Sarton. (Anon.) 37:77-8
S2'61. B          11733
Small war on Murray Hill.
by Robert E. Sherwood.
(Gibbs) 32:58-60 Ja12'57.
T          11734
Small world. (J. Lardner)
35:162-6 Ap18'59; 35:189-93
D12'59. TV          11735
The small world of Sammy
Lee. (Miller) 39:52-4 Ag17'63.
CC          11736
The smile on the face of the
lion. by P. M. Pasinetti.
(West) 41:178-81 Mr27'65.
B          11737
Smiles of a Summer night.
(McCarten) 33:103 Ja11'58.
CC          11738
Smiling, the boy fell dead.
by Ira Wallach, David
Baker, and Sheldon
Harnick. (Balliett) 37:94-5
Ap29'61. T          11739
Smoke Island. by Antony
Trew. (Anon.) 40:244 N14'64.
B          11740
The smokeweaver's daughter.
by Thomas Barbour. (Mal-
colm) 35:87-8 Ap25'59. T
          11741
Snake man. by Alan Wykes.
(Anon.) 37:175 Ap8'61. B
          11742
Snow gods. by Frederic
Morton. (Anon.) 44:88 Ja11
'69. B          11743
The snow was black. (Mc-
Carten) 32:159 O27'56. CC
          11744

So excellent a fishe. by
Archie Carr. (Anon.) 43:
246-7 N25'67. B          11745
So fell the angels. by Thomas
Graham Belden and Marva
Robins Belden. (Anon.) 32:
87*S1'56. B          11746
So human an animal. by René
Dubos. (Anon.) 45:139
My24'69. B          11747
Soap operas. (J. Lardner)
34:131-5 S13'58. TV          11748
Socialism in one country, 1924-
26. by Edward Hallett
Carr. (Anon.) 34:143-4
F7'59. B          11749
Socialism reëxamined by
Norman Thomas. (Anon.)
39:119-20 Ja18'64. B          11750
The society I live in is mine.
by Paul Goodman. (Anon.)
39:74 Jy6'63. B          11751
Sodom and Gomorrah. (Gill)
38:101-102 F2'63. CC          11752
The soft skin. (Gill) 40:149-50
O24'64. CC          11753
Sold for silver. by Janet
Lim. (Anon.) 35:177 Mr21'59.
B          11754
The soldier and the rose. by
Marcel Haedrich. Monroe
Sterns, trans. (Anon.)
38:84 Jy7'62. B          11755
Soldier in the West: the Civil
War letters of Alfred Lacey
Hough. by Alfred Lacey
Hough. Robert G. Athearn,
ed. (Anon.) 33:164-5 My11
'57. B          11756
Soldier of fortune. (McCarten)
31:124 Je11'55. CC          11757
Soldier: the memoirs of Mat-
thew B. Ridgway. by
Matthew B. Ridgway. (Anon.)
32:145*Ap28'56. B          11758
A soldier with the Arabs. by
John Bagot Glubb. (Liebling)
34:182-90 O4'58. B          11759
Soldiers. by Rolf Hochhuth.
(Gill) 44:83-4 My11'68. T
          11760
The soldier's art. by Anthony

Powell. (Anon.) 43:145
Je3'67. B                11761
The solid gold Cadillac.
(McCarten) 32:174-5 N3'56.
CC                       11762
The solitary singer: a critical
biography of Walt Whitman.
by Gay Wilson Allen. (Bogan)
31:106-108 F26'55. B     11763
Solomon and Sheba. (McCarten)
35:75 Ja9'60. CC         11764
Some angry angel. by Richard
Condon. (Balliett) 36:156-8
Ap2'60. B                11765
Some beasts no more. by
Kenneth Giles. (Anon.) 44:239-
40 N9'68. B              11766
Some came running. by James
Jones. (Anon.) 33:102-105
Ja18'58. B               11767
Some came running. (McCarten)
34:94-7 Ja31'59. CC      11768
Some classic trains. by Arthur
D. Dubin. (Anon.) 43:72
D23'67. B                11769
Some corner of an English
field. by Dannie Abse.
(Anon.) 32:72-3 Ja5'57.
B                        11770
Some late Victorian attitudes.
by David Daiches. (Anon.)
45:211-12 N29'69. B      11771
Some like it hot. (McCarten)
35:142-3 Ap4'59. CC      11772
Some prefer nettles. by Junichirō
Tanizaki. (West) 31:101-102
Je18'55. B               11773
Some trees. by John Ashbery.
(Bogan) 32:85-6*S1'56. B
                         11774
Someone waiting. by Emlyn
Williams. (Gibbs) 32:89-
90*F25'56. T             11775
Someone will die tonight in
the Caribbean. by René
Puissesseau. Stephen
Becker, trans. (Anon.)
34:202-203 O25'58. B     11776
Someone's comin' hungry. by
McCrea Imbrie and Neil Selden.
(Oliver) 45:131-2 Ap12'69.
T                        11777

Something about a soldier. by
Ernest Kinoy. (McCarten)
37:62 Ja13'62. T         11778
Something different. by Carl
Reiner. (McCarten) 43:93-4
D9'67. T                 11779
Something more! by Nate
Monaster. (McCarten) 40:
143-4 N21'64. T          11780
Something of value. (McCarten)
33:146-7 My18'57. CC     11781
Something to answer for.
by P.H. Newby. (Sheed)
45:125-8 S6'69. B        11782
Something wicked this way
comes. by Ray Bradbury.
(Anon.) 38:216 O27'62. B
                         11783
Something wild. (Gill) 37:45
D30'61. CC               11784
Sometimes, but not always.
by James Stevenson. (Anon.)
43:82 Ag5'67. B          11785
Son of dust. by H.F.M.
Prescott. (Anon.) 32:101-102
Ja12'57. B               11786
Son of Oblomov. by Ricardo
Aragno. (Panter-Downes)
40:62 Ja2'65. T          11787
Son of Talleyrand. by
Françoise de Bernardy.
Lucy Norton, trans. (Anon.)
33:166 My4'57. B         11788
Sondra. by Frederick Feirstein.
(Oliver) 43:138-40 My20'67.
T                        11789
A song at twilight. by Noёl
Coward. (Panter-Downes)
42:70 Jy23'66. T         11790
A song of sixpence. by A.J.
Cronin. (Anon.) 40:222-3
O3'64. B                 11791
Song of songs. by Jean
Giraudoux. (Malcolm) 34:63
Ja31'59. T               11792
The song of the grasshopper.
by Alfonso Paso. (McCarten)
43:131-2 O7'67. T        11793
Song of the Lusitanian bogey.
by Peter Weiss and Coleridge-
Taylor Perkinson. (Oliver)
43:57-8 Ja13'68. T       11794

Song without end. (Balliett) 36:73
Ag20'60. CC            11795
Sons and lovers. (Balliett) 36:56-8
Ag13'60. CC            11796
Sons of the shaking earth. by
Eric R. Wolf. (Anon.)
36:162-3 Ap2'60. B     11797
Soon, one morning: new writing
by American Negroes, 1940-62.
Herbert Hill, ed. (Anon.)
39:92 Ag10'63. B       11798
Sophie. by Phillip Pruneau
and Steve Allen. (McCarten)
39:82-4 Ap27'63. T     11799
Sophokles' Women of Trachis: a
version by Ezra Pound. by
Ezra Pound. (Anon.) 33:200
N2'57. B               11800
Soul clap hands and sing. by
Paule Marshall. (Anon.) 37:180
S23'61. B              11801
The soul of China. by Amaury
de Riencourt. (Anon.) 34:238-9
N29'58. B              11802
The soul of kindness. by
Elizabeth Taylor. (Balliett)
40:118 Ja23'65. B      11803
The sound. by Ross Russell.
(Balliett) 37:68-9 Jy8'61. B
                       11804
The sound and the fury.
(McCarten) 35:143 Ap4'59. CC
                       11805
The sound of laughter. (J.
Lardner) 34:78-82 Je7'58.
TV                     11806
The sound of music. by
Richard Rodgers and Oscar
Hammerstein, II. (Tynan)
35:106-10 N28'59. T    11807
The sound of music. (Gill)
41:96 Mr6'65. CC       11808
A sound of silence. by Harold
Willis. (Oliver) 41:84 Mr20
'65. T                 11809
The sound of trumpets. (Gill)
39:205-206 O26'63. CC
                       11810
The sounds of Eden. (J. Lardner)
35:203 D5'59. TV       11811
The source. by James A.
Michener. (Anon.) 41:106-
109 Je26'65. B         11812

The South and the Southerner.
by Ralph McGill. (Anon.)
39:176-7 Ap27'63. B
                       11813
South from Granada. by Gerald
Brenan. (West) 33:111-12
Ja11'58. B             11814
South of the moon. by Blaine
Littell. (Anon.) 42:83-4
Jy30'66. B             11815
South Pacific. (McCarten)
34:105 Mr29'58. CC     11816
South seas adventure.
(Hamburger) 34:48-9 Ag2'58.
CC                     11817
South to the Pole: the early
history of the Ross Sea
Sector, Antarctica. by L.B.
Quartermain. (Anon.)
43:189-90 O7'67. B     11818
A Southern reader. by
Willard Thorp, ed. (Anon.)
31:134 *O1'55. B       11819
A souvenir from Qam. by
Marc Connelly. (Anon.)
41:119 Ag14'65. B      11820
Soviet Russian nationalism. by
Frederick C. Barghoorn.
(Anon.) 32:187-8 O6'56. B
                       11821
Soviet scientist in Red China.
by Mikhail A. Klochko.
(Anon.) 40:228-30 O17'64.
B                      11822
The Soviet world. by Luca
Pietromarchi. Lovett F.
Edwards, trans. (Anon.) 41:
117-18 Ja15'66. B      11823
Sowing. by Leonard Woolf.
(Anon.) 36:202-203
O8'60. B               11824
The Spanish Civil War. by
Hugh Thomas. (N. Bliven)
37:200-205 O21'61. B
                       11825
The Spanish gardener. (Mc-
Carten) 33:77 S21'57. CC
                       11826
Spanish Harlem: anatomy of
poverty. by Patricia Cayo
Sexton. (Hentoff) 41:74-8
Jy31'65. B             11827
The Spanish inquisition. by

Henry Kamen. (Anon.) 42:237-
8 S24'66. B          11828
Spanish leaves. by Honor
Tracy. (Anon.) 40:246-7
N7'64. B             11829
Sparrows can't sing. (Gill)
39:169-70 My18'63. CC  11830
Spartacus. (Gill) 36:133-4
O15'60. CC           11831
Speaking of murder. by
Audrey Roos and William
Roos. (Gibbs) 32:45 D29'56.
T                    11832
Speaking of pianists. by Abram
Chasins. (Anon.) 33:198
N2'57. B             11833
The special friendship. (Gill)
43:137-8 N18'67. CC  11834
Speculations about Jakob. by
Uwe Johnson. Ursule Molinaro,
trans. (Anon.) 39:177-8
My18'63. B           11835
The spider's house. by Paul
Bowles. (West) 31:208-10*D
3'55. B              11836
Spindrift. by John J. Rowlands.
(Anon.) 36:184 O1'60. B
                     11837
Spinster. by Sylvia Ashton-
Warner. (Wain) 35:169-70
Ap11'59. B           11838
The spirit of St. Louis.
(McCarten) 33:88 Mr2'57.
CC                   11839
Spirits of the dead. (Gilliatt)
45:144-5 S13'69. CC  11840
Spiro who? by William
Meyers. (Oliver) 45:77 My31'69.
T                    11841
Spitting image. by Colin
Spencer. (Oliver) 45:134-5
Mr15'69. T           11842
The splendid pauper. by
Allen Andrews. (Anon.) 44:
80 Ag3'68. B         11843
Splendor in the grass. (Gill)
37:177-8 O14'61. CC  11844
The split. (Kael) 44:199-201
N23'68. CC           11845
Spofford. by Herman Shumlin.
(McCarten) 43:43 J23'67.
T                    11846

The sponge room. by Keith
Waterhouse and Willis Hall.
(Oliver) 40:124 Mr7'64.
T                    11847
Spopono. by Alan Paton and
Krishna Shah. (McCarten)
40:95 Ap11'64. T     11848
Spoon River anthology. by
Edgar Lee Masters. Charles
Aidman, adapt. (McCarten)
39:89 O12'63. T      11849
Spring on an Arctic island.
by Katharine Scherman.
(Anon.) 32:201-202 O20'56.
B                    11850
Spring song and other stories.
by Joyce Cary. (Anon.)
36:160 D17'60. B     11851
The springtime of freedom.
by William McCord. (Anon.)
41:111-12 Je26'65. B 11852
The spy who came in from the
cold. (Gill) 41:46 Ja1'66.
CC                   11853
The square. by Marguerite
Duras. Ann Borchardt,
trans. (Balliett) 37:100 Ap
1'61. T              11854
Square in the eye. by Jack
Gelber. (Oliver) 41:56-8
My29'65. T           11855
The square pegs. by Irving
Wallace. (Anon.) 33:110
Ag24'57. B           11856
The square root of wonderful.
by Carson McCullers. (Gibbs)
33:103-105 N9'57. T  11857
Squat Betty. by Keith Water-
house and Willis Hall. (Oliver)
40:122-4 Mr7'64. T   11858
Stage struck. (McCarten) 34:
62 My3'58. CC        11859
Staircase. by Charles Dyer.
(Gill) 43:82 Ja20'68. T
                     11860
Staircase. (Gilliatt) 45:74
Ag30'69. CC          11861
Stalingrad. by Hans Schröter.
Constantine FitzGibbon,
trans. (Anon.) 34:237-8
N29'58. D            11862
The stalking moon. (Kael) 44:
74-7 F1'69. CC       11863

Stanton: the life and times
of Lincoln's Secretary of
War. by Benjamin P.
Thomas and Harold M.
Hyman. (Anon.) 38:142
Mr31'62. B          11864
Star! (Kael) 44:206-209 O
26'68. CC          11865
The stars grow pale. by Karl
Bjarnhof. Naomi Walford,
trans. (Anon.) 34:106 My31
'58. B          11866
The star-spangled girl. by
Neil Simon. (McCarten) 42:59
D31'66. T          11867
Starting from tomorrow. by
Tony Gray. (Anon.) 41:108
Jy17'65. B          11868
State fair. (Gill) 38:172-3
Ap14'62. CC          11869
State of possession. by Edith
deBorn. (Anon.) 39:91
Ag17'63. B          11870
The stature of man. by Colin
Wilson. (Anon.) 35:122-3
Ja16'60. B          11871
The stature of Theodore Dreiser.
by Alfred Kazin, and
Charles Shapiro, eds. (Anon.)
31:154*D17'55. B          11872
The status seekers. by Vance
Packard. (Anon.) 35:192
My16'59. B          11873
Stauffenberg. by Joachim
Kramarz. R.H. Barry,
trans. (Anon.) 43:177-8
S23'67. B          11874
Steam's finest hour. by David
P. Morgan, ed. (Anon.)
35:135*D19'59. B          11875
Stella. (McCarten) 33:73
Je29'57. CC          11876
Step on a crack. by Bernard
Evslin. (McCarten) 38:148
O27'62. T          11877
Stephen Crane: a biography.
By R.W. Stallman. (Anon.)
44:180 S28'68. B          11878
Stephen Crane: letters. by
Stephen Crane. R.W. Stallman
and Lillian Gilkes, ed.
(Liebling) 37:48-72 Ag5
'61. B          11879

Stephen Crane: Sullivan County
tales and sketches. by
Stephen Crane. R.W.
Stallman, ed. (Anon.) 44:
249 N23'68. B          11880
Stephen D. by Hugh Leonard.
(Oliver) 43:132-3 O7'67.
T          11881
Stephen Hero. by James Joyce.
John J. Slocum and Herbert
Cahoon, eds. (Anon.) 32:143
*Mr10'56. B          11882
The stepmother. by R.C.
Hutchinson. (Anon.) 31:94
*Ag27'55. B          11883
The sterile cuckoo. (Kael)
45:138-40 N1'69. CC 11884
The Steve Allen show. (J.
Lardner) 34:113-14 Ap19'58.
TV          11885
The stick and the stars. by
William King. (Anon.) 34:
178 S27'58. B          11886
Stolen kisses. (Kael) 45:114-15
Mr8'69. CC          11887
Stomp. Anon. (Oliver) 45:88
N29'69. T          11888
The stone bridal bed. by
Harry Mulisch. Adrienne
Dixon, trans. (Anon.)
39:164-5 My25'63. B 11889
Stoner. by John Williams.
(Anon.) 41:155-6 Je12'65.
B          11890
Stop the world--I want to get
off. by Anthony Newley and
Leslie Bricusse. (McCarten)
38:180 O13'62. T          11891
Stop, you're killing me. by
James Leo Herlihy. (Oliver)
45:99-100 Mr29'69. T 11892
Stop-time. by Frank Conroy.
(S. Lardner) 43:106-11
F3'68. B          11893
The stories of William Sansom.
by William Sansom. (Anon.)
39:246 O19'63. B          11894
Stories to remember. Thomas
B. Costain and John
Beecroft, eds. (Anon.)
32:238 N17'56. B          11895
Stormy passage. by W.S. Woy-
tinsky. (Anon.) 38:192 My5
'62. B          11896

The story of a life. by Konstantin Paustovsky. Joseph Barnes, trans. (N. Bliven) 40:70-2 Ja2'64. B     11897

The story of a three day pass. (Gilliatt) 44:78 Jy20'68. CC     11898

Story of a year: 1848. by Raymond Postgate. (Anon.) 31:131*F18'56. B     11899

The story of jazz. by Marshall Stearns. (Anon.) 32:241 N17'56. B     11900

The story of mankind. (McCarten) 33:108-109 N16'57. CC     11901

The story of medicine. by Kenneth Walker. (Anon.) 31:87-8*Ag20ª55. B     11902

The story of Ruth. (McCarten) 36:70 Je25'60. CC     11903

The story of Vickie. (McCarten) 33:126-9 F8'58. CC     11904

The story of Walt Disney. by Diane Disney Miller. (Anon.) 34:143-6 Mr15'58. B     11905

The story on page one. (McCarten) 35:120-1 Ja23'60. CC     11906

Stover at Yale. (J. Lardner) 33:145-6 N16'57. TV     11907

Stowaway in the sky. (Gill) 38:68 Je30'62. CC     11908

The straight and narrow path. by Honor Tracy. (Gill) 32: 181-2 D15'56. B     11909

Strange bedfellows. (Gill) 41:154 Mr20'65. CC     11910

The strange career of Jim Crow. by C. Vann Woodward. (Anon.) 31:71*S3'55; 41:143 F12'66. B     11911

The strange enchantment. by Geoffrey Cotterell. (Anon.) 33:163-4 Ap6'57. B     11912

Strange interlude. by Eugene O'Neill. (McCarten) 39:73 Mr23'63. T     11913

The strange one. (McCarten) 33:134-5 Ap20'57. CC     11914

The strange ordeal of the Normandier. by H. L. Tredree.

(Anon.) 35:178 Mr21'59. B     11915

The stranger. (Gill) 43:48 D30'67. (Kael) 43:105 F10 '68. CC     11916

Stranger in two worlds. by Hugh Clevely. (Anon.) 35:120-1 Ja16'60. B     11917

A stranger knocks. (Gill) 41:106 Ap3'65. CC     11918

The stranger's hand. (McCarten) 31:73-4 Mr5'55. CC     11919

Strangers in the city. (Oliver) 38:73 Jy28'62. CC     11920

Strangers when we meet. (Gill) 36:168-9 S24'60. CC     11921

The stranglers: the cult of Thugee and its overthrow in British India. by George Bruce. (Anon.) 45:120 Mr1'69. B     11922

Strategic air command. (McCarten) 31:116-17 Ap30'55. CC     11923

Strategy in the missile age. by Bernard Brodie. (B. Bliven) 36:186-95 Mr12'60. B     11924

The straw man. by Jean Giono. (West) 35:114-16 Je20'59. B     11925

Stray dog. (Gill) 40:169-70 Mr7'64. CC     11926

The street where the heart lies. by Ludwig Bemelmans. (Anon.) 38:97 Ja5'63. B     11927

A streetcar named Desire. by Tennessee Williams. (Gibbs) 32:86-9*F25'56. T     11928

The streets of New York. by Barry Allen Grael and Richard B. Chodosh. (Oliver) 39:95-8 N9'63. T     11929

Streetwalker. Anon. (Anon.) 36:182 Ap16'60. B     11930

Stride toward freedom: the Montgomery story. by Martin Luther King, Jr.

(Anon.) 34:173-4 S20'58.
B                        11931
Strike a blow and die. by
George Simeon Mwase.
(Hyman) 44:85-8 Jy27'68.
B                        11932
Strike for a kingdom. by
Menna Gallie. (Balliett)
36:140-1 F27'60. B       11933
Strike out where not applicable.
by Nicolas Freeling.
(Anon.) 44:126-7 Je8'68.
B                        11934
The Striker portfolio. by
Adam Hall. (Anon.) 45:175-6
Ap26'69. B               11935
String. by Alice Childress.
(Oliver) 45:131 Ap12'69. T
                         11936
String too short to be saved.
By Donald Hall. (Anon.)
37:181-2 S23'61. B       11937
The strings are false: an un-
finished autobiography. by
Louis MacNeice. (Anon.)
43:192 Mr11'67. B        11938
The strong breed. by
Wole Soyinka. (Oliver)
43:133-4 N18'67. T       11939
The struggle of the modern.
by Stephen Spender. (Anon.)
39:98 F1'64. B           11940
The Stuarts. by J.P.
Kenyon. (Anon.) 35:171-2
Ap11'59. B               11941
The Stuarts in love. by
Maurice Ashley. (Anon.)
40:223-4 O3'64. B        11942
A student's diary: Budapest,
October 16-November 1,
1956. by Laszlo Beke.
Leon Kossar and Ralph M.
Zoltan, eds. & trans.
(Anon.) 33:166 My4'57. B
                         11943
Studies in European realism. by
Georg Lucáks. Edith Bone,
trans. (Anon.) 40:247-8
O10'64. B                11944
The subject was roses. by
Frank D. Gilroy. (McCarten)
40:86 Je6'64. T          11945

The subject was roses.
(Kael) 44:215 O19'68.
CC                       11946
The subterraneans. by
Jack Kerouac. (Malcolm)
34:137-42 Ap5'58. B
                         11947
Subways are for sleeping. by
Betty Comden and Adolph
Green. (McCarten) 37:56
Ja6'62. T                11948
Success story: the life and
times of S.S. McClure.
by Peter Lyon. (Anon.)
39:242-3 N16'63 B        11949
The successor. by Seymour
Epstein. (Anon.) 37:78-81
S2'61. B                 11950
The sudden and accidental
re-education of Horse
Johnson. by Douglas
Taylor. (Gill) 44:50
D28'68. T                11951
Suddenly, last Summer.
by Tennessee Williams.
(Gibbs) 33:66-8 Ja18'58.
T                        11952
Suddenly, last Summer.
(McCarten) 35:74-5 Ja9
'60. CC                  11953
Suez. by Hugh Thomas.
(Anon.) 43:82 Ag5'67. B
                         11954
The Suez war. by Paul
Johnson. (Anon.) 33:177
Ap13'57. B               11955
The sugar pill: an essay on
newspapers. by T.S.
Matthews. (Anon.) 34:94-7
Ja17'59. B               11956
The suitor. (Gill) 39:112-13
S21'63. CC               11957
Summer and smoke. (Gill)
37:205-206 N25'61. CC
                         11958
The Summer intrigue. by
Frank Swinnerton. (Anon.)
31:206*D10'55. B         11959
The Summer lovers. by
Hollis Alpert. (Anon.)
34:74-5 Jy26'58. B       11960
A Summer night. by Alan

Moorehead. (Anon.) 31:151
Mr19'55. B            11961
The Summer of Daisy Miller.
by Bertram Greene. (Oliver)
39:126-8 Je8'63. T    11962
Summer of the seventeenth
doll. by Ray Lawler.
(Panter-Downes) 33:53-4 Jy13'57
(Gibbs) 33:53-4 F1'58
(Oliver) 44:82-4 Mr2'68. T
                      11963
A Summer place. by Sloan
Wilson. (Anon.) 34:160
Ap12'58. B            11964
A Summer place. (McCarten)
35:174 O31'59. CC     11965
A Summer to remember. (Gill)
37:131-2 N11'61. CC   11966
A Summer world. by Richard
Dougherty. (Anon.) 36:141-2
F27'60. B             11967
Summerhill: a radical approach
to child rearing. by A.S.
Neill. (Anon.) 37:151-2 Ap
29'61. B              11968
Summer's lease. by John
Rothenstein. (Anon.) 42:
192-3 Ap23'66. B      11969
Summerskin. (Gill) 38:79
Je2'62. CC            11970
Summertime. (McCarten)
31:64-5 Je25'55. CC   11971
Summertree. by Ron Cowen.
(Oliver) 44:130-4 Mr16'68.
T                     11972
The sun also rises (Hamburger)
33:54 Ag31'57. CC     11973
The sun in scorpio. by
Margery Sharp. (Anon.) 41:
242 N20'65. B         11974
The sun king: Louis XIV at
Versailles. by Nancy
Mitford. (Anon.) 42:245-6
O29'66. B             11975
The sun on the snow. by Rodrigo
Royo. (West) 32:115-16*Je
16'56. B              11976
Sunday in New York. by Norman
Krasna. (McCarten) 37:
160 D9'61. T          11977
Sunday in New York. (Gill)
40:114-16 F22'64. CC 11978

Sundays and Cybele. (Gill)
38:209 N17'62. CC   11979
The sundowners. (Angell)
36:137-8 D17'60. CC
                    11980
The sunken garden. by
Douglass Wallop. (Anon.)
31:105*Ja21'56. B   11981
Sunrise at Campobello. by
Dore Schary. (Gibbs) 33:
93-5 F8'58. T        11982
Sunrise at Campobello.
(Gill) 36:106-107 O8'60.
CC                   11983
Sunrise semester. (J.
Lardner) 33:210-12 D14'57;
35:140-5 My23'59. TV
                     11984
Sunset. by Isaac Babel.
(Oliver) 42:96 My21'66.
T                    11985
Sunset and evening star. by
Sean O'Casey. (Pritchett)
31:147-56 Ap16'55. B
                     11986
The sunset of the splendid
century. by W.H. Lewis.
(Anon.) 31:215*N12'55. B
                     11987
A sunset touch. by Moira
Pearce. (Anon.) 36:204-205
S10'60. B            11988
The supreme choice: Britain
and Europe. by Drew Mid-
dleton. (Anon.) 39:181 My11
'63. B               11989
Surface at the Pole. by
James Calvert. (Anon.)
36:102-103 Ag27'60. B
                     11990
The surprise party complex.
by Ramona Stewart. (Anon.)
38:133 Ja26'63. B    11991
Susy and Mark Twain. Edith
Colgate Salsbury, ed.
(Anon.) 41:245 O23'65.
B                    11992
Sut Lovingood: yarns spun by
a nat'ral born durn'd fool. by
George Washington Harris.
Brom Weber, ed. (Wilson)
31:150-9 My7'55. B  11993

Swamp fox: the life and campaigns of General Francis Marion. by Robert D. Bass. (Anon.) 35:170 Ap4'59. B 11994

The swan. (McCarten) 32:139 *My5'56. CC 11995

The swastika and the eagle. by James V. Compton. (Anon.) 43:86 S2'67. B 11996

Swedish wedding night. (Gill) 41:233-4 N27'65. CC 11997

The Sweeniad. by Victor Purcell. (Wilson) 34:119-50 My24'58. B 11998

Sweet and sour. (Gill) 40: 104-105 Ja9'65. CC 11999

Sweet bird of youth. by Tennessee Williams. (Tynan) 35:98-100 Mr21'59. T 12000

Sweet bird of youth. (Gill) 38:148 Ap7'62. CC 12001

Sweet Charity. by Neil Simon, Dorothy Fields and Cy Coleman. (McCarten) 41:84 F5'66. T 12002

Sweet Charity. (Gilliatt) 45: 138 My10'69. CC 12003

The sweet enemy. by Joyce Carol Oates. (Oliver) 41:99 F27'65. T 12004

Sweet Eros. by Terrence McNally. (Oliver) 44:140-2 D7'68. T 12005

Sweet light in a dark room. (S. Lardner) 42:92 Jy16'66. CC 12006

Sweet love, bitter. (Gill) 42:135 F11'67. CC 12007

Sweet medicine. by Peter J. Powell. (Anon.) 45:88 Ja31'70. B 12008

Sweet Miani. by Ed Tyler. (Oliver) 38:183-4 O13'62. T 12009

Sweet November. (Kael) 43: 109-10 F17'68. CC 12010

Sweet smell of success. (McCarten) 33:57-8 Jy6'57. CC 12011

Swift in the night. by William Byron Mowery.

(Anon.) 32:84*Je30'56. B 12012

The swimmer. (Gilliatt) 44: 84-7 My25'68. CC 12013

Swinburne: a selection. by Algernon Charles Swinburne. Edith Sitwell, ed. (Anon.) 37:135-6 F25'61. B 12014

The Swinburne letters. by Algernon Charles Swinburne. Cecil Y. Lang, ed. (Wilson) 38:165-200 O6'62. B 12015

The Swiss banks. by T.R. Fehrenbach. (Anon.) 42:203-204 My14'66. B 12016

Sylva. by Jean Bruller. Rita Barisse, trans. (Anon.) 37:90-1 Ja6'62. B 12017

Sylvia. (Gill) 40:90-2 F13'65. CC 12018

Symphony for a massacre. (S. Lardner) 41:102 Je 12'65. CC 12019

Synanon. (Gill) 41:167-8 My8 '65. CC 12020

The system: the misgovernment of modern Britain. by Max Nicholson. (Anon.) 45:173 Ap26'69. B 12021

T

T. E. Lawrence; or, the search for the absolute. by Jean Beraud Villars. Peter Dawnay, trans. (Anon.) 35:163-4 My2'59. B 12022

T. H. White. by Sylvia Townsend Warner. (Anon.) 44:202-203 N2'68. B 12023

T. S. Eliot: a symposium for his seventieth birthday. Neville Braybrooke, ed. (Anon.) 34:179 N1'58. B 12024

T. S. Eliot: the man and his work. Allen Tate, ed. (Anon.) 43:195 Mr18'67. B 12025

Ta, ta, tan, tan--"fight fight, talk talk": the inside story

TABLE                    -364-                    TALE

of Communist China. by
Valentin Chu. (Anon.) 39:122-3
Je15'63. B              12026
Table number seven. by
Terence Rattigan. (Gibbs)
32:68-70 N3'56. T       12027
The tailor's maid. (McCarten)
35:123 S12'59. CC       12028
Take a giant step. (Oliver)
37:162-3 Mr18'61. CC
                        12029
Take a girl like you.
by Kingsley Amis. (N.
Bliven) 37:162-4 Ap15'61.
(Sissman) 45:164-5 Ap26'69. B
                        12030
Take heed of loving me: a
novel about John Donne. by
Elizabeth Gray Vining. (Anon.)
39:117 Ja18'64. B       12031
Take her, she's mine. by
Phoebe Ephron. and Henry
Ephron. (McCarten) 37:57-8
Ja6'62. T               12032
Take me along. by Joseph
Stein, Robert Russell and
Bob Merrill.    (Tynan)
35:134-5 O31'59. T      12033
No entry.               12034
Take hands at Winter. by John
Peter. (Anon.) 42:162-3
F11'67. B               12035
Take the money and run.
(Gilliatt) 45:74-5 Ag30'69.
(Kael) 45:149-50 O4'69. CC
                        12036
Taken at the flood. by John
Gunther. (Anon.) 36:107-108
S3'60. B                12037
Taken care of : the auto-
biography of Edith Sitwell.
by Edith Sitwell. (Anon.)
41:156-7 Je12'65. B     12038
The takers. by Max Ehrlich.
(Anon.) 36:91 Ja28'61.
B                       12039
A tale for midnight. by
Frederic Prokosch. (Anon.)
31:85*Ag20'55. B        12040
Tale of a hero. by Stella
Wilchek. (Anon.) 41:201-202
Mr13'65. B              12041

A tale of two cities.
(Hamburger) 34:70 Ag16'58.
CC                      12042
Tales of Paris. (McCarten)
38:82 S8'62. CC         12043
Tales of ten worlds. by
Arthur C. Clarke.
(Bernstein) 38:94-7 Ja5'63.
B                       12044
Talk about America. by
Alistair Cooke. (Anon.)
44:251 N23'68. B        12045
Talking of music. by Neville
Cardus. (Anon.) 33:135-6
F8'58. B                12046
Tall story. by Howard Lind-
say and Russel Crouse. (Ty-
nan) 34:87-8 F7'59. T
                        12047
Tambourines to glory. by
Langston Hughes. (Mc-
Carten) 39:95 N9'63. T
                        12048
Tambourines to glory. by
Langston Hughes. (Anon.) 34:
124-5 Ja24'59. B        12049
Tamburlaine the great. by
Christopher Marlowe. (Gibbs)
31:52*Ja28'56. T        12050
The taming of the shrew. by
William Shakespeare.
(Oliver) 39:137-8 Mr16'63
(Tynan) 44:144-9 N9'68. T
                        12051
The taming of the shrew.
(Gill) 43:181 Mr11'67. CC
                        12052
Tangaroa's godchild. by
Olaf Ruhen. (Anon.) 39:151
F23'63. B               12053
Tango. by Slawomir Mrozek.
(Oliver) 44:50-1 F1'69.
T                       12054
Taras Bulba. (Gill) 38:62
D29'62. CC              12055
Target for three. (J. Lardner)
35:167 O17'59. TV       12056
Targets. (Gilliatt) 44:85
S7'68. CC               12057
The tarnished angels.
(McCarten) 33:95 Ja18'58.
CC                      12058
Tartuffe. by Molière.

(McCarten) 37:112-14
Mr11'61. T         12059
A taste of honey. by Shelagh
Delaney. (Panter-Downes)
34:98 F7'59 (McCarten)
36:73 O15'60. T     12060
A taste of honey. (Gill)
38:164-5 My12'62. CC  12061
The tavern. by George M.
Cohan. (Oliver) 38:108-109
Ap14'62. T         12062
Taxi for Tobruk. (Gill)
41:159-60 Ap10'65. CC
                   12063
Tchin-tchin. by Sidney Michaels.
(McCarten) 38:111 N3'62. T
                   12064
Tea and sympathy. (McCarten)
32:90-1 O6'56. CC   12065
Tea party. by Harold Pinter.
(Oliver) 44:140-1 O26'68.
T                  12066
Teacher's pet. (McCarten)
34:106 Mr29'58. CC  12067
The teahouse of the August
moon. (McCarten) 32:144-5
D8'56. CC          12068
Teenage rebel. (McCarten)
32:179 D15'56. CC   12069
Telemachus Clay. by Lewis
John Carlino. (Oliver) 39:244-5
N23'63. T          12070
Television. (Miller) 39:115-16
N16'63. TV         12071
Tell no tales. by Gina Day.
(Anon.) 44:148 Je8'68. B
                   12072
Tell them Willie boy is here.
(Kael) 45:47-8 D27'69. CC
                   12073
The tempering years. by
Edwin P. Hoyt. (Anon.) 39:
182 My11'63. B      12074
Tempest in the flesh.
(McCarten) 32:94-5 Ja26
'57. CC            12075
The temple of the golden
pavilion. by Yukio Mishima.
Ivan Morris, trans. (West)
35:113-14 Je20'59. B  12076
Tempo di Roma. by Alexis
Curvers. (West) 35:102-103
Jy18'59. B         12077

The temptation of Don Volpi.
by Alfred Hayes. (Anon.)
36:86-7 Ja7'61. B   12078
The temptress and the monk.
(Gill) 39:56 Je15'63. CC
                   12079
The ten commandments.
(McCarten) 32:101-102 N17
'56. CC            12080
Ten North Frederick. by John
O'Hara. (McKelway) 31:
146-50*D17'55. B    12081
Ten North Frederick. (Mc-
Carten) 34:59-60 My31'58.
CC                 12082
The ten pains of death. by
Gavin Maxwell. (West)
36:164-73 F20'60. B  12083
Ten Rillington Place. by
Ludovic Kennedy. (Anon.)
37:243 N11'61. B    12084
1066: the story of a year.
by Denis Butler. (Anon.)
42:166-7 Je4'66. B   12085
10:30 p.m. Summer. (Gill)
42:198-9 N5'66. CC   12086
The ten thousand things. by
Maria Dermoût. (Balliett)
34:144-6 My3'58. B   12087
Ten years of prelude: the
story of integration since
the Supreme Court's 1954
decision. by Benjamin
Muse. (Anon.) 40:124-5
Ag22'64. B         12088
Tender and violent Elizabeth.
by Henri Troyat. Mildred
Marmur, trans. (Anon.)
36:239-40 N12'60. B  12089
Tender is the night. (Gill)
37:83-4 Ja27'62. CC  12090
Tender scoundrel. (Gill)
43:154 D2'67. CC     12091
The tender trap. (McCarten)
31:184*N19'55. CC    12092
Tenderloin. by George Abbott
and Jerome Weidman.
(McCarten) 36:86 O29'60.
T                  12093
The tenth man. by Paddy
Chayefsky. (Tynan) 35:118-
21 N14'59. T        12094
A tenth of an inch makes the

difference. by Rolf Forsberg.
(Oliver) 38:118 N24'62. T 12095
The 10th victim. (Gill)
41:56 D25'65. CC      12096
The tents of wickedness. by Peter
DeVries. (Balliett) 35:201-203
O10'59. B            12097
Teorema. (Gilliatt) 45:91-4
Ap26'69. CC          12098
Term of trial. (Gill) 38:82-3
F9'63. CC            12099
The terrace. (Gill) 40:158
D5'64. CC            12100
Terrible swift sword. by
Bruce Catton. (Anon.)
39:167 My25'63. B    12101
The territorial imperative.
by Robert Ardrey. (Anon.)
42:247 N5'66. B      12102
Terror and resistance: a study
of political violence. by
Eugene Victor Walter. (Anon.)
45:95 Ag9'69. B      12103
The terrorists. by Robert
Payne. (Anon.) 33:199 O12
'57. B               12104
Test ban and disarmament: the
path of negotiation. by Arthur
H. Dean. (Anon.) 42:203 My
14'66. B             12105
Testament of Orpheus. (Gill)
38:171-2 Ap21'62. CC 12106
The testimony of the spade.
by Geoffrey Bibby. (Anon.)
32:185-6 D15'56. B   12107
Tête d'or. by Paul Claudel.
(Flanner) 44:100-103 Mr2
'68. T               12108
Texas. by Stanley Walker.
(Anon.) 38:247 N17'62.
B                    12109
Texas across the river. (Gill)
42:161-2 D3'66. CC   12110
Textures of life. by Hortense
Calisher. (Anon.) 39:190
My4'63. B            12111
Thackeray: the age of
wisdom, 1847-63. by Gordon
N. Ray. (Anon.) 33:106-107
Ja18'58. B           12112
Thaddeus Stevens. by Ralph
Korngold. (Anon.) 31:222-3
*N19'55. B           12113

Thalia. by Frances Faviell.
(Anon.) 33:161-2 S28'57.
B                    12114
Thank heaven for small
favors. (Gill) 40:104-107
Ja23'65. CC          12115
Thank you and other poems.
by Kenneth Koch. (Bogan)
39:210-11 O12'63. B  12116
Thank you, Miss Victoria.
by William Hoffman. (Oliver)
42:126 Ap23'66. T    12117
That awful mess on Via
Merulana. by Carlo Emilio
Gadda. William Weaver,
trans. (West) 41:63-4 D25'65.
B                    12118
That certain feeling. (Mc-
Carten) 32:49*Je30'56. CC
                     12119
That cold day in the park.
(Gilliatt) 45:84-5 Je14'69. CC
                     12120
That darn cat. (Gill) 41:222-3
D11'65. CC           12121
That kind of woman. (McCarten)
35:89-91 S19'59. CC  12122
That man from Rio. (McCarten)
40:123 Je20'64. CC   12123
That Summer in Paris. by
Morley Callaghan. (Wilson)
39:139-48 F23'63. B  12124
That Summer--that Fall. by
Frank D. Gilroy. (McCarten)
43:119 Mr25'67. T    12125
That thing at the Cherry Lane.
by Jeff Harris. (Oliver)
41:58-61 My29'65. T  12126
That touch of mink. (Gill)
38:90 Je23'62. CC    12127
That uncertain feeling. by
Kingsley Amis. (Wilson)
32:129-35*Mr24'56. B
                     12128
That was the week that was.
(Panter-Downes) 39:180
My4'63. TV           12129
That was Yvette: the biography
of Yvette Guilbert, the
great diseuse. by Bettina
Knapp and Myra Chipman.
(Anon.) 40:247 D12'64. B
                     12130

That wilder image. by
James Thomas Flexner.
(Anon.) 38:246-7 D8'62.
B                    12131
The theatre abroad: England.
by Kenneth Tynan. 35:101-25
S26'59. T           12132
The theatre abroad: France.
by Kenneth Tynan. 35:42-55
Ag1'59; 42:120-44 O15'66. T
                    12133
The theatre abroad: Germany.
by Kenneth Tynan. 35:90-
119 S12'59. T       12134
The theatre abroad: Italy. by
Kenneth Tynan. 43:86-118
O21'67. T           12135
The theatre abroad: London. by
Kenneth Tynan. 44:123-59
N9'68. T            12136
Theatre abroad: Prague. by
Kenneth Tynan. 43:99-123
Ap1'67. T           12137
Them. by Joyce Carol Oates.
(Sissman) 45:238-42 D6'69. B
                    12138
Theodore Roosevelt and the
rise of America to world
power. by Howard K.
Beale. (Rand) 33:143-51 Ap20
'57. B              12139
Theodore Roosevelt: the
formative years. by Carleton
Putnam. (Anon.) 34:144-5
Ap5'58. B           12140
Theodore Roosevelt the naturalist.
by Paul Russell Cutright.
(Anon.) 32:75-6*Jy21'56. B
                    12141
The Theodore Roosevelt treasury.
by Theodore Roosevelt.
Hermann Hagedorn, ed.
(Anon.) 33:242-3 D7'57. B
                    12142
There was a little girl. by
Daniel Taradash. (Tynan)
36:114-16 Mr12'60. T  12143
There's a girl in my soup. by
Terence Frisby. (McCarten)
43:105-106 O28'67. T  12144
Theresa's choice. by Rachel
Cecil. (Anon.) 35:175-6
Ap25'59. B          12145

Thérèse. (Gill) 39:231-2
N16'63. CC          12146
These are the British. by
Drew Middleton.
(Anon.) 33:83 Ag31'57. B
                    12147
These are the damned.
(Arlen) 41:88 Jy24'65. CC
                    12148
These ruins are inhabited. by
Muriel Beadle. (Anon.)
37:71-2 Jy8'61. B    12149
These were the hours. by Nancy
Cunard. (Flanner) 45:207-
208 N15'69. B        12150
They came to Cordura.
(McCarten) 35:173-4 O31'59.
CC                   12151
They fought for the sky.
by Quentin Reynolds.
(Anon.) 33:126 Je15'57. B
                    12152
They saw it happen: 1485-1688.
C.R.N. Routh, ed. (Anon.)
33:75*Jy27'57. B     12153
They shoot horses, don't
they? (Kael) 45:62-8 D20'69.
CC                   12154
They were there: the Civil
War in action as seen by
its combat artists. by
Philip Van Doren Stern.
(Anon.) 35:247-8 D5'59. B
                    12155
The thief of Paris. (Gilliatt)
43:74-6 S2'67. CC    12156
Thieves' carnival. by Jean
Anouilh. Lucienne Hill,
adapt. (Gibbs) 31:77-8 F19
'55. T               12157
Thin ice. by Compton Mac-
kenzie. (Anon.) 33:133-4 Mr
9'57. B              12158
The thing desired. by Lalage
Pulvertaft. (Anon.) 33:175
S14'57. B            12159
Things of this world. by
Richard Wilbur. (Bogan)
32:180 O6'56. B      12160
Thinking about the unthinkable.
by Herman Kahn. (Anon.)
38:89 Je30'62. B     12161
Third best sport. by Eleanor

Bayer and Leo Bayer.
(Tynan) 34:70-2 Ja10'59. T
                                    12162
The third book about Achim. by
Uwe Johnson. (Steiner)
43:210-12 O28'67. B      12163
The third choice. by Elizabeth
Janeway. (Anon.) 35:150-1
My23'59. B               12164
Third girl. by Agatha Christie.
(Anon.) 43:248 N25'67. B
                                    12165
The third key. (McCarten)
33:70-2 Je15'57. CC      12166
The third lover. (Oliver) 39:42
Jy6'63. CC               12167
Third man in the ring. by Ruby
Goldstein and Frank Graham.
(Anon.) 35:242-3 N28'59. B
                                    12168
The third policeman. by Flann
O'Brien. (Moss) 44:174-80
S28'68. B                12169
The Third Republic of France;
the first phase, 1871-94.
by Guy Chapman. (Anon.)
39:120-1 Je15'63. B      12170
The third rose: Gertrude
Stein and her world. by John
Malcolm Brinnin. (Anon.)
35:107-108 Ja30'60. B    12171
The third secret. (Gill) 40:86
My2'64. CC               12172
The third voice. (McCarten)
36:173 Mr19'60. CC       12173
13 daughters. by Eaton
Magoon, Jr. (McCarten) 37:
112 Mr11'61. T           12174
13 days to glory. by Lon
Tinkle. (Anon.) 34:151 Ap
19'58. B                 12175
30 is a dangerous age. (Kael)
44:156-7 Mr16'68. CC     12176
Thirty years that shook physics:
the story of quantum theory.
by George Gamow. (Anon.)
42:166 Ap30'66. B        12177
Thirty-eight witnesses. by
A. M. Rosenthal. (Anon.) 40:
91 Jy25'64. B            12178
The thirty-eighth floor. by
Clifford Irving. (N. Bliven)
41:89-94 Ag7'65. B       12179

36 children. by Herbert Kohl.
(Hentoff) 44:166-8 Mr16'68.
B                        12180
36 hours. (Gill) 40:120
F6'65. CC                12181
This animal is mischievous.
by David Benedictus.
(Anon.) 42:247 N19'66. B
                                    12182
This could be the night.
(McCarten) 33:129 My25
'57. CC                  12183
This fiery night. by Joan
Vatsek. (Anon.) 35:170-1
Ap18'59. B               12184
This green and pleasant land.
by Dudley Barker. (Anon.)
32:99-100*Mr31'56. B
                                    12185
This hallowed ground. by
Bruce Catton. (West) 32:92-
100 Ja12'57. B           12186
This happy feeling. (McCarten)
34:62-3 ·Je28'58. CC     12187
This high man. by Milton
Lehman. (Anon.) 39:97-8
D21'63. B                12188
This is Moscow speaking and
other stories. by Yuli Daniel.
Stuart Hood, Harold Shuk-
man and John Richardson,
trans. (Anon.) 45:139 My24
'69. B                   12189
This is our world. by Louis
Fischer. (Anon.) 32:154-5
*Ap14'56. B              12190
This is the castle. by
Nicolas Freeling. (Anon.)
45:118 Mr1'69. B         12191
This is the rill speaking.
by Lanford Wilson. (Oliver)
42:126 Ap23'66. T        12192
This is your life. (J. Lardner)
35:165-6 O24'59. TV      12193
This property is condemned.
(Adler) 42:88 Ag27'66. CC
                                    12194
This side Jordan. by
Margaret Laurence. (Anon.)
36:86 Ja7'61. B          12195
This side of paradise. by
Sidney Sloane. (Oliver) 38:
93-4 Mr3'62. T           12196

This sporting life. (Oliver)
39:72 Jy20'63. CC       12197
This strange passion.
(McCarten) 31:102*D10'55.
CC                      12198
This stubborn soil. by William
A. Owens. (Anon.) 42:246
O8'66. B                12199
This timeless moment. by
Laura Archera Huxley. (Anon.)
44:183 O5'68. B         12200
This U.S.A.: an unexpected
family portrait of 194,067,296
Americans drawn from the
census. by Ben J. Watten-
berg and Richard M. Scam-
mon. (Anon.) 42:158 Mr5'66.
B                       12201
This view of life. by George
Gaylord Simpson. (Anon.)
40:179-80 Je6'64 . B
                        12202
This was burlesque. by Joe
Dimona, et al. (Oliver) 38:117-
18 Mr17'62. T           12203
Thistle in my bed. by Gudrun
Powers. (Oliver) 39:110-12
N30'63. T               12204
Thomas Becket. by Richard
Winston. (Anon.) 43:223-4
O14'67. B               12205
The Thomas Crown affair.
(Gilliatt) 44:82-5 Jy13'68.
CC                      12206
Thomas Howard: fourth duke
of Norfolk. by Neville
Williams. (Anon.) 41:189-90
My1'65. B               12207
Thomas Wolfe. by Elizabeth
Nowell. (Anon.) 36:105
Ag13'60. B              12208
Thomas Woodrow Wilson: a
psychological study. by
William C. Bullitt and
Sigmund Freud. (Steiner)
42:111-18 Ja21'67. B
                        12209
Thoroughly modern Millie.
(Gill) 43:94 Ap1'67. CC
                        12210
Those Americans. by N.N.
Mikhailov and Z.V. Kossenko.
(Anon.) 39:207-208 Mr16'63.
B                       12211

Those cursed Tuscans. by
Curzio Malaparte. Rex
Benedict, trans. (Anon.)
40:247-8 N14'64. B      12212
Those days. by Hamilton
Fish Armstrong. (Anon.)
39:191 S21'63. B        12213
Those extraordinary Blackwells.
by Elinor Rice Hays.
(Anon.) 43:178-9 S9'67. B
                        12214
Those magnificent men in
their flying machines.
(S. Lardner) 41:114 Je19'65.
CC                      12215
Those without shadows. by
Françoise Sagan. (Balliett)
33:100-101 Ja18'58. B
                        12216
A thousand clowns. by Herb
Gardner. (McCarten) 38:
106-108 Ap14'62. T      12217
A thousand clowns. (Gill)
41:162 D17'65. CC       12218
The thousand doors. by
Abraham Rothberg. (Anon.)
41:219-20 My15'65. B 12219
3 bags full. by Jerome
Chodorov. (McCarten)
42:160 Mr19'66. T       12220
The three banners of China.
by Marc Riboud. (Anon.)
42:96 Ja7'67. B         12221
3 brave men. (McCarten)
33:103-104 Mr23'57.
CC                      12222
3 x 3. by Arnold Weinstein,
Kenneth Koch and Elaine
May. (Oliver) 38:83-4
Mr10'62. T              12223
Three by Thurber. by James
Thurber. Paul Ellwood and
St. John Terrell, adapt.
(Gibbs) 31:68-70 Mr19'55.
T                       12224
The three faces of Eve.
(McCarten) 33:145-6 O5'57.
CC                      12225
Three faces of love. by Emile
Zola. Roland Gant, trans.
(Anon.) 45:184 Ap12'69. B
                        12226
Three for the show. (McCarten)
31:74 Mr5'55. CC        12227

3 for tonight. by Robert Wells
and Walter Schumann.
(Gibbs) 31:74-6 Ap16'55. T
    12228
Three hand reel. by Paul
Avila Mayer. (McCarten)
42:178 N19'66. T    12229
Three in the attic. (Kael)
45:115-16 Mr8'69. CC  12230
3 into 2 won't go. (Gilliatt)
45:74-5 Jy12'69. CC   12231
Three men on a horse. by John
Cecil Holm and George
Abbott. (Gill) 45:138-9
O25'69. T    12232
Three modern Japanese plays.
by Yokio Mishima. Donald
Keene, trans. (Balliett) 36:78-
80 F11'61. T    12233
Three saints and a sinner. by
Louise Hall Tharp. (Anon.)
32:188 D15'56. B    12234
Three sides to the sea. by
David Patten. (Anon.) 32:
70-2*Ag11'56. B    12235
Three sisters. by Anton
Chekhov. (Panter-Downes) 34:
80 Jy12'58 (Malcolm) 35:96-8
O3'59 (McCarten) 40:56 Jy4
'64 (Oliver) 41:96-9 F27'65
(Gill) 45:149 O18'69. T
    12236
Three stripes in the sun.
(McCarten) 31:178*D3'55. CC
    12237
The three worlds of Captain
John Smith. by Philip L.
Barbour. (Anon.) 40:108
Ag29'64. B    12238
Three years in Mississippi.
by James Meredith. (Anon.)
42:208 My21'66. B   12239
Three years with Grant, as re-
called by war correspondent
Sylvanus Cadwallader. by
Sylvanus Cadwallader.
(Wilson) 32:126-9
*Je9'56. B    12240
The threepenny opera. (McCarten)
36:54-5 Jy30'60. CC  12241
Threescore and ten. by Walter
Allen. (Anon.) 35:149-50
My23'59. B    12242

Thrones 96-109 de los
Cantores. by Ezra Pound.
(Anon.) 36:188 O29'60. B
    12243
Through a glass darkly. (Gill)
38:122-3 Mr17'62. CC
    12244
Through the fields of clover.
by Peter DeVries. (Wain)
37:130-3 F25'61. B   12245
Through the hoop. by Michel
del Castillo. (West) 39:170-
3 Ap27'63. B    12246
Through the minefield. by
Constantine FitzGibbon.
(Anon.) 43:214 O28'67.
B    12247
Through the Russian Revolu-
tion. by Albert Rhys Williams.
(Anon.) 44:114 Je15'68. B
    12248
Thrush Green. by Dora Jessie
Saint. (Anon.) 35:122 Ja23
'60. B    12249
A thunder of drums. (Gill)
37:141-2 S30'61. CC  12250
Thunderball. by Ian Fleming.
(Anon.) 37:136 My27'61.
B    12251
Thunderball. (Gill) 41:101-103
Ja8'66. CC    12252
A Thurber carnival. by
James Thurber. (Tynan)
36:125-6 Mr5'60. T  12253
Thursday's child. by Eartha
Kitt. (Anon.) 32:198 O20'56.
B    12254
The ticket-of-leave man. by
Tom Taylor. (Oliver) 37:58
Ja6'62. T    12255
Tides of crisis. by Adolph A.
Berle. (Anon.) 33:166-7
My18'57. B    12256
Tides of fortune, 1945-1955.
by Harold Macmillan. (Anon.)
45:60 D27'69. B   12257
The tiger. by Murray Schisgal.
(Oliver) 38:116 F16'63. T
    12258
Tiger at the gates. by Jean
Giraudoux. Christopher Fry,
adapt. (Panter-Downes) 31:57
*Jy30'55 (Gibbs) 31:72-5

*O15'55 (Gill) 44:130-2
Mr9'68. T                12259
Tiger Bay. (McCarten) 35:55-6
D26'59. CC               12260
The tiger makes out. (Gill)
43:93-5 S23'67. CC       12261
The tiger of Ch'in. by
Leonard Cottrell. (Anon.)
38:107 Je23'62. B        12262
Tiger, tiger, burning bright.
by Peter S. Feibleman.
(McCarten) 38:75-7 Ja12'63. T
                         12263
A tigress in the village. by
Frank Swinnerton. (Anon.)
35:117-18 Je20'59. B     12264
Tike, and five stories. by
Jonathan Strong. (Anon.)
45:166 My10'69. B        12265
Till we have faces. by C. S.
Lewis. (Anon.) 32:124-5
F9'57. B                 12266
The time between the wars. by
Jonathan Daniels. (Anon.)
42:230 S17'66. B         12267
A time for burning. (Gill)
43:132-5 F25'67. CC      12268
A time for singing. by John
Morris and Gerald Freedman.
(McCarten) 42:72 My21'66. T
                         12269
A time in Rome. by Elizabeth
Bowen. (Anon.) 36:164 Mr26'60.
B                        12270
Time limit! by Henry Denker
and Ralph Berkey. (Gibbs)
31:54-5*F4'56. T         12271
Time limit. (McCarten)
33:165-6 N2'57. CC       12272
Time lost and time remembered.
(Gill) 42:71 S3'66. CC   12273
The time machine. (Balliett)
36:54-6 Ag27'60. CC      12274
Time of parting. by Anton
Donchev. (West) 44:101-103
Ja25'69. B               12275
The time of the dragons. by
Alice Ekert-Rotholz. (Anon.)
34:100 Jy12'58. B        12276
The time of your life. by
William Saroyan. (Gill)
45:163-4 N15'69. T       12277

A time on Earth. by Vilhelm
Moberg. Naomi Walford,
trans. (Anon.) 41:108 Jy17
'65. B                   12278
Time out for love. (Gill)
39:102-104 My4'63. CC
                         12279
Time remembered. by Jean
Anouilh. Patricia Moyes,
trans. (Gibbs) 33:77-8
N23'57. T                12280
A time to love and a time to
die. (McCarten) 34:82-5
Jy19'58. CC              12281
Timothy Dexter revisited. by
John P. Marquand. (Anon.)
36:203-204 O8'60. B
                         12282
The tin drum. by Günter Grass.
(West) 39:169-70 Ap27'63.
B                        12283
Tinkers and genius. by Edmund
Fuller. (Anon.) 31:168-9
*O22'55. B               12284
Tiny Alice. by Edward Albee.
(McCarten) 40:84 Ja9'65
(Gill)45:85-6 O11'69. T
                         12285
Tip on a dead jockey.
(McCarten) 33:93-4 S14'57.
CC                       12286
'Tis pity she's a whore. by
John Ford. (Malcolm)
34:111-12 D13'58. T      12287
The Titans. by André Maurois.
(Anon.) 34:123 Mr1'58. B
                         12288
Titicut follies. (Gill) 43:166-7
O28'67. CC               12289
To a young actress: the letters
of Bernard Shaw to Molly
Tompkins by George Bernard
Shaw. Peter Tompkins, ed.
(Anon.) 37:134 F25'61. B
                         12290
To be a crook. (Gill) 42:134-5
F11'67. CC               12291
To be a politician. by Stimson
Bullitt. (Rovere) 35:147-9
My23'59. B               12292
To be young, gifted, and
black. by Lorraine Hansberry.

Robert Nemiroff, adapt.
(Oliver) 44:58 Ja11'69. T
                              12293
To be young was very heavenly.
by Marian Lawrence Peabody.
(Anon.) 43:74-5 Jy1'67. B
                              12294
To bed... or not to bed. (Gill)
39:73-4 Ja4'64. CC    12295
To catch a thief. (McCarten)
31:47*Ag13'55. CC     12296
To change China: Western ad-
visers in China, 1620-1960.
by Jonathan Spence. (Anon.)
45:140 My24'69. B     12297
To clothe the naked. by Luigi
Pirandello. (Oliver) 43:155-6
My6'67. T             12298
To criticize the critic. by T.S.
Eliot. (Anon.) 42:208-209
Mr19'66. B            12299
To Damascus. by August
Strindberg. (Balliett) 37:77
F25'61. T             12300
To die in Madrid. (Gill)
41:168 S25'65. CC     12301
To hell with culture. by
Herbert Read. (Anon.) 39:
122 Je1'63. B         12302
To kill a mockingbird. by
Harper Lee. (Anon.) 36:203-
204 S10'60. B         12303
To kill a mockingbird. (Gill)
39:125-6 F23'63. CC   12304
To love. (Gill) 40:204 N28'64.
CC                    12305
To mix with time. by May
Swenson. (Bogan) 39:175
Ap27'63. B            12306
To move a nation. by Roger
Hilsman. (Anon.) 43:84
Jy29'67. B            12307
To Paris with love. (McCarten)
31:110-11 Ap9'55. CC  12308
To Sir, with love. by E.R.
Braithwaite. (Anon.) 36:160
Mr26'60. B            12309
To Sir, with love. (Gilliatt)
43:92 Je17'67. CC     12310
To the castle. by Dorothea
Malm. (Anon.) 33:138 Je8
'57. B                12311
To the one I love the best.

by Ludwig Bemelmans.
(Anon.) 31:118 Mr5'55. B
                              12312
To the precipice. by Judith
Rossner. (Anon.) 42:68
D31'66. B             12313
The toadstool millionaires. by
James Harvey Young. (Anon.)
37:183 S23'61. B      12314
Tobruk. (Gill) 42:143 F18'67.
CC                    12315
The toilet. by LeRoi Jones.
(Oliver) 40:52 D26'64. T
                              12316
Toinette. by J.I. Rodale.
(Oliver) 37:121 D2'61. T
                              12317
Tolbecken. by Samuel
Shellabarger. (Anon.) 32:
150*S15'56. B         12318
Tolstoy. by Henri Troyat.
(Flanner) 41:182-3 Ap17'65.
B                     12319
Tolstoy. by Henri Troyat.
Nancy Amphoux, trans.
(Anon.) 43:115 Ja20'68. B
                              12320
Tolstoy remembered. by
Sergei Tolstoy. Maura
Budberg, trans. (Anon.)
38:185-6 Ap14'62. B   12321
Tom Jones. (Panter-Downes)
39:98-100 S7'63. (Gill) 39:
169-70 O12'63. CC     12322
Tom Paine. by Paul Foster.
(Oliver) 44:110-11 Ap6'68.
T                     12323
Tomorrow and tomorrow and
tomorrow. by Aldous Huxley.
(Anon.) 32:203-204 O13'56.
B                     12324
Tomorrow is my turn. (Gill)
37:77-8 F3'62. CC     12325
Tomorrow's fire. by Jay
Williams. (Anon.) 40:223
O3'64. B              12326
Toni. (Gilliatt) 45:98-9 S6'69.
CC                    12327
Tonight at 8:30. by Noël Coward.
(McCarten) 43:158 My13'67.
T                     12328
Tonight in Samarkand. by
Jacques Deval and Lorenzo

Semple, Jr. (Gibbs) 31:50-2
F26'55. T            12329
Tonight we improvise. by
Luigi Pirandello. (Malcolm)
35:122-4 N14'59. T      12330
Too bad she's bad. (McCarten)
31:48*Ja7'56. CC       12331
Too true to be good. by George
Bernard Shaw. (McCarten)
39:73-4 Mr23'63. T      12332
Too late the Phalarope. by
Robert Yale Libott. (Gibbs)
32:106-108 O20'56. T    12333
Too many crooks. (McCarten)
35:157 My2'59. CC       12334
Too much Johnson. by William
Gillette. Burt Shevelove,
adapt. (Oliver) 39:74-6
Ja25'64. T              12335
Too much, too soon. (McCarten)
34:91-2 My17'58. CC     12336
Too near the sun. by Gordon
Forbes. (Anon.) 31:86-7
Jy16'55. B              12337
Top secret affair. (McCarten)
32:108 F9'57. CC        12338
Topaz. (Kael) 45:48-50 D27'69.
CC                      12339
Topkapi. (Gill) 40:194
S26'64. CC              12340
Torero! (McCarten) 33:95
*Je1'57. CC             12341
Tormented loyalty. by
Christopher Sykes. (Anon.)
45:92 Jy12'69. B        12342
Torn curtain. (Adler) 42:84
Ag6'66. CC              12343
Torregreca: life, death,
miracles. by Ann Cornelisen.
(Anon.) 45:173 Ap26'69. B
                        12344
The tortured earth. by Gert
Ledig. (West) 32:114*Je16'56.
B                       12345
Toscanini: an intimate portrait.
by Samuel Chotzinoff. (Anon.)
32:102*Mr31'56. B       12346
The Toscanini musicians knew.
by B.H. Haggin. (Anon.)
43:179-80 S23'67. B     12347
A touch of innocence. by
Katherine Dunham. (Anon.)
35:227-8 O17'59. B      12348

A touch of larceny. (McCarten)
36:148-9 Mr26'60. CC
                        12349
A touch of the dragon. by
Hamilton Basso. (Anon.)
40:185-6 My23'64. B     12350
A touch of the poet. by Eugene
O'Neill. (J. Lardner) 34:87
O11'58 (McCarten) 43:158
My13'67. T              12351
Tourist in Africa. by Evelyn
Waugh. (Anon.) 36:238-9
N26'60. B               12352
Tovarich. by Jacques Deval
and Robert E. Sherwood.
(McCarten) 39:108-10
Mr30'63. T              12353
Tower in the West. by Frank
Norris. (Gill) 32:137-40
F16'57. B               12354
The towers of love. by
Stephen Birmingham. (Anon.)
37:242-3 N11'61. B      12355
The towers of Trebizond.
by Rose Macaulay. (Anon.)
33:104-105*Je1'57. B    12356
The town. by William
Faulkner. (Podhoretz) 33:
101-104*Je1'57. B       12357
The town behind the wall. by
Elie Wiesel. Stephen Becker,
trans. (N. Bliven) 40:115-16
Ja9'65. B               12358
Town burning. by Thomas
Williams. (Anon.) 35:235-6
D12'59. B               12359
The town in bloom. by Dodie
Smith. (Anon.) 41:119-20
Ag14'65. B              12360
Town without pity. (Gill)
37:178-9 O14'61. CC     12361
Toynbee and history. M.F.
Ashley Montagu, ed. (Anon.)
32:201 O13'56. B        12362
Toynbee in Elysium: a fantasy
in one act. by Victor
Purcell. (Anon.) 35:247
D5'59. B                12363
Toys in the attic. by Lillian
Hellman. (Tynan) 36:124-5
Mr5'60. T               12364
Toys in the attic. (Miller) 39:
60-1 Ag10'63. CC        12365

Track of the bear. by William
Bixby. (Anon.) 41:110-11
Je26'65. B            12366
Trafalgar. by René Maine.
Rita Eldon and B.W.
Robinson, trans. (Anon.) 33:
166 S28'57. B          12367
Tragedy in Dedham: the story
of the Sacco-Vanzetti case.
by Francis Russell. (N. Bliven)
38:235-43 D8'62. B     12368
The trail of the dinosaur and
other essays. by Arthur
Koestler. (Anon.) 31:75-6*Ja
7'56. B                12369
The train. (Gill) 41:152-3 Mr20
'65. CC                12370
The train was on time. by
Heinrich Böll. (West) 32:
113-15*Je16'56. B      12371
The traitor. by André Gorz.
Richard Howard, trans.
(Anon.) 35:121-2 Ja16'60. B
                       12372
The transatlantic persuasion: the
liberal-democratic mind in
the age of Gladstone. by
Robert Kelley. (Anon.) 45:92
Jy12'69. B             12373
The transatlantic Smiths. by
Robert Allerton Parker.
(Anon.) 35:170 Je6'59. B
                       12374
Trans-Europ-express. (Gilliatt)
44:153-4 My18'68. CC   12375
Transfers. by Conrad Bromberg.
(Oliver) 45:56-8 Ja31'70. T
                       12376
Transport from paradise. (Gill)
42:143 F18'67. CC      12377
The trap. (McCarten) 34:120-1
F7'59. CC              12378
Trapeze. (McCarten) 32:64
*Je23'56. CC           12379
A traveller in Italy. by H.V.
Morton. (Anon.) 40:248 N28'64.
B                      12380
A traveller in Rome. by
H.V. Morton. (Anon.)
33:243-4 N16'57. B     12381
Traveller without luggage.
by Jean Anouilh. (McCarten)
40:160 S26'64. T       12382

The travels of Jaimie Mc
Pheeters. by Robert Lewis
Taylor. (Anon.) 34:154 Mr22
'58. B                 12383
Travels with Charley in search
of America. by John Stein-
beck. (Anon.) 38:152 S8'62.
B                      12384
Treason in the twentieth century.
by Margret Boveri. Jonathan
Steinberg, trans. (Anon.)
39:178 Mr30'63. B      12385
Treasures of the Vatican. by
Maurizio Calvesi. James
Emmons, trans. (Anon.)
38:184 S15'62. B       12386
A treasury of birdlore. Joseph
Wood Krutch and Paul S.
Eriksson, eds. (Anon.)
38:163 F16'63. B       12387
The tree witch. by Peter
Viereck. (Bogan) 38:175-6
Mr24'62. B             12388
Tremor of intent: an
eschatological spy novel.
by Anthony Burgess. (N.
Bliven) 42:159-60 F11'67. B
                       12389
Trenchard. by Andrew Boyle.
(Anon.) 38:98-9 Ja5'63. B
                       12390
The trend is up. by Anthony
West. (Anon.) 36:200-201
O8'60. B               12391
Trepleff. by MacDonald
Harris. (Anon.) 45:58-9 D27'69.
B                      12392
Trial. (McCarten) 31:138
*O22'55. CC            12393
The trial. (Flanner) 38:104-
106 Ja12'63. (Gill) 39:132
Mr2'63. CC             12394
Trial and error. (Gill)
38:133-4 D1'62. CC     12395
The trial begins. by Abram
Tertz. (Balliett) 36:84-6
Ja7'61. B              12396
The trial of Callista Blake. by
Edgar Pangborn. (Anon.)
37:111 Ja13'62. B      12397
The trial of Dr. Adams. by
Sybille Bedford. (Anon.) 35:
119 F28'59. B          12398

The trial of Dr. Spock, the
Reverend William Sloane
Coffin, Jr., Michael Ferber,
Mitchell Goodman, and
Marcus Raskin. by Jessica
Mitford. (Anon.) 45:202
O11'69. B          12399
Trial of Joan of Arc. (Gill)
41:137-8 F20'65. CC    12400
The trial of Marie Besnard.
by Marie Besnard. Denise
Folliot, trans. (Anon.)
39:177-8 Ap27'63. B    12401
The trial of Marshal Ney. by
Harold Kurtz. (Anon.) 33:83
Ag31'57. B           12402
The trials of Brother Jero.
by Wole Soyinka. (Oliver)
43:133-4 N18'67. T     12403
The trials of Oscar Wilde.
(McCarten) 36:56 Jy2'60. CC
                     12404
The triangle fire. by Leon
Stein. (Anon.) 38:194 My5'62.
B                    12405
The tribe that lost its head.
by Nicholas Monsarrat. (West)
32:222-4*N10'56. B     12406
A tribute to Busby Berkeley.
(Gill) 41:110-12 D4'65. CC
                     12407
A tribute to Governor Smith. by
Robert Moses. (Anon.) 38:
140 Je9'62. B          12408
The trigon. by James Broom
Lynne. (Oliver) 41:196-7
O16'65. T            12409
The trip. (Gilliatt) 43:109-10
S9'67. CC            12410
Tristessa. by Jack
Kerouac. (Balliett) 36:97-8
Ag27'60. B           12411
Triumph in the West. by
Arthur Bryant. (Anon.)
35:121 Ja16'60. B      12412
Troilus and Cressida. by
William Shakespeare. (Gibbs)
32:50-2 Ja5'57 (Flanner)
40:142-3 Mr7'64. T     12413
The Trojan women. by Euripi-
des. Edith Hamilton, trans.
(Oliver) 39:70 Ja11'64. T
                     12414

The Trojan women. by Euripides.
Jean-Paul Sartre, trans.
(Flanner) 41:183-4 Ap17'65.
T                    12415
Tropic of Capricorn. by
Henry Miller. (Balliett)
38:74-6 D29'62. B      12416
Tropical Africa. by
George H. T. Kimble. (Anon.)
36:91-2 Ja28'61. B     12417
The troublemaker. (McCarten)
40:59 Jy4'64. CC       12418
The trouble makers: dissent
over foreign policy, 1792-1939
by A. J. P. Taylor. (Anon.)
34:164 S13'58. B       12419
True grit. (Gilliatt) 45:67-8
Jy26'69. CC          12420
A true story. by Richard Kurt.
(West) 41:106-108 Ja29'66.
B                    12421
The Truman administration. by
Barton J. Bernstein and
Allen J. Matusow, eds.
(Anon.) 42:246-7 O15'66. B
                     12422
The Truman presidency: the
history of a triumphant suc-
cession. by Cabell Phillips.
(Anon.) 42:104 Jy16'66.
B                    12423
Trumbull Park. by Frank
London Brown. (Anon.) 35:
174-5 Ap25'59. B       12424
The trumpet shall sound. by
H. M. Tomlinson. (Anon.)
33:141-2 Ap27'57. B    12425
The trumpet unblown. by
William Hoffman. (Anon.) 31:
55*D31'55. B          12426
Trumpets from Montparnasse.
by Robert Gibbings. (Anon.)
31:206*D10'55. B       12427
Trumpets from the steep. by
Diana Cooper. (Anon.) 36:
161 D17'60. B          12428
Trumpets of the Lord. by
Vinnette Carroll. (Oliver)
39:60-1 Ja4'64. T      12429
Trustee from the toolroom.
by Nevil Shute. (Anon.)
34:160 Ap2'60. B       12430
The truth. (Gill) 37:58 Jy8
'61. CC              12431

The truth about cancer. by
Charles S. Cameron. (Anon.)
32:166*My12'56. B      12432
Tsar Nicholas I. by Constantin
de Grunwald. (Anon.) 31:
214-15*D3'55. B      12433
The Tudors. by Christopher
Morris. (Anon.) 32:143*S8'56.
B      12434
The tumbled house. by
Winston Graham. (Anon.)
36:173 F20'60. B      12435
The tumbler. by Benn W.
Levy. (Tynan) 36:123-4 Mr
5'60. T      12436
Tunes of glory. by James
Kennaway. (Balliett) 33:94-5
*Je22'57. B      12437
Tunes of glory. (Angell)
36:50-1 D24'60. CC      12438
The tunnel of love. by Joseph
Fields and Peter DeVries.
(Gibbs) 33:69 F23'57. T
12439
The tunnel of love. (McCarten)
34:205-206 D6'58. CC      12440
Turgenev, a life. by David
Magarshack. (Wilson)
33:163-216 O19'57. B      12441
The Turgenev family. by
Varvara Zhitova. (Wilson)
33:163-216 O19'57. B      12442
Turmoil and tradition: a study of
the life and time of Henry
L. Stimson. by Elting E.
Morison. (Anon.) 36:206-207
O15'60. B      12443
Turn again tiger. by Samuel
Selvon. (Balliett) 35:107-108
My30'59. B      12444
The turn of the screw. (Gill)
37:72 Ja6'62. CC      12445
The turn of the screw. (J.
Lardner) 35:203-204 D5'59.
TV      12446
The turn of the tide. by
Arthur Bryant. (B. Bliven)
33:130-8 Je8'57. B      12447
Turn of the wheel. by Roger
Vailland. Peter Wiles, trans.
(Anon.) 37:141-2 F17'62.
B      12448
Turned on. by Dick Schaap.

(Anon.) 43:155-6 Ap1'67. B
12449
The turning point: Jefferson's
battle for the presidency.
by Frank van der Linden.
(Anon.) 38:98-9 Ag18'62. B
12450
The Tweed ring. by Alexander
B. Callow, Jr. (Anon.)
42:122-3 Ja14'67. B      12451
Twelfth night. by William
Shakespeare. (Tynan)
34:52-5 D27'58. T      12452
The twelfth step. by Thomas
Randall. (Anon.) 33:198-200
O26'57. B      12453
The twelve. by Carlos Franqui.
Albert B. Teichner, trans.
(Anon.) 44:127 Je1'68. B
12454
12 angry men. (McCarten)
33:66-8 Ap27'57. CC      12455
Twelve girls in the garden.
by Shane Martin. (Anon.)
33:125 Je15'57. B      12456
The twelve pictures. by
Edith Simon. (Anon.) 31:125-6
My28'55. B      12457
The twenties. by John Mont-
gomery. (Anon.) 33:141
Je8'57. B      12458
The twentieth Maine. by
John J. Pullen. (Anon.)
33:201-202 O5'57. B      12459
20 July. by Constantine Fitz-
Gibbon. (Anon.) 31:105*Ja21
'56. B      12460
Twenty letters to a friend. by
Svetlana Alliluyeva.
Patricia Johnson McMillan,
trans. (Wilson) 43:232-44
D9'67. B      12461
The 25th hour. (Gill) 43:135
F25'67. CC      12462
Twenty-one . (J. Lardner) 33:
147-59*N30'57. TV      12463
21 stayed. by Virginia Pasley.
(Anon.) 31:87*Ag20'55. B
12464
Twenty-one years. by
Randolph S. Churchill.
(Anon.) 41:125 Je19'65. B
12465

27 wagons full of cotton. by
Tennessee Williams. (Gibbs)
31:69-70 Ap30'55. T    12466
Twilight for the gods. by
Ernest K. Gann. (Gill)
32:140 F16'57. B    12467
Two are guilty. (Gill) 40:156
Mr14'64. CC    12468
2 by Saroyan. by William
Saroyan. (Oliver) 37:129-30
N4'61. T    12469
Two by two. by Martha
Gellhorn. (Anon.) 34:144 Mr8
'58. B    12470
Two centuries of Russian verse:
an anthology from Lomonosov
to Voznesensky. Avraham
Yarmolinsky, ed. Babette
Deutsch, trans. (Anon.)
42:248 D3'66. B    12471
Two daughters. (Gill) 39:101-
102 My11'63. CC    12472
The two deaths of Christopher
Martin. by William Golding.
(Podhoretz) 33:189-90
S21'57. B    12473
Two Dreisers. by Ellen
Moers. (Anon.) 45:80 Ag30'69.
B    12474
The two executioners. by
Fernando Arrabal. (Oliver)
40:79 Ap4'64. T    12475
Two for the road. (Gill) 43:172
My6'67. CC    12476
Two for the seesaw. by
William Gibson. (Gibbs) 33:
56-8 Ja25'58. T    12477
Two for the seesaw. (Gill)
38:203-204 N24'62. CC
    12478
The two French revolutions.
by Guglielmo Ferrero. Luc
Monnier, ed. Samuel J.
Hurwitz, trans. (Anon.)
44:190-3 Ap20'68. B    12479
Two gentle men: the lives of
George Herbert and Robert
Herrick. by Marchette
Chute. (Anon.) 36:196 My7'60.
B    12480
Two in the far North. by
Margaret E. Murie. (Anon.)
39:178-9 Mr30'63. B    12481

Two lovers in Rome: extracts from
the journal and letters of
Etienne-Jean Delécluze.
by Etienne-Jean Delécluze. Louis
Desternes, ed. Gerard
Hopkins, trans. (Anon.)
34:209 O18'58. B    12482
Two minutes till midnight.
by Elmer Davis. (Anon.)
31:137 Mr12'55. B    12483
Two minutes to noon. by
Noel F. Busch. (Anon.)
38:177-8 S22'62. B    12484
The two of us. (Kael) 44:122-5
Mr2'68. CC    12485
Two studies in constitutional
interpretation. by Telford
Taylor. (Anon.) 45:179-80
Ap19'69. B    12486
2001: a space odyssey. by
Arthur C. Clarke.
(Bernstein) 44:180-4 S21'68.
B    12487
2001: a space odyssey. (Gilliatt)
44:150-2 Ap13'68. CC
    12488
The two towers. by J.R.R.
Tolkien. (Anon.) 31:170-3
My14'55. B    12489
Two tudor portraits. by
Hester W. Chapman. (Anon.)
39:91 Jy20'63. B    12490
Two under the Indian sun. by
Jon Godden and Rumer
Godden. (Anon.) 42:118
S3'66. B    12491
Two views. by Uwe Johnson.
Richard Winston and Clara
Winston, trans. (Updike)
42:92-4 Ja7'67. B    12492
Two women. (Oliver) 37:152-3
My20'61. CC    12493
The two-ocean war. by
Samuel Eliot Morison. (Anon.)
39:114 Je22'63. B    12494
Two-way stretch. (Angell) 36:71
Ja28'61. CC    12495
Tynan right & left. by Kenneth
Tynan. (Anon.) 43:71 D23'67.
B    12496
The typists. by Murray Schisgal.
(Oliver) 38:114-16 F16'63.
T    12497

U

US. by Peter Brook, et al.
(Panter-Downes) 42:208-13
D3'66. T          12498
U. S. A. by John Dos Passos
and Paul Shyre. (Malcolm)
35:88 N7'59. T          12499
U. S. camera '62. Tom
Maloney, ed. (Malcolm)
37:198-205 D16'61. B    12500
UTBU. by James Kirkwood
(McCarten) 41:74 Ja22'66.
T          12501
The ugly American. by William
J. Lederer and Eugene
Burdick. (Anon.) 34:207-208
O18'58. B          12502
The ugly American. (Gill)
39:112-13 Ap20'63. CC 12503
Ulendo. by Archie Carr.
(Anon.) 40:192 Ap4'64. B
          12504
Ulterior motives. by David
Garnett. (Anon.) 42:167
F18'67. B          12505
The ultimate Viking. by Eric
Linklater. (Anon.) 32:87-8
*S1'56. B          12506
Ultramarine. by Malcolm
Lowry. (Anon.) 38:230
O20'62. B          12507
Ulysses. (Hamburger) 31:76
*Ag27'55. (Gill) 43:93-4
Ap1'67. CC          12508
Umberto D. (McCarten) 31:90
*N12'55. CC          12509
The umbrellas of Cherbourg.
(Flanner) 40:141-2 Mr7'64.
(Gill) 40:151 D19'64. CC
          12510
Un adolescent d'Autrefois. by
François Mauriac. (Flanner)
45:144-5 Ap19'69. B    12511
Un caso clinico. by Dino
Buzzati. (Flanner) 31:115
Mr26'55. T          12512
Un certain regard. (Flanner)
43:81-2 F3'68. TV    12513
Unarmed in paradise. by Ellen
Marsh. (Anon.) 35:173
Mr14'59. B          12514

An unavoidable delay and other
stories. by Diana Athill.
(Anon.) 38:186 My19'62. B
          12515
The uncertain trumpet. by
Maxwell D. Taylor. (Anon.)
35:103 Ja9'60. B    12516
The uncle. (S. Lardner)
42:66 Jy30'66. CC    12517
Uncle Vanya. by Anton Chekhov.
(Panter-Downes) 34:80
Jy12'58. T          12518
Uncle Vanya. (McCarten)
34:141 My10'58. CC   12519
Uncle Willie. by Julie Berns
and Irving Elman.(Gibbs)
32:52-3 Ja5'57. T    12520
The uncompromising heart:
a life of Marie Mancini,
Louis XIV's first love.
by Françoise Mallet-Joris.
Patrick O'Brian, trans. (Anon.)
42:187 My7'66. B    12521
The undefeated. by George
Paloczi-Horvath. (Anon.)
35:207 O10'59. B    12522
Under a colored cap. by Sean
O'Casey.(Anon.) 39:70-1
Ag3'63. B          12523
Under Milk Wood. by Dylan
Thomas. (Gibbs) 33:95-6
O26'57 (Balliett)37:132-4
Ap8'61 (Oliver) 38:132 D15'62.
T          12524
Under six reigns. by G. P.
Gooch. (Anon.) 35:155
Mr28'59. B          12525
Under the sycamore tree.
by Samuel Spewack. (Malcolm)
36:121-2 Mr19'60. T 12526
Under the weather. by Saul
Bellow. (McCarten) 42:127-8
N5'66. T          12527
Under the yum yum tree. by
Lawrence Roman. (McCarten)
36:106-107 N26'60. T
          12528
Under the yum yum tree. (Gill)
39:138 N30'63. CC    12529
Understanding media. by
Marshall McLuhan.
(Rosenberg) 41:129-36 F27'65
B          12530

Unfair to Goliath. by Herbert
Appleman and Menachem Zur.
(Oliver) 45:76 F7'70. T
                            12531
An unfinished autobiography.
by Gilbert Murray. (Anon.)
36:191 O22'60. B     12532
Unfinished funeral. by Niccolò
Tucci. (Anon.) 41:194-5
Ap17'65. B           12533
The unforgiven. (McCarten)
36:148-9 Ap16'60. CC  12534
Unheard witness. by Ernst
Hanfstaengl. (Anon.) 33:243
N16'57. B            12535
Unholy desire. (Gill) 40:149-
50 N21'64. CC        12536
The uninvited envoy. by James
Leasor. (Anon.) 38:112-13
Ja12'63. B           12537
The unknown Degas and Renoir.
by Denis Rouart. (Anon.)
41:111-12 Ja22'66. B  12538
The unknown soldier and his
wife. by Peter Ustinov.
(Oliver) 43:94 Jy15'67. T
                            12539
Unofficial history. by
William Joseph Slim. (Anon.)
38:178 S22'62. B     12540
An unofficial rose. by Iris
Murdoch. (Balliett) 38:178-9
S15'62. B            12541
The unpossessed. by Edward
Hyams. (Anon.) 36:177
Ap23'60. B           12542
Unpublished correspondence of
Henri de Toulouse-Lautrec.
by Henri de Toulouse-
Lautrec. Lucien Goldschmidt
and Herbert Schimmel, eds.
Edward B. Garside, trans.
(Anon.) 45:238-9 N15'69. B
                            12543
The unquiet Germans. by
Charles W. Thayer. (Anon.)
33:165 S28'57. B     12544
The unrepentant pilgrim: a
study of the development of
Bernard Shaw. by J. Percy
Smith. (N. Bliven) 42:175-6
Mr12'66. B           12545

The unsilent generation. Otto
Butz, ed. (Anon.) 34:127
Mr29'58. B           12546
The unsinkable Molly Brown.
by Meredith Willson.
(McCarten) 36:103-104 N12'60.
T                    12547
The unspeakable Skipton.
by Pamela Hansford
Johnson. (Balliett) 35:167
-70 Mr21'59. B       12548
The unstrung harp. by
Edward Gorey. (Wilson)
35:60 D26'59. B      12549
The unvanquished. (McCarten)
35:159-60 My9'59. CC
                            12550
Up above the world. by Paul
Bowles. (Anon.) 42:90 Jy9
'66. B               12551
Up Eden. by Robert Rosenblum
and Howard Schuman.
(Oliver) 44:142 D7'68. T
                            12552
Up from the beach. (S. Lardner)
41:104 Je12'65. CC   12553
Up the down staircase.
(Gilliatt) 43:76-7 Ag26'67.
CC                   12554
Up the junction. (Kael) 44:141-2
Mr23'68. CC          12555
Up to his ears. (Gill)
42:101-102 My21'66. CC
                            12556
Up to Thursday. by Sam
Shepard. (Oliver) 41:56-8
F20'65. T            12557
The urban guerrilla. by Martin
Oppenheimer. (Anon.) 45:
104 Je21'69. B       12558
Utamaro, painter of women.
(Gill) 40:200 D12'64. CC
                            12559
Utopia, Ltd. William S. Gilbert
and Arthur Sullivan. (Oliver)
37:99 N18'61. T      12560
Utrillo. by Waldemar George.
(Anon.) 36:247-8 D10'60.
B                    12561

V

V. by Thomas Pynchon. (Balliett) 39:113-17 Je15'63. B                              12562
The V.I.P.s (Gill) 39:104-106 S28'63. CC                      12563
Va donc chez torpe.(Flanner)] 37:154 N25'61. CC          12564
The vagabond. by Sidonie Gabrielle Colette. Enid McLeod, trans. (Flanner) 31:137-41 Ap2'55. B      12565
The Valadon drama. by John Storm. (Anon.) 35:174 Ap18 '59. B                               12566
Vali. (Gilliatt) 43:94-5 Je17 '67. CC                            12567
The valley of bones. by Anthony Powell. (N. Bliven) 40:75 D26'64. B                           12568
Valley of the dolls. (Gill) 43:48 D23'67. CC              12569
The valley of the Latin bear. by Alexander Lenard. (Anon.) 41:158-9 Je12'65. B      12570
Valmouth. by Sandy Wilson. (Panter-Downes) 34:168-9 N1'58 (Balliett) 36:75-6 O15'60. T                      12571
Vanity fair. Cleveland Amory and Frederic Bradlee, eds. (Gill) 36:154-8 D17'60. B                               12572
Valparaiso. by Nicolas Freeling. (Anon.) 41:196-7 Ap24'65. B                         12573
The vamp. by John LaTouche and Sam Locke. (Gibbs) 31:115*N19'55. T          12574
Van Gogh, a self-portrait: letters revealing his life as a painter. by Vincent Van Gogh. W.H. Auden, ed. (Anon.) 37:171 S30'61. B                               12575
Van Meegeren: master forger. by John Raymond Godley Kilbracken. (Anon.) 44:96 Ag10'68. B                    12576
Vanished. by Fletcher Knebel. (Anon.) 43:134 F17'68. B                         12577

Vanished cities. by Hermann Schreiber and Georg Schreiber. Richard Winston and Clara Winston, trans. (Anon.) 33: 153-4 S7'57. B         12578
Vanishing Cornwall. by Daphne du Maurier. (Anon.) 43:178 S23'67. B                       12579
Variety lights. (Gill) 41:167 My8'65. CC                    12580
Variety of men. by C.P. Snow. (Anon.) 43:152 My27'67. B                               12581
Varvara. by Dennis Parry. (Anon.) 32:81-2*Je30'56. B                               12582
Venceremos! by Ernesto Ché Guevara. John Gerassi, ed. (Anon.) 44:87-8 Je29'68. B                            12583
The vendor of sweets. by R.K. Narayan. (West) 43:222-3 O14'67. B                      12584
Venetian red. by P.M. Pasinetti. (Balliett) 36:100-101 Ag27'60. B             12585
The Venetian twins. by Carlo Goldoni. (Gill) 44:112 Je8'68. T                                 12586
Venice, Vicenza, and Verona. by George Campbell Dixon. (Anon.) 36:72 Jy2'60. B                               12587
Venus at large. by Henry Denker. (McCarten) 38:85 Ap21'62. T          12588
Verandah: some episodes in the crown colonies, 1867-89. by James Pope-Hennessy. (Anon.) 40:206-207 Ap25'64. B                               12589
Verdict for the doctor: the case of Benjamin Rush. by Winthrop Nielson and Frances Neilson. (Anon.) 34:103 Ja31'59. B                               12590
Verdict on Schweitzer. by Gerald McKnight. (N. Bliven) 41:190-6 Ap24'65. B          12591
Vermont general: the unusual war experiences of Edward Hastings Ripley, 1862-1865. by Edward Hastings Ripley.

Otto Eisenschiml, ed.
(Anon.) 36:143 F27'60. B
12592
Versailles and the Trianons.
by G. Van der Kemp and J.
Levron. Ethel Whitehorn, trans.
(Anon.) 34:76 Ja3'59.
B          12593
Vertigo. (McCarten) 34:65
Je7'58. CC          12594
Very personal Presidency:
Lyndon Johnson in the White
House. by Hugh Sidey.
(Anon.) 44:95-6 Ag10'68.
B          12595
A very private affair. (Gill)
38:191 O13'62. CC          12596
A very private life. by Michael
Frayn. (Anon.) 44:138-9 S7'68.
B          12597
A very rich woman. by Ruth
Gordon. (McCarten) 41:184
O9'65. T          12598
A very special baby. by Robert
Alan Aurthur. (Gibbs) 32:123-
4 N24'56. T          12599
The viceroys. by Federico
De Roberto. Archibald
Colquhoun, trans. (Anon.)
38:176 My12'62. B          12600
Vicky: a biography of Victoria
C. Woodhull. by M.M. Mar-
berry. (Anon.) 43:195
Ap15'67. B          12601
Victim. (Gill) 37:130-3 F10'62.
CC          12602
Victims of duty. by Eugène
Ionesco. (Oliver) 40:88-9
Je6'64. T          12603
Victor Herbert: a life in
music. by Edward N.
Waters. (Anon.) 31:139-40
Je11'55. B          12604
Victor, ou les enfants au pouvoir.
by Roger Vitrac. (Flanner)
38:191-2 O20'62. T          12605
Victoria. by Knut Hamsun.
Oliver Stallybrass, trans.
(Updike) 45:90-5 Je28'69.
B          12606
Victoria, Albert, and Mrs.
Stevenson. by Sallie Coles
Stevenson. Edward Boykin, ed.

(Anon.) 33:137 Mr30'57. B
12607
Victoria R.: a biography with
four hundred illustrations
based on her personal photo-
graph albums. by Helmut
Gernsheim and Alice Gern-
sheim. (Anon.) 35:134-5
*O19'59. B          12608
A Victorian canvas: the memoirs
of W.P. Frith, R.A. by
W.P. Frith. Nevile Wallis, ed.
(Anon.) 33:99-100 D21'57. B
12609
A Victorian poacher. by James
Hawker. (Malcolm) 37:62-6
D30'61. B          12610
Victorian scandal: a biography
of the right honourable
gentleman Sir Charles Dilke.
by Roy Jenkins. (Anon.)
41:246-7 N20'65. B          12611
Victorian vista. by James Laver.
(Anon.) 31:75*Ja7'56. B
12612
The Victorians. by Charles
Petrie. (Anon.) 37:167-8
S30'61. B          12613
The Victorians and their read-
ing. by Amy Cruse.
(Anon.) 39:118-20 Je15'63.
B          12614
The victors. (Gill) 39:52
D28'63. CC          12615
Victory in Papua. by Samuel
Milner. (Kahn) 33:74-82
Je29'57. B          12616
Vie du Marquis de Sade. by
Gilbert Lely. (Wilson) 41:
175-224 S18'65. B          12617
Vie privée. (Flanner) 38:127-8
Mr3'62. CC          12618
Vienna and the young Hitler.
by William A. Jenks. (Anon.)
36:159-60 Mr26'60. B
12619
Viet Cong. by Douglas Pike.
(Alsop) 42:112-26
Ja28'67. B          12620
Vietnam: between two truces.
by Jean Lacouture. Konrad
Kellen and Joel Carmichael,
trans. (Anon.) 42:167 Je11'66.
B          12621

Vietnam perspective: air war in
the North. (Arlen) 43:148-53
Mr4'67. TV            12622
Vietnam reporting. (Arlen)
43:173-86 O21'67. TV
12623
Vietnam: the logic of with-
drawal. by Howard Zinn.
(Anon.) 43:179-80 S9'67.
B                     12624
Vietnam weekly review.
(Arlen) 43:139-45 My27'67.
TV                    12625
Viet-Nam witness, 1953-66.
by Bernard B. Fall. (Anon.)
42:165 Je4'66. B      12626
The Vietnamese. by Susan
Sheehan. (Anon.) 43:150-3
Ap1'67. B             12627
The view from Pompey's Head.
(McCarten) 31:90 N12'55. CC
12628
A view from the bridge. by
Arthur Miller. (Gibbs) 31:
86-9*O8'55. (Panter-Downes)
32:79 Ja12'57 (Gill) 37:82-3
Ja27'62 (Oliver) 40:94 F6'65.
T                     12629
A view of the spree. by Alson
J. Smith. (Anon.) 38:184-5
Ap14'62. B            12630
View to the southeast. by
Santha Rama Rau. (Anon.)
33:71 D28'57. B       12631
Vigilante justice. by
Alan Valentine. (Anon.) 31:102-
103*Ja14'56. B        12632
The Viking book of aphorisms:
a personal selection.
W.H. Auden and Louis Kronen-
berger, eds. (Anon.) 38:
147-8 F9'63. B        12633
The Viking book of folk ballads
of the English-speaking
world. Albert Friedman, ed.
(Anon.) 32:244 N17'56. B
12634
The Vikings. (McCarten) 34:68-
9 Je21'58. CC         12635
A villa in Summer. by
Penelope Mortimer. (Gill)
31:170 My14'55. B     12636

Villa Mimosa. by Jerrard
Tickell. (Anon.) 37:163
Mr25'61. B            12637
Village in the Vaucluse. by
Laurence Wylie. (Anon.)
33:135-6 Mr9'57. B    12638
The vinegar works. by Edward
Gorey. (Anon.) 39:71 Ag31'63.
B                     12639
The vintage Mencken. by H.L.
Mencken. Alistair Cooke, ed.
(McKelway) 31:217-21*
N19'55. B             12640
Vintage '60. by Jack Wilson,
Alan Jeffreys and Maxwell
Grant. (McCarten) 36:97
S24'60. T             12641
Violent Saturday. (McCarten)
31:130 My21'55. CC    12642
Violent Summer. (Oliver)
37:121-2 Je3'61. CC   12643
Violin and roller. (Balliett)
38:56 S1'62. CC       12644
Virgil Thomson. by Virgil
Thomson. (Anon.) 42:248
N19'66. B             12645
The virgin queen. (McCarten)
31:47*Ag13'55. CC     12646
The virgin Spring. (Gill)
36:152-4 N19'60. CC
12647
The Virginia dynasties. by
Clifford Dowdey. (Anon.)
45:167-8 My10'69. B   12648
Viridiana. (Gill) 38:147-8
Mr24'62. CC           12649
The virtuous bigamist.
(McCarten) 35:125 Je6'59.
CC                    12650
Visa for Avalon. by Winifred
Bryher. (Anon.) 41:156
Je12'65. B            12651
A vision of battlements. by
Anthony Burgess. (Anon.)
42:186 My7'66. B      12652
A vision of Paris: the photographs
of Eugène Atget. by Eugène
Atget. (Anon.) 39:238-40
D14'63. B             12653
Visions rise and change. by
Pierre van Paassen.
(Anon.) 31:177*O15'55. B
12654

The visit. by Friedrich Duerrenmatt. Maurice Valency, adapt. (Gibbs) 34:87 My17'58 (Tynan) 36: 118-20 Mr19'60. T    12655
The visit. (Gill) 40:135-6 O31'64 CC    12656
A visit to a small planet. by Gore Vidal. (Gibbs) 32:78-80 F16'57. T    12657
The visitor. by Anthony Gilbert. (Anon.) 43:248 D9'67. B    12658
The visitors. by Mary McMinnies. (Anon.) 34:238-9 D6'58. B    12659
Vitelloni. (McCarten) 32:175 N3'56. CC    12660
Viva Madison Avenue! by George Panetta. (Tynan) 36:132-4 Ap16'60. T    12661
Viva Maria. (Gill) 41:56-8 D25'65. CC    12662
Vivaldi, genius of the baroque. by Marc Pincherle. Christopher Hatch, trans. (Anon.) 34: 163 Ap12'58. B    12663
Vive moi! by Sean O'Faolain. (Anon.) 40:245-6 O10'64. B    12664
The voice at the back door. by Elizabeth Spencer. (Gill) 32:180-1 D15'56. B    12665
A voice from the attic. by Robertson Davies. (Anon.) 36:246 D10'60. B    12666
Voice of Israel. by Abba Eban. (Anon.) 33:141-2 My25'57. B    12667
The voice of Latin America. by William Benton. (Anon.) 37:224 N4'61. B    12668
The voice of the desert. by Joseph Wood Krutch. (Anon.) 31:160-1*S24'55. B    12669
Voice of the hurricane. (McCarten) 40:90 Je13'64. CC    12670
A voice through a cloud. by Denton Welch. (Updike) 42:236-41 O29'66. B    12671

Voices from the sky. by Arthur C. Clarke. (Anon.) 41:202-203 D18'65. B    12672
Voices in court: a treasury of the bench, the bar, and the courtroom. William H. Davenport, ed. (Anon.) 34:244-5 N15'58. B    12673
Voices of dissent. Dissent (Periodical) (Macdonald) 35:150-1 Mr28'59. B    12674
The voices of others. by Ruth Tabrah. (Anon.) 35:167-8 Je6'59. B    12675
Voltaire. by Theodore Besterman. (Gay) 45:71-5 Ja10'70. B    12676
Voltaire and the Calas case. by Edna Nixon. (Anon.) 39:191-2 My4'63. B    12677
Voltaire in love. by Nancy Mitford. (Anon.) 34:139 F22'58. B    12678
Von Ryan's express. (Arlen) 41:59-60 Jy17'65. CC    12679
Voss. by Patrick White. (Anon.) 33:197-8 O5'57. B    12680
The voyage home. by Richard Church. (Anon.) 42:173-4 Ap2'66. B    12681
The voyage of Magellan: the journal of Antonio Pigafetta. by Antonio Pigafetta. Paula Spurlin Paige, trans. (Anon.) 45:102-103 F7'70. B    12682
Voyage of silence. (Gilliatt) 44:194-8 S14'68. CC    12683
Voyage to America: the journals of Thomas Cather. by Thomas Cather. Thomas Yoseloff, ed. (Anon.) 37:211-12 O7'61. B    12684
Voyage to the amorous islands. by Newton A. Rowe. (Anon.) 32:137-8*Mr24'56. B    12685
Voyage to the bottom of the sea. (Gill) 37:70-1 Ag12'61. CC    12686

Voyager Belsky. by Monroe
Engel. (Anon.) 38:214-15
O27'62. B            12687
The voyages of Joshua Slocum.
by Joshua Slocum. Walter
Magnes Teller, ed. (Anon.)
34:215 D13'58. B       12688

W

W.J. Cash: Southern prophet.
by Joseph L. Morrison.
(Anon.) 43:62-5 D30'67. B
                     12689
W. Somerset Maugham. by
Karl G. Pfeiffer. (Anon.)
34:126-7 Ja24'59. B   12690
The wackiest ship in the Army.
(Angell) 37:98-9 F18'61.
CC                   12691
The wages of fear. (McCarten)
31:88-9 F26'55. CC    12692
Waging peace. by Dwight D.
Eisenhower. (Rovere)
41:244-6 D11'65. B     12693
The waif. by Nicholas Voinov.
(Anon.) 31:198-9*N5'55.
B                    12694
The wailing mountain. by Mihailo
Lalić. (West) 41:217-18
S25'65. B            12695
The waist-high culture. by Thomas
Griffith. (Anon.) 35:176 Mr
14'59. B             12696
Wait a minim! by Leon
Gluckman and Andrew Tracey.
(McCarten) 42:160 Mr19'66.
T                    12697
Wait till the sun shines, Nellie.
by Audrey Gellen Maas. (Anon.)
42:94-5 Ja7'67. B     12698
Wait until dark. by Frederick
Knott. (McCarten) 41:112
F12'66. T            12699
Wait until dark. (Gill) 43:
167-8 N4'67. CC      12700
Waiting for Godot. by Samuel
Beckett. (Gibbs) 32:83-4
*My5'56. T           12701
Waiting for the end. by Leslie
A. Fiedler. (Anon.) 40:180
Je6'64. B            12702

Waiting for the Mahatma. by
R.K. Narayan. (Anon.)
31:204*D10'55. B      12703
Wai-Wai: through the forests
north of the Amazon. by
Nicholas Guppy. (Anon.) 34:
165 S13'58. B         12704
Wake up darling. by Alex
Gottlieb. (Gibbs) 32:76-7
*My12'56. T          12705
Waldo. by Paul Theroux. (Anon.)
43:246 N11'67. B      12706
Waldorf. by James Goldman.
(Anon.) 41:243-4 N6'65.
B                    12707
Walk, don't run. (Gill) 42:71
S3'66. CC            12708
Walk down mah street! by
Norman Curtis and Patricia
Taylor Curtis. (Oliver) 44:59
Je22'68. T           12709
Walk Egypt. by Vinnie
Williams. (Anon.) 36:106
S3'60. B             12710
The walk home. by Gwyn
Jones. (Anon.) 38:98 Ja5'63.
B                    12711
Walk in darkness. by William
Hairston. (Oliver) 39:99
N9'63. T             12712
A walk in the mountains. by
Ralph Izzard and Molly
Izzard. (Anon.) 36:161-2 D17
'60. B               12713
A walk on the wild side. by
Nelson Algren. (Podhoretz)
32:120-7*Je2'56. B    12714
Walk on the wild side. (Gill)
38:111 F24'62. CC     12715
A walk through Britain. by
John Hillaby. (Anon.) 45:
152 My17'69. B        12716
Walk together children. (Oliver)
44:129-30 N23'68. T   12717
A walk with love and death.
(Kael) 45:159-60 O11'69. CC
                     12718
Walking to Waldheim. by
Mayo Simon. (Oliver) 43:
149 D2'67. T         12719
The wall. by Millard Lampell.
(McCarten) 36:89-90 O22'60

(Flanner) 38:94-6 Je23'62.
T                  12720
Walleyed Nippon. (McCarten)
39:118-19 S14'63. CC
                   12721
Walt Whitman reconsidered. by
Richard Chase. (Anon.) 31:
84 Jy9'55. B       12722
Walt Whitman's New York.
by Walt Whitman. Henry M.
Christman, ed. (Anon.)
39:140 F15'64. B   12723
Walter Bagehot. by Norman
St. John-Stevas. (Anon.)
35:172-3 Ap11'59. B   12724
Walter Lippmann and his
times. Marquis Childs and
James Reston, eds. (Anon.)
35:170-1 O3'59. B   12725
The waltz of the toreadors. by
Jean Anouilh. (Gibbs) 32:68-
70 Ja26'57. T      12726
Waltz of the toreadors.
(Balliett) 38:67-8 Ag25'62.
CC                 12727
Wandering. (Gilliatt) 43:57-8
Jy1'67. CC         12728
The wandering years: diaries,
1922-1939. by Cecil Beaton.
(Anon.) 37: 139-40 F10'62.
B                  12729
Wanted: an Asian policy. by
Edwin O. Reischauer.
(Anon.) 31:135-6 Mr26'55.
B                  12730
The wanting seed. by
Anthony Burgess. (Anon.)
39:209-10 N2'63. B   12731
The Wapshot chronicle. by
John Cheever. (Brennan) 33:
154-62 My11'57. B   12732
The war: a concise history 1939-
1945. by Louis L. Snyder.
(Anon.) 36:198-9 S17'60. B
                   12733
War and peace. by Alfred
Neumann, Edwin Piscator
and Guntram Prufer. Robert
David MacDonald, trans.
(Oliver) 40:92-4 Ja23'65.
T                  12734
War and peace. (Hamburger)
32:56*S1'56 (Flanner) 42:72
Jy30'66 (Gilliatt) 44:163-7

My4'68. CC         12735
War and peace in the space
age. by James M. Gavin.
(Anon.) 34:94 Ag16'58. B
                   12736
The war dispatches of Stephen
Crane. by Stephen Crane.
R.W. Stallman and E.R.
Hagemann, eds. (Anon.)
40:214-15 S19'64. B   12737
The war game. (Gill) 43:94-6
Ap1'67. CC         12738
War hunt. (Balliett) 38:68-9
Ag18'62. CC        12739
The war lord. (Gill) 41:112
D4'65. CC          12740
The war lover. by John
Hersey. (Balliett) 35:132-3
*D19'59. B         12741
The war of the buttons. (Gill)
39:39-90 D21'63. CC   12742
War within a war: the Con-
federacy against itself. by
Carleton Beals. (Anon.)
41:94-5 Ag7'65. B   12743
The war years, 1939-1945. by
Harold Nicolson. Nigel Nicol-
son, ed. (N. Bliven) 43:170-
6 S9'67. B         12744
Warhorse. by John Cunningham.
(Anon.) 32:138-9*Mr10'56.
B                  12745
Warlock. by Oakley Hall.
(Anon.) 34:163 S13'58. B
                   12746
Warlock. (McCarten) 35:104-
106 My16'59. CC    12747
Warm bodies. by Donald Mor-
ris. (Malcolm) 33:233-6
D7'57. B           12748
The warm peninsula. by Joe
Masteroff. (Tynan) 35:135-6
O31'59. T          12749
Warrendale. (Gilliatt) 44:147-8
S21'68. CC         12750
The wars of America. by
Robert Leckie. (Anon.) 44:
139-40 Mr30'68. B   12751
The Warsaw Hersey. by S.L.
Shneiderman. (Anon.) 35:
204-205 O31'59. B   12752
The washing of the spears. by
Donald Morris. (West) 41:
129-34 F5'66. B    12753

Washington and the American
Revolution. by Esmond
Wright. (Anon.) 33:106
Ja18'58. B                 12754
The Washington papers. Saul
K. Padover, ed. (Anon.)
31:152-3 Mr19'55. B
                           12755
Washington wife: journal of
Ellen Maury Slayden from
1897-1919. by Ellen Maury
Slayden. (Anon.) 39:177 Mr
9'63. B                    12756
The waste makers. by Vance
Packard. (N. Bliven) 36:
234-9 N12'60. B            12757
The watch that ends the night.
by Hugh MacLennan. (Anon.)
35:117-18 F28'59. B    12758
A watcher on the Rhine. by
Brian Connell. (Anon.) 33:
165-6 Ap6'57. B            12759
Watchman, what of the night?
by Jed Harris. (Anon.)
39:206-207 Mr16'63. B
                           12760
Water of life. by Henry Morton
Robinson. (Anon.) 36:103-104
Je25'60. B                 12761
A water walk by the Villa
d'Este. by Jean Garrigue.
(Bogan) 36:154-7 Mr26'60.
B                          12762
Watercolor. by Philip Mag-
dalany. (Gill) 45:56 Ja31'70.
T                          12763
The waterfall. by Margaret
Drabble. (Anon.) 45:158-9
O4'69. B                   12764
The watering place. by Lyle
Kessler. (Gill) 45:87 Mr22
'69. T                     12765
Waterloo: day of battle. by
David Howarth. (Anon.)
44:242 N30'68. B           12766
The waters of Kronos. by
Conrad Richter. (Anon.)
36:166-7 My21'60. B
                           12767
The waters under the earth.
by John Moore. (Anon.)
41:243 N6'65. B            12768

Wavell: scholar and solider.
by John Connell. (Anon.)
41:216 My15'65. B      12769
The way back. by Vincent
Brome. (Anon.) 34:162
Ap12'58. B                 12770
A way of looking. by Elizabeth
Jennings. (Bogan) 32:179-80
O6'56. B                   12771
The way we live now. by War-
ren Miller. (Balliett) 34:
104-105 My31'58. B     12772
The way West. (Gill) 43:104
My27'67. CC                12773
The wayward bus. (McCarten)
33:72 Je15'57. CC          12774
The wayward saint. by Paul
Vincent Carroll. (Gibbs)
31:69-70 Mr5'55. T     12775
The wayward wife. by Alberto
Moravia. (West) 36:144-5
Je11'60. B                 12776
We are all murderers.
(McCarten) 32:95-6 Ja19
'57. CC                    12777
We are not alone. by Walter
Sullivan. (Bernstein) 42:
117-32 My28'66. B      12778
We bombed in New Haven. by
Joseph Heller. (Gill) 44:
139 O26'68. T              12779
We, comrades three. by Richard
Baldridge. (McCarten)
42:59 D31'66. T            12780
We die alone. by David Howarth.
(Anon.) 32:142*Mr10'56. B
                           12781
We have always lived in the
castle. by Shirley Jackson.
(Anon.) 38:231-2 O13'62.
B                          12782
We have always lived in the
castle. by Hugh Wheeler.
(McCarten) 42:95-6 O29'66.
T                          12783
We have seen the best of our
times. by Nancy A.J. Potter.
(Anon.) 44:126-7 F8'69. B
                           12784
We shall march again. by
Gerhard Kramer. (West)
31:102-104 Je18'55. B
                           12785

We still kill the old way. (Kael)
44:150 Mr9'68. CC    12786
Wealth and power in America.
by Gabriel Kolko. (Mac-
donald) 38:84-6 Ja19'63.
B                    12787
The weather of February.
by Hollis Summers. (Anon.)
33:190-1 S21'57. B    12788
The web of victory. by Earl
Schenck Miers. (Anon.)
31:128 Ap30'55. B    12789
Webster's new international
dictionary (third edition).
Philip Gove, ed. (Mac-
donald) 38:130-60 Mr10'62. B
                     12790
Weddings and babies. (Gill)
36:100-101 O22'60. CC
                     12791
Weekend. by Gore Vidal.
(Gill) 44:101-102 Mr23'68.
T                    12792
Weekend. (Flanner) 43:80-1
F3'68 (Kael) 44:141-5
O5'68. CC            12793
A weekend in September. by
John Edward Weems. (Anon.)
33:154-5 Ap20'57. B    12794
Welcome to hard times.
(Gill) 43:181 My13'67. CC
                     12795
The well of the saints. by
John Millington Synge.
(Malcolm) 35:82-3
Ap18'59. T           12796
Wellington at war: 1794-1815
by Arthur Wellesley.
Antony Brett-James, ed.
(Anon.) 37:120 Je17'61. B
                     12797
Wellington at Waterloo. by Jac
Weller. (Anon.) 43:190-1
O7'67. B             12798
We're civilized? by Alfred
Aiken and Ray Haney.
(Oliver) 38:148 N17'62. T
                     12799
We're no angels. (McCarten)
31:59 Jy16'55. CC    12800
West Side story. by Leonard
Bernstein and Stephen Sond-
heim. (Gibbs) 33:64 O5'57.
T                    12801

West Side story. (Gill)
37:196-7 O21'61. CC
                     12802
The Western mind in
transition. by Franz Alexander.
(Anon.) 36:143 My28'60.
B                    12803
Westward vision: the story of
the Oregon Trail. by David
Lavender. (Anon.) 39:247
D7'63. B             12804
Wet paint. (Oliver) 41:85-6
Ap24'65. T           12805
Whale off! by Everett J.
Edwards and Jeannette
Edwards Rattray. (Anon.)
32:154-5*S15'56. B    12806
What a kingdom it was. by
Galway Kinnell. (Bogan)
37:130 Ap1'61. B     12807
What a way to go! (Gill)
40:191 My16'64. CC   12808
What about Ronald Reagan?
(Arlen) 43:59-60 D30'67.
TV                   12809
What did we do wrong?
by Henry Denker. (McCarten)
43:162 N4'67. T      12810
What did you do in the war,
Daddy? (Gill) 42:103
S10'66. CC           12811
What Dr. Spock didn't tell us.
by B.M. Atkinson, Jr.
(Anon.) 35:174-5 Ap11'59.
B                    12812
What end but love. by Gordon
Webber. (Anon.) 35:241
N28'59. B            12813
What ever happened to Baby
Jane? (Gill) 38:209-10
N17'62. CC           12814
What I think. by Adlai E.
Stevenson. (Anon.) 32:170
*Mr17'56. B          12815
What is remembered. by Alice
B. Toklas. (Flanner) 38:66-8
D29'62. B            12816
What makes Sammy run? by
Budd Schulberg, Stuart
Schulberg and Ervin Drake.
(McCarten) 40:118-20 Mr7'64.
T                    12817
What makes Sammy run? (J.
Lardner) 35:166-7 O17'59

TV                    12818
What shall we tell Caroline?
   by John Mortimer. (Oliver)
   37:120 D2'61.  T      12819
What the butler saw: two
   hundred and fifty years of
   the servant problem. by
   E.S. Turner. (N. Bliven)
   39:82-8 Ag10'63. B    12820
What's new pussycat? (Oliver)
   41:78 Je26'65. CC     12821
What's up, Tiger Lily?
   (Gill) 42:122 N26'66. CC
                         12822
The wheel of earth. by Helga
   Sandburg. (Anon.) 34:156-
   7 My17'58. B          12823
The wheeler dealers. (Gill)
   39:236 N23'63. CC     12824
Wheels West. by Homer
   Croy. (Anon.) 31:175-6 My14
   '55. B                12825
When in Greece. by Emma
   Lathen. (Anon.) 45:160
   S13'69. B             12826
When London walked in terror.
   by Tom A. Cullen. (Anon.)
   41:235 O9'65. B       12827
When the kissing had to stop.
   by Constantine FitzGibbon.
   (West) 36:179-80 O1'60. B
                         12828
When the war is over. by
   Stephen Becker. (Anon.)
   45:210 N29'69.
   B                     12829
When the wolves howl. by
   Aquilino Ribeiro. (West)
   39:73-6 D28'63. B     12830
Whence all but he had fled. by
   L.J. Davis. (S. Lardner)
   44:188-9 Ap20'68. B   12831
"Where did you go?" "Out"
   "What did you do?" "Nothing".
   by Robert Paul Smith.
   (Anon.) 33:168-9 My18'57. B
                         12832
Where people gather. by Peter
   Copani. (Oliver) 43:163
   N4'67. T              12833
Where the air is clear. by
   Carlos Fuentes. (West) 37:
   123-5 Mr4'61. B       12834

Where the boys are. (Angell)
   36:71 Ja28'61. CC     12835
Where the hot wind blows.
   (Gill) 36:152 N19'60. CC
                         12836
Where the lion trod. by
   Gordon Shepherd. (N. Bliven)
   37:238-44 D2'61. B    12837
Where the sea breaks its
   back. by Corey Ford.
   (Anon.) 42:245-6 O15'66.
   B                     12838
Where the spies are. (Gill)
   41:142 F12'66. CC     12839
Where were you when the
   lights went out? (Gilliatt)
   44:96-7 Ag24'68. CC
                         12840
Where's Daddy? by William
   Inge. (McCarten) 42:110
   Mr12'66 T             12841
Where's the melody?
   by Martin Williams. (Anon.)
   42:84 Jy30'66. B      12842
While the city sleeps.
   (McCarten) 32:109*My26'56.
   CC                    12843
Whipple's castle. by Thomas
   Williams. (Anon.) 44:122-3
   F15'69. B             12844
Whisper into my good ear.
   by William Hanley. (Oliver)
   38:182-3 O13'62. T    12845
Whisper to me. by Greer
   Johnson. (Balliett) 36:104
   D3'60. T              12846
The whisperers. (Gilliatt)
   43:72-4 Ag12'67. CC
                         12847
Whistle down the wind. (Gill)
   38:142 Ap28'62. CC    12848
A whistle in the dark. by
   Thomas Murphy. (Oliver)
   45:150-1 O18'69. T    12849
White and black: test of a
   nation. by Samuel Lubell.
   (Anon.) 40:124 Ag22'64.
   B                     12850
The white desert. by Noel
   Barber. (Anon.) 35:200
   S12'59. B             12851
The White House. by A.E.
   Hotchner. (McCarten)

40:78-80 My30'64. T
                        12852
White nights. (Oliver) 37:
130-1 Je10'61. CC      12853
The white rajahs. by Steven
Runciman. (Anon.) 36:241
N12'60. B              12854
White voices. (Gill) 41:165
Ap24'65. CC            12855
The white voyage. by John
Christopher. (Anon.) 37:
170 Mr11'61. B         12856
White wilderness. (McCarten)
34:68 Ag23'58. CC      12857
Who killed Mr. Crittenden?
by Kenneth Lamott. (Anon.)
39:246-7 N23'63. B     12858
Who killed society? by Cleveland
Amory. (Anon.) 36:58-9
D31'60. B              12859
Who speaks for the Negro?
by Robert Penn Warren.
(Anon.) 41:126-7 Je19'65.
B                      12860
Who was that lady I saw you
with? by Norman Krasna.
(J. Lardner) 34:89-90
Mr15'58. T             12861
The whole creation. by
Theodore Morrison. (Anon.)
37:117 Ja20'62. B      12862
Who'll save the plowboy?
by Frank D. Gilroy. (Oliver)
37:69 Ja20'62. T       12863
Wholly communion. (Gilliatt)
43:92-4 Je17'67. CC    12864
Whoop-up. by Cy Feuer,
Ernest H. Martin and Dan
Cushman. (Tynan) 34:50-3 Ja
3'59. T                12865
Who's afraid of Virginia Woolf?
by Edward Albee. (Mc-
Carten) 38:85-6 O20'62
(Flanner) 40:67-8 D26'64.
T                      12866
Who's afraid of Virginia
Woolf? (Oliver) 42:64-5
Jy2'66. CC             12867
Who's got his own. by Ronald
Milner. (Oliver) 42:86
O22'66. T              12868
Who's happy now? by Oliver
Hailey. (Oliver) 45:86-8

N29'69. T              12869
Who's who, Baby? by Gerald
Frank and Johnny Brandon.
(Oliver) 43:90-1 F10'68. T
                       12870
Why men confess. by O. John
Rogge. (Anon.) 35:176-7
Ap25'59. B             12871
The wicked cooks. by
Günter Grass. (Oliver)
42:93-4 F4'67. T       12872
The wicked scheme of
Jebal Deeks. (J. Lardner)
35:207 D5'59. TV       12873
Wide wide world. (J. Lardner)
33:199-201 N23'57. TV
                       12874
Widowers' houses. by
George Bernard Shaw.
(Malcolm) 35:102-103
Mr21'59. T             12875
The widowing of Mrs. Holroyd.
by D.H. Lawrence. (Panter-
Downes) 44:102 My11'68.
T                      12876
A wife for the pretender.
by Peggy Miller. (Anon.)
42:245 O15'66. B       12877
The wild bunch. (Gilliatt) 45:
74 Jy5'69. CC          12878
The wild duck. by Henrik
Ibsen. Eva Le Gallienne,
trans. (McCarten) 42:69
Ja21'67. T             12879
Wild flowers. by Homer D.
House. (Anon.) 37:248
D2'61. B               12880
The wild hunters. by Gene
Caesar. (Anon.) 33:135
F8'58. B               12881
Wild is the wind. (McCarten)
33:52 D21'57. CC       12882
Wild 90. (Kael) 43:90-5
Ja20'68. CC            12883
The wild oat. (McCarten)
32:59*Jy7'56. CC       12884
Wild ocean. by Alan Villiers.
(Anon.) 33:95-6*Je22'57. B
                       12885
Wild river. (McCarten) 36:
99-100 Je4'60. CC      12886
Wild strawberries. (McCarten) 35:
44-6 Jy25'59. CC       12887

Wild train: the story of the Andrews raiders. by Charles O'Neill. (Anon.) 32:83*D22 '56. B                    12888

Wildcat. by N. Richard Nash, Carolyn Leigh and Cy Coleman. (McCarten) 36:38 D24'60. T                    12889

Wilderstone. by John Leggett. (Balliett) 36:139-40 F27 '60. B                    12890

Wilderness kingdom: the journals and paintings of Father Nicolas Point. by Nicolas Point. Joseph P. Donnelly, trans. and ed. (Anon.) 44:188 My4'68. B                    12891

A wilderness of mirrors. by Max Frisch. (West) 42:172-3 Ap2'66. B                    12892

Wildlife in America. by Peter Matthiessen. (Anon.) 35: 198-9 O24'59. B                    12893

Will success spoil Rock Hunter? by George Axelrod. (Gibbs) 31:82-4*O22'55. T                    12894

Will success spoil Rock Hunter? (McCarten) 33:75 S21'57. CC                    12895

William Glackens and the ash-can group. by Ira Glackens. (Anon.) 33:202-203 O26'57. B                    12896

William Hazlitt. by Herschel Baker. (Anon.) 38:99-100 Ag18'62. B                    12897

William Herschel and the con-struction of the heavens. by Michael A. Hoskin. (Anon.) 40:79 Ag1'64. B                    12898

William Howard Taft: Chief Justice. by Alpheus Thomas Mason. (Anon.) 41:182-3 My8'65. B                    12899

A William March omnibus. by William March. Robert Loomis, ed. (West) 32:97-9*Mr31'56. B                    12900

William Morris: his life, work, and friends. by Philip Henderson. (Gill) 44:201-204 S14'68. B                    12901

William of Orange: a personal portrait--Volume II: 1674-1702. by Nesca A. Robb. (Anon.) 42:126-7 Ag27'66. B                    12902

William the conqueror: the Norman impact upon England. by David C. Douglas. (Anon.) 40:100 My8'64. B                    12903

William III and the defense of European liberty, 1650-1702. by Stephen B. Baxter. (Anon.) 42:246-7 O29'66. B                    12904

William Wetmore Story and his friends. by Henry James. (Anon.) 33:170 My18'57. B                    12905

Wilson: confusions and crises, 1915-16. by Arthur S. Link (Anon.) 40:77-8 D26'64. B                    12906

Wilson: the new freedom. by Arthur S. Link. (Anon.) 32: 143-4 F16'57. B                    12907

Wilson's night thoughts. by Edmund Wilson. (Anon.) 37: 118-20 Ja20'62. B                    12908

Wind across the Everglades. (McCarten) 34:86 S20'58. CC                    12909

The winds of revolution: Latin America today--and tomorrow. by Tad Szulc. (Anon.) 39:79 Ja4'64. B                    12910

Windsor revisited. by Edward VIII. (Anon.) 36:119-20 Ja 14'61. B                    12911

The windward road. by Archie Carr. (Anon.) 31:117-18 *F11'56. B                    12912

Winesburg, Ohio. by Christopher Sergel. (Gibbs) 33:55-8 F15'58. T                    12913

The wings of the dove. by Christopher Taylor. (Panter-Downes.) 39:118-19 F15'64. T                    12914

The winners. by Julio Cortázar. Elaine Kerrigan, trans. (West) 41:177-8 My8'65. B                    12915

Winning. (S. Lardner) 45:80-1 My31'69. CC                    12916

Winslow Homer at Prout's Neck. by Philip C. Beam. (Anon.)

42:166-7 Ap30'66. B   12917
Winston Churchill: an intimate
    portrait. by Violet Bonham
    Carter. (Anon.) 41:159
    Je12'65. B          12918
Winston Churchill: British bull-
    dog. by Emrys Hughes.
    (Anon.) 31:127-8 My28'55.
    B                   12919
Winston S. Churchill. by
    Randolph S. Churchill.
    (Steiner) 42:238-45 N5'66
    (Anon.) 43:247-8 N18'67. B
                        12920
The Winter beach. by
    Charlton Ogburn, Jr. (Anon.)
    42:95 Ja7'67. B     12921
Winter light. (Gill) 39:173
    My18'63. CC         12922
The winter of our discontent.
    by John Steinbeck. (Anon.)
    37:177 S16'61. B    12923
The winter of the bombs.
    by Constantine FitzGibbon.
    (Anon.) 33:105-106 Ja18'58.
    B                   12924
The Winter people. by Gilbert
    Phelps. (Anon.) 40:182
    Ap11'64. B          12925
Winter quarters. by Alfred
    Duggan. (Gill) 32:234-6
    N17'56. B           12926
Winterset. (J. Lardner) 35:
    204 D5'59. TV       12927
Wise child. by Simon Gray.
    (Tynan) 44:126-9 N9'68. T
                        12928
The wisest fool in Christendom:
    the reign of King James I
    and VI. by William McElwee.
    (Anon.) 34:212-13 N8'58. B
                        12929
The witches. by Jay Williams.
    (Anon.) 33:93-4 Jy13'57.
    B                   12930
Witches of Salem. (McCarten)
    34:209-10 D13'58. CC
                        12931
Witches' sabbath. by Harry
    Granick. (Oliver) 38:97-8
    Ap28'62. T          12932
The witching ship. by Frederic
    Morton. (Anon.) 35:122 Ja23
    '60. B              12933

With dearest love to all: the
    letters and life of Lady Jebb.
    by Caroline Jebb. Mary
    Reed Bobbitt, ed. (Anon.)
    36:185-6 O29'60. B   12934
With gall and honey. by R.
    Leslie Gourse. (Anon.) 37:
    94-5 Je24'61. B      12935
With Kennedy. by Pierre
    Salinger. (Anon.) 42:238-9
    S24'66. B            12936
With love from Gracie. by
    Grace Hegger Lewis. (Anon.)
    32:172 S22'56. B     12937
Without a city wall. by
    Melvyn Bragg. (Anon.) 45:
    151 Je7'69. B        12938
Witness. by Terrence McNally.
    (Oliver) 44:142 D7'68. T
                         12939
Witness for the prosecution.
    (McCarten) 33:80 F15'58.
    CC                   12940
The wives. by Lionel Abel.
    (Oliver) 41:161 My29'65.
    T                    12941
Wives and lovers. (McCarten)
    39:147-8 S7'63. CC   12942
The Wobblies: the story of
    syndicalism in the United
    States. by Patrick Renshaw.
    (Anon.) 43:86-7 S2'67. B
                         12943
Wolf Willow: a history, a story,
    and a memory of the last
    plains frontier. by Wallace
    Stegner. (Anon.) 38:244-6
    D1'62. B             12944
The woman from Sarajevo.
    by Ivo Andrić. Joseph Hitrec,
    trans. (West) 41:181-2 My8'65.
    B                    12945
Woman in a dressing gown.
    (McCarten) 33:75-7 S21'57. CC
                         12946
Woman in the dunes. (Gill)
    40:202-203 N7'64. CC
                         12947
A woman is a woman. (Gill)
    40:150 N14'64. CC    12948
Woman is my idea. by Don C.
    Liljenquist. (Gill) 44:96-7
    O5'68. T             12949

Woman obsessed. (McCarten)
35:125-6 Je6'59. CC    12950
Woman of Rome. (McCarten)
32:198 N24'56. CC    12951
Woman times seven. (Gilliatt)
43:52 Jy8'67. CC    12952
The woman with the little fox.
by Violette Leduc.
(Brennan) 43:181-4 My6'67.
B    12953
Women and Thomas Harrow.
by John P. Marquand. (Anon.)
34:232-3 N22'58. B    12954
Women are weak. (McCarten)
35:74 Je20'59. CC    12955
The women at the tomb. by
Michel de Ghelderode.
(Balliett) 37:123 My6'61.
T    12956
Women of the world. (Miller)
39:64-5 Ag24'63. CC
12957
The wonderful clouds. by
Françoise Sagan. Anne Green,
trans. (Anon.) 38:71 Ag4
'62. B    12958
The wonderful O. by James
Thurber. (Anon.) 33:104
*Je1'57. B    12959
The wonderful world of the
brothers Grimm. (Balliett)
38:56 S1'62. CC    12960
A wondrous moment then. by
Rowena Rutherford Farrar.
(Anon.) 44:154 Mr9'68.
B    12961
The wooden dish. by Edmund
Morris. (Gibbs) 31:75-7
*O15'55. T    12962
A word carved on a sill.
by John Wain. (Bogan)
34:161 S13'58. B    12963
The word "cop". (J. Lardner)
35:55-61 Jy18'59. TV
12964
The words. by Jean-Paul
Sartre. Bernard Frechtman,
trans. (Rosenberg) 40:131-6
F6'65. B    12965
Words are stones. by Carlo
Levi. (West) 34:158
S13'58. B    12966
Words for the wind. by

Theodore Roethke. (Bogan)
35:195-6 O24'59. B    12967
The workhouse donkey. by John
Arden. (Panter-Downes) 39:
69 Ag3'63. T    12968
The workhouse ward. by
Isabella Augusta Gregory.
(Malcolm) 35:82-3 Ap18'59.
T    12969
World alive. by Robert Dunn.
(Anon.) 32:87-8*Jy14'56
B    12970
The world and William Walker.
by Albert Z. Carr. (Anon.)
39:194-5 S28'63. B    12971
The world in Vogue.
Vogue magazine and Viking
Press, eds. (Anon.) 39:247
N9'63. B    12972
A world more attractive. by
Irving Howe. (Adler) 40:60-2
Jy4'64. B    12973
The world of Apu. (Gill)
36:107-108 O8'60. CC
12974
The world of bees. by
Gilbert Nixon. (Anon.) 32:
158*Ap14'56. B    12975
The world of Carl Sandburg.
by Norman Corwin. (McCarten)
36:97 S24'60. T    12976
The world of Carnegie Hall. by
Richard Schickel. (Anon.)
36:60 D31'60. B    12977
The world of Günter Grass. by
Dennis Rosa. (Oliver) 42:120
My7'66. T    12978
The world of Henry Orient.
(Gill) 40:144-7 Mr28'64. CC
12979
The world of Herodotus. by
Aubrey de Sélincourt. (Anon.)
39:178 Mr9'63. B    12980
The world of James McNeill
Whistler. by Horace
Gregory. (Anon.) 35:123-4 Ja
23'60. B    12981
The world of Paul Slickey. by
John Osborne. (Panter-Downes)
35:97-8 Je20'59. T    12982
The world of Ray Bradbury. by
George Voskovec. (Oliver)
41:197-8 O16'65. T    12983

A world of strangers. by
Nadine Gordimer.
(Balliett) 34:230-2 N29'58.
B            12984
The world of Suzie Wong. by
Paul Osborn. (J. Lardner)
34:88-90 O25'58.  T    12985
The world of Suzie Wong.
(Gill) 36:153-4 D10'60.  CC
             12986
The world of the atom. by
Henry A. Boorse and Lloyd
Motz, eds. (Anon.) 42:84
Jy30'66.  B        12987
The world of the coyote. by Joe
Van Wormer. (Anon.) 41:
218 My15'65.  B      12988
The world of the great horned
owl. by G. Ronald Austing
and John B. Holt, Jr.
(Anon.) 42:168 Je4'66.  B
             12989
The world of the moon. by
Henry C. King. (Anon.)
43:148 Je3'67.  B     12990
The world of the past. Jacquetta
Hawkes, ed. (Anon.) 39:220
O26'63.  B         12991
The world of the red-tailed
hawk. by G. Ronald Austing.
(Anon.) 40:119 S5'64.
B            12992
The world of the shining
prince: court life in ancient
Japan. by Ivan Morris.
(Anon.) 40:108 Ag29'64.  B
             12993
The world of the white-tailed
deer. by Leonard Lee Rue,
III. (Anon.) 38:114-15 Ja12
'63.  B         12994
The world, the flesh, and the
devil. (McCarten) 35:91
My30'59.  CC       12995
The world through my eyes.
by Andreas Feininger.
(Anon.) 39:80 Ja4'64.  B
             12996
World War 2-1/2. by Roger
O. Hirson.(Oliver) 45:132
Ap12'69.  T        12997
World without sun. (Gill) 40:
64 Ja2'65.  CC      12998

The worlds of Robert E.
Sherwood: mirror to his
times. by John Mason Brown.
(Anon.) 41:107-108 Ja22'66.
B            12999
The worlds of William Shakespeare.
by Marchette Chute and
Ernestine Perrie. (Oliver) 39:
80-2 D14'63.  T      13000
The world's one clock. by
Louise Townsend Nicholl.
(Bogan) 35:236-7 N28'59.  B
             13001
A worm in the horseradish.
by Esther Kaufman. (Balliett)
37:114-15 Mr25'61.  T
             13002
Wozzeck. (Gill) 38:90 Mr10
'62.  CC         13003
A wreath for Udomo. by
Peter Abrahams. (West) 32:
78-81 Je30'56.  B     13004
The wreck of the Golden Mary.
by Charles Dickens and
Wilkie Collins. (Anon.) 31:
74-5*Ja7'56.  B      13005
The wreck of the Mary Deare.
(McCarten) 35:127-8 N14'59.
CC           13006
The wreck of the Memphis. by
Edward L. Beach. (Anon.)
42:247 O29'66.  B     13007
The wretched of the Earth. by
Frantz Fanon. (Hentoff) 41:
115-17 Ja15'66.  B    13008
Write me a murder. by
Frederick Knott. (McCarten)
37:126-8 N4'61.  T    13009
Writer by trade. by Dudley
Barker. (Pritchett) 43:189-93
Ap15'67.  B        13010
The wrong arm of the law.
(Gill) 39:176-7 Ap6'63.  CC
             13011
The wrong box. (S. Lardner)
42:64 Jy30'66.  CC    13012
The wrong man. (McCarten)
32:61-2 Ja5'57.  CC   13013
The wrong way light bulb. by
Leonard Spigelgass. (Gill)
45:132-3 Mr15'69.  T
             13014
Wyndham Lewis. by Hugh Kenner.

(Woodcock) 31:124-5 Je4'55.
B                    13015
Wyndham Lewis. by Geoffrey
Wagner. (Anon.) 33:106
*Je1'57. B                    13016

### X

Xmas in Las Vegas. by Jack
Richardson. (McCarten)
41:154-6 N13'65. T    13017

### Y

The Yalu flows. by Mirok Li.
H.A. Hammelmann, trans.
(Anon.) 32:238-9 N17'56.
B                    13018
Yanco. (Balliett) 40:56 Jy25'64.
CC                    13019
Yang kwei fei. (McCarten)
32:160 S22'56. CC    13020
Yankee nomad. by David
Douglas Duncan. (Ross) 42:
236-45 D10'66. B    13021
Yankee reporters: 1861-1865
by Emmet Crozier. (Anon.)
32:171-2*Mr17'56. B
13022
The year Boston won the
pennant. by John Ford
Noonan. (Oliver) 45:77-8
My31'69. T            13023
Year of decisions. by
Harry S. Truman. (Rovere)
31:205-11*N12'55. B 13024
The year of the gorilla. by
George Schaller. (N. Bliven)
40:96-9 Jy18'64. B    13025
The year of the whale. by
Victor B. Scheffer. (Anon.)
45:182-4 S20'69. B    13026
The year of the yield. by
March Cost. (Anon.) 41:
241-2 N20'65. B    13027
The year 2000: a framework
for speculation on the next
thirty-three years. by Herman
Kahn and Anthony J. Wiener.
(Anon.) 43:62 D30'67. B
13028
The years between: diaries
1939-1944. by Cecil Beaton.

(N. Bliven) 41:102-106
Ja22'66. B            13029
The years of Alison. by Warren
Chetham Strode. (Anon.)
37:88 Ag12'61. B    13030
Years of trial and hope: 1946-
1952. by Harry S. Truman.
(Anon.) 32:140-1*Mr10'56.
B                    13031
Yellow back radio broke-down.
by Ishmael Reed. (Sissman)
45:200-202 O11'69. B
13032
Yellow flowers in the antipodean
room. by Janet Frame.
(S. Lardner) 45:146-50 My17
'69. B                    13033
The yellow Rolls-Royce.
(Gill) 41:167-8 My22'65.
CC                    13034
Yellow submarine. (Kael)
44:153-6 N30'68. CC
13035
Yerma. by Federico García
Lorca. W.S. Merwin, trans.
(McCarten) 42:118 D17'66.
T                    13036
Yes I can. by Sammy Davis,
Jr., Jane Boyar and Burt
Boyar. (Anon.) 41:246-7
O30'65. B            13037
Yes is for a very young man.
by Gertrude Stein. (Oliver)
39:139 Mr16'63. T    13038
Yesterday. by Maria Dermoût.
(N. Bliven) 35:162-5 O3'59.
B                    13039
Yesterday, today, and tomorrow.
(Gill) 40:173-4 Mr21'64. CC
13040
Yevtushenko: selected poems.
by Yevgeny Yevtushenko.
Robin Milner-Gulland
and Peter S.J. Levi, trans.
(Anon.) 38:148 F9'63. B
13041
Yoga. by Mircea Eliade.
Willard R. Trask, trans.
(Anon.) 34:67 D27'58. B
13042
The yoke and the arrows. by
Herbert L. Matthews. (Anon.)
33:164 My11'57. B    13043

The Yorkist age: daily life during the wars of the roses. by Paul Murray Kendall. (Anon.) 38:84 Jy7'62. B          13044
The Yoshida memoirs. by Shigeru Yoshida. Kenichi Yoshida, trans. (Anon.) 38: 138 Je9'62. B          13045
You are what you eat. (Kael) 44:169-70 O12'68. CC          13046
You can't take it with you. by Moss Hart and George S. Kaufman. (McCarten) 41:106 D4'65. T          13047
You know I can't hear you when the water's running. by Robert Anderson. (McCarten) 43:119 Mr25'67. T          13048
You never can tell. by George Bernard Shaw. (Panter-Downes) 42:85 Jy9'66. T          13049
You only live twice. by Ian Fleming. (Anon.) 40:216 S19'64. B          13050
You only live twice. (Gilliatt) 43:74-6 Je24'67. CC          13051
You only love once. (Gilliatt) 45:87 Je28'69. CC          13052
The young and beautiful. by Sally Benson. (Gibbs) 31:86*O8'55. T          13053
Young Aphrodites. (Gill) 42:90 Ja7'67. CC          13054
Young Cassidy. (Gill) 41: 169-70 Mr27'65. CC          13055
The young doctors. (Gill) 37:75-6 Ag26'61. CC          13056
The young Hilaire Belloc. by Marie Belloc Lowndes. (Anon.) 32:142*Mr10'56. B          13057
Young in New York: a memoir of a Victorian girlhood. by Nathalie Dana. (Anon.) 39:118 Ja18'64. B          13058
The young lions. (McCarten) 34:147-8 Ap12'58. CC          13059

The young one. (Angell) 36:89 Ja21'61. CC          13060
The young provincials. by Ben Levinson. (Malcolm) 34:80 S27'58. T          13061
Young Sam Johnson. by James L. Clifford. (Anon.) 31: 160-1 My7'55. B          13062
The young savages. (Oliver) 37:130 Je10'61. CC          13063
The young Stalin. by Edward Ellis Smith. (Anon.) 43:65 D30'67. B          13064
The young stranger. (McCarten) 33:135 Ap20'57. CC          13065
Young Törless. (Gilliatt) 44:80 Jy27'68. CC          13066
A young world. (Gill) 42:87 Je4'66. CC          13067
Youngblood Hawke. by Herman Wouk. (Anon.) 38: 186 My19'62. B          13068
Youngblood Hawke. (Gill) 40:158-9 D5'64. CC          13069
Your own thing. by Donald Driver, Hal Hester and Danny Apolinar. (Oliver) 43: 86 Ja27'68. T          13070
Your past is showing! (McCarten) 34:85 Jy19'58. CC          13071
You're a big boy now. (Gill) 43:153 Mr25'67. CC          13072
You're a good man, Charlie Brown. by John Gordon and Clark Gesner. (Oliver) 43: 121-3 Mr18'67. T          13073
You're never too young. (Hamburger) 31:51*S3'55. CC          13074
Yours, mine and ours. (Gilliatt) 44:68 Je22'68. CC          13075
Yuan Mei: eighteenth-century Chinese poet. by Arthur Waley. (Anon.) 33:203 O5'57. B          13076

Z

Z. (Kael) 45:168-75 D13'69. CC          13077
Zazie. (Gill) 37:204-205 N25 '61. CC          13078

Zelda. by Sylvia Regan.
  (Gill) 45:133 Mr15'69.
  T                    13079
Zen: a rational critique.
  by Ernest Becker. (Anon.)
  37:223-4 O14'61. B      13080
Zero in the universe. (Gill)
  42:204 O15'66. CC      13081
Ziegfeld follies. by Jack
  Lawrence, et al. (Gibbs)
  33:64 Mr9'57. T        13082
Zita. (Gilliatt) 44:92 Ag24'68.
  CC                    13083
Zone of emptiness. by Hiroshi
  Noma. (Anon.) 32:181
  O6'56. B               13084
A zoo in my luggage. by
  Gerald Durrell. (Anon.)
  36:186-7 O29'60. B     13085
The zoo story. by Edward Albee.
  (Malcolm) 35:75-6 Ja 23
  '60. T                 13086
Zorba. by Joseph Stein,
  John Kander and Fred Ebb.
  (Gill) 44:124-9 N23'68. T
                         13087
Zorba the Greek. (Gill) 40:
  151 D19'64. CC         13088
Zulu. (Balliett) 40:93
  Jy18'64. CC            13089
The Zulu and the zayda. by
  Howard Da Silva and Felix
  Leon. (McCarten) 41:149-50
  N20'65. T              13090

# Name Index

Abbey, Edward
7046
Abbott, Claude Colleer
7813
Abbott, Elisabeth
9881
Abbott, George
5859, 6318, 6907, 7613,
7670, 10242, 11419, 12093,
12232
Abel, Elie
9978
Abel, Lionel
12941
Abelson, Ann
9389
Abrahams, Beth-Zion
7957
Abrahams, Peter
10296, 13004
Abrams, Charles
6640
Abse, Dannie
4075, 4686, 5516, 11770
Accoce, Pierre
9663
Ace, Goodman
6286
Achard, Marcel
23, 10712
Acheson, Dean
6638, 7034, 10069, 10942,
10958
Ackland, Rodney
7547
Acomb, Evelyn M.
11201
Acton, Harold
9093
Adams, Alice
1779
Adams, Charles Francis
7104
Adams, J. Donald
10188

Adams, Henry
8273
Adams, John
7088
Adams, Lee
5716, 6407, 7986, 8746
Adams, Ruth M.
2393
Adams, Samuel Hopkins
1862, 1863
Adams, Sherman
7634
Adamson, Joy
6295, 9411
Addison, John
6845
Adler, Edward
10374
Adler, Lucile
4984
Adler, Renata
1609, 2603, 2634, 2668, 2684,
3287, 4887, 5711r, 6113r,
6526r, 7180r, 7919r, 7967r,
7990r, 8728r, 9048r, 9517r,
9603r, 10022r, 10631r, 10891r,
11381r, 11538r, 11694r,
11709r, 12194r, 12343r,
12973r
Adler, Richard
8991
Agar, Herbert
10968
Agee, James
4169, 5258, 5679, 6998
Agee, Joel
2205
Aidman, Charles
11849
Aiken, Alfred
12799
Aiken, Conrad
11195
Aiken, Henry D.
10792

Aıkman, Ann
10597
Ainslie, Kenneth
10630
Aird, Catherine
10075
Akrigg, G. P. V.
8759
Albee, Edward
83, 5766, 6032, 6059, 6313,
7007, 7029, 7455, 9643,
11080, 12285, 12866, 13086
Aldington, Richard
9087, 9144
Alexander, Franz
12803
Alexander, Harold R. L.
5701
Alexander, Ronald
8392, 10349
Alexander, Sidney
8362
Alexandra, Queen of
Yugoslavia
7686
Alexandrov, Victor
7380
Alfred, William
92, 8386
Algren, Nelson
10375, 12714
Allan, Gene
6197
Alland, Mitchell
3608
Alleg, Henri
11068
Allegro, J. M.
6976
Allen, Donald M.
10231
Allen, Fred
10098
Allen, Gay Wilson
5780, 11763
Allen, Jay
7711, 10331, 10971
Allen, John
10446, 10592
Allen, John Alexander
36
Allen, Steve
11799

Allen, Tom
11588
Allen, Walter
7400, 12242
Allen, Woody
1073, 1207, 1853, 2756, 3036,
3239, 3391, 4568, 5539, 7195,
10845
Allerton, Robert
6832
Alliluyeva, Svetlana
10537, 12461
Allsop, Kenneth
8201
Almagor, Dan
8570
Alpert, Hollis
4303, 11960
Alsberg, Arthur
8181
Alsop, Joseph
906, 1100, 1171, 2422, 2899,
3936, 9126r, 9634r, 10203r,
11172, 12620r
Alsop, Stewart
11172
Amabile, George
3575, 4458, 4679, 5052
Amado, Jorge
7820, 8407
Ambler, Eric
10694
Amen, Grover
943, 1206, 1380, 3062, 4259,
4641, 5471
American Heritage
5760
Ames, Delano
9087
Ames, Evelyn
5412
Ames, Winslow
10974
Amichai, Yehuda
3235, 4515, 10366
Amis, Kingsley
6487, 8524, 8534, 9571,
10497, 12030, 12128
Amory, Cleveland
12572, 12859
Amosoff, Nikolai M.
10541

Amphoux, Nancy
12320
Andersch, Alfred
10290
Andersen, Victor
6607
Anderson, Alston
3198
Anderson, Carl S.
10472
Anderson, Elizabeth
9972
Anderson, Jack
6482
Anderson, Jessica
10571
Anderson, John M.
7128
Anderson, John Q.
6354
Anderson, Jon
3650
Anderson, Marian
10151
Anderson, Maxwell
5519, 6959, 7995
Anderson, Patrick
10961
Anderson, Quentin
5774
Anderson, Robert
8529, 11669, 13048
Anderson, Sherwood
11619
Andreski, Stanislav
10671
Andrews, Allen
11843
Andrews, Beth
10422
Andrews, J. Cutler
10359
Andrews, Wayne
6153, 7886
Andrić, Ivo
12945
Angell, Robert
4610
Angell, Roger
34, 48, 78, 493, 603, 711,
712, 945, 1035, 1101, 1268,
1422, 1458, 1529, 1653, 1882,
2102, 2354, 2426, 2499, 2711,

3146, 3237, 3250, 3297, 3302,
3624, 3766, 3993, 4304, 4663,
4729, 4871, 5566, 5826r,
6030r, 6628r, 6870r, 7190r,
7470r, 7503r, 7767r, 8049r,
9189r, 9889r, 9521r, 9630r,
9786r, 9944r, 9970r, 10025r,
10761r, 11327r, 11393r,
11980r, 12438r, 12495r, 12691r,
12835r, 13060r
Angle, Paul M.
9414
Anglesey, George Charles
10529
Anouilh, Jean
5847, 6584, 7600, 9086,
9209, 9300, 10723, 10894,
11146, 11164, 12157, 12280,
12382, 12726
Ansel, Walter
8383
Ansell, Jack
8352
Anthony, Rock
8757
Antin, David
3670, 4017
Antrobus, John
6092
Apolinar, Danny
13070
Apollinaire, Guillaume
5696, 8304
Appell, Don
7924, 9940
Appleby, John T.
7397
Appleman, Herbert
12531
Appleman, Philip
11668
Apstein, Theodore
8663
Aragno, Ricardo
11787
Aragon, Louis
8354, 8397, 9033
Arbó, Sebastian Juan
6538
Arbuzov, Aleksei
11008
Archer, W. G.
9559

Archibald, William
6447, 6875, 8665
Arciniegas, Germán
5793
Ardayne, Julia Collins
4910
Arden, John
5896, 11548, 12968
Ardrey, Robert
11585, 12102
Arendt, Hannah
574, 1158, 1310, 5022,
5284, 5367, 8078, 8490,
10474
Ariès, Philippe
6532
Ariss, Jean
11073
Aristophanes
9584, 10728
Arlen, Harold
8211, 8457, 8762, 11406
Arlen, Michael J.
55, 242, 837, 2101, 3142,
3564, 4534, 5683r, 6000r,
6036r, 7035r, 8220r,
9130r, 9594r, 10067r,
10323r, 11027r, 11174r,
11315r, 11397r, 12148r,
12622r, 12623r, 12625r,
12679r, 12809r
Arluck, Elliot
9852
Armour, Richard
336, 3174, 4982
Armstrong, Christa
10290
Armstrong, Hamilton Fish
12213
Arnaldi, Jean
7569
Arnheim, Rudolf
7603
Arno, Owen G.
10487
Arnold, Matthew
7857
Arnothy, Christine
11549
Aron, Raymond
7748, 10730
Aronson, Theo
7985

Arrabal, Fernando
5989, 9000, 9025, 9084, 9154,
9168, 10810, 12475
Arrighi, Mel
10572
Arvin, Newton
9464
Asch, Sholem
11013
Ashbery, John
11774
Ashe, Geoffrey
9074
Ashford, Daisy
8890
Ashley, Maurice
10465, 11942
Ashley, Robert
7566
Ashmead, John
10089
Ashton, E. B.
5809
Ashton-Warner, Sylvia
8637, 11838
Ashworth, Mary Wells
7881
Asimov, Isaac
10432, 11640
Asinof, Eliot
7317
Asprey, Robert B.
4161
Asquith, Cynthia
7087, 9791, 10920
Astley, Thea
11731
Aston, Benjamin Gwilliam
10743
Aston, Margaret
7593
Astrachan, Sam
7382
Asturias, Miguel Angel
7327
Aswell, Mary Louise
3196, 3940
Atget, Eugène
12653
Athearn, Robert G.
11756
Atherton, John
1102, 3701, 4744, 4879, 5155

Athill, Diana
8680, 12515
Atkins, John
7877
Atkinson, Alex
6178, 6406
Atkinson, B.M., Jr.
12812
Atkinson, James Blakely
8359
Atlas, James
2726
Atwell, Lester
10984
Aub, Max
8889
Aubrey, John
6340
Auchincloss, Louis
867, 8094, 8456, 10912.
11042, 11127
Aucoin, Clifford
362, 1170, 1677, 2302
Auden, W.H.
56, 255, 638, 819, 1371,
1451, 1559, 2063, 3133,
3499, 3511, 3833, 4795,
5531, 5590, 5702r, 5918r,
6108r, 6301r, 6340r, 6410r,
6857, 7257, 7977r, 8398,
8737, 9281r, 9289r, 9395r,
9434r, 9834r, 10133r, 10317,
10663r, 11058r, 11210r,
11373r, 11478, 11528,
11621, 12575, 12633
Audubon, John James
7320
Aulicino, Armand
11627
Aurthur, Robert Alan
6474, 8991, 12599
Austin, A.M.
3506
Austin, Oliver L., Jr.
6207
Austin, Paul Britten
7166
Austin, William W.
10115
Austing, G. Ronald
12989, 12992
Axelrod, George
8020, 12894

Ayckbourn, Alan
11150
Ayer, Ethan
3910, 4987
Ayer, Fred, Jr.
6104
Aymé, Marcel
5606, 8110, 9018, 10062
Azad, Maulana Abul Kalam
8647
Azrael, Gabriella
10258

B

Babel, Isaac
2371, 5553, 11985
Babington-Smith, Constance
9103, 9292
Bacchelli, Riccardo
10382
Bacharach, Burt
11011
Badaut, Marie-Louise
9023
Bagley, Ben
9405, 11632
Bagnold, Enid
6545, 6611
Bagrow, Leo
8357
Bailey, Anthony
98, 995, 1890, 2301, 2586,
2694, 2941, 3440, 4122, 4190,
4882, 5136, 5454, 8674
Bainbridge, John
820, 1092, 1156, 1499, 2375,
2456, 2623, 2644, 2728,
4227, 4357, 4700, 5549, 7837
Baines, Jocelyn
8834
Baird, Bil
10750
Baker, Carlos
7416, 7776
Baker, David
6710, 6797, 10794, 11739
Baker, Dorothy
6490
Baker, Elliott
10745
Baker, Herschel
12897

Baker, J. A.
  10763
Baker, Sheridan
  3178
Balabanoff, Angelica
  8590
Balchin, Nigel
  7555, 8615
Baldick, Robert
  6066, 6532, 7243, 10042,
  10635, 11654, 12780
Baldridge, Richard
  12780
Baldwin, James
  2583, 5751, 5834, 6260,
  7923, 10347, 10377
Baldwin, Michael
  9958
Ballard, Bettina
  8607
Balliett, Whitney
  409, 517, 1288, 1295, 1375,
  1398, 1773, 2945, 2996,
  3210, 3370, 3606, 4001,
  4103, 4450, 5276, 5733r,
  5738r, 5766r, 5820r, 5834r,
  5876r, 6005r, 6033r, 6046r,
  6059r, 6084r, 6149r, 6208r,
  6213r, 6235r, 6247r, 6248r,
  6290r, 6308r, 6346r, 6361r,
  6425r, 6446r, 6472r, 6511r,
  6514r, 6522r, 6600r, 6627r,
  6652r, 6658r, 6672r, 6692r,
  6715r, 6716r, 6725r, 6784r,
  6846r, 6864r, 6883r, 6943r,
  6950r, 7007r, 7014r, 7077r,
  7121r, 7193r, 7194r, 7204r,
  7227r, 7234r, 7238r, 7357r,
  7374r, 7375r, 7392r, 7410r,
  7426r, 7431r, 7448r, 7458r,
  7462r, 7524r, 7598r, 7626r,
  7649r, 7705r, 7828r, 7917r,
  7936r, 7978r, 8002r, 8009r,
  8061r, 8075r, 8115r, 8116r,
  8148r, 8149r, 8163r, 8184r,
  8185r, 8254r, 8294r, 8385r,
  8388r, 8447r, 8464r, 8550r,
  8613r, 8624r, 8629r, 8667r,
  8733r, 8864r, 8885r, 8953r,
  8976r, 8989r, 9057r, 9190r,
  9192r, 9333r, 9442r, 9447r,
  9485r, 9593r, 9608r, 9612r,
  9642r, 9693r, 9720r, 9721r,

9765r, 9776r, 9785r, 9852r,
9893r, 9913r, 9934r, 10013r,
10054r, 10059r, 10094r, 10144r,
10174r, 10208r, 10355r, 10358r,
10381r, 10412r, 10413r, 10430r,
10460r, 10461r, 10503r, 10540r,
10559r, 10689r, 10791r, 10863r,
10899r, 10996r, 11081r, 11127r,
11131r, 11164r, 11181r, 11184r,
11212r, 11285r, 11295r, 11306r,
11330r, 11395r, 11424r, 11490r,
11502r, 11541r, 11544r, 11555r,
11583r, 11610r, 11627r, 11647r,
11650r, 11658r, 11715r, 11732r,
11739r, 11765r, 11795r, 11796r,
11803r, 11804r, 11854r, 11933r,
12087r, 12097r, 12216r, 12233r,
12274r, 12300r, 12396r, 12411r,
12416r, 12437r, 12444r, 12524r,
12541r, 12548r, 12562r, 12571r,
12585r, 12644r, 12727r, 12739r,
12741r, 12772r, 12846r, 12890r,
12956r, 12960r, 12984r, 13002r,
12019r, 12089r
Balmain, Pierre
  10170
Bamm, Peter
  5704
Banfield, Edward C.
  6641
Banks, Nathaniel
  11472
Bantry, Michael
  57
Barasch, Norman
  9629, 11536
Barber, Noel
  11695, 12851
Barbour, Philip L.
  12238
Barbour, Thomas
  11741
Barca, Calderón de la
  See Puigvert Calderón de la
  Barca, Alfredo
Barer, Marshall
  9596, 10492, 10940
Barghoorn, Frederick C.
  11821
Bargy, Jeanne
  8116
Baring-Gould, Ceil
  5833
Baring-Gould, William S.
  5833

Barisse, Rita
6069, 12017
Barkeley, Richard
11244
Barker, Dudley
9685, 12185, 13010
Barker, George
4541
Barker, Richard H.
9754
Barlow, James
6378, 9523, 10718
Barnard, Mary
3804, 10177
Barnes, Djuna
3944
Barnes, Elizabeth
1241
Barnes, Joseph
11897
Barnes, Kate
854, 1977, 2953, 3678
Barnes, Malcolm
10704
Barnouw, Victor
2271
Barnstone, Willis
2498
Baro, Gene
504, 823, 1016, 1543, 1603,
1760, 2212, 2241, 2249,
2473, 3271, 3332, 3737,
3906, 4012, 4423, 4457,
4643, 4863, 4892, 4981,
5035, 5265, 5280
Barolini, Antonio
585, 1335, 1872, 2509,
2514, 2749, 3645, 3710
Baron, Stanley
1772, 2155
Barr, Beryl
5920
Barr, Pat
7022
Barrault, Jean-Louis
9066, 11383
Barrett, Michael
11203
Barrett, William
8714, 10792
Barry, Philip
8294

Barry, R. H.
8671, 11874
Barsha, Tony
8230
Barsley, Michael
10577
Bart, Benjamin F.
7655
Bart, Lionel
6241, 9037, 9426, 10462
Barth, John
7917
Barth, Karl
5838, 7031, 8467
Barthelme, Donald
220, 294, 356, 359, 813, 916,
1191, 1213, 1392, 1429, 1462,
1512, 1728, 2285, 2438, 2773,
2934, 2955, 2956, 3487, 3652,
3736, 3739, 3754, 3759, 3818,
3819, 3881, 4036, 4295, 4382,
4447, 4456, 4731, 4841, 5213,
6702
Bartlett, Vernon
11166
Barton, John
5915, 8393
Baruch, Bernard M.
6060
Barzini, Luigi
8741
Barzun, Jacques
7449, 10114, 11444, 11525
Bass, Jules
10052
Bass, Robert D.
11994
Bassani, Giorgio
8000
Basso, Hamilton
1342, 3963, 4529, 4599, 4794,
4814, 12350
Bate, Walter Jackson
8814
Bates, H. E.
6902, 7368, 8048, 11725
Bates, Marston
6936, 10965
Battersby, Martin
7020
Battershaw, Brian
6217

Battiscombe, Georgina
11056
Baudelaire, Charles
6075, 7676, 9963
Bauer, Raymond
10311
Baur, John I. H.
10234
Bawden, Nina
7068
Baxter, Stephen B.
12904
Bay, Ellen
3700
Bayer, Eleanor
12162
Bayer, Leo
12162
Bayley, John
8597
Bazin, Germain
8355
Bazna, Elyesa
8536
Beach, Edward L.
13007
Beach, Stewart
11388
Beach, Sylvia
11590
Beadle, George
9082
Beadle, Muriel
9082, 12149
Beal, Anthony
6899
Beale, Howard K.
12139
Beals, Carleton
12743
Beam, Lura
9624
Beam, Philip C.
12917
Beard, James Franklin
9268
Beardmore, George
6572
Beaton, Cecil
12729, 13029
Beauchamp, Emerson
3305, 4612

Beaumarchais, Pierre Augustin
9171
Beaverbrook, William Maxwell Aitken
5585, 7017, 9891
Beck, Simone
9814
Becker, Ernest
13080
Becker, George J.
10678
Becker, Stephen
8876, 11776, 12358, 12829
Beckett, J. C.
9633
Beckett, Samuel
6728, 7387, 8186, 8469, 8985, 10460, 10844, 12701
Beckingsale, B. W.
6379
Bedford, Sybille
7500, 9204, 12398
Beebe, William
5630
Beecroft, John
11895
Beerbohm, Max
550, 648, 1866, 1945, 1959, 2168, 2357, 2449, 2539, 2980, 3137, 3778, 3857, 4160, 4355, 5037, 5445, 5532, 9835
Begner, Edith P.
8891
Behan, Brendan
6300, 8431, 11052, 11428
Beheler, Laura
10656
Behrend, Jeanne
10378
Behrman, S. N.
421, 550, 648, 925, 1866, 1945, 1959, 2030, 2168, 2357, 2449, 2539, 2980, 3137, 3778, 3857, 4160, 4355, 5037, 5445, 5532, 6386, 6392, 6673, 6958r, 8306r, 9479
Beiber, Ethel
8421
Beich, Albert
9671
Beigel, Uli
4448

Beke, Laszlo
11943
Belden, Marva Robins
11746
Belden, Thomas Graham
11746
Belfrage, Sally
11287
Belgion, Montgomery
9740
Belitt, Ben
2527, 3508, 3647, 5205,
5474, 7384, 10875
Bell, Clive
10454
Bell, Daniel
6763, 10232, 11087
Bell, Harold
6411
Bell, Marvin
2040, 2234
Bellew, Peter
9804
Bellonci, Maria
10977
Bellow, Saul
3164, 8272, 8315, 9088,
9996, 10072, 11509, 12527
Bellson, Louis
10910
Beloff, Nora
7858
Bemelmans, Ludwig
11927, 12312
Bemis, Samuel Flagg
8818
Benchley, Nathaniel
637, 964, 1547, 1558, 1717,
2051, 2149, 2417, 2490, 2920,
3480, 3628, 3707, 4113, 5159
Bender, Marylin
6085
Bendiner, Robert
10407
Benedict, Rex
12212
Benedictus, David
7734, 12182
Benjamin, Joseph
11236
Benkovitz, Miriam J.
11281

Bennett, Alan
7713
Bennett, Arnold
5898
Bennett, Jack
8771, 10411
Bennett, John
3489
Bennett, John C.
10392
Benson, Sally
257, 2068, 3563, 3597, 4171,
5295, 13053
Bentley, Beth
238, 5289
Bentley, Eric
8017, 9679
Bentley, Phyllis
6357, 9682
Bentley, W. A.
7956
Benton, Robert
8746
Benton, William
12668
Berberova, Nina
8743
Berckman, Evelyn
8257
Berczeller, Richard
1505, 3124, 3162, 3603, 4009,
4087, 5006
Berenson, Bernard
6135, 7427, 9484, 11510
Berg, Stephen
459, 1230, 1911, 2041, 4927,
5120, 5436
Berger, Meyer
9916
Berger, Ted
11628
Berger, Thomas
8931
Berger, Yves
9184
Bergersen, Baldwin
6875
Berkey, Ralph
12271
Berkowitz, Sol
10391
Berle, Adolph A.
10951, 12256

9091r, 9093r, 9098r, 9112r,
9219r, 9323r, 9335r, 9401r,
9429r, 9482r, 9520r, 9661r,
9686r, 9794r, 9795r, 9386r,
9921r, 9932e, 10097r, 10243r,
10268r, 10302r, 10331r,
10474r, 10527r, 10555r,
10652r, 10660r, 10743r,
10758r, 10820r, 10822r,
10839r, 11015r, 11059r,
11216r, 11230r, 11682r,
11726r, 11825r, 11897r,
12030r, 12179r, 12358r,
12368r, 12389r, 12545r,
12568r, 12591r, 12744r,
12757r, 12820r, 12837r,
13025r, 13029r, 13039r

Blochman, Lawrence G.
10949

Bloch-Michel, Jean
7664

Block, Anita Rowe
10213

Block, Herbert
8292

Blondin, Antoine
10042

Bloom, Harry
6427, 7409, 8945

Bloomstein, Henry
657a

Blue, Dan
7248

Bluestone, George
10387

Blum, Daniel
10814

Blum, Edwin Harvey
11418

Blum, Ralph
696, 1040, 1675, 2642, 3795,
7701

Blunt, Wilfrid
6668

Bly, Robert
8495

Blyth, Henry
10865

Blythe, Ronald
5686

Boas, Louise Schutz
8215

Boas, Marie
11445

Bobbitt, Mary Reed
12934

Bocca, Geoffrey
8966

Bock, Frederick
468, 1590

Bock, Jerry
5879, 6265, 7589, 7613,
11608

Bodard, Lucien
11074

Bode, Carl
9902

Boesiger, W.
9156

Bogan, Louise
2950, 3005, 3816, 4875, 5190,
5648r, 5654r, 5725r, 5780r,
6277r, 6292r, 6311r, 6368r,
6421r, 6471r, 6487r, 6678r,
6680r, 6681r, 6682r, 6683r,
6684r, 6686r, 6721r, 6841r,
6857r, 6890r, 7354r, 7502r,
7696r, 7696r, 7945, 8099r,
8112r, 8246r, 8256r, 8398r,
8506r, 8596r, 8617r, 8815r,
8841, 9087r, 9124r, 9198r,
9203r, 9254r, 9266r, 9337r,
9346r, 9729r, 9966r,
10113r, 10231r, 10233r,
10251r, 10252r, 10291r,
10394r, 10419r, 10501r,
10506r, 10608r, 10868r,
10869r, 10870r, 10872r,
10878r, 10938r, 10955r,
10956r, 11254r,
11501r, 11520r, 11521r,
11526r, 11576r, 11621r,
11763r, 11774r, 12116r,
12160r, 12306r, 12388r,
12762r, 12771r, 12807r,
12963r, 12967r, 13001r

Bohannan, Paul
5650

Bohner, Paul Hyde
5912

Bolcom, William
7259

Boles, Paul Darcy
7952

Boles, Robert
5387, 10757

Bolitho, Hector
7956

Böll, Heinrich
12371
Bolling, Richard
8461
Bologna, Joseph
9553
Bolt, Robert
7674, 9665
Bolton, Guy
5828, 5859, 5862, 6596,
9195
Bond, Edward
11417
Bond, Harold
1806
Bone, Edith
11571, 11944
Bongartz, Roy
1167, 1620, 1804, 1984,
4824, 5044
Bonner, John Tyler
8547
Bonner, Paul Hyde
255a
Bontly, Thomas
6741
Bony, Jean
7776
Boorse, Henry A.
12987
Boorstin, Daniel J.
8573
Booth, Philip
949, 1308 , 2356, 2958,
4269, 4777, 4954
Booy, D. M.
11257
Borchardt, Ann
11854
Borchsenius, Poul
8378
Bordeaux, Henry
9497
Boretz, Allen
8434
Borges, Jorge Luis
1045, 1657, 1665, 1993,
2196, 2199, 2335, 2338,
3595, 4408, 4877, 4913,
7586, 10590
Borland, Hal
8339
Borowik, Ann
9375

Boruff, John
9505
Bory, Robert
9574
Bosanquet, Mary
9311
Bost, Pierre
10945
Bostock, Anna
10747
Boswell, James
6305, 6306, 6307, 6308
Bosworth, Allan R.
2460, 3280, 3771
Botsford, S. B.
4518
Bottari, Stefano
5854
Bottome, Phyllis
7964
Boucicault, Dion
10413
Boulle, Pierre
10345, 10593, 10796, 11358
Boulnois, Luce
11675
Boulton, Agnes
10684
Boulton, James T.
9143
Bouquet, A. C.
7437
Bourjaily, Vance
1664, 1850, 3961, 5143, 9696
Bovasso, Julie
7954, 10057
Bove, Charles F.
10677
Boveri, Margret
12385
Bovill, E. W.
7997
Bovini, Giuseppe
11109
Bowen, Catherine Drinker
7749, 9368
Bowen, Croswell
2496, 6885
Bowen, Elizabeth
12270
Bowen, John
5662, 6529, 9388
Bowers, Q. David
11043

Bowers, Faubion
  1345, 2591, 2639, 2643,
  6353
Bowles, Chester
  10237
Bowles, Jane
  6690
Bowles, Paul
  11836, 12551
Bowman, John S.
  1015
Bowra, C.M.
  9887
Boxer, Charles R.
  7254
Boyajian, Ned R.
  7526
Boyar, Burt
  13037
Boyar, Jane
  13037
Boyd, Robert
  6535
Boyington, Gregory
  6001
Boykin, Edward
  7898, 12607
Boyle, Andrew
  12390
Boyle, Kay
  11464
Boyle, Sarah Patton
  7043
Brace, Gerald Warner
  6122
Brackman, Jacob
  1860, 3934, 8035r
Bradbury, Bianca
  3623
Bradbury, Malcolm
  103, 7282
Bradbury, Ray
  11783
Bradlee, Frederic
  12572
Bradley, John Lewis
  9279
Brady, Frank
  6306, 6307
Bragg, Melvyn
  12938
Braider, Donald
  10643

Brain, Leonard
  8748
Braine, John
  7789, 8783, 11285
Braithwaite, E.R.
  12309
Brand, Millen
  600, 1072, 5499
Brand, Oscar
  7301, 8481, 8865
Brand, Phoebe
  10925
Brandon, Johnny
  6630, 12870
Brandon, William
  9892
Brant, Irving
  8769, 8770
Braque, Georges
  6467
Brasillach, Robert
  9029
Brata, Sasthi
  10142
Bray, Barbara
  9064
Braybrooke, Neville
  12024
Brecher, Michael
  10217
Brecht, Bertolt
  5926, 6002, 6333, 6516,
  7237, 7825, 8017, 8624,
  9679, 10082, 11180
Bredt, James
  8190
Breit, Harvey
  7136, 8130
Breitbach, Joseph
  11169
Brenan, Gerald
  8391, 9329, 11814
Brennan, Donald G.
  5893
Brennan, Maeve
  297, 430, 524, 698, 769,
  770, 1027, 1174, 1205,
  1248, 1317, 1673, 1754,
  2157, 2219, 2503, 2507,
  2572, 4152, 4343, 4464,
  4469, 4617, 5043, 5560,
  5855r, 8458r, 8997r,
  10458r, 12732r, 12953

Brereton, Geoffrey
8693
Breton, André
9228, 9733
Brett-James, Antony
7856, 12797
Bricusse, Leslie
10807, 11251, 11891
Bridenbaugh, Carl
6636
Briffault, Herma
7570, 8662
Brill, Marty
6420
Brinig, Myron
9471
Brinnin, John Malcolm
265, 682, 1681, 2072,
2173, 2587, 3041, 3224,
3311, 3536, 4421, 4510,
10021, 12171
Brinton, Crane
8380
Brion, Marcel
7251, 11440
Briscoe, Robert
7690
Broad, Jay
11136
Brock, Van K.
3172, 4267
Brockett, Eleanor
8395
Broder, David S.
11173
Brodeur, Paul
2144, 2876, 4385, 4454,
4561, 5294
Brodie, Bernard
11924
Brodkey, Harold
13, 536, 709, 1024, 1554,
2036, 3531, 3781, 3943,
4319, 4373, 5463
Brodrick, Alan Houghton
11469
Brogan, D. W.
7768
Bromberg, Conrad
12376
Brome, Vincent
7751, 12770

Bronson, William
7267
Brook, Peter
12498
Brooke, Dinah
2578
Brooke, Jocelyn
7177
Brooke, John
6569
Brooks, Colleen
952, 2318, 3566, 3850
Brooks, Gladys
6302
Brooks, John
40, 173, 174, 175, 890, 901,
932, 933, 1023, 1161, 1214,
1244, 1271, 1359, 1584, 1606,
1697, 1755, 1820, 1933, 2224,
2889, 2994, 3424, 3545, 3604,
3663, 3918, 3998, 4286, 4607,
4653, 4493, 4749, 4802, 4845,
5016, 5428, 5431, 5529, 9695
Brooks, Mel
5716, 11622
Brooks, Robert A.
165, 1950
Brooks, Van Wyck
6967, 7224, 7577, 8259,
8820, 10599
Brophy, Brigid
7612, 7660, 8949, 10097
Brosnan, Jim
9458, 10744
Brough, James
5975
Brown, Alec
10954
Brown, Allen
9206
Brown, Claude
9720
Brown, D. C.
3059, 4367
Brown, Frank London
12424
Brown, Gifford
1729, 3312
Brown, Harry
3661
Brown, Jeff
3232

Brown, John Mason
12999
Brown, Kenneth H.
6342
Brown, Mark H.
7665
Brown, Maurice J. E.
11439
Brown, Milton W.
5779
Brown, Oscar, Jr.
6369
Brown, Spencer
507, 519, 3259
Brown, Wallace L.
7388
Brown, William F.
8481
Browne, Malcolm W.
10240
Browne, Michael Dennis
1091, 1742, 1920, 2320,
2443, 3310, 3730, 4141,
4374
Brownjohn, J. Maxwell
5704, 6419, 7518
Broyard, Anatole
327
Bruce, George
11922
Bruce, Maurice
11600
Bruce, Michael
10328
Bruce, Renaud
8372
Bruller, Jean
6069, 12017
Bryan, C. D. B.
798, 4466, 5360
Bryant, Arthur
7615, 12412
Bryher, Winifred
6672, 12651
Buchan, Perdita
2349, 5470, 7933
Buchanan, Marcia Darrah
2800
Buchwald, Art
11612
Buck, Pearl S.
6619, 7044

Buckner, Robert
11663
Budberg, Moura
12321
Buechner, Frederick
11188
Buechner, Georg
6922
Bufano, Rocco
8428
Bulgakov, Mikhail
6978
Bullins, Ed
7334
Bullitt, Stimson
12292
Bullitt, William C.
12209
Bullock, Michael
6770, 8568, 9774, 10609
Burckhardt, Joseph
9280
Burdick, Eugene
4138, 7726, 12502
Burger, Otis Kidwell
2215, 2316, 3975, 4580
Burgess, Anthony
7386, 11112, 11216, 12389,
12652, 12731
Burgess, Charles
5393
Burgett, Donald R.
6884
Burgie, Irving
6029
Burke, James
7658
Burke, Johnny
7192
Burke, Norah
8886
Burland, Brian
7516
Burlingame, Roger
7196, 8277
Burn, Michael
9992
Burnham, Alan
10262
Burns, James MacGregor
6981, 11294
Burns, Robert Grant
627

Burr, Anne
8504
Burr, Gray
4188, 5223
Burroughs, William
10183, 10386
Burrows, Abe
6416, 8482, 10969, 11676
Burrows, Millar
6977
Burt, Kendal
10522
Burt, Nathaniel
10764
Burton, Elizabeth
10634
Burton, Maurice
7956
Burwell, Basil
6473
Busch, Francis X.
6488
Busch, Fritz-Otto
8395
Busch, Harald
8031
Busch, Niven
6423
Busch, Noel F.
1513, 2592, 12484
Bush, Douglas
7394
Bush, Geoffrey
2403
Bush, Josef
6972
Butler, Denis
12085
Butler, E. M.
11144
Butler, Ewan
7096, 9566
Butler, Samuel
7531
Butler, William
11222
Butor, Michel
9017, 10012, 10700
Butterfield, L. H.
5615, 7088
Buttle, Myra
See Purcell, Victor

Butz, Otto
12546
Buxton, John
7342
Buzzati, Dino
9085, 12512
Byatt, A. S.
11582

C

Cabaud, Jacques
11682
Cabell, James Branch
5929, 6159
Cabell, Margaret Freeman
6159
Cable, Mary
267, 383, 2243, 2974, 4664, 5329, 5994, 7223
Cabot, Samuel, Jr.
4583
Cabriès, Jean
8758
Cadell, James
8902
Cadwallader, Sylvanus
12240
Cady, Edwin H.
10160
Caesar, Gene
12881
Caffarelli, Ernesto Vergara
6380
Cahn, Sammy
11714
Cahoon, Herbert
11882
Cailler, Pierre
10924
Cain, Emily
710
Cain, James M.
9613
Calamette, Joseph
7982
Calder, Angus
10760
Calder, John
11068
Calderisi, David
7473

Calderón, Pedro
8657
Caldwell, Erskine
8613
Calisher, Hortense
2185, 7484, 12111
Callaghan, Morley
9543, 9742, 12124
Callahan, Thomas
5778
Callow, Alexander B., Jr.
12451
Calmer, Ned
5730
Calvert, James
11990
Calvesi, Maurizio
12386
Calvino, Italo
6055
Cameron, Charles S.
12432
Cameron, James
8296, 9723, 10314, 10880
Cameron, Kenneth
10664
Camoletti, Marc
6267
Campbell, Joseph
5910, 9807
Campbell, Michael
10778
Campbell, Roy
9319, 11518
Campbell-Johnson, Alan
7293
Camus, Albert
6424, 7466, 7515, 9246,
9583, 10176, 10370
Canetti, Elias
5988
Cannan, Denis
10945
Cannon, Alice
8064
Capa, Robert
8576
Capek, Karel
9639
Caplan, Ralph
4950
Capote, Truman

1257, 2220, 3835, 6327, 8457
Capovilla, Don Loris
8559
Caputo, Giacomo
6380
Caraman, Philip
8280
Caras, Roger
6887
Cardozo, Nancy
4842
Cardus, Neville
12046
Carew Hunt, R.N.
8132
Carlino, Lewis John
7208, 7463, 12070
Carlson, Marcia
429
Carmichael, Joel
5892, 6541, 7904, 11355,
11599, 12621
Carmines, Al
8600, 11006
Carner, Mosco
11031
Carney, Frank
11219
Caroe, Olaf
10714
Carpentier, Alejo
9500
Carr, Albert Z.
6724, 8809, 12971
Carr, Archie
11745, 12504, 12912
Carr, Edward Hallett
11749
Carr, Leon
11486
Carrier, Constance
502, 866, 1325, 3372, 4973
Carrière, Anne
5536
Carrington, C.E.
9332
Carroll, Gordon
7053
Carroll, John Alexander
7881
Carroll, Joseph
6058

Carroll, June
8318
Carroll, Paul Vincent
5475, 12775
Carroll, Vinnette
12429
Carruth, Hayden
32, 1586, 3404, 4540, 4672,
5876
Carse, Robert
11333
Carson, Hampton L.
8299
Carson, Josephine
11671
Carson, Rachel
1299, 4392
Carson, Robert
9510
Carter, Angela
8415, 9611
Carter, Anne
10020
Carter, Dan T.
11451
Carter, John.
5581
Carter, Randolph
7434
Carter, Richard
9703
Carter, Violet Bonham
12918
Carthy, J. D.
10203
Cartier-Bresson, Henri
10572
Cary, Joyce
570, 986, 3247, 3896, 5685,
5784, 5905, 6750, 8454,
11851
Casares, Adolfo Bioy
2199
Casart, Julian
10139
Case, L. L.
2294, 4231
Casey, John
2922, 3144
Cassill, R. V.
6652, 10962
Cassini, Marguerite
10224

Cassou, Jean
6540
Castelot, André
8952
Casteret, Norbert
7042
Castillo, Bernal Díaz del
See Díaz del Castillo, Bernal
Castle, Irene
6497
Castle, John
10709
Catharine II
9875a
Cather, Thomas
12684
Cather, Willa
6689
Catherine of Cleves
8444
Catton, Bruce
6720, 8047, 12101, 12186
Cau, Jean
9253, 9907
Cauley, Harry
10639
Cavaliero, Glen
533
Cecil, David
9834, 9860
Cecil, Rachel
12145
Cela, Camilo José
7533
Céline, Louis-Ferdinand
6495
Ceram, C. W.
9758, 11492
Cerulli, Dom
8782
Cesari, Isotta
8590
Chamberlain, Dennis
11675
Chamberlain, John
7405, 11297
Chambers, Ernest
8318
Chamberlain, Samuel
8734
Chamberlain, Samuel E.
10132

Chambers, Ernest
8318
Chambers, Jessie
6896
Chambers, Robert
7147
Chamfort, Sebastien Roch
Nicholas
10994
Chancellor, Robin
7325, 9686
Chandler, David
6434
Chandler, Raymond
11110
Chandos, Oliver Lyttelton
9880
Chapler, Harold J.
9542
Chaplin, Charles
10129
Chapman, Guy
7229, 10705, 12170
Chapman, Hester W.
12490
Chapman, John Jay
11525
Chapman, William McK.
11158
Char, René
8506
Charlap, Moose
8907
Charles, Gerda
11715
Charnin, Martin
8437
Charrière, Henri
10662
Charters, Samuel B.
6824
Chase, Mary
9925
Chase, Richard
12722
Chase, Salmon P.
8673
Chasins, Abram
11833
Chaudhuri, Nirad C.
10695a
Chavchavadze, Paul
4256, 7565, 9773, 10537

Chayefsky, Paddy
7908, 9922, 10702, 12094
Cheever, John
158, 210, 436, 586, 613, 623,
776, 793, 831, 833, 1255, 1303,
1332, 1405, 1821, 1912, 2086,
2310, 2387, 2415, 2416, 2842,
2959, 3022, 3032, 3067, 3128,
3216, 3429, 3644, 3712, 4081,
4250, 4278, 4479, 4722, 4977,
5010, 5226, 5504, 5528, 12732
Chein, Isador
11241
Chekhov, Anton
6586, 6827, 7448, 8208, 8722,
8754, 11372, 11462, 12236,
12518
Cheslock, Louis
8146
Chesnut, Mary
7089
Chester, Alfred
419, 5291 .
Chester, Edward W.
7436
Chevalier, Haakon
8397, 11264
Chevallier, Gabriel
6656
Chichester, Francis
5741
Chidsey, Donald Barr
7340
Child, Julia
9814
Childress, Alice
11936
Childs, Marquis
7324, 12725
Chilton, C. W.
11413
Chilton, Charles
10447
Chin, Tsao Hsueh
7226
Chipman, Myra
12130
Chodorov, Jerome
8518, 10892, 12220
Chodosh, Richard B.
11929
Chomsky, Noam
9081

Chotzinoff, Samuel
9494, 12346
Chou, Eric
9680
Christiansen, Arthur
8235
Christie, Agatha
10094, 10647, 12165
Christman, Henry M.
5777, 12723
Christopher, John
9402, 10930, 11091, 12856
Christopher, Milbourne
10650
Chu, Valentin
12026
Chukovskaya, Lydia
7047
Church, Richard
12681
Churchill, Randolph S.
12465, 12920
Churchill, Winston S.
8374, 8375, 8376, 8377
Chute, Marchette
12480, 13000
Ciardi, John
278, 333, 554, 922, 2736
Clad, Noel
9518
Claman, Julian
5681, 9646
Claraso, Mercedes
11319
Clare, John
11615
Clark, Alan
6051
Clark, Gerald
6719
Clark, Kenneth
6928, 10393, 11342
Clark, R. T.
6776
Clark, Tom
3774
Clark, William
9286
Clarke, Arthur C.
7953, 12044, 12487, 12672
Clarke, John
1797

Claudel, Paul
12108
Clavell, James
8957
Clay, George R.
768, 809, 4983
Cleary, Jon
8329
Cleator, P. E.
9493
Cles-Reden, Sibylle
6382
Cleugh, James
7251, 7706, 10171
Clevely, Hugh
11917
Clifford, James L.
13062
Clifton, John
9711
Cline, Barbara Lovett
11069
Clinton-Baddeley, V. C.
10138
Cloete, Stuart
5651, 7857
Clough, Wilson O.
8510
Clune, Henry W.
7861
Clurman, Harold
9308
Clurman, Robert
1104
Coates, Robert M.
50, 687, 810, 1157, 1341,
1759, 1931, 2210, 2278, 2314,
2537, 2917, 3012, 3157, 3327,
3649, 4069, 4331, 4626, 4811,
5279, 6165, 7281, 7551
Cobbs, Price M.
6232
Coburn, Kathleen
10373
Cochran, Hamilton
6243
Cockburn, Claud
7127'
Coburn, Kathleen
10373
Cocteau, Jean
5848, 8654, 8691, 10582

Conference on Econ. Progress.
10941
Conklin, Bill
10404
Conlon, Kathleen
5871
Conn, William
6840
Connell, Brian
12759
Connell, John
10438, 12769
Connelley, William Elsey
11051
Connelly, Marc
11820
Connolly, Cyril
6305r, 9245
Conover, Grandin
10692
Conquest, Robert
8088, 10711, 10944
Conrad, Barnaby
6918
Conrad, Joseph
8835, 8836
Conroy, Frank
689, 1923, 3344, 11893
Constable, Rosalind
5042
Cook, Fred J.
6810
Cooke, Alistair
1105, 12045, 12640
Cookridge, E. H.
10222, 11553
Cooper, Clarence L.
11429
Cooper, Diana
9345, 11093, 12428
Cooper, Douglas
8067
Cooper, Giles
7454, 7455, 9060
Cooper, Henry S. F., Jr.
2468, 2686, 3020
Cooper, Irving
8228
Cooper, James Fenimore
9268
Cooper, Jane
2947, 3160, 3355, 5340

Cooper, Kent
11217
Cooper, Louise Field
223, 2034, 2137, 2550,
2722, 3938, 4776, 4815
Cooper, Norton
6031
Cooper, Simon
11090
Cooper, Susan
6110
Cooper, William
11430
Coopersmith, Jerome
6023
Copani, Peter
12833
Cope, Jack
2421, 3256
Copi
9013
Coppel, Alec
7849
Corbett, Scott
1522
Cordell, Alexander
11103
Corey, Herb
8116
Corke, Hilary
58, 118, 661, 740, 780, 886,
1071, 1143, 1471, 1680, 1705,
1766, 2341, 3155, 3405, 3809,
4548, 4625, 4940, 5008, 5286
Cornelisen, Ann
12344
Cornish, Roger
10544
Cortázar, Julio
3326, 12915
Corwin, Edward
10959
Corwin, Norman
11234, 12976
Cory, Daniel
9276
Coser, Lewis A.
9897
Cost, March
5659, 8687, 13027
Costa, Margaret
7684

Costain, Thomas B.
11895
Costigan, James
6008, 9399
Costikyan, Edward N.
6109
Cotler, Gordon
225, 1197, 2754, 2895, 3143,
4300, 4949, 5201
Cotterell, Geoffrey
11912
Cottrell, Leonard
7116, 8174, 11065, 12262
Coulette, Henri
499, 2409, 3844, 4386
Coulson, Jessie
7203
Court, Alfred
10149
Courthion, Pierre
10924
Courtney, C. C.
11384
Courtney, Marguerite
9131
Cousteau, Jacques-Yves
9418
Coward, Noël
7522, 8231, 9465, 10351,
10395, 10890, 10987, 11364,
11790, 12328
Cowen, Ron
11972
Cowen, William Joyce
7534
Cowles, Calvin D.
10441
Cowles, Virginia
7848, 8896, 10315, 10784
Cowley, Malcolm
7567
Cox, Cynthia
11117
Cox, Donald W.
5790
Cox, Joseph A.
11124
Cox, William
2873
Coxe, Louis O.
1516, 1702, 2005, 3442,
4577, 4904
Coxhead, Elizabeth
9055

Coyle, J. J.
10319
Cozzens, James Gould
6403, 10070
Craig, David
6797, 10794
Craig, Dennis
5631
Crane, Stephen
11879, 11880, 12737
Cranko, John
6845
Crankshaw, Edward
7895, 8921, 11351
Cranston, Maurice
8816
Crawford, Cheryl
8005
Cray, Ed
6174
Creal, Margaret
9256
Creatore, Luigi
9609
Creekmore, Hubert
852
Creighton, Anthony
7410
Crewe, Quentin
8774
Crews, Frederick C.
10893
Crichton, Kyle
8177
Crichton, Robert
11490
Crick, Francis
10428
Crittenden, Jordan
3784, 4878
Crompton, John
9419
Cromwell, John
6046, 9830, 10545
Cronin, A. J.
8869, 11791
Cronin, Vincent
7675, 9067, 9506, 11269
Crosland, C. A. R.
6774
Cross, Beverley
8157, 9793, 10515
Cross, Colin
7519

Cross, Wilbur
7899
Crossman, R. H. S.
6574, 10888
Croswell, Anne
7417, 8570
Crouse, Russel
5862, 8085, 8188, 9995,
12047
Crowley, Harriet Hughes
4199
Crowley, Mart
6319
Crown Princess of Prussia
See Victoria Adelaide Mary
Louisa
Crowther, Bosley
9374
Croy, Homer
12825
Crozier, Brian
9817
Crozier, Emmet
13022
Cruse, Amy
12614
Cruse, Harold
6855
Cryer, Gretchen
9114, 10389
Cucci, Frank
10435
Cuddon, J. A.
10102
Cullen, Tom A.
7363, 12827
Cullinan, Elizabeth
3, 2544, 3340, 3466, 3862,
4082, 4690, 4719, 4903,
5248, 8458
Cuming, Cecile Lamalle
5430
Cummings, E. E.
4772, 10320
Cummings, Parke
5476
Cummins, P. D.
11167
Cunard, Nancy
12150
Cuneo, Ernest
9340
Cunningham, John
12745

Cuomo, George
6344
Curley, James Michael
8544
Current, Richard N.
9361
Currie, Ellen
4890
Currimbhoy, Asif
7963
Curry-Lindahl, Kai
7435
Curtis, Charles P.
10556
Curtis, Norman
12709
Curtis, Patricia Taylor
12709
Curtiss, Mina
6220, 10140
Curvers, Alexis
12077
Cushman, Dan
12865
Cushman, Howard
3165
Cutright, Paul Russell
12141

D

Da Costa, Morton
11406
Dahl, Roald
743, 2491, 8418
Daiches, David
2026, 2482, 2576, 3946,
4397, 4924, 6858, 11771
Dain, Martin J.
7568
Dale, Edwin L., Jr.
6775
Dallin, David J.
6554
Dalton, Elizabeth
766
Daly, Maria
7098
Dana, Nathalie
13058
Dana, Robert Patrick
5481
Dangerfield, George
6550

Daniel, Hawthorne
10566
Daniel, Yuli
12189
Daniels, Guy
11084
Daniels, Jonathan
10976, 12267
Daninos, Pierre
6920, 10372
Dante, Ron
6197
Danzig, Allison
8356
Da Ponte, Lorenzo
9881
Darcy, Louise
3426
Darion, Joe
8567, 9683, 11622
da Rocha Miranda, Edgard
5810
Darring, Walter
4705
Dart, Raymond A.
5631
Darwin, Charles
6936
Dash, Samuel
7285
Da Silva, Howard
13090
Dasmann, Raymond F.
7060
Dassin, Jules
8567
Davenport, Marcia
6779
Davenport, Russell W.
7115
Davenport, William H.
12673
Davey-Hill, Leonard
4822
David, Hal
11011
David-Neel, Alexandra
9610
Davidson, Angus
7364, 8310
Davidson, Basil
6228, 10417

Davie, Donald
2716
Davie, Michael
8993
Davies, A. Powell
9843
Davies, Margaret
5869
Davies, Rhys
106, 786, 2163, 2752, 3449
Davies, Robertson
9515, 10011, 12666
Davis, Bertram H.
9333
Davis, Burke
8051
Davis, Catherine
2442
Davis, Christopher
6124
Davis, Clyde Brion
11583
Davis, Eddie
5828
Davis, Elmer
12483
Davis, Gwen
6146
Davis, Jefferson
8787
Davis, Kenneth S.
11014
Davis, L.J.
12831
Davis, Nuel Pharr
9141
Davis, Olivia
9106
Davis, Ossie
11035
Davis, Richard Beale
7879
Davis, Sammy, Jr.
13037
Davis, Samuel
5486
Davison, Ann
10158
Davison, Peter
2886, 3799
Dawnay, Peter
12022

Dickinson, Edward
7353
Dickinson, Emily
9274, 10872
Dickson, Lovat
5842, 8460
Didion, Joan
11336
Diehl, Charles
6411
Dietrich, Otto
8382
Dietz, Howard
7847, 8790
Dietz, Robert S.
11566
di Giovanni, Norman Thomas
1045, 1657, 1665, 1993,
2196, 2199, 2335, 2338,
3595, 4408, 4913
Dillon, Richard
9908
Dimona, Joe
12203
Dinesen, Isak
7315, 9115, 11589
Dinneen, Joseph F.
5744
Diolé, Philippe
7843
DiSalle, Michael V.
10949
Dissent (periodical)
12674
Dixon, Adrienne.
11889
Dixon, George Campbell
12587
Dixon, Pierson
10722
Dizenzo, Charles
7442
Djilas, Milovan
5800, 6789, 9076, 10236,
10324
Dobrée, Bonamy
7399
Dobzhansky, Theodosius
8300, 9735
Dodds, Baby
6005
Doenitz, Karl
9884

Dolci, Danilo
9701, 11167
Dolson, Hildegarde
1793, 2434, 5268
Domino, Ruth
3910
Donald, Aïda Di Pace
7104
Donald, David
6568, 7104, 8673
Donaldson, Frances
9763
Donchev, Anton
12275
Doner, Dean
424, 1349, 1795, 2279
Donleavy, J.P.
1668, 7919, 7920, 11361,
11694
Donnelly, Dorothy
512, 1219, 1786, 1800, 2548,
4326, 4442, 4459, 5390
Donnelly, Joseph P.
12891
Donovan, John
11235
Donovan, Robert
7816
Dooley, John
8385
Dooley, Thomas A.
2030
Dorian, Marguerite
4109
Dos Passos, John
8065, 9899, 9919, 12499
Dostoevski, Fyodor
7203, 8549, 10371
Dougherty, Richard
6730, 7510, 11967
Douglas, David C.
12903
Douglas, Ellen
3517
Douglas, Jerry
11282
Douglas, Norman
7720, 11703
Douglas, Paul H.
5757
Douglas, William O.
10169, 11352

Douglass, Jane
435a
Dourado, Autran
8320
Dowdey, Clifford
12648
Downing, Ronald
9461
Doyle, Richard M.
361
Drabble, Margaret
7840, 8793, 9946, 12764
Drake, Ervin
8288, 12817
Drake, Stillman
7826
Draper, Theodore
11296
Drayton, Mary
7012, 10851
Dreiser, Theodore
9287
Dresden, Donald William
11
Drexler, Rosalyn
8408
Driver, Donald
13070
Drouet, Minou
10867
Drowne, Tatiana Balkoff
10669
Dru, Alexander
9280
Drucker, Peter F.
5791
Druon, Maurice
6886
Drury, Allen
11534, 11580
Duberman, Martin B.
8633, 9888
Dubin, Arthur D.
11769
Du Bois, W. E. B.
5987
Du Bois, William,
7514
Dubos, René
11747
Dubus, André
154, 1181
Duby, Georges
8359

Du Cros, Janet Teissier
7149
Duckworth, Sophia
6531
Dudintsev, Vladimir
10258, 10364
Duerrenmatt, Friedrich
7752, 10484, 10861, 11054,
12655
Dufault, Peter Kane
122, 217, 291, 501, 849,
962, 992, 1563, 1803, 2369,
2582, 2786, 3193, 3396, 3470,
3486, 3780, 3847, 4068, 4165,
4177, 4858, 5379, 5483, 5561
Duffy, Gordon
8195
Duffy, John
8428
Duffy, Maureen
10668
Dufresne, Frank
10337
Dugan, Alan
4650, 10869
Dugan, James
9418, 9692, 10862
Duggan, Alfred
7529, 12926
Duhrssen , Alfred
9862
Duke, Vernon,
9405, 10708
Dulles, Allen
6843, 11494
Dumas, Alexandre
5624, 5626, 5707, 11245
du Maurier, Daphne
7950, 8655, 11423, 12579
Dumitriu, Petru
9854
Dumond, Dwight Lowell
5852
Dumont, René
8496a
Dunbar, Janet
7991
Duncan, David Douglas
8986, 10804, 11530, 13021
Duncan, Jane
10141
Duncan, Ronald
7008

Dunham, Katherine
  12348
Dunn, Robert
  12970
Dunnett, Dorothy
  7139
Dupee, Frederick W.
  11511
Durant, Ariel
  5671, 5674, 11318
Durant, Mary
  8611
Durant, Will
  5671, 5674, 11318
Duras, Marguerite
  6079, 9064, 9178, 9183, 10017,
  11854
Durdin, Peggy
  5116
Durrell, Gerald
  11313, 13085
Durrell, Lawrence
  1090, 3648, 4206, 4608
  5709, 6218, 6222, 6679,
  9142, 11017
Duthuit, Georges
  9121
Dutourd, Jean
  7636, 8425, 9251, 9686
Duveen, James Henry
  11229
Dyer, Charles
  11107, 11860
Dyer, Richard
  8394
Dyer, William
  8802
Dyne, Michael
  11215

E

E.F.K.
  1539
E.T.
  See Chambers, Jessie
Eager, Edward
  8190
Earle, Edward
  7014
East, P.D.
  9618

Eastlake, William
  7960
Eastman, Max
  8063
Eaton, Evelyn
  1794, 7959, 8532
Eban, Abba
  12667
Ebb, Fred
  6414, 7670, 8194, 10071, 13087
Eberhart, Richard
  1142, 1320, 1360, 1918, 2975,
  3111, 3422, 4268, 4368, 4964,
  5224
Ebling, F.J.G.
  10203
Ebright, Frederick
  719, 3741
Eby, Cecil D.
  11655
Eckert, Allan W.
  8057, 11670
Edel, Leon
  7099, 8281, 8283, 8284,
  9383, 11025, 11514
Edelman, Maurice
  7756
Eden, Anthony
  7801, 9785, 11123
Edie, James M.
  11353
Edisford, Rosemary
  2018
Editors
  1131
Editors of Look
  9466
Editors of Year
  10812
Edman, Irwin
  8810
Edward VIII
  12911
Edwardes, Michael
  6068
Edwards, Everett J.
  12806
Edwards, Lovett F.
  6186, 10220, 11823
Edwards, Maurice
  10836
Edwards, Sherman
  11573

Eells, George
9338
Ehrenburg, Ilya
10747, 10935
Ehrenzweig, Anton
8395
Ehrlich, Blake
11179
Ehrlich, Max
12039
Einaudi, Marìo
11293
Einhorn, Abe
5665
Einstein, Alfred
7429
Eiseley, Loren
7623
Eisenhower, Dwight D.
9725, 12693
Eisenschiml, Otto
12592
Eisenstein, Sergei
7604, 7605
Ekert-Rotholz, Alice
9774, 12276
Elder, Donald
11223
Elder, Lonne, III
6533
Eldon, Rita
12367
Elegant, Robert S.
7220
Eliade, Mircea
13042
Elias, Robert H.
9287
Eliot, Elizabeth
8258
Eliot, George
7874
Eliot, T. S.
6669, 7328, 7329, 7535,
10473, 10873, 12299
Eliscu, Edward
6045
Elizabeth, Countess of Longford
See Longford, Elizabeth
Pakenham
Ellin, Stanley
10648

Ellington, Duke
10940
Elliott, George P.
8630
Elliott, Janice
5822, 7972
Elliott, Sumner Locke
6464
Ellis, A. E.
11085
Ellis, H. F.
246, 537, 782, 918, 920,
1618, 2513, 3255, 3375, 3379,
3495, 3948, 4033, 4353, 4401,
4576, 5237, 5270, 5338, 5406,
5442, 5488, 5563
Ellison, James Whitfield
9813
Ellmann, Richard
5918, 7354, 7902, 8767,
9278, 10131
Ellul, Jacques
11012
Ellwood, Paul
12224
Elman, Irving
12520
Elman, Richard E.
10900
Elsner, Gisela
7904
Elton, Godfrey
7855
Elward, James
7774
Elwell, Robert
299
Elwin, Malcolm
9475
Emmet, L. D.
10302
Emmons, James
12386
Engel, Leonard
10548
Engel, Monroe
12687
Engle, Paul
355, 1351, 4118, 10877
Engvick, William
6084
Ennis, Philip
5778

Enright, Elizabeth
    4216
Ephron, Henry
    12032
Ephron, Phoebe
    8483, 12032
Epstein, Edward Jay
    1741
Epstein, Jacob
    7413
Epstein, Julius J.
    6394
Epstein, Seymour
    9190, 10823, 11950
Epton, Nina
    9520
Eriksson, Paul S.
    12387
Errington, Paul L.
    10426
Ervine, St. John
    6136
Escholier, Raymond
    9827
Espey, John J.
    1106
Estang, Luc
    6157
Estivals, Gabrielle
    7836
Estrin, Herman A.
    10255
Etcherelli, Claire
    7338
Etiemble, René
    10681
Euripides
    8707, 9252, 12414, 12415
Evans, Abbie Huston
    1445, 1694, 1715, 3512,
    4989, 7502
Evans, Bergen
    1154a
Evans, Dan
    5342
Evans, Joan
    5623
Evans, Ray
    10443
Evans, Walker
    9911
Evanson, Elizabeth Moss
    7770

Evarts, Esther
    1906, 3728
Evreinov, Nikolai
    6592
Evslin, Bernard
    7885, 11877
Ewart, Gavin
    4782
Ewen, Frederic
    10925

F

Fabbri, Jacques
    9182
Faber, Geoffrey
    8860
Fabre-Luce, Alfred
    8226
Fadiman, Clifton
    834, 5783, 10691
Fain, Samuel
    6619
Fain, William
    1941, 6581
Fair, C. M.
    1097, 2930, 3205, 3381, 3529,
    3569, 3632
Fairbairn, Douglas
    7852
Fairbrother, Nan
    8448
Fairlie, Henry
    1416, 9330
Falk, Minna R.
    8360
Fall, Bernard B.
    8261, 8384, 12626
Fallaci, Oriana
    8555
Falls, Cyril
    8090
Faltermayer, Edmund K.
    11139
Fandel, John
    1011, 1734, 2286
Fanon, Frantz
    13008
Fant, Joseph L., III
    7566
Faralla, Dana
    6602
Farber, Norma
    1969

Finney, Jack
  5945
Firbank, Ronald
  10253a
Fischer, Louis
  9327, 11349, 12190
Fisher, Agnes Adams
  6964
Fisher, John
  7319
Fisher, M. F. K.
  746, 2821, 3472, 4287,
  5059, 8290r, 9747r, 10779r,
  11050r, 11487r, 11488r
Fisher, M. H.
  8396
Fisher, Michael
  6156
Fisher, Robert
  8181, 8589
Fisher, Roger
  8684
FitzGerald, Edward
  9272
Fitzgerald, Edward
  5843, 7037, 8514, 9272,
  11614
Fitzgerald, F. Scott
  9275
Fitzgerald, Robert
  47, 1621, 2368, 2405, 3684,
  8412
FitzGerald, Xavière Desparmet
  8032
FitzGibbon, Constantine
  7508, 7979, 8914, 9323,
  11862, 12247, 12460, 12828,
  12924
FitzLyon, April
  9304
Flagler, J. M.
  748, 1474, 1756, 2116, 2669,
  3925, 3996, 4053, 4646, 5011,
  5278, 11278
Flanagan, William
  6059
Flanders, Michael
  5956, 5957
Flanner, Hildegarde
  3013
Flanner, Janet
  228, 393, 445, 534, 535,
  562, 669, 805, 827, 1003,

1246, 1488, 1509, 1869, 2330,
2497, 2541, 2656, 2661, 2782,
2891, 2972, 3675, 3919, 4030,
4099, 4186, 4205, 4225, 4704,
4804, 4938, 5045, 5189, 5251,
5573, 5604r, 5743r, 5815r,
5851r, 5962r, 6048r, 6079r,
6131r, 6132r, 6280r, 6332r,
6467r, 6516r, 6536r, 6543r,
6577r, 6584r, 6660r, 6728r,
6729r, 6848r, 6920r, 6953ar,
7040r, 7100r, 7112r, 7121r,
7184r, 7308r, 7336r, 7367r,
7515r, 7525r, 7746r, 7752r,
7775r, 7900r, 7914r, 7998r,
8155r, 8196r, 8226r, 8254r,
8351r, 8353r, 8354r, 8431r,
8551r, 8558r, 8594r, 8633r,
8657r, 8713r, 8760r, 8797r,
8840r, 8853r, 8941r, 8994r,
8997r, 9000r, 9001r, 9003r,
9005r, 9006r, 9009r, 9012r,
9013r, 9014r, 9016r, 9017r,
9018r, 9021r, 9023r, 9025r,
9028r, 9029r, 9030r, 9031r,
9033r, 9034r, 9038r, 9041r,
9045r, 9046r, 9047r, 9049r,
9066r, 9084r, 9122r, 9151r,
9152r, 9153r, 9154r, 9155r,
9157r, 9163r, 9164r, 9165r,
9166r, 9167r, 9168r, 9170r,
9172r, 9174r, 9175r, 9177r,
9178r, 9179r, 9181r, 9182r,
9183r, 9184r, 9185r, 9186r,
9188r, 9204r, 9220r, 9224r,
9228r, 9230r, 9232r, 9233r,
9236r, 9237r, 9238r, 9240r,
9241r, 9244r, 9246r, 9247r,
9249r, 9250r, 9251r, 9253r,
9262r, 9263r, 9300r, 9350r,
9605r, 9424r, 9551r, 9603r,
9756r, 9863r, 9867r, 9928r,
10012r, 10062r, 10110r,
10191r, 10193r, 10215r,
10219r, 10447r, 10560r,
10575r, 10583r, 10585r,
10662r, 10681r, 10687r,
10723r, 10787r, 10853r,
10866r, 10867r, 10868r,
10908r, 11070r, 11071r,
11180r, 11183r, 11214r, 11298r,
21540r, 11590r, 11672r, 12108r,
12150r, 12319r, 12394r, 12413r,

12415r, 12510r, 12511r,
12512r, 12513r, 12564r,
12565r, 12605r, 12618r,
12720r, 12735r, 12793r,
12816r, 12866r
Flaubert, Gustave
9599
Fleischman, Harry
10356
Fleming, Ian
9715, 12251, 13050
Fleming, John
11309
Fleming, Peter
7560, 10553
Fleming, Seamus
2089, 4969
Fleming, William
5922
Fletcher, Colin
6748, 9709
Fletcher, Lucille
6942
Flexner, James Thomas
7882, 10027, 12131
Flexner, Stuart Berg
7110
Flicker, Theodore J.
10221
Flint, Emily
8868
Flint, R.W.
11523
Flood, Charles Bracelen
1544, 7143, 10064
Florit, Eugenio
11526
Flory, Sheldon
4260
Foley, Charles
6727
Folliot, Denise
10215, 12401
Fontaine, André
8372
Foot, Michael
5819, 10740
Forbes, Elliot
9321
Forbes, Gordon
12337
Forbes-Robertson, Diana
10128
Ford, Alice
7320

Ford, Corey
12838
Ford, Daniel
10388
Ford, Ford Madox
7594
Ford, Gerald R.
10926
Ford, Hilary
7575
Ford, John
12287
Ford, Nancy
9114, 10389
Ford, Ruth
11177
Forester, C.S.
5619, 5668, 7555, 9449
Forgue, Guy Jean
8145
Fornes, Maria Irene
11006
Forrest, George
5859, 8904
Forsberg, Rolf
12095
Forster, E.M.
5708, 9771, 10785
Forster, Margaret
9977
Forsyth, James
7357, 8269
Fort, Harriet
4310
Fosdick, Dorothy
6736
Foster, Elizabeth
6603
Foster, James R.
8069
Foster, Paul
6035, 12323
Fothergill, Brian
11702
Foulke, Adrienne
6813, 7764, 9739
Fowler, John M.
7523
Fowler, H.W.
7109
Fowles, John
6692, 9619
Fowlie, Wallace
11465

Fox, Paula
7054
Fox, Ruth
206, 5221
Fraenkel, Heinrich
8348
Frame, Donald M.
10047
Frame, Janet
3901, 4060, 5468, 5545,
5616, 13033
France, Pierre Mendès
10020
Francis, Robert
880, 5001
Francis, William
10918
Frank, Gerold
6125, 6303, 7021, 12870
Frank, Melvin
9348
Frank, Pat
5691
Frank, Philipp
7323
Frankau, Pamela
5936, 10615
Frankel, Charles
168, 3869, 8332
Frankfurter, Felix
7574
Franqui, Carlos
12454
Franzero, Carlo Maria
6082, 9314
Fraser, Antonia
8379, 9802
Fraser, Douglas
10973
Fraser, Kathleen
744, 2115, 2753, 2979
Fraser, Kennedy
9310r, 11156r,
Frater, Alexander
313, 937, 1250, 2977, 3867
Frayn, Michael
12597
Frechtman, Bernard
7563, 9403, 9955, 10458,
12965
Fredericks, Claude
6562
Freed, Fred
7015

Freedman, Gerald
12269
Freedman, Morris
726
Freeling, Nicolas
11934, 12191, 12573
Freeman, Arthur
3258, 4972
Freeman, Bud
6107
Freeman, Ira Henry
10610
Freeman, Stan
8518
Freidel, Frank
7754
Freidin, Seymour
7554, 7707
Freitag, George H.
1735, 4490
Fremantle, Anne
216, 357, 792, 950
Frenaye, Francis
5672, 9497, 11226
Freuchen, Dagmar
6288
Freuchen, Peter
5886, 6288
Freud, Ernst L.
9285
Freud, Sigmund
9285, 12209
Freund, E. Hans
7128
Friar, Kimon
10418
Friedenberg, Edgar Z.
6722
Friedman, Albert
12634
Friedman, Bruce Jay
10085, 11455
Friedman, Elizabeth S.
11593
Friedman, William F.
11593
Friel, Brian
135, 1074, 1176, 1215,
1413, 1490, 1650, 1819,
3243, 3248, 3854, 4237,
4417, 5435, 9549, 9557,
10789
Friend, Robert
1423, 2698

Friendly, Fred W.
7242
Frings, Ketti
9454, 9469
Frisbie, Johnny
7781
Frisby, Terence
12144
Frisch, Max
5814, 7620, 12892
Frith, W. P.
12609
Fritsch, Charles T.
11079
Fritz, Jean
1980
Froman, Robert
539
Frost, Raymond
6017
Frost, Robert
7447, 8617, 9284, 11515
Froud, Nina
6544
Fruchter, Norman
6664
Fry, Christopher
6930, 7633, 12259
Fuchida, Mitsuo
9930
Fuentes, Carlos
5977, 6551, 7006, 12834
Fugard, Athol
6246, 8264
Fulbright, J. William
5901
Fulford, Roger
6991, 6993
Fuller, Charles H., Jr.
10765
Fuller, Dean
10492
Fuller, Edmund
6808, 12284
Fuller, Hoyt
546
Fuller, J. F. C.
9937, 9938
Fuller, John
1075

Fuller, Roy
6368, 7542
Furbank, P. N.
8744
Furlaud, Maxime
6216, 7635
Furnas, J. C.
8026
Furneaux, Robin
5746
Furneaux, Rupert
8696

G

Gabel, Leona C.
9869
Gadda, Carlo Emilio
12118
Gaddis, Thomas E.
6204
Gaddis, William
11125
Gagliano, Frank
6757, 7564, 10287
Gail, Marzieh
5995
Gainham, Sarah
10280, 10837
Galbraith, John Kenneth
1107, 5649, 5748, 7290,
7296r, 8648r, 9100r,
9302, 10243
Gale, John
6649
Galen, Nina
11165
Gallagher, Barrett
7654
Gallagher, John F.
10146
Gallagher, Thomas
7616, 10540
Gallant, Mavis
16, 18, 236, 304, 310, 312,
446, 457, 527, 688, 693,
808, 942, 1334, 1350, 1379,
1404, 1828, 1899, 2136, 2171,
2230, 2268, 2370, 2384, 2890,
3099, 3228, 3290, 3323, 3456,
3540, 3590, 3907, 3955, 4020,
4037, 4149, 4228, 4591, 4682,

4683, 4791, 4980, 5067, 5142,
5152, 5171, 5222, 5344, 5397,
5447
Galler, David
1613, 2367, 2795, 2884, 3141,
4301, 4306, 4933, 4961
Gallico, Paul
2161, 10001
Gallie, Menna
11933
Gallois, Pierre
6024
Galton, Ray
11258
Gammond, Peter
7247
Gamow, George
10840, 12177
Gann, Ernest K.
7558, 8618, 12467
Gannon, Robert I.
10897
Gant, Roland
12226
Gara, Larry
6005
Gardener, William
643
Gardiner, Dorothy
11110
Gardner, Brian
5736, 11066
Gardner, Herb
8025, 12217
Gardner, Isabella
279
Gardner, John
6747
Gardner, John W.
10326
Gardner, Martin A.
11487, 11488
Garinei, Pietro
6953a, 11329
Garland, Joseph E.
9436
Garland, Madge
6553
Garland, Patrick
6341
Garnett, Constance
10156
Garnett, David
5938, 7677, 12505

Garnett, Richard
10482
Garraty, John A.
11220
Garrett, Zena
8449
Garrigue, Jean
140, 939, 1193, 1384,
3333, 3382, 3392, 3438,
4513, 5135, 5551, 12762
Garside, Edward B.
12543
Garson, Barbara
9590
Gary, Romain
7438, 9058, 11009, 11298
Gascar, Pierre
6080, 6802, 11503
Gaskin, Catherine
8523
Gassner, John
10207
Gaster, Theodor H.
6975
Gatteschi, Giuseppe
8044
Gavin, James M.
12736
Gay, Peter
6209r, 7366r, 12676r
Gazzo, Michael V.
8222, 10277
Gehrecke, Frank
8116
Geiger, Milton
7307
Geismar, Maxwell
8282
Gelb, Arthur
10527
Gelb, Barbara
10527
Gelbart, Larry
6768
Gelber, Jack
5877, 6766, 6876, 11855
Gelber, Lionel
5737
Gelber, Stanley Jay
9514
Geller, Bruce
5722, 9410
Gellhorn, Martha
12470

Gendel Evelyn
  10398
Genet, Jean
  6025,  6235,  7011,  9244,
  9622,  9623,  9955,  10891
Geoffrey, Christopher
  314
George, Peter
  6726
George, Waldemar
  12561
Gerard, Donald L.
  11241
Gerassi, John
  8068,  12583
Gerber, Merrill Joan
  2534,  5334
Gérin, Winifred
  6323
Gershe, Leonard
  6399,  7063
Gernsheim, Alice
  12608
Gernsheim, Helmut
  8365,  12608
Gershwin, George
  10431
Gershwin, Ira
  10431
Gesner, Clark
  13073
Gethers, Steven
  6791
Geymonat, Ludovico
  7826
Ghali, Waguih
  6099
Gheerbrant, Alain
  8636
Ghelderode, Michel de
  6048,  8422,  10651,  12956
Gibbings, Robert
  12427
Gibbs, Barbara
  1738,  3753,  4742,  5378
Gibbs, Margaret
  6893
Gibbs, Wolcott
  947, 1504,  3556,  5524,  5578,
  5644r,  5828r,  5878r,  5976r,
  6013r,  6120r,  6145r,  6265r,

6388r,  6439r,  6463r,  6505r,
6509r,  6521r,  6543r,  6545r,
6547r,  6588r,  6596r,  6651r,
6661r,  6750r,  6797r,  6828r,
6845r,  6907r,  6925r,  6930r,
6949r,  6959r,  6979r,  7012r,
7051r,  7055r,  7102r,  7206r,
7509r,  7522r,  7628r,  7633r,
7729r,  7863r,  7942r,  8005r,
8017r,  8085r,  8096r,  8120r,
8177r,  8188r,  8198r,  8222r,
8250r,  8323r,  8325r,  8389r,
8418r,  8434r,  8439r,  8542r,
8654r,  8658r,  8663r,  8683r,
8685r,  8724r,  8762r,  8772r,
8773r,  8803r,  8946r,  9086r,
9150r,  9255r,  9392r,  9405r,
9410r,  9452r,  9467r,  9469r,
9505r,  9550r,  9588r,  9625r,
9639r,  9753r,  9811r,  9821r,
9838r,  9845r,  9922r,  9973r,
9974r,  9975r,  9991r,  9999r,
10041r,  10051r,  10058r,
10078r,  10116r,  10135r,
10209r,  10241r,  10242r,  10341r,
10395r,  10443r,  10493r,  10583r,
10794r,  10830r,  10892r,  10910r,
11018r,  11135r,  11153r,  11207r,
11219r,  11266r,  11278r,  11288r,
11300r,  11334r,  11369r,  11419r,
11542r,  11586r,  11622r,  11631r,
11632r,  11676r,  11685r,  11705r,
11710r,  11724r,  11735r,  11775r,
11832r,  11857r,  11928r,  11952r,
11963r,  11982r,  12027r,  12050r,
12157r,  12224r,  12228r,  12259r,
12271r,  12280r,  12329r,  12333r,
12413r,  12439r,  12466r,  12477r,
12520r,  12524r,  12574r,  12599r,
12629r,  12655r,  12657r,  12701r,
12705r,  12726r,  12775r,  12801r,
12894r,  12913r,  12962r,  13053r,
13082r
Gibson, Walker
  1493,  1877
Gibson, William
  1108,  6873,  7122,  7986,
  9956,  11506,  12477
Gidney, James B.
  7193

Giedion, Siegfried
7432
Gilbert, Anthony
12658
Gilbert, Dorothy
287, 1676, 2927
Gilbert, Edwin
8443, 11678
Gilbert, Martin
5875
Gilbert, Michael
5660, 7833
Gilbert, Sandra M.
1992
Gilbert, Stuart
9277, 9914
Gilbert, William S.
8003, 8148, 12560
Gilbert, Willie
6510, 8437, 8482
Giles, Kenneth
11766
Gilkes, Lillian
6801, 11879
Gill, Brendan
341, 1109, 2048, 3295, 3708,
4026, 4498, 4726, 4935, 5582r,
5598r, 5599r, 5609r, 5636r,
5646r, 5661r, 5669r, 5682r,
5690r, 5717r, 5732r, 5734r,
5743r, 5732r, 5767r, 5787r,
5794r, 5799r, 5808r, 5825r,
5836r, 5856r, 5858r, 5866r,
5872r, 5881r, 5889r, 5897r,
5927r, 5993r, 6004r, 6007r,
6009r, 6015r, 6020r, 6026r,
6037r, 6041r, 6043r, 6044r,
6054r, 6064r, 6076r, 6088r,
6090r, 6094r, 6095r, 6105r,
6106r, 6112r, 6116r, 6148r,
6172r, 6180r, 6182r, 6196r,
6197r, 6198r, 6200r, 6205r,
6226r. 6244r, 6251r, 6262r,
6263r, 6268r, 6273r, 6281r,
6310r, 6313r, 6320r, 6328r,
6343r, 6348r, 6369r, 6376r,
6390r, 6394r, 6398r, 6399r,
6403r, 6404r, 6431r, 6433r,
6440r, 6445r, 6454r, 6459r,
6474r, 6475r, 6480r, 6489r,
6492r, 6524r, 6539r, 6546r,
6558r, 6559r, 6560r, 6575r,
6586r, 6589r, 6591r, 6595r,

6605r, 6606r, 6622r, 6625r,
6626r, 6629r, 6632r, 6633r,
6639r, 6650r, 6655r, 6659r,
6665r, 6669r, 6670r, 6674r,
6706r, 6710r, 6711r, 6712r,
6759r, 6765r, 6767r, 6783r,
6792r, 6793r, 6796r, 6818r,
6820r, 6822r, 6847r, 6856r,
6861r, 6873r, 6876r, 6878r,
6892r, 6906r, 6926r, 6932r,
6934r, 6944r, 6948r, 6951r,
6956r, 6957r, 6958, 6959,
6969r, 6974r, 6982r, 6986r,
6990r, 7023r, 7025r, 7066r,
7067r, 7078r, 7082r, 7084r,
7091r, 7118r. 7152r. 7170r,
7171r, 7173r, 7176r, 7181r,
7814r, 7199r, 7211r, 7217r,
7219r, 7230r, 7256r, 7279r,
7288r, 7289r, 7301r, 7316r,
7322r, 7326r, 7330r, 7333r,
7345r, 7246r, 7365r, 7373r,
7406r, 7418r, 7452r, 7463r,
6469r, 7474r, 7489r, 7505r,
7506r, 7508r, 7521r, 7525r,
7528r, 7538r, 7540r, 7543r,
7546r, 7559r, 7561r, 7562r,
7572r, 7584r, 7585r, 7590r,
7597r, 7599r, 7610r, 7614r,
7619r, 7622r, 7640r, 7644r,
7652r, 7657r, 7666r, 7673r,
7710r, 7712r, 7719r, 7723r,
7724r, 7728r, 7750r, 7755r,
7711r, 7772r, 7782r, 7787r,
7796r, 7806r, 7811r, 7824r,
7829r, 7831r, 7834r, 7853r,
7876r, 7884r, 7915r, 7922r,
7929r, 7932r, 7935r, 7937r,
7944r, 7954r, 7965r, 7993r,
7998r, 8000ar, 8004r, 8019r,
8025r, 8030r, 8035r, 8040r,
8041r, 8058r, 8060r, 8080r,
8091r, 8093r, 8098r, 8111r,
8123r, 8125r, 8127r, 8128r,
8130r, 8131r, 8134r, 8135r,
8137r, 8138r, 8143r, 8151r,
8155r, 8162r, 8163r, 8164r,
8175r, 8178r, 8181r, 8182r,
8194r, 8196r, 8200r, 8207r,
8212r, 8214r, 8224r, 8229r,
8245r, 9251r, 8270r, 8276r,
8288r, 8303r, 8315r, 8328r,
8337r, 8345r, 8402r, 8414r,

8420r, 8438r, 8440r, 8445r,
8451r, 8452r, 8465r, 8468r,
8470r, 8474r, 8474r, 8478r,
8486r, 8498r, 8501r, 8502r,
8503r, 8525r, 8529r, 8545r,
8560r, 8570r, 8586r, 8588r,
8601r, 8604r, 8605r, 8622r,
8626r, 8635r, 8638r, 8651r,
8569r, 8669r, 8694r, 8704r,
8710r, 8717r, 8729r, 8732r,
8740r, 8750r, 8794r, 8800r,
8801r, 8804r, 8811r, 8812r,
8822r, 8826r, 8828r, 8861r,
8870r, 8871r, 8874r, 8877r,
8880r, 8881r, 8884r, 8895r,
8899r, 8934r, 8938r, 8946r,
8951r, 8958r, 8964r, 8970r,
8974r, 8980r, 8983r, 8995r,
8990r, 8996r, 9004r, 9011r,
9019r, 9037r, 9039r, 9040r,
9042r, 9044r, 9051r, 9059r,
9061r, 9078r, 9108r, 9122r,
9129r, 9145r, 9147r, 9148r,
9149r, 9158r, 9194r, 9200r,
9213r, 9222r, 9239r, 9261r,
9264r, 9265r, 9267r, 9277r,
9316r, 9339r, 9344r, 9351r,
9367r, 9376r, 9379r, 9407r,
9432r, 9438r, 9439r, 9446r,
9453r, 9463r, 9473r, 9476r,
9477r, 9487r, 9491r, 9509r,
9513r, 9522r, 9525r, 9526r,
9528r, 9532r, 9539r, 9541r,
9544r, 9548r, 9549r, 9553r,
9556r, 9561r, 9564r, 9567r,
9570r, 9587r, 9589r, 9602r,
9609r, 9615r, 9617r, 9627r,
9640r, 9644r, 9645r, 9664r,
9666r, 9672r, 9706r, 9708r,
9722r, 9749r, 9779r, 9787r,
9788r, 9800r, 9801r, 9805r,
9809r, 9851r, 9857r, 9918r,
9927r, 9935r, 9949r, 9957r,
9960r, 9967r, 9969r, 9983r,
9985r, 9988r, 10004r, 10009r,
10018r, 10030r, 10036r,
10037r, 10043r, 10061r,
10066r, 10068r, 10084r,
10092r, 10095r, 10105r,
10107r, 10110r, 10119r,
10126r, 10129r, 10136r,
10148r, 10159r, 10168r,
10179r, 10181r, 10226r,

10229r, 10249r, 10271r,
10272r, 10273r, 10282r,
10285r, 10289r, 10301r,
10306r, 10307r, 10321r,
10329r, 10333r, 10336r,
10350r, 10351r, 10354r,
10367r, 10380r, 10401r,
10415r, 10423r, 10434r,
10442r, 10444r, 10449r,
10485r, 10518r, 10523r,
10525r, 10531r, 10534r,
10536r, 10539r, 10543r,
10576r, 10588r, 10600r,
10603r, 10605r, 10612r,
10614r, 10616r, 10637r,
10654r, 10672r, 10673r,
10676r, 10679r, 10697r,
10703r, 10713r, 10717r,
10726r, 10742r, 10745r,
10746r, 10771r, 10775r,
10782r, 10806r, 10811r,
10833r, 10845r, 10848r,
10849r, 10853r, 10854r,
10879r, 10881r, 10909r,
10918r, 10923r, 10960r,
10966r, 10971r, 11002r,
11011r, 11034r, 11036r,
11053r, 11055r, 11080r,
11092r, 11105r, 11108r,
11130r, 11136r, 11141r,
11155r, 11175r, 11176r,
11180r, 11187r, 11232r,
11252r, 11255r, 11258r,
11265r, 11272r, 11323r,
11339r, 11356r, 11359r,
11366r, 11369r, 11382r,
11385r, 11390r, 11394r,
11396r, 11398r, 11402r,
11408r, 11409r, 11435r,
11448r, 11453r, 11466r,
11471r, 11480r, 11500r,
11509r, 11551r, 11556r,
11559r, 11562r, 11572r,
11573r, 11574r, 11579r,
11592r, 11597r, 11607r,
11612r, 11626r, 11629r,
11637r, 11664r, 11667r,
11690r, 11711r, 11720r,
11723r, 11727r, 11752r,
11753r, 11760r, 11784r,
11808r, 11810r, 11830r,
11831r, 11834r, 11844r,
11853r, 11860r, 11869r,

Ginger, Ray
5745

Ginnes, Abram S.
7231, 9258

Ginsberg, Allen
5267

Ginsburg, Mirra
4425

Ginsbury, Norman
7628

Ginzburg, Eugenia Semyonovna
8848

Giono, Jean
11925

Giovannini, Sandro
6953a, 11329

Giovannitti, Len
7015

Girae, David
4670

Giraudoux, Jean
7244, 8873, 11792, 12259

Gironella, José María
6891, 10513

Girsberger, H.
9156

Gisler, Claude
8133

Gittings, Robert
8815

Glackens, Ira
12896

Glanville, Brian
7083

Glasgow, Ellen
9273

Glassman, Stephen
6197

Glaze, Andrew
2033, 3083

Glaze, Eleanor L.
10097a

Glazer, Nathan
6169

Glazier, Lyle
1562

Glenville, Peter
8439

Glickman, Will
6265, 9999

Glinn, Burt
10922

Glissant, Edouard
11226

Glubb, John Bagot
7362, 8056, 9489, 11759

Glück, Gustav
10777

Glück, Louise
2531, 2660, 3964

Gluckman, Leon
12697

Godden, Jon
12491

Godden, Rumer
6071, 8113, 8632, 12491

Godley, John
521, 1390

Goethe, Johann Wolfgang von
8706, 8737

Goetz, Augustus
8323

Goetz, Ruth
8323

Gogol, Nikolai
7095, 9605

Gold, Ernest
8570

Gold, Herbert
4905, 9710, 10559, 11381

Golden, Ray
6509

Goldhurst, William
7492

Golding, William
7759, 12473

Goldman, Eric F.
6867

Goldman, James
6249, 7527, 9371, 12707

Goldman, Michael
420, 966, 2733, 5235

Goldman, Robert
10969

Goldman, William
6249, 6317, 7527

Goldoni , Carlo
11552, 12586

Goldschmidt, Lucien
12543

Goldsmith, Oliver
10403, 11610

Goldstein, Ruby
12168

Goldston, Robert C.
6508, 9105, 11638
Gollin, A. M.
10993
Gombrich, E. H.
5904, 9848
Gombrowicz, Witold
7579, 10907
Goncourt, Jules de
10678
Goneim, M. Zakaria
9495
Gonzáles, Pancho
9712
González, Luis J.
8082
Gooch, G. P.
12525
Goodale, Alfred M.
3617
Goodfield, June
7134
Goodhart, Philip
9669
Goodhart, William
7860
Gooding, John
10753
Goodman, George J. W.
1194, 1849
Goodman, Jules Eckert
11245
Goodman, Mitchell
7375
Goodman, Paul
8124, 8831, 9347, 9631,
10758, 11751
Goodman, Walter
5718
Goodrich, Frances
7102
Goodrum, Charles A.
2189
Goodspeed, D. J.
6777
Goodwin, Richard N.
190, 2657, 3520, 4016,
4526, 5890r
Goolrick, Chester
3401, 5256
Goran, Lester
9769

Gordimer, Nadine
51, 579, 794, 2717, 2767,
3601, 3613, 3729, 3883,
4246, 4313, 4488, 4779,
5211, 5409, 10409, 12984
Gordon, Arthur
8421
Gordon, Caroline
9647
Gordon, Charles George
7855
Gordon, Daniel
2012
Gordon, John
13073
Gordon, Ruth
12598
Gordon, W. J. J.
1165
Gordone, Charles
10336
Gorer, Geoffrey
6996, 7480
Gorey, Edward
7209, 9381, 10406, 12549,
12639
Gorge, Peter
8031
Gorky, Maxim
6544, 9563
Görlitz, Walter
8898
Gorst, Frederick John
10422
Gorz, André
12372
Gosling, Nigel
9214
Gott, Richard
5875
Gottheimer, Stanley
997
Gottlieb, Alex
12705
Gottlieb, H. J.
166
Gottschalk, Louis Moreau
10378
Goudeket, Maurice
6660
Gourse, R. Leslie
12935

Gove, Philip
12790
Gover, Robert
10503
Goyen, William
7511, 8593
Graber, Richard F.
1145
Grael, Barry Allen
11929
Grafton, Samuel
10076
Gragg, Florence A.
9869
Graham, Frank
12168
Graham, Phyllis
4176
Graham, Ronny
6326, 9258
Graham, Sheilah
6125
Graham, Winston
5821, 12435
Grainger, Ron
12435
Graña, César
6269
Granick, Harry
12932
Grant, Bruce
578, 3618
Grant, Maxwell
12641
Grant, Michael
6211
Grant, Ulysses S.
10661
Grass, Günter
6501, 7179, 12283, 12872
Grau, Shirley Ann
2799, 4619
Graves, Robert
126, 250, 466, 498, 549,
832, 934, 1363, 1414, 1442,
1535, 1999, 2003, 2374,
2512, 2822, 3252, 3339,
3476, 3895, 3950, 3991,
4360, 4409, 4659, 4775,
4936, 5013, 5048, 5051,
5197, 5498, 5538, 5562,
6680, 6866, 8100, 10251
Gray, Anthony
See Aston, Benjamin Gwilliam

Gray, E. J.
5158
Gray, Francine du Plessix
565, 1856, 2847, 3153
Gray, Paul Edward
3241
Gray, Peter
2801
Gray, Simon
12928
Gray, Timothy
8336
Gray, Tony
8708, 11868
Grayson, Cecil
9324
Gréban, Arnoul
9188
Greeman, Richard
9894
Green, Adolph
6120, 7156, 7504, 8161, 11948
Green, Anne
7090, 10693, 12958
Green, Benny
11152
Green, Carolyn
8773
Green, F. Pratt
46, 337, 2141, 2762, 3794
4076
Green, Gerald
9089
Green, Hannah
1062, 4551, 4661
Green, Joseph
10574
Green, Julian
7090, 10687
Green, Martin
11443
Green, Peter
8911, 9366
Greenburg, Dan
5888, 8054
Greene, Bertram
11962
Greene, Graham
6387, 6477, 6742, 10601
10937, 11075, 11539
Greene, John C.
7004
Greene, Mary Francis
11438

Greene, Will
11225
Greener, Leslie
8331
Greenfeld, Josh
6645
Greet, Anne Hyde
2, 252, 4570
Gregg, Edith W.
10498
Gregg, Jess
11643
Gregor, Arthur
660, 1752, 2327, 2730, 4034, 4345, 4558, 4992, 5110
Gregory, Horace
7202, 12981
Gregory, Isabella Augusta
12969
Greig, Desmond
6826
Gressieker, Hermann
11321
Greville, Charles Cavedish Fulke
8095
Grier, William H.
6232
Grierson, Edward
7557
Griffin, Bulkley S.
10437
Griffin, Gwyn
10554, 11660
Griffin, John Howard
6225
Griffin, Jonathan
11298
Griffith, Richard
10096
Griffith, Samuel B.
3225, 4142, 4752
Griffith, Thomas
12696
Grimble, Arthur
11193
Grisman, Arnold E.
6279, 7265
Grodin, Charles
8421
Grodzins, Morton
5968
Grollenberg, L. H.
5966

Gronow, Rees Howell
11161
Groslier, Bernard-Philippe
5921
Grosser, Morton
2812, 7131
Grossman, Alfred
5602, 9745
Grossman, Sylva
1151, 1930, 3376, 3459, 3705
Grossman, William L.
7820
Grosz, George
7286
Grotowski, Jerzy
5868
Groueff, Stephane
9730
Groves, Leslie R.
10390
Guare, John
6796, 8402, 10127
Guerard, Albert J.
7467
Guerrero, Margarita
2196
Guevara, Ernesto Ché
6744, 12583
Guicciardini, Francesco
8362
Guillain, Robert
11706
Guirand, Felix
9087
Gulbenkian, Nubar
10913
Gullans, Charles
9102
Gumina, Shirley
1687
Gun, Nerin E.
7440
Gunn, Bill
9765
Gunn, Elizabeth
9112
Gunther, John
8668, 8670, 8675, 8676, 9490, 12037
Guppy, Nicholas
12704
Gurney, A. R., Jr.
6945, 7988

Gussman, Boris
10607
Guterman, Norbert
6285, 8050, 11374
Guth, Dorothy L.
4371
Guthrie, A.B., Jr.
6256
Gutman, Robert W.
11210
Gutmann, Assia
3235, 4515
Gwaltney, Francis Irby
10031
Gwyther, John
6452

H

H.D.
3132
H.P.F.
2965, 3718
Haag, John
4002
Haase, John
948, 2973
Habe, Hans
6821, 8568
Hackett, Albert
7102
Hadjidakis, Manos
8567
Hadley, Arthur T.
10200
Haedrich, Marcel
11755
Hagedorn, Hermann
8505, 12142
Hagemann, E.R.
12737
Haggin, B.H.
6790, 9380, 12347
Hague, Albert
6420
Hahn, Emily
82, 112, 320, 470, 492,
747, 799, 887, 1038, 1049,
1150, 1297, 1382, 1514,
1976, 2162, 2295, 2420,
2508, 2607, 2898, 3119, 3501,
3642, 3656, 3688, 3714, 3990,
4600, 4706, 4783, 4816, 4851,
4896, 4947, 5117, 5544, 6609,

8973, 11268
Hahn, Otto
10598
Haig, Alec
11659
Haight, Gordon S.
7873, 7874
Hailey, Oliver
7632, 8317, 12869
Haimsohn, George
6905
Hairston, William
12712
Halasz, Nicholas
6453
Halberstam, David
9632
Haldane, Harry M.
8195
Hale, John
8972
Hale, Nancy
251, 366, 401, 751, 767, 848,
885, 1006, 1018, 1110, 1406,
1436, 1550, 1570, 1601, 1776,
1790, 1835, 1958, 2217, 2292,
2315, 2401, 2444, 3094, 3104,
3168, 3236, 3261, 3284, 3397,
3425, 3596, 3621, 3685, 3758,
3765, 3831, 4106, 4295, 4673,
4691, 4813, 5365, 5520, 6984,
10238
Hale, Robert
2011
Hale, Robert Beverly
1096, 2852
Halévy, Daniel
10140
Haley, Alex
5983
Haley, Glen
5564
Halifax, Edward Frederick
7803
Hall, A. Rupert
7785
Hall, Adam
11935
Hall, Donald
788, 797, 846, 1042, 1242,
1262, 1427, 2365, 2903,
3025, 4383, 4412, 4429,
5441, 7447, 10252, 11937

Hall, Oakley
10857, 12746
Hall, Rémy Ingles
8304
Hall, Willis
6199, 8271, 9448, 11847, 11858
Halliwell, David
7473, 8154
Hallmundsson, Hallberg
5846
Halper, Albert
7733
Halperin, Morton H.
9352
Halsband, Robert
9326
Hamburger, Michael
2303
Hamburger, Philip
495, 501, 626, 750, 905, 917,
1052, 1099, 1136, 1152, 1210,
1260, 1331, 1377, 1391, 1450,
1642, 1667, 1765, 1839, 2061,
2071, 2105, 2138, 2289, 2407,
2458, 2478, 2480, 2500, 2957,
2989, 3050, 3100, 3151, 3262,
3304, 3448, 3479, 3709, 3839,
3909, 3921, 3965, 4132, 4178,
4182, 4187, 4195, 4198, 4208,
4210, 4213, 4214, 4220,
4222, 4239, 4562, 4575, 4798,
4998, 5322, 5432, 5449, 5450,
5462, 5652, 6537, 8730r,
8751r, 8784r, 8912r, 9020r,
9133r, 9529r, 9531r, 9667r,
9676r, 9681r, 9687r,
10178r, 10588r, 10640r,
10776r, 10788r, 11817r,
11973r, 12042r, 12508r,
12735r, 13074r
Hamilton, Alastair
10907
Hamilton, Alexander
5698, 10660
Hamilton, Edith
12414
Hamilton, Gerald
7356
Hamilton, Horace
425
Hamilton, L.D.
3915

Hamilton, Peter
11185
Hamilton, Wallace
6384
Hamm, Harry
6607
Hammarskjöld, Dag
9781
Hammelmann, H.A.
13018
Hammerstein, Oscar, II
7672, 10830, 11807
Hammond, Harold Earl
7098
Hampton, Max
8195
Hamsun, Knut
8495, 10472, 12606
Han Suyin (pseud.)
581, 1940, 4539, 6854, 10090
Handlin, Oscar
5688
Haney, Ray
12799
Hanff, Helene
3599
Hanfstaengl, Ernst
12535
Hangen, Welles
2466
Hankinson, Norman
5206
Hanley, Gerald
7232, 7918
Hanley, James
6544, 8661, 11420
Hanley, William
10002, 11730, 12845
Hansberry, Lorraine
11097, 11657, 12293
Hansen, Agnes Camilla
8045
Hansen, Joseph
1013, 2829, 3102
Hansen, Thorkild
5882
Hanson, Philip
10013
Hanssen, Hans Peter
7092
Harari, Manya
7172
Harburg, E.Y
6934, 8762, 8176

Harding, Walter
  6966
Hardwick, Elizabeth
  826, 3423, 3933, 4291,
  11517, 11684
Hardy, G.H.
  9825
Hardy, René
  6219
Hardy, Thomas
  6992
Hare, Humphrey
  6597, 6886, 7844
Hare, Richard
  10928
Harnack, Curtis
  9511
Harnick, Sheldon
  5879, 6265, 7589, 7613,
  11608, 11739
Harrer, Heinrich
  8514
Harrington, Alan
  9317, 11495
Harrington, Michael
  5600, 10589
Harris, Frank
  10146
Harris, George Washington
  11993
Harris, Jed
  12760
Harris, Jeff
  5835, 12126
Harris, Leon
  10538
Harris, MacDonald
  10985, 12392
Harris, Mark
  9780
Harris, Phyllis
  1719
Harris, Richard
  185, 186, 187, 188, 191,
  1087, 1293, 1640, 2119,
  2174, 4318, 4818, 5154,
  5351
Harris, Seymour
  8817
Harris, Ted
  9852, 11674, 12760
Harrison, Gilbert A.
  7892

Harrison, Harry P.
  6880
Harss, Luis
  9398
Hart, Howard
  10355
Hart, Lorenz
  6318, 6402
Hart, Moss
  5611, 13047
Hart, Robert A.
  8092
Hart, Stan
  9596
Hart-Davis, Rupert
  9281
Hartford, Huntington
  8772
Hartley, L.P.
  8349, 10137, 10767
Harvey, Harriet
  3822
Harwell, Richard B.
  7059
Hasek, Jaroslav
  8013
Haslip, Joan
  9441
Hassall, Christopher
  5749, 6201, 11340
Hassett, William D.
  10436
Hassler, Warren W., Jr.
  7854
Hatch, Alden
  7690, 10091
Hatch, Christopher
  12663
Hatch, James
  7679
Hatfield, Weston P.
  373
Hatsumi, Reiko
  946, 2363
Hauptmann, Gerhart
  7111
Havel, Václav
  8641, 9885
Havoc, June
  9750
Hawes, Elizabeth
  2555, 5458
Hawker, James
  12610

Hawkes, Jacquetta
8847, 12991
Hawkins, John
9333
Hawley, Cameron
9360
Hayes, Alfred
12078
Hayes, Douglas
6713
Hayes, Joseph
6422, 7055
Hayes, Rutherford B.
8232
Haygood, William Converse
8548
Hayman, Jane
2391, 3199
Hays, Elinor Rice
12214
Hays, H. R.
11526
Hayward, John
10622
Hayward, Max
2371, 5553, - 5853, 7172,
8159, 8848
Hayward, William
1575
Haywood, Charles
7681
Haywood, Richard Mansfield
10175
Hazelton, Nika Standen
1169, 2880
Hazzard, Shirley
680, 836, 882, 1401, 1409,
1605, 1942, 2551, 3007,
3398, 3444, 3609, 3664,
3757, 3785, 4309, 4322,
4627, 4727, 5214, 5238,
5346, 5512, 5523
Hearne, John
9072
Hearne, Samuel
6800
Hecht, Anthony
821, 2019, 2579
Hecht, Ben
7796
Heckscher, August
11029

Heckstall-Smith, Anthony
6740
Heer, Friedrich
9847
Heidegger, Martin
7128
Heilbrun, Carolyn G.
7839
Heinrich, Willi
6860
Heinrichs, Waldo H., Jr.
5761
Heinsheimer, Hans W.
6151
Heller, Joseph
6511, 12779
Hellman, Geoffrey T.
42, 132, 452, 481, 650, 671,
672, 734, 1008, 1111, 1163,
1187, 1204, 1312, 1362, 1410,
1480, 1510, 1571, 1784, 1943,
2100, 2106, 2110, 2111, 2112,
2113, 2114, 2184, 2201, 2358,
2961, 3173, 3176, 3447, 3559,
3560, 3561, 3927, 3928, 3935,
4172, 4257, 4258, 4339, 4475,
4660, 4760, 4817, 4901, 4902,
5161, 5194, 5212, 5241, 5242,
5288, 5302, 5366, 5381, 5507
Hellman, Lillian
9086, 9391, 10054, 10153,
12364
Helm, Thomas
11602
Helmore, Thomas
5642
Helprin, Mark Henry
415
Helps, Arthur
6158
Hemenway, Robert
2145, 2530, 3457, 4616, 4734
Hemingway, Ernest
6409
Hemingway, Mary
1112, 1987
Heminway, John Hylan, Jr.
8581
Hemsley, Stuart
4180
Henderson, Archibald
7870

Henderson, Ian
9669
Henderson, Jean
11319
Henderson, Philip
11206, 12901
Henderson, Robert
62, 318, 360, 472, 695,
742, 851, 857, 893, 968,
1047, 1188, 1192, 1237,
1264, 1340, 1475, 1536,
1809, 1973, 2052, 2069,
2083, 2084, 2198, 2568,
2742, 2755, 2789, 2875,
3048, 3057, 3060, 4083,
4547, 4615, 4694, 4743,
5141, 5354
Heneker, David
8157, 8709
Henriques, Robert
8494
Hentoff, Nat
136, 923, 967, 1113, 2254,
2990, 3892, 4988, 5684r,
6928r, 6995r, 7428, 8238,
9043r, 10266r, 10729,
10900r, 11827r, 12180r,
13008r
Heppenstall, Rayner
11111
Her Majesty's Stationery Office
11168
Herbert, F. Hugh
6145
Herbert, John
7709
Herlihy, James Leo
6254, 11892
Herman, Jerry
6990, 8265, 9598, 9650,
9940, 10665
Herman, William
9689
Herold, J. Christopher
5673, 10006
Herrmann, Paul
6770
Hersey, John
1731, 2397, 3625, 11693,
12741
Hervé, Pierre
9030
Herzen, Alexander
10156

Herzing, Albert
4436
Hess, Stephen
11173
Hesse, Hermann
6130, 8856, 10196
Hester, Hal
13070
Hetherington, John
9859
Heurgon, Jacques
6903
Heuvelmans, Bernard
10482
Hewins, Ralph
9989, 11078
Heydenreich, Ludwig H.
9218
Hibbert, Christopher
6812, 7062, 8042, 8557,
8947
Hickey, William
10996
Higgins, Aidan
9079
Hilberry, Conrad
1982
Hileman, Sam
6551, 7006
Hill, Elizabeth Starr
4907
Hill, Errol
9662
Hill, Frank Ernest
7698, 7699
Hill, Herbert
11798
Hill, Lucienne
11477, 12157
Hill, Pati
10832
Hillaby, John
8858, 12716
Hillcourt, William
6021
Hillier, J.
8387
Hills, L. Rust
2104
Hillyer, Robert
365, 1387, 1902, 2353, 2944, 3019,
3195, 3916, 4162, 4249, 5198
Hilsman, Roger
12307

Honegger, Arthur
8510
Hong, Edna
10663
Hong, Howard
10663
Honig, Edwin
3406
Honour, Hugh
6612
Hood, Stuart
10735, 12189
Hook, Sidney
6735
Hooker, Nancy Harvison
10026
Hoopes, Townsend
9354
Hoover, Herbert
5771, 10567
Hoover, James
3543
Hopkins, Gerard
7797, 8758, 12482
Hopkins, Gerard Manley
7813, 9365
Hopkins, Harry
10246
Hoppe, Arthur
569, 2178
Horan, James D.
11474
Horia, Vintila
7112
Hornbein, Thomas F.
7451
Horner, Joyce
2993
Horovitz, Israel
8413, 8649, 10068
Horsley, E. M.
7087
Horthy, Nicholas
5620
Horwitt, Arnold B.
7938
Hoskin, Michael A.
12898
Hoskins, Katherine
1396, 5041, 10608
Hosokawa, Bill
10322
Hotchner, A. E.
12852

Hough, Alfred Lacey
11756
Hough, Henry Beetle
10239
Hough, Richard
195, 199, 1346, 5621, 7009, 9457
House, Homer D.
12880
Household, Geoffrey
5664
Housman, A. E.
5581
Houtchens, Carolyn Washburn
9211, 9212
Houtchens, Lawrence Huston
9211, 9212
Howard, Anthony
11247
Howard, Eleanor Harris
9826
Howard, Elizabeth Jane
1020, 5655, 6158, 9459
Howard, Frances Minturn
353, 3760
Howard, Maureen
10362
Howard, Richard
531, 1473, 2495, 4071, 5989,
6024, 6970, 7618, 7685, 7697,
7747, 8368, 8497, 8625, 9015,
9524, 9731, 9767, 9785, 9854,
9907, 10202, 10593, 10642,
11256, 12372
Howarth, David
7045, 12766, 12781
Howe, George
10087
Howe, Helen
7621
Howe, Irving
12973
Howe, Mark De Wolfe
11601
Howells, William Dean
7130
Howes, Barbara
395, 1281, 1595, 1619, 1724,
1939, 2679, 3088, 3436, 3496,
4174, 4275
Hoyer, Linda Grace
620, 2021a, 3871, 3872, 4974
Hoyle, Fred
7370, 7798, 7822, 9677,
10425, 10586

Hoyt, Edwin P.
5705, 8459, 12074
Hubal, Victor J., Jr.
5119
Hubbell, Albert
1802, 2121, 5928r, 6453r,
9961r, 10399r
Huddleston, Trevor
10210
Hudson, Deatt
2245, 3505, 4480
Hudson, Derek
9299
Hudson, Helen
9917
Hudson, Lois Phillips
1368
Hughes, Cledwyn
11326
Hughes, David
7512, 8240
Hughes, Dorothy
71, 4624
Hughes, Emmet John
10565
Hughes, Emrys
12919
Hughes, H. Stuart
10408
Hughes, John
8653
Hughes, Langston
5653, 6229, 8539, 9080, 10997,
11591, 11683, 12048, 12049
Hughes, Richard
7740
Hughes, Ted
614, 644, 1658, 1663, 2021,
2479, 3213, 3687, 4284, 4365,
4594, 4605, 4853, 4941, 4993
Hughes, V. E.
10147
Hulme, Kathryn
10399
Humes, H. L.
9893
Humphrey, Philip S.
6936
Humphrey, William
3181, 8404, 10573
Humphreys, J. R.
9501
Humphries, Rolfe
739, 1689, 2404, 2828,

3024, 4508, 5125, 6681
Hunt, Hamlin
543
Hunt, Leigh
9212
Hunt, Morton M.
170, 193, 706, 1768, 2095,
2293, 3313, 3773, 3824,
5151, 5358
Hunter, Charlayne
2132, 5007
Hunter, Ian McLellan
7742
Hunter, Jim
10838
Hunter, Kristin
9077
Hunter, N. C.
6949
Hürlimann, Martin
7766, 9815
Hurnscot, Loran
10981
Hurwitz, Samuel J.
12479
Husson, Albert
8250
Hutchens, John K.
10512
Hutchinson, Alfred
11240
Hutchinson, R. C.
9760, 11883
Hutchison, Harold F.
8943
Hutter, Catherine
6821
Huws, Daniel
1467
Huxley, Aldous
7862, 7863, 8248, 9386, 12324
Huxley, Elspeth
7653, 10478
Huxley, Francis
5639
Huxley, Julian
5679, 6563, 10235
Huxley, Laura Archera
12200
Huxley, Matthew
7549
Hyams, Edward
6862, 9107, 9111, 10256,
10257, 12542

Hyland, Stanley
6881
Hyman, Harold M.
8239, 11864
Hyman, Stanley Edgar
8722r, 9085r, 11523, 11932
Hyslop, Francis E., Jr.
6075
Hyslop, Lois Boe
6075

I

Ibsen, Henrik
6322, 7182, 7393, 7901,
8254, 9390, 9811, 10738,
11311, 12879
Idell, Albert
6134
Iglauer, Edith
125, 411, 745, 904, 1519,
3086, 3183, 3788, 3886,
4077
Ignatow, David
4293
Ik, Kim Yong
See Kim, Yong-ik
Imbrie, McCrea
11777
Inge, William
6388, 6925, 9488, 10201,
12841
Inglis, Brian
5586
Ingram, Bowen
1716
Ingram, Kenneth
8370
Ingrams, Richard
10008
Ingstad, Helge
9075
Innes, Hammond
7200
Ionesco, Eugène
6027, 6543, 6729, 7469,
8928, 8941, 9012, 9034, 9176,
9255, 11204, 12603
Irons, Evelyn
1403, 5511
Irvine, William
5867

Irving, Clifford
12179
Irving, David
7061, 7887
Irwin, Ray
838
Irwin, Will
10910
Isaacs, Harold R.
134, 335, 1435, 7349
Isherwood, Christopher
7213, 9855, 11099
Ismay, Hastings Lionel
9878
Israel, Fred L.
11470
Ito, Teiji
6662
Izis
8726
Izzard, Molly
12713
Izzard, Ralph
5589, 12713

J

J.U.
3416, 3451
Jackson, C.
7679
Jackson, Charles
11479
Jackson, Donald
9286
Jackson, Josephine
6115
Jackson, Norman
514
Jackson, Richard
10410
Jackson, Shirley
8225, 12782
Jackson, Stanley
11407
Jackson, W.G.F.
11567
Jacob, Bill
8800
Jacob, Patti
8800
Jacobs, Florence B.
3853

Jacobs, Hayes B.
  244, 485, 2080, 4867,
  5299, 5326, 5572
Jacobsen, Josephine
  2833, 3203, 4272, 5311
Jacobsohn, Annette
  8367
Jacobsohn, Peter
  8367
Jacobson, Dan
  1243, 1782, 2557, 2797,
  3010, 6910, 7458, 10330
Jacobson, Jan
  1014a
Jacobson, Lenore
  11047
Jacquemard, Simonne
  10302
Jaffa, Alisa
  6540
James, Alice
  7099
James, Daniel
  6744
James, Henry
  7398, 8281, 11514, 12905
James, Robert Rhodes
  9480, 11304
James, William
  11517
Jameson, Storm
  7264, 8322, 10053, 11238
Jamiaque, Yves
  10108
Janeway, Elizabeth
  5597, 12164
Janowitz, Morris
  11000
Jarrell, Randall
  303, 2235, 3103, 3314,
  11519
Jarry, Alfred
  11522
Jaspers, Karl
  8078
Javabu, Noni
  7222
Javits, Joan
  8441
Jeal, Tim
  7689
Jeanneret-Gris, Charles Edouard
  10866

Jebb, Caroline
  12934
Jefferson, Thomas
  8789
Jeffreys, Alan
  12641
Jellicoe, Ann
  8977
Jencks, Christopher
  5595
Jenkins, Elizabeth
  7339, 7341
Jenkins, John Holland
  11126
Jenkins, John Holmes, III
  11126
Jenkins, Robin
  7253
Jenkins, Romilly
  6412
Jenkins, Roy
  9984, 12611
Jenks, William A.
  12619
Jennings, Elizabeth
  4139, 12771
Jennings, John
  11236
Jhabvala, R. Prawer
  428, 456, 488, 1318, 2231,
  2281, 2313, 2560, 2919,
  3460, 3672, 4413, 5434,
  7426, 8464, 10208
Jiménez, Juan Ramón
  10843, 11526
John, Errol
  10060
John XXIII
  8559
Johnson, Gerald W.
  9577
Johnson, Greer
  12846
Johnson, James Weldon
  11591
Johnson, Laurie
  9426
Johnson, Lee
  7028
Johnson, Nora
  479, 1037, 1777
Johnson, Nunnally
  8287

Johnson, Pamela Hansford
  6804, 7422, 8491, 10275,
  11021, 11458, 12548
Johnson, Paul
  11955
Johnson, Richard
  7981
Johnson, Robert Owen
  8644
Johnson, Samuel
  7168
Johnson, Stewart
  1847, 3095, 5494
Johnson, Thomas H.
  7352, 9274, 10872
Johnson, Uwe
  11835, 12163, 12492
Johnston, Denis
  8614, 10059, 10310
Johnston, George
  2169, 3415, 4158
Johnston, Johanna
  10005
Jolas, Maria
  6160, 7990, 8636
Jonah, Dolly
  11662
Jonas, Florence
  9270
Jonas, Gerald
  212, 1114, 2236, 3334,
  3900, 4097, 4273, 4667,
  5070, 5477
Jonas, Hans
  7958
Jones, A. H. M.
  9126
Jones, David
  5798, 7412
Jones, Ernest
  9315
Jones, Gwyn
  12711
Jones, Howard Mumford
  10405
Jones, James
  10831, 11767
Jones, Joseph M.
  7592
Jones, Katherine M.
  8314
Jones, L. E.
  7305, 7883

Jones, LeRoi
  7255, 11718, 11719, 12316
Jones, Tom
  6524, 7541, 8515, 10507
Jones, Virgil Carrington
  8052
Jonson, Ben
  5694
Jordan, Hal
  11282
Jordan, John Alfred
  7337
Joseph, Robert L.
  8725
Josephson, Hannah
  5689
Josephson, Matthew
  5689
Joubert de la Ferté, Philip
  Bennet
  11259
Joudry, Patricia
  11532
Jourdain, E. F.
  5623
Joyce, James
  6662, 7263, 7902, 9277,
  9278, 10938, 11882
Joyce, James Avery
  6450
Joyce, Stanislaus
  7263, 10131
Juenger, Ernst
  7945
Jung, Carl Gustav
  9886
Jungk, Robert
  6187, 6347
Junkins, Donald
  5266
Jupp, Kenneth
  6391
Jurkowski, John
  1313
Justice, Donald
  463, 487, 907, 989, 1232,
  2840, 3068, 4934, 5183

K

Kadison, Luba
  6583

Kael, Pauline
532, 3189, 5614r, 5712r,
5729r, 5831r, 5900r, 6049r,
6093r, 6132r, 6215r, 6261r,
6283r, 6304r, 6315r, 6360r,
6373r, 6395r, 6408r, 6443r,
6561r, 6571r, 6573r, 6608r,
6615r, 6717r, 6718r, 6909r,
6971r, 7165r, 7216r, 6245r,
7246r, 7379r, 7499r, 7611r,
7650r, 7738r, 7809r, 7819r,
7821r, 7930r, 8015r, 8024r,
8119r, 8153r, 8158r, 8164r,
8234r, 8262r, 8266r, 8298r,
8233r, 8417r, 8430r, 8479r,
8526r, 8527r, 8541r, 8552r,
8631r, 8692r, 8805r, 8807r,
8930r, 8988r, 8998r, 9002r,
9135r, 9225r, 9372r, 9373r,
9586r, 9607r, 9783r, 9790r,
9829r, 9839r, 9929r, 9942r,
10016r, 10028r, 10288r,
19297r, 10344r, 10448r,
10463r, 10470r, 10625r,
10636r, 10720r, 10841r,
10895r, 10901r, 10964r,
10972r, 10998r, 11060r,
11141r, 11149r, 11279r,
11325r, 11463r, 11475r,
11483r, 11491r, 11497r,
11546r, 11595r, 11596r,
11630r, 11680r, 11845r,
11863r, 11865r, 11884r,
11887r, 11916r, 11946r,
12010r, 12036r, 12073r,
12154r, 12176r, 12230r,
12339r, 12485r, 12555r,
12718r, 12786r, 12793r,
12883r, 13035r, 13046r,
13077r
Kafka, Franz
9152
Kahn, E. J., Jr.
108, 402, 474, 690, 771,
841, 1009, 1115, 1162,
1166, 1291, 1389, 1431,
1511, 1622, 1695, 1837,
1844, 1857, 1960, 2032,
2202, 2216, 2328, 2593,
2602, 2613, 2629, 2654,
2690, 2912, 2914, 2968,
3031, 3040, 3053, 3117,
3231, 3428, 3439, 3662,

3859, 4005, 4041, 4048, 4062,
4104, 4437, 4471, 4527, 4572,
4632, 4701, 4792, 4833, 4861,
5015, 5140, 5259, 5550, 8218,
12616r
Kahn, Herman
12161, 13028
Kaiser, Walter
2837
Kalb, Marvin L.
7277
Kalcheim, Lee
9823, 10690
Kallen, Lucille
9838
Kalven, Harry, Jr.
5778
Kamen, Henry
11828
Kaminsky, Max
10147
Kamp, Irene
8074
Kander, John
6414, 7527, 7670, 8194, 13087
Kaneko, Hisakazu
9734
Kanin, Fay
7847, 11106
Kanin, Garson
6709, 7156, 7913, 8014, 11159
Kanin, Michael
7847, 11106
Kaplan, Justin
9988
Kaplan, Milton
1482
Kaplan, Sol
6045
Kaplon, Morton F.
8399
Kapp, Yvonne
10747
Karamzin, N. M.
9270
Karli, Simon Peter
3234
Karmon, Jonathan
10249
Károlyi, Michael
9882
Karp, David
5719, 9196

Kasrils, Ronald
6985
Kass, Jerome
10045, 11410
Katcher, Leo
6238
Katel, Helen
10947
Katkov, George
11348
Katz, Shlomo
10366
Kauffman, Lane
8419
Kaufman, Esther
13002
Kaufman, George S.
204, 3014, 3294, 5398,
6397, 7120, 10431, 11676,
13047
Kaufman, Shirley
423
Kaufman, Sue
7093, 8104, 8193
Kaufmann, Edgar
5762
Kavaler, Lucy
5950, 10989
Kavanagh, Patrick
6682
Kayne, Richard
11692
Kaz, Fred
7791
Kazan, Molly
5738, 11306
Kazantzakis, Helen
10304
Kazantzakis, Nikos
6383, 7762, 10418, 11171,
11256
Kazin, Alfred
11264r, 11872
Kazin, Pearl
5331
Keane, John B.
11603
Keating, William J.
9703
Kee, Robert
10439
Keefe, Frederick L.
207, 597, 1216, 1515, 2311,
4125, 5287, 5502

Keen, Benjamin
9313, 9335
Keene, Donald
5844, 5845, 8776, 12233
Keep, Anne E.
5906
Kellen, Konrad
11012, 12621
Keller, Martha
1612
Kelley, Reeve Spencer
61, 2298, 3027, 3977, 4524,
4636
Kelley, Robert
12373
Kelley, William Melvin
7234
Kelly, George
11644
Kelly, Gerald R.
9972
Kelly, Tim
6931
Kemal, Yashar
9861
Kemelman, Harry
11412
Kemp, Lysander
715, 1815, 5977
Kempton, Murray
10685
Kendall, Paul Murray
11208, 13044
Kendrick, T. D.
9378
Kennan, George F.
7016, 9866, 11345, 11347,
11350, 11647
Kennaway, James
12347
Kennedy, Adrienne
6635, 7812
Kennedy, Ellen Conroy
9583
Kennedy, Gerta
758
Kennedy, John F.
11005
Kennedy, Ludovic
12084
Kennedy, Margaret
5610, 10365
Kennedy, Michael
10921

Kennedy, X. J.
 1369, 1827, 2751, 3482,
 3586, 10394
Kenner, Hugh
 13015
Kent, Rockwell
 8114, 8753
Kentfield, Calvin
 435, 1833, 1840, 1885, 2296,
 2774, 3163, 4154, 4193,
 5113, 5695
Kenyon, J. P.
 11941
Kepler, Johannes
 8913
Kerans, J. S.
 7425
Kerensky, Alexander
 11344
Kerman, Joseph
 10547
Kerman, Sheppard
 6889, 9998
Kermode, Frank
 11046
Kern, Alfred
 9067
Kern, Jerome
 9195
Kerouac, Jack
 7080, 9445, 11947, 12411
Kerr, Jean
 7999, 9799, 10898
Kerr, Walter
 7018, 7999, 8471
Kerrigan, Anthony
 4877, 7533, 11186
Kerrigan, Elaine
 11437, 12915
Kersh, Gerald
 7737
Kersten, Felix
 8914
Kesey, Ken
 10499
Kessel, Joseph
 9366
Kesselring, Alfred
 8915
Kessler, Edward
 3159
Kessler, Lyle
 12765

Kessler, Robert
 10403
Kesten, Hermann
 6478
Ketchum, Richard
 10579
Kettlewell, H. B. D.
 6563
Khaldun, Ibn
 10103
Khan, Ismith
 8883
Khosla, G. D.
 8347
Kidd, David
 102, 144, 983, 1190, 2087,
 4010, 4196, 4393
Kidder Smith, G. E.
 8745
Kiel, Hanna
 6135
Kiely, Benedict
 1189, 1875, 2002, 2077, 2088,
 2394, 4379, 5207, 5418, 5440, 6455
Kieran, John
 10204, 10368
Kierkegaard, Søren
 9123, 10663
Kilbracken, John Raymond Godley
 12576
Kilmartin, Terrence
 6556
Kilty, Jerome
 6987
Kilvert, Francis
 8932
Kim, Richard E.
 9798
Kim, Yong-ik
 4298
Kimble, George H. T.
 12417
Kimche, David
 6648
Kimche, Jon
 6648
King, Francis
 1491, 6929, 9688
King, Henry C.
 12990
King, Larry L.
 10526
King, Martin Luther, Jr.
 11931

King, William
11886
Kingsley, Sidney
10284
Kingston, Jeremy
1172, 1218
Kinkead, Eugene
3602, 4648, 4906
Kinkead, Katharine T.
587, 2339, 4153, 4497, 5330
Kinnell, Galway
1648, 2470, 4035, 4553,
6219, 12807
Kinoy, Ernest
6022, 7993, 11778
Kinross, Patrick
391, 2932, 4072, 4751 6163
Kipphardt, Heinar
8626
Kirk, Russell
6166, 8682, 10456
Kirkland, Edward Chase
6566
Kirkland, Jack
9726
Kirkpatrick, B. L.
8046
Kirkpatrick, Irone
10122
Kirkpatrick, Lyman B., Jr.
11116
Kirkup, James
60, 477, 1285, 2364, 3458,
4305, 4770, 6903, 10799
Kirkwood, James
12501
Kirkwood, Patricia Frueh
8913
Kirst, Hans Hellmut
11198, 10439
Kirschenbaum, Leo
2167
Kissinger, Henry A.
5772
Kitt, Eartha
12254
Klass, Rosanne
9071
Klee, Ernst
6210
Klee, Felix
10721

Klein, Alexander
6819, 7360
Klein, Martin J.
9291
Klein, Paul
10071
Klein, William
11271
Kline, George L.
11353
Klochko, Mikhail A.
11822
Klyhn, Joan
3207
Knapp, Bettina
12130
Knebel, Fletcher
12577
Knight, Arthur
9408
Knott, Frederick
12699, 13009
Knowles, Horace
7867
Knowles, John
11541
Knowlton, Robert A.
81
Knowlton, Robert E.
7285
Kober, Arthur
1808, 2060, 2166, 3830,
5380, 9933
Kobler, John
5567
Koch, Kenneth
6140, 12116, 12223
Koenig, Laird
7217
Koenig, Louis W.
8699, 10959
Koestler, Arthur
9504, 11143, 11726, 12369
Kohl, Herbert
12180
Kolko, Gabriel
12787
Koningsberger, Hans
777, 2632, 2651
Kopit, Arthur
6960, 8651, 10445

Kops, Bernard
7141, 8166
Korall, Burt
8782
Korbonski, Stefan
7601
Korngold, Ralph
12113
Koš, Erih
6186
Kossar, Leon
11943
Kossenko, Z. V.
12211
Kotker, Norman
4564
Kovach, Nora
9191
Koven, Stanley
4340, 6927, 9990
Kozodoy, Neal
8799
Kozol, Jonathan
6995, 7804
Kraft, Hy
6420
Kraft, Ken
1534
Kramarz, Joachim
11874
Kramer, Arthur
4595
Kramer, Gerhard
12785
Kramer, Jane
1785, 2915, 3680, 4422
Kramer, Lawrence
3061
Kramm, Joseph
1778a
Kramrisch, Stella
5909
Kraslow, David
6535, 11493
Krasna, Norman
9527, 11977, 12861
Krepps, Robert W.
7269
Kristol, Irving
6763
Kroeber, Theodora
8719

Kroll, Ernest
1524, 1541, 3069
Kronenberger, Louis
8095, 12633
Kropotkin, Peter
9871
Krott, Peter
7037
Kruger, Rayne
8023
Krutch, Joseph Wood
8290, 12387, 12669
Kubie, Nora Benjamin
11246
Kubly, Herbert
5775, 7276
Kuby, Erich
11305, 11704
Kuh, Katherine
6331
Kumin, Maxine W.
1556, 1669, 1913, 1972,
2055, 2985, 3179, 3917,
4116, 5319
Kummer, Clare
8289
Kunitz, Stanley
1636, 11521
Kunstler, William M.
9951
Kürenberg, Joachim von
8897
Kurnitz, Harry
10488, 11641
Kurt, Richard
12421
Kurtz, Harold
12402
Kuzma, Greg
2232

L

La Farge, Oliver
145, 602, 800, 976, 1932,
2390, 2766, 3220, 4308,
10813
La Rochelle, Pierre Drieu
7618
La Touche, John
6033, 12574
Labin, Suzanne
5843

Laborde, Jean
 7512, 10992
Lacouture, Jean
 7311, 12621
Lacouture, Simonne
 7311
Lady Gregory
 See Gregory, Isabella Augusta
Lafore, Laurence
 9455
Laforgue, Jules
 11527
Lagerkvist, Pär
 8311, 11648
Lagus, Charles
 10551
Lahr, John
 10379
Laird, Bailey
 3820
Lait, Robert
 9810
Lake, Carlton
 1627, 2816, 9341
Lalić, Mihailo
 12695
Lambert, Derek
 5823
Lamkin, Speed
 6714
Lamming, George
 7350
Lamont, Lansing
 6954
Lamott, Kenneth
 1924, 2855, 4468, 5333, 12858
Lampedusa, Giuseppe di
 9219
Lampell, Millard
 12720
Lamport, Felicia
 1981
Lanahan, Frances
 3026
Lancaster, Osbert
 8297
Lanchberry, Edward
 10170
Land, Barbara
 2557a
Land, Myrick
 2557a, 7608

Landesman, Fran
 10221
Landesman, Jay
 10221
Lane, Burton,
 10468
Lane, Helen R.
 8082, 9229, 9733
Lane, Richard
 9819
Lang, Cecil Y.
 12015
Lang, Daniel
 59, 714, 1274, 1284, 1415,
 1463, 2151, 2297, 2626,
 2631, 2636, 2902, 3131,
 3170, 3218, 3691, 3764,
 4054, 4263, 4645, 4839,
 4999, 5162, 5168, 5181
Lang, Paul Henry
 7875
Lang, Theo
 6933
Langdon-Davies, John
 6466
Langer, Susanne K.
 9947
Langfus, Anna
 9499
Langland, Joseph
 938, 969, 1408, 1761, 4183,
 4270, 5464, 10877
Langui, Emile
 7596
Lansing, Alfred
 7390
Lape, Esther Everett
 9846
Lapierre, Dominique
 8716, 10562
Lapp, Ralph E.
 8927
Lardner, John
 431, 1910, 2682, 3038, 3731,
 4333, 4800, 5576, 5622r,
 5625r, 5758r, 6133r, 6189r,
 6254r, 6264r, 6432r, 6437r,
 6498r, 6695r, 6714r, 6975r,
 6851r, 7169r, 7183r, 7231r,
 7292r, 7410r, 7434r, 7482r,
 7595r, 7940r, 7999r, 8059r,
 8071r, 8139r, 8165r, 8171r,

8227r, 8253r, 8319r, 8483r,
8516r, 8813r, 8910r, 8922r,
9120r, 9298r, 9629r, 9671r,
9789r, 9833r, 9853r, 9896r,
9965r, 10055r, 10104r,
10120r, 10276r, 10459r,
10467r, 10488r, 10516r,
10606r, 10629r, 10712r,
10751r, 10772r, 10774r,
10846r, 10850r, 10858r,
10904r, 10937r, 11145r, 11565r,
11652r, 11687r, 11708r, 11735r,
11748r, 11806r, 11811r, 11885r,
11907r, 11984r, 12056r, 12193r,
12351r, 12446r, 12463r, 12818r,
12861r, 12873r, 12874r, 12927r,
12985r, 19964r,

Lardner, Ring, Jr.
7742
Lardner, Susan
5946r, 6234r, 6296r, 6690r,
7389r, 7402r, 7439r, 7609r,
8016r, 8340r, 8480r, 8837r,
8863r, 8920r, 9320r, 9652r,
9926r, 9958r, 10186r,
10223r, 10360r, 10902r,
11495r, 11717r, 11893r,
12006r, 12019r, 12215r,
12517r, 12553r, 12831r,
12916r, 13012r, 10727r,
13033r
Larimer, Robert
8954
Larkin, Margaret
11568
Larkin, Philip
9254
Larrabee, Eric
2673
Larsen, Otto
10303
Larson, Mervin W.
5715
Larson, Peggy Pickering
5715
Lasker, Harvey
10453
Laski, Audrey
7187
Lathen, Emma
12826
Latour, Anny
6293, 8962

Lattimore, Owen
10352
Lattimore, Richmond
202, 386, 1732, 1841, 2461,
3371, 4115, 4344, 4416,
4517, 5069, 8099, 10419
Lauer, Stefanie
8406
Laurence, Dan H.
6138, 8476
Laurence, Margaret
12195
Laurence, William L.
9889
Laurents, Arthur
5861, 6651, 8142, 8161,
8702
Lavender, David
12804
Laver, James
6161, 7304, 9736, 10023,
10111, 12612
Lavin, Mary
577, 1001, 1884, 1927, 1971,
2206, 2256, 2768, 2841,
2850, 3552, 4290, 5533
Lawder, Donald, Jr.
3792, 4279, 5439
Lawler, Ray
11963
Lawrence, Barbara
1173
Lawrence, D. H.
6696, 6745, 6899, 6938,
9053, 9143, 12876
Lawrence, Eddie
8907
Lawrence, Jack
8518, 13082
Lawrence, Jerome
5976, 6426, 6990, 7835,
8658, 9650, 10535
Lawrence, Merloyd
7121
Lawrence, Reginald
9208
Laws, Maury
10052
Lazar, Nicolas
8726
Lazard, Naomi
161, 5283

Le Clézio, J. M. G.
7582
Le Comte, Edward
10384
Le Corbusier
See Jeanneret-Gris, Charles
Edouard
Le Gallienne, Eva
12879
Lea, Tom
8956
Leary, Paris
1061, 1557
Leasor, James
6657, 9945, 10522, 11132,
12537
Léautaud, Paul
6597, 8840
Leavis, F. R.
6898, 9199, 11454
Leavis, Q. D.
9199
Lebeck, Michael
6788
Leckie, Robert
12751
Lederer, William J.
12502
Ledig, Gert
12345
Leduc, Violette
8994, 12953
Lee, Alwyn
940, 1909
Lee, C. Y.
2908, 4241, 4242, 4243, 4244,
4245
Lee, Gypsy Rose
6883
Lee, Harper
12303
Lee, Laurie
260, 7295, 11302
Lee, Leonard
6979
Lee, Robert E.
5976, 6426, 6990, 7835, 8658,
9650, 10535
Lee, Robert S.
11241
Lefebvre, Georges
7770

Leffland, Ella
1315
Leggett, John
12890
Lehane, Brendan
11067
Lehman, Leo
7275
Lehman, Milton
12188
Leigh, Carolyn
8472, 9397, 12889
Leigh, Mitch
9683
Leishman, J. B.
11524
Leitch, David
7135
Leites, Nathan
11332
Leivick, H.
8001
Lely, Gilbert
12617
Lemon, Richard
150, 665, 910, 1116, 2096,
2097, 2839, 3410
Lenard, Alexander
12570
L'Engle, Madeleine
9534
Lengyel, Jozsef
7783
Lennon, Peter
38
Lenormand, H. R.
7507
Leon, Felix
13090
Leonard, Hugh
10882, 11881
Leonard, John
10185
Leonard, Michael
8474
Leonhard, Wolfgang
6599
Leopold, Nathan F., Jr.
9336
Lerner, Alan Jay
6430, 6670, 10135, 10468
Lerner, I. Michael
11228

Lerner, Jean
11012
Lerner, Max
5753
Leroux, Etienne
11558
Leslie, Anita
10003
Lessing, Doris
3046, 3245, 4883, 6604,
7730, 7992, 8610, 10847
Lethaby, W.R.
5885
Levaillant, Maurice
10704
Levenson, J.C.
9948
Leverson, Ada
9401
Levi, Carlo
9363, 12966
Levi, Peter S.J.
13041
Levi, Primo
11120
Levi, Stephen
6923
Leviant, Curt
2469
Levin, Harry
6785
Levin, Ira
6859, 7162, 7221, 7859,
8683, 10341
Levin, Martin
7639
Levine, Issac Don
9950
Levine, Philip
732, 1010, 2865
Levine, Robert A.
5894
Levinson, Ben
13061
Levitt, Saul
5813
Levron, J.
12593
Levy, Benn W.
11102, 12436
Levy, Newman
10189

Lewin, John
8452
Lewin, Ralph A.
2567
Lewine, Richard
7938
Lewis, Allen Jack
6805
Lewis, Anthony
183, 10914
Lewis, Arthur H.
6962
Lewis, Bernard
5944
Lewis, C.S.
9271, 12266
Lewis, C. Day
See Day Lewis, C.
Lewis, David L.
8937
Lewis, Edward
10725
Lewis, Flora
3282, 3522
Lewis, Grace Hegger
12937
Lewis, Meriwether
9286
Lewis, Norman
1000, 2014, 2062, 2598,
2633, 3959, 5929
Lewis, Oscar
7642, 8334, 9043
Lewis, R.W.B.
10800
Lewis, Robert
9915
Lewis, W.H.
5947, 9271, 9507, 11422,
11987
Lewis, Wilmarth Sheldon
8424
Lewis, Wyndham
7036, 9290, 11529
Ley, Willy
10598
Leyda, Jay
7604, 7605
Leymarie, Jean
9752
Lhote, Henri
11469

Li, Mirok
13018
Liberman, Alexander
5919
Libott, Robert Yale
12333
Licht, Fred S.
5229
Liddell Hart, B. H.
9306, 9307
Lidman, Hans
10754
Lieberman, Herbert
9832
Lieberman, Laurence
4975, 5111, 5144, 5484
Lieberman, Leo
1470, 6456
Liebling, A. J.
29, 77, 93, 116, 258, 331,
433, 467, 510, 708, 847,
861, 970, 1048, 1180, 1235,
1298, 1372, 1883, 1886,
1968, 2022, 2290, 2621,
2625, 2628, 2678, 2683,
2802, 2982, 3015, 3082,
3122, 3123, 3298, 3317,
3318, 3394, 3443, 3469,
3689, 3815, 3855, 3866,
4044, 4015, 4089, 4090,
4091, 4092, 4093, 4094,
4095, 4096, 4380, 4522,
4533, 4596, 4638, 4821,
4921, 4956, 5254, 5335,
5392, 5802r, 6252r, 6801r,
7744r, 8915r, 9309r, 9435r,
9936r, 10103r, 10370r,
10862r, 11075r, 11172r,
11452r, 11759r, 11879r,
Lieris, Michel
9731
Lifton, Robert Jay
6997
Lilienthal, David E.
8842
Liljenquist, Don C.
12949
Lilly, John C.
9655
Lim, Janet
11754
Lin Tai-yi
7284, 8900, 9349

Lincoln, Abraham
9414
Lincoln, Victoria
6919
Lind, Jakov
6823, 7415
Lindbergh, Anne Morrow
7910
Lindley, Denver
6230
Lindner, Robert
10123
Lindop, Audrey Erskine
9982
Lindsay, Howard
5862, 8085, 8188, 9995,
12047
Linell, Rosamund
8496a
Link, Arthur S.
12906, 12907
Link, Peter
11384
Linklater, Eric
7555, 11449  12506
Linson, Corwin K.
10160
Lippa, Louis A.
6329, 11555
Lippmann, Walter
6737, 11030
Lipsky, Eleazar
11446
Lipton, James
10391, 11618
Lissner, Ivar
6419
Lister, R. P.
10, 139, 162, 308, 413, 528,
685, 842, 899, 963, 1029,
1085, 1146, 1272, 1638,
1873, 1891, 1898, 2134,
2158, 2247, 2757, 2788,
3217, 3363, 3365, 3453,
3483, 3491, 3502, 3510,
3528, 3534, 3674, 3686,
3721, 3761, 4351, 4461,
4504, 4554, 4684, 4746,
5038, 5467, 5478, 8202
Littell, Blaine
11815
Little, Malcolm
5983

Lowell, Amy
6746
Lowell, Robert
7385, 7691, 8580, 9337,
10212, 10455
Lowenstein, Elsa B.
9659
Lowndes, Marie Belloc
13057
Lowrie, Donald A.
8499
Lowry, Malcolm
1252, 12507
Lubell, Samuel
12850
Lucáks, Georg
11944
Lucas, F. L.
8097, 11468
Lucas-Dubreton, J.
6294
Lucie-Smith, Edward
2291
Ludwig, Jack
5591
Luethy, Herbert
7746
Lukacs, John
8371
Luke, Peter
8151
Lumet, Baruch
10493
Lunt, James D.
11426
Lurie, Alison
11118
Lustig, Theodore H.
11704
Luttwak, Edward
6830
Lutyens, Emily
6442
Lyford, Joseph P.
5684
Lynd, Staughton
10353
Lynes, Russell
7186
Lynn, Kenneth S.
7225
Lynne, James Broom
12409

Lyon, Mary
8046
Lyon, Peter
11949

M

Maas, Audrey Gellen
12698
Maass, John
7921
MacArthur, Charles
7796
MacArthur, Douglas
11160
Macaulay, Pauline
5952
Macaulay, Rose
9103, 9292, 10860, 12356
McAvity, Helen
9826
MacBeth, George
387, 2563, 4070, 4584, 5297
McCague, James
7588
McCardell, Lee
8564
McCarten, John          1778ar,
2324, 5592r, 5607r, 5629r,
5635r, 5637r, 5641r, 5647r,
5658r, 5662r, 5665r, 5670r,
5687r, 5693r, 5694r, 5703r,
5710r, 5721r, 5731r, 5747r,
5797r, 5751r, 5801r, 5811r,
5814r, 5829r, 5837r, 5840r,
5857r, 5859r, 5861r, 5863r,
5865r, 5873r, 5879r, 5887r,
5899r, 5926r, 5935r, 5941r,
5952r, 5957r, 5972r, 5991r,
5997r, 6006r, 6008r, 6010r,
6012r, 6014r, 6019r, 6022r,
6023r, 6032r, 6034r, 6040r,
6050r, 6053r, 6057r, 6063r,
6070r, 6078r, 6083r, 6086r, 6089r,
6091r, 6097r, 6098r, 6111r,
6117r, 6121r, 6128r, 6131r,
6146r, 6154r, 6167r, 6168r,
6171r, 6176r, 6179r, 6181r,
6184r, 6185r, 6195r, 6214r,
6223r, 6231r, 6233r, 6255r,
6260r, 6267r, 6272r, 6282r,
6325r, 6326r, 6339r, 6350r,
6358r, 6363r, 6374r, 6389r,

6392r, 6393r, 6401r, 6414r,
6415r, 6416r, 6420r, 6422r,
6426r, 6429r, 6430r, 6436r,
6456r, 6461r, 6469r, 6470r,
6484r, 6485r, 6491r, 6500r,
6506r, 6510r, 6512r, 6516r,
6548r, 6552r, 6580r, 6601r,
6611r, 6613r, 6631r, 6653r,
6701r, 6703r, 6709r, 6732r,
6742r, 6751r, 6756r, 6768r,
6769r, 6791r, 6815r, 6828r,
6835r, 6836r, 6838r, 6839r,
6844r, 6859r, 6871r, 6874r,
6901r, 6908r, 6911r, 6922r,
6923r, 6940r, 6946r, 6952r,
6980r, 6988r, 7026r, 7029r,
7038r, 7040r, 7048r, 7050r,
7052r, 7056r, 7071r, 7072r,
7074r, 7081r, 7103r, 7120r,
7148r, 7153r, 7156r, 7157r,
7159r, 7162r, 7167r, 7174r,
7175r, 7178r, 7189r, 7192r,
7195r, 7221r, 7228r, 7250r,
7258r, 7270r, 7272r, 7275r,
7294r, 7297r, 7309r, 7318r,
7343r, 7347r, 7377r, 7391r,
7403r, 7408r, 7444r, 7453r,
7455r, 7481r, 7491r, 7496r,
7497r, 7504r, 7510r, 7527r,
7547r, 7548r, 7553r, 7571r,
7589r, 7630r, 7632r, 7638r,
7647r, 7670r, 7694r, 7695r,
7700r, 7703r, 7715r, 7722r,
7725r, 7742r, 7765r, 7771r,
7777r, 7794r, 7800r, 7802r,
7807r, 7808r, 7810r, 7825r,
7841r, 7847r, 7850r, 7859r,
7860r, 7894r, 7903r, 7907r,
7908r, 7911r, 7914r, 1713r,
7924r, 7925r, 7926r, 7927r,
7931r, 7939r, 7947r, 7948r,
7949r, 7971r, 7980r, 7981r,
7986r, 7897r, 8011r, 8039r,
8053r, 8064r, 8074r, 8076r,
8077r, 8107r, 8108r, 8109r,
8121r, 8141r, 8154r, 8157r,
8160r, 8161r, 8163r, 8170r,
8173r, 8176r, 8179r, 8183r,
8187r, 8192r, 8204r, 8223r,
8228r, 8233r, 8249r, 8260r,
8263r, 8265r, 8271r, 8287r,
8302r, 8313r, 8324r, 8433r,
8335r, 8336r, 8437r, 8344r,

8350r, 8351r, 8381r, 8390r,
8393r, 8401r, 8405r, 8410r,
8416r, 8429r, 8431r, 8436r,
8463r, 8472r, 8475r, 8477r,
8482r, 8484r, 8487r, 8508r,
8509r, 8515r, 8518r, 8533r,
8535r, 8538r, 8540r, 8551r,
8553r, 8556r, 8561r, 8567r,
8569r, 8577r, 8578r, 8579r,
8591r, 8506r, 8619r, 8634r,
8639r, 8652r, 8660r, 8679r,
8688r, 8697r, 8702r, 8703r,
8709r, 8711r, 8715r, 8721r,
8723r, 8746r, 8747r, 8754r,
8779r, 8790r, 8823r, 8827r,
8844r, 8865r, 8866r, 8878r,
8879r, 8901r, 8904r, 8905r,
8907r, 8908r, 8917r, 8925r,
8929r, 8939r, 8946r, 8950r,
8960r, 8968r, 8971r, 8991r,
9007r, 9024r, 9036r, 9038r,
9052r, 9054r, 9056r, 9060r,
9062r, 9069r, 9073r, 9088r,
9090r, 9092r, 9099r, 9101r,
9109r, 9117r, 9118r, 9134r,
9136r, 9161r, 9193r, 9202r,
9235r, 9257r, 9258r, 9269r,
9301r, 9343r, 9371r, 9377r,
9391r, 9397r, 9399r, 9400r,
9406r, 9416r, 9422r, 9443r,
9456r, 9468r, 9470r, 9479r,
9483r, 9575r, 9527r, 9533r,
9536r, 9537r, 9546r, 9551r,
9552r, 9555r, 9557r, 9572r,
9578r, 9579r, 9580r, 9588r,
9595r, 9596r, 9616r, 9643r,
9649r, 9650r, 9651r, 9653r,
9665r, 9670r, 9674r, 9675r,
9683r, 9697r, 9698r, 9700r,
9711r, 9714r, 9716r, 9719r,
9726r, 9748r, 9750r, 9756r,
9762r, 9766r, 9778r, 9797r,
9799r, 9818r, 9822r, 9826r,
9842r, 9845r, 9850r, 9895r,
9901r, 9909r, 9923r, 9995r,
9940r, 9951r, 9952r, 9953r,
9995r, 10000r, 10002r,
10010r, 10014r, 10015r,
10048r, 10056r, 10082r,
10088r, 10093r, 10108r,
10117r, 10152r, 10153r,
10161r, 10164r, 10180r,
10184r, 10198r, 10201r,

10205r, 10225r, 10227r,
10228r, 10274r, 10284r,
10286r, 10287r, 10292r,
10293r, 10295r, 10299r,
10308r, 10313r, 10319r,
10339r, 10342r, 10349r,
10363r, 10391r, 10400r,
10414r, 10416r, 10421r,
10424r, 10447r, 10450r,
10457r, 10462r, 10468r,
10475r, 10487r, 10489r,
10494r, 10500r, 10507r,
10521r, 10532r, 10550r,
10552r, 10558r, 10569r,
10602r, 10618r, 10619r,
10639r, 10641r, 10651r,
10653r, 10675r, 10675r,
10696r, 10702r, 10707r,
10715r, 10716r, 10791r,
10762r, 10766r, 10770r,
10781r, 10783r, 10789r,
19795r, 10799r, 10707r,
10808r, 10826r, 10855r,
18864r, 10826r, 10855r,
10864r, 10894r, 10898r,
10905r, 10906r, 10911r,
10931r, 10934r, 10936r,
10940r, 10970r, 10975r,
10982r, 10986r, 10988r,
10990r, 10995r, 11008r,
11019r, 11020r, 11024r,
11026r, 11028r, 11037r,
11041r, 11064r, 11076r,
11086r, 11094r, 11095r,
11096r, 11101r, 11102r,
11107r, 11113r, 11115r,
11121r, 11146r, 11154r,
11189r, 11199r, 11204r,
11209r, 11211r, 11214r,
11215r, 11218r, 11225r,
11231r, 11250r, 11251r,
11278r, 11280r, 11283r,
11286r, 11290r, 11299r,
11303r, 11307r, 11310r,
11312r, 11316r, 11320r,
11324r, 11329r, 11335r,
11337r, 11362r, 11369r,
11370r, 11371r, 11389r,
11404r, 11416r, 11421r,
11425r, 11432r, 11434r,
11460r, 11462r, 11499r,
11508r, 11533r, 11536r,
11543r, 11545r, 11547r,

11557r, 11564r, 11570r,
11575r, 11578r, 11611r,
11617r, 11618r, 11641r,
11642r, 11644r, 11645r,
11657r, 11672r, 11677r,
11679r, 11696r, 11697r,
11714r, 11716r, 11729r,
11730r, 11738r, 11744r,
11757r, 11762r, 11764r,
11768r, 11772r, 11778r,
11779r, 11780r, 11781r,
11793r, 11799r, 11805r,
11816r, 11826r, 11839r,
11846r, 11848r, 11849r,
11859r, 11867r, 11876r,
11877r, 11891r, 11901r,
11903r, 11904r, 11906r,
11913r, 11914r, 11919r,
11923r, 11945r, 11948r,
11953r, 11965r, 11971r,
11977r, 11995r, 12002r,
12011r, 12028r, 12032r,
12043e, 12048r, 12058r,
12059r, 12060r, 12064r,
12065r, 12067r, 12068r,
12069r, 12075r, 12080r,
12082r, 12092r, 12093r,
12119r, 12122r. 12123r,
12125r, 12144r, 12151r,
12166r, 12173r, 12174r,
12183r, 12187r, 12198r,
12217r, 12220r, 12222r,
12225r, 12227r, 12229r,
12226r, 12237r, 12241r,
12260r, 12263r, 12269r,
12272r, 12281r, 12285r,
12286r, 12296r, 12308r,
12328r, 12331r, 12332r,
12334r, 12336r, 12338r,
12341r, 12349r, 12351r,
12353r. 12378r, 12379r,
12382r, 12393r, 12404r,
12418r, 12440r, 12455r,
12501r, 12509r, 12519r,
12527r, 12528r, 12534r,
12547r, 12550r, 12588r,
12594r, 12598r, 12628r.
12635r, 12641r, 12642r,
12646r, 12650r, 12660r,
12670r, 12692r, 12697r,
12699r, 12720r, 12721r,
12747r, 12774r, 12777r,
12780r, 12783r, 12800r,

12810r, 12817r, 12841r,
12843r, 12852r, 12857r,
12866r, 12879r, 12882r,
12884r, 12886r, 12887r,
12889r, 12895r, 12909r,
12931r, 12940r, 12942r,
12946r, 12950r, 12951r,
12955r, 12976r, 12995r,
13006r, 13009r, 13013r,
13020r, 13036r, 13047r,
13048r, 13059r, 13065r,
13071r, 13090r
McCarthy, Cormac
   10611
McCarthy, Mary
   269, 815, 2073, 3554, 3823,
   4088, 4324, 8490r
McClellan, George B., Jr.
   7865
McCloskey, Mark
   3055
McClure, James G.
   2731
MacColl, René
   11261
McComb, A. K.
   11510
McConkey, James
   1383, 1411
McConnell, Will
   3817
McCord, David
   349, 1537
McCord, William
   11852
McCormick, Carolyn
   4820
McCormick, Harold W.
   11588
McCoubrey, John W.
   5923
McCoy, Donald R.
   6428
MacCuish, David
   7154
McCullers, Carson
   6658, 11857
McCullough, David G.
   8824
MacDermot, Galt
   8155
MacDiarmid, Hugh
   6686

MacDonagh, Donagh
   8185, 10621
MacDonald, Betty
   10533
Macdonald, Dwight
   72, 713, 1552, 1649, 2399,
   2971, 3186, 3725, 4426,
   5040, 5770r, 5984r, 6998r,
   7109r, 7603r, 7604r, 7605r,
   8640r, 8767r, 9374r, 9408r,
   9860r, 9872, 10096r,
   10145r, 10387r, 10589r,
   10613r, 10682, 10941r,
   11249r, 11355r, 12674r,
   12787r, 12790r,
MacDonald, Malcolm
   6299
MacDonald, Robert David
   12734
McDougall, Colin
   7462
MacDougall, Roger
   8325
McElwee, William
   12929
McEnroe, Robert E.
   7192
McEwen, John
   7576
McFarlane, James
   5882
McFarlane, Kathleen
   5882
MacFarquhar, Roderick
   8493
McGahern, John
   4662
McGill, Ralph
   11813
McGinley, Phyllis
   298, 540, 736, 1226, 1661,
   1792, 2398, 2485, 3386,
   4537, 4545, 4546, 4880,
   4957, 5180, 5300
McGinniss, Joe
   11531
MacGrath, Leueen
   11676
McGrath, Russell
   8701
McGurn, Barrett
   7013
McHugh, Heather
   1178

McHugh, Robert
6062
MacInnes, Colin
7396
McIver, Ray
7970
MacKaye, Percy
2260
McKee, Alexander
7786
McKelway, St. Clair
66, 181, 254, 450, 701, 702,
703, 704, 705, 764, 840, 850,
1117, 1225, 1300, 1542, 1555,
1713, 1957, 2103, 2307, 2425,
2713, 3116, 3296, 3300, 3301,
3303, 3498, 3821, 3877, 3878,
3879, 3880, 3891, 3897, 3962,
4212, 4391, 4400, 4465, 4758,
4799, 4819, 4846, 5030, 5153,
5370, 7145r, 8409r, 12018r,
12640r
Macken, Walter
1744, 2450, 3353
MacKendrick, Paul
10125
McKenna, Richard
11395
MacKenzie, Compton
12158
McKisack, May
7732
McKnight, Gerald
12591
McLanathan, Richard
8574
McLaughlin, Robert
10383
MacLean, Alistair
11498
Maclean, Fitzroy
8305, 10773
MacLean, Joan
10513
MacLeish, Archibald
8755, 8756
MacLennan, Hugh
12758
McLeod, Enid
12565
Macleod, Iain
10230

McLiam, John
11685
MacLiammóir, Micheál
8528
McLuhan, Marshall
12530
Macmillan, Harold
6237, 12257
McMillan, Patricia Johnson
12461
McMinnies, Mary
12659
McMullen, Henry T.
5521
McNally, Terrence
5811, 9060, 10265, 10354,
12005, 12939
MacNeice, Louis
6683, 11938
MacNeil, Neil
7704
McNevin, Michael
1764
McNulty, Faith
865, 1118, 1691, 2329,
4560, 4860, 5260
McNulty, John
2204, 2860, 5363
McPhee, John
380, 1517, 1521, 1634,
1964, 2336, 2538, 2703,
3576, 3777, 4147, 4314,
4767
MacQueen, John
10623
Macrory, Patrick A.
7591
Maddux, Rachel
8105
Magalaner, Marvin
8768
Magarshack, David
7977, 9293, 9385, 12441
Magaziner, Sari
2747
Magdalany, Philip
6856, 12763
Magidoff, Robert
7490
Magnus, Philip
8975
Magoon, Eaton, Jr.
12174

Magurn, Ruth Saunders
9282
Mahoney, Bill
10167
Mailer, Norman
1388, 1855, 5633, 7023, 7024
Maine, René
12367
Maisky, Ivan
9873
Majdalany, Fred
6065, 6067
Malamud, Bernard
4674, 5948, 7649, 10245
Malanga, Gerard
4764
Malaparte, Curzio
12212
Malcolm, Angus
11163
Malcolm, Donald 1119, 1154ar,
5810r, 5847r, 5850r,
5920r, 5967r, 6025r, 6031r,
6087r, 6300r, 6329r, 6377r,
6520r, 6557r, 6666r, 6766r,
6827r, 6875r, 7008r, 7019r,
7027r, 7122r, 7146r, 7257r,
7310r, 7332r, 7393r, 7417r,
7433r, 7507r, 7523r,
7534r, 7535r, 7541r,
7552r, 7680r, 7716r, 7846r,
7885r, 7896r, 7909r, 7919r,
7995r, 8001r, 8003r, 8028r,
8148r, 8156r, 8166r, 8206r,
8269r, 8272r, 8278r, 8279r,
8665r, 8706r, 8754r, 8757r,
8854r, 8867r, 8928r, 8946r,
8985r, 9032r, 9053r, 9195r,
9209r, 9302r, 9396r, 9420r,
9431r, 9575r, 9584r, 9592r,
9621r, 9631r, 9699r, 9744r,
10112r, 10183r, 10245r,
10330r, 10343r, 10347r,
10420r, 10427r, 10492r,
10646r, 10665r, 10738r,
10798r, 10896r, 10945r,
10948r, 10989r, 10994r,
11052r, 11137r, 11298r,
11321r, 11357r, 11377r,
11378r, 11380r, 11472r,
11476r, 11535r, 11554r,
11577r, 11580r, 11591r,
11609r, 11620r, 11663r,
11692r, 11741r, 11792r,

11947r, 12236r, 12287r,
12330r, 12499r, 12500r,
12526r, 12610r, 12748r,
12796r, 12875r, 12969r,
13061r, 13086r
Malcolm, Janet
4854
Malcolm X
See Little, Malcolm
Malgonkar, Manohar
10979
Mallan, Lloyd
9898
Mallet, Marie
9342
Mallet, Victor
9342
Mallet-Joris, Françoise
7570, 12521
Malm, Dorothea
12311
Malone, Dumas
8785
Maloney, Tom
12500
Malraux, André
5851, 9016, 9914, 11413
Malraux, Clara
9865
Maltby, Richard
11403
Maltz, Maxwell
8324
Manceron, Claude
5978
Manchester, Joe
11486
Manchester, William
5895, 7001, 7145
Mandat-Grancey, Edmond
6840
Mandel, Loring
5635
Mandrou, Robert
8359
Manet, Edouard
10924
Manet, Eduardo
9241
Mangione, Jerre
10701
Manheim, Ralph
6495, 6501, 8078, 9656

Manhoff, Bill
  10618
Mankowitz, Wolf
  6667, 10807
Mann, Arthur
  9008
Mann, Neil
  6293
Mann, Stanley
  8325, 11289
Mannering, Eva
  6150
Mannes, Marya
  10261
Manning, Helen Taft
  11197
Manning, Olivia
  6435, 7212
Mannix, Dan
  9096
Manvell, Roger
  8348
Manville, Bill
  11380
Manville, W.H.
  10645
Maraini, Dacia
  5672
Maraini, Fosco
  8902, 9856
Marberry, M.M.
  12601
Marceau, Félicien
  6848, 7308, 7309, 8014, 8240,
  9263
March, William
  12900
Marchand, Leslie A.
  6410
Marchant, William
  7051
Marckwardt, Albert H.
  5770
Marcus, Alan
  10430
Marcus, Frank
  8929
Mariano, Nicky
  7714
Marine, Gene
  5759
Maritain, Jacques
  11142

Markandaya, Kamala
  11665
Markham, Felix
  10192
Marks, Edward B.
  5054
Marks, S.J.
  2090
Marks, Walter
  6022, 7993
Marlowe, Christopher
  7164, 12050
Marlowe, Derek
  6916
Marmur, Mildred
  12089
Maroger, Dominique
  9875a
Marples, Morris
  11270
Marquand, John P.
  11688, 12282, 12954
Marques, René
  10619
Marquess of Anglesey
  See Anglesey, George Charles
Marr-Johnston, Diana
  8027
Marriott, Alice
  471, 2165, 3585, 4204, 5320
Marsh, Edward
  5749
Marsh, Ellen
  12514
Marsh, Ngaio
  6999
Marshall, Herbert
  9837
Marshall, Jack
  404, 2031, 4330
Marshall, Margaret
  4997
Marshall, Paule
  6364, 11801
Marshall, S.L.A.
  10279, 11686
Martelli, George
  9705
Martin, Ernest H.
  12865
Martin, Henno
  11614
Martin, Herbert
  8474

Martin, Hugh
6143, 8336
Martin, John Bartlow
10617
Martin, Ralph G.
8792
Martin, Robert Dale
6349
Martin, Shane
12456
Marwick, Arthur
7033
Marx, Arthur
8589
Maschler, Tom
7019
Mason, Alpheus Thomas
12899
Mason, Ellsworth
7263
Mason, Kenneth
5588
Mason, Loys
5638
Mason, Marie-Jacqueline
8240
Massey, Valgene
6557
Massie, Robert K.
10268
Massiker, Frances
5645
Masteroff, Joe
6414, 11608, 12749
Masters, Dexter
5598
Masters, Edgar Lee
11849
Masters, John
6371, 6479, 7537, 7545,
11239
Mather, Berkeley
11237
Mathews, Jackson
7676
Mathews, Marthiel
7676
Mathieu, William
7792
Matshikiza, Todd
8945
Matthews, Herbert L.
13043

Matthews, T. S.
3129, 11956
Matthiessen, Peter
2520, 3582, 3616a, 3734,
4215, 4932, 5455, 10688,
11089, 12893
Matusow, Allen J.
12422
Matute, Ana Marie
11437
Matz, Mary Jane
9743
Maudslay, A. P.
7129
Maugham, Robin
9718
Maugham, W. Somerset
5907
Maund, Alfred
6175
Maurel, Micheline
10570
Mauriac, Claude
6788, 7121, 9785
Mauriac, François
6970, 7797, 8662, 9065,
9365, 12511
Maurois, André
5706, 8354, 8565, 9334,
10466, 11007, 12288
Max, Jerome
7465
Maximov, Vladimir
9690
Maxwell, Gavin
6042, 8455, 9481, 10755,
11224, 12083
Maxwell, William
7, 1531, 1678, 1722, 1739,
3148, 3149, 5061, 5062,
5177, 5708r, 6576, 6660r,
7215r, 7260r, 7295r, 7531r,
8038r, 8046r, 8932r, 9295r,
9599r
May, Elaine
5617, 7444, 12223
Mayakovsky, Vladimir
9028, 9837
Mayer, Arno J.
10886

Mayer, Arthur
10096
Mayer, Elizabeth
7945, 8737
Mayer, Grace M.
10491
Mayer, Martin
9604
Mayer, Paul Avila
12229
Mayer, Tom
3748
Mayfield, Sara
6778
Mayhew, Henry
9434
Mazor, Julian
358, 559, 4133, 5306
Mazzetti, Lorenza
11712
Mazzucchelli, Mario
10398
Mead, Margaret
6879
Meader, Duncay Y.
149
Mecklin, John
9980
Medaris, John B.
6816
Medawar, P. B.
7814
Mednick, Murray
8230
Medvedev, Zhores A.
11228
Meehan, Thomas
31, 241, 437, 622, 828, 862,
1279, 1357, 1632, 1682, 2186,
2250, 2382, 2510, 2523, 3242,
3400, 3481, 3903, 4008, 4232,
4265, 4581, 5541
Meeker, Oden
4889
Meerloo, Joost A. M.
11104
Mehdevi, Anne Sinclair
1082, 2867, 2881, 3084, 3182
Mehdevi, Mohamed
1094, 1712, 4489
Mehnert, Klaus
10739

Mehta, Ved
99, 388, 1088, 1132, 1597,
1656, 2056, 2282, 2284,
3211, 3289, 3884, 3958,
3982, 4288, 4832, 4968,
7975r, 11422r
Meissner, Hans-Otto
9717
Melfi, Leonard
6203, 10271
Mellaart, James
7261
Melvin, Mel
11628
Memmi, Albert
10824
Menashe, Samuel
4364
Mencken, H. L.
6062, 6468, 8146, 8147,
9954, 12640
Mendelsohn, Jack
7966
Mengin, Robert
10331
Menninger, Karl
6853
Mercer, Johnny
11406
Mercier, Mary
8823
Meredith, James
12239
Meredith, William
4, 390, 1307, 1591, 1623,
1814, 2517, 3454, 3492, 3808,
4855, 5264, 5285, 5339, 5480,
5696
Meriwether, James B.
9370
Merk, Frederick
9732
Merrill, Bob
6469, 7808, 8287, 10242, 12033
Merrill, James
54, 443, 593, 1007, 1685, 1763,
4723, 4859, 4996, 5247, 5515,
5518, 7107, 11544
Merk, Otto
6210
Merlin, Frank
7680, 8517

Merton, Robert K.
10481
Merwin, W. S.
20, 213, 259, 268, 482, 506,
621, 760, 781, 873, 1077,
1081, 1254, 1302, 1438, 1496,
1567,1579,1614,1672,1995,2124,
2172, 2380, 2562, 2630, 2806,
2843, 3468, 3697, 3791, 3798,
3838, 3893, 4003, 4025, 4061,
4191, 4285, 4399, 4827, 5115,
5126, 5324, 5327, 5343, 5350,
5433, 10999, 13036
Metaxas, Alexandre
11343
Metzger, Walter P.
7065
Meyer, Donald
10929
Meyer, Stanton M.
2323
Meyers, William
11841
Meynell, Viola
1159, 3096, 3667, 5187
Mezey, Robert
68, 2180, 2439, 2524
Mian, Mary
2866
Michael, Donald
10266
Michael, Maurice
8627
Michaels, Sidney
6128, 7258, 12064
Michaels, Walter Benn
7338
Michal, Mira
282
Michel, Georges
9238
Michelfelder, William
6077
Michener, James A.
6338, 6457, 11812
Middleton, Christopher
11513
Middleton, Drew
5792, 5964, 11713, 11989,
12147
Middleton, Thomas
6552

Middleton, William D.
8689
Miers, Earl Schenck
9414, 12789
Migeo, Marcel
11375
Mihaly, Csikszentmihalyi
5460
Mikhailov, N. N
12211
Milbert, J.
10816
Miles, Bernard
9426
Miles, Hamish
8565
Miles, Josephine
692, 1466, 4404, 10956
Millar, George
10624
Millar, Ronald
5641, 11253
Millard, George
8738
Millay, Edna St. Vincent
9545
Miller, Arthur
5658, 7393, 8639, 10966,
12629
Miller, Bob
10404
Miller, David Humphreys
6888
Miller, Diane Disney
11905
Miller, Edgar H., Jr.
8320
Miller, Edwin Haviland
11001
Miller, Francis Trevelyan
10797
Miller, Fred R.
2870
Miller, Henry
6190, 8285, 12416
Miller, Jane
10801
Miller, John C.
5699
Miller, Jonathan
5943r, 6634r, 7273r, 7731r,
7983r, 8066r, 8778r, 9220r,
9478r, 9994r, 10402r, 11736r,
12071r, 12365r, 12957r

Miller, Max
2280, 5394, 11623
Miller, Merle
6950, 7845
Miller, Nina Hull
11646
Miller, Peggy
12877
Miller, Perry
6753
Miller, Robin
6905
Miller, Sigmund
9808
Miller, Townsend
6496
Miller, Walter M., Jr.
6446
Miller, Warren
2911, 6872, 7678, 11721,
12772
Miller, Wright W.
11357
Millgate, Michael
5601 9370
Milligan, Spike
6092
Mills, Hugh
9392
Milner, Roger
8484
Milner, Ronald
12868
Milner, Samuel
12616
Milner-Gulland, Robin
13041
Minney, R.J.
10397
Minoff, Lee
6708
Minogue, Kenneth R.
9303
Mins, Leonard
8707
Mishima, Yukio
5657, 7693, 11368, 12076,
12233
Miss Read
See Saint, Dora Jessie
Mitchell, Adrian
21, 9748
Mitchell, Broadus
5700

Mitchell, James
9057
Mitchell, Joseph
412, 2377, 3080, 4120
Mitchell, Julian
8307
Mitchell, Loftin
6029
Mitchell, S.
7530
Mitchell, William
9883
Mitchell-Hedges, F.A.
6917
Mitchner, Stuart
9259
Mitford, Jessica
5785, 6941, 12399
Mitford, Nancy
10346, 11975, 12678
Mitgang, Herbert
9358, 9704
Mittelholzer, Edgar
10451
Mizener, Arthur
11538
Moberg, Vilhelm
12278
Moberly, C.A.E.
5623
Moeckel, Fred
2131
Moers, Ellen
6915, 12474
Moffat, Jay Pierrepont
10026
Moffitt, John
2809, 3433, 4571
Mohrt, Michel
9777
Moinot, Pierre
5805, 11323
Moley, Raymond
7631
Molière
7184, 8577, 8591, 9040, 9150,
9966, 9967, 9969, 10798,
11425, 12059
Molinard, Patrice
11275
Molinaro, Ursule
8106, 11835
Moll, Elick
11508

Molli, Jeanne
6385
Molloy, Robert
10594
Monaghan, Jay
6643
Monaster, Nate
11780
Monnier, Luc
12479
Monsarrat, Nicholas
10825, 12406
Monsey, Derek
8309
Montagu, M. F. Ashley
12362
Montague, James L.
783, 2027
Montand, Yves
7446
Monteiro, Luís de Sttau
9684
Montgomery, Bernard Law
5795, 9877
Montgomery, Bruce
136a
Montgomery, John
12458
Montherlant, Henry de
6556, 9151
Moody, R. Bruce
5312
Mooney, Stephen
3756, 5313
Moore, Archie
5884
Moore, Brian
5839
Moore, Carroll
9629, 11536
Moore, Doris Langley
7260, 9772
Moore, Henry
8237
Moore, John
12768
Moore, Marianne
240, 378, 511, 667, 749, 872,
1120, 1220, 1364, 1426, 1805,
1865, 2566, 2729, 3023, 3051,
3450, 4058, 4200, 4203, 4763,
5255, 9346, 9770, 10955
Moore, Patrick
10247

Moore, Richard
232, 1247, 2885, 4654
Moore, Samuel Taylor
5131
Moore, Sharon
4428
Moore, T. Inglis
6284
Moorehead, Alan
177, 179, 180, 542, 1245,
1399, 1725, 2343, 2540,
2590, 4043, 4074, 4311,
4766, 4930, 6974, 7556,
7827, 11354, 11961
Moorhouse, Geoffrey
5663
Moos, Malcolm
6468
Moraes, Frank
8646, 11196
Moran, Charles McMoran Wilson
5803, 6624
Morath, Max
7443
Moravia, Alberto
7364, 9661, 12776
Mordell, Albert
7130
More, Julian
8709
Morgan, Al
9953, 10443, 10520
Morgan, Berry
152, 376, 1602, 3064, 3072,
3074, 3581, 3711, 4130, 4337,
11038
Morgan, David P.
11875
Morgan, James N.
8640
Morgan, Murray
10511
Morgan, Sarah
6758
Morgenbesser, Sidney
10793
Morgenstern, Joseph
9560
Morison, Elting E.
12443
Morison, Samuel Eliot
8695, 10680, 12494
Morley, Helena
7105

Moross, Jerome
6033
Morrill, Katherine
7142
Morris, Aldyth
6463
Morris, Christopher
12434
Morris, Donald
12748, 12753
Morris, Edmund
12962
Morris, Herbert
4536
Morris, Ira
10659
Morris, Ivan
12076, 12993
Morris, Jackson
1447, 5209
Morris, James
6807, 8720
Morris, John
12269
Morris, John N.
3464
Morris, Rebecca
1834
Morris, Richard B.
5698, 5781, 10733
Morris, Taylor
4067
Morris, Willie
3016, 10360
Morris, Wright
1895, 7590, 7974
Morrison, Joseph L.
12689
Morrison, Ray
5739
Morrison, Renate
5739
Morrison, Theodore
12862
Morros, Boris
10162
Morse, Samuel French
2463, 2737, 3719, 10561
Mortimer, John
7158, 12819
Mortimer, Penelope
2160, 2445, 2759, 3657,
3747, 4029, 4234, 5112, 5357,
5416, 6346, 6522, 12636

Morton, David
5055
Morton, Frederic
11314, 11433, 11743, 12933
Morton, H. V.
12380, 12381
Morton, J. B.
8343
Mosbacher, Eric
7579, 8536, 9856
Mosby, John Singleton
9876, 10073
Mosel, Tad
5731, 9598
Moses, Robert
12408
Moses, W. R.
557, 4406
Mosley, Leonard
6503, 7955, 9095
Mosley, Nicholas
8587
Moss, Grant, Jr.
427
Moss, Howard
208, 253, 286, 354, 397, 399, 553,
568, 571, 609, 806, 896, 991,
1059, 1231, 1261, 1263, 1395,
1430, 1453, 1494, 1538, 1600,
1704, 1710, 1757, 1781, 1817,
2183, 2221, 2266, 2721, 2778,
2810, 3008, 3021, 3058, 3187,
3518, 3637, 3660, 3724, 3755,
3922, 3967, 3971, 4131, 4140,
4219, 4271, 4323, 4414, 4439,
4455, 4476, 4604, 4665, 4721,
4796, 4951, 4959, 5019, 5160,
5185, 5301, 5315, 5403, 5443,
5465, 6582r, 10821r, 11512r,
11625r, 12169r
Moss, Norman
9900
Moss, Stanley
5176
Mossiker, Frances
11062
Mossner, Ernest Campbell
9322
Motley, Willard
9260
Motz, Lloyd
12987
Mount, Charles Merrill
8819

Mountzoures, H.L.
405, 496, 1033, 1338, 1370,
1419, 1421, 1486, 2269,
2556, 2823, 3212, 3346,
3767, 4084, 5049
Mowat, Farley
6800, 10563, 10883, 11550
Mowatt, Anna Cora
7552
Mowery, William Byron
12012
Moyes, Patricia
10106, 12280
Moyles, Lois
4039, 4736, 4847
Moynahan, Julian
10638
Moynihan, Daniel P.
6169, 9836, 10483
Mrozek, Slawomir
10884, 12054
Mueller, Lisel
1693, 1859, 2785, 3493,
3690, 3947, 3995, 4688
Muhlen, Norbert
8642
Muir, Edwin
5981, 10501
Muir, Willa
9421
Mulisch, Harry
11889
Muller, Herbert J.
7760, 7761, 8727, 9472
Muller, Romeo
10052
Mulvihill, William
11401
Mumford, Lewis
1393, 4757, 5762r,
5782r, 5885r, 6636r, 6639,
7432r, 8062r, 8369r, 8745r,
9886r
Munro, Eleanor
4567
Munro, James
10040
Murch, A.E.
6385
Murch, Alma Elizabeth
5624, 5626
Murchie, Guy
10118

Murdoch, Iris
6366, 7663, 8735, 11577,
11578, 12541
Murfen, James V.
7951
Murie, Margaret E.
12481
Murphy, Gardner
5934
Murphy, Jack
3118
Murphy, Joseph Francis
2519
Murphy, Lois B.
5934
Murphy, Thomas
12849
Murphy, William J.
2222, 2300, 3494
Murray, A.A.
5860, 6236
Murray, Angus Wolfe
7376
Murray, Gilbert
12532
Murray, Ken
8908
Murray, William
1031, 1290, 2489, 2653, 2662,
3570, 5245, 11330
Murry, John Middleton
8833
Muse, Benjamin
12088
Muste, A.J.
7428
Mwase, George Simeon
11932
Myers, Henry
8176
Myrdal, Gunnar
5765, 5933, 6170
Myrer, Anton
6193, 10486

N

Nabokov, Dmitri
2727, 4786
Nabokov, Vladimir
49, 346, 2727, 2857, 2859,
3435, 3806, 3807, 3972,
4786, 5000, 5200, 5612,

7909, 8700, 8955, 9431, 10646
Nacenta, Raymond
  11436
Nadeau, Maurice
  8368
Naguib, Mohammed
  7312
Naipaul, V.S.
  8447, 9924, 9934, 10174
Namier, Lewis
  6569, 6863
Nanda, B.R.
  9620
Narayan, R.K.
  2066, 4338, 5114, 7975,
  8129, 9728, 12584, 12703
Nasatir, Mort
  8782
Nash, Mary
  2376, 3092
Nash, N. Richard
  7942, 8171, 8194, 10507,
  12889
Nash, Ogden
  94, 100, 101, 113, 146, 148,
  224, 262, 334, 339, 523,
  582, 583, 624, 645, 683, 858,
  876, 990, 1025, 1196, 1201,
  1203, 1228, 1309, 1498, 1506,
  1811, 1889, 2092, 2108, 2177,
  2182, 2188, 2190, 2192, 2333,
  2344, 2381, 2413, 2414, 2488,
  2735, 2897, 2938, 3145, 3175,
  3265, 3349, 3359, 3387, 3413,
  3420, 3421, 3651, 3803, 3846,
  3856, 3987, 4114, 4352, 4384,
  4563, 4601, 4633, 4634, 4635,
  4793, 5024, 5133, 5146, 5236,
  5332, 5352, 5382, 5384, 5385,
  5408, 5420, 5422, 5424, 5527,
  5557, 9405
Nassau, Paul
  7301, 8865
Nasser, Gamal Abdul
  7313
Nathan, John
  11368
Nathan, Leonard
  489, 2805
Nathan, Paul
  7206
Naughton, Bill
  5710, 5721, 8905
Naydler, Merton
  10741

Neame, Alan
  7475
Negin, Louis
  9516
Nehls, Edward
  6894, 6895
Neider, Charles
  5984, 10604
Neill, A.S.
  11968
Neilson, Frances
  12590
Neilson, Winthrop
  12590
Nekrasov, Viktor
  8967, 9047
Nel, Elizabeth
  9987
Nelson, Dale
  3417
Nemerov, Howard
  157, 285, 515, 897, 1149,
  1323, 1635, 2127, 2392,
  2406, 2526, 2942, 2964,
  2983, 3109, 3192, 3525,
  3882, 3888, 4218, 4550,
  5203, 5526, 6733, 10233
Nemiroff, Robert
  10934, 12293
Neruda, Pablo
  11520
Nestroy, Johann
  7322
Netboy, Anthony
  5965
Nettl, J.P.
  11301
Neumann, Alfred
  12734
Nevins, Allan
  7698, 7699
New York Times
  10914
Newby, Eric
  8037
Newby, P.H.
  6052, 10517, 10809, 11200,
  11782
Newcomb, Richard F.
  5583
Newgarden, Albert
  1532
Newhall, Beaumont
  9816

Newhall, Nancy
9816
Newhouse, Edward
123, 594, 1080, 2118, 2133,
2546
Newley, Anthony
11251, 11891
Newman, Al
1699
Newman, Andrea
9959
Newman, David
8746
Newman, James R.
8214
Newman, Montgomery
829, 1443, 4078, 4579, 4945
Newman, Preston
45, 5411
Newman, Robert
6803
Newton, Isaac
8718
Ney, Richard
10910
Nicholl, Louise Townsend
996, 13001
Nichols, Mike
4240, 7444
Nichols, Peter
6951
Nichols, Roy F.
6259
Nicholson, Max
12021
Nicholson, Margaret
7109
Nicol, Eric
9952
Nicolaeff, Ariadne
11008
Nicolson, Harold
7086, 8006, 11373, 12744
Nicolson, Nigel
7086, 12744
Nietzsche, Friedrich
11513
Nims, John Frederick
4852
Nin, Anaïs
6675, 6897, 7101
Nirumand, Bahman
8707

Nixon, Edna
12677
Nixon, Gilbert
12975
Nixon, John, Jr.
235, 3320
Nkrumah, Kwame
7897
Noah, Robert
5637
Noakes, David
8780
Noble, William
6254
Nogly, Hans
8536
Noll, Bink
155
Nolte, Charles
7155, 8147
Nolte, William H.
8147
Noma, Hiroshi
13084
Nomad, Max
5940
Noonan, John Ford
13023
Norman, Charles
2549, 4995, 5508, 7864, 9614
Norman, Monty
8709
Norris, Frank
12354
Norris, John
11613
North, Jessica Nelson
3378
Norton, Lucy
11788
Noss, Murray
5137
Nossal, Frederick
6937
Nourissier, François
7764
Novak, Joseph
10340
Nowell, Elizabeth
9288, 12208
Nugent, Elliot
7450

Nussbaum, Arthur
8373
Nutting, Anthony
10327

O

O.N.
2345
Oates, Joyce Carol
12004, 12138
Oberth, Hermann
9678
Obler, Paul C.
10255
O'Brady, Frédéric
5735
O'Brian, Patrick
9865, 11074, 12521
O'Brien, Edna
878, 2827, 2830, 2834,
4170, 5410, 6825
O'Brien, Flann
12169
O'Brien, Justin
7790, 10176
O'Brien, Kate
5930
An observer
9910
O'Casey, Sean
6096, 6665, 6666, 10863,
10939, 11135, 11581, 11986,
12523
O'Connell, Richard
564, 4613
O'Connor, Edwin
5723, 7296, 8537, 8538, 9100
O'Connor, Flannery
7457, 8010, 10172
O'Connor, Frank
25, 26, 133, 330, 588, 762,
930, 1046, 1133, 1258, 1425,
1561, 1810, 1878, 2153,
2909, 2970, 3056, 3215, 3544,
3615, 3654, 3665, 4052, 4207,
4261, 4328, 4647, 4656, 4754,
5348, 8961, 9962, 11594
O'Connor, Jack
8426
O'Connor, Richard
8268, 8825, 9496

Oddie, Bill
6429
O'Donnell, Eugene
10278
Oerke, Andrew
1951, 1961, 2148, 4013, 4542
O'Faolain, Julie
2826
O'Faolain, Sean
8247, 8531, 12664
Offenbach, Jacques
8176, 9021, 9045
Ogburn, Charlton, Jr.
9751, 12921
O'Gorman, Ned
10291
O'Hara, John
69, 107, 274, 295, 606, 655,
728, 795, 1134, 1418, 1483,
1487, 1588, 1726, 1787, 1836,
2093, 2099, 2159, 2194, 2350,
2378, 2564, 2780, 2910, 2918,
2921, 2969, 3115, 3273, 3926,
4233, 4378, 4597, 4692, 5004,
5071, 5337, 5466, 5506, 5571,
7793, 12081
Okumiya, Masatake
9930
Oliver, Edith
136ar, 435ar, 675ar,
5587r, 5593r, 5604r, 5617r,
5628r, 5694r, 5716r, 5720r,
5722r, 5723r, 5724r, 5740r,
5755r, 5795r, 5817r, 5818r,
5824r, 5835r, 5848r, 5849r,
5862r, 5868r, 5877r, 5888r,
5891r, 5989r, 5998r, 6002r,
6003r, 6027r, 6028r, 6029r,
6035r, 6038r, 6045r, 6058r,
6061r, 6115r, 6129r, 6140r,
6143r, 6183r, 6188r, 6192r,
6199r, 6203r, 6216r, 6227r,
6229r, 6240r, 6246r, 6249r,
6253r, 6258r, 6270r, 6318r,
6319r, 6333r, 6336r, 6341r,
6342r, 6349r, 6356r, 6383r,
6384r, 6391r, 6397r, 6400r,
6402r, 6427r, 6444r, 6447r,
6465r, 6473r, 6476r, 6477r,
6502r, 6504r, 6518r, 6521r,
6533r, 6534r, 6562r, 6579r,
6583r, 6586r, 6592r, 6594r,
6616r, 6630r, 6635r, 6645r,

6662r, 6691r, 6693r, 6697r,
6699r, 6708r, 6752r, 6757r,
6780r, 6787r, 6805r, 6811r,
6849r, 6900r, 6905r, 6927r,
6931r, 6945r, 6960r, 6965r,
6968r, 6972r, 6978r, 6983r,
7024r, 7049r, 7064r, 7095r,
7111r, 7114r, 7137r, 7155r,
7158r, 7164r, 7182r, 7188r,
7208r, 7218r, 7237r, 7248r,
7249r, 7255r, 7259r, 7314r,
7321r, 7334r, 7358r, 7359r,
7373r, 7385r, 7387r, 7395r,
7415r, 7421r, 7442r, 7443r,
7445r, 7447r, 7465r, 7473r,
7487r, 7501r, 7564r, 7596r,
7620r, 7635r, 7637r, 7641r,
7446r, 7679r, 7682r, 7708r,
7709r, 7727r, 7736r, 7745r,
7753r, 7774r, 7791r, 7792r,
7796r, 7812r, 7818r, 7893r,
7901r, 7906r, 7920r, 7946r,
7961r, 7963r, 7970r, 7988r,
7994r, 8012r, 8013r, 8029r,
8054r, 8155r, 8163r, 8167r,
8169r, 8172r, 8180r, 8186r,
8190r, 8191r, 8197r, 8210r,
8211r, 8216r, 8221r, 8230r,
8264r, 8289r, 8317r, 8318r,
8386r, 8400r, 8403r, 8408r,
8413r, 8421r, 8422r, 8428r,
8431r, 8541r, 8457r, 8481r,
8504r, 8513r, 8517r, 8522r,
8528r, 8530r, 8554r, 8585r,
8591r, 8600r, 8616r, 8633r,
8641r, 8649r, 8661r, 8681r,
8691r, 8701r, 8705r, 8725r,
8777r, 8802r, 8831r, 8832r,
8850r, 8855r, 8873r, 8890r,
8919r, 8953r, 8969r, 8977r,
8978r, 8982r, 8987r, 9001r,
9045r, 9104r, 9114r, 9128r,
9132r, 9171r, 9176r, 9255r,
9305r, 9319r, 9369r, 9388r,
9390r, 9400r, 9425r, 9448r,
9450r, 9514r, 9516r, 9538r,
9542r, 9547r, 9554r, 9560r,
9653r, 9573r, 9590r, 9598r,
9606r, 9622r, 9628r, 9641r,
9658r, 9662r, 9674r, 9679r,
9689r, 9713r, 9727r, 9782r,
9823r, 9830r, 9831r, 9832r,
9858r, 9885r, 9888r, 9904r,

9943r, 9964r, 9990r, 9998r,
10002r, 10007r, 10038r,
10045r, 10050r, 10052r,
10057r, 10060r, 10065r,
10071r, 10127r, 10154r,
10167r, 10265r, 10267r,
10269r, 10283r, 10294r,
10336r, 10338r, 10361r,
10385r, 10389r, 10403r,
10404r, 10431r, 10435r,
10445r, 10446r, 10453r,
10455r, 10477r, 10496r,
10504r, 10519r, 10524r,
10544r, 10545r, 10546r,
10572r, 10582r, 10587r,
10592r, 10627r, 10628r,
10664r, 10667r, 10683r,
10690r, 10692r, 10699r,
10728r, 10750r, 10759r,
10765r, 10786r, 10810r,
10815r, 10819r, 10836r,
10844r, 10847r, 10852r,
10856r, 10859r, 10882r,
10884r, 10925r, 10932r,
10997r, 11006r, 11033r,
11035r, 11057r, 11063r,
11098r, 11122r, 11129r,
11135r, 11221r, 11235r,
11236r, 11242r, 11267r,
11282r, 11284r, 11289r,
11311r, 11328r, 11361r,
11364r, 11383r, 11384r,
11387r, 11403r, 11410r,
11411r, 11418r, 11420r,
11425r, 11427r, 11431r,
11434r, 11462r, 11486r,
11548r, 11560r, 11585r,
11587r, 11603r, 11608r,
11628r, 11634r, 11635r,
11643r, 11662r, 11674r,
11689r, 11705r, 11718r,
11719r, 11728r, 11777r,
11789r, 11794r, 11809r,
11841r, 11842r, 11847r,
11855r, 11858r, 11881r,
11888r, 11892r, 11920r,
11929r, 11936r, 11939r,
11962r, 11963r, 11972r,
11985r, 12004r, 12005r,
12009r, 12029r, 12051r,
12066r, 12070r, 12095r,
12117r, 12126r, 12167r,
12192r, 12196r, 12197r,

12203r, 12204r, 12223r,
12255r, 12258r, 12293r,
12298r, 12316r, 12317r,
12323r, 12335r, 12376r,
12403r, 12409r, 12414r,
12429r, 12469r, 12475r,
12493r, 12497r, 12524r,
12531r, 12539r, 12552r,
12557r, 12560r, 12603r,
12629r, 12643r, 12709r,
12712r, 12717r, 12719r,
12734r, 12799r, 12805r,
12819r, 12821r, 12833r,
12845r, 12849r, 12853r,
12863r, 12867r, 12868r,
12869r, 12870r, 12872r,
12932r, 12939r, 12941r,
12978r, 12983r, 12997r,
13000r, 13023r, 13038r,
13063r, 13070r, 13073r,
Oliver, James
  8914
Olivier, Fernande
  10801
Olivier-Michel, Françoise
  8133
Oljača, Mladen
  10954
Ollard, Richard
  7424
Olson, Elder
  245, 1164, 2225, 2453
Olson, Sigurd F.
  11691
O'Malley, Tom
  435a
O'Meara, Walter
  11415
O'Neill, Charles
  12888
O'Neill, Eugene
  7049, 7114, 8072, 8487, 8542,
  9452, 9762, 10058, 10065,
  11913, 12351
O'Neill, William L.
  7287
Oparin, A.
  9318
Ophir, Shai K.
  7716
Opie, Iona
  9482
Opie, Peter
  9482

Oppen, George
  342
Oppenheimer, George
  9933
Oppenheimer, J. Robert
  10542, 12558
Oppenheimer, Martin
  12558
Ordish, George
  9412
Origo, Iris
  9903
Ormond, Jacques F.
  7661
Ornadel, Cyril
  10807
Ortega y Gasset, José
  9654, 10471
Orton, Joe
  7408, 7421, 9473, 11328
Orwell, George
  6654, 6677, 8906, 11249
Osaragi, Jiro
  8843
Osborn, James M.
  5985
Osborn, Millicent
  2075
Osborn, Paul
  12985
Osborne, John
  7407, 7410, 8634, 9467,
  9579, 10717, 12982
Osgood, Laurence
  10819
Osk, Richard
  2150, 3800
Osofsky, Gilbert
  8205, 11045
Ostroff, Anthony
  2808
Ostrovsky, Erika
  6525
Ostrow, Joanna
  731, 5165
O'Sullivan, Lawrence
  9968
Oswald, Robert L.
  2557a, 9201
Ottenheimer, Albert M.
  2710
Owen, Wilfred
  6688
Owens, Rochelle
  7818

Owens, William A.
  12199

P

Pack, Robert
  676, 2209, 3811, 3980, 10252
Packard, Frederick
  345, 2154, 3733, 4826, 4848
Packard, Vance
  8321, 11048, 11873, 12757
Packard, William
  10786
Packe, Michael St. John
  10584
Packer, Herbert L.
  7461
Padover, Saul K.
  8789, 12755
Padula, Edward
  8865
Page, Evelyn
  6587
Page, Thornton
  10578
Paige, Paula Spurlin
  12682
Paisey, D. L.
  8357
Pakenham, Simona
  10820
Pakington, Humphrey
  6513
Paléologue, Maurice
  8690
Palmer, Eve
  10839
Palmer, R. R.
  5677
Palmer, Winthrop
  10836
Paloczi-Horvath, George
  8923, 9746, 12522
Panama, Norman
  9348
Panetta, George
  8954, 8969, 9935, 12661
Pangborn, Edgar
  8872, 12397
Panichas, George A.
  11010
Panizza, Oscar
  9155

Panter-Downes, Mollie
  89, 219, 590, 1053, 1054,
  1339, 1641, 2309, 2448,
  2476, 2604, 2608, 2615,
  2618, 2645, 2646, 2667,
  2670, 2671, 2676, 2677,
  2787, 2935, 2946, 3263,
  3427, 3565, 3593, 3786,
  3920, 4197, 4289, 4834,
  2687, 5546, 5713r, 5896r,
  3427, 5941r, 5976r, 6092r,
  6223r, 6241r, 6322r, 6465r,
  6516r, 6586r, 6614r, 6624r,
  6696r, 6742r, 6913r, 6938r,
  6941r, 6951r, 7072r, 7328r,
  7407r, 7454r, 7463r, 7713r,
  7741r, 8152r, 8163r, 8231r,
  8410r, 8569r, 8634r, 8660r,
  8882r, 8945r, 8978r, 9203r,
  9426r, 9431r, 9579r, 9748r,
  9974r, 10008r, 10135r,
  10267r, 10447r, 10462r,
  10497r, 10524r, 10587r,
  10696r, 10717r, 10795r,
  10971r, 11093r, 11417r,
  11153r, 11168r, 11204r,
  11209r, 11253r, 11279r,
  11295r, 11310r, 11312r,
  11324r, 11340r, 11533r,
  11551r, 11578r, 11787r,
  11790r, 11963r, 12060r,
  12129r, 12236r, 12259r,
  12322r, 12498r, 12518r,
  12571r, 12629r, 12876r,
  12914r, 12968r, 12982r,
  13049r
Paolotti, John
  11191
Papaleo, Joseph
  4064
Papashvily, Helen Waite
  5728
Parfit, Derek
  3750
Paris, Peter
  8584
Paris Review
  6152
Parker, Dorothy
  363, 2783
Parker, James Reid
  478, 1954, 2317, 2933, 5147
Parker, Robert Allerton
  12374

Parker, Stephen
5469
Parker, Tony
6832
Parkes, Henry Bamford
7973
Parkinson, C. Northcote
7271, 7459, 9138
Parkman, Francis
7132, 10680
Parks, Gordon
6617, 9192
Parmenter, Ross
5996
Parone, Edward
2050, 2521
Parr, Charles McKew
7578
Parry, Dennis
12582
Parry, J. H.
5675
Parsons, Elizabeth
796
Pascal, Fran
7876
Pascal, John
7876
Pasinetti, P. M.
11732, 12585
Pasley, Virginia
12464
Paso, Alfonso
11793
Pasternak, Boris
7172, 9293
Patch, Stephen
1789
Paton, Alan
9068, 11848
Patrick, John
7453, 8005, 9532
Patrick, Marsena Rudolph
8672
Patten, David
12235
Patterson, R. M.
6370
Patton, Frances Gray
263, 2906
Paustovsky, Konstantin
11897
Pavese, Cesare
6385, 11523
Paxton, Glenn

10969
Payne, Robert
9312, 12104
Peabody, Marian Lawrence
12294
Pearce, Moira
11988
Pearsall, Phyllis
3238
Pearson, Drew
6482
Pearson, Hesketh
6100, 7163, 7916, 8286,
8316, 9409, 11701
Pease, Deborah
1212
Pease, Robert
5949
Peaslee, Richard
10269
Peck, Charles K., Jr.
6619, 9037
Peck, David W.
8118
Pedrick, Jean
2874
Peel, Doris
159, 3848
Peissel, Michel
10124
Pellegrini, Angelo M.
5788
Penn, Irving
10032
Penrose, Roland
10802
Perec, Georges
9229
Perelman, S. J.
65, 147, 169, 243, 325, 398,
438, 604, 653, 656, 722, 725,
877, 953, 1002, 1068, 1148,
1253, 1292, 1314, 1577,
1589, 1706, 1743, 1879, 1915,
1938, 1965, 1974, 1983, 2001,
2008, 2146, 2179, 2181, 2242,
2332, 2334, 2472, 2574, 2575,
2779, 3121, 3135, 3194, 3229,
3254, 3316, 3348, 3360, 3361,
3446, 3507, 3539, 3542, 3568,
3614, 3636, 3677, 3805, 3843,
3932, 3986, 4031, 4085, 4100,
4238, 4341, 4362, 4407, 4431,
4440, 4470, 4717, 4725, 4761,
4774, 4840, 4870, 4885, 4919,

4946, 5273, 5399, 5407, 5530,
6086
Perera, Padma
1184, 2981, 4262, 4869,
4944,
Perera, Victor
4925
Peretti, Hugo
9609
Pergament, Lola
10403
Perkins, Bradford
8081
Perkins, Dexter
6565
Perkinson, Coleridge-Taylor
9662, 11794
Perlberg, Mark
2023, 2085
Perowne, Stewart
6418, 8150
Perrie, Ernestine
13000
Perrin, Noel
215, 864, 1121, 1199, 1651,
1825, 1990, 2359, 2487,
3343, 3461, 3562, 4136, 4398,
4403, 4762, 5262, 7160
Perruchot, Henri
7844
Perry, Tom
1625
Perse, St. -John
11465
Peter, John
12035
Peterkiewicz, Jerzy
7817
Peters, Fritz
6316
Petersen, Don
7176
Peterson, Merrill D.
8788
Peterson, Virgilia
10695
Petrie, Charles
7306, 12613
Petrie, Paul
580, 802, 1267, 1361, 1703,
3201, 3467, 4658, 5005
Petrov, Evdokia
7361
Petrov, Vladimir
7361

Petrovich, Michael B.
6789, 10324
Petrovskaya, Kyra
8992
Petry, Ann
1953, 3283
Pettet, E. C.
10479
Pettit, Norman
8242
Peyrefitte, Roger
9230
Pfaff, William
10253, 10887
Pfeiffer, Karl G.
12690
Phelan, Francis Joseph
4628
Phelps, Gilbert
12925
Phelps, Lyon
1324
Phelps, Mary
4803, 5036
Phelps, Robert
8312, 9384
Philipe, Anne
9185
Phillips, C. E. Lucas
7425
Phillips, Cabell
12423
Phillips, Harlan B.
7574
Phillips, Irving
11334
Phillips, John
8742
Phipps, Thomas W.
7729
Picard, Jacques
11566
Pick, Robert
6478
Pietri, Arturo Uslar
11133
Pietromarchi, Luca
11823
Pigafetta, Antonio
12682
Pike, Douglas
12620
Pilat, Oliver
9364

Pincherle, Marc
12663
Pinget, Robert
8666, 10460
Pinkus, Oscar
7779
Pinter, Harold
6061, 6214, 6465, 6691,
7249, 8410, 9165, 9547,
11284, 11728, 12066
Pinto, Vivian de Sola
6734, 6745
Pinza, Ezio
7490
Pippett, Aileen
10080
Pirandello, Luigi
8777, 9305, 9713, 11218,
11705, 12298, 12330
Piscator, Erwin
12734
Pitchford, Kenneth
79, 3548, 3945
Pitt, Barrie
10312, 11194
Pittman, Arthur
10932
Pius II
9869
Plagemann, Bentz
548
Plant, Michael
9973
Plant, Richard
1783
Plath, Sylvia
503, 2900, 3218, 3277,
3337, 3490, 4334, 5031,
5314, 5482
Plimpton, George
10657
Plomer, William
2263, 5272, 5953, 6292,
7207
Plumb, J. H.
7627, 11699
Pober, Leon
6107
Pockriss, Hal
7310
Pockriss, Lee
7417

Podhoretz, Norman
6749r, 6772r, 7180, 7466r,
7827r, 9724r, 10364r,
11200r, 12357r, 12473r,
12714r,
Pogodin, Nikolai
8987
Pogue, Forrest C.
7871
Point, Nicolas
12891
Polite, Frank
3052
Pollack, Barbara
6694
Pomerans, A. J.
11119, 11148
Pomeroy  Ralph
2016, 2765, 3431, 4166,
4451, 4923, 5063
Poncins, Gontran de Montaigne
7563
Pope, Dudley
5959, 8036
Pope-Hennessy, John
8736, 10035, 11058, 12589
Popper, Karl R.
9429
Porter, Cole
5862, 7846, 11676
Porter, Katherine Anne
11625
Portmann, Adolf
10250
Posner, David
480, 668, 1304, 2273, 3484,
4507, 4785, 5231
Post, Charles Johnson
9404
Postgate, Raymond
11899
Potter, Jeffrey
1533, 2346, 4844
Potter, Jeremy
6912
Potter, Nancy A. J.
12784
Potter, Stephen
11537
Pottle, Frederick A.
6305, 6306, 6307, 6308
Pottle, Sam
5794

Pound, Ezra
1696, 8583, 9540, 9576,
10724, 10938, 11501, 11800,
11243
Powdermaker, Hortense
6799
Powell, Anthony
5596, 5954, 6481, 8935,
9939, 11761, 12568
Powell, Dawn
7996
Powell, John
4110
Powell, John Wesley
7477
Powell, Peter J.
12008
Powell, Richard
10790, 10829
Powers, Gudrun
12204
Powers, J. F.
473, 957, 1812, 1892, 2435,
2818, 3885, 5525
Powledge, Fred
4487
Pratolini, Vasco
6365
Pratt, Fletcher
6642, 6738
Praz, Mario
8310
Prebble, John
7126
Preger, Paul, Jr.
5575
Prescott, H. F. M.
9492, 11786
Prescott, William H.
6771
Press, John
4505
Prettyman, Barrett, Jr.
6994
Previn, André
6670
Price, Francis
5805, 8851, 10992
Price, Reynolds
9447
Price, Stanley
6708
Price, Victor
7002, 10591

Priestley, J. B.
6564, 8571, 8752, 8847,
9387, 9660, 9768, 10978,
11578, 11698
Princess Royal
See Victoria Adelaide Mary
Louisa
Prior, Allan
9562
Pritchett, V. S.
686, 752, 811, 1079, 1454,
2410, 2433, 2704, 3270,
3276, 3366, 3367, 4415,
5388, 5626r, 6206r, 6413,
9417, 9435, 9565r, 10263,
11367, 11375r, 11986r,
13010r
Prittie, Terence
7888, 7890
Proctor, Maurice
7464
Prokosch, Frederic
12040
Proudfoot, Merrill
7097
Proust, Marcel
9755
Prufer, Guntram
12734
Pruneau, Phillip
11799
Prunier, Simone B.
11023
Pryce-Jones, David
11400
Przibram, K.
9291
Pudney, John
4603
Puigvert Calderón de la Barca,
Alfredo
6780
Puissesseau, René
11776
Pullen, John J.
12459
Pulvertaft, Lalage
12159.
Purcell, John Francis
6155
Purcell, J. Q.
2373
Purcell, Victor
6417, 11998, 12363

Purdom, C.B.
6139
Purdy, James
6, 6699, 9642
Putnam, Carleton
12140
Pynchon, Thomas
12562

Q

Quarles, Benjamin
9357
Quaroni, Pietro
7124
Quartermain, L.B.
11818
Queen Victoria
See Victoria, Queen of Great
Britain
Quennell, Peter
5702, 10710, 10996
Quenneville, Freda
5317
Quentin, Ames Rowe
4023
Quet, Pierre
9663
Quigly, Isabel
7460, 8000, 11481
Quint, Beverly Baff
1564, 3246, 5204
Quirk, John
8203

R

R.A.L.
5391
Rabinowitch, Eugene
5968
Rabovsky, Istvan
9191
Rachleff, Owen
8779
Racine, Jean Baptiste
5818, 5962, 10786
Radano, Gene
10546
Radin, Edward D.
9423
Rado, James
8155
Ragni, Gerome
8155

Raine, Kathleen
635, 903, 2486, 3029, 4247,
4410, 4801, 4872
Rambach, Pierre
7984
Ramsbotham, Michael
11156
Ramshaw, Molly
1905
Rand, Ayn
5967
Rand, Christopher
271, 611, 733, 817, 954,
1182, 1316, 1654, 1701,
1888, 2054, 2325, 2609,
2638, 2640, 2650, 2655,
3605, 3634, 3852, 3930,
4389, 4424, 4496, 4652,
4712, 4866, 5108, 5277,
5321, 12139r
Randal, Vera
95
Randall, J.G.
9361
Randall, John Herman, Jr.
6462
Randall, Ruth Painter
6837
Randall, Thomas
12453
Randhawa, Mohinder Singh
8648
Randolph, John
10925
Raphael, Chaim
9874
Raphael, Frederic
9355
Raposo, Joseph
11689
Ratti, John
1177, 3762
Rattigan, Terence
7931, 8206, 9653, 11312,
11542, 11724, 12027
Rattray, Jeannette Edwards
11624, 12806
Rau, Santha Rama
2535, 2883, 10696, 11157,
12631
Rawicz, Piotr
6245
Rawicz, Slavomir
9461

Rawson, Geoffrey
10649, 11243
Ray, Cyril
6743
Ray, Gordon N.
8281, 12112
Rayfiel, David
10198, 10627
Raymond, Jack
10946
Raymond, John
11161
Read, Bill
10021
Read, Conyers
9474, 9997
Read, Forrest
10938
Read, Herbert
6663, 6786, 12302
Read, Kenneth E.
8338
Reade, Brian
5974
Reardon, Frank
11334
Reavey, Jean
10836
Reboux, Paul
7684
Record, Jane Cassels
1289
Redding, William Jay
396
Redgrave, Michael
5941
Redlich, H. F.
5692
Redman, Ben Ray
3841
Reed, Henry
8724, 9085
Reed, Henry Hope
5782, 6531
Reed, Ishmael
13032
Reed, J. D.
1580
Reed, Kit
5960, 10083
Rees, Goronwy
6375, 10101
Rees, Richard
7878

Reeve, F. D.
88, 439, 1464, 4909, 5336,
5345
Reeves, Ambrose
11636
Regan, Sylvia
13079
Reichler, Joe
8356
Reid, Alastair
305, 651, 1005, 1012, 1122,
1209, 1455, 1526, 1626,
1730, 1748, 1767, 1904, 2237,
2570, 2571, 2595, 2620, 2622,
2648, 2675, 2820, 2991, 3004,
3299, 3380, 3941, 3949, 3976,
4441, 4544, 4555, 4797, 4876,
4928, 4978, 5234, 5361, 5386,
5485, 5555
Reid, B. L.
9668
Reid, Joyce M. H.
5966
Reilly, Helen
6448
Reiner, Carl
11779
Reischauer, Edwin O.
12730
Remak, Joachim
11405
Remarque, Erich Maria
6230
Remini, Robert V.
7331
Remy
See Renault-Roulier, Gilbert
Renard, Jules
8841, 10202
Renault, Mary
7617, 9806
Renault-Roulier, Gilbert
10919
Renoir, Jean
10585
Renshaw, Patrick
12943
Resnik, Muriel
5857
Reston, James
12725
Révai, Andrew
7325

Reverdy, Pierre
9121
Reverzy, Jean
6862
Rewald, John
8361, 10933
Rexroth, Kenneth
10505, 10506
Reynaud, Paul
8628
Reynolds, Butch
6355
Reynolds, Quentin
6405, 7587, 8236, 12152
Ribeiro, Aquilino
12830
Ribman, Ronald
6534, 8216, 8850, 10699
Riboud, Marc
12221
Rice, Elmer
6877
Rice, Robert
461, 801, 830, 1723, 2408,
2720, 2984, 3321, 3722, 3727,
4897, 4955, 5199, 5423
Rice, Tamara Talbot
11456
Rich, Adrienne Cecile
110, 283, 289, 684, 1698,
2213, 2372, 3190, 3763,
4126, 4709, 5026
Rich, Norman
8396
Richardson, Dorothy
10822
Richardson, Francis
951
Richardson, Howard
9128, 11018
Richardson, Jack
7828, 9483, 10994
Richardson, Joanna
10980
Richardson, John
12189
Richardson, William
7554
Richie, Donald
6739
Richmond, Jane
4432

Richter, Conrad
12767
Richter, Harvena
1894
Richter, Werner
6217
Rickover, H. G.
5769, 7299
Rideout, W. B.
5780
Ridgway, Matthew B.
11758
Ridland, John M.
3555
Ridolfi, Roberto
9324
Rienow, Leona Train
10029
Rienow, Robert
10029
Riesenberg, Felix, Jr.
11461
Riesman, David
5594, 5595
Rilke, Rainer Maria
9283, 11524
Rinehart, Patricia
8130
Ringelbaum, Emmanuel
10376
Ripley, Edward Hastings
12592
Riskin, Robert
2848
Riter, Faye
1036
Ritner, Peter
7005
Ritter, Margaret
11681
Rives, Hallie Erminie
7185
Roach, Eloise
10843
Roazen, Paul
6359
Robb, Nesca A.
12902
Robbe-Grillet, Alain
7685, 8625, 9015
Roberts, F. Warren
6745

Roberts, Meade
9621
Roberts, William David
2740, 4512
Robertson, Don
7651
Robertson, E. Arnot
8893
Robertson, Ian W.
5838
Robertson, Martin
8102
Robertson, Strowan
1674
Robertson, Terence
6555
Robinson, B.W.
12367
Robinson, Edgar Eugene
11292
Robinson, Eric
11615
Robinson, Henry Morton
12761
Robinson, J.K.
5780
Robinson, Lennox
10621
Robson, William A.
8062
Roc, John
7614
Roche, France
9424
Roche, Paul
576, 4236
Rochefort, Christiane
9179
Rodale, J.I.
8028, 12317
Roddy, Joseph
229
Rodell, Fred
10309
Rodgers, Mary
9596
Rodgers, Richard
6318, 6402, 7153, 7672,
10338, 10830, 11807
Roditi, Edouard
9861
Rodman, Selden
7486

Rodway, Allan Edwin
6734
Rodway, Stella
10270
Roethke, Theodore
233, 679, 1221, 1276, 1947,
2193, 2396, 2455, 2724,
2772, 2796, 2939, 2967,
3000, 4029, 4032, 4066,
4150, 4325, 4411, 4435,
4445, 4620, 4823, 4991,
5243, 5269, 6687, 12967
Roffey, Jack
8433
Rogers, David
10508
Rogers, Thomas
11040
Roget, Elizabeth
8841
Rogge, O. John
12871
Rogin, Gilbert
293, 754, 1138, 1327, 1378,
1518, 2098, 2288, 2402,
2569, 3797, 4377, 4474,
4492, 4809, 4898, 4931,
5060, 5121, 5122, 5377, 5556
Rogow, Arnold A.
8765
Rojo, Ricardo
10139
Rokkan, Elizabeth
10644
Rolfe, Frederick
8152
Rollins, Alfred B., Jr.
11291
Rollnick, Sonia
486, 556, 1446, 1747,
3171, 3274, 3643
Rolo, P.J.V.
7872
Romains, Jules
7193
Roman, Jean
10674
Roman, Lawrence
12528
Romanowicz, Zofia
10695
Rome, Harold
7063, 8513

Romulo, Carlos P.
6868
Ronan, Colin A.
7298
Rooney, Frank
8061, 9591
Roos, Audrey
11832
Roos, William
11832
Roosenburg, Henriette
197, 198
Roosevelt, Theodore
8500, 12142
Root, John Wellborn
9844
Root, Wm. Pitt
807
Rorem, Ned
10259
Rosa, Dennis
12978
Rose, Arnold M.
5765, 10950
Rose, Reginald
6227
Rose, W.K.
9290
Rose, Willie Lee
11147
Rosen, Elliot A.
7631
Rosen, Norma Stahl
5369, 8864
Rosenberg, Harold
2305, 5902, 7100r, 7412r,
8549r, 9897r, 10371r,
11454r, 12530r, 12965r,
Rosenberg, James L.
2130
Rosenberg, John
7100
Rosenblum, Robert
12552
Rosenfeld, Eva
11241
Rosenthal, A.M.
12178
Rosenthal, Laurence
11618
Rosenthal, M.L.
3240
Rosenthal, Raymond
6365

Rosenthal, Robert
11047
Roshwald, Mordecai
9297
Rosier, Bernard
8496a
Roske, Ralph J.
9362
Ross, Albion
8849
Ross, Carmel
11311
Ross, David
3488
Ross, Donald
11634
Ross, George Maxim
10791
Ross, Irwin
8572
Ross, Ishbel
11673
Ross, J.A.
8179
Ross, James E.
6973
Ross, Lillian
143, 465, 1017, 1503, 1830,
1985, 2998, 3308, 3324,
3402, 3578, 3796, 3875,
3979, 4768, 5192, 5359,
5389, 5535, 5554, 13021r
Ross, Malcolm
6449
Ross, Michael
10924
Ross, Nancy Wilson
2532, 11190
Ross, Ralph,
7494
Rossen, Robert
6872
Rossiter, Clinton
6773
Rossner, Judith
12313
Rostand, Edmond
6892
Rosten, Norman
4916, 5496, 9991
Rosvall, Toivo David
9841
Roth, Henry
3732, 4707

Roth, Philip
  1084, 2440, 3407, 8021,
  9296, 10909
Rothberg, Abraham
  5800, 12219
Rothenstein, John
  6324, 6351, 11969
Rothschild, Pauline de
  8713
Rothstein, Andrew
  9873
Rouart, Denis
  12538
Roueché, Berton
  87, 209, 338, 640, 707,
  738, 915, 1043, 1060, 1336,
  1548, 1876, 2010, 2203, 2246,
  2275, 2431, 2511, 2554, 2705,
  2851, 2907, 3167, 3550, 3574,
  3749, 3789, 4049, 4107, 4108,
  4179, 4372, 4485, 4486, 4528,
  4720, 4769, 4874, 5274, 5489,
  5503, 6882
Rouse, Blair
  9273
Roussin, André
  9236
Routh, C. R. N.
  12153
Rovere, Richard H.
  192, 276, 662, 663, 664, 666,
  1123, 1135, 1917, 2379, 2385,
  2386, 2441, 2589, 2599, 2605,
  2616, 2619, 2627, 2647, 2652,
  2666, 2687, 2696, 2741, 3249,
  3286, 4675, 5074, 5138, 5139,
  5748r, 7001r, 7383r, 7634r,
  8209r, 8668r, 8909r, 9637r,
  9723r, 9725r, 9866r, 10565r,
  10685r, 10706r, 11030r,
  11143r, 11294r, 11391r,
  11535, 11601r, 12292r,
  12693r, 13024r
Rowan, Carl T.
  7962
Rowan, Helen
  10326
Rowe, Newton A.
  12685
Rowen, Hobart
  7758
Rowlands, John J.
  11837

Rowley, H. H.
  5966
Rowley, William
  6552
Rowse, A. L.
  4229, 5874, 6621, 7262,
  7472, 11700
Roy, Claude
  10530
Roy, Jules
  6066, 8851, 9009
Royo, Rodrigo
  11976
Ruark, Robert
  10896
Rubens, Peter Paul
  9282
Rubin, Larry
  4621
Rudd, Mary D.
  3619
Rudnik, Raphael
  2477, 3703
Rudofsky, Bernard
  8933
Rudorff, Raymond
  8133
Rue, Leonard Lee, III
  12994
Rugoff, Milton
  8089
Ruhen, Olaf
  12053
Rukeyser, Muriel
  1352
Runciman, Steven
  7517, 11649, 12854
Rush, James
  10361
Ruskin, John
  9279
Russ, Martin
  8189, 9110
Russell, A. J.
  6326
Russell, Bertrand
  5982, 6141, 10927
Russell, Charlie L.
  7646
Russell, Edward Frederick
  11452
Russell, Francis
  11584, 12368

Russell, Franklin
11484
Russell, Robert
7670, 12033
Russell, Ross
11804
Russell, William Howard
10134
Russoli, Franco
11163
Rutenborn, Guenter
11658
Ryan, Cornelius
9091, 9462
Ryan, Orletta
11438
Ryland, George
5680
Rynne, Xavier
2692, 7735
Ryscamp, Charles
6308
Ryskind, Morrie
10431

S

Sabartés, Jaime
10803
Sacharow, Lawrence
6752
Sachs, Albert Louis
8761
Sachs, Barbara Turner
5920
Sachs, Maurice
8497
Sachs, Nelly
4773
Sack, John
270, 1337, 1832, 2147, 2849,
3161, 5253
Sackler, Howard
8093
Saerchinger, César
5925
Safire, William
10244
Sagan, Françoise
6280, 6281, 6536, 6577, 8244,
8594, 8997, 9031, 9153,
12216, 12958
Sahl, Hans
7583

Saidy, Fred
8176, 8762
Sainsbury, Geoffrey
7596
Saint, Dora Jessie
12249
St. Aubyn, Giles
11322
Sainte-Beuve, Charles Augustin
11374
St. George, George
10541
St. John, Bruce
8821
St. John-Stevas, Norman
12724
Salamanca, J.R.
11459
Salazar, Gustavo A. Sánchez
8082
Salinger, J.D.
1934, 3978, 4342, 5574
Salinger, Pierre
12936
Salisbury, Harrison E.
5776, 10074, 10254, 11633
Salisbury, Ralph J.
2248
Salmon, André
10024
Salomon, I.L.
765
Salomonsen, Finn
5886
Salsbury, Edith Colgate
11992
Salter, Elizabeth
9124
Sampson, Anthony
5802, 5804, 7236
Samuels, Charles
8936
Samuels, Ernest
8274, 8275
Samuels, Lesser
8117
Sancton, Thomas
6814
Sandburg, Helga
5497, 12823
Sandeen, Ernest
761, 3268
Sanders, Joan
9784

Sanderson, Ivan T.
9415
Sandrich, Mark, Jr.
6128
Sandstrom, Flora
10596
Sandy, Stephen
1386, 2135, 2304
Sanford, Marcelline Hemingway
5958
Sankey, Tom
7994
Sann, Paul
9140
Sansom, William
8018, 11894
Santayana, George
9276
Santucci, Luigi
10574
Sansom, William
8018, 11894
Sapin, Louis
6900
Sargeant, Winthrop
75, 451, 566, 994, 1055,
1501, 1700, 1881, 2053, 2129,
2348, 2553, 2871, 3138, 3587,
3744, 3801, 3863, 3908, 4134,
4157, 4252, 4535, 4787, 4952,
4963, 5500, 5547, 5753r,
5919r, 6101r, 7161r,
7692r, 7875r, 8079r, 8366r,
8380r, 8476r, 8766r, 8986r,
9321r, 9331r, 9472r, 9867r,
9947r, 10378r, 10471r,
10633r, 11031r, 11413r,
Sargent, E. N.
1824, 4224, 4828, 4873
Saroyan, William
6521, 8295, 12277, 12469
Sarraute, Nathalie
6160, 7990, 9172, 9177,
9181, 9232, 9795
Sarrazin, Albertine
5951, 11338
Sarton, May
1897, 2079, 2267, 3002,
3475, 6208, 7513, 8806,
10874, 11733
Sartre, Jean-Paul
6113, 6756, 9240, 9250, 9382,
10219, 12415, 12965

Saunders, David
4943
Saunders, Edith
8492, 10195
Saunders, James
10267, 11431
Saunders, Josephine
2187, 2739, 4315
Sauter, Joe
5740, 6630
Savage, Henry, Jr.
11504
Savage, Frances Higginson
2853
Savage, Joe
2798
Savill, Mervyn
6963, 8898, 8962, 11706
Sawyer, Mike
6630
Sayre, Joel
4332
Sayre, Woodrow Wilson
7721
Scaglia, Gustina
5854, 11109
Scammell, Michael
2857
Scammon, Richard M.
12201
Scanlon, James P.
11353
Scarfe, Francis
7311, 8355
Schaap, Dick
12449
Schack, William
5903
Schafer, Milton
6326, 7221
Schakovskoy, Zinaïda
7518
Schaller, George
13025
Schary, Dore
6348, 7074, 8341, 10494,
11982
Schechner, Richard
9628
Scheffer, Victor B.
13026
Schéhadé, Georges
8353

Schell, Jonathan
3942, 5217
Schelling, Thomas C.
5890
Scherman, Katharine
11850
Schickel, Richard
7138, 12977
Schiddel, Edmund
7070
Schiller, Johann Christoph
7188
Schimmel, Herbert
12543
Schisgal, Murray
7745, 8801, 9580, 12258,
12497
Schlesinger, Arthur M., Jr.
5676, 6723, 8612, 10889
Schlitt, Robert
7309
Schmidt, Dana Adams
8845
Schmidt, Harvey
6524, 7541, 8515, 10507
Schmitz, Ettore
See Svevo, Italo
Schmoe, Floyd
7688
Schnabel, Ernst
5830
Schneider, Franz
9102
Schnitzler, Arthur
9032
Schochen, Seyril
10056
Schoenberg, Robert J.
1202
Schoenbrun, David
5928
Schoenstein, Ralph
6242
Schoeters, T.
6210
Scholer, Patricia
3504
Scholes, Kenneth
4007, 5107
Scholes, Percy A.
7161
Schonberg, Harold C.
8079

Schreiber, Georg
12578
Schreiber, Hermann
12578
Schrödinger, Erwin
10166
Schröter, Hans
11862
Schulberg, Budd
7136, 12817
Schulberg, Stuart
12817
Schüller, Sepp
7706
Schulman, Arnold
8389, 8790
Schulthess, Emil
5841
Schulze-Holthus
6963
Schuman, Howard
12552
Schumann, Walter
12228
Schutz, Anton
9804
Schuyler, George S.
6221
Schwab, Arnold T.
8766
Schwartz, Arthur
7847, 8790
Schwartz, Bernard
11003
Schwartz, Delmore
1022, 1266, 2760, 4965,
5239
Schwartz, Jerome J.
8441
Schwartz, Richard F.
7285
Schwarz, Eugene
7218
Schweikert, Ernest G.
11334
Sciascia, Leonardo
6813, 9739
Scott, Harold
6754
Scott, J.D.
10963
Scott, J.M.
8087

Scott, Paul
8798
Scott, Peter
7488
Scott, Tom
10623
Scott, Virgil
8521, 11414
Scott, Winfield Townley
5053
Scully, James
377, 980, 1472, 1770, 1799,
1864, 2533, 3044
Seager, Allan
3319, 3858, 7780
Seager, Robert, II
5812
Seaman, L. C. B.
7795
Searle, Ronald
6178, 6406
Seaver, Richard
9733, 10017
Sedgwick, Peter
9870
Seff, Richard
10676
Segal, Erich
11689
Segal, Frau Glückel
7957
Segal, Lore
85, 97, 774, 2706, 2966,
3063, 3097, 3293, 4223,
4521
Seidel, Frederick
7606
Selby, John
9597
Selden, Neil
11777
Seldes, Gilbert
7193
Seligman, Germain
9905
Selmark, George
6334
Selvon, Samuel
8520, 9442, 12444
Semmel, Bernard
8763

Semple, Lorenzo, Jr.
7989, 12329
Semprun, Jorge
9460
Sender, Ramón J.
6103
Senhouse, Roger
6257
Serge, Victor
9870, 9894
Sergeant, Elizabeth Shepley
11254
Sergel, Christopher
12913
Servan-Schreiber, Jean-
Jacques
5763, 9157, 9309
Sevareid, Eric
6438, 10163
Severin, Timothy
7479
Sexton, Anne
1051, 1592, 1624, 1643,
2340, 2701, 2751, 3134,
3635, 4123, 4678, 4680,
4868, 5164, 5565, 5725
Sexton, Patricia Cayo
11827
Seymour, John
10509
Shadbolt, Maurice
4640
Shaffer, Peter
6223, 7643, 10986, 11028,
11324
Shah, Krishna
11848
Shahn, Ben
11598
Shakespeare, William
5931, 8276, 8278, 8279,
8882, 9588, 9845, 9904,
9928, 10099, 10587, 11207,
11278, 12051, 12413, 12452
Shalit, Sherna
490
Shapiro, Charles
11872
Shapiro, Fred C.
182, 449, 3272
Shapiro, Harvey
1929

Shapiro, Karl
652, 659, 1581, 2229, 2928,
3751, 5355, 6311
Shapiro, Nat
8238, 10903
Shaplen, Robert
121, 124, 194, 332, 544,
788, 902, 1089, 1344, 1955,
2197, 2287, 2462, 2584,
2585, 2594, 2612, 2617, 2641,
2649, 2663, 2664, 2672, 2674,
3035, 3693, 4046, 4047, 4181,
4282, 5149, 5166
Shapley, Harlow
10429
Sharnik, John
730
Sharp, Margery
8609, 9796, 11974
Shattuck, Katharine
10197
Shattuck, Roger
6047, 11522
Shaw, David
11138
Shaw, George Bernard
5634, 5817, 5878, 5891, 6013,
6138, 6139, 6377, 7896, 8243,
8288, 8476, 9625, 9658,
9943, 9964, 10007, 10133,
11369, 11604, 11606, 11620,
12290, 12332, 12875, 13049
Shaw, Irwin
6601, 10712
Shaw, Robert
6458, 8326, 9672
Shaw, Wilbur
7868
Sheaffer, Louis
10528
Shebunina, Tatiana
10935
Sheean, Vincent
6164, 7201, 7624, 10218
Sheed, Wilfrid
1994, 6234, 8149, 9921,
11782r
Sheehan, Edward R. F.
8959
Sheehan, Susan
1353, 2545, 12627
Sheldon, Sidney
11138, 11263

Shellabarger, Samuel
12318
Shelton, Richard
115, 912, 3291, 3500, 3913
Shepard, Sam
11129, 12557
Shepherd, Gordon
12837
Shepherd, Jean
8603
Sheppard, Lancelot C.
10919
Sher, Jack
10766
Sheridan, Richard Brinsley
5722, 11434
Sherlock, John
10564
Sherman, Allan
7599
Sherman, Constance D.
10816
Sherman, William T.
9879
Sherriff, R. C.
8423
Sherwood, Robert E.
5587, 11734, 12353
Shevelove, Burt
12335
Shevrin, Alizah
2699
Shiffert, Edith
1286
Shigenori, Togo
6517
Shine, Ted
6787
Shipton, Eric
9070
Shiragian, Sonia
5230
Shire, David
11403
Shirer, William L.
6676, 11230
Shirley, Glenn
9139
Shneiderman, S. L
12752
Sholokhov, Mikhail
8219

Shrubb, Peter
1774
Shub, Elizabeth
1684, 2699
Shukman, Harold
12189
Shulman, Max
8472
Shultz, Gladys Denny
8791
Shuman, Earl
11486
Shumlin, Herman
11846
Shurtleff, Michael
6425
Shuster, George N.
8122
Shute, Nevil
6330, 12430
Shyre, Paul
6594, 7238, 8522, 10815,
12499
Sidney, Hugh
12595
Siebel, Julia
3571
Siegel, Larry
9596
Siegfried, André
11319
Sigal, Clancy
7978
Sillitoe, Alan
3970, 7010, 8918, 9437
Sillman, Leonard
9216, 10241
Silone, Ignazio
7683, 7739, 11489
Silver, Arnold
7531
Silver, James W.
9981
Simckes, Seymour
11560
Simenon, Georges
6123, 7057, 9224, 9403,
10458
Simmons, Ernest J.
6582
Simms, Ruth L. C.
10590
Simon, Claude
10642

Simon, Edith
8070, 10817, 12457
Simon, Hilda
11496
Simon, Joan
10915
Simon, John Y.
7857, 10661
Simon, Kathrin
11162
Simon, Mayo
8180, 12719
Simon, Mina Lewiton
560, 1607, 1711
Simon, Neil
6053, 9108, 9397, 10414,
10854, 11011, 11867, 12002
Simpson, Alan
11258
Simpson, George Gaylord
2835, 12202
Simpson, Louis
775, 871, 914, 1227, 1479,
1848, 1896, 2342, 2559,
2825, 3003, 3209, 3222,
3551, 3622, 4192, 4390,
4829, 10252
Simpson, N. F.
8388, 10524, 11181
Sinclair, Andrew
10666
Sinclair, Marianne
11178
Sinclair, Upton
5986, 6627
Singer, Charles
8369
Singer, Isaac Bashevis
647, 1058, 1684, 1908,
2419, 2432, 2699, 4425
7430, 9738
Singh, Khushwant
9737
Singleton, Betty
10369
Sissman, L. E.
1032, 1223, 1269, 1322,
1367, 1816, 1988, 2218, 2709,
2846, 3281, 3292, 3515, 3682,
4185, 4253, 4502, 4693, 4716,
4864, 5046, 5057, 5058, 5195,
5233, 5292, 5353, 5487, 7430r,
8534r, 9571r, 9738r, 9996r,
10638r, 11118r, 11531r,

12030r, 12138r, 13032r
Sitwell, Edith
  5963, 6685, 10113, 11061,
  12014, 12038
Sitwell, Osbert
  4004
Sitwell, Sacheverell
  8857
Skelton, Geoffrey
  9748
Skelton, R. A.
  7478, 8357
Skinner, Cornelia Otis
  6309
Sklar, Robert
  7493
Skolle, John
  5999
Skulnik, Menasha
  7715
Slade, Susan
  11115
Slate, Joseph
  4063, 4849
Slayden, Ellen Maury
  12756
Slenczynska, Ruth
  7692
Slessor, John
  6530
Slim, William Joseph
  12540
Sloan, Jacob
  10376
Sloane, Eric
  11473
Sloane, Sydney
  12196
Slocum, John J.
  11882
Slocum, Joshua
  12688
Smart, Mae
  3471
Smart, Sue
  3626
Smith, A. J. M.
  10620
Smith, A. M. Sheridan
  9663
Smith, Alexander H.
  10112
Smith, Alice Kimball
  10769

Smith, Alson J.
  12630
Smith, Betty
  8862
Smith, Denis Mack
  8366
Smith, Dodie
  10243, 12360
Smith, Edward Ellis
  13064
Smith, Emma
  6806
Smith, Frank E.
  6764
Smith, Glenn Allen
  8400
Smith, Harold W.
  2493
Smith, J. Percy
  12545
Smith, Janet Adam
  8808
Smith, Lillian
  10502
Smith, M. J.
  720
Smith, Margoret
  2558
Smith, Paul
  6829
Smith, Pauline
  9394
Smith, Robert C.
  5923
Smith, Robert Paul
  12832
Smith, Ronald Gregor
  9123
Smith, Stevie
  4917
Smith, Sydney
  10079, 11528
Smith, William Jay
  460, 1328, 2125, 2549a,
  3085, 3150, 3984, 4144,
  5472, 10870, 11527
Snapp, Thomas
  28
Snell, Graham
  8008
Snodgrass, W. D.
  2777, 2836, 2858, 3865,
  4503, 5654, 8246

Stafford, William
  33, 290, 2228, 2987, 3018,
  3114, 3126, 3580, 4024, 4573,
  5172, 5396
Stallings, Laurence
  7210
Stallman, R. W.
  11878, 11879, 11880, 12737
Stallybrass, Oliver
  5937, 12606
Stampfer, J. L.
  2191
Stampp, Kenneth M.
  7414
Standish, Jean Sewell
  1751
Stanford, Ann
  406, 888, 3329, 5109
Stanford, Donald E.
  10871
Stanley. H. M.
  7475
Stanley, Richard
  7475
Stanton, Will
  1019, 5025
Starbuck, George
  272, 352, 529, 860, 892,
  1434, 3607, 3782, 4294,
  4420, 4589, 4756, 4922,
  5134, 5191, 6277
Stark, Freya
  7252, 8859, 11213, 11277
Starkie, Enid
  6074, 7656
Starkie, Martin
  6445
Starrett, Vincent
  6297
Stavis, Barrie
  9699
Stead, Philip John
  6294
Stearns, Marshall
  11900
Steegmuller, Francis
  156, 211, 803, 2253, 2542,
  2624, 2761, 2791, 3177,
  3418, 4073, 4146, 4730, 5870,
  6285r, 6618, 8038, 9599r,
  11374
Steel, Ronald
  5763

Steele, Max
  716
Steen, Marguerite
  6441
Stegner, Wallace
  2888, 7477, 12944
Steichen, Edward
  7532
Stein, Gertrude
  5742, 6694, 7892, 7893,
  8600, 13038
Stein, Jess
  11100
Stein, Joseph
  6265, 7403, 7589, 8888,
  9999, 12033, 13087
Stein, Leon
  12405
Stein, Sol
  11586
Steinbeck, John
  10427, 10490, 12384, 12923
Steinberg, Jonathan
  12385
Steiner, George
  418, 727, 2006, 2007, 4164,
  4711, 5832, 5982r, 6130r,
  6202r, 6525r,
  6677r, 6761r, 6762r, 6997r,
  7140r, 7355r, 7416, 8587r,
  8744r, 8856, 9081r, 9585,
  9813, 10156r, 10196, 10730,
  10760r, 11111r, 11722r,
  12163r, 12209r, 12920r
Stendhal
  See Beyle, Marie Henri
Stenton, Doris Mary
  7401
Stephan, Ruth
  7662
Stephensen, P. R.
  11365
Sterba, Editha
  6101
Sterba, Richard
  6101
Sterling, Thomas
  167, 3345
Stern, David S.
  4463
Stern, James
  6478, 9285
Stern, Philip Van Doren
  7381, 12155

Stern, Richard G.
  8002, 8598
Stern, Richard Martin
  8916
Stern, Tania
  9285
Sterner, Richard
  5765
Sterns, Monroe
  11755
Stevens, Ann
  9684
Stevens, Edmund
  10357
Stevens, Leslie
  6547, 9550, 9789
Stevens, Wallace
  10561
Stevens, William
  10736
Stevenson, Adlai E.
  7778, 12815
Stevenson, Elizabeth
  8273
Stevenson, Fanny
  10604
Stevenson, James
  227, 3388, 3390, 3706, 4549,
  4703, 11785
Stevenson, Paul
  8848
Stevenson, Robert Louis
  10604
Stevenson, Sallie Coles
  12607
Steward, Ron
  11387
Stewart, Carroll
  10862
Stewart, Desmond
  7356
Stewart, Donald
  348, 1508, 1647, 4850, 5404,
  6864
Stewart, George R.
  10805
Stewart, J. I. M.
  8125
Stewart, Jean
  6123, 8101, 10700
Stewart, John D.
  3054, 4167

Stewart, Mary
  10305
Stewart, Michael
  6407, 6469, 7876, 8265
Stewart, Natacha
  14, 525, 547, 630, 784,
  985, 2255, 2261, 2577,
  2864, 3845, 4396, 4519,
  4737, 5371
Stewart, Ramona
  11991
Stewart, Sidney
  7943
Stiles, John R.
  10926
Stillman, Edmund
  10253, 10887
Stipp, John L.
  7076
Stirling, Monica
  7607, 9600
Stock, Dennis
  8781
Stock, Noel
  9450, 11114
Stockton, Frank R.
  5879
Stoddard, Haila
  6078
Stokesbury, Leon
  2483
Stoloff, Carolyn
  1160
Stone, David
  8007
Stone, Edward Durell
  7302
Stone, Gillian
  1822
Stone, Kate
  6354
Stone, Peter
  8904, 11573, 11714
Stone, Ruth
  1979, 2536, 4452, 5308,
  5438, 8596
Stone, Walter
  956, 3264, 3533, 3997,
  4771
Stopp, Frederick J.
  7441
Stoppard, Tom
  11310

Storey, R. L.
 7378
Storm, John
 12566
Storm, Lesley
 11250
Storry, G. R.
 6486
Stoutenburg, Adrien
 24, 109, 221, 315, 591,
 804, 3430, 3530, 4102,
 4651, 4976, 4979, 4990
Stoye, John
 11656
Strachey, James
 9295
Strachey, John
 10480
Strachey, Julia
 678
Strachey, Lytton
 7355, 9295
Strand, Mark
 323, 1014, 1222, 2451,
 2504, 2580, 2901, 2904,
 2905, 2940, 3136, 3230,
 3812, 4021, 4430, 4582,
 4657, 5220, 5376, 5395,
 5543
Strandberg, Olle
 8764
Stratton, Arthur
 8083
Straus, Dorothea
 647, 1908
Strauss, Lewis L.
 9890
Strausz-Hupé, Robert
 9890
Stravinsky, Igor
 4201
Strindberg, August
 6849  6913  7227, 7900,
 9974, 12300
Stringfellow, William
 10157
Strode, Hudson
 8786, 8787
Strode, Warren Chetham
 13030
Strong, Jonathan
 12265
Strouse, Charles
 5716, 6407, 7986, 8746

Stuart, Dabney
 491, 1249, 2175, 4056,
 4117, 4321, 4958
Stuart, Eddie
 10453
Stubbs, Jane
 4394
Stuhlmann, Gunther
 7101, 8285
Styne, Jule
 6934, 7156, 7504, 7808,
 8142, 8161
Styron, William
 6761, 11554
Sukhanov, N. N.
 11355
Sullivan, Arthur
 8003, 8148, 12560
Sullivan, Frank
 724, 1900, 2070, 2107,
 2331, 3073, 3939, 4283,4296
Sullivan, Walter
 12778
Sully, Ruby
 8434
Sulzberger, C. L.
 6191
Summerfield, Geoffrey
 11615
Summers, Hollis
 12788
Summers, Margaret S.
 10570
Sundgaard, Arnold
 2427, 8976, 10424
Sundquist, James L.
 10469
Sutcliffe, R. B.
 8496a
Sutcliffe, William
 7380
Sutherland, Monica
 9508
Svevo, Italo
 6762
Swados, Harvey
 5786, 7524, 11088
Swain, Joseph Ward
 7303
Swan, Jon
 633, 814, 891, 958, 959,
 1004, 1456, 1485, 1644,
 2057, 2227, 2446, 2877,
 2951, 3278, 3571a,

3836, 3957, 4038, 4086, 4569,
4735, 4807, 7622
Swan, Michael
9761
Swanberg, W. A.
6637, 7625, 11032, 11651
Swann, Donald
5956, 5957
Sward, Robert
3188
Swartz, Roberta Teale
63
Sweet, Frederick A.
9976
Swenson, Karen
1476, 5501
Swenson, May
8, 114, 119, 292, 721, 812,
869, 1066, 1500, 1576, 1585,
1610, 1637, 2211, 2321, 2452,
2764, 2811, 2844, 3253,
3309, 3393, 3497, 3547, 3589,
3612, 3770, 3834, 3864, 3912,
3974, 4299, 4530, 4681, 4891,
5123, 5318, 5325, 5456, 5537,
6421, 12306
Swift, Joan
3630, 3752
Swinburne, Algernon Charles
12014, 12015
Swinglehurst, Pamela
8555
Swinnerton, Frank
6016, 6345, 7000, 7602,
7823, 8034, 11049,
11140, 11392, 11959,
12264
Sydow, Jack
8550
Sykes, Christopher
7555, 12342
Synge, John
7968
Synge, John Millington
7027, 12796
Syrett, Harold C.
7865, 10660
Szogyi, Alex
6827, 11462
Szulc, Tad
2610, 12910

T

Tabori, George
5814, 6444, 10269
Tabrah, Ruth
12675
Tagore, Rabindranath
8953
Talbot, Toby
10471
Tanizaki, Junichirō
7094, 9638, 11773
Tao-Kim-Hai, André M.
3584
Taper, Bernard
41, 567, 700, 729, 785,
1259, 1366, 1829, 2492,
2614, 2658, 2689, 2832,
3011, 4481, 5426
Taradash, Daniel
12143
Tardieu, Jean
8919, 9554
Tarloff, Frank
8313
Tarr, Yvonne
7014
Tarver, Ben
9711
Tate, Allen
12025
Tate, James
855
Tate, Neal
11387
Taton, R.
11119
Tatu, Michel
10947
Tatum, George B.
5923
Taubenslag, Elliott
11427
Tavel, Ronald
8029
Taves, Isabella
11072
Taylor, A. J. P.
7788, 10580, 12419
Taylor, Christopher
12914

Taylor, Douglas
11951
Taylor, D..ight
839, 6250, 7846
Taylor, Edmund
7520
Taylor, Edward
10871
Taylor, Elizabeth
127, 442, 518, 1083, 1439,
1788, 1935, 2208, 2264,
2700, 3037, 3087, 3717,
3876, 4156, 4402, 4669,
4741, 4790, 5017, 5246,
5252, 5558, 5820, 8595, 11803
Taylor, Gordon Rattray
6202
Taylor, James L.
7820
Taylor, Maxwell D.
11182, 12516
Taylor, Peter
960, 1093, 1907, 1966, 3065,
3091 3275, 3598, 3638, 4059,
4320, 5065, 5132
Taylor, Renée
9553
Taylor, Richard
7059
Taylor, Robert Lewis
90, 1417, 1645, 1686, 1807
2471, 2702, 3042, 3351,
3541, 4065, 4585, 4738,
8854, 12383
Taylor, Samuel
5993, 6098, 7630, 10338,
10858
Taylor, Simon Watson
5955, 11522
Taylor, Telford
9759, 12486
Taylor, Tom
12255
Taylor, William R.
6519, 7132
Teale, Edwin Way
5990
Teichmann, Howard
7940, 8878, 9975, 11096
Teichner, Albert B.
12454
Teitel, N.R.
6129

Teitelbaum, Maurice
8421
Teller, Edward
1124, 9206
Teller, Walter Magnes
7648, 11467, 12688
Tempel, Gudrun
7889
Templeton, Edith
444, 1026, 1034, 1234
1282, 1311, 1321, 1373,
2845, 3695, 4739
Tennen, Laura
3658
Terkel, Studs
7150
Terpak, Luba
8722
Terpak, Michael
8722
Terrell, John Upton
9702
Terrell, St. John
12224
Terry, Megan
10759
Tertz, Abram
7539, 12396
Thayer, Alexander Wheelock
9321, 9328
Thayer, Charles W.
7123, 8126, 12544
Thayer, Tiffany
10034
Tharp, Louise Hall
5632, 12234
Theroux, Paul
12706
Thesiger, Wilfred
5883, 9794
Thielen, Benedict
5219
Thirlwall, John C.
11516
Thody, Philip
9583, 10370
Thom, Robert
6750, 7268
Thomas, Benjamin P.
11864
Thomas, Bob
8940
Thomas, Caitlin
9203

Thomas, Dana Lee
10677
Thomas, Dylan
5627, 9294, 11512
Thomas, Edward
6028
Thomas , Elizabeth Marshall
1996, 8209
Thomas, Hugh
11825, 11954
Thomas, Lately
7032, 9840, 11386
Thomas, Louis
8008
Thomas, Norman
9986, 11750
Thomas, Rosemary
1278, 1326, 2819
Thomas, Ross
11505
Thomas, Sydney
10207
Thompson, A. A.
8342
Thompson, Ariadne
6798
Thompson, C. J. S.
10173
Thompson, Dorothy
6833
Thompson, Dunstan
3627
Thompson, E. P.
9635
Thompson, Hunter S.
8267
Thompson, Jay
7204, 10492
Thompson, Kate
8073
Thompson, Kay
7344
Thompson, Lawrance
11515
Thompson, R. W.
5961
Thomsen, Alexander
8627
Thomson, David
10756
Thomson, Margaret
2949
Thomson, Virgil
12645
Thoreau, Henry David

6753
Thorne, Joan
1273
Thornton, Michael John
10194
Thornton, Willis
351
Thorp, Willard
11819
Thorpe, Peter
3485
Throckmorton, Peter
9498
Thubron, Colin
8346
Thuna, Lee
10205
Thurber, James
329, 382, 516, 561, 628,
717, 844, 924, 981, 993,
1030, 1130, 1484, 1617,
1662, 1688, 1851, 1903,
1937, 2042, 2126, 2351,
2352, 2360, 2447, 2474,
2505, 2738, 2831, 2878,
2929, 3043, 3152, 3184,
3477, 3692, 3743, 3924,
4151, 4155, 4566, 4893,
4894, 5012, 5020, 5039,
5056, 5073, 5184, 5310,
5341, 5364, 5461, 5492,
5493, 12224, 12253, 12959
Thurman, Richard
3374
Thwaite, Anthony
3825
Tickell, Jerrard
12637
Tillich, Paul
7815, 10063, 10476
Tillion, Germaine
7747
Tindall, George B.
7348
Tingom, Elizabeth
4556
Tinkle, Lon
12175
Tisdall, E. E. P.
9775
Tobias, Fred
10940
Tobias, Fritz
11148

Todd, A. L.
5584
Todd, Ruthven
1740, 1962, 3009
Toklas, Alice B.
12816
Toland, John
6072, 7117, 9098
Tolbert, Frank X.
6312
Tolkien, J. R. R.
12489
Tolstoy, Leo
10948
Tolstoy, Sergei
12321
Tomkins, Calvin
129, 184, 234, 464, 737,
921, 977, 1376, 1523,
2028, 2258, 2516, 2771,
2896, 3090, 3191, 3377,
4825, 5163, 5193, 5216,
5419, 5513, 5570
Tomlinson, Charles
280, 3341
Tomlinson, H. M.
12425
Tompkins, Molly
11605
Tompkins, Peter
11605, 12290
Tonkin, Mel
9838
Topkins, Katharine
1069
Torn, Jesse
7598
Toulmin, Stephen
7134
Toulouse-Lautrec, Henri de
12543
Tournier, Michel
7773, 7775
Towers, Robert
10044, 10214
Towne, Anthony
1063
Townsend, Emily
1560
Toynbee, Arnold J.
7274
Toynbee, Philip
10652
Tracey, Andrew

12697
Tracy, Honor
7626, 11829, 11909
Trask, Willard R.
13042
Traven, B.
10300
Treadwell, Sophie
9592
Trease, Geoffrey
8043, 8739
Treat, Id a
469, 723, 790, 1492, 3769
4194, 4467, 4918
Tredree, H. L.
11915
Treece, Henry
9812
Trefousse, Hans Louis
6127
Tremayne, Penelope
6126
Trevelyan, George Otto
5781
Trevelyan, Raleigh
8308
Trevor, Meriol
10264
Trevor, William
10452
Trew, Anthony
11740
Trillin, Calvin
368, 369, 370, 371, 372,
608, 868, 1305, 1628, 1633,
2152, 2600, 2637, 2665,
3358, 4137, 4835, 5075,
5076, 5077, 5078, 5079,
5080, 5081, 5082, 5083,
5084, 5085, 5086, 5087,
5088, 5089, 5090, 5091,
5092, 5093 , 5094, 5095,
5096, 5097, 5098, 5099,
5100, 5101, 5102, 5103,
5104, 5105, 5106, 5263,
5290, 5548, 5579, 9981r
Trilling, Lionel
10557
Triolet, Elsa
9167
Trotsky, Leon
10145
Trovaiola, Armando
11329

Trowbridge, John T.
7053
Troyat, Henri
5750, 7369, 12089, 12319,
12320
Truax, Hawley
281, 513, 835, 1050, 2776,
3158, 3408, 4538, 4630,
4939, 5415
Truman, Harry S.
13024, 13031
Trypanis, C. A.
4781
Tucci, Giuseppe
10220
Tucci, Niccolò
203, 410, 1076, 1139, 1652,
4788, 5002, 6102, 12533
Tuchman, Barbara W.
8136
Tucker, Don
11136
Tucker, Ellen Louisa
10498
Tucker, Glenn
6947
Tugwell, Rexford Guy
5914, 6321
Tullius, F. P.
475, 1692, 1798, 1970,
2015, 2803, 2887, 3347,
3474, 3610, 4280, 4718
Tumarin, Boris
8550
Tunley, Roul
5773
Tunnard, Christopher
5782
Tunney, Kieran
7968
Tuohy, Frank
1599
Tuotti, Joseph Dolan
6192
Turco, Lewis
3579
Turgenev, Ivan
9385, 10050, 10051
Turnbull, Andrew W.
1572, 1721, 4264
9275, 11450

Turnbull, Colin M.
7702
Turnell, Martin
5908
Turner, Arlin
7880
Turner, David
11533
Turner, E. S.
12820
Turner, Wallace
7830
Turton, Godfrey
10150
Tusiani, Joseph
911
Twain, Mark
5879, 7857
Tyler, Anne
264, 1495, 5064
Tyler, Ed
12009
Tynan, Kenneth
5611r, 5680r, 5813r, 5931r,
5956r, 6096r, 6107r, 6147r,
6353r, 6372, 6407r, 6424r,
6585r, 6619r, 6673r, 6872r,
6877r, 6889r, 6913r, 6951r,
6983r, 6987r, 7044r, 7063r,
7119r, 7136r, 7142r, 7244r,
7307r, 7446r, 7600r, 7613r,
7643r, 7672r, 7674r, 7835r,
7849r, 7938r, 7968r, 7989r,
8014r, 8020r, 8072r, 8117r,
8142r, 8163r, 8195r, 8208r,
8243r, 8276r, 8341r, 8756r,
8829r, 8875r, 8888r, 8903r,
9022r, 9208r, 9308r, 9454r,
9465r, 9488r, 9545r, 9588r,
9626r, 9808r, 9915r, 9933r,
9956r, 10062r, 10099r,
10221r, 10277r, 10442, 10515r,
10535r, 10693r, 10917r, 10939r,
10969r, 11097r, 11106r,
11138r, 11150r, 11177r,
11234r, 11263r, 11406r,
11477r, 11506r, 11552r,
11532r, 11581r, 11669r,
11807r, 12000r, 12033r,
12047r, 12051r, 12094r,
12132r, 12133r, 12134r, 12135r,
12136r, 12137r

12162r, 12253r, 12364r,
12436r, 12452r, 12496,
12655r, 12661r, 12749r,
12865r, 12928r
Tyner, Paul
    2117
Tyrmand, Leopold
    128, 1394, 3384, 4098

## U

Udall, Stewart L.
    11077
Uhlan, Edward
    11262
Uhry, Alfred
    8303
Ulam, Adam B.
    6271, 7471
Ullman, James Ramsey
    5789, 6955
UNESCO
    5979
Unger, Robert
    6270
Unwin, George
    5978
Updike, John
    1, 22, 70, 111, 117, 131, 137,
    151, 160, 218, 226, 275, 277,
    317, 322, 416, 417, 440,
    447, 453, 497, 505, 509,
    541, 612, 681, 789, 894,
    908, 931, 941, 1021, 1039,
    1065, 1098, 1137, 1185,
    1224, 1238, 1256, 1287, 1397,
    1420, 1432, 1433, 1469, 1478,
    1497, 1546, 1596, 1660,
    1690, 1775, 1796, 1801, 1880,
    1921, 1926, 1949, 2000,
    2017, 2020, 2025, 2035, 2049,
    2120, 2128, 2156, 2164, 2176,
    2195, 2226, 2240, 2272, 2277,
    2306, 2355, 2428, 2430, 2437,
    2484, 2552, 2588, 2714, 2719,
    2763, 2868, 2894, 2952, 2963,
    2992, 3001, 3076, 3079, 3101,
    3105, 3106, 3156, 3166, 3202,
    3206, 3214, 3233, 3306, 3385,
    3434, 3452, 3473, 3523, 3532,
    3549, 3616, 3631, 3655, 3666,
    3723, 3742, 3768, 3793, 3828,
    3851, 3929, 3960, 3966, 4000,

4014, 4015, 4040, 4057,
4105, 4145, 4248, 4255,
4274, 4276, 4312, 4317,
4376, 4381, 4395, 4460,
4473, 4478, 4511, 4514,
4516, 4587, 4606, 4629,
4649, 4655, 4671, 4695,
4696, 4697, 4702, 4745,
4748, 4759, 4857, 4862,
4908, 4915, 4942, 4948,
4960, 5003, 5009, 5027,
5050, 5145, 5148, 5156,
5157, 5170, 5188, 5196,
5225, 5250, 5257, 5305,
5414, 5431, 5437, 5473,
5490, 5559, 5569, 5612r,
5838r, 5951r, 6011r, 6471,
6526, 7579r, 7618r, 7902r,
7941r, 8469r, 8495r, 8666r,
9015r, 9123r, 9524r, 9530r,
9835r, 9955r, 10070r,
10086r, 10472r, 10682r,
10899, 10907r, 11038r,
11081, 11338r, 11522r,
12492r, 12606r, 12671r,
Uphaus, Willard
    6731
Urbont, Jacques
    5722, 9410
Urdang, Laurence
    11100
Urquhart, Brian
    9781
Ussher, Arland
    8852
Ustinov, Peter
    8160, 10795, 11266, 12539
Uxkull, Boris
    5892

## V

Vagts, Alfred
    8363
Vail, Amanda
    9535
Vailland, Roger
    7581, 9014, 12448
Valency, Maurice
    12655
Valenti, Michael
    8890
Valentine, Alan
    12632

Valentine, Jean
4953
Valentinov, Nikolay
7371
Valéry, Paul
5913
Vall, Seymour
8474
Vallentin, Antonina
7325, 8256
van den Haag, Ernest
7494
Van der Kemp, G.
12593
van der Linden, Frank
12450
van der Post, Laurens
9503, 10922
Van Doren, Charles
9362
van Druten, John
1448
Van Gogh, Vincent
12575
Van Heusen, James
11714
van Itallie, Jean-Claude
5755
Van Keuren, W.G.
4022
van Paassen, Pierre
12654
Van Puyvelde, Léo
8485
van Warmer, Joe
12988
Vane, Norman
8198
Vansittart, Peter
10568
Vari, John
7547
Varna, Andrew
7912
Vatsek, Joan
12184
Vaughan-Thomas, Wynford
5864
Vauthier, Jean
9175
Veevers-Carter, Wendy
4316
Vegtel, Maddy
1277

Veiel, Christopher
8245
Vennewitz, Leila
10739
Venturi, Lionello
11707
Vercors
See Bruller, Jean
Vesaas, Tayei
10644
Vian, Boris
7359, 9166
Viansson-Ponté, Pierre
9233
Vickery, Walter N.
8967
Victoria Adelaide Mary Louisa
6991, 6993
Victoria, Queen of Great Britain
6991, 6993, 9197
Vidal, Gore
6147, 11260, 11280, 12657,
12792
Viereck, Peter
12388
Viertel, Joseph
9116
Viking Press
12972
Vilar, Jean
9163
Villars, Jean Beraud
12022
Villiers, Alan
12885
Villiers, Marjorie
6567
Vinaver, Stephen
7146, 9596
Vining, Elizabeth Gray
7669, 12031
Violett, Ellen
6797
Viorst, Milton
8432
Visnevsky
10560
Vitrac, Roger
12605
Vittorini, Elio
6924
Vivante, Arturo
37, 163, 328, 379, 476, 592,
646, 675, 1457, 1481, 1553,

1565, 1615, 1780, 1791, 2037,
2274, 2389, 2515, 2725, 2746,
2893, 3078, 3110, 3342, 3463,
3577, 3669, 3889, 3968, 3981,
3989, 4121, 4143, 4173, 4291,
4375, 4586, 4642, 4970, 5186,
5215, 5228, 5261
Vogue magazine
  12972
Voinov, Nicholas
  12694
Volodin, Alexander
  7641
Volponi, Paolo
  10163
Voltaire
  6439
von Abele, Rudolph
  10689
von Cles-Reden, Sibylle
  See Cles-Reden, Sibylle
von Closen, Ludwig
  11201
von Doderer, Heimito
  7039
von Frisch, Karl
  9659
von Kardorff, Ursula
  7096
von Müller, Georg Alexander
  8898
Vonnegut, Kurt, Jr.
  6514, 7969, 11717
von Pückler-Muskau, Hermann
  11144
von Rauch, Georg
  8367
von Rezzori, Gregor
  3017
von Salomon, Ernst
  7744
von Schlabrendorff, Fabian
  11496
von Schramm, Wilhelm
  6776
von Sternberg, Josef
  7805
von Thurn, Marie
  9283
von Uexküll, Detlev
  5892
von Weidinger, A.R.
  3842

Voros, Sandor
  4971, 5764
Vorres, Ian
  9097
Voskovec, George
  12983
Voysey, Michael
  6401
Voznesensky, Andrei
  5853
Vroom, Barbara
  2038, 5347

W

Waagenaar, Sam
  9820
Wade, Allan
  9289
Wade, Rosalind
  6707
Wagenknecht, Edward
  11569
Wagner, Esther R.B.
  4598
Wagner, Geoffrey
  5942, 9063, 13016
Wagoner, David
  52, 284, 649, 843, 1566,
  1708, 2045, 3330, 3331,
  3790, 4593, 5174, 5349
Wain, John
  6784, 7793r, 9413, 9920r,
  10568r, 11838r, 12245r,
  12963
Wakoski, Diane
  677, 2299
Walcott, Derek
  9641
Walden, William
  589, 1582, 1616, 3403, 3873,
  4168
Walder, Francis
  10215
Waldman, Marguerite
  11712
Waldman, Robert
  8303
Waldron, Eli
  1125, 4042, 4050
Waldrop, Keith
  927
Waley, Arthur
  13076

Walford, Naomi
8311, 9075, 11866, 12278
Walker, Augusta
7283, 9931
Walker, Dale L.
9496
Walker, David
988
Walker, Frank
8488, 9694
Walker, John
6119
Walker, Joseph A.
6115, 8197
Walker, Kathrine Sorley
11110
Walker, Kenneth
11902
Walker, Mildred
6266
Walker, Richard L.
6610
Walker, Stanley
1998, 8409, 12109
Walker, Ted
53, 551, 572, 636, 697,
978, 1195, 1358, 1385,
1583, 1867, 1916, 1944,
2004, 2059, 2388, 2561,
3197, 3208, 3509, 3694,
3787, 3937, 4226, 4419,
4491, 4552, 4685
Wall, Bernard
9661
Wallace, Edward S.
7058
Wallace, Irving
7495, 11856
Wallace, Kevin
1355, 1989, 2807, 4006,
4209, 4434
Wallace, Robert A.
347, 973, 1155, 1608,
1736, 2252, 2361, 2494,
2892, 3904, 4588, 4622
Wallach, Ira
5592, 7231, 10794, 11739
Wallant, Edward Lewis
6600
Waller, George
8926
Wallis, Dave
7934

Wallis, Nevile
12609
Wallop, Douglass
6907, 11981
Walter, Eugene Victor
12103
Walton, Eda Lou
1952, 3269
Walton, Su
8293
Wang, Chi-Chen
7226
Wangermée, Robert
7659
Wanshel, Jeff
7137
Warburg, Fredric J.
4433
Ward, Barbara
8645, 8686, 10199, 11205
Ward, Douglas Turner
6952, 8187, 11122
Ward, Edmund
4668
Ward, Theodora
9274
Ware, Eugene F.
8671
Waren, Helen
6583
Warlimont, Walter
8671
Warner, Denis
9094
Warner, Rex
10768
Warner, Sylvia Townsend
27, 73, 76, 367, 385, 458,
584, 674, 755, 1236, 1265,
1356, 1520, 1611, 1720, 1823,
1928, 1967, 2214, 2244, 2312,
2347, 2383, 2781, 2790, 3223,
3465, 3503, 3553, 3629, 3639,
3713, 3827, 3941, 3951, 4202,
4346, 4477, 4520, 4557, 4715,
4755, 4808, 4865, 5021, 5023,
5210, 5227, 5444, 5457, 5517,
5568, 9755, 12023
Warnke, Janet
11039

Warren, Harris Gaylord
8291
Warren, Joyce
91, 316, 972, 1126, 3098,
3357, 5118
Warren, Robert Penn
302, 1452, 1459, 2047,
3395, 3683, 5405, 6039,
6520, 7668, 9207, 11507,
12860
Warrington, John
7042
Washburn, Deric
9538
Wasiolek, Edward
10371
Waskow, Arthur I.
9353
Wasserman, Dale
9410, 9683, 10500
Waterfield, Gordon
9146
Waterfield, Lina
6493
Waterhouse, Keith
6199, 7456, 8271, 8867,
11847, 11858
Waters, Edward N.
12604
Watkins, Edward
1525
Watkins, Vernon
67, 414, 900, 935, 984,
1283, 1437, 1659, 1718,
2140, 2712, 2995, 3257,
4079, 4361, 4453, 4713,
5648, 6890, 9294
Watney, John
1428
Watson, Barbara Bellow
2528, 3154
Watson, Donald
8666
Watson, George L.
5580
Watson, James D.
7205
Watson, Ralph
2366
Watson, Robert
2013
Watt, Douglas
11011

Watt, Hannah
8989
Watt, W.W.
15, 432, 1198, 1569, 1604,
2046, 2692, 3704
Wattenberg, Ben J.
12201
Watts, C.T.
8836
Watts, Stephen
74, 3034
Waugh, Alec
7266, 7799, 9519
Waugh, Auberon
7741
Waugh, Evelyn
9395, 10046, 10440, 12352
Weaver, Dorothy
10024
Weaver, Helen
10555
Weaver, Randolf
10024
Weaver, William
8643, 12118
Webb, Denis
9973
Webb, Kenneth
7846
Webb, Paddy
4387
Webber, Gordon
12813
Webber, Howard
1733, 5293
Weber, Brom
11993
Weber, Carl J.
6992
Webster, Margaret
6356
Webster, Paul
6509, 6619
Webster, Tony
8096
Wechsberg, Joseph
12, 17, 80, 288, 422, 500,
607, 779, 816, 975, 1229,
1354, 1402, 1655, 1746,
1858, 2065, 2074, 2200,
2597, 2601, 2606, 2611,
2659, 2693, 2695, 2697,
2784, 2792, 3033, 3226,

3251, 3368, 3572, 3890,
3954, 4045, 4111, 4124,
4501, 4565, 4765, 4985,
5240, 5275, 5328, 5413,
5992, 10109
Wedekind, Frank
5998, 9575
Wedgwood, C.V.
6671, 8963, 8965, 10464
Weekes, C.P.
8698
Weeks, Edward
8868
Weeks, Robert Lewis
231
Weems, John Edward
10734, 11082, 12794
Weesner, Theodore
153
Weidman, Jerome
6528, 7392, 7613, 8513,
10084, 10940, 12093
Weightman, Doreen
7982
Weinberg, Arthur
5973
Weinberg, Lawrence
6188
Weiner, J.S.
10827
Weiner, Leslie
8619
Weiner, Norbert
8511
Weingarten, Romain
9262
Weinstein, Arnold
7708, 11131, 12223
Weinstock, Herbert
7191, 8889
Weinstock, Jack
6510, 8437, 8482
Weintraub, Stanley
11604
Weisgal, Meyer W.
6541
Weismiller, Edward
4698
Weiss, George David
9609, 10969
Weiss, Irving J.
4472

Weiss, Neil
5514
Weiss, Peter
8697, 9748, 11794
Weiss, Theodore
2715
Weiss, W.A.
1365
Weisslitz, E.F
344, 3746
Welch, Denton
12671
Welch, Holmes
10686
Welch, Robert H.W., Jr.
6252
Welch, William
8477
Wellard, James
5643, 8084
Wellek, René
8364
Weller, Jac
12798
Welles, Orson
10014
Wellesley, Arthur
12797
Wells, Anna Mary
4920, 6989
Wells, Calvin
6278
Wells, H.G.
5898, 8281
Wells, John
10008
Wells, Robert
12228
Wellwarth, George
8919, 9554
Welty, Eudora
1095, 1598, 3573, 5400
Wendt, Herbert
10609
Wentworth, Harold
7110
Werfel, Alma Mahler
5809
Werner, M.R.
1183
Wertenbaker, William
897, 1578, 2506, 3905, 4221

Wescott, Glenway
8575, 10821
Wesker, Arnold
6613, 6614, 7727, 11295
West, Anthony
394, 2467, 2691, 3066, 3081,
3089, 3093, 4358, 4637,
5208, 5602r, 5657r, 5695r,
5784r, 5832r, 5867r, 5938r,
5977r, 5988r, 6039r, 6052r,
6074r, 6080r, 6099r, 6103r,
6136r, 6157r, 6220r, 6245r,
6365r, 6460r, 6551r, 6556r,
6570r, 6598r, 6802r, 6813r,
6860r, 6862r, 6891r, 6895r,
6910r, 6924r, 6935r, 7006r,
7039r, 7062r, 7094r, 7127r,
7179r, 7226r, 7262r, 7327r,
7350r, 7423r, 7533r, 7539r,
7565r, 7582r, 7636r, 7668r,
7683r, 7693r, 7701r, 7720r,
7734r, 7739r, 7759r, 7762r,
7779r, 7783r, 7797r, 7832r,
7836r, 7848r, 7862r, 7870r,
7895r, 7923r, 7979r, 8094r,
8100r, 8110r, 8129r, 8219r,
8306r, 8407r, 8425r, 8454r,
8520r, 8630r, 8643r, 8771r,
8834r, 8843r, 8883r, 8906r,
8952r, 8981r, 9058r, 9100r,
9144r, 9287r, 9326r, 9398r,
9437r, 9460r, 9499r, 9518r,
9638r, 9656r. 9710r. 9728r,
9739r, 9741r, 9907r, 10006r,
10035r, 10081r, 10163r,
10296r, 10300r, 10310r,
10324r, 10366r, 10451r,
10466r, 10495r, 10513r,
10517r, 10571e, 10590r,
10635r, 10644r, 10767r,
10824r, 10831r, 10928r,
11007r, 11085r, 11133r,
11157r, 11167r, 11169r,
11186r, 11198r, 11220r,
11233r, 11245r, 11368r,
11430r, 11437r, 11489r,
11503r, 11648r, 11651r,
11673r, 11703r, 11712r,
11737r, 11773r, 11814r,
11836r, 11925r, 11976r,
12076r, 12077r, 12083r,
12118r, 12186r, 12246r,
12275r, 12283r, 12345r,
12371r, 12391r, 12406r,

12421r, 12441r, 12584r,
12695r, 12753r, 12776r,
12785r, 12828r, 12830r,
12834r, 12892r, 12900r,
12915r, 12945r, 12966r,
13004r
West, E.J.
5634, 11606
West, Morris L.
6939, 6940, 7073
West, Nathanael
6749
West, Rebecca
3659, 6206, 6834, 7719
West, Richard
11247
Westbrook, Robert
8846
Westheimer, David
10161
Westhoff, Robert
8244, 8997
Westin, Alan F.
10983
Westlake, Donald E.
10835
Westminster, Loelia Grosvenor
8033
Weston, Christine
3524, 3696, 4159
Weston, Mildred
1956, 2999, 4911
Wevill, David
2322, 3125
Weyer, Edward, Jr.
8887
Whalen, Richard J.
7717
Wharton, Edith
6153
Whedon, Tom
5724
Wheeler, Hugh
6181, 9470, 12783
Wheeler, Keith
10732
Wheeler, Mortimer
11273
Wheeler, Post
7185
Wheeler-Bennett, John W.
8942
Wheelock, John Hall
120, 300, 384, 1067, 1175,

Wilk, Max
  6661
Wilkins, Sophie
  7889
Wilkins, Thurman
  6647
Willans, Geoffrey
  10165
Willard, John
  6502
Willcox, William B.
  10916
Williams, Albert Rhys
  12248
Williams, C.K.
  3521, 5522
Williams, Edward Bennett
  10510
Williams, Emlyn
  7869, 11775
Williams, Gene
  1144, 2568, 2986, 3646,
  4202, 5534
Williams, Glanville
  11391
Williams, Heathcote
  9425
Williams, Hugh
  8715, 9857
Williams, Jay
  7705, 12326, 12930
Williams, John
  11890
Williams, Kenneth P.
  9359
Williams, Margaret
  8715, 9857
Williams, Martin
  5911, 12842
Williams, Maslyn
  7645
Williams, Neville
  8979, 12207
Williams, Pat
  8945
Williams, Raymond
  6291
Williams, T. Harry
  8232
Williams, Tennessee
  979, 6433, 6505, 7947,
  8616, 9941, 10293, 10583,
  10770, 10917, 11562,

11716, 11928, 11952, 12000,
12466
Williams, Thomas
  4418, 4462, 4710, 12359,
  12844
Williams, Vinnie
  12710
Williams, William Carlos
  3931, 9744, 11516
Williams, Winifred
  1468, 3952
Williams, Wirt
  5613
Williamson, Hugh Ross
  6961
Willingham, Calder
  5373, 7431
Willis, Harold
  11809
Willis, William
  7976
Willman, Allan
  8510
Willson, D. Harris
  8944
Willson, Meredith
  8302, 10116, 12547
Wilner, Daniel M.
  11241
Wilson, Angus
  3147, 3537, 5825, 9125,
  9920, 11561
Wilson, Carter
  8519
Wilson, Colin
  6137, 10613, 11233, 11871
Wilson, Edmund
  230, 632, 641, 642, 657,
  1064, 1154, 1329, 1573,
  1852, 1946, 3389, 3414,
  3514, 3868, 3874, 4184,
  4266, 4631, 4724, 5034,
  5451, 5452, 5768, 5929r,
  5940r, 6125r, 6354r, 6417r,
  6519r, 6758r, 6778r, 7047r,
  7053r, 7059r, 7089r, 7110r,
  7209r, 7880r, 7996r, 8088r,
  8145r, 8147r, 8314r, 8848r,
  8931r, 9464r, 9543r, 9742r.
  9773r, 9876r, 9879r, 9954r,
  10073r 10406r, 10537r, 10818r,
  11345r, 11993r, 11998r,
  12015r, 12124r, 12128r,

Young, Stanley
    3338
Young, Wayland
    7419
Young, William E.
    11588
Yurasov, Vladimir
    10669
Yurick, Sol
    7580

Zur, Menachem
    12531

Z

Zachary, Frank
    1449, 5175
Zavin, Benjamin Bernard
    7301
Zeigler, Philip
    5618
Zeisel, Hans
    5778
Zeldin, Mary-Barbara
    11353
Zeno, (Pseudo.)
    9310
Zerbe, Jerome
    9245
Zetterling, Mai
    10281
Zhitova, Varvara
    12442
Ziegler, Gilette
    5955
Ziegler, Philip
    7240
Zilles, Luke E.
    381, 616, 965, 1333,
    3130, 4011, 5316
Zimmer, Heinrich
    5910
Zinn, Howard
    12624
Zoffer, G.
    7372
Zohn, Harry
    5284
Zola, Émile
    9050, 12226
Zoltan, Ralph M.
    11943
Zuckerman, Solly
    11447